Montgomery County Maryland

Marriage Licenses

1798-1898

Compiled by
Janet Thompson Manuel

HERITAGE BOOKS
2007

HERITAGE BOOKS
AN IMPRINT OF HERITAGE BOOKS, INC.

Books, CDs, and more—Worldwide

For our listing of thousands of titles see our website at
www.HeritageBooks.com

Published 2007 by
HERITAGE BOOKS, INC.
Publishing Division
65 East Main Street
Westminster, Maryland 21157-5026

Copyright © 1987, 1998 Janet Thompson Manuel

Other books by the author:

Abstracts of Wills, Montgomery County, Maryland, 1776-1825
Mary Gordon Malloy, Jane C. Sween and Janet D. Manuel

Abstracts of Wills Montgomery County, Maryland, 1826-1875
Mary Gordon Malloy, Jane C. Sween and Janet D. Manuel

All rights reserved. No part of this book may be reproduced or transmitted in any form or by any means, electronic or mechanical, including photocopying, recording or by any information storage and retrieval system without written permission from the author, except for the inclusion of brief quotations in a review.

International Standard Book Number: 978-1-58549-489-7

INTRODUCTION

In September of 1776 Montgomery County, Maryland, was formed from the lower portion of Frederick County. A few months later, in February of 1777, the Maryland General Assembly passed an act requiring marriage licenses be issued by the clerks of the county courts.

The date of the first marriage license issued in Montgomery County is unknown, because the first license record book has been missing since the early 1800's. The earliest extant record book begins February 9, 1798. The marriages in this volume begin with that date and end December 30, 1898. During this hundred year period approximately 8,725 licenses were issued.

The entries appear in the books by date of license, name of male and name of female. After April 1844 the cost of the license is entered. At that time the charge was $4.50. In 1885 this was reduced to $4.00 and in 1886 was lowered to $.50. During the year 1888 the clerk stopped entering the license fee. Some of the clerks indicated the race of the couple by entering "c" for colored and "w" for white, but this was not done consistently until December 1855; even then, a few appear without the race notation. In this book that notation appears after the date.

As with many old records, the handwriting in these books has sometimes been difficult to read; several were impossible. Some of the pages are partially missing and those containing the licenses from October 11, 1798 to April 13, 1799 are completely missing. Several earlier transcriptions have been made and these have been consulted for those missing licenses and for the names which are only partially readable because of torn pages. The following are the earlier readings which were consulted:

1. J. Thomas Scharf, History of Western Maryland, Philadelphia, 1882.
2. Clifford Robertson, typed manuscript located at the Montgomery County Historical Society Rockville, Md. Transcription of licenses 1798-1830 made in 1899; transcription of licenses 1830-1839 made in 1904.
3. Ella R. Plummer, Typed manuscript located at the Montgomery County Historical Society. Date unknown.

Montgomery County, Maryland, Marriages, 1796-1850 was published in 1966 by Tressie Nash Bowman. This volume contains a number of additions and corrections to Bowman's work.

Another problem encountered in early records is the variations in the spelling of names; many are recorded as the clerk heard them spoken or as he thought they should be spelled. As an added help in locating an individual, liberal cross-indexing of surnames has been done. First names can also cause problems. Frequently the name by which the person was known appears in the record; be sure to check under a nickname or middle name if the entry cannot be found under the known given name.

There is always the question of accuracy in a project such as this. Mistakes are bound to occur, but every precaution has been taken to avoid as many as possible. The entire work has been double proofed. Jane C. Sween, the librarian at the Montgomery County Historical Society, and Mary Gordon Malloy gave many hours of their time to this task. When a reading was questionable we tried to reconcile it by consulting the earlier transcriptions and the numerous other records at the Society.

Beginning in the year 1865, ministers were required to return to the clerk of the court proof of marriages which they performed. These returns are recorded in a separate set of books, which are titled Record of Marriages and give additional information, such as: the ages, occupations and marital status of the couple. The earliest entries are not complete, because the ministers failed to file the returns. They do, however, contain a few marriages which were performed by church banns and for which no license was issued. These records were not abstracted and those marriages are not included here. If you are interested in a marriage which occurred after 1865, searching these records may give additional information. Copies of marriages in the return books may be obtained from the Office of the Clerk of the Circuit Court, Montgomery County Courthouse, Rockville, Maryland 20850.

At the present time, the marriage license books from which the licenses in the following pages were taken are not available at the Office of the Clerk of the Circuit Court. Mary Gordon Malloy has graciously deposited a photocopy of the record books at the Montgomery County Historical Society, 103 W. Montgomery Avenue, Rockville, Maryland 20850. Copies may be ordered from the Society for a fee of $.25 per marriage plus postage.

NOTE: In the alphabetical list of names on the following pages all names beginning with "Mc" are treated as though they begin with "Mac".

THE AUTHOR

Janet Thompson Manuel is a native of Montgomery County, Maryland. She is an avid family genealogist and has been on the staff of the Montgomery County Historical Society library for the past 16 years. Mrs. Manuel has coauthored <u>Abstracts of Wills, Montgomery County, Maryland, 1776-1825</u>, <u>Abstracts of Wills, Montgomery County, Maryland, 1826-1875</u> and <u>Gaithersburg, The Heart of Montgomery County</u>. She has also compiled the 1850 census for Montgomery County, Maryland and is currently completing recording the tombstones in the county. Both of these will be published in the near future.

MARRIAGE LICENSES
Montgomery County, Maryland

AARON, Sarah H.	George A. Hinsch	29 Aug 1892 w
ABBE, Edward H.	Lillian J. Prescott	16 Sep 1889 w
ABEL, Mary F.	Reuben Slater	14 Feb 1853
ABELL, Bessie M.	William H. Standiford	21 Feb 1891 w
John R.	Mary E. Wylie	23 Dec 1859
ABERT, Charles Jr.	Martha W. Stonestreet	12 Jan 1880 w
Maria Bache	William D. Baldwin	2 Aug 1884 w
Mary C.	George E. Cook	28 Jul 1896 w
Sophie B.	James S. Mallory	8 Nov 1878
ACRES, James W.	Mary E. Jarvis	8 Sep 1841
ACTION, Jennie	Joseph Nicholson	3 Feb 1879 w
William E.	Mollie E. Young	3 Jan 1881
ACTON, Offy	Moses Padgett	23 Dec 1817
A'DALE, Alan	Bessie E. Poley	18 Nov 1890 w
ADAMS, Alice	Joshua Duffin	13 Feb 1874
Alice	George W. Bellows	13 Jul 1881 c
Andrew J.	Clero Duvall	20 Oct 1850
Ann	James Lyddan	19 Mar 1812
Annie	Addison Ormstead	17 Aug 1887 c
Bennedict	Catherine Richards	27 Jan 1807
Caroline	John Rainer	28 Aug 1838
Caroline	Caleb Poole	23 Dec 1874
Carrie	John Chunn	7 Sep 1893 c
Catharine	Henry Johnson	4 May 1878 c
Charles A.	Sarah E. Thomas	4 Apr 1888 c
Charles Francis	Eleanor Williams	21 Dec 1868
Edith May	Marshall V. Bowman	21 May 1896 w
Edward	Mary L. Mason	2 Jan 1890 c
Eleanor	Henry Paul	28 Jan 1801
Elizabeth	James Rawlings	1 Jun 1840
Emma	Edward Sims	8 Dec 1898 c
Emma A.	Nathan B. Warthen	15 Sep 1870
Ernest N.	Sarah H. Janney	27 Feb 1894 w
Fannie	Benjamin C. H. Johnson	13 Feb 1888 c
Florence E.	J. C. W. Kemp	19 Nov 1870
George A.	Harriet A. R. Lancaster	7 Apr 1888 c
George E.	Mary S. Brown	31 May 1888 c
George S.	Martha A. Johnson	3 Mar 1886 c
Harriett	Basil Ragan	11 Nov 1813
Henny	Thomas W. Trundle	18 Mar 1823
Jane E.	Caleb Musgrove	18 Nov 1845
John Jr.	Eleanor Colyer	21 Jan 1799
John	Rosanna Day	7 Feb 1804
John	Malinda Benton	3 Jul 1804
John	Anne Maria Beall	1 Feb 1866
John	Catharine Smith	14 Oct 1869
John Edward	Mary Ellen Duvall	15 Oct 1842
Joseph R.	Laura J. Tilley	27 Apr 1882 c
Josephine	Remus Boswell	16 Nov 1871
Josias	Ann House	1 Sep 1810
Lorenzo D.	Elizabeth Iglehart	9 Mar 1837

ADAMS, Lucinda	Asbury Johnson	6 Apr 1885	c
Margaret	Boyd Travers	22 Jan 1817	
Mary	Elias Young	13 Jun 1891	c
Mary A.	Charles A. Stanley	31 Oct 1863	
Mary Ann	Basil Warren	13 Oct 1827	
Mary F.	Charles W. Shern	20 Nov 1890	c
Mary F. C.	Benjamin F. Pickett	25 Aug 1891	w
Mary J.	Milton B. Lewis	22 Sep 1890	c
Milly	Milburn Howard	29 Jul 1870	
Philip	Margarett Harper	25 Feb 1811	
Rachel A.	Thomas Owens	27 Jul 1874	
Robert	Rachel Dorsey	6 Oct 1882	c
Turner S.	Martha Clark	21 Aug 1878	c
Turner S.	Emma Nickens	14 May 1898	c
Walter	Amanda White	5 Aug 1898	c
William H.	Georgiana Magruder	4 Jul 1888	c
ADAMSON, Clara S.	James B. Henderson	10 Aug 1870	
Eleanor	Benedick H. Duley	13 Feb 1811	
Elisha	Catharine Simms	2 May 1833	
Elizabeth	William Prather	2 Jun 1798	
Elizabeth J.	George E. Gilpin	5 Jul 1870	
Frederick	Sarah Summers	25 Jan 1803	
Frederick	Martha Palmore	28 Feb 1809	
Hinda	John W. Fraley	7 Nov 1892	w
Ida	John W. Chappell	* Oct 1881	w
John	Rebecca Duley	18 Jan 1816	
Kesiah	Sykes Beckwith	22 Jan 1801	
Lloyd	Jane Smith	7 Jan 1813	
Narcissa	Archibald S. Magruder	19 Jan 1844	
Sarah Elizabeth	Alfred H. Wells	2 Jan 1836	
Victoria C.	Samuel Rabbitt	12 Dec 1855	
Walter H.	Margaret Ann Alby	8 Oct 1844	
ADDISON, Lucinda	John Bradley	16 Jun 1875	
Richard	Anna Mariott	22 Dec 1873	
ADKINS, Cary (female)	Justus Colburg	8 Oct 1814	
ADRAIN, John M.	Mary E. Greenlease	6 Sep 1866	
ADRIAN, James A.	Olivia Elizabeth Havener	7 Jun 1869	
AGER, Charles B.	India Marlow	24 Nov 1885	w
AHALT, Charles L.	Lillie B. Bean	18 Feb 1888	w
AIKENS, Walter H.	Catherine S. Wiley	5 Dec 1871	
AIRESS - also see AYRES			
AIRESS, Sarah	John Browning	13 Apr 1802	
ALBURGER, William J.	Anna M. Croasdale	8 Dec 1882	w
ALBY, Cassandra	Joshua Davis	16 Oct 1832	
Margaret Ann	Walter H. Adamson	8 Oct 1844	
ALCORN - also see ELCORN, ELLCORN			
ALCORN, Edward	Hattie Shipley	19 Nov 1891	c
Joseph G.	Mary Manakee	5 Oct 1869	
ALDER, Elizabeth	Greenbury Warfield	13 Mar 1817	
William Henry	Emma Grady	26 Jul 1869	
ALDRICH, Edwin R.	Lizzie Smith	29 Sep 1885	w
ALDRIDGE, Dorothy	Richard Murray	1 Feb 1802	
Elizabeth	Charles Soaper	13 Jan 1801	
Jacob	Martha Jones	5 Feb 1805	

* The day has been written over; could be 1 or 3

ALEXANDER, Charles G.	Victorine Williams	28 Dec 1874	
Kitty	William H. Triplett	3 Mar 1806	
Lucy	George Conrad	27 Nov 1867	
Mahanty	Robert Dodge	12 Sep 1871	c
Nannie	James H. Gross	22 Aug 1881	c
Nellie	Wesley Watts	28 Nov 1872	
Ruthy	John B. James	*22 May 1798	
ALL, John	Comforte Young	12 Jul 1798	
ALLAN - also see ALLEN			
ALLAN, Edgar	Olive Estelle Bennett	10 Jan 1898	w
ALLEGER, Walter W.	Edith Hanzsche	22 Oct 1884	w
ALLEN - also see ALLAN			
ALLEN, Albert W.	Eliza A. Gray	1 Dec 1877	w
Alice G.	Joseph F. Bateman	14 Apr 1868	
Charlotte	Henry Lyday	29 Oct 1861	
Effie May	William T. Drowns	18 Oct 1894	w
Grace B.	Harry B. Richards	17 Mar 1898	w
Henry	Sarah Groom	21 Nov 1816	
Henry	Kitty Ann Gantt	4 Aug 1845	
James	Grace Lomax	13 Sep 1897	c
James F.	Lillie B. Maus	28 Aug 1888	w
Kate H.	John G. Tennent	2 Sep 1898	w
Lizzie A.	Hary C. King	8 Aug 1872	
Robert H.	Charlotte Hardt	4 Feb 1851	
Sarah	Peter Kirkwood	5 Jun 1806	
Sarah E.	L. H. Crown	29 Dec 1873	
Sarah E.	J. Gilbert Burnell	30 Mar 1874	
Sidonia	Julian M. House	29 Jan 1878	w
Virginia C.	Timothy Caton	15 Nov 1886	w
William E.	Sarah C. Gates	19 Aug 1890	w
William W.	Catharine Hessey	31 Mar 1838	
ALLENS, Eliza Ann	Richard Budd	24 Nov 1841	c
ALLIS - also see ELLIS			
ALLIS, Carrie	Charles Brown	16 Apr 1898	c
ALLISON, Ann	James B. Crawford	14 Mar 1799	
Cora	Charles A. Clagett	18 Jul 1895	w
Elijah	Sally Caldwell	18 Dec 1819	
Elizabeth M.	Harry C. Wolford	15 Jul 1898	w
Horatio C.	Hester E. O'Neale	22 Oct 1890	w
Presha	William Golding	9 Mar 1809	
William	Ann Waters	28 Sep 1819	
ALLGOOD, Sarah	Anthony Liver	23 Aug 1800	
ALLNUTT - also see ALNUTT			
ALLNUTT, Aden Darby	Martha Virginia Duvall	21 Jun 1875	
Anna	Reubin Howes	5 Nov 1816	
Avilda A.	William Wallace Poole	23 Aug 1855	
Benjamin W.	Rachel White	10 Jan 1866	
Binoni	Emily A. Dawson	17 Nov 1860	
Caroline	John H. Thompson	6 Oct 1845	
Charles E.	Mary E. Clagett	25 Oct 1887	w
Clarence B.	Katie V. Thompson	8 Nov 1893	w
Elizabeth	Alexander B. Knott	22 Dec 1846	
Elizabeth Jane	Hanson Allnutt	31 May 1838	
Estelle	Thomas C. Darby	3 Dec 1895	w

* Page torn; only one 2 visible; 22 from earlier readings

ALLNUTT,	Eva W.	Edward J. Chiswell	4 Dec 1865
	Evie W.	George D. Jones	12 Dec 1891
	George H.	Jane Darby	7 Dec 1812
	Gertie M.	Arthur C. Haney	17 Oct 1896 w
	H. Clinton	Josephine Veirs	23 Oct 1877 w
	Hanson	Elizabeth Jane Allnutt	31 May 1838
	Henry C.	Clara E. Bowman	20 Dec 1894 w
	Jacob M.	Exerline Warfield	22 Feb 1881 w
	James	Eleanor Gott	12 Sep 1801
	James N.	Barbara Ann Dawson	3 Dec 1832
	James W.	Mary J. Groomes	14 Jun 1870
	John	Elizabeth Ann Miller	1 Nov 1837
	John B.	Anna M. Marlow	3 Nov 1863
	John H.	Bettie M. Padgett	21 Aug 1895 w
	Joseph N.	Lucy W. Williams	9 Dec 1890 w
	Lawrence	Eleanor White	7 Dec 1825
	Lydia	Ephraim B. G. Ayton	3 Jul 1839
	Maggie E.	Thomas J. Brown	21 Dec 1891 w
	Margaret A.	Benjamin F. White	19 Dec 1851
	Mary Ann	Horatio Crawford	31 Oct 1844
	Mary Effie	John W. Poole	3 Mar 1884
	Mary J.	James S. Benson	20 Dec 1866
	Nathan W.	Margaret E. White	23 Dec 1850
	Sarah E.	Henry Young	27 Oct 1860
	Valeria W.	Samuel E. Veirs	23 Jan 1886 w
	Verlinda	George Darby	12 Jan 1822
ALMONEY,	Albert J.	Miriam Prettyman	10 Dec 1884
	Alice A.	William Veirs Bouic, Jr.	5 Jul 1870
ALNUTT - also see ALLNUTT			
ALNUTT,	Aden D.	Amelia Bowman	30 Dec 1812
	Anne	James M. Dawson	17 Dec 1801
	Daniel	Virlinda Dawson	20 Dec 1809
	Elizabeth	William Dawson	21 Nov 1808
	Jane	John Perry	18 Dec 1799
	Mary	Thomas Harper	19 Dec 1801
	Rebecca D.	Thomas Darby	4 Jan 1816
	Robert D.	Mary Dawson	7 Jan 1807
	Susannah	Thomas Dawson	15 Feb 1812
	Thomas	Elizabeth Gott	27 Jan 1801
ALSOP,	Benjamin B.	Eva McWhirt	28 Apr 1891 w
ALVEY,	Joseph	Elizabeth Ramsay	16 Jan 1821
ALVORTH,	Annie	Peter A. Schladt	18 Nov 1892 w
AMBLER,	Vincent L.	Mary E. Hutchison	31 Aug 1833
AMBROSE,	St. Cloud	Dora M. A. Dufour	19 Jun 1894 w
AMBUSH,	Mortimer	Annie Higgins	27 Feb 1878 c
	Mortimer	Lucy Jackson	15 Dec 1883
	Mortimer	Mary Overs	16 Feb 1897 c
	Patrick	Henrietta Coats	20 Dec 1866
AMERICA,	Susie A.	Charles Thomas	5 Aug 1897 w
AMISS,	Edmund L.	Angie Green	28 Jan 1879
	Oscie L.	Fred S. Yount	28 Jul 1898 w
ANAWALT,	James W.	Ella A. Sweeney	27 Jul 1893 w
ANCARROW,	Carrie C.	Thomas A. Gibson	25 Mar 1898 w
ANCHORS,	Anne	James Harvey	10 Dec 1808
	Francis	Elizabeth Hervy	7 Jan 1807
	Snowden	Delilah Harvey	9 Dec 1805

ANCHORS, Snowden	Margarett Beall	23 Feb 1814
ANDERS, Doris C.	John F. Fisher	27 Dec 1893 w
Sarah	John Woollard	7 May 1816
ANDERSON, Altie (female)	Willie W. Dronenburg	9 Jul 1878 w
Anna M.	Nacey W. Smith	26 May 1846
Augusta	William L. G. Appleby	27 Sep 1875
C. T.	Eliza A. Hurley	10 Nov 1857
Charles	Martha Toogood	19 May 1866
Charles H.	Lavinia Brown	24 May 1847
Clarence E.	Bertha G. Hall	8 Jan 1896 w
David	Margaret Thompson	5 Feb 1799
Elizabeth	Evan Thompson	27 Dec 1813
Elizabeth	James Duff McKay	16 Jun 1890 w
Elizabeth A.	Philemon Griffith	6 Jun 1857
F. Virginia	Francis W. Rozer	19 Sep 1860
Fannie	William Jones, Jr.	20 Nov 1871
George W.	Sarah Frances Mount	19 Oct 1846
Hanson C.	Rachel A. Shipley	1 Nov 1847
James	Rachel Hopkins	2 May 1801
James F.	Fannie E. Leishear	25 Mar 1867
John H.	Mary F. Andrew	1 Jan 1883 w
John W.	Mira C. Magruder	15 Feb 1831
John W.	Cecilia B. Scott	19 Oct 1896 w
Joseph	Mildred Thompson	10 Mar 1814
Joseph	Mary Ann Talbott	10 Mar 1823
Joseph	Charlotte Knott	22 Jan 1845
Joseph	Ann V. Sprigg	28 Nov 1867
Kitty Anne	Edward A. Gantt	2 Oct 1827
Laura V.	Thomas O. Smith	18 Jan 1847
Lucinda B.	George Bibb Brown	18 Nov 1895 w
Margarett	James Parsley	28 Sep 1808
Martha L.	Joshua Brown	22 Nov 1860
Mary	Zach Thompson	12 Sep 1822
Mary E.	Charles B. Rozer	29 Dec 1882 w
Mary Ellen	William H. Howser	30 Nov 1876
Mary Louisa	Nicholas D. Offutt	24 Sep 1867
Minerva S.	James H. Brown	29 Sep 1857
Nathan	Lizzie Shedrick	16 May 1893 c
Polly	John Ray	30 Jan 1822
Robert	Margaret Hamilton	14 Mar 1879 c
Robert H.	Amanda L. Bowie	7 Nov 1877 c
Robert T.	Rose V. Curtis	4 Dec 1884 w
Rosa	Richard H. Williams	14 Nov 1864
S. E.	Nicholas Worthington	18 Oct 1847
Sarah Ann	Otho H. Duvall	20 Mar 1847
Sarah Ellen	Thomas S. Nicholls	29 Jul 1846
Sophronia	Joseph F. Williams	22 Oct 1874
Stephen	Mary Ann Noland	24 Dec 1824
Stephen	Rebecca Brown	28 Oct 1845
Stephen H.	Sarah A. Boswell	18 Oct 1871
Susan	Joseph Cephas	31 Oct 1873
Thomas	Mary J. Hurley	13 Apr 1850
Thomas	Martha Wootton	7 Feb 1873
Thomas	Ella Darne	18 Apr 1887 w
William Alonzo	Corrilla J. Byrne	27 Jan 1891 w
ANDREW, Mary F.	John H. Anderson	1 Jan 1883 w

ANDREWS,	Charles	Acka Thompson	13 Sep 1824
	Christopher	Henrietta Webb	12 Apr 1814
	Elizabeth	Isaiah Phelps	10 May 1800
	Frank	Josephine Davis	24 Aug 1898 w
	George M.	Emily A. Hawkins	3 Jun 1889 w
	Ida E.	George W.B. Turner	21 Jan 1890 w
	James*	Mary Cecil	5 Mar 1822
	James	Marion G. Macgill	7 Oct 1845
	James	Ellen Shipley	16 Sep 1847
	James T.	Minnie Perkins	19 Apr 1888 w
	John	Martha Bennet	21 May 1862
	Lydia E.	James A. S. Nichollson	10 Jan 1848
	Margaret E.	Edward Thomas Keith	20 Jan 1869
	Martha	William D. Welling	6 May 1871
	Mary	John Flood	13 Mar 1820
	Mary G.	William M. Newman	12 Mar 1896 w
	Mary P.	Jacob Pickens	19 Apr 1865
	Samuel C.	Caroline R. Keith	26 Aug 1858
	Sarah	Edward Phelps	25 Apr 1807
	William	Verlinda Peters	25 Feb 1813
ANGEL,	Thomas	Mary C. Earp	30 Sep 1857
APPLEBY,	A. O.	Mary J. Cashell	5 Nov 1870
	Florence M.	William T. Thomspon	** Feb 1879 w
	Frances C.	Richard C. Carlisle	5 Jan 1870
	George W.	Mary A. Dove	10 Apr 1851
	Harriet A.	Thomas L. Phillips	19 Jan 1859
	Harriett	Westly Burdett	6 Jun 1816
	Ida May	John L. Best	22 Apr 1893 w
	James B.	Maggie E. Leaman	29 Oct 1877 w
	James C.	Susanna R. Leaman	31 Jan 1850
	Levi T.	Sarah A. Lizier	10 Jan 1857
	Lula M.	Willoughby Santman	12 Sep 1895 w
	Maria	John Richerd	30 Mar 1835
	Mary	John Leaman	21 Oct 1818
	Mary J.	Rufus E. G. Hilton	20 Mar 1877 w
	Nicholas W.	Mary W. Fitch	26 Feb 1856
	Phares	Thomas L. Case	17 Jan 1814
	Rufus H.	Martha A. Bennett	6 Nov 1854
	Samuel	Elizabeth Lemmon	12 Dec 1821
	Sarah	Brice Lowry	28 Jan 1799
	Sarah	Henry H. Brown	17 Feb 1835
	Susen M.	Robert H. Leamon	28 Mar 1860
	W. C.	Mollie Ball	14 Jan 1882 w
	Walter	Deborah Watkins	10 Mar 1827
	Washington	Tabitha Mockbee	7 Nov 1827
	William L. G.	Augusta Anderson	27 Sep 1875
APSEY,	George	Ann C. D. Swann	17 Feb 1829
	George	Mary J. Swann	15 Oct 1832
	Jacob	Mary Poole	24 Jan 1835
ARCHBOLD,	James	Elizabeth Penn	18 Apr 1817
ARCHER,	Adele T.	Arthur C. Small	14 Sep 1898w
	Ann	Lafayette Lunsford	24 Jan 1883 w
ARCHY,	James	Ruth Jones	28 Dec 1803

* Both last names are written over; look like the above
** The day has a blot on it; is either 25 or 26

ARGENT, Samuel J.	Jennie Wilkerson	25 May 1892 w
ARMIGER, John W.	Rosa M. Crawford	6 Apr 1897
ARMSTEAD - also see ORMSTEAD		
ARMSTEAD, Amanda	Richard P. Budd	28 Nov 1887 c
ARMSTRONG, Annie I.	R. Lee Horten	29 Jun 1898 w
Clara E.	Henry T. Harvey	4 Feb 1889 w
ARNOLD, Andrew B.	Emma A. Wade	28 Dec 1891 w
Andrew J.	Sarah M. Smith	2 Aug 1856
D. W.	Mattie E. Duley	14 Jul 1869
Elizabeth H.	George W. Oden	3 Jan 1852
Henry	Elizabeth Oden	11 Nov 1826
James	Sidney Johnson (female)	29 Dec 1870
Julia	Samuel T. Mobley	18 Aug 1853
Lucinda	Uriah Majors	22 Dec 1879 w
Malinda	Thomas McDonnough	27 Feb 1860
Mary Catharine	Samuel Phillips	27 Feb 1860
Nettie	Robert Taylor	1 Mar 1893 w
Richard H.	Henrietta Norris	10 Jan 1866
Sarah J.	William W. Washburn	26 Mar 1867
Teresa J.	Nicholas E. Selby	24 Apr 1897 w
Thomas	Mary Frazer	26 Oct 1798
ARTHUR, Annie	Wesley Coleman	4 Jun 1889 c
Charles E.	Nora L. Beans	5 Sep 1884
Mary	Frederick D. Simms	8 Oct 1898 c
ARTIS, Stephen	Eleanor Walker	15 Dec 1829
ARTIST, Anne	Justice Ridgeway	7 Aug 1798
ARUNDELL, Mahala	James Wiley	16 Jan 1840
ARVIN - also see IRVIN		
ARVIN, John	Elizabeth Duvall	18 Feb 1799
ASHBURN, Jerry S.	Alma R. Knowles	6 Sep 1892 w
ASHBY, Lilly	Henry J. Norris	1 Mar 1898 w
Margaret E.	Marshall Miller	31 Jan 1889 w
ASHLEY, Henry C.	Mary E. Padgett	29 May 1878 w
ASHTON, Becra	Rachel Perry	23 Nov 1798
Helen W.	James W. Brown	30 May 1898 w
John E.	Roberta Corn	23 Nov 1885 c
John W.	Susie E. Lawson	17 Mar 1884 w
Mary R.	George A. Dyer	24 Apr 1854
ASKEN, John M.	Susannah Beall	6 Dec 1827
ASKINS, Alex	Sarah Linn	24 Aug 1871
George	Mary Bacon	3 Jan 1888 c
George W.	Frances Carter	2 Feb 1891 c
George Washington	Mariah Dorsey	11 Dec 1886 c
Isabella S.	Julian Diggs	13 Jan 1874
Robert	Susie C. Nucey	21 Feb 1895 c
ASLIN - also see HASLIN		
ASLIN, Daniel	Carey Etcherson	30 Sep 1812
ASTLEN, Joseph	Rachel Chiswell	12 Dec 1798
ASTLIN, George R.	Mary Mildred Matthews	* Apr 1879
Richard B.	Eliza Ann Hinton	5 May 1838
Sarah E.	Richard H. Lowe	22 Dec 1865
ASLUN, Charles	Susan Snowden	18 Mar 1869
ATCHERSON - also see ATCHESON, ATCHISON, ETCHISON, ETCHERSON		
ATCHERSON, Ann	Thomas Sedgwick	20 Feb 1799

* Day too light to read; between 14 and 21

ATCHERSON, John	Sylvia Perkins	16 Jan 1800
ATCHESON, Elisha	Elizabeth Simpson	15 Dec 1801
ATCHISON, Ephraim	Ruth Simpson	11 Sep 1800
ATHEY, Annie E.	Willaim H. Miles	2 Sep 1886 w
George B. McClellan	Rebecca Norris	11 Jun 1884 w
ATSTERE, Teresa	Christian Hafner	23 Feb 1860
ATWELL, Samuel T.	Laura F. Kirby	9 May 1889 w
Thomas	Eleanor Wathan	24 May 1800
ATWOOD, Ann E.	Benjamin Thompson	7 Jan 1833
Annie L.	Henry C. James	25 Sep 1889 w
George P.	Anne Clements	5 Nov 1813
James T.	Pearlie J. Howser	18 Dec 1890 w
AUD, William T.	Susan Ann Veirs	31 Jul 1862
AUGUSTUS, Charley	Mary Dates	5 Nov 1874
AULT, Charles F.	Mary J. McKenney	17 Mar 1871
John W.	Susan A. McKenney	18 Jun 1863
AUSTIN, Ann	Israel Case	30 Dec 1830
Brooke	Rachael Benton	28 Nov 1815
Cassander	John B. Lewis	5 Feb 1821
Eleanor	Patrick Connelly	28 Jan 1804
Guy F.	Martha Yost	15 Apr 1834
James M.	Margarett West	15 Feb 1831
James W.	Lucy V. Byrne	28 Jun 1892 w
John	Cassandra Odle	13 Feb 1799
John H.	Hetty Knott	22 Nov 1827
John H.	Louisa Knott	21 Sep 1840
John H.	Jeratia Ann Rabbitt	23 Aug 1846
Jonas	Ann Hoggins	15 Jan 1799
M. H.	Lizzie Rawlins	10 Nov 1864
Mahlon R.	Mamie C. Beatty	18 Dec 1888 w
Milly Ann	John Boswell	22 Dec 1812
Prissilla	Frederick Golden	29 Nov 1810
Stacey	Edward Cooley	19 Feb 1828
Stephen R.	Mary E. Wade	22 Jan 1878 w
Tabitha	George Braddock	1 Sep 1840
Virgnia	Theophilus Talbott	27 Apr 1875
Virlinda	Daniel Beall	27 Nov 1804
William N.	Eleanor Busey	17 May 1847
William Nelson	Elizabeth Cushman	8 Apr 1818
William R.	Mary A. Nichols	14 Jan 1879 w
William W.	Rachel McCoy	11 Jan 1823
AUTHOR, William	Annie Fisher	27 Oct 1896 c
AVEY, Henry	Rebecca Livers	6 Jun 1832
AWKARD, Elijah	Ann Beall	23 Mar 1833*c
James Anna	Dennis W. Lee	16 Oct 1894 c
Jerry P.	Sarah E. Holt	29 Feb 1892 c
AWKWARD, Eliza	Archie M. Hopkins	9 May 1889 c
Jeremiah	Frances Mason	22 Oct 1855
Mary	William Lewis	8 Aug 1866
Robert	Caroline Thomas	2 Nov 1858
Robert	Annie Holland	19 May 1890 c
Rosie	Augustus S. Hill	20 Oct 1892 c
Sarah A.	Singleton H. Billows	20 Jun 1878 c

* This entry reads "coloured free persons"

AYLER, Annie P.	William W. Jones	16 Apr 1889	
AYLMER, James R.	Kate J. Robinson	11 Jul 1885	
AYRES - also see AIRESS			
AYRES, Susan	William A. Holland	8 Nov 1867	
William J.	Margaret V. Sisson	15 Dec 1893	w
AYTON, Beale	Eleanor Redman	20 Jun 1803	
E. Victoria	Z. Windsor Kessler	6 Feb 1866	
Edward M.	Eleanor R. Ayton	24 Dec 1833	
Eleanor E.	Edward Hughes	5 Jul 1813	
Eleanor R.	Edward M. Ayton	24 Dec 1833	
Ellen R.	David L. Pugh	10 Dec 1844	
Ephraim B. G.	Lydia Allnutt	3 Jul 1839	
Ephraim G.	Laura V. Fisher	9 May 1881	
James E.	Frances E. King	11 Nov 1870	
Jane	Gabriel G. Vanhorn	23 Jul 1803	
John S.	Elizabeth E. Burriss	29 Aug 1870	
Samuel	Anne Howard	26 Feb 1802	
Warnetta A.	J. W. Wallich	25 Sep 1877	w
BACHERS, Tilghman	Catharine Lee	30 Nov 1870	
BACKET - also see BECKETT			
BACKET, Alexander	Bertie Tyler	24 Apr 1894	c
BACKHANON, Fenton	Annie Hull	31 Aug 1878	c
BACON -also see BAKON, BAKEN, BAKIN			
BACON, Charles	Rosie Walker	14 May 1885	c
Georgiana	Franklin W. Murphy	3 Feb 1890	c
John	Caroline Inconie	30 Aug 1867	
John	Mary Scott	27 Dec 1883	c
Martha	Horace T. Pumphrey	8 Apr 1880	
Mary	George Askins	3 Jan 1888	c
Newman	Susannah Madden	26 Jan 1824	
Samuel	Josephine Prettyman	5 Nov 1879	c
Sofie	John White	13 Nov 1878	
BADGER, O. C.	Margaret Johnston	27 Oct 1852	
BAGBY, Richard	Daisy V. Price	2 Jun 1896	w
BAGEOT, Lily	Robert B. Reeves	13 Aug 1890	w
BAGGERLY - also see BEGGARLY			
BAGGERLY, James	Elizabeth Smith	17 Oct 1798	
BAGIN, Emma J.	James E. Whalen	2 Jan 1879	w
BAGON, Rose	Robert L. Weber	19 Jan 1897	w
BAILER, Mira	Wesley J. Green	10 Mar 1870	
BAILEY - also see BAILY, BALEY, BALLY, BAYLEY			
BAILEY, Addie E.	George R. McMannus	10 Jun 1890	w
Charles	Nellie Copeland	16 Aug 1890	c
Cora	Joseph W. Chase	22 May 1895	c
Irene	Thomas W. Entwistle	5 Nov 1867	
Joseph T.	Jane L. Noland	21 Feb 1843	
Joseph T. Jr.	Attelia Clagett	2 May 1871	
Nicholas	Rachel Fitzgerald	23 Sep 1809	
Oregeri V.	Thomas H. Lynch	27 Oct 1869	
Stephen	Lucinda Maria Willson	2 Dec 1845	
Thomas N.	Kate Lyddane	17 Jan 1895	w
Walter	Sarah Beall	29 Nov 1804	
Walter	Millie Young	20 Sep 1882	c
Zachariah	Susannah Lizier	1 Mar 1808	
BAILY, Isaac	Lucy Douglass	27 Dec 1873	

BAILY, Mary	Raife Branison	12 Nov 1872	
BAIRD, Lydia A.	Francis Barnes	30 Apr 1898	w
BAKEN - also see BACON			
BAKEN, Allen - see Allen Baker			
BAKEN, Samuel T.	Rebecca Miles	5 Nov 1896	c
BAKER, Adam	Sophia Williams	* Jun 1877	c
Alice C.	W. H. Boroughs	20 Aug 1879	
Allen**	Jane Bowie	9 Nov 1882	c
Ann	Amon Bowman	13 Jan 1825	
Annie A.	Jacob J. Kemp	5 Dec 1882	w
Benjamin	Sophia Crown	9 Jan 1834	
Catharine	James W. Davis	24 Dec 1863	
Catherine E.	William W. Magruder	1 Mar 1860	
Charles H.	Catharine V. Cissell	20 Mar 1850	
Clara L.	Charles Carter	4 Oct 1887	c
Cordelia	Adam Royer	1 Jan 1812	
Delia	Joseph Duvall	13 Nov 1897	c
Edward	Harriet A. Hays	11 Sep 1874	
Edward C.	Sarah Earpe	24 Sep 1864	
Eliza A.	George A. Beall	21 Feb 1870	
Eliza E.	James A. Thompson	18 Jul 1878	w
Elizabeth	John T. Baker	7 Mar 1843	
Elizabeth A.	Thomas Rabbitt	19 Nov 1846	
Enoch	Sarah Hurley	17 Nov 1825	
Harriet	Joshua Spurrier	19 Feb 1799	
Henry T.	Mary M. Cook	27 Apr 1882	
Isaac H.	Anne E. Wilburn	25 Sep 1871	
J. M.	Caroline Cashell	8 May 1875	
James	Sarah Rhodes	2 Nov 1875	
James	Ida Carroll	30 Jan 1896	c
James A.	Ida V. Harding	18 Dec 1897	w
John	Elizabeth Brashears	24 Dec 1801	
John	Mary C. Miles	3 Apr 1852	
John E.	Rebecca Rabbitt	29 Jul 1847	
John George	Amelia Jackson	21 Mar 1799	
John H.	Eliza Colston	27 Feb 1883	
John H.	Mollie Johnson	29 Oct 1891	c
John M.	Rosalie H. Lewis	27 Oct 1897	w
John T.	Elizabeth Baker	7 Mar 1843	
John W.	Elizabeth Ricketts	8 Jan 1824	
John W.	Mary Ann Burdett	26 Apr 1865	
Jonathan	Keziah Penn	14 Dec 1858	
Kate L.	Luther W. Charlton	14 Jan 1886	w
Kitty	John Price	1 Nov 1879	c
Laura	James F. Braddock	3 May 1866	
Laura	William F. Lazenby	24 Feb 1868	
Laura V.	James Crawford	16 Sep 1879	
Leanna	Edward T. Ricketts	30 Mar 1875	
Louisa N.	Jesse L. Burns	20 Sep 1876	
Levy	Catharine Sears	30 Mar 1815	
Lydia A.	James F. Marshall	17 Jun 1885	c
Margaret E. T.	James L. West	21 Jun 1855	
Margarett	James R. Lewis	20 Dec 1827	

* Day has blot on it; between 12 and 27
** This could be Allen Baken

BAKER,	Maria Isabella	William Stewart	18 May 1892 c
	Martha	Nathan B. Mullican	27 Jan 1841
	Martha E.	William H. Downs	6 May 1868
	Martha V.	Richard Parsley	25 Apr 1844
	Mary	Evan Bowman	24 Dec 1827
	Mary E.	Elias P. Soper	12 Apr 1859
	Mary Elizabeth	Hezekiah Metz	15 Dec 1841
	Mary G.	Robert H. Burnell	29 Jun 1896 w
	Mary J.	William Henry Stewart	6 Jun 1876
	Matilda	Basil Beall	20 Feb 1834
	Octavius O.	Sallie M. Johnson	14 Oct 1880
	Ollie C.	Florence E. Waters	15 Jun 1896 w
	Reuben	Elizabeth Beall	22 Dec 1819
	Reuben	Susan Shaw	31 Dec 1839
	Reuben A.	Laura Bevan	20 Aug 1861
	Reuben T.	Mary F. Belt	2 Feb 1886 w
	Rufus F.	Emma E. Kemp	17 Dec 1889 w
	Samuel	Elizabeth Barnes	24 Feb 1819
	Sarah	William Mount	3 Aug 1831
	Sarah Ann	Hezekiah Trail	14 Dec 1841
	Sarah E.	William M. Glaze	5 May 1891 w
	Thomas P.	Mary A. C. Chambers	4 Sep 1833
	Tyson B.	Edith Sullivan	7 Sep 1881 w
	William	Elizabeth Parsley	23 Apr 1800
	William	Elizabeth Robertson	28 Feb 1824
	William	Rachel A. Rabbitt	7 Aug 1855
	William A.	Mary R. Brown	8 Feb 1888 w
	William E.	Mary Ann Selby	21 Jul 1848
	William L.	Mary E. Rabbitt	3 Sep 1872
	Zachariah	Sarah Beall	25 Jan 1823
BAKIN - also see BACON			
BAKIN,	Samuel	Elizabeth A. Bell	4 Mar 1875
BAKON,	Luvinia J.	John W. Dorsey	8 Jan 1896 c
BALDWIN,	Susan R.	Allen Reed	10 Sep 1869
	William D.	Maria Bache Abert	2 Aug 1884 w
BALEY - also see BAILEY			
BALEY,	John S.	Lydia Hicks	10 Sep 1832
BALL,	Amanda	Josephus Hardy	15 Feb 1858
	Andrew F.	Sarah L. Jackson	8 Apr 1867
	Anne	William O'Neale	6 May 1804
	Bertha L.	Edgar R. Perry	27 Apr 1891 w
	Cassandra V.	William Thomas Fisher	26 Jan 1854
	Clem	Blanche Creamer	21 Jan 1895 w
	Daniel	Elizabeth Carroll	5 Feb 1799
	Eleanor	Samuel Tarman	15 Dec 1829
	Eliza A.	Richard Collins	8 Jan 1851
	Elizabeth	John Crown	1 Dec 1803
	Elizabeth A.	Osborn S. Willson, Jr.	28 Feb 1854
	George W.	Jetta Ricks	14 Nov 1876
	Henry	Susan Ball	14 Sep 1808
	Hilleary	Matilda Riggs	7 May 1822
	James R.	Annie L. Schiller	26 Oct 1896 w
	Joanna	Zachariah Bogely	10 Mar 1821
	John	Delyla Medley	9 Feb 1828
	John L.	Cora Perry	15 Nov 1898 w
	John S.	Eletha Riggs	15 Feb 1831

BALL, Laura J.	Claude O. Cooley	26 Oct 1896	w
Laurence	Cassandra Spates	5 May 1814	
Laurence	Eliza Willson	13 Jan 1824	
Lavenia C.	Robert A. Magruder	1 Mar 1858	
Lewis H.	Ellen Robinson	21 Mar 1840	
Mary	Thomas Whalan	17 Oct 1816	
Mary Catherine	Thomas H. Rabbitt	15 Apr 1841	
Mary Ellen	Jesse Hyatt	3 Sep 1845	
Mollie	W. C. Appleby	14 Jan 1882	w
Priscilla	Charles Shook	27 Feb 1805	
Richard Lewis	Rachel Jackson Lahy	20 Feb 1850	
Susan	Henry Ball	14 Sep 1808	
Turner*	Lethana Seares	12 Jan 1818	
William	Ann Harry	24 Dec 1816	
BALLY - also see BAILEY			
BALLY, Jesse	Leanah Cole	12 Jul 1812	
BALTIMORE, Lucinda	Nathan R. Cromwell	21 Jul 1879	
BALTZER, George	Susan Webb	28 Dec 1808	
BANE, Howard K.	Mary A. Murray	24 Jun 1896	w
BANK, Susanna Brooke**	John Markham	14 Jan 1804	
BANKS, Thomas O.	Mary A. Crawford	30 Jan 1888	w
BARBER, Ann	Edward Willett	28 Oct 1813	
Charles H.	Nora Watkins	6 Apr 1898	w
Courtney	Samuel Shipley	22 Jan 1814	
Edward H.	Mary E. Burriss	21 Dec 1888	w
Greenberry E.	Sarah E. Beall	19 Feb 1858	
Greenberry E.	Cora C. Bowman	17 Dec 1891	w
Hezekiah	Nancy Williams	8 Dec 1831	
Hezekiah	Ruth Ann Campbell	23 Apr 1875	
James	Mary E. Barber	27 Feb 1873	
Lewis	Jamima Summers	19 Jun 1821	
Lewis	Mary Saffell	16 Feb 1831	
Lewis	Henrietta Mason	29 Jun 1878	
Margaret E.	George N. Beall	24 Nov 1856	
Matilda	John Fowler	26 Dec 1814	
Mary E.	James Barber	27 Feb 1873	
Rachel A.	William S. Sheckles	20 Feb 1866	
Rezin	Eleanor Williams	7 Jun 1832	
William	Mary Hudson	22 Oct 1817	
Zadok	Miranda Gue	22 May 1835	
BARCLAY, Sally	Singleton Ricketts	22 Aug 1805	
BARGUS, Ida V.	John M. Ricks	15 Dec 1897	c
BARKER, Eliza	James Coleman	6 Dec 1826	
John H.	Julia A. Lazenby	7 Dec 1863	
Gertrude A.	Snowden Southerland	5 Jul 1898	w
BARKS, Malcolm	Anna Turner	30 Oct 1878	
BARLOW, James	Keziah Davis	3 Mar 1801	
BARNARD, William E.	Alverda Thomas	16 Nov 1887	w
BARNECLO, Elizabeth Emily	John Thomas Caho	1 Jun 1829	
John M.	Eliza H. Edmonstone	16 Sep 1834	
William H.	Elizabeth L. Bean	22 Aug 1839	
BARNECLOW, Andrew	Delilah Trundle	21 Jan 1807	

* His last name and her first name from earlier reading
** Part of last name from earlier reading

BARNES - also see BARNS

BARNES, Abraham	Margarett St. Claire Patterson	28 Nov 1831	
Alexander	Henrietta Storridge	13 Jan 1877	
Amanda	Charles Collinsgrue	21 Sep 1858	
Benjamin	Susannah Jones	17 Apr 1802	
Bettie	Sloter Bishop	31 Oct 1895	c
Catharina M.	John A. Schlenther	28 Oct 1895	w
Clement	Harriet Cooley	4 Jan 1888	c
Daniel G.	Lucy C. Roberson	19 May 1896	c
Daniel W.	Hattie Day	23 May 1890	w
Eleanora	Hanson Gittings	26 Dec 1883	c
Eliza	Isaac Bruner	12 Apr 1898	c
Elizabeth	Samuel Baker	24 Feb 1819	
Francis	Lydia A. Baird	30 Apr 1898	w
Gainor M.	Thomas B. Linkins	14 Nov 1866	
George F.	Johanna A. Joy	6 Jun 1896	w
Henry C.	Cornelia Marlow	8 Feb 1881	
Henry C.	Ella Gross	16 Dec 1890	c
Jane	Charles H. Folwell	13 Mar 1873	
John	Milly Bassford	4 Sep 1799	
John	Polly Fling	8 Apr 1809	
Jonathan	Nettie W. Walter	13 Nov 1894	w
Patience	Eli Poole	5 Mar 1825	
Ruth	John Soper	10 Jun 1800	
Thomas	Elizabeth Fenwick	22 May 1800	

BARNESLEY - also see BARNSLEY, BARNESLY

BARNESLEY, Elizabeth C.	Thomas Barnesley	19 Feb 1851	
George	Deborah Holland	3 Feb 1812	
John J.	Juliet A. Price	22 Feb 1843	
Thomas	Elizabeth C. Barnesley	19 Feb 1851	
BARNESLY, James	Susan Gaither	5 Oct 1838	
Mary E.	Reuben W. Young	29 Dec 1883	w
Moses	Elizabeth Duley	17 Mar 1812	

BARNETT - also see BURNETT

BARNETT, Charles S.	Laura Gesford	31 Jul 1888	w
Eleanor*	John Miller	14 Apr 1798	
Solomon	Verlinda Lanham	6 Nov 1812	
William H.	Emma Long	12 May 1896	w
BARNETTE, Fannie T.	Frank J. Fidler	19 Sep 1881	w
BARNHOUSE, Ellen H.	Raphael T. Jarboe	6 Nov 1893	w
Sidney	Mary Lusette C. Smith	23 Dec 1864	
BARNITZ, Richard H.	Leona S. West	11 Aug 1884	

BARNS - also see BARNES

BARNS, John T.	Martha E. Trucks	19 Jan 1855	
Mary C.	James F. Fedeline	7 Jan 1859	

BARNSLEY - also see BARNESLEY, BARNESLY

BARNSLEY, Ellen T.	Richard Torpin, Jr.	15 Feb 1897	w
George T.	Susa G. Jones	10 Jun 1890	w
James N.	Carrie E. Cashell	26 Nov 1881	
Jonathan D.	Mary E. Owens	16 May 1864	
Kate	George C. Cashell	12 Feb 1866	
Lewis R. W.	Evie V. Bell	9 Nov 1897	w
Mary E.	Josiah W. Jones	30 May 1864	

* Could be Barrett

BARNSKEY, Samuel G.	Laura Umstead	16 Oct 1877	w
BARRATT, Catharine	Ludowick Young	27 Dec 1817	
BARRETT, Andrew J.	Luretta Simms	3 Jan 1840	
Benjamin	Elizabeth Beckwith	17 Dec 1846	
Cassandra	Walter Semmes	12 Nov 1804	
Darkey	John Jacobs	22 Dec 1802	
Eleanor - see Eleanor Barnett			
Elizabeth	William Clarke	29 Jan 1806	
Honora	John McMahen	7 Aug 1883	
Lewis	Anne Carr	27 May 1816	
Lewis	Jemima Robey	25 Sep 1869	
Margaret Ann	John W. Radcliff	18 Mar 1846	
Mary	Francis Brown	30 Dec 1805	
Mary	William Swann	19 Apr 1815	
Mary Ann	Nicholas Lyddane	7 Feb 1831	
Rebecca	John Rabbett	5 Jan 1808	
Richard	Ann Bonnifield	14 Oct 1820	
Richard	Martha Redman	22 Oct 1840	
Ruth	James Connell	13 Feb 1817	
Samuel	Elizabeth Jarboe	21 Aug 1815	
Sarah	William H. H. Brown	10 Aug 1898	c
Susie E.	Wilton Robey	17 Dec 1878	w
BARRICK, Roderick A.	Addie E. Getzendanner	10 May 1881	
BARRON, Albert W.	Nettie H. Lauxmann	20 Aug 1885	w
Henry C.	Mary V. Clements	24 Nov 1887	w
William H.	Sarah C. Zeigler	13 May 1873	
BARRY - also see BERRY			
BARRY, Basil	Martha W. Magruder	25 Oct 1830	
David	Eliza Coote	20 Mar 1833	
Jacob	Elizabeth Orme	2 Apr 1828	
BARTELMES, Mary C.	Charles I. Webster	2 Mar 1895	w
BARTHLOW, Elizabeth	William Reid	28 Dec 1808	
BARTHOLOMEW, Mary E.	William Erhart	12 Mar 1892	w
BARTOLETTE, Sarah L.	James G. Boss	13 Aug 1878	w
BARTON, Elizabeth	Thomas Walter	16 Jul 1828	
BARWISE, Thomas H.	Harriet E. Vinson	29 Nov 1856	
BASEMAN, Ernest	Minnie Young	17 Feb 1888	w
BASFORD - also see BASSFORD			
BASFORD, Alfred	Eleanor Smith	12 Feb 1824	
Alice	John L. Burch	23 Feb 1876	
Cordeny	Asa Nicholson	9 Sep 1813	
John	Jane Welling	4 Apr 1827	
BASIL, Elizabeth	Perry G. Bowman	24 Aug 1876	
BASSFORD - also see BASFORD			
BASSFORD, Alfred	Matilda Larman	29 May 1818	
Eleanor	John Peters	2 Aug 1813	
Milly	John Barnes	4 Sep 1799	
BAST, Charles L.	Mary Degnin	13 Feb 1882	
BASTEN, Laura	Frederick A. Finacom	21 Oct 1891	w
BATCHELOR, Charles	Mary Ann Taylor	28 Feb 1859	
Lizzie L.	William H. Rapley	9 Nov 1885	
Lucretia	Edgar P. Watkins	22 Apr 1878	w
Mary	J. C. Lay	5 Feb 1868	
BATEMAN, Joseph F.	Alice G. Allen	14 Apr 1868	
BATES, Charles Mason	Helen N. Burgess	12 Nov 1892	w
Polly	Upton King	13 Dec 1817	

BATH, William	Mary Johnson	11 Apr 1804
BATTEY - also see BEATTY		
BATTEY, James Collinson	Elizabeth Reynolds	26 Sep 1846
BATSON, Maria	Claibron Lang	13 Aug 1828
BATTIS - also see BETTUS		
BATTIS, Frances	John Rozier	26 Dec 1873
BAUGHER, Sallie F.	John W. Stearn	12 Jan 1887 w
BAUGHMAN, Hattie S.	Louis A. Schwartzbeck	1 Jul 1893 w
BAULLAUF, Louisa	Charles D. Boland	16 Jun 1881 w
BAUSE, Frederick William	Marian G. Johns	3 Nov 1884 w
BAXTER, Andrew J.	Fanny Metzgar	4 Jan 1863
Frank S.	Mary B. Klug	7 May 1895 w
BAYLEY - also see BAILEY		
BAYLEY, James	Drusilla Leasure	11 Aug 1806
BEALE, George W.	Mary A. Bouic	3 Dec 1879 w
BEALL - also see BELL, BEALLE		
BEALL, Ada	Charles H. McNaughton	4 Apr 1865
Adam	Eleanora Fyffe	20 Feb 1828
Agnes	Charles King	10 May 1826
Alexander	Crecilla Harvy	12 Dec 1799
Amos	Tabathy O'Brian	14 Dec 1802
Angeline R.	Claiborne H. Mannar, Jr.	10 Feb 1892 w
Ann	John Wilmington	4 Apr 1816
Ann	John B. Browning	17 Jan 1831
Ann	Elijah Awkard	25 Mar 1833*c
Anne Maria	John Adams	1 Feb 1866
Annie M. V.	James T. Brown	20 Jan 1873
Avory C.	Sarah Ann Stone	21 Jun 1841
Basil	Anne Jourdan	13 Dec 1801
Basil	Matilda Mark	20 Feb 1819
Basil	Matilda Baker	20 Feb 1834
Basil D.	Elizabeth Townsend	14 Oct 1806
Basil M.	Verlinder Wright	17 Apr 1850
Benjamin	Ann Jarboe	7 Dec 1816
Benjamin	Susan Ann Connelly	2 Dec 1845
Cecilia E.	Charles H. Vinson	21 Apr 1865
Charity	Thomas Lanham	10 Jan 1803
Charles	Sarah Orme	2 Feb 1816
Charles	Charlott White	10 Oct 1818
Charles A.	Catherine Perry	9 May 1864
Cornelius W.	Lucy Conner	19 Aug 1874
Daniel	Virlinda Austin	27 Nov 1804
Daniel	Fannie Wotons	4 Aug 1891 w
Deborah	Basil Roby	13 Dec 1832
Eden	Matilda Perry	19 Jan 1813
Eden	Priscilla P. Beall	25 May 1830
Edmund D.	Annie E. Davis	22 Apr 1891
Edward T.	Imogene Poole	9 Nov 1897 w
Effy I.	Jacob C. Norwood	12 Jan 1892 w
Elbridge W.	Annie E. Hager	23 Dec 1897 w
Eleanor	William T. Beall	30 Jan 1799
Eleanor	Robert Jones	18 Aug 1812
Elema (male)	Leonary Marbury Beall	17 May 1831
Eleven	Katie Hutchinson	24 Aug 1872

* Entry reads "coloured free persons"

BEALL,	Elias	Ida Pyles	9 Nov 1880
	Elisha	Lethe Ann Lewis	12 Dec 1823
	Eliza	John Mines	26 Mar 1822
	Elizabeth	Richard Turner	10 Jan 1799
	Elizabeth	Richard Lewis	1 Feb 1799
	Elizabeth	Henry Winrod	24 Feb 1819
	Elizabeth	Reuben Baker	22 Dec 1819
	Elizabeth C.	James Stephenson	4 May 1835
	Elizabeth C.	William H. Vinson	14 Sep 1848
	Elizabeth E.	Thomas Hall	30 Dec 1848
	Ella E.	Otto C. Meem	21 Feb 1876
	Ella V.	George Miles	17 Oct 1877 w
	Ellen	Charles Johnson	29 Sep 1879 c
	Ellmaria	John R. Champayne	28 Feb 1854
	Ellvira M.	James H. Miles	30 Dec 1830
	Ely	Octava Owen (female)	5 Jun 1802
	Emeline B.	Richard H. Jones	16 Jun 1833
	Emory M.	Margaret Piles	9 Jan 1832
	Fannie M.	George Miles	10 Jan 1882
	Frances R.	John E. Clagett	2 Nov 1886 w
	Francis	Sarah Shaw	25 Nov 1806
	Francis L.	Amanda M. M. Peddicord	13 Sep 1850
	George A.	Eliza A. Baker	21 Feb 1870
	George N.	Margaret E. Barber	24 Nov 1856
	George W.	Mary Ellen Willson	9 Sep 1875
	George W.	Savannah E. Brown	9 Nov 1885
	Grant	Lizzie Brooks	26 Dec 1888 c
	Harriet A.	Richard T. Burdett	19 Nov 1868
	Harriett	Jacob Green	25 Nov 1822*c
	Hattie E.	Gilbert D. Norwood	12 Jan 1892 w
	Hellen	William Stewart	22 May 1798
	Henry	Margarett Lanham	2 Oct 1815
	Hezekiah	Prissilla Keith	18 Nov 1811
	Hiram **	Elizabeth Roche**	26 Jan 1824
	Horatio	Evelina Offutt	2 Jun 1825
	Ida C.	John C. Owens	8 Jan 1895 c
	Isaiah F.	Elizabeth A. Cashell	15 Oct 1856
	James Alexander	Eleanor Culver	2 Jan 1804
	James H.	Susan C. Hoyle	14 Nov 1854
	James H.	Josephine R. Fenwick	4 Feb 1861
	James J.	Jennie Peter	5 Oct 1885 w
	James J.	Hattie A. Miller	28 Nov 1888 w
	James M.	Catharine V. Morrison	23 Dec 1873
	Jenny	Thomas Prather	22 Feb 1800
	John	Charlotte Jones	28 Dec 1807
	John H.	Louisa G. Darne	27 Jul 1825
	John Thomas	Mary Elizabeth Whiter	7 Sep 1868
	John W.	Catharine Rine	9 Sep 1831
	John William	Emily M. C. Cashell	4 Feb 1864
	Kitty	Lewis G. Burdett	14 May 1841
	Laura W.	American A. S. Day	7 Dec 1886 w
	Lavinia	Charles G. DuFief	18 Feb 1878 w

* Entry reads "colored and free"
** Insert in a different handwriting has been made after Hiram and another before Elizabeth; not clear enough to be read

BEALL, Leonary Marbury	Elema Beall	17 May 1831	
Lethey P.	Luther T. Beall	20 Jan 1887	w
Lewis	Eliza Wootton	9 Jul 1801	
Lizzie T.	Alfred C. Pigett	22 Jan 1884	w
Lloyd	Elizabeth Greentree	18 Nov 1812	
Lurecia	John Gartrell	26 Feb 1798	
Luther T.	Lethey P. Beall	20 Jan 1887	w
Margaret	John E. Selby	18 May 1820	
Margaret D.	Samuel Schissel	20 Jan 1825	
Margaret Jane	Thomas Stone	10 Apr 1844	
Margarett	Snowden Anchors	23 Feb 1814	
Margary	James Lazenby	18 Jan 1808	
Martha	Nathan Holland, Jr.	12 Dec 1798	
Martha	Henry Lizear	26 Apr 1815	
Mary	John B. Magruder	20 Dec 1803	
Mary	Cephas Lazenby	21 Jun 1803	
Mary Ann	Francis Gittings	4 Jul 1859	
Mary E.	Peter H. Clements	1 May 1848	
Mary J.	Charles W. Brady	11 Nov 1852	
Mary L.	Isaac T. Jones	26 Nov 1863	
Mary M.	Joshua L. Riggs	7 Jan 1889	w
Melvina	William H. Prather	23 Oct 1879	
Nathan	Ellen E. Edelen	2 Jun 1866	
Nathan F.	Marceline Burton	7 Nov 1867	
Nehemiah	Eleanor Palmore	2 Mar 1810	
Nelson	Verlinda Browning	27 Jun 1833	
Nettie F.	Joseph G. Watkins	17 Feb 1893	w
Otho	Emma Langster	8 Dec 1876	
Polly	Nathan Orme	21 Jan 1800	
Priscilla P.	Eden Beall	25 May 1830	
Rachel	Simon Gillispie	13 Aug 1817	
Richard	Katie Johnson	22 May 1883	c
Richard D.	Cecelia Darne	15 Feb 1831	
Rignald W.	Florenc Mae Grady	21 Jun 1895	w
Ruth Elizabeth	William F. Piles	11 Jun 1845	
Ruth M.	Simon D. Best	26 Dec 1891	w
Sabra	Joseph C. Duley	23 Apr 1811	
Sallie M.	Southey Carroll	21 Oct 1893	w
Samuel	Elizabeth W. Berry	26 Nov 1801	
Samuel M.	Mary Ann Candler	18 Jan 1826	
Sarah	Walter Bailey	29 Nov 1804	
Sarah	Gassaway Perry	9 Jan 1817	
Sarah	Zachariah Baker	25 Jan 1823	
Sarah	Richard M. Downes	19 Dec 1825	
Sarah A.	Charles I. Poole	8 Jan 1895	w
Sarah E.	Greenberry E. Barber	19 Feb 1858	
Sarah F.	George W. Hoyle	8 Nov 1877	w
Sarah M.	William R. Iglehart	22 Apr 1873	
Selea	Eden Benson	22 Jul 1819	
Shedereck	Jemima Brown	25 Sep 1822	
Susannah	John M. Asken	6 Dec 1827	
Teresa	Lloyd S. Jones	25 Jan 1836	
Thomas	Dorcas Beddo	22 Dec 1814	
Thomas	Mary K. Hedley	17 Jan 1822	
Thomas G.	Mary F. Burdette	12 Nov 1884	w
Thomas J.	Catherine G. Owen	4 Jan 1858	

BEALL, Tyson	Willey Beddo	31 Mar 1804	
Upton	Jane N. Robb	6 Dec 1810	
Verdie	Samuel Turley	25 Dec 1882	c
Verlinna	William H. Ward	28 Nov 1833	
William	Elizabeth Ray	12 Nov 1800	
William E.	Martha E. Merson	12 Oct 1895	w
William F.	Sarah E. Cross	4 Nov 1872	
William L.	Annie E. Shaw	19 Dec 1871	
William M.	Cassandra E. Burdett	29 Jul 1885	
William M.	Ida F. Newman	13 Apr 1887	w
William R.	Martha E. McAttee	20 Jul 1839	
William R.	Eliza C. West	25 Jan 1860	
William T.	Eleanor Beall	30 Jan 1799	
William V.	Mollie Purdum	27 Nov 1878	
Willietta	Julian Magruder	23 Nov 1895	w
Winfield S.	Melissa Moulden	26 Oct 1875	
BEALLE, Annie J.*	Samuel T. Grimes	19 Mar 1891	w
BEAMER, Lulie B.	Joseph M. Thompson	10 Aug 1895	w
BEAN - also see BEEN, BEANS, BEENS			
BEAN, Agnes	James Reed	6 Jan 1897	w
Annie C.	William E. Paxton	30 Apr 1872	
Basil T.	Mary A. Ricketts	6 Jan 1852	
Charles O.	Lelia E. Trevy	7 Mar 1888	w
Charlotte	Jacob Ricketts	14 Nov 1840	
Columbus G.	Effie Mullican	23 Feb 1897	w
Cornelius M.	Lucinda Thompson	17 Nov 1861	
Elizabeth L.	William H. Barneclo	22 Aug 1839	
Frances	Aaron Burress	14 Aug 1827	
Frances S.	James F. Gittings	5 Jan 1882	
George	Caroline A. Ricketts	22 Mar 1860	
George F.	Mary C. Kelly	9 Nov 1892	w
George H.	Mary J. Hamilton	5 Dec 1893	w
Henry T.	Georgianna B. Kelly	21 Dec 1888	w
Henry T.	Annie L. Johnson	10 Nov 1896	w
Ida E.	George H. Ricketts	27 Apr 1882	
James C.	Sallie E. Lewis	2 Mar 1891	w
James T.	Mary R. Mullinix	16 Dec 1889	w
Jane	Charles Stewart	28 Sep 1869	
John	Rachael Waters	5 Dec 1820	
John	Mary Ryan	4 Dec 1828	
John	Ann Reynold	1 Jan 1839	
John W.	Elizabeth V. Selby	3 Jun 1875	
John W.	Mary M. Lewis	11 Aug 1887	w
Josiah Jr.	Elenor Wilson	23 Oct 1801	
Leonard	Cassandra Thompson	1 Oct 1816	
Lethea	William Kisner	19 Feb 1827	
Lillie B.	Charles L. Ahalt	18 Feb 1888	w
Maggie D.	Lee Hutchinson	25 Feb 1891	w
Maggie J.	Louis M. Greaves	18 Aug 1876	
Mary	Edwin Wallace Chick	2 Jun 1886	w
Mary A.	John T. Crown	1 Jun 1871	
Mary C.	John R. Carey	24 Jul 1889	w
Mary Ann	Perry Trail	17 Nov 1846	
Mary Ellen	James English	26 Dec 1837	

* Last name could be Bealte

BEAN, Nancy	Isaac Ricketts	2 Feb 1837	
Prudence A.	George C. Patterson	18 Jul 1848	
Richard	Margaret V. Harriss	16 May 1861	
Richard B.	Mary G. Robertson	10 May 1882	w
Roberta E.	Albert Darcey	30 Oct 1894	w
Rosie B.	Harry Riley	5 Jul 1897	w
Serena A.	Zadok Ricketts	21 Jan 1862	
Sophronia J.	Jonathan Magruder	7 Sep 1880	
Treasa	Thomas Dean	14 Nov 1808	
William E.	Ada L. Burroughs	7 Apr 1887	w
William N.	Georgie A. Webster	25 Mar 1878	w
Windsor L.	Grace E. Thompson	2 Feb 1898	w
BEANDER, Archibald	Sarah Ellen Whims	18 Jul 1866	
Elijah	Henrietta Mason	24 Dec 1879	w
Ida E.	Frederick Dyson	28 Nov 1883	c
Jane	William Lee	23 Dec 1865	
John T.	Glendora Webster	13 Jan 1891	c
Martha	Samuel Lee	18 Sep 1878	c
Mary	Charles Johnson	19 May 1869	
Mary E.	William Thomas	17 May 1877	c
Rachel	Philip Johnson	26 Sep 1877	c
Samuel	Florence Hall	7 May 1887	c
BEANMAN, Mary E.	Thomas Stewart	4 Nov 1892	c
BEANS - also see BEAN, BEEN, BEENS			
BEANS, Nora L.	Charles E. Arthur	5 Sep 1884	
Tabatha	Joseph Gittings	11 Feb 1809	
Harriet	John Mullican	27 Dec 1818	
BEARD, Elizabeth	Lewis Knott	6 Jan 1806	
Harriet	Nathan L. Trail	13 Dec 1843	
Jacob	Matilda Lazier	21 Oct 1813	
John	Harriet Lyles	2 Feb 1815	
Mary	Joseph Haslin	21 Jul 1802	
Mary	Alexander E. Soper	20 Sep 1841	
Stephen	Mary Amo Gott	31 Jan 1879	w
William H.	Fanny Ridgely	12 Aug 1895	c
BEATON, Mary H.	Frank M. Thomas	9 Oct 1894	w
BEATTY - also see BATTEY			
BEATTY, Charles	Virlinder Offutt	13 Apr 1799	
James E.	Helen A. Strow	10 Aug 1896	w
Laura	H. Bradley Magruder	8 Dec 1869	
Mamie C.	Mahlon R. Austin	18 Dec 1888	w
BEAVERS, George N.	Sarah L. Gray	18 Jul 1867	
George T.	Bessie J. Selby	29 Dec 1896	w
James W.	Sarah E. Weaver	11 Dec 1895	w
Joseph W.	Carrie Ann Matthews	27 Dec 1866	
Mary C.	Sylvester Thompson	30 Jan 1866	
Mary L.	William R. Chick	7 Apr 1893	w
BEAVIN - also see BEVIN			
BEAVIN, Mary	William Smith	3 Nov 1801	
BECK, Ann	Nathan Walker	20 Jul 1798	
BECKARD, Mary E.	Otho ?. Thompson	20 Aug 1884	c
BECKET, Maria Ann	Dennis Brown	24 Oct 1876	
BECKETT, Martha	Franklin Mason	6 Jun 1881	c
Mary	Jesse Smackum	19 Dec 1870	
Mary E.	Paul Starks	15 Oct 1892	c
BECKLEY, Lydia	William Butler	14 Jul 1894	c

BECKS, Henry	Elizabeth Harrison	3 Jan 1821	
BECKWITH, Aletha	Levi Mason	31 Oct 1895	c
Ann	John B. Belt	16 Feb 1837	
Ann Maria	James W. Campbell	10 Jun 1845	
Benedict	Elizabeth White	28 Jan 1800	
Benjamin R.	Mary E. Williams	24 Mar 1868	
Charles	Mary Rabbitt	21 Jul 1819	
Eliza L.	William T. Fisher	10 Jan 1843	
Elizabeth	Hazel S. Butt	30 May 1816	
Elizabeth	Benjamin Barrett	17 Dec 1846	
Frances	Edward H. Briggs	29 May 1862	
Georgeanna	James Beckwood	16 Jan 1877	c
Greenbury C.	Lizzie Burriss	17 Mar 1873	
Helen	Augustus W. Rhine	21 Sep 1871	
Isaac J.	Charity Ann Humes	27 Dec 1886	c
John A.	Eliza Ann Ricketts	10 Mar 1834	
Joseph B.	Sarah Leizear	13 Jan 1877	
Martha J.	Andrew J. Hoskins	26 Oct 1847	
Nannie	James McRoy	10 Jan 1872	
Mary E.	Alexander F. Boswell	30 Oct 1845	
Nicholas	Mary Butt	10 Aug 1799	
Permelia A.	Edward Craycroft	2 Feb 1829	
Rebecca G.	Matthew Fields	30 Dec 1850	
Robert O.	Dorathy Ann Belt	6 Feb 1841	
Samuel	Sarah Summers	22 Mar 1826	
Sandy	Laura Johnson	26 Dec 1878	c
Sykes	Kesiah Adamson	22 Jan 1801	
Sykes	Lucy Prather	14 Jun 1820	
Thomas	Maggie Rhine	13 Jun 1871	
Virlinda*	Benjamin Summers	11 Oct 1798	
William	Rachel Coats	17 Oct 1868	
William	Maria Taylor	29 Oct 1879	c
William T.	Bertie Garnett	29 Nov 1895	c
Zachariah	Julia M. Hughes	17 Dec 1878	w
BECKWOOD, James	Georgeanna Beckwith	16 Jan 1877	c
James H.	Jane Lee	20 Feb 1873	
BECRAFT, Abraham	Anne Nesbit	24 Nov 1803	
Ann	John Mackelfresh	4 Sep 1817	
Clara E.	Thomas L. Willson	26 Aug 1889	w
Harriett	Samuel Magruder	22 Feb 1814	
Florence L.	James R. Hilton	14 Nov 1887	w
Jonathan	Luraner Higgins	10 Jun 1800	
Kesiah V.	William Oden	21 Sep 1881	
Margaret Ellen	Valentine Tobias Trout	6 Oct 1869	
Mary	Henry Crockett	17 Nov 1836	
Mary	Willis Burriss	23 Aug 1880	
Minerva	Andrew M. Stephenson	21 Apr 1841	
BEDDO, Dorcas	Thomas Beall	22 Dec 1814	
Eleanor	William Downes	20 Dec 1817	
Elizabeth	Richard Watkins	8 Mar 1800	
Sarah	Zachariah Wellmore	22 Dec 1806	
Willey (female)	Tyson Beall	31 Mar 1804	
BEDFOFD, Rebecca	Allen Bowman	4 Jan 1808	
BEEDING, Catharine J.	James D. Norman	7 Dec 1836	

* Part of last name and day from earlier reading

BEEDING, Craven V.	Rosetta L. Lackland	27 May 1816
Elic L.	Ann Hickman	22 Feb 1842
Nancey	Jonathan Munroe	23 Mar 1801
Patsey	James Cooke	29 Jan 1802
BEEDLE, Agnes N.	Charles G. Miller	25 Nov 1891 w
Samuel	Elizabeth Edmonston	13 Jul 1808
BEEDLEY, Mary Ann	Obedia Gray	1 Mar 1819
BEEN - also see BEAN, BEANS, BEENS		
BEEN, Elizabeth	William Gray	20 Jul 1811
BEGGARLY - also see BAGGERLY		
BEGGARLY, John	Ruth Lazenby	17 Nov 1806
BEENS - also see BEAN, BEEN, BEANS		
BEENS, Jemimah	Dawson Cash	3 Oct 1798
BEHRENS, Louis	Mary Keese	26 Mar 1860
BELFORD, Hesther	James Jamison	6 Apr 1813
BELL - also see BEALL		
BELL, Alfred H.	Eleanora Hopkins	19 Oct 1889 c
Ann	John Thomas Day	11 Feb 1846
Anna	Jerry Coats	9 Sep 1870
Annie L.	Joseph C. Higgins	27 Apr 1885 w
Charlotte	George Hackett	15 Oct 1874
Elizabeth A.	Samuel Bakin	4 Mar 1875
Ellen	John Henry Diggs	25 Dec 1873
Emma	William Butler	7 Aug 1890 c
Evie V.	Lewis R. W. Barnsley	9 Nov 1897 w
George R.	Lavinia Myers	17 Jun 1885
Grace Jane	---ewell Wheeler	13 Feb 1890 w
Isaiah	Ida Brunner	22 May 1895 c
James W.	Ida J. Prather	4 Feb 1891 c
John	Lucetta D. Belt	31 Jul 1855
John	Susan Daden	11 Nov 1876
John S.	Annie A. Hettinger	17 Jan 1898 w
Josiah	Mary Ellen Harding	16 Oct 1879 w
Lemuel	Mary E. Hilliard	7 Dec 1860
Levin	Julia Hamilton	9 Apr 1891 c
Maria - see Maria Belt		
Mary F.	G. W. Mobley	23 Oct 1876
Mary V.	Thomas S. Hopkins	29 May 1895 c
Maurice	Julia F. Bettice	13 Apr 1892 c
Mollie V.	James A. Sutton	24 Sep 1890 w
Rebecca	Andrew Soper	13 Oct 1886 w
Robert H.	Florence E. Wright	15 Mar 1898 w
Rosa	Washington Dorsey	16 Jan 1874
Sarah E.	William F. Dorsey	4 Nov 1897 c
Sarah L.	John G. Cashell	2 May 1861
Silas A.	Emma R. Cashell	29 Apr 1873
Theodore C.	Martha V. Miller	26 Aug 1886 w
William D.	Della Warfield	8 Nov 1887 w
William H.	Ruth Ann Oldfield	28 Dec 1869
William H.	Emma Washington	9 May 1887 c
BELLIS, Charity	Rezin Boswell	5 Dec 1876
BELLISON, Edward L.	Hattie V. Moxley	7 Nov 1887 w
John H.	Julia A. Watkins	8 Dec 1891 w
Martha A.	Garrison Moxley	17 Dec 1895 w
Minnie J.	Willie B. Moxley	17 Jan 1888 w

BELLOWS - also see BILLOWS

BELLOWS, George W.	Alice Adams	13 Jul 1881	c
William	Lucy Calton	22 Dec 1891	c
BELMEAR, Elizabeth	William C. W. Veirs	30 Jan 1816	
Susan	Leonard Green	11 Feb 1822	
BELMERE, Samuel	Priscilla Williams	24 Nov 1802	
BELT, Aeneas	Jane Clagett	7 Dec 1816	
Alfred	Charlott Trundle	18 Dec 1809	
Ann	William Trail	30 Mar 1807	
Ann	Warren King	21 Dec 1824	
Anne	Richard Wells	10 Sep 1799	
Anne	Nicholas Harding	28 Aug 1812	
Basil	Nancy Orme	28 Jan 1808	
Benjamin	Jane Cecill	23 Feb 1805	
Benoni	Keziah Thompson	16 Jan 1813	
Carlton Jr.	Elizabeth Jones	25 Feb 1799	
Clarissa	Joshua Stewart	24 Jun 1806	
Dolly	Walter Williams	6 Jan 1819	
Dorathy Ann	Robert O. Beckwith	6 Feb 1841	
Dorothy E.	Charles W. Bready	19 Oct 1874	
Elizabeth	Samuel Cecill	27 Oct 1802	
Ellen S.	Charles A. Thompson	5 Dec 1877	w
Esther	Daniel Trundle	18 Nov 1802	
Evan	Sarah Hobbs	26 Jul 1803	
Greenby	Margaret Lansdale	25 Feb 1808	
Henry Franklin	Mary F. Davis	10 Oct 1866	
Isabell	Samuel Cecill	28 Feb 1806	
John	Rebecca Scissel	5 Nov 1806	
John	Statira Higgins	15 Feb 1812	
John B.	Ann Beckwith	16 Feb 1837	
John S.	Laura P. Belt	19 Oct 1867	
John W.	Anna Maria Stewart	24 Feb 1834	
Laura P.	John S. Belt	19 Oct 1867	
Lucetta D.	John Bell	31 Jul 1855	
M. W.	Deborah Thompson	27 Feb 1877	w
Maria*	George McCormick	24 Oct 1799	
Maria L.	Aurelius Coe	** Oct 1858	
Mary E. P.	James Orme	16 Jan 1854	
Mary F.	Reuben T. Baker	2 Feb 1886	w
Matilda Jane	Benjamin Wells	21 Dec 1832	
Rebecca	James Turnbull	9 Jan 1812	
Rufus M.	Annie E. Thompson	22 Dec 1873	
Samuel S.	Mary E. Wilson	19 Feb 1879	w
Sarah	Samuel Cecil	4 Dec 1798	
Sarah M.	Marshall Brown	15 Dec 1857	
Tresey J.	Jesse O. Mathias	24 Jul 1894	w
Virginia L.	Bushrod L. Fose	28 Oct 1857	
William	Elizabeth Waters	22 Feb 1804	
William D.	Elizabeth Mills	3 Jan 1810	
William T.	Mary E. Stewart	29 Feb 1848	
BENDER, Minnie G.	George A. Kirk	10 May 1894	w
BENNA, Leanna	William Henry Gray	30 Dec 1897	c
BENNET, Martha	John Andrews	21 May 1862	

* Page torn; this could be Bell
** Day has blot on it; between 20 and 27

BENNETT,	Charles D.	Eveline Carter	18 Mar 1879	c
	Allen H.	Ann B. Holland	13 Feb 1826	
	Ann H.	Leonard D. Shaw	23 Mar 1832	
	Annie R.	James E. Wallich	28 Nov 1875	
	Carrie V.	Charles F. Ricketts	22 Feb 1898	w
	Catharine V.	William Jefferson Thompson	16 Jan 1872	
	Clarence Lee	Mary E. Shaw	7 Sep 1898	w
	Deborah	Basil Burditt	23 Feb 1809	
	Deborah A.	John T. Mortimer	16 Feb 1861	
	Edna	Henry Cooley	26 May 1841	
	Eliza	Hezekiah Thompson	18 Aug 1817	
	Elizabeth	Jacob Feaster	31 Dec 1825	
	George M.	Emma J. Moss	22 May 1865	
	Helen M.	Samuel S. Carroll	20 Apr 1885	
	Henrietta	John Harriss	12 Nov 1825	
	Isabella C.	Richard H. Nicholson	29 Dec 1870	
	James T.	Annie Mary Cecil	24 Mar 1885	w
	Job M. C.	Amelia C. Molesworth	28 Feb 1887	
	John A.	Annie Milstead	21 Jan 1864	
	John W.	Mary E. Bennett	28 Jan 1851	
	John W.	Mary A. L. Welling	17 Mar 1869	
	Laura L.	Otho B. Williams	26 Apr 1898	w
	Margaret L.	W. C. R. Shipley	24 Dec 1851	
	Martha	Henry Gerheart	14 Nov 1825	
	Martha	Richard Purdy	25 May 1827	
	Martha A.	Rufus H. Appleby	6 Nov 1854	
	Mary	Joseph Galloway	27 Dec 1817	
	Mary	Jacob Miller	17 Oct 1843	
	Mary E.	John W. Bennett	28 Jan 1851	
	Mary Ellen	John William Matthews	16 Nov 1886	w
	Mary P.	Charles W. Hirsh	4 Nov 1895	w
	Nehemiah	Polly Cole	15 Jan 1820	
	Olive Estelle	Edgar Allen	10 Jan 1898	w
	Priscilla	Caleb Keeth	28 Jul 1834	
	Richard H.	Savilla Miller	20 Apr 1850	
	Richard H.	Mattie A. Trail	4 May 1881	
	Rose G.	William A. Hughes	31 Aug 1883	
	Samuel F.	Sarah C. Thompson	23 Feb 1846	
	Samuel F.	Ann E. Summers	14 Feb 1873	
	Sarah	Joseph Fiester	25 Nov 1834	
	Timothy	Maggie Wren	31 Aug 1876	
	Wesley	Anna Eliza Preston	1 Oct 1828	
	William	Henrietta Benton	2 Mar 1819	
	William Baker	Harriett Ann Winemiller	24 May 1827	
	William F.	Irene Earp	15 Mar 1875	
	William H.	Maggie A. Davis	20 Dec 1881	
BENSON,	Alice B.	Michael Wallace	20 Sep 1875	
	Allen M.	Mary E. Brashears	8 Feb 1853	
	Allen M.	Anne Walters	27 Aug 1879	w
	Ann	William Green	15 Mar 1821	
	Annie M.	Harry Brown	31 Oct 1893	w
	Ann Eliza	Henry W. Mossburg	19 May 1845	
	Arthur	Minnie Warren Grimes	27 Sep 1886	w
	Benjamin B.	Matilda Williams	20 Jan 1840	
	Catharine	Henry P. Dwyer	10 Sep 1845	

BENSON,	Catherine E.	Clarence Brown	8 Jan 1895 w
	Charles E.	Annie M. Marlow	18 May 1891 w
	Eden	Selea Beall	22 Jul 1819
	Harriet A.	Joseph Sibley	7 Jan 1863
	Henrietta	Zadok Talbert	22 Apr 1839
	James S.	Mary J. Allnutt	20 Dec 1866
	John E.	Rebecca A. Dowden	7 Dec 1872
	John T.	Kate Ritenour	1 Jun 1865
	John William	Emma Florence Miles	1 Feb 1879 w
	Julia Ann	Levi Dove	20 Oct 1832
	Lewin T.	Sarah Thomas King	13 Nov 1844
	Mary E.	Thomas Crawford	11 Nov 1840
	Minnie W.	Daniel W. Hammond	30 Dec 1895 w
	Mollie E.	James T. Trail	20 Dec 1870
	Nicholas	Debby Merrick	23 Feb 1838
	Ninian	Anne Crockett	8 Mar 1809
	Richard H.	Mary E. Girard	30 Aug 1888 w
	Richard J.	Elizabeth B. Murphy	21 Dec 1897 w
	Roberta J.	William T. Dowden	30 Nov 1886 w
	Ruthy	James Stone	23 Dec 1816
	Sarah	Allen Simpson	12 May 1802
	Sarah	Henry Talbot	18 Jul 1812
	Sarah	William H. Dove	20 Mar 1830
	Sarah	Benjamin E. Eller	19 Mar 1839
	Sarah A.	Uriah Miles	12 Feb 1853
	Sarah C.	James Lowe	19 Jun 1860
	Sarah F.	Richard C. Pindell	11 Jan 1875
	Sarah J.	Benjamin F. Watkins	11 Nov 1868
	Sarah T.	George W. Johnson	17 Sep 1872
	Susan	Richard Pyles	25 Feb 1847
	Thomas	Elizabeth Morgan	18 Jan 1811
	Thomas	Mary Ann Maginniss	22 Nov 1821
	Thomas B.	Isabella Broome	26 Dec 1828
	Thomas B.	Susan Veirs	10 Mar 1841
	Thomas B.	Barbara A. Broom	10 Aug 1867
	Thomas E.	Annie E. Green	21 Jan 1871
	William	Sarah Dowden	9 Nov 1803
	William H.	Jane Trail	5 Feb 1842
	William H.	Catharine Crawford	20 Apr 1843
	William H.	Cornelia Elizabeth Shriner	26 Aug 1875
	William H.	Nettie Grimes	24 Mar 1885 w
	William H.	Mary A. Pillsbury	2 Sep 1897 w
BENTLEY,	Anna M.	William J. Parker	11 Nov 1872
	Burton D.	Sarah B. Boteler	24 Feb 1896 w
	Edward N.	Hallie J. Chandlee	12 Jul 1880
	Louise H.	Frederick C. Gentner	14 May 1888 w
	Mary T.	Romulus L. Moore	1 Sep 1834
	Sarah	George W. Warfield	21 Oct 1835
BENTON,	Charity	Thomas Odle Offutt	16 Jul 1800
	Dorey	Henrietta Smith	14 Nov 1809
	Edward Willett	Hannah Duvall	7 May 1806
	Elizabeth	Richard Shipley	1 Jan 1825
	Emza Ann	John P. Connell	14 Sep 1853
	Henrietta	William Bennett	2 Mar 1819
	Horace	Susan P. Trammell	26 Oct 1837

BENTON,	Horace	Mary A. Carroll	2 Mar 1848
	James N.	Airy M. Thompson	12 Mar 1868
	James N.	Sarah E. Higgins	14 Feb 1872
	Jane E.	Richard P. Spates	11 Feb 1857
	John Joseph	Elizabeth Scott	23 Feb 1815
	Laura V.	Joseph T. Cater	17 Jan 1860
	Leanna	William Walter Magruder	4 Jun 1833
	Louisa	Samuel M. Fisher	27 Jan 1841
	Mahala	James Dowden	25 Dec 1809
	Malinda	John Adams	3 Jul 1804
	Martha Ann	William Henderson	3 Jan 1839
	Mary	William Clagett	20 Nov 1816
	Mary	John McDonald	7 Apr 1863
	Mordica	Martha Duley	23 Jan 1811
	Morgan S.	Cora B. Dutrow	29 Jan 1884
	Rachael	Brooke Austin	28 Nov 1815
	Rosetta	Samuel M. Fisher	22 Feb 1859
	Sarah	Hatton Fish	18 Feb 1801
	Sarah	Samuel M. Clagett	7 Dec 1813
	Theophilus L.	Sarah Ann Shaw	6 Mar 1843
	William	Caty G. Griffith	17 Apr 1828
	William	Ruth Shipley	16 Dec 1835
BERKLEY - also see BURKLEY			
BERKLEY,	Lucinda	Benjamin Duncan	25 Jul 1822
BERRY - also see BARRY			
BERRY,	Basil	Eleanor Lansdale	18 Sep 1821
	Edward	Polly Rawlings	1 Feb 1802
	Elisha D.	Elizabeth E. Higgins	3 Nov 1853
	Eliza	Nathaniel House	4 Oct 1803
	Elizabeth	John Selby	15 Nov 1806
	Elizabeth	Maurice W. Downs	29 Jun 1876
	Elizabeth W.	Samuel Beall	26 Nov 1801
	Emma	Levi Hopkins	4 May 1876 c
	Helen	Henry H. Huff	14 Nov 1878 c
	Hesther	Hezekiah Edmonstone	4 Jan 1819
	John D.	Angelina Griffith	5 Jan 1852
	John W.	Ann Maria Dorsey	27 Aug 1879
	Margaret	Columbus Williams	27 Oct 1879
	Martha R.	Edward E. Stonestreet	14 Oct 1852
	Mary V.	Thomas P. Collier	20 May 1874
	Michael R.	Barbary Lyles Higgins	12 Feb 1818
	Mariam	John M. Wheat	8 Nov 1826
	Nancy	John Thomas	19 Nov 1798
	Rachel E.	James G. House	5 Apr 1838
	Ruthy	Washington Owen	7 Jan 1806
	Sallie Murdock	Edwin Howard	17 Dec 1883
	Sarah*	Isaac Williams	5 Aug 1819
	Sarah E.	George T. Foreman	8 Feb 1872
	Sarah E.	Gassaway Sellman	27 Apr 1882
	Thomas	Annie M. Poole	4 Feb 1879
	Thomas	Laura V. Creamer	14 Sep 1886 w
	Thomas	Ella J. Ricketts	23 Jul 1889 w
	William H.	Norah J. Whalen	2 Dec 1860
	Zachariah	Mary B. Canby	7 Jun 1865

* Smeared; could be Perry

BERRYMAN, Alberta	Cyrus Hall	15 Apr 1889 c
BERTTON - also see BURTON		
BERTTON, Eliza	Larkin Shipley	4 May 1829
BESSANT, John	Magdalene Myers	9 Aug 1815
BEST, Emma C.	Richard L. Harman	25 Jan 1887 w
George M.	Florence Mulligan	10 Jun 1890 w
John L.	Ida May Appleby	22 Apr 1893 w
John T.	Catharine E. Carlyle	31 Oct 1860
Lydia R.	Richard F. Loy	29 Mar 1876
Martha E.	George F. Linthicum	5 Apr 1887 w
Sarah E.	Charles A. Poole	16 Oct 1897 w
Simon D.	Ruth M. Beall	26 Dec 1891 w
William H.	Ella E. Davis	15 Feb 1897 w
BETLER - also see BUTLER		
BETLER, Hepy E.	Nathan S. T. Naylor	30 Jul 1884 c
BETTAS - also see BATTIS, BETTICE, BETTIS, BETTUS		
BETTAS, Nannie	Thomas Williams	28 May 1884 c
BETTICE, Julia F.	Maurice Bell	13 Apr 1892 c
BETTIS, Isaac	Mary J. Posey	26 Dec 1883 c
Jacob	Anna Peters	15 Jul 1875
BETTITT, Amanda	Lewis Brooks	21 Jan 1870
BETTS - also see BETZ		
BETTS, Franklin C.	Adele E. Page	17 Dec 1890 w
BETTUS - also see BATTIS, BETTAS		
BETTUS, Alice	James Hamilton	5 Dec 1868
Martha	John C. Tyler	4 Jun 1881 c
BETZ - also see BETTS		
BETZ, Peggy	Robert Wright	7 Jul 1800
BEVAN - also see BEVIN, BEAVIN		
BEVAN, Laura	Reuben A. Baker	20 Aug 1861
Mary O.	Bernard Monday	6 Jun 1861
W. F.	Sallie D. Poole	2 Jun 1885
BEVANS, William	Margaret Casey	12 Apr 1869
BEVERIDGE, Charles C.	Myra Givler	10 Jan 1895 w
BEVIN - also see BEVAN		
BEVIN, Bennett	Sarah Dougherty	18 Dec 1798
Charles	Sophia Moore	20 Dec 1799
BEVINS, James	Ellen B. Deffer	27 Aug 1867
BIAYS, James P.	Rebecca Hodges	28 Oct 1867
BIBB, Caroline	Thomas J. Brown	10 Oct 1866
BICKET, Stephen	Catherine Cliver	30 Mar 1799
BICKFORD, Frederick A.	Bertha C. Glascott	2 Aug 1895 w
BIELASKI, Alexander	Roselle Israel	20 Sep 1879 w
BIGGS, Americus	Mary E. Whalan	28 Feb 1870
Andrew	Sarah Lewis	16 Dec 1817
Ann	John Truman	30 Dec 1859
Darkey	Thomas Biggs	21 Aug 1805
Elijah	Betsey Welling	28 Dec 1818
James A.	Martha A. Mire	24 Sep 1839
Linny	Gerrard Steel	27 Dec 1819
Martha J.	Charles E. Downs	19 Apr 1870
Sarah	Charles Bloyce	6 Oct 1824
Thomas	Darkey Biggs	21 Aug 1805
BIGHAM, John	Eliza Ann Dorsey	29 Aug 1836
BIKES, Rosa E.	Gilbert G. Fancher	22 Mar 1897 w

BILLOWS - also see BELLOWS			
BILLOWS, Arthur E.	Lucy E. Budd	13 Jan 1898	c
Singleton H.	Sarah A. Awkward	20 Jun 1878	c
BILLUPS, John W.	Mary C. Hughes	22 Jul 1861	
BIRCH - also see BURCH			
BIRCH, Carrie E.	Charles N. Ritter	14 Jan 1896	w
Thomas J.	Martha J. Rozier	26 Jun 1890	c
BIRD - also see BYRD			
BIRD, Eburn	Martha W. Glaze	9 Jan 1858	
Harold	Ellenor L. Luard	15 Dec 1887	w
Henry L.	Elizabeth G. Eler	7 Apr 1856	
Willie N.	Cora B. Day	12 Aug 1892	w
BIRDETT - also see BURDETTE			
BIRDETT, Notley	Rhody R. Holland	30 Jun 1836	
BIRDWHISTELE, William	Ann Sunnions	1 Apr 1820	
BIRDWHISTLE, Thomas	Elizabeth Nicholls	1 Jan 1806	
BIRGFELD, Frederica P.	Emil George Bruehl	24 Jan 1881	
BIRKHEAD, William	Mary Culver	14 Mar 1811	
BIRNSIDES - also see BURNSIDES			
BIRNSIDES, Mary Ann E.	John G. Cockey	1 May 1836	
BISER, Ira E.	Irene C. Walter	7 Jul 1898	w
Minnie	Milton Carter	16 Jun 1892	w
BISHOP, Arch	Caroline Hackett	3 Dec 1874	
Charles E.	Pocahontas Ryan	26 Jun 1889	w
Franklin T.	L. Anna Marshall	13 Sep 1866	
Sloter	Bettie Barnes	31 Oct 1895	c
Solomon	Elizabeth Fielding	13 Nov 1811	
BISSETT, Charles F.	Nettie Gibbs	23 Sep 1897	w
Cora L.	James E. Wheatley	28 Jul 1896	w
BLACK, Charles	Henrietta Haines	2 Jul 1881	
Charles	Jane Gilbert	28 Dec 1892	c
Hannah E.	Joseph T. Keiler	25 May 1885	
Henry M.	Palma Sheridan	3 Sep 1895	w
Mary Fannie	Robert Boston	18 Apr 1898	c
BLACKBURN, Jeremiah G.	Helen B. Duvall	21 Sep 1881	
Lethea	Larkin Warfield	14 Mar 1827	
Ruth	William Turner	27 Jan 1804	
BLACKFORD, Francis G.	Anna Maria Stone	14 Jan 1830	
BLACKLOCK, Gass	Susan E. Brewer	31 Dec 1883	c
Sarah	Alfred Scott	17 Oct 1868	
BLACKMAN, George A.	Maybell R. Sherwood	3 Jul 1894	c
Viola E.	George E. Dale	18 Jun 1894	w
BLACKSTON, Thomas	Ginnie Ross	17 May 1893	c
BLACKWELL, Robert	Julia Watts	5 Sep 1881	
BLAIR, Alexander	Nettie Carr	2 Jan 1883	w
Carrie	Reuben Hill	9 Jul 1879	c
George	Louiza Carroll	28 May 1870	
James R.	Sophia Powell	28 Mar 1889	c
Lillie	William Nelson	9 Jul 1895	c
BLAKE, Edward	Caroline Plummer	12 Oct 1871	c
BLAKES, Caroline	William Hebron	27 Dec 1881	
BLAKEMORE, David L.	Annie E. Poole	3 Mar 1890	w
BLAND, Aaaron	Amelia Thompson	15 Apr 1891	c
BLINCOE, William	Emily Johnson	27 Sep 1838	
BLINKOE, Katie	Wade Dunn	28 Nov 1888	w

BLOICE - also see BLOYCE			
BLOICE, Ann	William Jeanes	1 Oct 1836	
Miranda	Zachariah Lowe	10 Mar 1849	
BLOOM, Mary	John Sipe	24 Aug 1804	
BLOUNT, Samuel	Harriett W. Dorsey	19 Feb 1818	
BLOWERS, Anna	Richard H. Thompson	6 Feb 1835	
Elizabeth	Basil Johnson	1 Mar 1815	
Mahala	George W. Thompson	23 Feb 1835	
Mary Ann	Basil Johnson	7 Nov 1816	
Richard	Ann Cloud	18 Dec 1824	
Samuel	Susan W. Darby	8 Aug 1829	
BLOYCE - also see BLOICE			
BLOYCE, Charles	Sarah Biggs	6 Oct 1824	
BLUNDON, Ada E.	William J. Darcey	28 Apr 1887	w
George W.	Alhima Dougherty	6 Oct 1885	w
John Francis	Elizabeth A. Mullican	16 Nov 1880	
BLUNT - see BLOUNT			
BOARMAN, John R.	Annie V. Kelchner	27 Jun 1892	w
BODINE, Joseph Henry	Elizabeth Frances Stone	7 Sep 1861	
BOEMAN, Richard L.	Minnie L. Litzsinger	10 Nov 1891	w
BOGAN, John T.	Louisa M. Brunett	18 Sep 1842	
BOGELEY - also see BOGLEY			
BOGELEY, Ann Ellen	James H. Fowler	15 Nov 1864	
BOGELY, Zachariah	Joanna Ball	10 Mar 1821	
BOGGESS, Ann	Thomas Summers	22 Dec 1802	
John W.	Elizabeth A. Schaefer	1 Sep 1891	w
BOGLEY - also see BOGELEY, BOGELY			
BOGLEY, Alice V.	George F. Ray	23 Sep 1885	w
Isidora	William E. Ward	23 Jan 1889	w
John H.	Ritta C. Haney	5 Aug 1862	
John H.	Cappie V. Fields	16 Nov 1897	w
Nannie	James Morrison	26 Dec 1883	w
Olivia A.	Edwin M. West	6 Jun 1894	w
Mary V.	John D. Simpson	30 Dec 1885	w
Rosalie	Joseph A. Briggs	16 Dec 1895	w
William A.	Isabella A. Haney	21 Oct 1862	
William A.	Grace Penn	9 Oct 1895	w
BOHRER, Alex L.	Cornelia L. Fisher	9 Dec 1847	
Charles C.	Annie R. Hodges	12 Dec 1879	w
Edgar P.	Stattira Duvall	14 Dec 1870	
Eva P.	William R. Hodges	23 Oct 1882	w
Fannie May	Dionysius Hilton	2 Apr 1895	w
Hattie L.	Franklin L. Hilton	15 Oct 1895	w
Jacob L.	Margaret Perry	6 Dec 1855	
John G.	Elizabeth Renshaw	15 Oct 1850	
John S.	Louisa Duvall	21 Dec 1869	
Julius S.	Lucinda A. Brown	16 Nov 1848	
Martha L.	William Shoemaker	6 Dec 1887	w
Mary Elizabeth	John W. Weltberger	20 Nov 1843	
Mary Elizabeth	Charles Edwin Higgins	14 Oct 1875	
Minnie W.	Beall G. W. Unglesbee	29 Mar 1893	w
BOICE - also see BOYCE			
BOICE, Maria Ann	Benjamin Vermillion	18 Dec 1827	
Martha An	Eleven Reid	9 Mar 1829	
Richard	Ann James	15 Jan 1829	
Washington F.	Magarett James	18 Dec 1827	

BOLAND - also see BOWLAND, BOWLEN		
BOLAND, Charles D.	Louisa Baullauf	16 Jun 1881 w
BOLDEN, Laura	Charles W. Praiter	23 May 1885 c
BOLINGER, David C. Y.	Almira C. Thomas	17 Sep 1880 w
BOLTON, Annie M.	Joseph S. Lowe	12 Jun 1894 w
Frances E.	Downey M. Williams	31 Dec 1892 w
James	Lucy Shaw	23 Nov 1799
James H.	Elizabeth Johnson	11 Apr 1894 w
James Henry	Mary E. Oden	11 Jul 1872
Lewis E.	Ida Oden	19 May 1877 w
Martha	James H. Welling	26 May 1874
BOND, Ann	William Earp	13 Dec 1831
Annie	John Gaither	26 Nov 1889 c
Beverly W.	Elizabeth R. Lumsden	8 Nov 1876
Deborah	George Washington Russel	20 Aug 1885 c
Eliza Ann	William Howard	29 Dec 1803
Ella M.	Samuel D. Waters, Jr.	11 Dec 1871
George W.	Janey Campbell	13 Mar 1894 c
Hanson	Helen E. Warfield	20 Sep 1872
Hattie	Charles Harris	26 Sep 1883
James H.	Laura M. Shaw	4 May 1881
Jane	Robert Brown	13 Apr 1817
Jemima	Thomas J. Mitchell	9 Apr 1868
Lewis	Mary Swailes	23 Dec 1896 c
Martha	Jeffrey Warfield	22 Jul 1878 c
Martha	John Thornton	16 Dec 1887 c
Mary	Thomas Walker	19 Apr 1888 c
Mary E.	John F. Simms	25 Sep 1878 c
Rachel	John H. Harding	10 Dec 1828
Rebecca	Benjamin King	7 Mar 1827
Robert	Matilda Davis	19 Dec 1827
Sarah	Notley Wheat Lanham	30 Dec 1807
Susannah	John Lee	2 Jan 1896 c
Thomas	Julianna Sedgwick	20 Mar 1867
William	Marian J. Jonston	22 Nov 1870
BONIFANT - also see BONNIFANT		
BONIFANT, George	Helen Green	22 Mar 1875
Mary Ann	Thomas O. Willson	20 Apr 1841
BONN, Harriet Ann	George Albert Cave	6 Aug 1869
BONNIFANT - also see BONIFANT		
BONNIFANT, Eliza Ann	James Pope	11 Aug 1830
Samuel	Cassandra Henry	10 Jul 1818
Sarah	Thomas Willson	20 Nov 1850
BONNIFIELD, Ann	Richard Barrett	14 Oct 1820
BOODY, Elizabeth	James Henson	22 Jan 1801
BOOK, George W.	Alice J. Woodward	24 May 1888 c
George W.	Clara L. Carter	5 Nov 1896 c
Mary C. E.	John Higgins	5 Sep 1868
BOONE, Letitia	Joseph Brooke	17 Dec 1798
Rebecca*	Asa Sheckles	5 Apr 1811
BOOSE, Levi O.	Agnes C. Glover	5 Jan 1876
Mary	Daniel Miller	14 Apr 1810
Sarah Ann	Tobias Matthews	7 Sep 1810

* License has Boone; should be Bowman according to court records

BOOTH, Mamie C.	Richard H. Reamey	26 Nov 1896	w
BOREHAM, Nathaniel	Ann Langford	25 May 1805	
BOROUGHS - see BURROUGHS or BURRIS for other spellings			
BOROUGHS, Mamie M.	James A. Houser	23 Nov 1897	w
Millard S.	Minnie M. Slater	27 Feb 1888	w
Nicholas C.	Edna C. E. Good	12 Sep 1889	w
W. H.	Alice C. Baker	20 Aug 1879	
BORROUGHS - see BURROUGHS or BURRIS for other spellings			
BORROUGHS, Amos G.	Sarah C. Burroughs	26 Mar 1889	w
Sarah C.	Amos G. Borroughs	26 Mar 1889	w
BORUM, William D.	Alice V. Zeigler	14 Nov 1882	w
BOSART, Jacob M., Dr.	Jane V. Gruble	18 May 1896	w
BOSS, James G.	Sarah L. Bartolette	13 Aug 1878	w
BOSTON, Augustus	Harriet A. Holmes	28 Nov 1877	c
Robert	Mary Fannie Black	18 Apr 1898	c
BOSWELL, Alexander F.	Mary E. Beckwith	30 Oct 1845	
Ann	Nathan Soper	3 Nov 1807	
Anna Maria	Samuel W. Boswell	28 Dec 1853	
Caroline V.	Uriah Harden	25 Feb 1863	
Cenah	Judson Thompson	22 Jan 1811	
Chloe Ann	Alexander Campbell	1 Jan 1799	
Christiana	John S. Harding	8 Sep 1821	
Clement	Susannah Trail	24 Dec 1821	
Elizabeth	Edward Harper	27 Jan 1808	
George	Mary Ann Thompson	8 Mar 1820	
George W.	Laura J. Higgins	9 Jan 1856	
Henry	Johana Henry	19 May 1834	
James W.	Mary Ann Harper	17 Oct 1843	
James W.	Jennie Magruder	24 Jul 1894	w
Jennetter	Lewis F. Thompson	5 Apr 1881	
Jetson	Ann Keith	10 Apr 1838	
John	Polly Thompson	5 Mar 1800	
John	Milly Ann Austin	22 Dec 1812	
John	Sarah Ward	24 Dec 1823	
John	Airy Proctor	22 Aug 1876	
John H.	Ann Hurley	5 Jan 1842	
John H.	Elizabeth Truman	10 Feb 1853	
John H.	Laura C. Walker	6 Jan 1859	
John James	Elizabeth Campbell	19 Jan 1809	
Martha J.	William H. Mullican	26 Feb 1850	
Mary E.	Millard C. Fisher	20 May 1871	
Nicholas	Eleanor Thompson	3 Mar 1810	
Otho	Margaret Connelly	20 Dec 1826	
Otho	Serena Dawson	22 Nov 1857	
Rebecca Ann	Elias Bussard	9 May 1832	
Remus	Josephine Adams	16 Nov 1871	
Rezin	Charity Bellis	5 Dec 1876	
Samuel W.	Anna Maria Boswell	28 Dec 1853	
Samuel W.	Sarah Higgins	14 Oct 1879	
Sarah	Henry Thompson	30 Mar 1809	
Sarah A.	Stephen Anderson	18 Oct 1871	
Sarah Ann	Edward Harper	15 Apr 1800	
Sarah U.	James W. Parsley	5 Dec 1882	w
Susanna	Thomas Hood	9 Jul 1835	
Susie J.	John R. Taylor	4 Feb 1884	w
Thomas	Rachel Eveley	26 Apr 1843	

BOSWELL, Thomas H.	Nettie C. Carrington	5 Nov 1894	w
Volinder	William Heath	30 Jan 1799	
William	Margaret Duley	13 Dec 1820	
William	Jane Burress	18 Jun 1828	
BOTELER - also see BUTLER			
BOTELER, Benjamin F.	Fannie J. H. Hulings	6 Sep 1876	
Sarah B.	Burton D. Bentley	24 Feb 1896	w
BOTTLEMAY, John J.	Susie Axia Thompson	1 Oct 1880	w
BOTTOMY, Mary E.	John W. Swartzback	15 Apr 1874	
BOUIC - also see BOWIC			
BOUIC, D. H.	Mary L. Higgins	26 Oct 1875	
David H.	Jane R. Hall	12 Sep 1853	
David H.	Sarah Renneberger	5 Jul 1864	
Ella C.	Nathan S. White	19 Oct 1882	w
Mary A.	George H. Beale	3 Dec 1879	w
Peter	Darky Fletchall	7 Apr 1812	
Rosa V.	Charles W. Prettyman	7 Dec 1881	
Rosetta	Edward C. Gott	18 May 1832	
Sarah E.	Samuel R. White	10 Nov 1862	
William V.	Mary A. M. Veirs	2 Jan 1844	
William Veirs Jr.	Alice A. Almoney	5 Jul 1870	
BOUIE - also see BOWIE			
BOUIE, Charles	Eliza Warren	26 Dec 1892	c
BOWEN - also see BOWENS			
BOWEN, Ann M.	John W. Hill	10 Jan 1878	c
Anna	William King	15 Nov 1884	c
Anna J.	Caleb Pumphry	3 May 1869	
Annie	Thomas Scott	5 Sep 1868	
Bettie E.	Charles H. Trout	8 May 1896	w
Carrie E.	Henry Powell	1 May 1894	c
Cyrus	Louisa Dorsey	11 Sep 1873	
Cyrus Jr.	Laura Burford	24 Nov 1859	
Edith B.	Nathan E. Sheckles	5 Oct 1893	w
Ella	Joshua Sedgwick	6 Apr 1883	
Ellen	Peter Williams	8 Nov 1867	
Emma	Ralph Holman	31 Oct 1878	c
Emma A.	Clarence Hilton	1 Feb 1897	w
Ferris (male)	Olie M. Phebus	28 Sep 1896	w
Harriet A. M.	Wallace B. Price	12 Apr 1880	
Henry H.	Eliza Clarence	7 Nov 1894	c
Jehu	Rosina Young	27 Dec 1866	
Jesse C.	Grace Robertson	24 Oct 1898	w
John B. J.	Martha A. Swales	26 Dec 1881	c
Joseph P.	Mary Ann Johnson	1 Oct 1870	
Laura R.	Caleb Pumphrey	7 Sep 1897	c
Maria E. E.	George W. Johnson	24 Nov 1875	
Mary A.	Harrison Fraiser	21 Nov 1868	
Mary Ann	Daniel Shaw	21 Jun 1872	
Sarah	Joseph E. Camel	31 Dec 1890	c
Sarah Ann	Alexander Pointer	26 Nov 1867	
Thomas	Monnica C. Jones	11 Oct 1810	
Thomas	Lizzie Jackson	10 May 1894	c
Thomas R.	Lydia Rice	1 Mar 1889	c
BOWENS, Cora	Samuel Tyler	6 Aug 1892	c
BOWERS, Joseph B.	Catherine E. Hughes	24 Apr 1893	w

```
BOWIC - also see BOUIC
BOWIC, Mary Ann            Daniel V. Fletchall        24 Sep 1823
       Peter A.            Sarah H. Trundle           14 Jan 1824
BOWIE - also see BOUIE
BOWIE, Alcinda             William Johnson            27 Jun 1878 c
       Alvin T.            Rachel A. Brown            28 Oct 1891 c
       Amanda              Marshall Prather            1 Jan 1870
       Amanda L.           Robert H. Anderson          7 Nov 1877 c
       Catherine D.        Edward Trippe              29 Nov 1841
       Charles E.          Mary Hopkins               10 Jan 1889 c
       Elizabeth           Thomas Davis               18 Jan 1802
       Elizabeth H.        Thomas Worthington of      26 Feb 1839
                             William
       Ellen               Hilleary Lamar             25 Oct 1886 c
       Emma                Greenbury Camel            15 Dec 1881
       George W. W.        Martha J. Jackson          20 Nov 1875
       Harriet             Charles S. Hyson           22 Dec 1879 c
       Harriet B.          David L. Snowden           12 Feb 1868
       Harry C.            Anna Holland                1 Jan 1868
       Isabella            Enoch G. Howard            30 Jan 1895 c
       James A.            Mary Murphy                 2 Mar 1889 c
       Jane                Allen Baker*                9 Nov 1882 c
       John M. S.          Anna B. Crawford            7 Oct 1895 w
       Katie D.            James E. Trundle           10 Jun 1890 w
       Lucinda             William Williams           29 Nov 1897 c
       Lucy                George Williams             5 Jan 1866
       Margaret            Oscar F. McCauley          10 Nov 1857
       Margaret A.         Robert H. Randolph         21 Mar 1895 c
       Mary                George M. Chichester       16 Dec 1824
       Mary                James A. Warfield           1 Dec 1881
       Mary C.             William Lancaster          27 Aug 1894 c
       Mary C.             William G. P. Gambril      19 Nov 1896 c
       Nacy                Lizzie Frazier              5 Jul 1878 c
       Nathan              Angeline Snowden           17 Nov 1879
       Rachel V.           William F. Proctor          1 Oct 1888 c
       Richard J.          Catharine L. Williams       5 May 1833
       Sarah               Hilleary Lamar              8 Dec 1888 c
       Syney               Solomon Williams           14 Mar 1871
       Thomas John         Catharine W. Davis         14 Jan 1830
       Washington          Ann Crabb Chew             16 Sep 1799
       Washington M.       Hattie Ellen Potts         28 Feb 1872
       William             Lillie Brown               25 Dec 1889 c
BOWLAND - also see BOLAND
BOWLAND, Margarett         Joseph McKee               13 Nov 1813
BOWLEN, George             Margaret McFarland         18 Dec 1809
        Inez V.            Henry B. Gardiner           3 Dec 1888 w
        Mary A.            Lewis G. Gardiner          26 Oct 1889 w
BOWLES, Warren             Annie G. Carroll           11 Nov 1889 w
BOWMAN - also see BOEMAN
BOWMAN, Aden               Keziah Sedgwick             3 Jan 1809
        Aden McK.          Susie E. Duvall             7 Feb 1876
        Alcinda            John W. Dwyer              20 Aug 1855
        Allen              Rebecca Bedford             4 Jan 1808
        Amelia             Aden D. Alnutt             30 Dec 1812
```

* This could be Allen Baken

BOWMAN,	Amon	Ann Baker	13 Jan 1825	
	Ann	William Sedgwick	5 Dec 1811	
	Anne	Richard Gatrell	17 Feb 1802	
	Clara E.	Henry C. Allnutt	20 Dec 1894	w
	Clinton	Lilian A. Pope	28 Dec 1896	w
	Cora C.	Greenberry E. Barber	17 Dec 1891	w
	Elizabeth	James Case	25 Feb 1807	
	Elizabeth	Joseph Gew	26 Aug 1830	
	Erwin	Anne Molesworth	7 Aug 1827	
	Evan	Mary Baker	24 Dec 1827	
	Evan	Mary Ann Hopwood	15 Jan 1839	
	Evan	Sarah Ann Selby	25 Jan 1871	
	Evan T.	Marbara E. Earp	30 Nov 1887	w
	Francis A.	Melissa D. Riggs	13 Dec 1864	
	Frederick	Jane Gloyd	3 May 1823	
	Frederick	Ruth R. Darby	18 Dec 1832	
	Frederick	Elizabeth Cashell	17 Apr 1871	
	Frederick F.	Mattie S. Sibley	22 Mar 1893	w
	Gassaway	Mary E. Gue	20 Dec 1860	
	George	Deborah Smith	29 Jun 1805	
	George Gustavus	Margaret Smith	4 Jun 1868	
	George Robert	Agnes Gleeson	26 Sep 1885	w
	George W.	Eleanor Young	15 Dec 1834	
	Harriet A.	George Gibbs	26 Feb 1869	
	Ida S.	Charles K. Nichols	7 Mar 1893	w
	John	Mary Hittle	5 Jan 1799	
	John B.	Rosa M. Lovell	24 Sep 1895	w
	John E.	Martha V. Bukoffsky	9 Dec 1893	w
	Laura	Henry Prettyman	28 Sep 1870	
	Marcella A.	James E. Wallick	19 Dec 1867	
	Margaret Ann	John T. Selby	10 Jan 1861	
	Marshall V.	Edith May Adams	21 May 1896	w
	Martha J.	Randolph S. Hawkins	15 Dec 1874	
	Mary E.	Stephen C. Bowman	21 Dec 1870	
	Mary E.	William C. Dwyer	17 May 1897	w
	Matilda	Stephen W. Cross	24 Aug 1821	
	Nonie	Silas B. Burns	2 Nov 1895	w
	Perry	Caroline Snider	8 Nov 1827	
	Perry	Anne Rebecca Musgrove	4 Dec 1830	
	Perry G.	Elizabeth Basil	24 Aug 1876	
	Rebecca - see Rebecca Boone			
	Rezin	Ruth Gue	14 Feb 1809	
	Rezin H.	Mary Young	29 Apr 1845	
	Rezin W.	Mollie E. Hawkins	20 Dec 1872	
	Richard H.	Sarah A. Gue	7 Apr 1863	
	Richard H.	Elizabeth Jane Darby	13 Sep 1879	
	Rosa V.	William T. Gray	18 Nov 1890	w
	Samuel P.	Elizabeth Miles	2* Feb 1879	c
	Sarah Ann	Benjamin Franklin Sullivan	14 Jun 1858	
	Sarah E.	George H. Gew	11 Dec 1838	
	Sarah E.	Harry B. White	21 Dec 1897	w
	Sarah J.	James R. Creamer	1 Aug 1882	w
	Sarah L.	Albert B. Thompson	15 Apr 1856	

* Day has blot on it; either 25 or 26

BOWMAN,	Shadrack	Susannah Smith	24 Dec 1810	
	Shadrack A.	Mary J. Sullivan	28 Dec 1889	w
	Stephen C.	Mary E. Bowman	21 Dec 1870	
	Virlender	Michael Merrick	21 May 1800	
	William	Fannie Shorts	12 Jul 1871	
	William C.	Ann R. Wallace*	24 Dec 1861	
	William C.	Mary E. Poole	15 Jan 1867	
	William H.	Sarah Miller	20 Dec 1841	
	Willson	Matilda E. Hopwood	5 Jan 1836	
BOXALL,	James A.	Edith J. Nichols	26 Sep 1898	w
BOYCE - also see BOICE				
BOYCE,	Margaret E.	George Earl	10 Jun 1895	w
BOYD,	Charity D.	Horace Waters	10 May 1815	
	Elizabeth	George H. Gloud	27 Dec 1799	
	Elizabeth	Somerset Washington	22 Dec 1881	
	Elmore E.	Mary Martin	19 Jan 1888	c
	Henry P.	Mrs. Elizabeth L. Higgins	5 Apr 1872	
	John	Mary Parmer**	10 Mar 1798	
	Joseph	Harriet A. Washington	*** May 1883	
	Rachel	Joseph Owens	12 Feb 1805	
	Rufus E.	Bertha M. Zahn	31 Aug 1896	w
	Sarah	James Summers	15 Oct 1801	
	Sarah	John H. Posey	11 Sep 1878	w
	Thomas S. W.	Charlotte E. Frazier	17 May 1822	
	Wesley	Melinda Johnson	1 Apr 1879	c
	William	Emeline Prather	17 Oct 1836	
BOYER,	Basil E.	Elizabeth J. Warfield	30 Dec 1882	w
	Columbus	Leathan Miller	2 Apr 1884	
	Emma C.	Thomas G. Woodfield	29 Dec 1886	w
	J. Fletcher	Amanda W. Day	17 Dec 1881	
	J. Wellington	Alice H. Lewis	28 Jan 1844	
	Jesse D.	Carrie E. Watkins	9 Jan 1894	w
	John	Elizabeth Day	24 Feb 1816	
	John W.	Mary E. Warfield	12 Sep 1896	w
	Mary L.	Alonzo C. Watkins	26 Jul 1893	w
	Matilda****	Samuel Smith	19 Oct 1821	
	Sarah R.	Claude H. Burdette	3 Jun 1898	w
	William*****	Rebecca Norriss	23 Feb 1822	
BRACKETT - also see BROCKETT				
BRACKETT,	Eva A.	William G. Griffin	19 May 1897	w
BRADBURN,	Dolly	Rezin Wilburn	24 Jan 1807	
	Elizabeth	James Moore	31 Dec 1803	
	Elizabeth	William Steele	15 Oct 1817	
	John	Mary Wimsett	14 Nov 1803	
BRADDOCK - also see BRADOCK				
BRADDOCK,	Ann	William T. McCormick	1 Nov 1841	
	Elizabeth	John R. Miller	24 Feb 1838	
	George	Tabitha Austin	1 Sep 1840	
	Grace	James F. Green	24 Oct 1888	w

* As written; court records show Wallick to be correct
** As written; court records show Palmer to be correct
*** Cannot read complete day; between 16 and 19
**** Last name very light; earlier reading has Bryer
***** Blot on last 2 letters of last name; Boyer may be incorrect

BRADDOCK, Hannah	Isaiah Porter	2 Jun 1812	
James F.	Laura Baker	3 May 1866	
John	Sarah Ann Locke	27 Jul 1839	
Joseph	Laura Lock	6 Feb 1839	
Mary R.	Jetson Granger	13 Apr 1830	
Sarah H.	Charles Smith	8 May 1845	
William Perry	Elizabeth Locke	15 Jun 1843	
BRADFORD, Mabel	Edson B. Olds	1 Oct 1895	w
O. L.	Emmeline M. Talbott	1 Nov 1844	
BRADLEY, Alfred	Mary E. Jackson	25 May 1892	c
Caroline M.	John W. Magruder	3 Dec 1833	
George G.	Laura Gassaway	17 Aug 1863	
George G. Jr.	Katharine F. McDonald	8 Dec 1897	w
Guy B.	Rose B. Offutt	14 Dec 1896	w
John	Lucinda Addison	16 Jun 1875	
Joseph H. Jr.	Eliza M. Thomas	22 Nov 1856	
Sarah S.	James H. Davidson	11 Oct 1859	
Sylvia A.	G. W. Green	13 Aug 1874	
William P.	Mary H. Russell	6 Jan 1875	
BRADMAN, Mary Eleanor	Andrew Dumay	6 Jul 1816	
BRADOCK - also see BRADDOCK			
BRADOCK, Minty	Alexander Read	26 Oct 1801	
BRADY - also see BREADY			
BRADY, Charles W.	Mary J. Beall	11 Nov 1852	
Julia	James H. Redman	29 Mar 1875	
BRAN----ON, Daisy V.	John ?. Sullivan	* Oct 1896	w
BRANDBURG, Alice V.	Basil R. Burnes	20 Feb 1878	w
BRANDENBURG, Andrew J.	Carrie G. Watkins	4 Nov 1889	w
Charles J.	Mary V. Weaber	7 Nov 1892	w
George W.	Sarah F. Brown	29 Nov 1881	
Lottie E.	John W. Brown	26 Dec 1887	w
Sarah L.	Luther H. H. Browning	22 Apr 1861	
William B.	Minnie E. Watkins	31 Jan 1893	w
BRANDENSON, Warnetta	Richard Lee	21 Dec 1867	
BRANDISON - also see BRANISON			
BRANDISON, John	Mary Duffin	31 Oct 1868	
BRANHAM, Peter	Catharine Flaherty	8 Apr 1815	
BRANISON - also see BRANDISON, BRANSON			
BRANISON, John F.	Maggie Jackson	28 Dec 1898	c
Mary F.	Alex Hebron	30 Aug 1898	c
Raife	Mary Baily	12 Nov 1872	
BRANNON, Robert D.	Eleanor McBee	23 Nov 1824	
Sally	James O. Flaherty	2 Jan 1802	
BRANSON - also see BRANISON			
BRANSON, Arthur	Mary L. McDonald	30 Sep 1893	c
John F.	Ada Straighney	31 Jul 1889	c
Mary J.	John H. Duskins	13 May 1880	
BRASHEAR, Christopher H.	Sarah E. Hodges	27 Sep 1852	
James	Susan Hawker	3 May 1826	
BRASHEARS, Ann	William Thompson	19 Dec 1803	
Edward	Ann Dyson	22 Dec 1798	
Elizabeth**	Basil Ferguson	8 Oct 1798	
Elizabeth	John Baker	24 Dec 1801	

* Entire entry is blurred; day is before 9
** Part of last name from earlier reading

BRASHEARS, Emma C.	Frank M. Miller	24 Apr 1883
James	Mary M. Broome	22 Feb 1832
James	Mary Jane Taylor	27 Feb 1843
Lilburn	Mary Roberts	15 Jan 1803
Mary	Thomas Cross	14 Jan 1807
Mary E.	Allen M. Benson	8 Feb 1853
Milly	Richard P. Spates	20 Dec 1814
William	Anne Morrison	1 Jan 1810
BRASHERS, Ruth	Allin Harvey	14 Feb 1803
BRASSEL, Edward	Mary M. Guth	22 Sep 1897 w
BRAWNER, Julius	Lucinda Nelson	24 Dec 1872
BRAXTER, Ella	Charles McCallaster	22 May 1889 w
BRAXTON, Annie F.	William H. Eaglen	25 Apr 1890 c
Daniel	Mary Virginia Proctor	24 Oct 1883
Francis	Minnie L. Lee	30 Apr 1894 c
George	Lucy Jones	11 May 1877
John	Susan Waters	30 Aug 1897 c
Laurence	Airy Lucket	18 Jul 1877 c
Martha	David T. Nelson	8 Dec 1890 c
Sarah	William Lea	5 Dec 1894 c
William E.	Willie A. Nelson	13 Jul 1896 c
BRAY, Catherine	Hezekiah Trail	28 Dec 1811
Maurice W.	Ida M. Lowe	1 Jul 1893 w
Minnie	Robert E. L. Scott	5 Aug 1891 w
BRAYSHAW, Squire L.	Mary J. Winpenny	30 May 1871
BREADY - also see BRADY		
BREADY, Alice M.	Albert F. Rabbitt	23 Feb 1878 w
Calvin	Eliza Bready	7 Mar 1882
Charles W.	Dorothy E. Belt	19 Oct 1874
David F.	Octavia H. Cashell	16 Feb 1858
David J.	Ollie L. Hardy	26 Apr 1898 w
E. Tobias	Mary T. Hays	18 Aug 1876
Eliza	Calvin Bready	7 Mar 1882
Ida M.	Luther M. Duvall	15 Jun 1881 w
Laura	Franklin W. Price	23 Mar 1855
Samuel K.	Anne L. Rabbitt	25 Nov 1873
BREATHED - also see BRETHARD		
BREATHED, Isaac	Kitty Lyles	31 Dec 1811
BREATHILL, Cardwell	Rebecca Harwood	26 Mar 1810
BREEN, Hannah C.	George T. Garner	25 Jul 1892 w
BRELSFORD, Abner	Catharine Sullivan	30 Mar 1813
Amos	Sarah Sullivan	21 Apr 1814
Ann	John Brown	21 Sep 1811
BRENT, Harriet V.	John Thomas	28 May 1872
Jennie	Robert W. Hall	31 Jan 1895 c
Kate	John Washington	10 Sep 1884 c
Katie V.	Clarence Holman	12 Sep 1878 c
Mary	Theodore Mozier	22 Dec 1845
Peter	Eliza Williams	5 Dec 1868
William	Caroline Johnson	26 May 1881 c
BRETHARD - also see BREATHED		
BRETHARD, John T.	Ann M. Williams	12 Feb 1838
BRETT, Lelia S.	Harry A. A. Schroeder	6 May 1898 w
BREUER - also see BREWER		
BREUER, Eleanor	Joseph N. Burch	13 Jan 1825
Nathaniel N.	Mary E. Burch	15 Nov 1848

BREWELL, Isaac	Ann Henderfield	12 Sep 1815	
BREWER - also see BREUER			
BREWER, Amy C.	John M. King	16 Sep 1853	
Asenath R.	Benjamin W. Riggs	14 Feb 1844	
Eleanor I.	Oliver T. Watkins	23 Dec 1851	
Elizabeth	Charles Johnson	24 Aug 1897	c
Elizabeth W.	Charles Sutherland	2 Nov 1869	
Ellen	Spencer C. Jones	21 Dec 1871	
George	Alethea T. Young	28 Feb 1849	
Jennie P.	J. Lynn Davis	9 Nov 1875	
John	Delilah Burdictt	25 Apr 1805	
John	Elizabeth S. Buchanan	30 Jan 1838	
John B.	Virginia Russell	6 Oct 1874	
John H. C.	Fanny Cumming	29 Aug 1860	
John W.	Hettie W. Smith	14 Aug 1890	w
Joseph	Warnetter Sellman	10 Feb 1844	
Josephine	Wesley Garrison	1 May 1885	c
Mary	Amonadshanddai Moore	31 Dec 1832	
Mary R.	George R. Gott	25 Nov 1878	w
May G.	George L. Cramer	19 Mar 1895	w
Nicholas	Martha P. Williams	3 Sep 1849	
Susan E.	Gass Blacklock	31 Dec 1883	c
Vinson	Catharine Lewis	1 May 1827	
William	Mary R. Chiswell	5 Feb 1800	
William	Matilda P. Russell	12 Feb 1878	w
William	Carrie Green	20 Jul 1892	c
BREWINGTON, Nancy	Samuel Crawford	2 Jan 1802	
BRIAN - also see BRYAN			
BRIAN, Farnham	Eliza Keiler	7 May 1886	w
Henry	Martha Garnett	7 Nov 1883	
BRICE, Edward C.	Lucy L. Young	3 Nov 1894	w
BRIDGER, Aileen M.	Benedict W. Gheen	6 Jul 1897	w
BRIDGET, Thomas	Ruth Swearingen	26 Sep 1814	
BRIGGS, Clara E.	Francis B. Musgrove	21 Dec 1891	w
Edward H.	Frances Beckwith	29 May 1862	
Elizabeth	Thomas B. Scott	1 Jan 1824	
Elonzo M.	Rachel P. Snyder	4 Dec 1872	
Gideon D.	Ida V. Sparrow	3 Dec 1873	
J. W.	Mary C. Sparrow	14 Nov 1872	
James M. W.	Drusilla Snyder	8 Jan 1868	
Jesse E.	Carrie E. Crouse	14 Jan 1886	w
Joseph A.	Rosalie Bogley	16 Dec 1895	w
Lillie M.	George R. Stuart	9 Feb 1897	w
Maggie V.	James E. Duvall	21 Jun 1898	w
Mary E.	Thomas E. Peddicord	20 May 1889	w
Nettie M.	Ira I. Covert	26 Jul 1898	w
Oliver N.	Elberta Penn	20 Nov 1894	w
Robert	Sarah Williams	22 Dec 1804	
Robert B.	Leannah Snyder	9 Jun 1862	
Samuel S.	Eleanor W. S. Higgins	22 Oct 1835	
Samuel T.	Sarah E. Clagett	21 Dec 1864	
Thomas E.	Augusta I. Clagett	19 Oct 1895	w
William H.	Henrietta E. Thomas	4 May 1836	
Zachariah	Mary James Clagett	7 Dec 1870	
Zachariah T.	Elenora Power	6 Sep 1898	w
BRIGHAM, John H.	Annie A. Crown	24 Sep 1889	w

BRIGHT, Amanda	John Shreeves	24 Dec 1870	
Franklin M.	Cedalia M. Miles	27 Apr 1898	w
Ida J.	Harry Clay King	23 Dec 1884	c
Louisa	Richard Washington	19 Aug 1875	
William J.	Elizabeth E. Gray	24 Mar 1842	
BRIGHTWELL, John A.	Mary Owen	12 Nov 1834	
BRISCOE, Margaret M.	Matthew Dyson	30 Nov 1875	c
Mary E.	Jutson W. Phelps	21 Mar 1846	
Sarah Jane	Francis M. Weadon	6 Nov 1837	
BROADHURST, John N.	Cerita M. Mullinix	1 May 1896	w
BROADNIX, Martin	Lizzie Martin	24 Dec 1867	
BROADUS, John	Joan Johnson	11 Jun 1867	
BROCKETT - also see BRACKETT			
BROCKETT, Robert L.	Ann E. McCormick	11 Jun 1842	
BRODERICK, Nora C.	Michael C. Kelley	3 Aug 1895	w
BRODERS, Joseph*	A. E. Monroe	13 Nov 1856	
BROGDAN, Mary E.	Robert Neucy	19 Nov 1870	
BROGDEN, Anne	Jacob Grigg	22 Dec 1870	
Augustus	Mary Johnson	11 Sep 1879	c
Charlotte	James Brown	25 Nov 1893	c
Edward	Mary Jane Lee	2 Jan 1877	
Frances	William White	30 Nov 1882	c
James W.	Mary A. Thomas	4 Oct 1895	c
Josiah	Sophia Warren	29 Jun 1866	
Louisa	John T. Taylor	26 Oct 1887	c
Lydia	John G. Franklin	26 Aug 1891	c
BRONOUGH, Robert	Mary Ann Kindle	16 Dec 1828	
BROOK, Alice	William H. Thompson	28 May 1884	c
BROOKE, Alban	Sarah E. Pleasants	2 Jan 1878	w
Allice	James P. Stabler	18 Nov 1870	
Emilie T.	Robert O. Coulter	15 Oct 1896	w
Henrietta	Ellsworth Simmons	8 Mar 1896	c
Joseph	Letitia Boone	27 Dec 1798	
Margaret H.	William E. Magruder	21 May 1864	
Maria W.	Spencer Watkins	14 Jun 1870	
Martha	William Wallace	28 Dec 1800	
Martha R.	Frederick Stabler	5 Nov 1866	
Mary P.	Elisha J. Hall	3 Oct 1838	
William D.	Henrietta J. Trundle	25 Sep 1860	
William Irvin	Helen Holland	31 Jan 1882	
BROOKES - also see BROOKS			
BROOKES, William	Dolly Coombes	16 Feb 1801	
BROOKINS, Kassius	Elizabeth Dawes	22 Dec 1815	
BROOKS - also see BROOKES			
BROOKS, Charles	Eliza Neel	20 Jan 1873	
Daniel J.	Lavinia Johnson	16 Dec 1880	c
Edward	Mary A. Carr	11 Jan 1853	
Lewis	Amanda Bettitt	21 Jan 1870	
Lizzie	Grant Beall	26 Dec 1888	c
Martha L.	George Snowden	8 Apr 1873	
Mattie E.	Jerry D. Riley	3 Feb 1897	c
Millie	Henry Prator	8 Feb 1872	
Nannie F.	George A. Jeffries	3 Oct 1886	c
Rebecca	Franklin H. Dorsey	19 Jan 1888	c

* In brackets after names is "Alex. Co., Va."

BROOKS, Sarah	George Dorsey	8 Jun 1870	
Wesley	Florence Palmer	28 Jul 1897	c
BROOM, Barbara A.	Thomas B. Benson	10 Aug 1867	
BROOME, Alexander	Mary E. Darby	15 Jun 1830	
Alexander	Mollie L. Warfield	2 Dec 1878	
Dathan	Sarah E. Nicholls	4 Mar 1868	
Ella F.	William F. Connell	10 Mar 1884	
Issabella	Thomas B. Benson	26 Dec 1828	
Mary M.	James Brashears	22 Feb 1832	
Thomas	Columbia V. Nicholls	23 Feb 1875	
William H.	Ellen F. Purdum	30 Jan 1877	w
BROUGHTON, Charlotte	James E. Swick	22 Jul 1895	w
BROUN - also see BROWN			
BROUN, Elijah	Martha E. Tyler	14 Oct 1875	
BROWN - also see BROUN			
BROWN, Airah	Lancelot Wilson Ray	28 Mar 1811	
Albert	Ella Washington	31 Dec 1879	c
Albert	Matilda Cephas	13 May 1880	
Alexander	Lavinia Nelson	25 Aug 1875	
Alexander	Savanna Warren	1 Mar 1897	c
Alfred	Henrietta Zeigler	15 Aug 1848	
Alice	Joseph Green	1* Sep 1883	c
Amanda	William Henry Wims	16 Dec 1876	
Amelia A.	Richard H. Willson	26 May 1882	c
Amos	Sarah Ridgely Griffith	20 Jan 1808	
Ann	Thomas Mills	16 Nov 1840	
Annie E.	Joseph G. Brown	24 Oct 1891	w
Annie Mary	James C. Reid	29 May 1893	w
Annie R.	Richard I. Lea	22 Dec 1888	w
Augustus	Mary Ann Stephens	18 Nov 1835	
Basil	Anne Davis	18 Mar 1807	
Basil E.	Eveline Hood	23 Apr 1895	w
Belle	Charles Scott Jones	29 Nov 1893	w
Bettie	Adolphus Higgins	23 Dec 1873	
Bradley	Rosa M. Swann	8 Sep 1896	c
Bryant	Eliza A. Mack---**	22 Feb 1867	
Catharine E.	John S. Heckrote	26 Jun 1849	
Charles	Mary House	15 Dec 1808	
Charles	Carrie Allis	16 Apr 1898	c
Charles E.	Annie E. Harrity	20 Feb 1895	c
Charles H.	Mary Jane Onley	23 Dec 1869	
Clara	James H. Campbell	17 Aug 1889	c
Clarence	Catherine E. Benson	8 Jan 1895	w
Clemmie	George Clagett	3 Jan 1877	
Daniel A.	Mary E. Herbert	16 Dec 1886	c
Della	William Medley	2 May 1891	c
Dennis	Maria Ann Becket	24 Oct 1876	
Edith	Oliver L. Brown	25 Oct 1888	w
Edward	Edmonia Cooper	11 Dec 1884	c
Edward B.	Anna M. Phoebus	15 Jan 1883	w
Edward H.	Ann E. Stone	31 Oct 1863	
Edward L.	Rosie A. Lavalley	2 Jan 1895	w
Edward T.	Laura H. McCrossin	15 Jan 1883	w

* Cannot read complete day; between 10 and 19
** Remainder of name written over

BROWN,	Eleanor	Nicholas Mullican	28 Dec 1822	
	Elijah	Mary C. Turner	22 Nov 1886	c
	Elizabeth	Benjamin Burdett	8 Dec 1812	
	Elizabeth	Rezin Praither	10 Jun 1886	c
	Elizabeth Anne	Richard Harding	6 Jan 1824	
	Elizabeth E.	William Brown of J	22 Nov 1865	
	Ella F.	Henry W. Freeman	16 Sep 1897	c
	Emeline	Daniel Shaw	13 May 1876	
	Emeline	John Thompson	11 Dec 1878	c
	Ephraim	Julia Ann Waugh	5 Nov 1873	
	Ephraim Willson	Louisa Turner	4 Nov 1830	
	Fannie	Henry Johnson	7 Sep 1876	
	Fannie	George B. Curtis	18 Oct 1879	w
	Florence	Irwin Oliver Ridgely	27 Mar 1894	w
	Francis	Mary Barrett	30 Dec 1805	
	Francis S.	Lucinda R. Edmonstone	15 Sep 1829	
	Frederick T.	Ann Maria Worrell	19 Jan 1856	
	George A.	Mamie M. Lee	15 Jun 1896	c
	George Bibb	Lucinda B. Anderson	18 Nov 1895	w
	Gertrude	William H. Williams	11 Jul 1895	c
	Gertrude M.	George M. Miller	9 Apr 1898	w
	Gertrude V.	Clifford E. Price	29 Feb 1892	w
	Hannah	Llewellen Mackall	23 Sep 1870	
	Harriet	Peter H. Davis	26 Sep 1873	
	Harriet	John Mason	29 May 1882	c
	Harry	Annie M. Benson	31 Oct 1893	w
	Hatten	Deborah Shanks	11 Jul 1826	
	Henrietta	Harry Thomas	27 Dec 1883	c
	Henry	Sarah Ann Harris	29 Mar 1838	
	Henry	Matilda Marriott	4 Oct 1854	
	Henry	Mary Williams	21 Aug 1879	c
	Henry Clay	Anne Holland	12 Jan 1872	
	Henry H.	Sarah Appleby	17 Feb 1835	
	Henson	Janie Howard	21 Mar 1889	c
	Hervey Jr.	Sallie Willson	20 Sep 1892	w
	Hetty A.	George L. Dwyer	14 Apr 1890	w
	Hutchison	Rebecca Irvin	5 Nov 1867	
	Ida B.	Greenbury C. Poole	21 Sep 1881	w
	Ida J.	William P. Leizear	29 Nov 1877	w
	James	Nancy Leek	18 Jan 1803	
	James	Elizabeth Rawlins	16 Feb 1828	
	James	Charlotte Brogden	25 Nov 1893	c
	James	Hattie Mason	20 Mar 1895	c
	James C.	Mary Ellen Penn	6 Jan 1827	
	James Frank	Ida Veirs	8 Sep 1886	w
	James H.	Minerva S. Anderson	29 Sep 1857	
	James T.	Annie M. V. Beall	20 Jan 1873	
	James W.	Helen W. Ashton	30 May 1898	w
	Jane	William Diggs	15 Apr 1865	
	Jemima	Shedereck Beall	25 Sep 1822	
	Jennie	Luke Childs	24 Dec 1866	
	Jeremiah	Elizabeth Thompson	8 Jan 1816	
	Jesse D.	Annie M. Green	27 Nov 1888	w
	John	Ann Brelsford	21 Sep 1811	
	John	Louisa Hawkins	18 May 1877	c

BROWN, John	Maria Howard	* Jul 1882	c
John**	Agnes Snowden	9 Oct 1883	c
John	Mary E. Hall	6 Feb 1884	c
John F.	Helen Ritter	4 Sep 1896	w
John Fletcher	Martha Wheatly Groomes	16 Jan 1884	
John S.	Ann M. Wigton	26 Dec 1817	
John W.	Mary E. Shaw	22 Nov 1852	
John W.	Lottie E. Brandenburg	26 Dec 1887	w
John William	Alice A. Jason	6 Jul 1878	c
Joseph	Nancy Windsor	18 Dec 1799	
Joseph G.	Annie E. Brown	24 Oct 1891	w
Joshua	Martha L. Anderson	22 Nov 1860	
Joshua ***	Nancy H. Jones	12 Dec 1816	
Joshua W.	Laura V. Moxley	19 Dec 1891	w
Julia	Edward Sewell	19 May 1893	c
Laura V.	Upton Duston	30 Aug 1881	
Lavinia	Charles H. Anderson	24 May 1847	
Lavinia	William E. Howes	6 Sep 1894	w
Lee E.	Peter C. R. Erdman	19 Dec 1891	w
Lewis	Lizzie Jackson	24 Sep 1870	
Lillie	William Bowie	25 Dec 1889	c
Lorala Ann	William Harding	29 May 1840	
Lucinda A.	Julius S. Bohrer	16 Nov 1848	
Luther	Gracie Ann Hawkins	4 Jan 1893	c
Lydia	James Mitchell	1 Sep 1891	c
Lydia H.	W. B. Chichester	13 Jan 1854	
Maggie	William Carter	30 Dec 1872	
Margaret	Henry Tyler	3 Jan 1874	
Margaret	John Kinchen	13 Nov 1799	
Margaret A.	Uriah T. Watkins	26 Nov 1884	w
Margaret E.	John T. Ridgely	22 Nov 1877	w
Margarett	Berry Robey	19 May 1828	
Maria	John F. Rix	24 Dec 1869	
Marshall	Sarah M. Belt	15 Dec 1857	
Martha	? ? ?	17 Jun 1879	
Martha A.	John R. Harding	16 Mar 1863	
Martha E.	Dandridge Harriss	1 Mar 1888	c
Martha E.	Israel K. Phillips	18 Jul 1889	w
Martha E.	Robert P. Foreman	28 Dec 1892	c
Mary	Elias Power	16 Nov 1810	
Mary	Jasper Ridgley	19 Sep 1867	
Mary	John H. Tyler	7 Feb 1888	c
Mary E.	Richard E. Dorsey	3 Nov 1897	c
Mary O.	William Lyles	20 Jul 1893	c
Mary R.	George P. Hedrick	3 Sep 1887	w
Mary R.	William A. Baker	8 Feb 1888	w
Mary S.	George E. Adams	31 May 1888	c
Matilda	John W. Ridgely	18 Feb 1884	w
Matilda J.	Frank Offutt	12 Nov 1868	
Melvin D.	Emily Jackson	22 Nov 1897	w
Mercer	Charlotte Lewis	14 Feb 1825	
Mercer	Mary G. Linthicum	12 Dec 1831	

* Cannot read day; before 10
** Both last name very difficult to read; could be incorrect
*** Initial I or J

BROWN, Nathan	Eliza L. Leach	14 Apr 1818	
Nathaniel B.	Mary A. Jenkins	10 Mar 1870	
Oliver L.	Edith Brown	25 Oct 1888	w
Olivia J.	Marshall C. Watkins	29 May 1884	
Owen C.	Sallie Phillips	4 Jan 1888	w
Pleasant (male)	Irodine Franklin	9 Dec 1890	w
Rachel A.	Charles A. Clagett	16 Dec 1887	c
Rachel A.	Alvin T. Bowie	28 Oct 1891	c
Rebecca	John Congalton	1 May 1820	
Rebecca	Walter Carr	20 Nov 1833	
Rebecca	Stephen Anderson	28 Oct 1845	
Remus	Susan Clagett	31 Jan 1885	c
Reuben	Minerva Poole	9 Nov 1840	
Reuben	Jemimah P. King	30 Jan 1850	
Reuben M.	Annie G. King	10 Dec 1872	
Richard R.	Elizabeth T. Murphey	11 May 1846	
Robert	Jane Bond	13 Apr 1817	
Robert	Martha C. Thompson	13 Sep 1847	
Robert	Alice Nelson	21 Jan 1884	c
Robert	Charlotte Scott	1 Feb 1894	c
Sally	Allen Holland	6 Mar 1816	
Samuel	Hattie Mackabee	30 Jan 1879	c
Sarah	Moses W. Jones	15 Jan 1803	
Sarah	Uriah Brown	22 Dec 1823	
Sarah	Andrew Jackson	16 May 1868	
Sarah	Jeremiah Mackall	27 Dec 1883	c
Sarah Annie	Mortimer L. Price	27 Oct 1886	w
Sarah E.	William C. Harvey	22 Oct 1890	w
Sarah F.	George W. Brandenburg	29 Nov 1881	
Savannah E.	George W. Beall	9 Nov 1885	
Susan Ann	James Shreeves	6 Sep 1832	
Susan E.	Elijah Lancaster	5 Jun 1879	c
Susannah	Mahlin A. Pool	11 May 1857	
Thomas	Ann Sewell	13 Sep 1803	
Thomas	Anne Warfield	23 Jan 1883	c
Thomas E.	Eliza A. Chambers	8 Feb 1858	
Thomas J.	Caroline Bibb	10 Oct 1866	
Thomas J.	Maggie E. Allnutt	21 Dec 1891	w
Tilghman	Clara Mason	10 Dec 1885	c
Uriah	Sarah Brown	22 Dec 1823	
Verlinda	Jeremiah Mitchell	26 Dec 1811	
Wallace H.	Sarah Telley	11 May 1898	c
Walter	Frances Holman	12 Aug 1876	
William	Priscilla Hart	18 Feb 1801	
William	Sarah Leake	2 Apr 1821	
William	Jane Fletchall	5 Sep 1838	
William	Sarah A. Burriss	17 Nov 1857	
William	Rebecca Norris	26 Jun 1895	c
William of J	Elizabeth E. Brown	22 Nov 1865	
William C.	Mollie Darby	17 Feb 1876	
William E.	Margaret A. Warren	5 Nov 1896	c
William H.	Eliza Young	11 Feb 1898	c
William H. H.	Mary Hall	4 Mar 1875	
William H. H.	Sarah Barrett	10 Aug 1898	c
William T.	Elizabeth Campbell	17 Aug 1889	c
Zephaniah	Leannah Burress	27 Oct 1831	

BROWNING, Alice E.	William S. Reid	23 Apr 1894	w
Archibald	Eleanor Browning	30 Nov 1805	
Charles E.	Livenia E. Windsor	4 Mar 1887	w
Cornelius H.	Eveline R. Walker	25 Nov 1890	w
D. M., Rev.	Mallina V. Davis	11 Oct 1876	
Daniel	Axia Warfield	7 Feb 1801	
Dorcas	Berry Roby	6 Aug 1833	
Edith	Littleton Macklin	4 Jan 1833	
Eleanor	Archibald Browning	30 Nov 1805	
Elizabeth	Henry Roby	22 Dec 1800	
Elizabeth	Thomas Hillard	16 Dec 1806	
George R.	Louisa Clarke	26 Feb 1831	
George R.	Mary Elizabeth Clark	18 Jun 1833	
Greenbury	Darcus Hoskinson	8 Nov 1821	
Hessa	Aaron Poole	11 Dec 1798	
James	Mary Smith	23 Sep 1802	
Jeremiah	Elizabeth Summers	30 Apr 1803	
Jeremiah*	Drusilla Lewis	31 Dec 1808	
John	Sarah Airess	13 Apr 1802	
John B.	Ann Beall	17 Jan 1831	
Jonathan	Susannah Winroad	31 Nov 1804	
Jonathan	Polly Hobbs	5 Sep 1825	
Joseph	Sarah Veatch	18 Jan 1817	
Joseph	Rhoda Ann Harper	7 Nov 1826	
Luther H. H.	Sarah L. Brandenburg	22 Apr 1861	
Mahlon	Sarah F. Smith	24 May 1858	
Margaret	Arnold Warfield	21 Mar 1798	
Margarett Louisa	Thomas C. Cole	15 Sep 1831	
Martha	John ?. Harding	15 Feb 1826	
Mary	James A. E. Merritt	7 Sep 1836	
Mary E.	John D. Scott	14 Nov 1848	
Mary J.	Nathan Burdett	21 Jun 1890	w
Meshech	Sally C. Holmes	14 Dec 1805	
Rachel	Asher Layton, Sr.	20 Nov 1824	
Rachel	John Ramey	8 Dec 1830	
Reverdy	Sarah E. A. Purdum	29 Jan 1884	
Samuel H. W.*	Rosa B. Purdum	21 Dec 1896	w
Samuel P.	Rebecca Shipley	12 Jan 1807	
Silas	Serena S. Gittings	4 Feb 1858	
Verlinda	Nelson Beall	27 Jun 1833	
W. T.	Carolyn M. Cinnamond	31 Mar 1859	
Wesley	Martha Valdenar	22 Oct 1833	
William	Priscilla Buxton	1 Feb 1820	
BRUCE, Eliza Jane	Isaac White	15 Nov 1865	
Emily	Leonard Hebborn	19 May 1877	c
Hattie E.	Henry A. Lewis	18 Apr 1891	w
John	Maria Ridgeley	31 Jan 1874	
Mary	William C. Plummer	21 Dec 1877	c
Sarah E.	James W. Lyles	16 Sep 1880	c
BRUEHL, Emil George	Frederica P. Birgfeld	24 Jan 1881	
BRUMIDI, Lola V.	Columbus Kirkwood	23 Jul 1891	w
BRUNER - also see BRUNNER			
BRUNER, Amy F.	George McC. Offutt	28 Dec 1896	w

* Last names written in record as Browing; Browning is correct

BRUNER, Henry	Mary E. Dorsey	18 May 1891	c
Isaac	Eliza Barnes	12 Apr 1898	c
Matilda	Hilleary Piles	22 Dec 1827	
Mollie A.	Isaac N. Staub	5 Sep 1879	w
BRUNETT, John L.	Florence J. Clements	20 May 1884	w
Julian M.	Martha F. Shaw	27 Dec 1893	w
BRUNETT, Louisa M.	John T. Bogan	18 Sep 1842	
BRUNNER - also see BRUNER			
BRUNNER, Hattie A.	Charles S. Butler	24 Aug 1895	w
Ida	Isaiah Bell	22 May 1895	c
Rosa E.	Richard T. Butler	1 Feb 1896	w
Sallie E.	Joseph T. White	25 Nov 1889	w
BRYAN - also see BRIAN			
BRYAN, James A.	Mary V. Leizear	20 May 1881	
William	Eleanor Soper	4 Apr 1817	
BRYANT, Laura	Patrick McMahon	5 Dec 1891	w
BRYER, Matilda - see Matilda Boyer			
BUCHANAN, Elizabeth S.	John Brewer	30 Jan 1838	
Mary J.	Otis C. Wight	28 Jul 1847	
BUCK, Lavinia	Eleazer O. Earnest	21 Jul 1879	w
Wilson D.	Minnie S. Suter	23 Jun 1884	w
BUCKINGHAM, John W.	Elizabeth A. Guy	10 Jun 1881	w
Lemuel	Lizzie E. Stevens	30 Dec 1876	
BUCKMAN, Jonathan	Ann S. Payton	21 Feb 1833	
BUDD, Christiana	Benjamin F. Marriott	30 May 1889	c
Eliza E.	Matthew Stewart	7 Oct 1890	c
James A.	Lizzie L. Cook	1 Sep 1874	
John H.	Mary A. Rounds	28 Oct 1885	c
Joseph	Eliza Cook	4 Dec 1868	
Lizzie	George W. Russell	12 Jul 1877	c
Lucy	William Eli Thomas	28 Sep 1898	c
Lucy E.	Arthur E. Billows	13 Jan 1898	c
Martha Jane	William H. Thomas	17 Jan 1871	
Mary E.	John S. Powell	4 Oct 1887	c
Richard	Eliza Ann Allens	24 Nov 1841	c
Richard P.	Amanda Armstead	28 Nov 1887	c
Richard T.	Laura B. Snowden	24 Nov 1883	
Sadie R.	John W. Williams	2* Jan 1888	c
Samuel	Harriet A. Squirrel	12 Nov 1866	
Sarah	Frederick Nesbit	10 Apr 1871	
Walter	Lizzie Newcy	5 May 1892	c
William H.	Catharine A. Sedgwick	** Jan 1880	
BUECHLER, Frank H.	Mary L. Shedd	31 Aug 1897	w
BUKOFFSKY, Martha V.	John E. Bowman	9 Dec 1893	w
William H.	Martha Leizear	1 May 1866	
BUMBREY, James E.	Mary C. Morris	28 May 1897	c
BUNTING, Charles	Susan Fling	9 Apr 1819	
BURCH - also see BIRCH, BURCHE			
BURCH, Benjamin	Nancy Moore	16 May 1816	
Henry C.	Mary R. Hall	19 Apr 1887	w
James F.	Jennie E. Corson	27 Feb 1884	
John L.	Alice Basford	23 Feb 1876	
John T.	Annie M. Cecil	19 Apr 1898	w

* Cannot read complete day; either 25 or 28
** Day too light to read; between 21 and 29

BURCH, Joseph N.	Eleanor Breuer	13 Jan 1825	
Lewis B.	Marlena Hunter	25 Jan 1832	
Mary E.	Nathaniel N. Breuer	15 Nov 1848	
Nora L.	James R. Dove	18 Aug 1886	w
BURCHE, Margaret A.	James A. Dove	12 Jan 1880	w
Mary	William C. Mossburg	4 Aug 1879	
BURDEST - also see BURDETTE			
BURDEST, Martha	Philip Smallwood	26 Mar 1831	
BURDETT - also see BURDETTE			
BURDETT, Ann	George W. Gue	7 Mar 1836	
Ann H.	Richard Wheeler	13 Feb 1849	
Basil	Deborah J. Burdett	15 Jun 1861	
Benjamin	Elizabeth Brown	8 Dec 1812	
Benjamin	Mary A. Hickman	26 Feb 1848	
Betsey	Obed Leek	28 Oct 1801	
Carrie S.	Lorenzo Gue	10 Feb 1865	
Cassandra E.	William M. Beall	29 Jul 1885	
Courtney	George T. Nicholls	29 Jan 1879	w
Deborah	Moses Snider	5 Mar 1824	
Deborah Ann	Nathaniel Mills	11 Dec 1845	
Deborah J.	Basil Burdett	15 Jun 1861	
Elizabeth	Lloyd Gray	23 Oct 1832	
Emma F.	Remus G. Weaver	8 Aug 1887	w
Evan	Mary Ann Miller	13 Nov 1828	
George M.	Emma Reeder	6 Nov 1888	w
Greenbury W.	Martha E. Ward	25 Nov 1840	
Hamilton	Elizabeth R. King	25 Feb 1833	
Ida F.	Luther N. King	14 May 1884	w
Ida P.	Randolph H. Windsor	6 Nov 1888	w
James W.	Cassandra Purdom	14 Apr 1840	
John	Mary Hilton	9 Jan 1822	
John E.	Elizabeth King	6 Jun 1871	
John F.	Ella F. Turner	20 Feb 1883	w
Joseph	Sary Burdett	31 Dec 1803	
Josephine	John A. Lembrick	23 Oct 1874	
Julia A.	George E. King	30 Dec 1861	
Lewis G.	Kitty Beall	14 May 1841	
Lula D.	John O. Haynie	26 Feb 1883	w
Mary Ann	John W. Baker	26 Apr 1865	
Mary E.	James H. Watkins	22 Nov 1892	w
Nathan	Mary J. Browning	21 Jun 1890	w
Philip	Susannah Rebecca Clagett	17 Aug 1838	
Prudence V.	Dorsey W. Day	20 Dec 1895	w
Rhoda R.	Henry Gue	21 Dec 1866	
Richard H.	Louisa Ann Darby	20 Feb 1835	
Richard H.	Sarah A. Stallings	15 Dec 1863	
Richard T.	Harriet A. Beall	19 Nov 1868	
Richard T.	Laura V. Watkins	11 Jun 1875	
Sarah	Henry Gue	30 Nov 1843	
Sarah J.	James E. Williams	4 Oct 1856	
Sary	Joseph Burdett	31 Dec 1803	
Westly	Harriett Appleby	6 Jun 1816	
William G.	Bessie A. Gue	26 Oct 1895	w
William M.	Martha A. Shipley	13 Mar 1856	
Zachariah J.H.W.	Mary Ann Miles	20 Jan 1846	

BURDETTE - also see BIRDETT, BURDICT, BURDICTT, BURDIT,
          BURDITT, BURDETT, BURDEST

BURDETTE, Allen H.	Nellie A. Thompson	19 Feb 1884	
Charles W.	Rebecca N. Williams	24 Aug 1878	w
Claude H.	Sarah R. Boyer	3 Jun 1898	w
Deborah J.	Charles R. Israel	22 Dec 1884	w
Emma C.	William H. Warfield	22 Dec 1890	w
Emma Cole	James W. Johnson	17 May 1898	w
Emma J.	Richard W. Cain	18 Dec 1894	w
Fannie C.	Benjamin A. Mossburg	24 Dec 1890	w
Franklin E.	Henrietta R. Ward	13 Jan 1898	w
George F.	Marian H. Jones	20 Jul 1886	w
Greenbury W.	Ida M. Lewis	12 Apr 1887	w
Harry L.	Mary Lee Shea	26 May 1886	w
James F.	Iona M. Snyder	20 Feb 1897	w
James W.	Miranda E. Etchison	14 Oct 1895	w
Jerrie L.	Vivia C. Day	12 Aug 1892	w
John D.	Maggie M. King	14 Jan 1896	w
John J.	Cora I. King	27 Dec 1897	w
Joseph M.	Hattie A. Purdum	18 Dec 1882	
Lincoln	Georgie W. King	23 Feb 1886	w
Lillie M.	John W. Umberger	22 Oct 1898	w
Mary E.	H. M. Musser	20 Oct 1882	
Mary E.	Charles McGregor	19 May 1886	w
Mary F.	Thomas G. Beall	12 Nov 1884	w
Rebecca Z.	Bradley Watkins	9 Oct 1896	w
Richard T.	Laura W. Lewis	17 Jan 1880	w
Thomas A.	Sarah P. Darby	24 Jan 1881	w
Valinda C.	Jeremiah Lewis	26 May 1892	w
William C.	Nice Gue	1 May 1889	w
Willie H.	Mamie E. Peugh	20 Nov 1895	w
Willie H.	Beda C. King	9 Aug 1897	w
Willis B.	Lula B. Walker	6 Jun 1896	w

BURDICT - also see BURDETTE

BURDICT, Ann	Henry L. Moore	19 Jun 1817	
BURDICTT, Delilah	John Brewer	25 Apr 1805	

BURDIT - also see BURDETTE

BURDIT, Zachariah	Elizabeth Leeke	16 Dec 1825	
BURDITT, Basil	Deborah Bennett	23 Feb 1809	
Ezar (female)	Somerset T. Williams	9 May 1871	
Thomas	Elizabeth Moore	21 May 1811	
William	Ruth Fitzgerald	16 Feb 1804	
BURFORD, John A.	Sarah Silby	18 Sep 1813	
Laura	Cyrus Bowen, Jr.	24 Nov 1859	
William	Sarah Cecil	29 Nov 1842	

BURGESS - also see BURGISS

BURGESS, Andrew F.	Katie M. Wheeler	21 Oct 1897	w
Benjamin L.	Elizabeth H. Mobley	3 Jan 1832	
Eleanor	John McCann	6 Apr 1808	
Helen N.	Charles Mason Bates	12 Nov 1892	w
Henry W.	Ann E. Evelin	1 May 1850	
James	Annie McAllister	26 Aug 1896	c
John	Hellen Maccubbin	19 Mar 1800	
John	Elizabeth Thompson	10 Jan 1818	
Margarett	Ninian Clagett	5 Sep 1804	
Mary R.	Dennis McMahew	5 Apr 1858	

BURGESS, Nancy*	Joshua Lewis	18 Dec 1817
Owen	Alice Young	30 May 1883
Rachel Ann	Daniel F. Redman	1 Apr 1886 c
Rebecca ?.	Samuel E. Ryon	1 Jul 1867
Rebeccah	Thomas Selby	7 Aug 1810
Sarah E.	Thomas E. Carter	27 Oct 1898 c
William	Alley Seal	16 Jun 1801
BURGISS - also see BURGESS		
BURGISS, Elizur	James Vermillion	15 Oct 1821
BURK, Greenberry	Margarett Hickman	4 Oct 1814
BURKE, Greenbury	Elizabeth Dorsey	26 Mar 1841
Katie E.	Edward Welsh	25 May 1895 w
Nellie F.	Sylvester Reid	9 Feb 1887 w
BURKHEAD - also see BIRKHEAD		
BURKHEAD, John	Ann Trail	30 Nov 1813
William	Elizabeth Middleton	31 Mar 1814
BURKHOLDER, Mallie M.	Parke L. Cootes	26 Jul 1894 w
BURKITT, Mary A.	George Howard	9 Nov 1885 c
BURKLEY - also see BERKLEY		
BURKLEY, Louisa A.	Thomas R. Edwards	**28 Mar 1898 w
BURNELL, J. Gilbert	Sarah E. Allen	30 Mar 1874
Robert H.	Mary G. Baker	29 Jun 1896 w
BURNES - also see BURNS		
BURNES, Basil R.	Alice V. Brandburg	20 Feb 1878 w
John H.	Matilda Thompson	21 Apr 1829
Mary	John H. Thompson	3 Mar 1832
Nelson	Catharine Iglehart	16 Jan 1837
Thomas	Biddy Donohough	18 Apr 1802
William	Ann Darby	23 Jul 1804
BURNETT - also see BARNETT		
BURNETT, Carrie B.	Samuel S. Saxton	13 Jun 1891 w
Charles A.	Eleatha Lanham	18 Jul 1805
BURNS - also see BURNES		
BURNS, Amanda E.	Basil B. Iglehart	14 Mar 1865
Ann Virginia	Richard Plummer	1 Jan 1866
Anne	William Thompson	19 Apr 1832
Catharine M.	William C. Burns	18 Jan 1868
Clinton	Hattie A. Crawford	6 Feb 1889 w
Eleanor	Nicholas R. Darby	30 Jan 1837
Elizabeth	Otho Trundle	20 Jan 1804
Harry N.	Mary E. Waters	17 Oct 1889 w
Ida E.	Thomas O. King	*** Nov 1888 w
Jesse L.	Louisa N. Baker	20 Sep 1876
John	Virginia Mills	27 Feb 1871
Joshua R.	Alice V. Merson	19 Dec 1883
Leonard C.	Lillie S. Ward	18 May 1887 w
Lillie M.	John B. King	**** Oct 1881 w
Mina	Willie Unglesbee	30 Apr 1888 w
Ollie B.	Franklin E. Gue	21 Jul 1891 w
Oscar	Addie Duvall	20 Sep 1898 w
Sarah Ann	E. Columbus Thompson	12 Dec 1854

* Part of last name from earlier reading
** Date is written Mar 28, but is after Feb 26 and before Mar 4
*** Cannot read complete day; between 14 and 18
**** Day is written over; either 1 or 3

BURNS, Silas B.	Nonie Bowman	2 Nov 1895	w
Sylvester	Elizabeth A. Riggs	16 Mar 1856	
Verlinda	Edward Woodfield	20 Apr 1847	
William C.	Catharine M. Burns	18 Jan 1868	

BURNSIDES - also see BIRNSIDES

BURNSIDES, Margaret Ann	Amos Vanfossen	6 Aug 1823	
BURNSYDES, Mary	William Griffith	9 Apr 1812	
BURR, Louise S.	George G. Getty	3 Jun 1895	w
BURRELL, Emmitt Marcellus	Bettie Gardner	10 Nov 1886	c

BURRESS - see BURROUGHS or BURRIS for other spellings

BURRESS, Aaron	Frances Bean	14 Aug 1827	
Basil	Verlinda Burress	30 Sep 1819	
Basil	Verlinda Gray	31 Dec 1832	
Cassandra	Proverb Burress	5 Jan 1815	
Eliza Ann	William Swain	19 Dec 1828	
Jane	William Boswell	18 Jun 1828	
John	Margaret Swailes	1 Jan 1811	
Leannah	Zephaniah Brown	27 Oct 1831	
Letha	Robert Ricketts	26 Dec 1839	
Mary	Basil Butt	29 Oct 1814	
Nancy	William Tucker	18 Jan 1821	
Proverb	Cassandra Burress	5 Jan 1815	
Ruth	Ransel Mowyer	26 Jan 1830	
Sarah	John H. Wright	12 Oct 1825	
Thomas	Linny Butt	5 Nov 1798	
Verlinda	Basil Burress	30 Sep 1819	

BURRIS - also see BURRESS, BURRISS, BURROIS, BURROUGHS, BURROWS, BOROUGHS BORROUGHS

BURRIS, Eli Z.	Rebecca A. Burris	29 Dec 1852	
Harriet E. A.	Philip D. Howser	21 Mar 1867	
John G.	Harriet A. Tarman	7 Sep 1852	
Josephine	William E. Ward	1 Jan 1873	
Margaret Ann	William Henry Knight	23 May 1883	
Mary C.	Addison N. Ray	26 Jan 1876	
Mary Jane	Daniel Harvill	9 Jul 1866	
Milinda	William A. Gray	22 Jun 1852	
Rebecca A.	Eli Z. Burris	29 Dec 1852	
William McK.	Ann Elizabeth Case	31 Oct 1868	

BURRISS - see BURROUGHS or BURRIS for other spellings

BURRISS, Adella	Henry Chapman	2 Dec 1876	
Aggie	James Fling	21 Nov 1894	w
Arthur E.	Annie A. Shorts	16 Jan 1896	w
Caroline	William T. Burriss	25 Apr 1871	
Casander V.	Isaih Trundle	2* Oct 1844	
Clara	Hanson Plummer	9 Nov 1871	
Clarence E.	Icidean Ray	19 Sep 1893	w
Dorothy A.	William A. Lovell	4 Nov 1889	w
Eleanor R.	Asa Tarman	12 May 1829	
Eli	Catharine Ann Stewart	16 Jan 1837	
Elizabeth	Thomas Crown	15 Jan 1835	
Elizabeth E.	John S. Ayton	29 Aug 1870	
George W.	Mollie Thompson	11 Sep 1891	w
Ignatius	Hannah Kisner	12 Mar 1877	w

* Day is written over either 24 or 25

BURRISS,	James F.	Martha Fuss	2 Dec 1875
	Jennie	Joseph C. Pennifill	2 Sep 1869
	Jessie	John W. Henderson	23 May 1890 w
	John G.	Maggie A. Garrett	10 Aug 1867
	John W.	Elizabeth J. Gates	28 Dec 1868
	Josephine Catharine	George A. Phebus	12 Jun 1876
	Lemuel P.	Hester V. Hendley	21 Dec 1854
	Lizzie	Greenbury C. Beckwith	17 Mar 1873
	Lloyd	Catherine Ellen Duley	17 Feb 1841
	Lucinda	David Knight	16 Sep 1886 w
	Lucretia	Nicholas Butt	9 Jan 1840
	Luther E.	Mary V. Chezum	23 May 1864
	Marian E.	John W. Cooley	22 Feb 1882
	Marshall	Ellen Hill	3 Apr 1845
	Martha	Edward Knight	8 Jan 1886 w
	Martha C.	John J. Smith	29 Aug 1893 w
	Mary E.	Reuben P. Hines	25 Aug 1888 w
	Mary E.	Edward H. Barber	21 Dec 1888 w
	Reuben	Margaret A. Mullican	1 Mar 1855
	Richard J.	Mary Craycroft	17 Dec 1867
	Sarah A.	William Brown	17 Nov 1857
	Thomas H.	Sarah E. Henley	8 Jun 1854
	Thomas H.	Elizabeth Ray	19 Oct 1854
	Thomas H.	Mary Agnes Gray	8 Feb 1883 w
	Thomas Hilleary	Catherine Shaw	25 Oct 1841
	Washington	Jane Henley	20 Nov 1845
	William G.	Juliet S. Mullican	12 Oct 1848
	William T.	Caroline Burriss	25 Apr 1871
	Willis	Mary Becraft	23 Aug 1880
BURROIS - see BURROUGHS or BURRIS for other spellings			
BURROIS,	Elizabeth	Elias Elvill	18 Oct 1803
BURROUGHS - also see BURRESS, BURRIS, BURRISS, BURROIS, BURROWS, BOROUGHS, BORROUGHS			
BURROUGHS,	Ada L.	William E. Bean	7 Apr 1887 w
	Emma	Uriah Ricketts	15 Dec 1880 w
	George E.	Barbara U. Peter	27 Dec 1888 w
	Harry J.	Edith M. Magruder	11 Sep 1896 w
	James A.	Elizabeth A. Shaeffer	1 Aug 1872
	John T.	Mrs. Elizabeth Spreadbrough	29 Dec 1884 w
	John W.	Mary E. Posey	3 Apr 1852
	Lewis L.	Lilie Musgrove	24 Dec 1887 w
	Mary L.	John T. Johnson	18 Jan 1894 w
	Walter M.	Mary E. Peter	29 Dec 1896 w
BURROWS - see BURROUGHS or BURRIS for other spellings			
BURROWS,	Hilleary T.	Minnie G. Duvall	22 May 1894 w
	Mary	Tyson Burrows	18 Dec 1819
	Tyson	Mary Burrows	18 Dec 1819
BURSIDE,	James	Ann D. Richardson	3 Nov 1835
BURTON - also see BERTTON			
BURTON,	Addie	John W. Snowden	23 Nov 1878 c
	Ally	John Grantt	6 Apr 1801
	Edward E.	Mary N. White	12 Mar 1895 w
	Elizabeth	Joseph Lewis	22 Apr 1805

BURTON, Elizabeth J.*	Levi L. Watkins	20 Dec 1864	
Emma C.	George G. Burton	24 Dec 1864	
George G.	Emma C. Burton	24 Dec 1864	
Isaac	Keturah Duvall	14 Sep 1812	
Isaac Jr.	Sarah Carr	20 Sep 1842	
Jennie	Clinton Dustin	6 Jul 1887	w
Lucretia	Berry Robey, Jr.	19 Aug 1801	
Lucretia V.	Joseph T. Morgan	10 Dec 1863	
Marceline	Nathan F. Beall	7 Nov 1867	
Mary	Barton Soper	29 Dec 1812	
Mary	Cajor G. Holt	17 Mar 1892	c
Mary E.	Caleb Carr	4 Jan 1853	
Mary E.	William T. Coar	29 Feb 1896	w
Sallie	Henry Crusen	10 Jan 1872	
Sarah	Jesse Iglehart	5 Jan 1811	
Sarah Ann	Lemuel Butler	15 Jan 1833	
Thomas B.	Margaret E. Roby	21 Jan 1861	
William	Susannah Iglehart	13 Mar 1810	
BUSEY - also see BUSY			
BUSEY, Ann	John Rhodes	13 Dec 1816	
Eleanor	William N. Austin	17 May 1847	
Henry	Mary Lansdale	16 Jan 1827	
John	Rachel White	13 Jun 1827	
John	Annie Franklin	23 May 1898	c
John R.	Emily Lee	24 Dec 1875	
Martha	Robert Ivory	19 Aug 1880	c
Mary	Isaac Stoddart	31 Dec 1874	
Maud A.	William E. Onley	6 Apr 1896	c
Patrick	Elizabeth Joy	13 Jul 1829	
Samuel C.	Catharine A. M. Posey	1 May 1849	
Washington	Elizabeth Read	4 Oct 1809	
William	Idella Lee	5 Apr 1876	
BUSY, Hezekiah	Nellie Gibbons	2 Jun 1886	c
BUSH, Alice	Enoch Spencer	31 Dec 1874	
Monie	Charles Clagett	9 Jun 1881	c
BUSSARD, Elias	Rebecca Ann Boswell	9 May 1832	
Henry	Anna Todd	8 Oct 1817	
John R.	Delila E. Perry	15 Jan 1810	
BUSSON, Margaret	Benjamin Curran	26 Jan 1817	
Mary	Henry Lansdale	5 May 1808	
BUTCHER, Philip H.	Hannah Ann Lewis	12 Nov 1838	
Thomas H.	Kesiah F. Oden	13 Dec 1859	
BUTLER - also see BUTTLER, BOTELER, BETLER			
BUTLER, Altie M.	John E. Porter	26 Jan 1885	c
Ann	Richard Dorsey	** May 1881	
Atlantic	Robert S. Moore	10 Jul 1884	c
Charles M.	Fannie T. Spates	4 Jan 1867	
Charles H.	Sarah E. Johnson	16 Dec 1891	c
Charles S.	Hattie A. Brunner	24 Aug 1895	w
Daniel	Mary Culver	17 Jul 1868	
Eleanor	Robert Sullivan	24 Dec 1800	
Elijah	Mary Jane Frazier	21 Mar 1870	
Elizabeth	William H. King	2 Jan 1890	c

* Entry reads Burton; family researcher says should be Buxton
** Day has blot on it; after 28

BUTLER,	Estella	John Storrage	9 Nov 1896 c
	George W.	Sophia A. Stubinger	9 Mar 1886 w
	Henry	Rebecca Sprigg	11 Nov 1880 c
	Ignatius	Anne Neal	2 Nov 1885 c
	J. N.	Susan Johnson	21 Dec 1881
	John	Rachel Matthew	14 Dec 1869
	Lemuel	Sarah Ann Burton	15 Jan 1833
	Louis B.	Nannie B. Cormick	26 Jun 1894 w
	Margaret E.	Robertus Trundle	10 Feb 1871
	Mary	Vachel Snowden	12 Oct 1875 c
	Mary A.	William Thomas Harwood	1 Nov 1866
	Nancy	James E. Hodges	4 Nov 1885 c
	Richard T.	Rosa E. Brunner	1 Feb 1896 w
	Samuel *.	Jane Fredericks	25 Jan 1865
	Sarah	Edward Ellcorn	24 Aug 1865
	William	Mary Lowe	18 Dec 1810
	William	Emma Bell	7 Aug 1890 c
	William	Lydia Beckley	14 Jul 1894 c
	William H.	Mary E. Hyatt	28 Apr 1882
	William P.	Hollice Williams	7 Mar 1892 c
BUTT,	Anne	Lloyd Lanham	16 Mar 1810
	Basil	Mary Burress	29 Oct 1814
	Basil Thomas	Alice H. Crown	30 Nov 1874
	Elizabeth A.	Edward M. Henley	1 Feb 1866
	Gertie B.	Thomas T. Mullican	25 Apr 1895 w
	Hazel	Sary Richards	31 Dec 1803
	Hazel S.	Elizabeth Beckwith	30 May 1816
	Heath E.	Roberta C. Chapman	22 Dec 1896 w
	Henrietta	William E. Henley	24 Dec 1888 w
	Howard M.	Catharine A. Demude	19 Nov 1889 w
	Ida V.	John L. Mills	16 Dec 1889 w
	John L.	Matilda Offutt	19 Jun 1856
	John William	Martha E. Henley	1 Feb 1866
	Linny	Thomas Burress	5 Nov 1798
	Luther S.	Martha E. Carter	29 Jan 1889 w
	Mary	Nicholas Beckwith	10 Aug 1799
	Mary	William Engle	19 Jan 1814
	Mary	Patrick Conley	23 Sep 1847
	Mary Cornelia	James W. Daymude	3 Sep 1890 w
	Nicholas	Lucretia Burriss	9 Jan 1840
	Richard	Sarah Ann Richards	21 Dec 1814
	Robert McKendry	Rebecca Ricketts	26 Jan 1869
	Sarah	John W. Crown	11 Apr 1876
BUTTLER - also see BUTLER			
BUTTLER, Edward		Jemima Jones	2 Dec 1805
BUTTS, Eliza J.		John E. Walter	25 May 1881 w
BUXTON, Anna**		Nathan Jones	18 Jan 1800
	Elizabeth J. - see Elizabeth J. Burton		
	Francis	Catharine Northcraft	2 Apr 1809
	George	Mary Ann Trail	4 Dec 1802
	James	Janett Green	18 Apr 1815
	John T.	Sophia J. Reid	15 Jan 1872

* Initial written over
** Page torn; Bu is all that is visible; all earlier readings are different; other records show Buxton to be correct

BUXTON, Julia	Thomas *. Parker	23 Dec 1824	
Lloyd	Elizabeth Harper	23 Dec 1826	
Maggie E.	A. B. Rittenour	18 Aug 1873	
Margaret	Edward C. Cunningham	24 Jan 1831	
Margery	Samuel Griffith	15 May 1820	
Mary	James Trail	11 May 1811	
Mary R.	Zachariah Dowden	15 Apr 1893	w
Priscilla	William Browning	1 Feb 1820	
Richard L.	Mollie E. Easton	8 Jul 1879	w
Richard L.	James Annie Easton	15 Dec 1886	w
Sarah	Walter Fryer	5 Sep 1810	
Susanna	Nathan Trail	19 Dec 1801	
William	Rachel Trail	11 Apr 1806	
William	Elizabeth Green	9 Apr 1839	
BYE, Martha	William Warfield	12 Apr 1803	
BYRD - also see BIRD			
BYRD, George	Ann Dyson	24 Dec 1828	
John B.	Sally T. Veirs	4 Aug 1862	
John F.	Nannie Wootton	25 Apr 1885	w
BYRON, George W.	Rose Schwab	21 Nov 1896	w
BYRN, Elizabeth	Robert Alexander Whittaker	6 Jan 1817	
BYRNE, Corrilla J.	William Alonzo Anderson	27 Jan 1891	w
Ida J.	Edward E. Miller	29 Sep 1890	w
James F.	Sarah E. Jones	19 Nov 1892	w
Lucy V.	James W. Austin	28 Jun 1892	w
Mary H.	James E. Garrett	19 Apr 1884	
Rosa Lee	Edward W. Starnell	14 Feb 1890	w
BYROAD, Samuel M.	Lizzie Riley	14 Aug 1877	w
CADE, Paul A.	Ellen Casey	6 Sep 1890	w
CADY, William A.	Sarah E. Poole	1 May 1855	
CAFFERY, John M.	Mary Tabler	7 Jul 1871	
CAHILL - also see CAIHILL			
CAHILL, Francis T.	Isabel Trail	20 Dec 1877	w
James S.	Evadna A. Osmond	11 Mar 1895	w
Mary E.	William H. Trail	24 Jan 1898	w
CAHO - also see COHO			
CAHO, John Thomas	Elizabeth Emily Barneclo	1 Jun 1829	
Mary Eveline	William Mills	29 Dec 1836	
CAIHILL - also see CAHILL			
CAIHILL, Joseph	Elizabeth Green	28 Sep 1801	
CAIN - also see KEAN, KANE			
CAIN, Richard W.	Emily J. Burdette	18 Dec 1894	w
CALCLASER, Thomas	Elizabeth Wineberger	19 May 1800	
CALDWELL, Ann S.	William N. Caldwell	10 Jan 1842	
Charles W.	Catherine Lewis	5 Oct 1842	
David	Lottie H. Repp	24 Apr 1897	w
Sally	Elijah Allison	18 Dec 1819	
Samuel B. T.	Mary Haugh	31 Jan 1824	
William N.	Ann S. Caldwell	10 Jan 1842	
CALFUS, Robert	---ana Hilton	15 Sep 1885	w
CALHOUN, Mary C.	Harry W. Chew	22 Sep 1896	w
CALLICO, Alexander	Mary Sedgewick	4 Jan 1800	
	William Bellows	22 Dec 1891	c

* Initial I or J

CALTON, Lucy	William Bellows	22 Dec 1891	c
CALVERT, Caleb	Jane Leizear	23 Feb 1832	
Caleb	Ruth Ann Willson	9 Dec 1872	
Susan H.	Richard H. Turner	3 Jun 1867	
CALVITE, Catharine	Joseph Leizear	15 Oct 1872	
CALWIGHT, Lydia	Henry Thompson	31 Oct 1812	
CAMBASH - also see COMBUSH			
CAMBASH, Samuel	Elizabeth Toogood	30 May 1887	c
CAMEL - also see CAMPBELL			
CAMEL, Greenbury	Emma Bowie	15 Dec 1881	
Joseph E.	Sarah Bowen	31 Dec 1890	c
CAMLIN, Mary - see Mary Cumlin			
CAMPBELL - also see CAMEL			
CAMPBELL, Alexander	Chloe Ann Boswell	1 Jan 1799	
Ann	John B. Knott	25 Jan 1825	
Anne	Lloyd Key	10 Sep 1823	
Arthur *. A.	Elizabeth Hilton	5 Jun 1832	
Carrie E.	Charlie H. Snowden	6 May 1896	c
Catharine	Thomas W. Langdon	23 Nov 1824	
Charles	Martha Forman	3 Apr 1878	c
Chloe	Robert Soper	20 Jun 1807	
Columbus	Caroline Linn	4 Feb 1868	
Eliza	William Sparrow	20 Mar 1802	
Elizabeth	John James Boswell	19 Jan 1809	
Elizabeth	William Henry Williams	29 Apr 1873	
Elizabeth	William T. Brown	17 Aug 1889	c
Elizabeth Jane	William M. Lowe	3 Feb 1826	
Florence	James R. Tunia	3 Nov 1891	c
Francis	Elizabeth Harper	27 Jan 1810	
George	Eliza Marlow	14 Aug 1882	c
George W. H.	Leanah Williams	6 Nov 1890	c
James	Margaret Capp	24 Feb 1874	
James H.	Maria Jackson	23 Jun 1866	
James H	Clara Brown	17 Aug 1889	c
James W.	Ann Maria Beckwith	10 Jun 1845	
Janey	George W. Bond	13 Mar 1894	c
John	Priscilla Oden	24 Dec 1798	
John	Marcy Hobbs	27 Feb 1808	
John	Susan Ann Duley	14 Jun 1820	
John	Irene Wheatley	26 Dec 1891	c
John I.	Martha T. Mines	2 Jun 1836	
Lelita	Henry Jones	7 Jan 1885	c
Lethe	Greenbury W. Johnson	12 Mar 1885	c
Levin	Mary Heffner	11 Feb 1829	
Lillie E.	Frank S. Kleindienst	29 Oct 1878	
Louisa	John Handy	15 Oct 1883	c
Louisa	Thomas Noland	14 Feb 1890	c
Macy	Andrew A. Davis	25 May 1887	c
Maggie	Perry Russell	21 Mar 1898	c
Mary	Abraham Dawson	21 May 1822	
Mary	Dennis Jones	16 Mar 1824	
Mary	Samuel Pumphrey	25 Mar 1828	
Mary	Samuel Crown	5 Sep 1832	
Mary E.	William A. West	18 Feb 1879	w

* Initial I or J

CAMPBELL,	Mary M.	John Cook	24 Apr 1823
	Mortimer	Anna Smith	26 Dec 1888 c
	Perry	Sarah Spriggs	7 Apr 1891 c
	Robert Hamilton	Mary Louisa Offutt	27 Aug 1892 w
	Rosa	Joseph R. Rabbitt	3 Nov 1875
	Ruth Ann	Hezekiah Barber	23 Apr 1875
	Sarah	Miley Jackson	9 Mar 1886 c
	Sarah A.	John W. Clagett	24 Oct 1889 c
	Susan M.	G. F. Carter	25 Feb 1868
	William	Susannah Moulding	24 Dec 1806
	William T.	Mary O. Offutt	15 Jul 1891 c
CANBY,	Charles	Emma Johnson	16 Aug 1873
	Kate E.	Evan Hipsley	5 Apr 1861
	Laura	Richard T. Willson	18 Apr 1853
	Mary B.	Zachariah Berry	7 Jun 1865
	Thomas	Deborah Duvall	28 Jan 1824
	William	Mary Duley	12 Nov 1833
	William M.	Sallie J. Rust	8 Jan 1884
CANDLER,	Eveline	Ben A. Cunningham	5 Dec 1836
	John	Sarah Hays	19 May 1804
	John	Cecilia Ellen Getzendanner	13 Dec 1843
	Leonard W.	Ann Eliza Fisher	30 Jan 1834
	Martha	Charles A. Darby	22 Nov 1831
	Mary Ann	Samuel M. Beall	18 Jan 1826
	Rebecca	Samuel Leeke	27 Mar 1818
	Rosanna Eleanor	James Offutt	18 Jan 1826
	William	Rebeccah Ray	27 Jun 1803
CANTWELL,	John O.	Delia Laporte	14 Oct 1889 w
CAPP,	Margaret	James Campbell	24 Feb 1874
CARACRISTI,	Carlo F.L.Z.	Carrie Russell	3 Oct 1891 w
CAREY - also see CARY			
CAREY,	Eleanor	John Getty	14 Apr 1801
	Elizabeth A.	Artarcexes E. Fisher	15 Jul 1879
	Ellender	Thomas Whalin	19 Jan 1799
	George	Trecey Ann Padgett	10 Apr 1830
	James	Sarah Jane Carlyle	2 Aug 1826
	James	Elizabeth Ann Wells	21 Dec 1829
	John R.	Mary C. Bean	24 Jul 1889 w
	Mary Jane	Solomon V. Hall	19 May 1877 w
	Rachel Ellen	Dennis M. Howser	20 Dec 1882
CARLILE - also see CARLISLE			
CARLILE,	Penock	Sarah A. Hill	8 Jul 1862
CARLIN - also see CARLON			
CARLIN,	Annie B.	William D. Knott	23 Dec 1893 w
	John	Maria Knott	4 Feb 1836
	Mary R.	Stephen A. Reid	20 Dec 1895 w
	Sarah	Lawrence Hogan	4 Feb 1881
	William E.	Mary S. Pierce	7 May 1890 w
	William H.	Mary E. Lowe	18 Dec 1868
CARLISLE - also see CARLILE, CARLYLE, CARLYSLE			
CARLISLE,	Alexander G.	Mary W. Coomes	12 Jun 1895 w
	David	Mary Hoskins	25 Jan 1806
	James	Susie E. Carter	4 Aug 1880
	John Francis	Susie Coomes	29 Nov 1893 w
	Louisa	Henry Williams	24 Oct 1866

Name	Spouse	Date
CARLISLE, Nora J.	Thomas Whalen	22 Feb 1854
Richard C.	Frances C. Appleby	5 Jan 1870
William M.	Mamie Walker	19 Nov 1889 w
CARLON - also see CARLIN		
CARLON, Philip	Sarah Willson	22 Dec 1804
CARLYLE - also see CARLISLE, CARLYSLE, CARLILE		
CARLYLE, Ann	Zachariah Mandel	28 Jan 1813
Catharine E.	John T. Best	31 Oct 1860
David J.	Margarett McDade	12 Feb 1819
James A.	Christy A. Spalding	24 Feb 1840
Martha A.	Henson R. Ricketts	2 Feb 1858
Sarah Jane	James Carey	2 Aug 1826
William	Catherine Rabbitt	12 Feb 1831
CARLYSLE - also see CARLISLE		
CARLYSLE, David	Mary Smith	10 Nov 1817
David	Margaret Conley	4 Feb 1862
CARMODY, John D.	Florence M. Fulton	16 Oct 1897 w
CARR, Anne	Lewis Barrett	27 May 1816
Annie M.	William F. Flack	24 May 1870
Benjamin	Lucy Dever	22 Nov 1813
Caleb	Mary E. Burton	4 Jan 1853
Isabella E.	James L. Iglehart	6 Jan 1876
John C.	Dora I. Gott	12 Apr 1890 w
Joshua	Judy Jones	11 Apr 1826
Mary A.	Edward Brooks	11 Jan 1853
Mary A.	Cyrus S. Wilson	15 Dec 1891 w
Nettie	Alexander Blair	2 Jan 1883 w
Patrick	Sarah E. Curtin	27 Nov 1889 w
Richard	Anthanet Jacobs	29 Jan 1828
Richard C.	Mary E. Iglehart	20 Jul 1864
Samuel	Elizabeth Cecil	14 Feb 1832
Samuel	Sarah Linthicum	15 Jan 1834
Sarah	Archibald Edmonston	7 Mar 1801
Sarah	Philip Cissel	19 May 1838
Sarah	Isaac Burton, Jr.	20 Sep 1842
Walter	Rebecca Brown	20 Nov 1833
William H.	Emma E. V. Kleindenst	4 May 1878 w
CARRINGTON, Elizabeth	Stephen Cawood	12 Nov 1803
Nettie C.	Thomas H. Boswell	5 Nov 1894 w
Thomas	Elizabeth Cawood	3 Aug 1804
CARROLL, Agatha	Dennis Smith	16 Sep 1880 c
Annie G.	Warren Bowles	11 Nov 1889 w
Carrie	Lewis Yager	15 May 1889 c
Clarence F.	Carrie V. Turner	17 Dec 1895 w
Daniel	Ann McCubbin	10 Jan 1799
Elizabeth	Daniel Ball	5 Feb 1799
Elizabeth	James Totten	9 Jun 1890 w
Ella H.	Howard A. Garrett	16 Apr 1881
Ellen D.	Louis M. Paxton	3 Jul 1883
Emily	Samuel Hawkins	12 Oct 1896 c
Evelyn R.	Forrest A. Carroll	30 Dec 1897 c
Forrest A.	Evelyn R.	30 Dec 1897 c
George	Bertha Prater	21 May 1893 c
George P.	Clara Hyde	25 Jun 1887 w
Henson	Agatha Martin	18 Oct 1866
Ida	James Baker	30 Jan 1896 c

CARROLL,	James	Margaret B. Younger	13 Jun 1897 c
	James W. N.	Eulie Johnson	3 Nov 1887 c
	John W.	Laura R. Thrift	16 May 1863
	Joseph L.	Mary Ellen Fling	10 Oct 1857
	Joseph L.	Catherine E. Rabbitt	11 Jan 1866
	Leila	Vernon Warren	30 Apr 1891 c
	Lewis	Rachel Todd	17 Nov 1879
	Louiza	George Blair	28 May 1870
	Margaret A. V.	Zachariah Thompson	17 Feb 1893 w
	Mary A.	Horace Benton	2 Mar 1848
	Matilda	James Terry	9 Sep 1870
	Patrick	Ann Tarell	25 Jun 1798
	Samuel S.	Helen M. Bennett	20 Apr 1885
	Southey	Sallie M. Beall	21 Oct 1893 w
	Thomas	Sarah T. Connelly	15 Nov 1897 w
	Thomas H.	Martha McKenney	11 Apr 1887 c
	Virginia	Wesley Smith	21 Dec 1865
	William *.	Margaret A. Seek	24 May 1893 w
	Winny Morgan	Joseph Wimsett	17 Dec 1800
CARSON,	Thomas	Katie Mossburg	** Jan 1883
CARTENHOUR,	John	Sarah Offutt	27 Dec 1806
CARTER,	Addie	Charles Combash	14 Dec 1893 c
	Albert F.	Mary Emma Hopkins	18 May 1898 c
	Alexander	Kate Carter	11 Oct 1897 w
	Anna	Samuel H. Johnson	30 Dec 1889 c
	Bural M.	Lizzie A. Ford	10 Apr 1888 w
	Burl M.	Margaret V. Green	16 Dec 1880 w
	Caroline	Thomas Oden	8 Mar 1881 w
	Charles	Clara L. Baker	4 Oct 1887 c
	Charles	Annie Kindle	1 Sep 1890 w
	Clara L.	George W. Book	5 Nov 1896 c
	Cornelia	Martin Stang	3 Oct 1882
	Elizabeth Ann	John Maury Dove	5 Sep 1882 w
	Emily	Marion M. Riley	18 Nov 1889 w
	Eveline	Charles D. Bennett	18 Mar 1879 c
	Florence	Jacob Hall	29 Oct 1873
	Frances	George W. Askins	2 Feb 1891 c
	Frances	John Handy	25 Oct 1894 c
	G. F.	Susan M. Campbell	25 Feb 1868
	George	Harriet Gage	28 Dec 1875
	Henry	Mary D. Scott	17 May 1878 c
	Hester L.	Charles W. Jackson	6 Sep 1894 c
	James C.	Emma J. Davis	15 Jun 1897 c
	James H.	Jane E. Jeffers	21 Feb 1879 w
	Jane	William H. T. Moore	8 Nov 1866
	Jennie	Joseph Carter	28 Jun 1880 w
	John A.	Mary Catherine Holmes Magruder	11 May 1830
	Joseph	Jennie Carter	28 Jun 1880 w
	Kate	Alexander Carter	11 Oct 1897 w
	Laura	John W. Jarby	16 Sep 1891 c
	Lucy	Henson Martin	13 May 1893 c
	Martha E.	Luther S. Butt	29 Jan 1889 w

* Initial written over
** Cannot read day; before 9

CARTER, Martha E.	Charles E. Thomas	25 Sep 1890	c
Mary	Andrew Jackson	3 Aug 1867	
Mary	Henry Washington	24 Jul 1875	
Mary A.	Levi T. Jones	21 Sep 1895	c
Mary Jane	John Thomas Oden	2 Jul 1883	
Mary Jane	John Henry Ray	14 Jun 1898	w
Mary R.	Thomas R. Clagett	20 Sep 1898	c
Mary V.	Angelo Grimes	6 Aug 1889	w
Milton	Minnie Biser	16 Jun 1892	w
Minnie	Benjamin J. Cross	1 Sep 1890	w
Nellie	Charles D. Kinniel	11 Jan 1889	w
Presly	Mary Cordell	3 Mar 1813	
Remus G.	Jane S. Smallwood	19 Apr 1832	
Robert W.	Mary A. Harding	19 Nov 1839	
Ruth	Lewis Frazier	14 Nov 1883	c
Samuel	Frances Scott	1 Jun 1893	c
Susan C.	Nelson J. Trail	7 Mar 1872	
Susie	William H. Thomas	3 May 1883	
Susie A.	Horace F. Mills	15 May 1883	
Susie E.	James Carlisle	4 Aug 1880	
Tasker	Sarah E. Johnson	29 Jul 1880	
Thomas	Susanah Howard	1 Dec 1869	
Thomas E.	Sarah E. Burgess	27 Oct 1898	c
Turner	Lulie Redman	20 Apr 1896	w
Walter	Mamie E. Robinson	29 Nov 1897	c
William	Maggie Brown	30 Dec 1872	
William	Emily Lee	21 Jul 1881	c
CARTRYSSE, Sidonie	Gustav Joseph	16 Sep 1895	w
CARTWRIGHT, Bettie	George Smith	7 Aug 1895	c
Josephine	Budd F. Smith	4 Jun 1886	c
Mary L.	John T. Hutchison	21 Dec 1872	
Samuel	Ida Price	9 May 1891	c
CARTZDARFAR, Michael	Maria Connelly	14 Apr 1823	
CARVER, Patrick	Margaret Hanaphin	27 Feb 1871	
CARY - also see CAREY			
CARY, Tracey	Charles Worth Wood	8 Nov 1832	
William G.	Blanche Marshall	1 Apr 1889	w
CASE, Ann Elizabeth	William McK. Burris	31 Oct 1868	
Catharine	James Case	6 Sep 1875	
Charles A.	Emma D. Fisher	5 Jun 1880	w
Darkey	William Stewart	6 Nov 1820	
Eleanor R.	Thomas W. Case	26 Dec 1870	
Eliza	James Case	6 Jan 1803	
Elizabeth	Thomas Pope	12 Aug 1817	
Elizabeth Ann*	Alfred Reed	18 Dec 1826	
Ellen E.	Oliver S. Maus	26 Apr 1871	
Florence E. V.	William H. McCrossen	16 Oct 1888	w
Frederick T.	Mary A. Selby	18 Jun 1861	
George R.	Mary A. Gingell	23 Feb 1881	
George W.	Elizabeth J. Thrift	30 Dec 1850	
Hester J.	Charles C. Cooper	2 Aug 1860	
Israel	Ann Austin	30 Dec 1830	
James	Eliza Case	6 Jan 1803	
James	Elizabeth Bowman	25 Feb 1807	

* Middle name is written over, but looks like Ann

CASE,	James	Catharine Case	6 Sep 1875
	John S.	Minerva J. Harding	18 Apr 1873
	John T.	Mary E. Williams	14 Jan 1845
	John T.	Elizabeth Ridgely	21 Dec 1860
	John T.	Mary F. Kisner	25 Feb 1862
	Kate	Robert Case	5 Apr 1876
	Mackey	John T. Higdon	22 Dec 1837
	Margaret	Jonathan Fields	16 May 1843
	Margaret E.	George W. White	16 Oct 1879 w
	Martha	William Reid	21 Oct 1828
	Martha E.	George W. Shaw	25 Mar 1847
	Mary E.	Richard H. Owden	18 Jun 1887 w
	Mary S.	James W. Sparrow	22 Aug 1872
	Philip J.	Harriet E. Ray	8 Nov 1877
	Richard	Hester Ann Easton	1 Feb 1862
	Richard	Mary A. Federline	24 Feb 1868
	Robert	Ann Willett	10 Apr 1816
	Robert	Kate Case	5 Apr 1876
	Sarah	James Mackey	28 Dec 1811
	Sarah	James M. Crown	13 Sep 1881 w
	Sarah M.	John W. Shaw	16 Jan 1838
	Sarah R.	William N. Gantz	17 Feb 1872
	Shadrack B.	Mary Padgett	13 Nov 1855
	Susan R.	William T. Fisher	2 Jul 1857
	Thomas L.	Phares Appleby	17 Jan 1814
	Thomas W.	Eleanor R. Case	26 Dec 1870
	Walter	Patsy Pennifield	9 Jan 1822
	Walter L.	Mary Kisner	9 Jan 1813
	Walter R.	Matilda Gittings	25 Feb 1840
	William	Eliza Kelly	22 Dec 1798
	William H.	Marion E. Stearn	27 Oct 1886 w
	William Henry	Eleanor Pennifield	31 Dec 1839
	William W.	Sarah D. Cole	10 Jan 1849
	William W.	Sarah V. Herbert	28 May 1891 w
	Zadok	Sarah Dove	7 Apr 1846
CASEY,	Adelaide	Charles E. Foster	25 Jun 1891 w
	Elizabeth	Barton Harriss	25 Nov 1799
	Ellen	Paul A. Cade	6 Sep 1890 w
	James	Catharine Duffey	8 Nov 1862
	Margaret	William Bevans	12 Apr 1869
CASH,	Dawson	Jemimah Beens*	3 Oct 1798
CASHEL,	Elizabeth	Henson Grooms	17 Feb 1841
	Henrietta		
	Mary Rebecca	Richard T. Ray	25 Jan 1875
	Richard H.	Angeline Ewell	2 Jan 1834
CASHELL,	Amanda	William W. Metzgar	24 Oct 1876
	Ann E.	William Harrison Wiley	16 Oct 1861
	Ann H.	Isaiah Shaw	7 Dec 1852
	Ashsah A.	Charles W. Huguely	10 Jan 1876
	Caroline	J. M. Baker	8 May 1875
	Carrie E.	James N. Barnsley	26 Nov 1881
	Edgar H.	Marie C. Weller	6 Apr 1896 w
	Elizabeth	Frederick Bowman	17 Apr 1871
	Elizabeth	Thomas B. Cissell	19 Feb 1873

* Part of last name from earlier reading

CASHELL, Elizabeth A.	Isaiah F. Beall	15 Oct 1856	
Emily M.	Jacob Miller	11 Feb 1874	
Emily M. C.	John William Beall	4 Feb 1864	
Emma R.	Silas A. Bell	29 Apr 1873	
G. Francis	Sarah Shaw	8 Mar 1865	
George	Elizabeth B. Edmonstone	14 Jun 1804	
George C.	Kate Barnsley	12 Feb 1866	
George W.	Octavia A. Yewell	24 Mar 1831	
George W.	Mary Ann Yewell	22 Mar 1866	
George W.	Kate Hobbs	15 Dec 1873	
Gertrude	Elbert Nichols	10 Oct 1894	w
Hazel B.	Caroline Groomes	28 Jan 1834	
Hazel W.	Mary E. Davis	25 Apr 1876	
James W.	Mary Ann Grooms	1 Feb 1841	
John G.	Sarah L. Bell	2 May 1861	
Juliana J.	William Glover	2 Sep 1869	
Mary	William Wheatly	8 Jun 1804	
Mary J.	A. O. Appleby	5 Nov 1870	
Octavia B.	Bennett R. Wilkinson	24 Oct 1893	w
Octavia H.	David F. Bready	16 Feb 1858	
Samuel S.	Laura L. Dorsey	19 Nov 1874	
Thomas F.	Hester A. Jefferson	4 Jun 1856	
Thomas F. Jr.	Elizabeth E. Groomes	13 Feb 1874	
Walter F.	Mary A. Henderson	15 Jan 1895	w
William	Annie D. Fidler	23 Feb 1892	w
William L.	Ellen R. Groomes	23 Apr 1872	
CASSELL - also see CASTLE			
CASSELL, Nellie E.	James F. Filgate	21 Aug 1894	w
CASSIDY, Annie B.	Horatio G. O'Neal	2 Jun 1894	w
CASTER, Susan	Hamilton Wallace	10 Feb 1879	c
CASTLE - also see CASSELL			
CASTLE, Ellen Eugenia	James L. Elgin	18 Nov 1886	w
CASTLEMAN, George P.	Sarah A. Magruder	12 Jul 1888	w
CATER - also see CATOR			
CATER, Joseph T.	Laura V. Benton	17 Jan 1860	
Samuel	Mary Ann Cross	5 Feb 1834	
CATLETT, Grandison	Mary Dorsey	18 Apr 1808	
CATLIN, William	Elizabeth Davis	28 Feb 1809	
CATON, James H.	Annie M. Fenton	6 Feb 1888	w
Kitty	James King	17 Feb 1801	
Thomas	Martha Snell	12 Jan 1801	
Timothy	Virginia C. Allen	15 Nov 1886	w
CATOR - also see CATER			
CATOR, Samuel H.	Margaret S. Moulden	13 Dec 1881	
Samuel H.	Josephine A. Zeller	15 nov 1894	w
CAULFIELD, William S.	Elizabeth B. Hutton	25 Jan 1898	w
CAULIFLOWER - also see COLLIFLOWER			
CAULIFLOWER, John C.	Martha A. Gordon	16 Feb 1848	
CAVE, George Albert	Harriet Ann Bonn	6 Aug 1869	
CAVENAUGH, Patrick D.	Elizabeth Margaret Scott	29 Dec 1840	
CAWOOD, Elizabeth	Thomas Carrington	3 Aug 1804	
Mary	William Evely	23 Dec 1809	
Stephen	Elizabeth Carrington	12 Nov 1803	
Virlinda	Benjamin Umpstalld	30 Jan 1805	
CAYWOOD, Mary E.	Milton F. Embrey	19 Nov 1873	

CECIL - also see CISSELL, CISSEL, CISELL, SCHISSEL, SCISSEL			
CECIL, Annie M.	John T. Burch	19 Apr 1898	w
Annie Mary	James F. Bennett	24 Mar 1885	w
Catharine	Samuel Perry	21 Feb 1824	
Elizabeth	Samuel Carr	14 Feb 1832	
Everett H.	Julia M. Thompson	3 Jul 1880	
Lilian G.	Garrett Davis Wolfe	16 Jan 1888	w
Mary*	James Andrews *	5 Mar 1822	
Mary A.	Charles W. Hirsh	25 Jan 1889	w
Madora H.	Maurice W. Watkins	15 Nov 1887	w
Mary D.	Alexander Garrett	25 Oct 1887	w
Sabret	Margaret Osborn	20 Dec 1828	
Samuel	Sarah Belt	4 Dec 1798	
Sarah	William Burford	29 Nov 1842	
William	Lydia Ann Feaster	24 Aug 1825	
William	Rachel Sarah Williams	30 Dec 1829	
William W.	Maggie E. Kinna	11 Aug 1893	w
CECILL, Amey	Charles Peters	8 Mar 1803	
Jane	Benjamin Belt	23 Feb 1805	
John	Milly Ann Stewart	22 May 1801	
Mary	Osborn Crawford	20 Dec 1823	
Rachel	Samuel Pumphrey	23 Mar 1816	
Samuel	Elizabeth Belt	27 Oct 1802	
Samuel	Isabell Belt	28 Feb 1806	
CEICILL, Ann	Basil Warfield	16 Feb 1803	
CEPHAS, Anna	William Hinton	12 Dec 1872	
Henry	Anna Fisher	8 Feb 1889	c
Joseph	Susan Anderson	31 Oct 1873	
Matilda	Albert Brown	13 May 1880	
Phebe	Clifton Childress	20 Nov 1867	
Rebecca	Robert Johnson	15 May 1875	
CHADBURN, Elizabeth	Joseph Gardner	24 Dec 1802	
Margaret	Benjamin Garner	8 nov 1806	
CHADWELL, James	Christanna Welling	15 Jun 1875	
CHAMBERLAIN, Jonah	Susan Collins	21 Dec 1799	
CHAMBERS, ------ J.	Rachel A. Johnson	** Nov 1882	c
Cassandra	Amos Willcoxen	28 May 1800	
Elijah	Anne Willcoxen	21 Nov 1806	
Elisha	Elizabeth Patrick	23 Jan 1811	
Eliza A.	Thomas E. Brown	8 Feb 1858	
Elizabeth	Jeremiah Hazle	4 Jan 1808	
Elizabeth	Hezekiah Sparrow	4 Mar 1815	
Fanny	George Diggs	10 Feb 1875	
Henrietta	Samuel T. Johnson	28 Oct 1880	c
Henry	Pricey Mockbee	14 Dec 1803	
James	Elizabeth Lewis	28 Mar 1814	
James	Jennie Thompson	17 Mar 1883	c
Levi	Sary Peddicoart	15 Nov 1802	
Louisa	William Johnson	3 May 1886	c
Margaret	Rezin Willcoxen	22 Dec 1800	
Margaret	Richard Chambers	1 Mar 1864	
Mary A. C.	Thomas P. Baker	4 Sep 1833	
Precious	John Lucas	14 Dec 1801	

* Last names written over; look like above, but may be incorrect
** First name and day too light to read; day before 10

CHAMBERS,	Rachael	Zadock Warfield	23 Dec 1801
	Richard	Margaret Chambers	1 Mar 1864
	Robert	Eliza Jones	11 Feb 1871
	Susan E.	Michael Whalen	23 Dec 1848
	Thomas	Elizabeth Miller	5 Dec 1878 c
	William	Jane Davis	27 Dec 1870
	William ?.	Mary Wallace	* Jul 1882
	William E.	Rachel Ann Grant	11 Jun 1872
CHAMPAYNE,	John R.	Ellmaria Beall	28 Feb 1854
CHANDLEE,	Clara L.	Edward T. Leadbeater	7 Oct 1861
	Hallie	Edward N. Bentley	12 Jul 1880
	Lettitia G.	Charles E. Kummer	17 Jul 1860
CHANDLIE,	Ivory**	Rose Dorsey	5 Oct 1897 c
CHANDLER,	Allan M.	Ada S. Fairfax	3 Oct 1892 w
	Ivorey**	Lottie Hackett	3 Dec 1879 c
CHANEY - also see CHAYNEY, CHENY			
CHANEY,	Alliz B. D.	John Conrad Free	14 Feb 1809
	Catharine	Thomas Riney	25 Sep 1815
	Elizabeth	Richard Stewart	24 Jan 1821
	Margaret	James McCoy	11 Jan 1823
	Maybell	Alfred M. Earp	7 Dec 1896 w
	Mollie	Thomas J. C. Wiley	30 Mar 1875
	Rachel	Philip Nicholas	22 Aug 1815
	Sarah Jane	George W. Waters	14 Nov 1853
CHAPLINE,	Anna L.	James S. Phillips	27 Mar 1883
CHAPMAN - also see CHATMAN			
CHAPMAN,	Clarence A.	Lillie Kelley	2 Jun 1897 w
	Henry	Adella Burriss	2 Dec 1876
	Henry A.	Christy Henley	18 May 1869
	Leonard S.	M. Velinda Thompson	12 Sep 1864
	Roberta C.	Heath E. Butt	22 Dec 1896 w
CHAPPELL,	Edward F.	Maggie L. Thomas	3 Feb 1894 w
	John W.	Ida Adamson	*** Oct 1881 w
CHARGE,	Benjamin T.	Susan A. Nugent	13 Jan 1887 c
	Mary A. E.	George L. Gant	2 Dec 1882 c
CHARITY,	William	Rachel Ann Scott	24 Apr 1884 c
CHARLTON,	Luther W.	Kate L. Baker	14 Jan 1886 w
CHASE,	Annie V.	Thomas W. Clagett	28 Dec 1898 c
	David	Sophia Dorsey	24 Jul 1869
	Eliza	John Thomas	3 Jun 1873
	Francis	Mary Price	17 Apr 1867
	Jane	Richard Watts	21 Aug 1867
	Joseph W.	Cora Bailey	22 May 1895 c
	Perry	Elizabeth Noland	15 May 1869
	Rosie M.	Willis T. Snowden	25 Jun 1891 c
CHATMAN,	Abbariler****	Aquila Duvall	13 Aug 1800
CHAYNEY - also see CHANEY, CHENY			
CHAYNEY,	Thomas	Elizabeth Robertson	11 Jul 1805
CHE--Y,	Mary E.	Peter Williams	15 Nov 1883

* Initial and day too light to read; day before 10
** Both entries are as written
*** Day has been written over; either 1 or 3
**** Only Cha and evidence of a crossed "t"; remainder from earlier reading

CHENY - also see CHANEY, CHAYNEY			
CHENY, Simon	Frances E. Wheeler	14 Dec 1869	
CHESALDINE, James C.	Emma F. Scott	3 Sep 1896	w
CHESHIRE, Grace L.	Joseph A. Donohoe	3 Aug 1893	w
CHEW, Agnes	Hanson Clarke	4 Jan 1821	
Ann Crabb	Washington Bowie	16 Sep 1799	
Harry W.	Mary C. Calhoun	22 Sep 1896	w
Robert F.	Tabitha Willson	28 Jun 1820	
CHEZUM, Mary V.	Luther E. Burriss	23 May 1864	
CHICHESTER, George M.	Mary Bowie	16 Dec 1824	
Lydia W.	William S. Muir	1 Jun 1894	w
Margaret B.	Warrington G. Smith	23 Jan 1890	w
W. B.	Lydia H. Brown	13 Jan 1854	
Washington B.	Eliza M. Hallowell	21 Dec 1891	w
CHICK, Edwin Wallace	Mary Bean	2 Jun 1886	w
Janet	Reuben A. Ingalls	14 Nov 1888	w
Roberta	Alexander S. Soper	9 Mar 1883	
William R.	Mary L. Beavers	7 Apr 1893	w
CHILDRESS, Clifton	Phebe Cephas	20 Nov 1867	
CHILDS, Arietta J.	William Hamilton Pace	13 Oct 1877	w
Carrie B.	William P. Waters	21 Oct 1874	
Cephas	Anne Clagett	20 May 1812	
Eleanor	Samuel Magruder	23 Nov 1820	
Hannah	Jonathan Dennis	28 Mar 1822	
Luke	Jennie Brown	24 Dec 1866	
Maggie	George B. McCeney	2 Feb 1886	w
Mary	Walter Magruder	6 Dec 1823	
Mary A. E.	Joshua W. Dorsey	10 Apr 1841	
Mary F.	John H. Evans	10 Apr 1817	
Samuel B.	Ann M. W. Martin	16 Oct 1857	
Theodore E.	Emma W. Umstead	13 Nov 1882	w
Virginia L.	Peter H. Whisner	13 Apr 1874	
William H.	Octavia B. Owen	5 Oct 1874	
William H.	Rosa McCeney	13 Dec 1886	w
CHILTON - also see SHELTON			
CHILTON, A. W.	Martha M. Kilgour	21 Feb 1865	
Joshua	Sukey Green	2 Feb 1829	
Joshua	Ann Cooley	25 Jun 1840	
Matilda	David Young	11 Apr 1827	
CHISWELL, Ann Newton	Joseph James Wilkerson Jones	22 Dec 1806	
Edward J.	Eva W. Allnutt	4 Dec 1865	
Eleanor	William Marvin	22 Jan 1844	
Eleanor W.	Thomas N. Gott	25 Sep 1843	
Eleanor White	George Walter Fletchall	12 Dec 1814	
Elizabeth	Stephen N. C. White	4 Jul 1837	
Elizabeth S.	Charles Macklefresh	5 Feb 1800	
Frances E.	William Vincent	3 Mar 1804	
George W.	Leah Griffith	26 Apr 1847	
Jemima E.	Nathan Maynard	27 Nov 1854	
John	Eleanor Griffith	21 May 1823	
John A.	Sarah R. Phillips	21 Nov 1851	
John A.	Eleanor S. Gott	25 Oct 1876	
Joseph N.	Eleanor White	20 Nov 1840	
Joseph N.	Virginia White	16 Aug 1869	
Joseph T.	Linda C. Young	29 Nov 1887	w

CHISWELL,	Lawrence A.	Hattie M. Hersberger	29 Apr 1895 w
	Lizzie E.	James T. Trundle	14 Jan 1867
	Maggie	Samuel C. White	22 Jan 1874
	Margaret	Henry Young	28 Jan 1823
	Mary R.	William Brewer	5 Feb 1800
	Nettie	Remus R. Darby	28 Oct 1879
	Rachel	Joseph Astlen	12 Dec 1798
	Rachel	Benjamin White	4 Dec 1815
	Sally A.	Lawrence A. Darby	2 Jun 1856
	Sarah N.	Howard Griffith	11 Jan 1847
	Sarah Newton	Thomas Fletchall	13 Mar 1801
	Sarah R.	William Rolison	2 Jan 1865
	Thomas F.	Mary E. Jones	13 Feb 1833
	William	Sarah Fletchall	14 Nov 1809
	William A.	Rachel Ann Fletchall	26 Jan 1846
	William G.	Lulu H. Lyons	9 Nov 1880
CHORLEY,	Frederick C.	Rebecca J. Leaman	14 Oct 1896 w
CHUNN,	John	Louisa Lewis	14 Jun 1892 c
	John	Carrie Adams	7 Sep 1893 c
CHURCH,	Katie L.	Israel G. Warfield, Jr.	3 Nov 1897 w
CINNAMOND,	Carolyn M.	W. T. Browning	31 Mar 1859
CISELL,	Anny	James Davis	25 Apr 1799
CISSEL - also see CECIL, CECILL, CEICILL, SCISSEL, SCHISSEL			
CISSEL,	Ada M.	Byron V. Cissel	18 Jun 1897 w
	Byron V.	Ada M. Cissel	18 Jun 1897 w
	Byron V.	Ada M. Cissel	18 Jun 1897 w
	Corrie I.	William W. L. Cissel	9 Jun 1891 w
	David T.	Sarah S. Young	7 Jan 1859
	E. Belle	Arthur Young	18 Apr 1870
	Edward G.	Helen D. Wilson	26 Jun 1882
	Edward G.	Minnie Waters	24 Apr 1889 w
	Ernest Richard	Mamie Zeigler	12 Apr 1888 w
	Humphrey	Julia Griffith	26 Oct 1874
	James H.	Frances I. Clark	26 Oct 1897 w
	John Francis	Mollie D. Gaither	27 Nov 1883
	Mariel R.	Benjamin C. Gott	13 May 1858
	Martha	Henry Young	10 Nov 1871
	Philip	Sarah Carr	19 May 1838
	Sarah J.	Andrew J. Jones	5 Dec 1859
	William W. L.	Corrie I. Cissel	9 Jun 1891 w
	Zephaniah	Eliza A. Magruder	7 Sep 1831
CISSELL,	Benjamin	Charlotte Phelps	10 Feb 1836
	Benjamin G.	Eleanor W. Whitaker	23 May 1833
	Catharine V.	Charles H. Baker	20 Mar 1850
	Charlotte	Richard Cissell	6 Feb 1799
	Lizzie W.	Maurice J. Weller	8 Jan 1867
	Mary J.	Francis Knott	2 Jun 1862
	Philip	Rachell Lizure	21 Jan 1800
	Prissilla	Henry Fitzgerald	10 Jan 1827
	Richard	Charlotte Cissell	6 Feb 1799
	Samuel	Ann M. Nicholson	26 Mar 1864
	Samuel	Mary A. Herron	10 Feb 1874
	Sarah C.	Zephaniah Jones	9 Mar 1840
	Thomas B.	Elizabeth Cashell	19 Feb 1873
	William	Nancy Owens	21 Dec 1802
	Zepheniah	Rachel Jones	27 Nov 1809

CLABAUGH, Robert L.	Bertie S. Shearer	30 Nov 1896	w
CLAGET, Eleanor Elizabeth	William H. L. Fisher	17 Dec 1840	
CLAGETT - also see CLAGGETT, CLAGETTS			
CLAGETT, Addie	Nathan W. Saunders	24 Dec 1879	w
Alberda J.	D. W. Whiting	5 May 1860	
Alfred	Susan W. Clagett	1 Dec 1825	
Alice V.	Marvin E. Plummer	8 Jun 1881	
Alphonso M.	Ellen Othella Fraley	13 Jun 1893	w
Ann	Zachariah Linthicum	31 Oct 1803	
Ann	Robert Clagett	8 Jan 1807	
Ann E.	Nathaniel Clagett	3 Jan 1852	
Anne	Cephas Childs	20 May 1812	
Anne M.	David Hard?ock	9 Mar 1829	
Annie	Albert King	24 Jul 1890	c
Annie M.	John H. Hilton	10 Apr 1878	w
Annie M.	Edgar A. Thompson	21 Dec 1881	
Ara E.	Samuel Oliver	25 Nov 1851	
Ara M. S.	Samuel Thrift	24 Jan 1839	
Ara R.	Thomas J. Peddicord	27 Oct 1860	
Asa	Mary Higgins	31 Jan 1816	
Asa	Jane S. Gartrell	22 May 1844	
Attelia	Joseph T. Bailey, Jr.	2 May 1871	
Augusta I.	Thomas E. Briggs	19 Oct 1895	w
Blanche	Wilson Owens	16 Jul 1894	c
Charles	Monie Bush	9 Jun 1881	c
Charles	Bettie Weaver	15 Jan 1889	c
Charles A.	Rachel A. Brown	16 Dec 1887	c
Charles A.	Cora Allison	18 Jul 1895	w
Charles E.	Antonia Snowden	26 Sep 1895	c
Clara A.	Joseph T. Kengla	24 Oct 1870	
Cornelia	James Davis	3 Mar 1890	c
Eleanor H.	Basil Offutt	13 Nov 1805	
Eletha	Jospeh C. Offutt	27 Nov 1834	
Elizabeth	Edward O. Williams	3 Dec 1800	
Elizabeth	Aquila Fisher	17 Dec 1810	
Elizabeth	Joseph H. Jones	16 Jan 1821	
Elizabeth	James Thompson	16 Feb 1837	
Elizabeth Ann	Edward W. Owen	25 Dec 1830	
Elizabeth R.	Elbert Perry	23 Feb 1848	
Elizabeth S.	Thomas E. Peddicord	2 Feb 1861	
Ellen	Grafton Holland	4 Nov 1834	
Emma	William B. Hawkins	29 Oct 1884	w
Emma M.	Joseph E. Gilliss	19 Nov 1895	w
Erasmus	Lucretia A. Etchison	16 Apr 1853	
George	Clemmie Brown	3 Jan 1877	
George H.	Susan G. Heeter	22 May 1893	w
Grace	Brooke Vincent	31 Aug 1897	w
Harriet	Richard Steward	24 Dec 1867	
Henry	Harriet Ann Ross	3 Jan 1898	c
Henry M.	Mary E. Shaw	14 Jan 1873	
Henry T.	Elizabeth Dorsey	2 Jan 1896	c
Horatio	Mary Martin	16 Feb 1824	
Ida E.	Francis W. Higgins	19 Dec 1877	w
James	Lucretia Prather	13 Aug 1889	c
James O.	Fannie E. Hilton	17 Nov 1894	w
James W.	Maria L. White	19 Feb 1853	

CLAGETT, Jane	Aeneas Belt	7 Dec 1816	
John E.	Frances R. Beall	2 Nov 1886	w
John H.	Elizabeth Hawkins	3 Mar 1812	
John H.	Emily C. Ricketts	7 Nov 1848	
John Henry	Maria Williams	5 Mar 1875	
John W.	Alvertra A. Layton	1 Jan 1867	
John W.	Sarah A. Campbell	24 Oct 1889	c
Joseph B.	Mary A. V. Higgins	22 Dec 1852	
Joseph Lee	Grace Collins	25 Aug 1898	w
Laura L.	Oliver W. Thompson	20 Feb 1883	w
Lillie	Elbert Perry	17 Mar 1891	w
Lucy J.	Charles W. Newman	19 Feb 1889	c
Maggie A.	John O. Clark	5 Nov 1874	
Margaret E.	John G. Stone	4 Feb 1881	
Marshall	Leanna Wallace	* Jun 1877	c
Martha A.	John Heeter	13 Dec 1848	
Martha L.	Charles Diggs	25 Jan 1889	c
Mary A.	Robert Ivory	10 Jun 1889	c
Mary C.	J. T. Garner	17 Dec 1867	
Mary E.	Charles E. Allnutt	25 Oct 1887	w
Mary E.	William T. Pratt	24 Oct 1893	w
Mary R.	Robert L. Hammond	21 Sep 1898	c
Mary James	Zachariah Briggs	7 Dec 1870	
Matilda	Benjamin Mullican	17 Jan 1816	
Montgomery	Ida Stone	25 Jan 1870	
Nathaniel	Peggy Ann Willcoxen	14 Dec 1807	
Nathaniel	Ellen M. Hawkins	14 Aug 1847	
Nathaniel	Ann E. Clagett	3 Jan 1852	
Nathaniel	Bettie E. Offutt	17 Feb 1862	
Ninian	Margarett Burgess	5 Sep 1804	
Oratio	Margaret E. Scott	28 Feb 1832	
Rebecca M.	David Lewis	13 Feb 1829	
Richard	Ann Maria Ricketts	5 Nov 1860	
Richard D.	Mollie C. Phillips	4 Oct 1887	w
Robert	Ann Clagett	8 Jan 1807	
Robert E.	Ida Belle Watkins	3 Jul 1894	w
Rosa	Leonard Clark	9 Dec 1868	
Sallie E.	James H. Hawkins	7 Oct 1868	
Samuel	Mary Snowden	28 May 1896	c
Samuel H.	Prissilla Poole	18 Dec 1809	
Samuel M.	Sarah Benton	7 Dec 1813	
Samuel T.	Ada Florence Heeter	22 Dec 1874	
Sarah E.	Samuel T. Briggs	21 Dec 1864	
Susan	Remus Brown	31 Jan 1885	c
Susan H.	Thomas Hawkins	30 Jan 1849	
Susan W.	Alfred Clagett	1 Dec 1825	
Susannah Rebecca	Philip Burdett	17 Aug 1838	
Susie	George E. Warfield	7 Feb 1896	c
Thomas	Rachell Offutt	12 Jan 1802	
Thomas	Harriett White	28 Nov 1812	
Thomas John	Sophia Martin	3 Dec 1811	
Thomas R.	Mary R. Carter	20 Sep 1898	c
Thomas W.	Annie V. Chase	28 Dec 1898	c
William	Mary Benton	20 Nov 1816	

* Day has blot on it; between 12 and 27

CLAGETT,	William	Ruth H. Holland	21 Dec 1855	
	Willie E.	Mattie W. Davis	20 Dec 1882	
	Zachariah T.	Sarah A. Warfield	10 Jan 1861	
CLAGETTS,	Alphonzo M.	Mollie V. Thompson	26 Jul 1877	w
CLAGGETT - also see CLAGETT, CLAGGETS				
CLAGGETT,	Arah	James Hawkins	7 Jan 1819	
	David	Sally Odle	16 Feb 1801	
	Flavius	Mary E. Harrell	24 Sep 1890	c
	Honore M.	Mary E. White	26 Aug 1889	w
	James H.	Mary Thrift	24 Dec 1838	
	John	Sarah Winsor	15 Dec 1817	
	Mary	Leonard Wathan	27 Oct 1821	
	Mary Ann	Artaxerxes Fisher	13 Sep 1813	
	Nathan	Catharine Winsor	6 Dec 1816	
	Nathan B.	Sarah Ann Hilton	22 Jan 1840	
CLANCEY,	John	Katharine Larner	31 Jan 1801	
CLARENCE,	Eliza	Henry H. Bowen	7 Nov 1894	c
	John Henry	Eliza Ann Warren	3 Jan 1868	
	Susan	Edward Lomax	30 Dec 1886	c
CLARK,	Alice V.	Albert H. Tilley	21 Mar 1896	c
	Annie M.	Washington Tobtan*	14 Oct 1884	w
	Daniel L.	Margaret H. Hardisty	4 Dec 1894	w
	David W.	Florence A. Griffith	11 May 1897	w
	Edward Fletch	Margery Hill	2 Dec 1880	
	Emma V.	Elias P. Marlow	26 Nov 1878	
	Frances I.	James H. Cissel	26 Oct 1897	w
	Frank P.	Caroline V. Scholl	8 Jul 1887	w
	Isabella	George W. Hoyle	2 Jun 1858	
	James	Susannah Dorsey	9 Oct 1879	
	John	Elizabeth Green	25 Jan 1802	
	John G.	Mary E. Knott	29 Oct 1895	w
	John O.	Maggie A. Clagett	5 Nov 1874	
	Josiah H.	Emma G. White	12 Mar 1884	
	Martha	Ashton T. Cobourn	26 Mar 1873	
	Martha	Turner S. Adams	21 Aug 1878	c
	Mary	George D. Mullican	4 Jan 1875	
	Mary Ann	John M. Reid	8 Nov 1802	
	Mary Augusta	Frederick L. Kregel	30 May 1853	
	Mary Elizabeth	George R. Browning	18 Jun 1833	
	Mary Katherine	James B. Fenwick	1 Oct 1890	w
	Moses	Liza Matthews	13 Jun 1889	c
	Oliver B.	Mary A. Stubbs	** Jan 1883	
	Richard Henry	Maria Douglas	21 Sep 1866	
	Ruth L.	Thomas O. Warfield	24 Nov 1897	w
CLARKE,	Ann	Henry G. Sothoron	13 Jan 1823	
	Anne	Otho Willson	29 Sep 1812	
	Augusta	John Turner	13 Oct 1864	
	Betsy	Nathan Oram	24 May 1800	
	Charles	Frances A. Cooper	5 Dec 1848	
	Edwin	Nancy Piles	20 Jan 1841	
	Elizabeth	Robert Crawford	18 Jan 1806	
	Frances T.	James R. Creamer	26 Nov 1866	
	Hanson	Agnes Chew	4 Jan 1821	

* As written; other records show Topham to be correct
** Day too light to read; either 10 or 11

CLARKE,	Henry	Mary Collier	19 Mar 1823
	Jane	Charles Willson	5 May 1807
	Laura	J. Thomas Parker	18 Jun 1867
	Lawson	Lucy Jones	3 Aug 1802
	Leonard	Rosa Clagett	9 Dec 1868
	Louisa	George R. Browning	26 Feb 1831
	Mary	Middleton Thompson	15 Dec 1805
	Mary	William Willson	13 Jan 1809
	Nathan B.	Harriet E. Gould	7 Aug 1878 w
	Oliver H. P.	Catherine A. Cooper	12 Apr 1852
	Sarah	David Gu	7 Dec 1807
	William	Elizabeth Barrett	29 Jan 1806
CLARKSON,	William	Lucy Watson	3 Jan 1807
CLATON - also see CLAYTON			
CLATON,	Sarah	Christopher Coall	31 Mar 1798
CLAY - also see KLAY			
CLAY,	Henry	Catharine Henson	24 Dec 1896 c
	Lavinia	Thomas A. Jackson	26 Oct 1888 c
CLAYTON - also CLATON			
CLAYTON,	Albert T.	Cora V. Moulden	27 Jun 1892 w
	Eleanor	Jonas Parsley	30 Nov 1799
CLELAND,	Anne	William Wilcoxen	10 Jun 1801
	David G.	Vina D. Osmond	8 Nov 1897 w
CLEMENS,	Ann	James Fenwick	12 May 1852 *
CLEMENTS,	Andrew	Ann C. Howard	13 Aug 1831
	Ann Eliza	Jacob A. Gloyd	4 Sep 1876
	Ann Juliett	George H. Judey	18 Mar 1823
	Ann V.	John Gardener	29 Sep 1828
	Anne	George P. Atwood	5 Nov 1813
	C. C.	Perry W. Lowe	10 Jan 1867
	Eliza	Thomas Gray	29 Oct 1890 c
	Florence J.	John L. Brunett	20 May 1884
	George H.	Emily J. Jones	17 Nov 1876
	Henry	Minora Robertson	3 Mar 1887 c
	Henry L.	Ellen A. Nicholson	2 Dec 1881 w
	Henry Walter	Martha J. Howard	29 Sep 1880
	Jane	Charles B. Jones	1 Oct 1836
	John	Emily Livers	29 Sep 1835
	Lemuel S.	Elizabeth Gardner	9 Nov 1818
	Martha	James Coombs	30 May 1808
	Mary E.	Gerrard P. Crown	19 Oct 1824
	Mary E.	Jacob A. Gloyd	10 Aug 1857
	Mary E.	Lee Offutt	20 Nov 1888 w
	Mary V.	Henry C. Barron	24 Nov 1887 w
	Ozwald	Elizabeth Lowe	12 Jan 1817
	Peter H.	Mary E. Beall	1 May 1848
	Richard A.	Mary Ann Gittings	15 Aug 1826
	Samuel N.	Mary Ann E. Farre	7 Jan 1826
	Sarah	John Martin Ratcliff	26 Jan 1819
	Thomas N.	Lydia Ann Livers	29 Oct 1825
	Valetta	Charles B. Jones	3 Nov 1841
	Wesley	Nancy Thompson	29 Mar 1843
	William	Maggie King	26 Oct 1871
	William H.	Laura M. Hopewell	12 Dec 1889 c
CLEMONS - also CLEMENS			
CLEMONS,	John	Margaret Steward	15 Jul 1896 c

CLEVELAND, Harrison	Sarah Richard	8 Dec 1798
John Robert	Josephine L. Kane	10 Jun 1892 w
CLIENCE, Mary	John William Day	19 Dec 1865
CLIFTON, Lewis	Mary Robertson	30 Aug 1890 c
CLINE - also see KLINE		
CLINE, Mark D.	Annie Landrum	20 Dec 1888 w
Walter A.	Daisy V. Moxley	21 Dec 1897 w
William H.	Rosana N. Winsor	13 Dec 1830
CLINGAN, James	Mary Offutt	6 Mar 1810
Mary	Henry Crosby	8 Nov 1826
William	Sarah Darby	5 Aug 1803
CLIPPER, Barbara	Henry H. Jackson	15 Oct 1892 c
George W.	Lucy Jackson	4 Apr 1889 c
John	Emma Murray	1 Aug 1891 c
John	Martha A. M. Johnson	17 Jun 1895 c
CLIVER, Catherine	Stephen Bicket	30 Mar 1799
CLOPPER, Anna B.	Henry Warring, Jr.	31 Dec 1868
Mary Augusta	William R. Hutton	20 Aug 1855
CLOUD, Abner	Susanah Smallwood	9 Feb 1799
Ann	Richard Blowers	18 Dec 1824
Nola	Evrrard Gary	22 May 1800
Susan P.	William Roberts	29 Apr 1814
CLOUGH, William H.	Lillian L. Nichols	29 Jul 1889 w
CLOWE, William H.	Agnes May Darby	6 Dec 1881
COALE - also see COLE		
COALE, John	Susanna Crown	11 Sep 1823
Mary Elizabeth	William Manakee	28 Mar 1850
COALL, Christopher A.	Sarah Claton	31 Mar 1798
COAR, Henry L.	Mary E. Coar	27 Dec 1887 w
Isaiah	Amanda E. Gray	30 Aug 1871
COAR, Mary E.	Henry L. Coar	27 Dec 1887 w
William T.	Mary E. Burton	29 Feb 1896 w
COATES, Eliza	Robert Gross	8 Dec 1887 c
Lloyd	Maria Diggs	22 Jan 1869
Lloyd	Annie Terry	18 Nov 1890 c
Lloyd J. Jr.	Susan E. Mason	3 Feb 1897 c
Mary	William Digges	21 Nov 1892 c
Milly	Patrick Hebbun	25 Dec 1869
Townsend	Achsah Nailor	5 Apr 1879 c
Robert	Annie White	24 Oct 1878 c
COATS, Charles	Henrietta Holman	27 Nov 1876
Henrietta	Patrick Ambush	20 Dec 1866
Henrietta	George Mason	22 Jan 1869
Jerry	Anna Bell	9 Sep 1870
Rachel	William Beckwith	17 Oct 1868
COBBIN, Bettie	George T. Lea	20 Jul 1887 c
COBERTH, Adelia M.	William T. Hickman	9 May 1838
Ann	John Flemming	20 Oct 1825
Catharine M.	John F. Hughes	5 Apr 1853
COBURTH, Horace	Elizabeth F. Williams	19 Feb 1835
COBOURN, Ashton T.	Martha Clark	26 Mar 1873
COBURN, Charles H.	Martha J. Owens	28 Apr 1869
COCKERAL - also see COCKRELL		
COCKERAL, Parthenia	Edward Smith	21 Aug 1803
COCKEY, John G.	Mary Ann E. Birnsides	1 mAy 1836

COCKRAM, William	Elizabeth Hooker	9 Dec 1814	
COCHRANE, Elizabeth	James Read	23 Sep 1809	
Jane	Solomon Smith	22 Jan 1812	
COCKRELL - also see COCKERAL			
COCKRELL, Richard H.	Julia G. Lockwood	4 Apr 1898	w
COCLYN - also see COGLAN			
COCLYN, Thomas	Eletha Reid	12 Apr 1828	
COE, Aurelius	Maria L. Belt	2* Oct 1858	
Elizabeth	Heator B. Peacock	26 Nov 1844	
COFFEY, Clare B.	Benjamin F. George	4 Jun 1888	w
COGLAN - also see COCLYN			
COGLAN, John	Elizabeth Hoyle	23 Aug 1802	
COGSWELL, Frank B.	Lizzie M. Sparshott	11 Jun 1894	w
COHEN, Abbie	Mayer M. King	18 Oct 1887	w
COHO -also see CAHO			
COHO, Catherine	Levin Redman	17 Oct 1804	
COHOO, Basil	Nancy Phillips	17 Dec 1798	
COLBURG, Justus	Cary Adkins (female)	8 Oct 1814	
COLE - also see COALE, COALL			
COLE, Camisdella	Peter Hammond	23 Dec 1865	
Charles	Martha Squirrel	1 Dec 1881	
Charles	Annie Heisler	26 Jun 1895	w
Edward	Rebecca Smallwood	12 Apr 1819	
Elizabeth S.	James Marlow	27 Nov 1845	
Ellen	Samuel Martin, Sr.	26 Dec 1828	
Emma	Joseph Wildman	30 Oct 1895	w
James S.	Lila V. Gantt	29 Dec 1887	c
John	Bettie Heisler	26 Feb 1898	w
John C.	Ida M. Thompson	15 Jan 1889	w
John R.	Emma Dorsey	22 Oct 1874	
Laura	Mahlon F. Mobley	8 Nov 1882	w
Leanah	Jesse Bally	12 Jul 1812	
Martha Ann	George Kennill	17 Jun 1895	w
Mary E.	Perry Thornton	8 Feb 1894	c
Polly	Nehemiah Bennett	15 Jan 1820	
Samuel	Fannie Spriggs	16 Sep 1872	
Sophia	Lorenzo Walston	25 Oct 1893	c
Susannah	John Peter Hoffman	7 Oct 1800	
Sarah D.	William W. Case	10 Jan 1849	
Thomas C.	Margarett Louisa Browning	15 Sep 1831	
William H.	Rachel Powell	6 Sep 1888	c
William N.	Lucy A. Williams	9 Oct 1884	
COLEAGE, Mary A.	Charles A. Hammond	18 Jun 1879	c
COLEMAN, Anna Belle	Samuel S. Mebane	28 Mar 1878	
Charles H.	Rachel A. Cromwell	21 Oct 1876	
Charles W.	Katie L. Smith	15 Apr 1896	c
Frank G.	Carrie C. Duvall	26 Jul 1887	w
Harriet	Charles Grandison	24 Jul 1889	w
James	Eliza Baker	6 Dec 1826	
Jane C.	Joel Morgan	15 Mar 1819	
Mary E.	George W. Frazier	16 Dec 1889	c
Patrick	Mary Holland	1 Jan 1813	
Roy	Mary Wallace	29 Mar 1875	

* Day has a blot on in; before 27

COLEMAN, S. H.	Lavinia Magruder	2 Oct 1871	
Susan B.	George E. Sewall	26 Mar 1877	c
Wesley	Annie Arthur	4 Jun 1889	c
William E.	Maggie E. Haske	19 May 1892	w
COLIFLOWER - also see COLLIFLOWER, CAULIFLOWER			
COLIFLOWER, L. S.	L. A. Davis (female)	28 May 1870	
COLLEGINS, Massey	Peter Hays	23 Jun 1866	
COLLETAN, Peter	Elizabeth A. Parsley	26 Dec 1859	
COLLEY, James H.	Fanny Stewart	20 Apr 1891	c
COLLIAR - also see COLLYAR, COLYER			
COLLIAR, Rachel	Thomas Read	28 Dec 1824	
COLLIER, Fannie	John C. Whalen	10 Feb 1876	
John W.	Anna C. Padgett	18 Jan 1878	w
Mary	Henry Clarke	19 Mar 1823	
Rachel	Samuel Tuttle	13 Apr 1808	
Thomas P.	Mary V. Berry	20 May 1874	
COLLIFLOWER - also see COLIFLOWER, CAULIFLOWER			
COLLIFLOWER, Hattie M.	Artemus R. Griffith	24 Oct 1898	
Sarah E.	William McIntosh	24 Oct 1867	
COLLINGS, Janie	Charles Newman	25 Nov 1879	w
COLLINS, Alice A.	John R. Gibson	28 Sep 1891	w
Ann	Richard Jackson	17 Feb 1848	
Catharine	Martin V. Cutler	6 Jul 1896	w
Daniel	Susannah Vancosen	8 Dec 1802	
Daniel	Maria Sparrow	21 Jan 1826	
Daniel	Clara E. O'Neal	6 Nov 1883	
David E.	Mary Ann S. Williams	28 Oct 1829	
Elijah	Rebecca Selby	9 Sep 1800	
Elizabeth	John Williams	1 Jan 1821	
Emma R.	James H. Howser	25 Feb 1863	
Eva J.	James T. English	27 Feb 1890	w
George	Mary Gaither	21 Sep 1893	c
Grace	Joseph Lee Clagett	25 Aug 1898	w
James	Nancy Whetzel	12 Jan 1799	
John	Ruth Lasheare	9 Jan 1802	
John L.	Lois Eunice Offutt	7 Apr 1868	
John R.	Augusta Felis	19 Dec 1888	w
Joseph	Elizabeth Sparrow	9 Nov 1816	
Laura	George D. Immick	20 Nov 1879	w
Lydia J.	James F. Ingalls	22 Sep 1881	w
Mary Jane	William Dalzell	10 Oct 1838	
Nellie	Joseph M. Harriss	13 Oct 1896	w
Rebecca	James Younger	9 Jan 1810	
Reubin	Margarett Matilda Crockett	28 Jul 1820	
Richard	Eliza A. Ball	8 Jan 1851	
Richard	Sarah Ann Houser	17 Jul 1855	
Rosella V.*	James W. Ricketts	5 Sep 1871	
Sarah E.	William E. Ingalls	19 Jul 1883	w
Susan	Jonah Chamberlain	21 Dec 1799	
Susannah	Levi Tucker	23 Mar 1799	
Thomas	Sarah Mockbee	20 Feb 1810	
William A.	Mary E. Henley	8 Mar 1894	w
Zachariah	Linny Whelan	13 Aug 1823	

* This could be Rosetta

COLLINSGRUE, Charles	Amanda Barnes	21 Sep 1858
COLLIS, Josie M.	James E. Kelley	26 Oct 1892 w
COLLYAR - also see COLLIER		
COLLYAR, Eleanor	Peter Higdon	21 Dec 1808
COLSON, Rebecca	George Taylor	2 Aug 1860
COLSTON, Eliza	John H. Baker	27 Feb 1883
COLTER - also see COULTER		
COLTER, Michael	Margaret Green	25 May 1830
COLYER - also see COLLIER		
COLYER, Eleanor	John Adams, Jr.	21 Jan 1799
COMBASH - also see CAMBUSH		
COMBASH, Charles	Sarah Johnson	27 Nov 1890 c
Charles	Addie Carter	14 Dec 1893 c
Maria	Washington Lee	7 Apr 1877 c
Vernon	Viny Milton	13 Jan 1898 c
William	Maggie Toogood	23 Dec 1879 c
COMER - also see KUMMER		
COMER, George P.	Mary Dawson	27 Oct 1897 w
COMLEY, William	Elizabeth A. Vinson	2 Dec 1862
COMPHER, Samuel P.	Nellie Lee Cooley	25 Nov 1895 w
COMPTON, Joseph	Monarchy Tunnely*	13 Nov 1799
CONFREY, Jane Ann	Samuel H. Wiley	28 Dec 1870
CONGALTON, John	Rebecca Brown	1 May 1820
CONLEY - also see CONNELLY, CONNELY		
CONLEY, Elizabeth	William D. Hughes	15 Sep 1857
Margaret	David Carlysle	4 Feb 1862
Patrick	Mary Butt	23 Sep 1847
Sarah	Columbus Wallace	28 Sep 1858
CONNELL, Annie E.	Lewis M. Cramer	12 Aug 1884
Clara R.	Clarence L. Hickerson	17 Jan 1882
Eleanor	Samuel Cox	14 Sep 1816
Elizabeth Ann	William E. Pumphrey	17 Nov 1840
Ella F.	Amos West	23 Feb 1891 w
Florence	Franklin Higgins	15 Feb 1882
Helen J.	Charles F. Hogan	12 Nov 1877
James	Ruth Barrett	13 Feb 1817
John P.	Emza Ann Benton	14 Sep 1853
John S.	Minnie E. Cramer	12 Aug 1884
Julia Ann	Richard Ricketts	10 Oct 1839
Perry H.	Mollie C. Higgens	7 Jan 1884
Philip	Martha Cooke	15 Feb 1810
Philip J.	Mary J. Pumphrey	15 Feb 1853
Rebecca	Henry A. Pumphrey	23 Jan 1845
Robert	Ann Pumphrey	12 Feb 1816
Robert G.	Lucinda Wilson	3 Jan 1871
Samuel	Elizabeth C. Pumphrey	2 Feb 1841
Samuel	Elizabeth M. Heeter	18 Jan 1847
William	Marian Counselman	26 May 1862
William F.	Ella F. Broome	10 Mar 1884
CONNELLEY, Mary	Thomas Whalen	15 Nov 1807
CONNELLY - also see CONLEY, CONNELY		
CONNELLY, Anne	Nicholas Whealan	3 Feb 1812
Anne Catharine	Henry Nicholls	9 Jun 1842
Elizabeth*	William Henley	1 Apr 1823

* Part of last name from earlier reading

CONNELLY, Elizabeth	Benjamin F. Middleton	9 Dec 1833	
John	Sarah Welsh	11 Feb 1801	
John	Polly Cook	31 Dec 1825	
John T.	Barbara Wells	29 Dec 1841	
Margaret	Otho Boswell	20 Dec 1826	
Margarett	Burgess Culver	18 Feb 1811	
Maria	Michael Cartzdarfar	14 Apr 1823	
Martha J.	Benjamin F. Grimes	13 Oct 1863	
Mary	Patrick Duvane	8 Feb 1805	
Mattie M.	Geary A. Fisher	22 Nov 1897	w
Maud	Egbert J. Davis	23 Sep 1896	w
Michael	Rachel Culver	11 Jan 1814	
Michael	Lucinda Jones	22 Apr 1830	
Patrick	Eleanor Austin	28 Jan 1804	
Patrick	Elizabeth Henley	1 Dec 1885	w
Sally	Peter Whalan	14 Oct 1800	
Sarah T.	Thomas Carroll	15 Nov 1897	w
Stephen	Nancy Lyddan	22 Aug 1803	
Susan Ann	Benjamin Beall	2 Dec 1845	

CONNELY - also see CONNELLY, CONLEY

CONNELY, Michael	Biddy Liddan	25 Jan 1869	
CONNER, Bridget	Patrick Whelan	15 Apr 1816	
George W.	Mary Jane McKnight	19 Jan 1869	
Helen R.	Philemon M. Smith	23 Jan 1897	w
Judy	Thomas Crowley	12 Apr 1798	
Lucy	Cornelius W. Beall	19 Aug 1874	
Maggie	Albert T. Sherwood	24 Jun 1884	
Nelson	Elizabeth Price	11 Jun 1844	
Sarah	Stephen B. B. Geizler	5 Jul 1853	
William O.	Catharine Moulden	19 Sep 1827	
Mary*	George Riffle	17 Apr 1819	
CONNERS, Charles	Mary West	13 Aug 1888	w
CONNOWAY, Eleanor	William Miles	17 Feb 1817	
CONOVER, Flora W.	Charles F. Plumb	** Aug 1898	w

CONRAD - also see CUNROD

CONRAD, Alice	Thomas Muse	8 Oct 1898	c
George	Lucy Alexander	27 Nov 1867	
Maggie	Samuel Mason	30 Apr 1887	c
Mollie	John Green	22 Dec 1897	c
Georggie	Augustus Mason	18 Apr 1881	
CONROY, Catharine	Richard W. Hall	15 May 1889	w
Mary	Thomas H. Offutt	1 Feb 1880	
CONSTANTINE, Dominique B.	Louella M. Proctor	21 Mar 1898	w

CONTEE - also see COUNTEE

CONTEE, Samuel	Louisa Stewart	8 Aug 1878	c
CONWAY, Joseph S.	Mary A. Gloyd	31 May 1893	w
COOGLE, Kitty	Samuel Snider	27 May 1822	
COOK, Augustus	Elizabeth Jackson	18 Apr 1895	c
Brandon	Mary A. Pratt	27 Jan 1868	
Cassy	Alfred Johnson	7 Nov 1867	
Catherine	Caleb Hodges	11 Nov 1868	
Charles	Mary Williams	20 Oct 1879	c
Charles C.	Josephine L. Hanfmann	25 Oct 1897	w

* Part of last name from earlier reading
** Cannot read day; before 5

COOK, Eliza	Joseph Budd	4 Dec 1868	
Eliza J.	Samuel Jones	6 Oct 1870	
Emeline	William E. Johnson	21 Oct 1896	c
Emma	Horace Sedgwick	22 Dec 1887	c
Frances	Richard Gaither	31 Oct 1868	
George	Fannie Hill	15 Dec 1886	c
George E.	Mary C. Abert	28 Jul 1896	w
Hannah	William H. Harding	25 Oct 1880	c
Harriett	William Robertson	30 Sep 1813	
Helen	William H. Pratt	14 Sep 1878	c
James	Harriet Ann Smith	23 Oct 1873	
James	Ann Hodges	19 May 1887	c
John	Mary M. Campbell	24 Apr 1823	
John H.	Lucretia Dawson	29 Jun 1892	c
Lizzie L.	James A. Budd	1 Sep 1874	
Martha E.	Ignatius D. Read	27 Dec 1847	
Mary M.	Henry T. Baker	27 Apr 1882	
Nathan	Elizabeth Magruder	17 Nov 1825	
Nathan	Harriet A. Waters	14 Dec 1863	
Nathan P.	Katie St.C. Cooper	15 Jan 1878	w
Polly	John Connelly	31 Dec 1825	
Rachael	Zadok Magruder	28 Nov 1822	
Rosa	Joaias Webster	27 Feb 1879	c
Susanna	Jason Johnson	23 Feb 1870	
Thomas	Sally Maria Traverse	2 Jan 1800	
William H.	Nancy Smith	28 Feb 1865	
William H.	Josephine E. Stang	16 Feb 1869	
COOKE, Agnes	John Shelton	14 Feb 1893	c
Isabella	William Magruder	31 Oct 1872	
James	Patsey Beeding	29 Jan 1802	
Martha	Philip Connell	15 Feb 1810	
Mary Isabella	Albin Pratt	3 Feb 1874	
Mary W.	Robert B. Moore	16 Apr 1895	w
Rachel	Harry Woodward Dorsey	16 Jun 1807	
Verlinda	Nicholas Ray	5 Jan 1820	
Zadoc M.	Sarah M. Griffith	14 Dec 1895	
Zadok D.	Rebecca D. Magruder	27 Nov 1821	
Zedekiah	Tracy Anne Jones	3 Feb 1806	
COOKENDAFFER, Mary	Thomas Morriss	26 Mar 1800	
COOL, Peona	William Sands	14 Nov 1814	
COOLEY, Agnes Ella	John Calvin Cooley	22 May 1879	w
Amos J.	Elizabeth A. Mitchell	9 Jun 1857	
Andrew J. D.	Mary A. Leaman	6 Sep 1886	w
Ann	Joshua Chilton	25 Jun 1840	
Annie R.	John T. Reid	18 Apr 1893	w
Attilla	Benjamin Hawkins	14 Jan 1829	
Claude O.	Laura J. Ball	26 Oct 1896	w
Della May	Samuel M. Holmes	29 OCt 1895	w
Edward	Stacey Austin	19 Feb 1828	
Elizabeth	John Grantt	6 Jan 1825	
Ellen	William T. Hickman	25 Jan 1846	
Emeline	William F. Veirs	10 Mar 1841	
Fannie Frazier	Charles K. Noland	11 May 1894	c
Franklin	Mary C. Nicholson	6 Dec 1865	
Harriet	Clement Barnes	4 Jan 1888	c
Henry	Edna Bennett	26 May 1841	

COOLEY,	Henry	Jenny R. Nichols	13 Jun 1853
	John	Ellen Glissen	4 Feb 1834
	John Calvin	Agnes Ella Cooley	22 May 1879 w
	John W.	Marian E. Burriss	22 Feb 1882
	Joseph H.	Belle Nicholls	30 Oct 1883
	Julia	James Lawman	12 Dec 1840
	Nellie Lee	Samuel P. Compher	25 Nov 1895 w
	Robert T.	Annie M. Poole	6 Feb 1879
	Robert T. Jr.	Mary Rebecca Luhn	17 Aug 1872
	Ruth Ann	William Eagle	1 Jun 1837
	Sarah	John T. Lynch	22 Mar 1828
	Sarah A.	James S. Mills	30 Mar 1886 w
	Susan E.	John W. Poole	20 Feb 1849
	Susan E.	Richard H. Oden	7 Aug 1878
	Thomas A.	Anne Mitchell*	28 Feb 1811
COOMBES - also see COOMES			
COOMBES,	Dolly	William Brookes	16 Feb 1801
COOMBS,	James	Martha Clements	30 May 1808
	James	Mary Cross	23 Aug 1817
COOMES,	Benjamin F.	Alice W. Young	1 May 1872
	Kate M.	Carson Ward	29 Apr 1890 w
	Mary W.	Alexander G. Carlisle	12 Jun 1895 w
	Rebecca V.	Crittenden H. Walker	22 Jan 1884
	Sarah	William Dwyer	13 Apr 1846
	Susie	John Francis Carlisle	29 Nov 1893 w
	William H.	Mary E. Darby	27 Apr 1858
COONRY,	Patrick H.	Anabelle V. Thompson	26 Oct 1855
COOPARD - also see COOPHARD, COOPER			
COOPARD,	Charles H.	Isabella Thompson	6 Feb 1871
COOPER - also see COOPARD, COOPARD			
COOPER,	Ann	Nathan Thompson	24 Dec 1814
	Arra	Benjamin Fitzgerald	9 Nov 1803
	Arthur J.	Hettie J. Keeling	8 Oct 1894 w
	Catharine A.	Oliver H. P. Clarke	12 Apr 1852
	Charles	Ida Hawkins	29 Apr 1897 c
	Charles C.	Hester J. Case	2 Aug 1860
	Delia	Zadoc Mitchell	25 May 1866
	Edmonia	Edward Brown	11 Dec 1884 c
	Eremantha Z.	Joseph W. Esworthy	14 Apr 1863
	Frances A.	Charles Clarke	5 Dec 1848
	George W.	Anna Nelson	4 Jul 1891 c
	Jackson M.	Mollie Ann Redmon	11 Oct 1886 w
	John	Laura L. Warfield	3 Feb 1876 c
	Joseph	Anna Lyles	2 May 1895 c
	Judson C.	Sarah Downs	4 Aug 1888 w
	Katie St.C.	Nathan P. Cook	15 Jan 1878 w
	Mahlon E.	Mary E. Huddleston	26 Apr 1866
	Margaret R.	James W. Stedman	27 Nov 1864
	Mary C.	James W. Hickman	7 Sep 1854
	Mary Lizzie	Willis H. Gray	12 Jul 1884 c
	Robert	Josephine Stewart	18 Jan 1879
	Samuel Jr.	Clara Mason	2 Dec 1891 c
	Sarah E.	Samuel Benjamin Crown	26 Nov 1857
	Sophronia	John Jackson	7 Mar 1890 c

* Part of last name from earlier reading

COOPER, Thomas H.	Rosa Nelson	13 Jul 1895	c
William F.	Sarah V. Fry	5 Apr 1889	w
COOPHARD - also see COOPARD			
COOPHARD, Mary V.	Joseph Hopkins	12 Jan 1866	
COOTE, Eliza	David Barry	20 Mar 1833	
COOTES, Parke L.	Mallie M. Burkholder	26 Jul 1894	w
COPE, Joseph	Elizabeth Hennis	22 Apr 1799	
COPELAND, Grafton	Jersey Hardesty	2 Nov 1882	
James	Pattie Miles	24 Oct 1883	c
Nellie	Charles Bailey	16 Aug 1890	c
Susan	Amos W. Maginis	26 Dec 1835	
Thomas	Sarah Whiting	20 Apr 1886	
COPELIN, David	Mary Dorsey	17 Jul 1875	
Ginnie	Ephraim Frazier	4 Feb 1886	c
Martha	Henson White	24 Oct 1876	
COPLIN, Carrie	William H. Hamilton	15 Mar 1897	c
Isaac S.	Annie King	21 Jul 1897	c
John W.	Nettie Murphy	31 Dec 1885	c
CORBETT, Jacob M.	Alice E. Leamon	2 Mar 1891	w
Maggie A.	Charles F. Smith	20 Feb 1889	w
CORCORAN, Ann	John Smith	13 May 1815	
CORDELL, Collin	Mary Musgrove	10 Nov 1808	
Mary	Presly Carter	3 Mar 1813	
CORMICK, Nannie B.	Louis B. Butler	26 Jun 1894	w
CORN - also see KORN			
CORN, Alexander	Harriett Hamilton	20 May 1865	c
Daphne A.	Robert Randolph	23 Aug 1881	c
Jennie	Samuel Foreman	11 Nov 1897	c
John	Eleanor Scherin	25 Aug 1800	
Martha	Joseph Simpson	15 Jun 1866	
Roberta	John E. Ashton	23 Nov 1885	c
Rosanna	Alexander Johnson	18 Jun 1887	c
CORNELISON, Charles	Anna J. Graff	4 Mar 1865	
CORNWELL, Jeanette	Frank Esworthy	14 Nov 1898	w
Richard S.	Alice V. Norris	7 Nov 1887	w
CORRICK, Harry K.	Helen G. Wheatley	12 Nov 1889	w
CORSON, Jennie E.	James F. Burch	27 Feb 1884	
COSGRAVE, Mary E.	James F. Richardson	31 Oct 1896	w
COUGHLAN - also see COGLAN, COCLYN			
COUGHLAN, John D.	Nora Reidy	26 Nov 1897	w
COULTER - also see COLTER			
COULTER, Robert O.	Emilie T. Brooke	15 Oct 1896	w
COUNSELMAN, Charles	Eleanora C. Perry	25 Apr 1846	
John	Matilda Perry	5 Apr 1836	
Marian	William Connell	26 May 1862	
William	Charlotte Query	2 Mar 1826	
William	Edith Shoemaker	30 Nov 1829	
William G.	Julia A. Offutt	15 Feb 1864	
COUNTEE - also see CONTEE			
COUNTEE, Ellen	Nace Holland	8 Jan 1867	
George	Mary Gantt	18 Mar 1879	c
Sarah Ann	Daniel W. Washington	27 Dec 1870	
COVERT, Ira I.	Nettie M. Briggs	26 Jul 1898	w
COWLING, Thomas E.	Agnes Lanne----*	30 Oct 1878	w

* Remainder of last name has blot on it

COX, John	Matilda Smith	1 Sep 1800
John M.	Eleanor Gray	17 Dec 1798
Joseph	Susannah Hogan	18 Sep 1802
Samuel	Eleanor Connell	14 Sep 1816
Samuel Willett	Elizabeth Jones	2 Oct 1826
Thomas	Sally Freeman	27 May 1800
COY, Mary J.	George A. Stocker	22 Dec 1891 w
CRABB, Ann	Richard J. Orme	18 Nov 1800
Charles H.	Mary L. Summers	28 Nov 1811
Elizabeth	Thomas W. Howard	26 Mar 1807
Lydia	MIchael B. Griffith	28 Aug 1823
Matild	James C. Lackland	23 Dec 1817
Sarah G.	Philemon Griffith	27 Jan 1825
CRACROFT - also see CRAYCROFT		
CRACROFT, Benjamin	Nelly Prather	8 Dec 1798
CRADDICK, Lydia	Joaeph Gardiner	11 Jun 1822
CRAFFORD - also see CRAWFORD		
CRAFFORD, Rachel B.	Basil Mockbee	23 Mar 1804
Sarah	Aaron Henry	2 Feb 1807
CRAGIN, Ellen	Charles Scharer	22 Jan 1879 w
CRAIG, Christina	Joseph Taney	1 Mar 1874
CRAMER - also see CREAMER, KRAMER		
CRAMER, George L.	May G. Brewer	19 Mar 1895 w
Harry B.	Elizabeth M. Snouffer	21 Nov 1889 w
Lewis M.	Annie E. Connell	12 Aug 1884
Lewis M.	Annie E. Connell	12 Aug 1884
Minnie E.	John S. Connell	12 Aug 1884
William F.	Laura R. Windham	27 Nov 1883
CRAMLET, Matilda	Andrew J. Keith	7 Dec 1863
CRAMPFIELD, Jacob	Sophia Ponder	28 Dec 1864
CRAMPTON, John E.	Annie E. Miles	10 Apr 1890 w
Mollie	John Ivory	14 Apr 1888
CRANE, John	Sarah Easton	16 Nov 1878 w
Mary E.	John F. Ertter	13 Nov 1894 w
CRAVEN, Samuel	Harriet Trundle	30 Nov 1831
CRAVER, Charles W.	Jennie F. Myers	19 Dec 1892 w
CRAWFORD - also see CRAFFORD		
CRAWFORD, Alice V.	John T. Crawford	30 Aug 1892 w
Anna B.	John M. S. Bowie	7 Oct 1895 w
Asa	Elizabeth Penn	25 Mar 1829
Catharine	William H. Benson	20 Apr 1843
Charles A.	Ruth E. Thompson	21 Nov 1850
Elizabeth	George Willson	22 May 1804
Elizabeth	Enoch G. Ward	1 Sep 1851
Ellen V.	Zaccheus C. Thompson	24 Jan 1874
Eugenia	Claude Rogers	28 Jul 1894 w
Frances M.	John H. Windsor	23 Dec 1854
Hamilton	Elizabeth M. Higgins	5 Feb 1846
Hamilton	Sarah E. Thompson	22 Nov 1866
Hattie A.	Clinton Burns	6 Feb 1889 w
Horatio	Mary Ann Allnutt	31 Oct 1844
Ida R.	Howard A. Plummer	15 Dec 1890 w
James	Cenah Gray	1 Feb 1812
James	Laura V. Baker	16 Sep 1879
James B.	Ann Allison	14 Mar 1799

CRAWFORD, James Hanson	Caroline Elizabeth Thompson	25 Dec 1832	
John	Massy A. Thompson	27 Oct 1821	
John	Cassy Reid	17 Mar 1865	
John H.	Ella D. Hood	6 Sep 1886	w
John R.	Melvina A. Iglehart	21 Dec 1865	
John R.	Alcinda L. Duvall	24 Mar 1884	
John T.	Alice V. Crawford	30 Aug 1892	w
Laura M.	Theodore A. Sellman	2 Jan 1888	w
Lorenzo	Bertha P. Dove	21 Sep 1887	c
Mary A.	Thomas O. Banks	30 Jan 1888	w
Mary Jane	James B. Higgins	19 Feb 1852	
Matilda	Samuel Higgins	20 Dec 1843	
Osborn	Mary Cecill	20 Dec 1823	
Robert	Elizabeth Clarke	18 Jan 1806	
Rosa B.	Robert E. Nelson	25 Jun 1890	w
Rosa M.	John W. Armiger	6 Apr 1897	
Samuel	Nancy Brewington	2 Jan 1802	
Sarah A.	Robert L. Sellman	28 Jan 1892	w
Selah Ann	John Penn	15 Jan 1822	
Stacey	Margaret Thompson	2 Jun 1825	
Thomas	Mary E. Benson	11 Nov 1840	
Thomas C.	Annie P. Etchison	22 Nov 1897	w
William C.	Mary J. D. Ray	30 Dec 1878	
CRAWLEY, Elizabeth	George Lomax	11 Jul 1893	c
CRAYCRAFT - also see CRACROFT			
CRAYCRAFT, Edward	Rebecca Rabbitt	3 Jan 1871	
CRAYCROFT, Aaron	Harriet ?. Harriss	13 Oct 1838	
Catharine	Edward Jardine	30 Oct 1872	
Edward	Parmelia A. Beckwith	2 Feb 1829	
Edward	Ann A. Holland	22 Jan 1855	
Eliza Ann	Thomas G. Harriss	25 Oct 1836	
John P.	Jane M. Price	2* Nov 1844	
Mary	Richard J. Burriss	17 Dec 1867	
CREAMER - also see CRAMER, KRAMER			
CREAMER, Alice C.	John B. Heeter	21 Nov 1882	w
Blanche	Clem Ball	21 Jan 1895	w
Eliza Ann	William Mullican	13 Oct 1857	
Enoch S.	Annie M. Niple	12 Jan 1898	w
James R.	Frances T. Clarke	26 Nov 1866	
James R.	Sarah J. Bowman	1 Aug 1882	w
James T.	Annie B. Mullican	28 Sep 1886	w
John	Eliza Harry	22 Aug 1822	
John C. L.	Nancy Selby	2 Feb 1851	
John W.	Emily A. Offutt	25 Oct 1880	
Laura V.	Thomas Berry	14 Sep 1886	w
Richard S.	Lavinia E. Offutt	5 Feb 1884	
Susan	William Silence	30 Apr 1851	
CREIGHTON, W. F.	H. N. Vowell (female)	4 Apr 1862	
CRIM, Anna	Rezin Shaw	31 Jan 1799	
CROASDALE, Agnes	Frank Gates	17 Dec 1887	w
Anna M.	William J. Alburger	8 Dec 1882	w
CROCKETT, Anne	Ninian Benson	8 Mar 1809	
Charles	Susanah Hilton	28 Jul 1820	

* Day is written over; either 20 or 21

CROCKETT,	Edward E.	Annie E. Pyles	23 Jul 1884
	George A.	Lucinda Stewart	16 Aug 1892 c
	Henry	Mary Becraft	17 Nov 1836
	James	Millie Hawkins	25 Jan 1897 c
	James H.	Mary ?. Magruder	30 Jun 1898 c
	Julius A.	Sarah E. Warthan	31 Dec 1856
	Margaret Matilda	Reubin Collins	28 Jul 1820
	Nancy	William Sullivan	21 Dec 1835
	Ruth Ann	William H. Worthington	18 Dec 1839
CROMWELL,	Amanda D.	George Robertson	14 May 1883
	Maria C.	William Musser	5 Mar 1857
	Mary	Jeremiah Duvall	21 Mar 1804
	Nathan T.	Lucinda Baltimore	21 Jul 1879
	Rachel A.	Charles H. Coleman	21 Oct 1876
	Richard	Elizabeth Ann Williams	9 Sep 1833
	Stephen C.	Jame B. Veirs	7 Feb 1893 w
	William	Iarada A. Getzendaner	3 Apr 1837
CROPLY,	Mary Ann	Baker Nichollson	21 Jan 1842
CROSBY,	Henry	Mary Clingan	8 Nov 1826
	Joseph T.	Mary Ann McLaughlin	19 Feb 1833
CROSLEY,	Fanny E.	James Fitch	22 Oct 1857
CROSS,	Anna	John George	9 Feb 1824
	Benjamin	Margarett Walker	12 Sep 1798
	Benjamin	Priscilla Johnson	9 Mar 1801
	Benjamin	Ann Hickman	9 Feb 1803
	Benjamin	Rebeccah Soper	20 May 1812
	Benjamin J.	Minnie Carter	1 Sep 1890 w
	Carrie M.	Michael B. Cross	29 Dec 1897 w
	Delilah	Jacob Cross	29 Nov 1798
	Eleanor	Nelson Fisher	28 Jan 1825
	Elizabeth	John Howe	14 Jan 1812
	Gassaway	Elizabeth James	5 Feb 1806
	Isaiah	Mary Murphey	6 Nov 1832
	Jacob	Delilah Cross	28 Nov 1798
	James H.	Mary McDonald	11 Feb 1810
	John	Mary Sweny	19 Mar 1810
	Lewis P.	Martha V. Grimes	1 Sep 1877 w
	Lydia	George Janes	27 Nov 1832
	Maggie M.	William E. Green	25 Jun 1891 w
	Matilda	Philip Darby	3 Apr 1821
	Mary	James Coombs	23 Aug 1817
	Mary Ann	Samuel Cater	5 Feb 1834
	Mary Cecilia	Nicholas Gartrell	30 Mar 1841
	Michael B.	Carrie M. Cross	29 Dec 1897 w
	Rachel R.	Richard T. West	16 Nov 1846
	Rosa B.	Clarence J. Edmonson	29 Nov 1897 c
	Sarah E.	William F. Beall	4 Nov 1872
	Stephen W.	Matilda Bowman	24 Aug 1821
	Thomas	Sary Soper	25 Jan 1804
	Thomas	Mary Brashears	14 Jan 1807
	Tilghman	Jemima Murphey	28 May 1832
CROUSE - also see KROUSE			
CROUSE,	Carrie E.	Jesse E. Briggs	14 Jan 1886 w
	George V.	Fannie Power	16 Apr 1895 w
CROW,	Highley	David King	26 Aug 1816

CROWDER, Alexander N.	Deborah J. Warfield	10 Dec 1860	
CROWLEY, Anthony T.	Minerva E. Pennell	14 Sep 1897	w
Catharine*	Samuel Price	19 Nov 1816	
Thomas	Judy Conner	12 Apr 1798	
CROWN, Alice H.	Basil Thomas Butt	30 Nov 1874	
Ambrose L.	Ann R. Gloyd	26 Jan 1858	
Anna	George Harrington	3 Oct 1870	
Annie A.	John H. Brigham	24 Sep 1889	w
Elizabeth	Erasmus Duly	12 Jan 1807	
George F.	Laura Virginia Ricketts	2 Jan 1869	
Gerrard P.	Mary E. Clements	19 Oct 1824	
Henry C.	Annie A. Stevens	5 Oct 1882	
Hezekiah	Jane Jingle	12 Apr 1834	
James M.	Sarah Case	13 Sep 1881	w
John	Elizabeth Ball	1 Dec 1803	
John O.	Mary Mills	21 May 1895	w
John T.	Mary A. Bean	1 Jun 1871	
John W.	Sarah Butt	11 Apr 1876	
Joseph	Mary Slater	26 Nov 1798	
L. H.	Sarah E. Allen	29 Dec 1873	
Leanna	H. S. Donaldson	14 Jun 1858	
Lizzie E.	Zachariah T. Crown	27 Mar 1873	
Martha Ann	George E. White	10 Mar 1873	
Mary	William Manakee	30 Mar 1820	
Mary A.	Samuel V. Sparrow	30 Dec 1890	w
Mary E.	George W. Sparrow	21 May 1874	
Ruth D.	Samuel B. Crown	21 Jun 1866	
Samuel	Mary Campbell	5 Sep 1832	
Samuel B.	Ruth D. Crown	21 Jun 1866	
Samuel Benjamin	Sarah E. Cooper	26 Nov 1857	
Sophia	Benjamin Baker	9 Jan 1834	
Susan S.	Henry Mullican	15 Mar 1859	
Susanna	Joan Coale	11 Sep 1823	
Teresa E.	Thomas T. Rabbitt	12 Feb 1866	
Thomas	Elizabeth Burriss	15 Jan 1835	
William T.	Emma C. Harrison	23 Nov 1887	w
Zachariah T.	Lizzie E. Crown	27 Mar 1873	
CRUM, Lizzie R.	Burnham W. Manypenny	8 Feb 1896	w
CRUMBAUGH, John H.	Josephine Smith	31 Dec 1868	
Maggie	Edward T. Woody	24 Dec 1867	
CRUMMER, Leana	Henry Rolinson	15 Mar 1880	c
Tilghman	Clara Tucker	12 Oct 1874	
CRUMPTON, Charles	Annie Walker	15 Jul 1885	c
Thomas	Emily Johnson	25 Dec 1878	c
CRUSEN, Henry	Sallie Burton	10 Jan 1872	
CRUTCHLEY, Lucinda	Samuel P. Heffner	11 Dec 1850	
William E.	Lydia M. Hurley	22 Jun 1895	w
CUFF, Celea A.	Winfield J. Murphy	19 Jan 1880	w
John	Clara Walker	8 Nov 1886	w
Martin	Martha Thompson	26 Jun 1879	w
Patrick Jr.	Maggie Welsh	12 Dec 1883	
William	Bessee Hewitt	29 Jul 1884	w
CULP, George	Mary Sands	16 Feb 1803	
Sophia	Robert Thompson	28 Mar 1821	

* Part of last name from earlier reading

CULPEPPER, John	Abigal Lansdale	26 May 1828	
CULVER, Anne	Samuel Middleton	4 May 1809	
Burgess	Margarett Connelly	18 Feb 1811	
Eleanor	James Alexander Beall	2 Jan 1804	
Elizabeth	Francis Valdenare	28 Mar 1821	
George H.	Caroline D. Graf	6 Dec 1880	
Margaret	James Halpin	22 Feb 1895	w
Mary	William Birkhead	14 Mar 1811	
Mary	Daniel Butler	17 Jul 1868	
Mary A.	Samuel Shreve	10 Feb 1851	
Rachel	Michael Connelly	11 Jan 1814	
Thomas	Matilda Gettings	26 Jun 1852	
William	Ann Estep	6 Jan 1807	
CUMLIN, Mary*	Brantford Sewell	7 Dec 1803	
CUMMING, Fanny	John H. C. Brewer	29 Aug 1860	
CUMMINGS, George	Jane Dickey	25 Jul 1802	
Lucien S.	Elizabeth Pritchard	17 Oct 1831	
William T.	Louisa A. Lawrence	5 Jun 1888	w
CUMMINS, Franklin	Ann M. Jones	1 Apr 1850	
CUNNINGHAM, Ben A.	Eveline Candler	5 Dec 1836	
Charles L.	Ann Elizabeth Kidwell	11 Oct 1865	
Edward C.	Margaret Buxton	24 Jan 1831	
CUNROD - also see CONRAD			
CUNROD, Ida	John Dorsey	14 Mar 1891	c
CURLETT, Katie A.	George W. Kinder	16 Nov 1887	w
CURRAN, Benjamin	Margaret Busson	26 Jan 1817	
CURRENT, Nancy	William Langvill	7 Jan 1805	
CURTIN, Honora	John Markwalder	5 Feb 1873	
Katie	William Scherrer	14 Feb 1893	w
Mary A.	James P. Raney	18 Sep 1880	w
Sarah E.	Patrick Carr	27 Nov 1889	w
CURTIS, Anna E.	John C. Parker	17 Nov 1855	
Charles	Maggie A. Lyles	11 Aug 1881	c
George B.	Fannie Brown	18 Oct 1879	w
Henrietta H.	James Spencer	21 Oct 1872	
Jesse	Jane Green	4 Jan 1872	
Julius	Martha Thomas	10 Sep 1895	c
Lena	John Johnson	31 Dec 1889	c
Lillie M.	William A. Oldfield	** Mar 1890	w
Noah	Ann E. Jinkins	15 Dec 1897	c
Rose V.	Robert T. Anderson	4 Dec 1884	w
William H.	Sallie W. Willard	3 Sep 1887	w
CURTISE, Noah	Alice Peters	29 Apr 1876	
CUSHMAN, Elizabeth	William Nelson Austin	8 Apr 1818	
CUSIAK, Elizabeth M.	Martin E. Whittington	23 Jan 1895	w
CUSTER - also see KUSTER			
CUSTER, George D.	Barbara E. Nicholson	22 Nov 1881	
Mary E.	George E. Nicholson	7 Feb 1888	w
CUTLER, Martin V.	Catharine Collins	6 Jul 1896	w
CUTTS, James M.	Eleanor E. Oneale	16 Dec 1833	
DADE, Alexander	Susan Ann White	7 Jan 1850	
Columbus	Ann Mary Jones	16 Jan 1856	

* There is a blot on the last name; could be Camlin
** Cannot read day; either 1 or 2

DADE, Gertrude E.	James W. Darby	15 Oct 1887	w
John H.	Sarah E. Jones	25 Mar 1851	
Joseph T.	Susan R. Dade	9 Mar 1875	
Lee M.	Ann E. Veirs	21 Jan 1836	
Mary	Christian Hempstone	18 Dec 1839	
Mollie H.	James W. Darby	27 Sep 1875	
Sallie R.	Benjamin F. Piles	25 Jan 1873	
Sarah Ann	Robert Sellman	20 Dec 1841	
Sarena E.	Robert Sellman	12 Jul 1854	
Susan R.	Joseph T. Dade	9 Mar 1875	
DADEN, Susan	John Bell	11 Nov 1876	
DAFFNEY - also see DAPHNE, DAPHNEY			
DAFFNEY, Bertie	Ernest Davis	9 Dec 1893	c
Ida V.	James W. Howard	13 Jan 1883	
DAILEY - also see DALEY, DALY			
DAILEY, William H.	Sarah Ann Gordon	13 Dec 1880	
DAILY, Hannah A.	Ninian M. Perry	12 Feb 1877	w
James H.	Elizabeth J. Edelin	20 Dec 1854	
DALE, George E.	Viola E. Blackman	18 Jun 1894	w
DALEY - also see DAILEY			
DALEY, Andrew J.	Savillia B. Nicholson	25 Oct 1881	w
DALLAS, George W.	Helen L. Martin	12 Apr 1876	
DALY - also see DAILEY			
DALY, Ellen	James Plant	25 Jul 1885	w
Mary F.	Lancelot H. Patterson	30 Nov 1882	w
DALZELL - also see DELZELL			
DALZELL, Eliza Ann	William H. Piles	28 Sep 1846	
Mary C.	Patrick Duffy	1 Oct 1852	
William	Mary Jane Collins	10 Oct 1838	
DAMRON, William C.	Mary J. Peacock	21 Nov 1889	w
DAMUDE - also see DAYMUDE			
DAMUDE, George Washington	Jennie Nicholson	27 Dec 1876	
DANCLEE, Thomas*	Elizabeth Harress	31 Dec 1805	
DANEWOOD, Julia A.	John T. Nicholson	21 Nov 1895	w
DANGLER, Curtis J.	Lizzie T. Sullivan	14 Oct 1896	w
DANIEL, Wallace B.	Eliza B. Saylor	20 Feb 1826	
DANIELS, George	Ella Tyler	9 Jun 1892	c
DAPHNE - also see DAFFNEY			
DAPHNE, John	Jane Jackson	27 Dec 1865	
DAPHNEY, Maria F.	James H. McRoy	28 Jul 1897	c
Mary E.	James E. Jackson	5 Nov 1884	c
William E.	Bessie V. McRoy	8 Nov 1898	c
DARBEY - also see DARBY			
DARBEY, Aza	Sarah Riggs	20 Sep 1808	
Mary	William C. Dawson	21 Mar 1807	
Rezin	Mary Warfield	3 Dec 1799	
DARBY - also see DARBEY			
DARBY, Agnes May	William H. Clowe	6 Dec 1881	
Alice	Charles H. Nourse, Jr.	14 Jun 1871	
Ann	William Burnes	23 Jul 1804	
Anne	James Ward	20 Apr 1812	
Anne	Benjamin Mackall	29 Dec 1813	
Charles A.	Martha Candler	22 Nov 1831	
Darius	Ann Gardner	24 Nov 1823	

* This could be Danelee

DARBY,	Dathan	Susannah Mackall	19 Dec 1808
	Dentin	Elizabeth Veirs	11 Apr 1810
	Drusilla	Thomas Thompson	6 Oct 1828
	Edwin N.	Sarah Ann Holland	19 Mar 1836
	Elizabeth Jane	Richard H. Bowman	13 Sep 1879
	Ella E.	William A. Darby	14 Dec 1864
	Emily J.	James R. Mullineaux	6 Jul 1889 w
	George	Verlinda Allnutt	12 Jan 1822
	George A.	Lizzie A. Soper	23 Mar 1871
	George W.	Mary Riggs	13 Dec 1809
	George W.	Lucy Davis	27 Mar 1848
	George W. Jr.	Chloe Ellen Mackatee	23 Oct 1837
	Harrison D.	Lucretia M. Shaw	19 Nov 1864
	Honor M. (female)	Meredith R. Willett	12 May 1845
	Isabella A.	Robert J. Isherwood	6 May 1856
	James W.	Mollie H. Dade	27 Sep 1875
	James W.	Gertrude E. Dade	15 Oct 1887 w
	Jane	George H. Allnutt	7 Dec 1812
	Jesse	Cordelia Veirs	1 Mar 1852
	John N.	Columbia Knowles	22 Oct 1853
	John W.	Ruth Ellen Edelin	10 Dec 1844
	John W.	Virginia L. Dorsey	11 Dec 1888 w
	Juliann	Isaac Dawes, Jr.	20 Sep 1827
	Kate	Luther M. Watkins	18 Dec 1878 w
	Lawrence A.	Sally A. Chiswell	2 Jun 1856
	Louisa Ann	Richard H. Burdett	20 Feb 1835
	Margaret	William L. Lewis	15 Nov 1894 w
	Martha	Jonathan Duley	12 Apr 1815
	Martha	L. T. Warthan	8 Oct 1856
	Martha A. P.	R. S. Dean Heironimus	17 Nov 1857
	Martha W.	Robert G. Davis	10 Jun 1889 w
	Mary Ann	Mahlon Woodward	23 May 1825
	Mary E.	Alexander Broome	15 Jun 1830
	Mary E.	William H. Coomes	27 Apr 1858
	Mary E. T.	Upton S. Howser	23 Jan 1861
	Matilda C.	William F. Talbert	24 Mar 1862
	Mollie	William C. Brown	17 Feb 1876
	Nathan H.	Amanda E. Walker	26 Nov 1878
	Nicholas R.	Eleanor Burns	30 Jan 1837
	Philip	Matilda Cross	3 Apr 1821
	Rebecca	Benjamin White	16 Mar 1820
	Remus R.	Nettie Chiswell	28 Oct 1879
	Rhoda	Thomas Thompson	5 Apr 1814
	Rose M.	John A. Jones	3 Jan 1866
	Ruth	Richard Green	23 May 1821
	Ruth E.	A. C. H. Darne	22 Jan 1870
	Ruth R.	Frederick Bowman	18 Dec 1832
	Samual	Jane Veirs	24 Dec 1817
	Samuel	Hesse Ervin	29 Nov 1800
	Samuel	Mary J. Harriss	30 Nov 1848
	Sarah	William Clingan	5 Aug 1803
	Sarah Ann	Edwin Warfield	4 Jan 1847
	Sarah P.	Thomas A. Burdette	24 Jan 1881 w
	Sarah R.	James S. Windsor	9 Oct 1865
	Susan Ellen	Benjamin C. Gott	17 Dec 1849
	Susan W.	Samuel Blowers	8 Aug 1829

DARBY, Susanna	Elisha W. Swift	23 Feb 1835	
Thomas	Rebecca D. Alnutt	4 Jan 1816	
Thomas C.	Estelle Allnutt	3 Dec 1895	w
Thomas D.	Sarah E. Dawson	21 Nov 1861	
Walter	Sarah Penn	2 Mar 1814	
William A.	Ella E. Darby	14 Dec 1864	
William H.	Eliza J. Duvall	5 Mar 1877	w
William W.	Laura Jones	27 Aug 1882	
William W.	Carrie M. Murphy	17 Feb 1885	w
DARCEY, Albert	Roberta E. Bean	30 Oct 1894	w
George N.	Mary E. Stacks	2 Oct 1877	w
Mary E.	John H. Gingell	18 Dec 1883	
William J.	Ada E. Blundon	28 Apr 1887	w
DARNALE, Benedict	Cassandra Swann	6 May 1815	
Mary	Daniel Veirs	19 Jan 1813	
Robert	Henrietta Murphey	12 Jun 1815	
DARNALL - also see DARNALE, DARNELL			
DARNALL, Elizabeth	John Jones	18 Jan 1830	
Fielder	Elizabeth Young	7 Jun 1824	
Nancy*	William Dyson	18 May 1819	
DARNE - also see DARNES			
DARNE, A. C. H.	Ruth E. Darby	22 Jan 1870	
Alexander C. H.	Mary A. Gassaway	20 Oct 1846	
Ann E.	Joseph Smoot	8 May 1844	
Cecelia	Richard D. Beall	15 Feb 1831	
Daniel M.	Artamesia Magruder	23 Apr 1829	
Ella	Thomas Anderson	18 Apr 1887	w
Louisa G.	John H. Beall	27 Jul 1825	
Maria	Robert A. Lacey	13 Aug 1830	
Thomas F.	Isabel E. Mossburg	10 Sep 1895	w
DARNELL - also DARNALL			
DARNELL, Margarett E.	Benjamin T. Franklin	28 Jun 1834	
DARNES - also see DARNE			
DARNES, William	Betsey Gassaway	14 Mar 1798	
DASEY, Maria A.	William Johnson	13 Sep 1822	
DASHIEL, Alfred Henry	Ann Ridgely	25 Oct 1815	
DATCHER, Bailey E.	Mary V. Tucker	31 Dec 1890	c
DATES, Mary	Charley Augustus	5 Nov 1874	
DAUGHTON, Samuel S.	Mattie P. Mahagan	20 Jun 1892	w
DAVIDSON, H. Bradley	Mary D. Porter	2 Jan 1890	w
James H.	Sarah S. Bradley	11 Oct 1859	
Robert G.	Annie A. Saunders	18 Jan 1853	
Robert G.	Rebecca J. Magruder	24 Oct 1879	w
DAVIS, A. Thomas	Sallie E. Gott	23 May 1871	
Alverta	Ignatius H. Ward	1 Aug 1894	w
Alexander	Elizabeth Sedgwick	6 Feb 1802	
Allen Bowie	Rebecca Comfort Dorsey	5 Oct 1830	
Altonia	Edward W. Oram	30 Sep 1886	c
Alvina	William Perry	18 Nov 1875	
Andrew	Mary F. Wood	17 Sep 1873	
Andrew A.	Macy Campbell	25 May 1887	c
Andrew J.	Sarah H. English	20 Aug 1862	
Anna E.	Samuel A. Matlock	16 Feb 1857	
Anne	Jonathan Parker	14 Oct 1800	

* Part of last name from earlier reading

DAVIS, Anne	Basil Brown	18 Mar 1807	
Annie C.	George W. V. Whipp	17 Dec 1895	w
Annie E.	Edmund D. Beall	22 Apr 1891	
Basil	Betsey Penn	2 Feb 1805	
Benjamin	Elizabeth Thresher*	16 Feb 1798	
Beverly	Henrietta Dunlop	20 Jun 1871	
Caroline	Washington Lewis	26 May 1836	
Caroline	William Holley	19 Mar 1867	
Caroline	Richard Gaither	31 May 1894	c
Catharine W.	Thomas John Bowie	14 Jan 1830	
Charles	Lawrady House	3 Dec 1798	
Charles	Elizabeth Dinkins	1 Jul 1880	c
Charles E.	Catharine E. Trail	5 Sep 1867	
Charles G.	Laura A. Warfield	21 Nov 1882	
Clarence	Laura Plummer	2 Jul 1889	c
Cornelius	Alice L. Green	30 May 1884	c
Darcus S.	John **. Harding	23 May 1810	
Edmund C.	Lydia Green	2 Mar 1881	
Egbert J.	Maud Connelly	23 Sep 1896	w
Eliza	William H. Johnson	19 Apr 1866	c
Elizabeth	William Catlin	28 Feb 1809	
Elizabeth	Levi Howser	17 Nov 1868	
Elizabeth	Francis Dow	8 Sep 1886	c
Ella	U. Magruder Ricketts	9 Aug 1880	
Ella E.	William H. Best	15 Feb 1897	w
Ella J.	Joseph A. Nugent	29 Sep 1887	c
Ellen R.	David H. Stewart	22 Aug 1889	c
Emma A.	James M. Purdum	15 Oct 1895	w
Emma J.	James C. Carter	15 Jun 1897	c
Ernest	Bertie Daffney	9 Dec 1893	c
Florence P.	Francis W. Watkins	23 Aug 1897	w
Francis (female)	Robert Read	12 Nov 1822	
Francis E.	Lula H. Hager	15 May 1893	w
Frank	Maggie E. Lancaster	31 Dec 1889	c
Franklin	Maria Hall	23 Apr 1870	
George	Elizabeth Hiat	10 Aug 1804	
George	Emma Hall	22 Oct 1885	c
George V.	Clara P. Hays	16 Nov 1880	
Geveneur	Rachel Murphy	5 Sep 1868	
Grafton	Lucinda Dorsey	21 Nov 1894	c
Hannah	Hamilton Wallace	28 Dec 1893	c
Harriet	Perry Riggs	29 Jul 1874	
Harriet A.	Hilleary H. Hebron	10 Jul 1883	
Henrietta	Thomas W. Johnson	20 Dec 1893	c
Henry	Rosetta Duvall	1 Jun 1868	
Horace M.	Emma Williams	2 Jul 1878	w
Ignatius	Margaret Wootton	22 May 1798	
Ignatius	Catharine Lackland	22 Nov 1806	
Isaac H.	Eliza M. Talbott	12 Sep 1888	w
Isaac T.	Sarah A. Noland	12 Nov 1887	c
Isabella	Thomas Neal	19 Mar 1891	w
Isabella	Joseph M. Simpson	28 Aug 1893	c
J. Lynn	Jennie P. Brewer	9 Nov 1875	

* Part of last name from earlier reading
** Initial I or J

DAVIS, James	Anny Cisell	25 Apr 1799	
James	Cornelia Clagett	3 Mar 1890	c
James	Bertie Wise	23 Jan 1896	c
James C.	Mary E. Waters	27 Oct 1893	w
James N.	Mannie A. Jenkins	9 Nov 1897	c
James R.	Clara Grimes	21 Apr 1877	w
James W.	Catharine Baker	24 Dec 1863	
Jane	George Guszler	3 Jun 1800	
Jane	William Chambers	27 Dec 1870	
John	Hannah Kershner	28 May 1816	
John Thomas	Ardella M. Ricketts	29 Sep 1880	
John W.	Hattie A. Hays	15 Jan 1883	
Joseph H.	Rachel A. Fisher	3 Jul 1876	
Joseph W.	Ruth Duley	27 Apr 1816	
Josephine	Frank Andrews	24 Aug 1898	w
Joshua	Lavinia Spates	30 Dec 1824	
Joshua	Cassandra Alby	16 Oct 1832	
Joshua Jr.	Mollie E. Young	21 Jun 1869	
Keziah	James Barlow*	3 Mar 1801	
L. A. (female)	L. S. Coliflower	28 May 1870	
L. Jane	William H. Rabbitt	4 Jun 1867	
Laura May	Joseph J. Purdum	12 Apr 1897	w
Leonard Young	Achsah Worthington	2 Mar 1801	
Llewellyn Phipps	Ann W. Leach	3 Jan 1837	
Louisa F.	Henry H. Lyman	12 Oct 1894	w
Lucy	George W. Darby	27 Mar 1848	
Lydda	Hezekiah Saffell	8 Sep 1804	
Lydia	Henry Miles	12 Feb 1894	c
Maggie A.	William H. Bennett	20 Dec 1881	
Maggie M.	John E. Monred	13 Jan 1894	w
Mallina V.	Rev. D. M. Browning	11 Oct 1876	
Maria	William Fisher	31 Jan 1824	
Mark	Delia E. Johnson	24 Dec 1892	c
Mary	William Whelan	16 Dec 1824	
Mary	George Wolfe	26 Feb 1829	
Mary C.	Robert C. Lutton	19 Aug 1889	w
Mary E.	Hazel W. Cashell	25 Apr 1876	
Mary E.	John H. Hollman	28 Dec 1888	c
Mary E.	Wilson Johnson	7 Sep 1893	c
Mary F.	Henry Franklin Belt	10 Oct 1866	
Mary I.	David T. Wims	16 Oct 1888	c
Mary J.	Levi T. Young	16 Jan 1867	
Mary Josephine	Mordecai Morgan	16 Jan 1856	
Mary L.	Charles W. Montgomery	24 Jan 1894	w
Mary V.	Edward H. Prather	27 Oct 1887	c
Mary V.	James S. C. Wilson	19 Nov 1887	c
Matilda	Robert Bond	19 Dec 1827	
Matilda	Robert Marbry	3 May 1898	c
Mattie W.	Willie E. Clagett	20 Dec 1882	
Middleton	Mary Ann Roby	13 Sep 1821	
Milley	Van Swearingen	27 May 1806	
Mollie E.	Luther E. Harper	21 Jun 1892	w
Nimrod	Clarinda King	3 Jan 1827	
Perry	Jane Young	12 Dec 1866	

* First letter of last name is written over; looks like B

DAVIS, Peter H.	Harriet Brown	26 Sep 1873	
Rachel	Benjamin Lyon	27 Aug 1803	
Rebecca H.	Edward P. Reed	29 Oct 1867	
Rezin	Polly Batth Deselm	11 Feb 1805	
Richard	Ann C. Williams	28 Sep 1852	
Robert	Catharine Weldon	3 Mar 1886	c
Robert A.	Julia A. Trail	11 Apr 1861	
Robert G.	Martha W. Darby	10 Jun 1889	w
Roena B.	John L. Emmert	9 Dec 1895	w
Rosetta	Samuel Gaither	9 Oct 1890	c
Rufus H.	Victorine Smith	18 Jan 1876	
Sallie	Emory Jenus	5 Sep 1874	
Sallie	Zachariah Hale	10 Dec 1896	c
Sallie	Solomon Owens	29 Jun 1897	c
Sarah	Philip Warfield	28 Apr 1801	
Sarah	Allen Selby	9 Jan 1810	
Sarah	Samuel Fisher	14 Mar 1885	c
Sarah M.	Richard M. Minnis	22 Oct 1872	
Sarah R.	Albert C. Fawcett	2 Feb 1869	
Susan Clara	Martin Lynch	8 Jul 1871	
Susie A.	Zachariah McM. Waters	26 Oct 1897	w
Susie E.	James K. Kerr, Jr.	23 Dec 1896	w
Thomas	Elizabeth Bowie	18 Jan 1802	
Thomas	Amanda Jones	21 Jan 1889	c
Thomas	Elizabeth Waters	11 Aug 1892	c
Thomas S.	Cassie Swearingen	29 Nov 1806	
Tony Ann	Henson Taylor	4 Aug 1887	c
Vachel H.	Florida B. Watkins	26 Feb 1895	w
Vallie	James E. Jenkins	24 Dec 1889	c
William	Mary Sullivan	10 Feb 1809	
William	Charlotte Duvall	12 Feb 1833	
William	Rebecca Griffith	12 Feb 1835	
William	Maria Wayman	30 Jan 1869	
William	Anna Laura Washington	* Sep 1882	
William A.	Anna McDonald	12 May 1870	
William C.	Ruth A. Duley	27 Aug 1866	
William H.	Elizabeth O. Powell	14 Dec 1891	c
Zachariah J.	Mary Jane Shaw	17 Aug 1843	
DAWES, Benjamin B.	Rebecca Perry	18 Jun 1827	
Elizabeth	Kassius Brookins	22 Dec 1815	
Isaac Jr.	Juliann Darby	20 Sep 1827	
Marial E.	Everard G. Fisher	27 Nov 1844	
William	Maria Jackson	26 Dec 1876	
DAWKINS, Edward L.	Ophelia Peck	2 Jul 1894	c
DAWSON, Abraham	Mary Campbell	21 May 1822	
Annie	Arthur Williams	13 Jan 1882	w
Annie E.	William M. Wilson	27 Nov 1889	w
Barbara Ann	James N. Allnutt	3 Dec 1832	
Barbaray E.	Perry L. Trundle	17 Dec 1838	
Barbary	Archibald Henderson	17 Apr 1820	
Benoni	Sarah Jones	14 Jul 1827	
Dorcas Ann	Daniel Wilkinson	7 Apr 1827	
Eleza	Samuel Willson	10 Apr 1802	
Emily A.	Binoni Allnutt	17 Nov 1860	

* Cannot read day; either 2 or 4

DAWSON,	James F.	Jennie Miller	3 Jun 1864
	James M.	Anne Alnutt	17 Dec 1801
	John	Serena Garrett	19 Feb 1829
	John L.	Amelia H. Somervelle	7 Sep 1871
	Laurence A.	Mary E. Kiger	16 Jan 1844
	Lucretia	John H. Cook	29 Jun 1892 c
	Martha M.	Thomas Waters	5 Dec 1864
	Mary	Robert D. Alnutt	7 Jan 1807
	Mary	George P. Comer	27 Oct 1897 w
	Mary Ann	David T. Jones	20 Jan 1840
	Mary Ellen	Isaac R. Poole	10 Mar 1842
	Mary L.	Francis T. Williams	22 Oct 1896 w
	Samuel	Sarah Gassaway	5 Feb 1812
	Sarah E.	Thomas D. Darby	21 Nov 1861
	Serena	Otho Boswell	22 Nov 1857
	Stephen	Anne White	29 Sep 1815
	Thomas	Susannah Alnutt	15 Feb 1812
	Thomas	Mary A. Peter	3 Jan 1889 w
	Virlinda	Daniel Alnutt	20 Dec 1809
	William	Elizabeth Alnutt	21 Nov 1808
	William	Emma C. Veirs	5 Dec 1882 w
	William C.	Mary Darbey	21 Mar 1807
DAY,	Alice	Michael Whalen	13 Nov 1879
	Amanda W.	J. Fletcher Boyer	17 Dec 1881
	American A. S.	Laura W. Beall	7 Dec 1886 w
	Aquila	Amelia Etcherson	7 Jan 1805
	Christy	Frederick Etchison	16 Nov 1807
	Columbus W.	L. Adelaide Hobbs	19 Dec 1885 w
	Cora B.	Willie N. Bird	12 Aug 1892 w
	Dorsey W.	Prudence V. Burdett	20 Dec 1895 w
	Elizabeth	John Boyer	24 Feb 1816
	Fletcher A.	Jemimah R. Hobbs	20 Oct 1896 w
	Franklin	Cora D. Price	22 Mar 1893 w
	George W.	Joanna Reed	30 Jan 1879 w
	Harriet A.	John T. Ricketts	11 Jun 1851
	Hattie	Daniel W. Barnes	23 May 1890 w
	Hezekiah	Maggie B. Mills	10 Apr 1896 w
	Ida V.	Joseph D. Watkins	15 Nov 1893 w
	Jacob	Rebecca English	19 Jan 1808
	Jacob	Catharine Thompson	25 Nov 1817
	Jacob Jr.	Susan R. MIlls	24 Dec 1846
	James E.	Mary E. Mullinix	1 Mar 1886 w
	James W.	Rachel Ricketts	6 Aug 1878 w
	John H. W.	Rosalie Fish	18 Jan 1898 w
	John Thomas	Ann Bell	11 Feb 1846
	John William	Mary Clience	19 Dec 1865
	Joseph F.	Drusilla J. Ingle	29 Sep 1884 w
	Langdon S.	Maud O. Day	8 Nov 1897 c
	Laura	John Reed	* Feb 1878 w
	Laura A.	William Alfred B. Walker	22 Dec 1890 w
	Lawson	Margaret Nicholls	25 Dec 1849
	Lawson	Elizabeth E. Nicholls	8 Sep 1884 w
	Lizzie	John Price	3 Aug 1874

* No day given; 11 or before

DAY, Martha	Patrick Henley	21 Mar 1848
Mary E.	Charles Richard Mills	5 Nov 1879
Maud O.	Langdon S. Day	8 Nov 1897 c
Rosanna	John Adams	7 Feb 1804
Susan	Thomas Mills	14 Aug 1877 w
Susan Rebecca	Isaiah Easton	16 Jan 1834
Titus G.	Laura D. Watkins	16 Oct 1885 w
Titus J.	Ethel W. Mount	27 Jan 1894 w
Titus W.	Rosie B. King	2 Mar 1886 w
Vivia C.	Jerrie L. Burdette	12 Aug 1892 w
Washington	Mary E. Smith	17 Feb 1855
DAYMUDE - also see DAMUDE, DEMUDE		
DAYMUDE, James W.	Josephine Kendall	20 Aug 1879
James W.	Mary Cornelia Butt	3 Sep 1890 w
Mary	Richard Thomas Taylor	5 Aug 1879
DEAN - also see DEANE		
DEAN, John H.	Annie B. Gamble	10 Oct 1870
John Thomas	Rachel Shoemaker	31 Oct 1843
Louis	Sarah J. Price	19 Dec 1895 c
Martha	David S. Voleutyn*	6 Apr 1891 w
Mary A.	Frank Perna	18 Dec 1893 w
Peggy	Samuel Gartrell	3 Jan 1810
Sarah E.	Curtis W. Kisner	12 Nov 1873
Thomas	Treasa Bean	14 Nov 1808
DEANE, Ann	William Drudge	31 Dec 1803
DEBTOR - also see DETTER		
DEBTER, Charlotte Ellen	Amos Joppy	8 Oct 1868
DEBTOR, Artemus	Elizar Doyle	19 Jun 1865
Mary	Frederick Proctor	3 Nov 1866
Rose	Joseph Walker	14 Sep 1869
DECK, William M.	Anne L. Hendricks	12 Nov 1885 w
DECKER, Elmer G.	Charlotte C. Groshon	21 Aug 1897 w
John F.	Elizabeth Duvall	28 Jan 1820
DEETS, James Edward, Dr.	Sarah Isabella Henderson	10 nov 1886 w
DEFFER, Ellen B.	James Bevins	27 Aug 1867
DEGGES - also see DIGGS		
DEGGES, Florence N.	Joseph M. Hopkins	23 Sep 1898 w
DEGNIN, Mary	Charles L. Bast	13 Feb 1882
DEINS - also see DINES		
DEINS, Sophia	Camden Duffin	11 Oct 1882 c
DEITZ -also see DIETZ		
DEITZ, Maria A.	Harry C. Taylor	14 Dec 1887 w
DELAPLANE, John W.	Mollie L. Hopkins	7 Jun 1881 w
DELARN, Charles	Mary Soper	28 Mar 1812
DELIHUNT, Thomas	Eliza K. Fitzgerald	20 Jan 1875
DELLEHAY - also see DILLEHAY		
DELLEHAY, John T.	Charlotte Johnson	20 Apr 1864
DELLS, Mary	Nicholas Ridgeley	6 Dec 1805
DELZELL - also see DALZELL		
DELZELL, Sarah Ann	Nathaniel Watts	19 Sep 1855
DEMPAL, Jane A.	Solomon Gilbert	13 Oct 1883 c
DEMUDE - also see DAYMUDE		
DEMUDE, Catharine A.	Howard M. Butt	19 Nov 1889 w

** This could be Volentyn

DENISON, Edward J.	Eliza J. Oneale	28 Oct 1842
DENNEY, Grace	Hamlin Steele	11 Jun 1877 c
DENNIS, Abraham	Rebecca Headly	6 Dec 1819
Anderson T.	Harriet McCarty	9 Feb 1835
Elizabeth H.	Philip W. Leeke	10 Dec 1822
George W.	Allie May Dwyer	9 May 1885 w
Mariya	Samuel Rusk	27 Sep 1825
Jonathan	Hannah Childs	28 Mar 1822
DENT, Anna	William H. Kelley	15 Apr 1890 c
Asa	Martha Hays	20 Mar 1804
Hannah	Andrew Foreman	17 Aug 1802
Frances	John H. Norwood	* Jul 1882 w
Isiah	Sarah T. Warfield	10 Jul 1867
Robert	Mary Hays	4 Apr 1801
Sarah	John T. Thornton	21 Feb 1896 c
DESELLEM, James	Catharine Fulks	27 Dec 1805
DESELM, Gabriel	Kezanna Lishear	20 Apr 1805
Polly Batth	Rezin Davis	11 Feb 1805
DESPER, Joseph E.	Maggie W. Fix	25 Oct 1897 w
DETRICK, Paul E.	Florence N. Jeffries	20 Nov 1894 w
DETTER - also see DITTER, DEBTOR		
DETTER, Martha	Mat Stewart	13 May 1875
DEVAN, William	Harriet Green	25 Nov 1839
DEVER, Lucy	Benjamin Carr	22 Nov 1813
DEWAR, Thomas J.	Eliza Lupton	20 Feb 1826
DIAL - also see DYAL		
DIAL, Ann	Elie Sparrow	22 Oct 1816
Joshua	Susannah Lanham	16 Jan 1807
DIAMOND, John B.	Grace E. Ranney	6 Nov 1877 w
DICK, Thomas	Margaret Peter	3 Dec 1798
DICKENSON, Edward C.	Fannie J. Lea	30 Oct 1874
DICKERSON, Catharine	William Henry Dutch	2 Nov 1881
Elizabeth	Francis M. Griffith	8 Feb 1859
John	Elizabeth Turnbull	18 Sep 1806
Nathan	Margaret Turnbull	6 Dec 1801
Nathan C.	Christy A. Hempstone	1 Dec 1834
Rebecca	William D. Poole	11 Apr 1831
Sally	John Poole	19 Jun 1826
Samuel T.	Caroline Sedgwick	8 Nov 1866
DICKEY, Jane	George Cummings	25 Jul 1802
DIEDERICK, George W.	Alice M. Offutt	1 Jan 1878 w
DIETZ - also DEITZ		
DIETZ, William H.	Lydia A. Jenkins	4 Feb 1889 w
DIGGES - also see DIGGS, DEGGES		
DIGGES, David	Jemima Wallace	31 Dec 1874
DIGGES, Edward	Elizabeth Oneale	27 Apr 1809
Nathan	Sarah Jackson	15 Sep 1874
Nelson	Margaret McDavitt	19 Dec 1828
William	Mary Coates	21 Nov 1892 c
DIGGINS, Daniel	Rosetta Richardson	28 Dec 1896 c
Elizabeth	Noah Lee	19 Sep 1883
Harriet	Emory Jenus	8 Jan 1867
Isaac	Kate Dorsey	30 Oct 1877 c
Jennie	Charles Webster	17 Jul 1868

* Cannot read day; after 10

DIGGINS, Jesse	Louisa E. Owens	6 Apr 1892 c
DIGGS - also see DIGGES, DEGGES		
DIGGS, Charles	Martha L. Clagett	25 Jan 1889 c
George	Fanny Chambers	10 Feb 1875
George	Harriet Fisher	22 Mar 1886 c
Grace	John W. Hurst	22 Sep 1894 w
Jerry	Ada Hood	21 Dec 1898 c
John Henry	Ellen Bell	25 Dec 1873
John Henry	Drucilla Tyman	2 Jun 1881 c
John William	Isabella Thomas	23 Nov 1884 c
Joseph	Polly Driver	27 Sep 1895 c
Julian	Isabella S. Askins	13 Jan 1874
Maria	Lloyd Coates	22 Jan 1869
Nellie	John H. Hoes	9 Aug 1894 c
Robert	Rebecca Snowden	* Sep 1883
William	Jane Brown	15 Apr 1865
William	Kate Jackson	31 Oct 1894 c
William	Florence Washington	6 Dec 1897 c
DILL, Ellen B.	William T. McDonald	1 Oct 1894 w
Joshua B.	Florence S. Nehouse	12 Nov 1896 w
William E.	Georgie A. Sellman	4 Apr 1888 w
DILLAHA, Arthur	Mary Wheat	18 Nov 1805
Benjamin	Rachel Slater**	14 Oct 1799
DILLEHAY - also see DELLEHAY		
DILLEHAY, Anne	Henry Lowe	8 Oct 1823
Annie M.	Frank S. Nicholson	3 Mar 1890 w
Elizabeth	Hiram Reid	15 Dec 1828
Henrietta	Helkiah W. Willson	21 Apr 1838
James W.	Mary M. Taylor	13 Jan 1877 w
John A.	Bessie M. Keith	18 Feb 1896 w
Mary Ann	Henry Reid	21 Nov 1835
DILLON, Deborah	James White	18 Oct 1823
DILLORDER, Polly	Philip Welsh	8 Dec 1806
DIMES, Ignatius	Emma Powell	2 Oct 1886 c
DINES - also see DIENS		
DINES, William P.	Jane E. Doy	21 Sep 1897 c
DINKINS, Elizabeth	Charles Davis	1 Jul 1880 c
DISBRO, Earl	Mary Kramer	17 Jan 1894 w
DISHMAN, Mildred	John Sinclair	2 May 1831
DISNEY, Lydia E.	George W. Johnson	3 Feb 1872
Mary V.	William Frazier	24 Dec 1894 c
Owen W.	Elizabeth Johnson	16 Apr 1870
DISON - also see DYSON		
DISON, Hezekiah	Lucy Perry	23 Feb 1799
DITTER - also see DETTER		
DITTER, Rachel A.	Richard Proctor	10 Mar 1868
DIVINE, Charles F.	Mary M. Raney	17 Feb 1890 w
James E.	Mary L. Leaman	29 Jul 1893 w
Sallie M.	Lorenzo D. Poole	4 Dec 1878
DIXON, Thomas	Mary Young	22 Aug 1820
William T.	Mary C. Storrid	14 Aug 1897 c
DOBBINS, Samuel William Henry	Martha Terry	31 Dec 1896 c

* Cannot read day; before 19
** Last name from earlier reading

DODD, Addison F.	Lucretia J. Thompson	19 Jul 1877	w
Edgar	Sidonia L. Thompson	19 Jul 1877	w
DODGE, Robert	Mahanty Alexander	12 Sep 1871	
DODSON, H. Elizabeth	James H. Powell	16 Feb 1870	
Robert	Anna Parker	21 Sep 1881	c
DOER - also see DUER			
DOER, Elizabeth	Joshua Grimes	11 Nov 1813	
DOLL, Mettie W.	Walter B. Krantz	16 Oct 1878	w
DOLLY, Adam B.	Mary R. Talbert	23 Feb 1858	
DOMINI, Emanuel	Nancy Jarboe	15 Oct 1803	
DONALDSON, H. S.	Leanna Crown	14 Jun 1858	
Mary R.	Arthur M. Sullivan	7 Oct 1891	w
DONN, Francis C.	Nannie E. Sellman	28 Jul 1887	w
DONNELLY, Juliette S.	Elma E. Magruder	3 Sep 1889	w
Emily	William H. Hamilton	14 Nov 1868	
Ellen	Owen Donocho	13 Jul 1871	
DONNOHO, Sarah	Marty Fohy	6 Jan 1804	
DONOCHO, Owen	Ellen Donnely	13 Jul 1871	
DONOHOE, Joseph A.	Grace R. Cheshire	3 Aug 1893	w
DONOHOUGH, Biddy	Thomas Burnes	18 Apr 1802	
DORAN, John	Elizabeth Grantt	11 Apr 1799	
DORSETT, Walter	Sarah Stonestreet	22 Dec 1819	
DORSEY, Achsah	Nathaniel Waters	22 Jun 1809	
Agnes	Charles Straitner	3 Aug 1895	c
Alexander	Mary E. Hopkins	30 Dec 1879	c
Alfred	Martha Proctor	1 Feb 1867	
Amanda	Monroe Ricks	8 Sep 1868	
Angeline	John W. Hood	24 Jul 1875	
Ann	William B. Williams	19 Jun 1817	
Ann Eliza	James Otho Trundle	15 Feb 1864	
Ann Hammond	John Henry Worthington	1 Mar 1815	
Ann Maria	John W. Berry	27 Aug 1879	
Annie R.	William Simms	6 Dec 1890	c
Basil T.	Alice B. Storrid	13 Jul 1891	c
Caleb	Caroline E. Riggs	11 Jan 1834	
Caroline	Richard Dorsey	26 Mar 1877	w
Caroline	Jarret Lea	24 May 1888	c
Caroline H.	Horace T. Mitchell	7 Feb 1871	
Carrie	Samuel Johnson	16 May 1893	c
Catharine	James Gaither	20 May 1871	
Catharine	John T. Riggs	13 Oct 1897	c
Catherine	Upton Worthington	28 Nov 1832	
Charles	Mary Hebron	30 May 1887	c
Deborah R.	Charles G. Edwards	9 Feb 1814	
Eliza	John Gassaway	22 Aug 1820	
Eliza	Isaac Johnson	1 Sep 1865	
Eliza Ann	John Bigham	29 Aug 1836	
Elizabeth	Basil MacGill	6 Feb 1826	
Elizabeth	Greenbury Burke	26 Mar 1841	
Elizabeth	Singleton Franklin	17 Oct 1872	
Elizabeth	Henry T. Clagett	2 Jan 1896	c
Elizabeth A.	John Gardner	6 May 1828	
Ellen	Samuel Gibbs	6 Sep 1873	
Emma	John R. Cole	22 Oct 1874	
Everline	William Prince	20 Aug 1818	
Ezra	Betsey G. Griffith	7 Jun 1821	

DORSEY,	Fanny	George Snowden	11 Jun 1883
	Flora	Henry Ward	29 Jan 1869
	Frank	Charlotte Genus	9 Sep 1884 c
	Franklin H.	Rebecca Brooks	19 Jan 1888 c
	Frederick M.	Charlotte L. Hill	1 Apr 1891 c
	George	Sarah Brooks	8 Jun 1870
	George	Emily Mason	28 Sep 1876
	George	Martha Johnson	27 Dec 1883 c
	George E.	Eleanor M. Hall	16 Sep 1896 w
	George W.	Catherine Thomas	22 Aug 1894 c
	Gustavus W.	Margaret Owens	26 Nov 1866
	Hannah E.	Larkin Wallace	23 Jan 1890 w
	Harriet	William Turnbull	12 Dec 1826
	Harriett W.	Samuel Blount	19 Feb 1818
	Harry O.	Florence Townsend	31 Oct 1887 w
	Harry W.	Susan M. Waters	9 Apr 1844
	Harry Woodward	Rachel Cooke	16 Jun 1807
	Henrietta	Israel Hoskins	1 Jan 1870
	Henry	Martha Turley	28 Dec 1885 c
	Henry	Laura Johnson	2 Jun 1887 c
	Henry W. Jr.	Sarah Ann Waters	27 May 1829
	Hester	Charles H. Griffith	20 Oct 1864
	Jackson Ellsworth	Tabitha Kisner	21 May 1885 w
	James Henry	Josephine Green	10 May 1876
	Jane	Andrew Warfield	26 Aug 1882 c
	John	Ida Cunrod	14 Mar 1891 c
	John Henry	Treasy Ellen Hood	5 Apr 1898 c
	John L.	Mary E. Magruder	10 Apr 1889 c
	John W.	Catharine E. Johnson	4 Sep 1873
	John W.	Eliza Johnson	5 Feb 1891 c
	John W.	Julia Ellen Moore	19 Dec 1893 c
	John W.	Luvinia J. Bakon	8 Jan 1896 c
	Joshua	Vallie Pumphrey	26 Nov 1872
	Joshua C.	Rose Higgins	30 Jan 1888 w
	Joshua W.	Lucetta Plummer	21 Mar 1804
	Joshua W.	Catherine Waters	13 Feb 1833
	Joshua W.	Mary A. E. Childs	10 Apr 1841
	Kate	Isaac Diggins	30 Oct 1877 c
	Laura	Samuel S. Cashell	19 Feb 1874
	Lavinia H.	Franklin L. Knight	11 Aug 1851
	Louisa	Cyrus Bowen	11 Sep 1873
	Lucinda	Grafton Davis	21 Nov 1894 c
	Lydia Ann	Philip Wade	21 Aug 1882 c
	Mahala	Reuben T. Hanson	8 Sep 1874
	Mariah	George Washington Askins	11 Dec 1886 c
	Martha	George Prather	23 Dec 1872
	Martha A.	James H. Duvall	25 Nov 1891 c
	Mary	Grandison Catlett	18 Apr 1808
	Mary	George Williams	5 Jan 1872
	Mary	David Copelin	17 Jul 1875
	Mary	Nathan Johnson	4 Jun 1881 c
	Mary Anna	James E. Matthews	29 Dec 1890 c
	Mary C.	William O. Powell	25 Jul 1888 c
	Mary E.	Samuel W. Gooden	17 Apr 1872
	Mary E.	Jason Pratt	8 May 1889 c

DORSEY,	Mary E.	Dennis Owens	8 Jul 1890 c
	Mary E.	Henry Bruner	18 May 1891 c
	Mary Ellen	William W. Welling	19 Apr 1859
	Mary J.	Horace Waters	24 Jan 1850
	Matilda	Mordecai Griffith	12 Sep 1810
	Nelson	Rose Annie Warren	3 Mar 1876
	Patrick	Alethia Green	16 Feb 1881 c
	Peter M.	Emily Smith	7 Apr 1890 c
	Philemon W.	Ellen Williams	18 Oct 1879 c
	Rachel	Robert Adams	6 Oct 1882 c
	Rachel V.	John T. Warfield	1 Nov 1862
	Rebecca Comfort	Allen Bowie Davis	5 Oct 1830
	Rebecca H.	Horatio Griffith, Jr.	26 Nov 1855
	Remus	Jane T. Riggs	8 Feb 1826
	Richard	Julia Edwards	14 Jan 1869
	Richard	Caroline Dorsey	26 Mar 1877 w
	Richard	Ann Butler	2* May 1881 c
	Richard E.	Mary E. Brown	3 Nov 1897 c
	Rose	Ivory Chandlie	5 Oct 1897 c
	Sarah	John Huff	1 Dec 1880 c
	Solomon J.	Cassie Windeer	28 Sep 1892 c
	Sophia	David Chase	24 Jul 1869
	Susannah	James Clark	9 Oct 1879
	Teresa E.	Henry Nailor	29 Dec 1896 c
	Thomas	Jolina Isabella Jennies	14 Jan 1890 c
	Thomas W.	Mary E. Welling	17 Feb 1862
	Valeria	Horace D. Waters	7 Oct 1878 w
	Virginia	John Miller	24 Dec 1886 c
	Virginia L.	John W. Darby	11 Dec 1888 w
	Washington	Rosa Bell	16 Jan 1874
	William	Ann Hambleton	18 Nov 1868
	William	Louisa Green	9 Nov 1874
	William **.	Susan R. Robertson	31 Oct 1825
	William F.	Sarah E. Bell	4 Nov 1897 c
	William H.	Eliza Granson	12 Feb 1890 c
DOUBLEN - also see DUBLIN			
DOUBLEN,	Milly	Charles Howard	4 Apr 1878
DOUBLIN,	Aaron	Mary E. Johnson	27 Mar 1873
DOUD,	Mary Ann	John Harper	9 Mar 1829
DOUDEN - also see DOWDEN			
DOUDEN,	Elizabeth	William Mullican	29 Dec 1800
DOUGHERTY,	Alhima	George W. Blundon	6 Oct 1885 w
	Sarah	Bennett Bevin	18 Dec 1798
DOUGLAS,	Maria	Richard Henry Clark	21 Sep 1866
DOUGLASS,	Anna	Nelson Watts	29 Jul 1868
	Archibald O.	Priscilla J. Pollard	4 Sep 1821
	Charles	Liza Martin	24 Mar 1874
	Charlotte	Thomas Vowell	3 Apr 1806
	Edward	Eleanor Magr---***	5 Dec 1799
	Elizabeth	Jesse Leeke	31 Oct 1820

* Day has blot on it; 28 or before
** Initial I or J
*** Page torn; earlier readings have Maglus and Maglue, but Magr is what is left on the page

DOUGLASS,	Ella	James W. Hebron	11 Jul 1894	c
	Francis T.	Alice A. Selby	22 Jan 1870	
	Hugh	Sarah Fowler	26 Dec 1810	
	Jane	Erasmus Hogdon	26 Dec 1798	
	Jane	George Hoskinson	2 Nov 1815	
	John	Nancy Fowler	10 Sep 1806	
	Josias	Martha Shelton	5 Feb 1806	
	Lucy	Isaac Bailey	27 Dec 1873	
	Margaret	John Lyles	31 Dec 1873	
	Mary A.	Addison Tuttle	9 Oct 1822	
	Priscilla P.	Samuel S. Freeland	25 Apr 1840	
	Samuel	Rebecca Young*	22 Feb 1808	
	Samuel	Margaret Green	19 Nov 1819	
	Sarah**	Edward Godman	17 Dec 1799	
	William	Caroline Jones	28 Oct 1856	
DOVE,	--lford	Ellen Handy	25 Nov 1882	c
	Ann	Charles Fisher	5 Jun 1834	
	Ann E.	John R. Kinder	29 Jan 1862	
	Bertha P.	Lorenzo Crawford	21 Sep 1887	c
	Catharine A.	Bernard Monday	12 May 1852	
	Clora E.	William T. Lowe	11 Feb 1885	w
	Eliza	Wesley Duley	24 Nov 1825	
	George William	Mary Ellen Whalen	18 Dec 1861	
	Henry S.	Sarah A. Price	28 Jun 1871	
	Ishmael	Mary Whaley	19 Feb 1840	
	James A.	Margaret A. Burche	12 Jan 1880	w
	James R.	Nora L. Burch	18 Aug 1886	w
	John Maury	Elizabeth Ann Carter	5 Sep 1882	w
	Joseph	Margaret Shaerer	11 Mar 1878	w
	Joseph Ambrose	Mollie Shearer	6 Oct 1885	w
	Levi	Julia Ann Benson	20 Oct 1832	
	Mary A.	George W. Appleby	10 Apr 1851	
	Mary A.	George Trammell	1 Jan 1870	
	Mary E.	James R. Lowe	22 Dec 1884	w
	Mary J.	William O. Orndorff	9 Nov 1874	
	Samuel	Henrietta Mason	2 Apr 1892	c
	Sarah	Zadok Case	7 Apr 1846	
	Sarah	John Souders	8 Mar 1881	
	Tilghman E.	Jane R. Scott	1 Aug 1889	c
	Tilghman E.	Mary V. Johnson	10 Oct 1894	c
	Victorine	Richard Williams	18 Dec 1867	
	William	Rachael R. Howser	21 May 1860	
	William H.	Sarah Benson	20 Mar 1830	
	William H.	Lucy Wood	27 Dec 1878	c
DOW,	Francis	Elizabeth Davis	8 Sep 1886	c
DOWDEN - also see DOUDEN				
DOWDEN,	Alcinda J.	Joshua Sibley	20 Dec 1859	
	Annie E.	Benedict Wallace	27 Sep 1871	
	George L. (male)	Neville Gladman	26 Apr 1892	w
	James	Mahala Benton	25 Dec 1809	
	James H.	Eleanor West	5 Aug 1846	
	Juliet	Solomon Fulks	28 Dec 1815	
	Lucinda	John Mullican	18 Nov 1818	

* Name from earlier reading
** Both names from earlier reading

DOWDEN,	Mary	Nathan T. Peck	3 Jan 1802
	Mary	Adam Getzendanner	6 Feb 1810
	Mary R.	George F. Reber	15 Oct 1886 w
	Rebecca A.	John E. Benson	7 Dec 1872
	Sarah	William Benson	9 Nov 1803
	Sarah W.	Bradley T. King	14 Jun 1892 w
	Solomon	Jane E. Harriss	30 Jan 1849
	Virginia	Hezekiah Leaman	11 Nov 1861
	William T.	Robert J. Benson	30 Nov 1886 w
	Zachariah	Rebecca Miller	6 Feb 1852
	Zachariah	Mary R. Buxton	15 Apr 1893 w
	Zachariah Jr.	Elizabeth Fulks	15 Mar 1814
DOWELL,	Arthur E.	Marie L. Noyes	5 Apr 1892 w
DOWNES,	Elizabeth	John Wright	27 Nov 1799
	Leanah	William M. Jones	10 Apr 1819
	Richard M.	Sarah Beall	19 Dec 1825
	Richard M.	Tabitha Willson	6 Jan 1834
	William	Eleanor Beddo	20 Dec 1817
DOWNS,	Charles E.	Martha J. Biggs	19 Apr 1870
	John	Anne Smallwood	2 Jul 1832
	Maurice W.	Elizabeth Berry	29 Jun 1876
	Oliver E.	Julia Duley	22 Oct 1895 w
	Sarah	Judson C. Cooper	4 Aug 1888 w
	William H.	Martha E. Baker	6 May 1868
DOWNY,	Rosy	John Macknall	21 Apr 1815
DOY,	Brook	Susan Smith	28 Oct 1897 c
	Emma J.	Thomas Lucket	28 Nov 1878 c
	Jane E.	William P. Dines	21 Sep 1897 c
	Lillie M.	George W. Wims	4 Oct 1894 c
	Mary Bell	Daniel T. Jackson	14 Sep 1886 c
	Millard F.	Ida E. Lee	10 Jun 1885 c
	Nathan	Mary Willson	30 Jul 1877 c
	Richard	Mollie Jackson	22 Dec 1888 c
	Robert	Mary P. Snowden	11 Jul 1877 c
	William R.	Maria Lee	31 May 1879 c
DOYLE,	Elizar	Artemus Debtor	19 Jun 1865
	George W.	Rebecca Angelina Fling	25 Mar 1845
	James	Mary V. Soper	11 Mar 1896 w
	Kitty	James McGee	27 Aug 1806
	William	Ann Rebecca Thompson	1 Aug 1842
DRAKE,	Wallie T.	Florence M. Rache	16 Aug 1898 w
DRANE,	James H.	Mary D. White	12 Jan 1813
DRAPER,	Elizabeth	Thomas Norris	19 Feb 1869
RESCHER,	Bridget C.	John C. Gill	12 Aug 1884
DRIVER,	Elias	Mary L. Martin	24 Dec 1891 c
DRIVER,	Elias	Jane Green	30 May 1895 c
	Polly	Joseph Diggs	27 Sep 1895 c
DRONENBURG,	Reverdy	Ida J. Harriss	5 Mar 1889 w
	W. J.	Sarah E. Lewis	10 Jan 1865
	William J.	Margaret A. Rhodes	9 Jan 1849
	William J.	Catharine Young	24 Mar 1871
	William J.	Sophia B. Wade	31 Dec 1877 w
	Willie W.	Altie Anderson	9 Jul 1878 w
DROWNS,	William T.	Effie May Allen	18 Oct 1894 w
DRUDGE,	Ann	George William Logan	14 Jan 1803
	Anne	Richard Power	12 Jan 1810

DRUDGE, Cordelia	David H. King	12 Jul 1895	w
Edward	Delia Nichollson	21 Jan 1847	
Sallie	James J. Peters	18 Oct 1882	w
Susanah	William Knox	7 Sep 1800	
William	Ann Deane	31 Dec 1803	
DRURY, Ignatius	Harrett Reding	4 Dec 1799	
Ignatius	Mary Tenney	26 Apr 1800	
DUBLIN - also see DOUBLEN			
DUBLIN, Harry M.	Carrie L. Johnson	20 Oct 1896	c
Herbert	Amanda Hill	26 Dec 1883	c
Susan	George Lynn	2* Apr 1887	c
DUCKER, Ruth	Charles Jones	31 Jan 1803	
DUDDEROR - also see DUDROW, DUTROW			
DUDDEROR, Jacob W.	Jane R. Williams	4 Apr 1865	
DUDLEY, Richard	Elizabeth Jordan	16 Jan 1807	
DUDROW - also see DUDDEROR, DUTROW			
DUDROW, Annie L.	Franklin H. Karn	21 Jun 1892	w
DUER - also see DOER			
DUER, Elce	Isaac Miller	10 Sep 1812	
DUFF, Mount V.	Littie Tyler	27 Dec 1888	c
DUFFEN - also see DUFFIN			
DUFFEN, Henny M.	Dennis Hamilton	9 Sep 1867	
DUFFEY - also see DUFFY			
DUFFEY, Catharine	James Casey	8 Nov 1862	
DUFFIN - also see DUFFEN			
DUFFIN, Camden	Sophia Deins	11 Oct 1882	c
Camden	Henrietta Parker	7 Nov 1894	c
George	Sarah Jackson	3 Apr 1874	
Hanson T.	Mary Duffin	16 Apr 1872	
Hensy	Gilmore Lynch	3 Sep 1869	
John	Mattie Warren	18 May 1893	c
John G.	Martha Owens	9 Apr 1883	c
Joshua	Alice Adams	13 Feb 1874	
Maria E.	Warner Weems	31 Dec 1878	
Mary	Hanson T. Duffin	16 Apr 1872	
Mary	John Brandison	31 Oct 1868	
Nathan T.	Vina Harper	19 Feb 1880	c
Vachel	Rachel Ridout	17 Jul 1868	
William T.	Sarah T. Owens	11 Feb 1878	c
Wiiliam Washington	Harriet M. Leek	21 Aug 1885	c
DUFFY - also see DUFFEY			
DUFFY, Patrick	Mary C. Dalzell	1 Oct 1852	
DuFIEF, Charles G.	Lavinia Beall	18 Feb 1878	w
M. E.	E. P. Hays (male)	18 Sep 1877	w
DUFOUR, Dora M. A.	St. Cloud Ambrose	19 Jun 1894	w
DUGAN, Anne	James Welsh	2 Mar 1813	
Daniel	Polly Hall	6 Oct 1814	
Elizabeth	Barton Harris	25 Feb 1817	
Mary	Allen Warfield	26 Jul 1808	
DUHURST, William	Keziah Ann Willson	19 Apr 1808	
DUKES, Susan R.	William C. Henderson	11 Dec 1872	

* Cannot read complete day; between 25 and 28

DULEY - also see DULY			
DULEY, Amanda	Erie Higgins	18 Jan 1844	
Benedick H.	Eleanor Adamson	13 Feb 1811	
Benedict H.	Anne O. Prather	20 Jun 1816	
Benedict H.	Eliza Prather	7 Oct 1821	
Catherine Ellen	Lloyd Burriss	17 Feb 1841	
E. Gilmore	Ann Maria Spates	28 Sep 1869	
Edmond G.	Elizabeth Nicholls	23 Apr 1835	
Elemuel G.	Eliza Holland	30 Jul 1825	
Eliza E.	Burgess K. Gladman	8 May 1858	
Elizabeth	Moses Barnesly	17 Mar 1812	
Emily	John W. Furguson	26 Oct 1835	
Emily J.	Thomas N. Shipley	9 May 1871	
Henry	Jurussia Edmonstone	30 Aug 1832	
John	Elizabeth Ann Sands	2 Dec 1841	
John B.	Hattie L. Grimes	29 Jan 1884	
Jonathan	Martha Darby	12 Apr 1815	
Joseph C.	Sabra Beall	23 Apr 1811	
Julia	Oliver E. Downs	22 Oct 1895	w
Mahala	Jesse Townsend	29 Sep 1814	
Margaret	William Boswell	13 Dec 1820	
Martha	Mordica Benton	23 Jan 1811	
Martha	Robert Isherwood	21 Jul 1841	
Martha J.	John C. Myers	30 Nov 1848	
Mary	William Canby	12 Nov 1833	
Mary E. E.	Martin W. J. Higgins	25 Jul 1833	
Mattie	D. W. Arnold	14 Jul 1869	
Milly	Benjamin Sparrow	27 Dec 1805	
Rebecca	John Adamson	18 Jan 1816	
Ruth	Joseph W. Davis	27 Apr 1816	
Ruth A.	William C. Davis	27 Aug 1866	
Sarah	William Sear	27 Dec 1814	
Susan Ann	John Campbell	14 Jun 1820	
Thomas	Anne Hutton	15 Feb 1813	
Thomas	Mary Osborn	15 Nov 1823	
Wesley	Eliza Dove	24 Nov 1825	
William	Julia Ann Padgett	8 Jul 1847	
Zachariah	Ann Lazenby	1 Jun 1798	
Zachariah	Ruth Elson	6 Mar 1806	
DULIN, Elizabeth	Newton Keene	18 Feb 1824	
Francis	Margaret H. Hoskinson	21 Jan 1824	
James B.	Edna A. Spencer	29 Apr 1896	w
William E.	Laura V. Wheatley	27 Oct 1896	w
DULY - also see DULEY			
DULY, Erasmus	Elizabeth Crown	12 Jan 1807	
DUMAY, Andrew	Mary Eleanor Bradman	6 Jul 1816	
DUMHART - also see DUNHARDT			
DUMHART, Lizzie	Henry R. Merson	27 Sep 1890	w
DUNAWIN, William H.	Maggie M. Ward	11 Dec 1893	w
DUNCAN, Benjamin	Lucinda Berkley	25 Jul 1822	
DUNHARDT - also see DUMHART			
DUNHARDT, Ruth Ann	William Orlando Saffell	19 Nov 1879	
DUNLAP - also see DUNLOP			
DUNLAP, William	Alice Jackson	22 Aug 1868	
DUNLEY - also see DUNLY			
DUNLEY, Jane	Rezin Offutt	27 Nov 1875	

DUNLEY, Lucy	John W. Warfield	3 Jan 1889	c
William	Miranda Lee	6 Jun 1881	c
DUNLOP - also see DUNLAP			
DUNLOP, Arianna F.	William Laird	22 Jul 1834	
Harriet Margaret	John M. Thomas	15 Nov 1832	
Helen	William Laird	7 Oct 1822	
Henrietta	Beverly Davis	20 Jun 1871	
Mary	John Mines	1 Feb 1842	
William L.	Sarah L. Peter	30 Nov 1878	w
DUNLY - also see DUNLEY			
DUNLY, Marianne	Reuben Waters	25 Mar 1869	
DUNN, Elizabeth	Jessy Merchant	20 Nov 1799	
Thomas	Mary Wathing	23 Oct 1800	
Wade	Katie Blinkoe	28 Nov 1888	w
DUSKINS, John H.	Mary J. Branson	13 May 1880	
DUSTIN, Cinderella	Richard B. Johnson	18 Oct 1879	w
Clinton	Jennie Burton	6 Jul 1887	w
DUSTON, Upton	Laura V. Brown	30 Aug 1881	
DUTCH, Louisa	Nathaniel Ray	23 Dec 1867	
William Henry	Catharine Dickerson	2 Nov 1881	
DUTROW - also see DUDROW, DUDDEROR			
DUTROW, Cora B.	Morgan S. Benton	29 Jan 1884	
Harriet M.	Edward C. King	26 Jan 1895	w
Mary E.	George A. Merson	26 Dec 1893	w
Nonie E.	James H. Norris	30 Dec 1884	w
William H.	Minnie M. Murphy	23 Nov 1892	w
DUTTON, Margaret M.	Frederick S. Schab	19 Jul 1888	w
DUTY, Daniel	Elizabeth Jinkins	20 Mar 1799	
DUVALL, Addie	Oscar Burns	20 Sep 1898	w
Alcinda L.	John R. Crawford	24 Mar 1884	
Alexander	Eliza Musgrove	15 Mar 1819	
Alice A.	J. Franklin Finney	10 Mar 1885	w
Alice E.	Zachariah L. Magruder	30 Apr 1866	
Ann H.	Jasper M. Jackson	30 Oct 1846	
Annie	Charles F. Pickett	11 Sep 1876	
Aquila	Abbariler Chatman*	13 Aug 1800	
Basil of Jesse	Dalilah Duvall	2 Dec 1828	
Beal	Amelia Lin**	30 Jan 1818	
Bessie E.	James M. Kemp	24 May 1897	w
Carrie C.	Frank G. Coleman	26 Jul 1887	w
Catharine R.	John Warren	29 Oct 1885	c
Charles	Martha Stewart	11 Jun 1867	
Charlotte	William Davis	12 Feb 1833	
Cleora	William P. Palmer	14 May 1831	
Clero	Andrew J. Adams	20 Oct 1850	
Dalilah	Basil Duvall of Jesse	2 Dec 1828	
Deborah	Thomas Canby	28 Jan 1824	
Delilah H.	Joshua D. Warfield	17 Jan 1849	
Effie	Theodore C. Thompson	26 Dec 1888	w
Eliza	Richard W. Stewart	9 Apr 1891	c
Eliza J.	William H. Darby	5 Mar 1877	w
Elizabeth	John Arvin	18 Feb 1799	
Elizabeth	Zachariah Hughes	23 Mar 1805	

* See note at Chatman
** Part of last name from earlier reading

DUVALL, Elizabeth	Joseph Isaac Jones	22 Nov 1805	
Elizabeth	Lewis Owings	1 Jan 1817	
Elizabeth	John F. Decker	28 Jan 1820	
Elizabeth	Thomas Dwyer	12 Jan 1828	
Ely	Ann M. King	1 Nov 1810	
Emanuel Maddison	Susan A. Penn	5 Mar 1839	
Frances E.	Alpheus Middleton	17 Dec 1858	
Franklin	Mary Mockbee	15 Nov 1866	
Franklin	Verlinda Ward	14 Jan 1868	
Grafton	Harriet Sheckells	26 Feb 1834	
Hammond	Margarete Lovejoy	14 Jan 1806	
Hammond	Eleanor Sprigg	21 May 1834	
Hannah	Edward Willett Benton	7 May 1806	
Hattie L.	Charles W. Ward	1 Sep 1887	w
Helen B.	Jeremiah G. Blackburn	21 Sep 1881	
Henry	Eleanor Hammond	10 Jan 1817	
Henry H.	Ruth H. Wood	21 Jan 1807	
James E.	Alice E. Penn	27 Jan 1862	
James E.	Maggie V. Briggs	21 Jun 1898	w
James H.	Martha A. Dorsey	25 Nov 1891	c
Jefferson	Florence M. Williams	20 Dec 1887	w
Jeremiah	Mary Cromwell	21 Mar 1804	
John	Jane Wyvell	6 May 1809	
John G.	Jane Gloyd	30 Dec 1826	
John G.	Elizabeth Glaze	29 May 1827	
John G.	Jerusha A. Penn	15 Jun 1863	
John H.	Elizabeth Poole	2 Feb 1814	
John S.	Alcinda L. Thompson	1 Jun 1858	
Joseph	Augusta Penn	21 Dec 1881	
Joseph	Delia Baker	13 Nov 1897	c
Keturah	Isaac Burton	14 Sep 1812	
Lewis	Sarah Wyvill	2 Feb 1801	
Lewis H.	Elizabeth Ellis	14 Jul 1806	
Lillie V.	Edward L. Unglesbee	7 Sep 1892	w
Lloyd R.	Elizabeth Emily Wyvill	13 Feb 1833	
Lot B.	Nora V. Warfield	9 Jul 1895	c
Louisa	John S. Bohrer	21 Dec 1869	
Luther M.	Ida M. Bready	15 Jun 1881	w
M. F.	William J. Easton	23 Jan 1872	
Maggie A.	Francis W. Nehouse	9 Apr 1895	w
Margaret	George W. Penn	25 Mar 1841	
Margaret A.	James E. Eveley	23 Sep 1891	w
Marine	Elizabeth Ann Etchison	1 Nov 1847	
Martha	Washington Tyler	21 Dec 1896	c
Martha Virginia	Aden Darby Allnutt	21 Jun 1875	
Mary	Henson Tyler	9 Jun 1881	c
Mary A.	John Rex	10 Mar 1853	
Mary A.	William E. Marlow	13 Apr 1896	w
Maryann*	Daniel Golden	10 May 1819	
Mary Ellen	John Edward Adams	15 Jan 1842	
Mary Ellen	Uriah H. Peugh	26 Jun 1849	
Mary F.	Thomas G. Penn	13 Apr 1883	w
Maurice E. ?.	Martha R. Thompson	11 Jun 1883	
Melvin L.	Matilda J. Herrell	8 Nov 1883	

* Last name from earlier reading

DUVALL,	Minnie G.	Hilleary T. Burrows	22 May 1894	w
	Nettie E.	Joseph C. Hawkins	16 Dec 1885	w
	Otho H.	Sarah Ann Anderson	20 Mar 1847	
	Otho H.	Rhoda Selby	22 Dec 1849	
	Owen S.	Maria V. Ray	16 Jun 1869	
	Philip	Mary LoveJoy	27 Feb 1802	
	Philip H.	Comfort Phelps	30 Apr 1822	
	Rachel Ann	William Sears	15 Nov 1842	
	Rebecca	Hiram Whirl	19 Dec 1825	
	Rezin	Kitty Shipley	19 Feb 1828	
	Rezin	Harriet A. Thompson	21 Feb 1849	
	Rezin	Mary Penn	27 Jul 1875	
	Richard	Mary Jane Weems	9 Sep 1867	
	Richard L.	Mary A. Herrell	8 Nov 1883	
	Rosetta	Henry Davis	1 Jun 1868	
	Ruth	Henry C. Wyvall	15 Jan 1799	
	Ruth	William Shields	5 Mar 1803	
	Sarah*	Walter Duvall	17 May 1798	
	Sarah	Philip Gardner Hammon	13 Mar 1807	
	Sarah E.	James T. Snyder	14 Jul 1873	
	Sarah E.	John W. Kelley	19 Jan 1878	w
	Selas B.	Sarah Catharine King	16 Dec 1865	
	Stattira	Edgar P. Bohrer	14 Dec 1870	
	Susan	Zach Thompson	10 Jan 1848	
	Susie E.	Aden McK. Bowman	7 Feb 1876	
	Thomas O.	Catharine E. Kelly	23 Nov 1880	
	Walter*	Sarah Duvall	17 May 1798	
	Washington	Eliza Ann Perry	11 Dec 1824	
	William C.	Fannie E. Grimes	12 Nov 1894	w
	William E.	Mary E. Washington	3 Oct 1895	c
	William F.	Harriet E. Purdum	10 Dec 1875	
	William H.	Mary Evely	10 Jul 1843	
	William R.	Mary Ann Whiteside	30 Oct 1842	
	William S.	Idie E. Rich	26 Nov 1877	w
	Willson O.	Priscilla Wyvill	18 Sep 1832	
	Zachariah T.	Marian L. Ward	11 Nov 1889	w
DUVANE,	Patrick	Mary Connelly	8 Feb 1805	
DWIRE,	John	Jane Elms	7 Mar 1835	
DWYER - also see DWYRE, DWIRE				
DWYER,	Alice E.	Richard E. Harris	15 Oct 1858	
	Allie May	George W. Dennis	9 May 1885	w
	Ann E.	Edward H. Houck	25 Feb 1859	
	Caroline Virginia	William F. House	26 Dec 1876	
	Carrie	William T. Ridgley	17 Oct 1894	w
	Clara E.	Julian E. Osmond	25 Jan 1890	w
	Delila A.	William E. Groomes	23 Oct 1880	
	Edward A.	Susie R. Hilton	14 Nov 1864	
	Eliza V.	Joseph R. Knode	2 Jan 1843	
	Frank	Magge E. Weeks	19 Mar 1892	w
	George L.	Hetty A. Brown	14 Apr 1890	w
	Henry	Harriet R. Sage	17 May 1880	
	Henry P.	Catharine Benson	10 Sep 1845	
	James	Mary Price	17 Aug 1805	
	John W.	Alcinda Bowman	20 Aug 1855	

* Both last names from earlier reading

DWYER, Lafayette M.	Joanna Nicholson	13 Aug 1874	
Lucy A.	James A. Linkins	6 Jun 1870	
Martha E.	Robert Small	25 Nov 1881	w
Mary	Benjamin Farquahar	17 Aug 1805	
Mary A.	John Shearrer	19 Dec 1868	
Mary A.	Theophilus Wilcoxen	10 Feb 1872	
Susie	Richard Hebron	14 May 1891	c
Thomas	Elizabeth Duvall	12 Jan 1828	
William	Sarah Coomes	13 Apr 1846	
William C.	Martha E. Rannie	5 Dec 1868	
William C.	Mary E. Bowman	17 May 1897	w
Willie A.	James E. Howes	30 Jan 1879	
DWYRE, Ellen S.	Caleb Griffin	17 Apr 1843	
DYAL - also see DIAL			
DYAL, Ignatius	Anne Tracy Ratliff	22 Dec 1809	
DYALL, Annastatia	Jacob Marshberger	17 Dec 1819	
DYAN, Benjamin	Margaret Lee	17 May 1817	
DYER - also see DYUR			
DYER, George A.	Mary R. Ashton	24 Apr 1854	
DYKES, Grace M.	Henry Lowry	10 Feb 1883	w
DYOTT, Samuel H.	Margaret O. Ricketts	20 Mar 1894	w
DYSON - also see DISON			
DYSON, Ann	George Byrd	24 Dec 1828	
Ann	Edward Brashears	22 Dec 1798	
Benjamin F.	Catharine J. Piles	8 Apr 1863	
Charles	Belle Thornton	2 Sep 1890	c
Charles H.	Anna E. Smith	22 Mar 1887	c
Eliza	Thomas Rhodes	24 Mar 1875	
Frederick	Ida E. Beander	28 Nov 1883	c
Ida	Harvey Jones White	28 Nov 1893	w
Jeremiah	Tafa Veirs	29 Dec 1806	
John	Priscilla Pearson	24 Feb 1832	
Lydia	Scott Veirs	17 Aug 1839	
Mary Jane	Richard W. Williams	*17 Dec 1844	
Matthew	Margaret M. Briscoe	30 Nov 1875	c
Milly	Ignatius Higdon	4 Jan 1806	
Vernon H., Dr.	Lena M. Warfield	25 Oct 1898	w
William	Nancy Darnall**	18 May 1819	
William	Mary Hebron	20 Nov 1888	c
DYUR - also see DYER			
DYUR, Elizabeth	Joshua Shelton	22 Feb 1810	
EAGLE, Florence	David C. Hoyle	2 Dec 1896	w
William	Ruth Ann Cooley	1 Jun 1837	
EAGLEN, William H.	Annie F. Braxton	25 Apr 1890	c
EARHART, Clara M.	John F. Harriss	20 Oct 1886	w
EARL, George	Margaret E. Boyce	10 Jun 1895	w
EARNEST, Eleazar O.	Elizabeth Penn	10 Mar 1862	
Eleazer O.	Lavinia Buck	21 Jul 1879	w
Henry T.	Mary L. Ward	3 Feb 1868	
EARP - also see EARPE, ERP, EARPT, HARP			
EARP, Alfred M.	Maybell Chaney	7 Dec 1896	w
Eliza	Eleazar Ray	24 Aug 1865	

* Day reads 17, but is entered after 21
** Part of last name from earlier reading

EARP, Elizabeth	Walter Earpt	30 Jan 1841	
Elizabeth Axsha	George L. Hutchinson	29 Oct 1889	w
Erasmus	Margaret Moland	29 Dec 1824	
Erasmus	Elizabeth Moulden	28 Jan 1837	
Irene	William F. Bennett	15 Mar 1875	
Jennie	Zadock Summers	22 Oct 1868	
Marbara E.	Evan T. Bowman	30 Nov 1887	w
Mary C.	Thomas Angel	30 Sep 1857	
Matilda	William H. Gordon	8 Jan 1852	
Nelson W.	Cassandra Reed	8 Aug 1853	
Washington	Catharine Thompson	4 Aug 1824	
William	Ann Bond	13 Dec 1831	
William J.	Mary Ray	17 Sep 1874	
Willson L.	Elizabeth Thompson	28 Jan 1863	
EARPE, Charles N.	Lulu Jeffries	18 Aug 1890	w
Sarah	Edward C. Baker	24 Sep 1864	
EARPT, Walter	Elizabeth Earp	30 Jan 1841	
EASTON, Andrew E.	Eliza F. Musgrove	26 Dec 1889	w
Annie E.	James Madigan	18 Nov 1890	w
Benjamin	Sarah Saffell	21 Dec 1826	
Caroline	John Easton	1 Dec 1866	
Carrie B.	Tony T. Unglesbee	17 Jul 1893	w
Catharine	Richard Lowe	12 Jun 1855	
Catharine	James H. Hazen	18 Jul 1889	w
Elizabeth	Nathan Lowe	28 Jul 1830	
Elizabeth	Richard Parsley	12 Feb 1862	
Emily J.	Lewis M. Leizear	2 Mar 1893	w
Giles	Elizabeth Nolen	2 Apr 1799	
Giles W.	Ann E. Hilton	3 Apr 1856	
Giles Washington	Sarah Elizabeth Lowe	10 Nov 1886	w
Harriet L.	Charles A. VanHorn	20 Apr 1886	w
Hattie V.	James A. Moxley	23 Oct 1895	w
Hester Ann	Richard Case	1 Feb 1862	
Hilleary	Kitty Murphy	7 Feb 1821	
Isaiah	Charlotte Haney	27 Jul 1825	
Isaiah	Susan Rebecca Day	16 Jan 1834	
Isaiah	Rebecca Easton	22 May 1865	
James Annie	Richard L. Buxton	15 Dec 1886	w
Jeffry	Dolly Haney	20 May 1831	
John	Louisa Low	1 Oct 1856	
John	Caroline Easton	1 Dec 1866	
Levin	Drusilla Ricketts	27 Feb 1801	
Lewis	Hesther Ann Henly	7 Jul 1827	
Louis B.	Laura C. Moxley	5 Dec 1893	w
Mamie B.	Harry G. Merson	1 Sep 1897	w
Marshall	Martha A. Johnson	18 Dec 1883	
Mary E.	Daniel W. Hazen	27 Dec 1876	
Mittie W.	Clarence M. Winemiller	5 Aug 1889	w
Mollie E.	Richard L. Buxton	8 Jul 1879	w
Ninian V. W.	Ruth Haney	12 Sep 1834	
Obias	Dolly Jacobs	30 May 1807	
Rebecca	Isaiah Easton	22 May 1865	
Robey	Sophia Easton	6 Feb 1847	
Rosa A.	Samuel S. Saumenig	7 Mar 1889	w
Samuel H.	Frances V. Thompson	13 Apr 1868	
Sarah	John Crane	16 Nov 1878	w

EASTON	Sarah Y.	Michael H. Swiger	1 Jun 1837
	Sophia	Robey Easton	6 Feb 1847
	Thomas	Elizabeth Kidwell	25 Sep 1855
	William	Ann Kidwell	26 Dec 1838
	William J.	M. F. Duvall	23 Jan 1872
EALY,	Walter P.	Elizabeth E. Shaw	21 Dec 1897 w
EBERT,	Edward C.	Annie H. Neff	17 Feb 1891 w
ECKER,	Ellen E.	Alexander Kemp	16 Dec 1886 w
EDELEN,	Ellen E.	Nathan Beall	2 Jun 1866
	Salva	John M. Smith	22 Dec 1884 w
	William	Julian Knott	20 Jan 1829
EDELIN,	Elizabeth	Elstan A. Edelin	21 May 1817
	Elizabeth J.	James H. Daily	20 Dec 1854
	Elstan A.	Elizabeth Edelin	21 May 1817
	Nathan R.	Mary E. Shipley	7 Apr 1849
	Richard	Susan Knott	19 Sep 1843
	Ruth Ellen	John W. Darby	10 Dec 1844
EDMONDS,	Benjamin F.	Mary J. Knode	14 Jul 1858
EDMONSON,	Clarence J.	Rosa B. Cross	29 Nov 1897 c
	John B.	Harriet D. Holt	5 Oct 1870
EDMONSTON,	Archibald	Sarah Carr	7 Mar 1801
	Brooke	Deborah Orme	7 Mar 1799
	Dorithy	Benjamin Waters, Jr.	25 Apr 1812
	Eden	Lucretia Waters	31 May 1809
	Edward O.	Julianna Veirs	12 Mar 1857
	Elijah	Elizabeth Orme	30 Mar 1807
	Elizabeth	Samuel Beedle	13 Jul 1808
	Elizabeth	Thomas Steward	12 Nov 1883
	Enoch	Sarah Turner	2 Jan 1809
	Hosea	Mary Orme	4 Jun 1808
	Lucy	Samuel Steel	19 Oct 1808
	Robert	Elizabeth Waters	17 Sep 1816
	William	Elizabeth Jones	2 Mar 1802
EDMONSTONE,	Angelina	Chandler Keys	11 Nov 1834
	Dolly	John Waters	18 Nov 1820
	Eliza H.	John M. Barneclo	16 Sep 1834
	Elizabeth	John G. Wood	1 Jan 1825
	Elizabeth B.	George Cashell	14 Jun 1804
	Hezekiah	Hesther Berry	4 Jan 1819
	Jurussia	Henry Duley	30 Aug 1832
	Lucinda R.	Francis S. Brown	15 Sep 1829
	Mary Ann K.	Joshua C. Higgins	30 Jan 1850
	Mary Ann Matilda	Martin F. Higgins	1 Apr 1823
	Nathan	Elizabeth Penn	10 Feb 1823
	Owen J.	Caroline Mannake	29 Jun 1843
	Robert	Polly Waters	25 Nov 1804
	Sarah	Joseph Levelle	2 Feb 1803
EDWARDS,	Anne	William Fishback	1 Jun 1809
	Charles G.	Deborah R. Dorsey	9 Feb 1814
	George A. W.	Sarah R. Powell	25 Jun 1891 c
	George T.	Mary E. Meem	3 Jun 1887 w
	Henry C.	Ida M. Watkins	10 Jul 1884 w
	James E.	Elizabeth Lyne	30 Dec 1829
	John W.	Hattie A. Frazier	21 Sep 1897 c
	Julia	Richard Dorsey	14 Jan 1869

EDWARDS, Katie	George E. Fuller	24 Nov 1885	c
Mary*	Henry Robert Whittaker	19 Sep 1798	
Nathan	Sarah Hill	15 Nov 1876	
Ninian	Elvira Lane	20 Feb 1803	
Sarah	William Wright	** Sep 1883	c
Thomas	Mary Laurens	29 Jul 1831	
Thomas R.	Louisa A. Burkely	***28 Mar 1898	w
William H.	May M. Smoot	29 Sep 1897	w
EICHLER, Frederick	Marie Enzle	15 Mar 1898	w
ELBERT, Mary J.	Harry Turner	11 Oct 1894	w
ELCORN - also see ALCORN, ELLCORN			
ELCORN, Tobias R.	Hester J. Ray	12 May 1898	c
ELD, Mary E.	Lewis E. Shoemaker	13 Nov 1862	
ELDER, Elizabeth	James McAtee	18 May 1814	
James M.	Rose Anna Selby	18 May 1879	w
ELER - also see ELLER, ELLAR			
ELER, Elizabeth G.	Henry L. Bird	7 Apr 1856	
ELFREY, Philip	Annie E. Watkins	5 Oct 1895	w
ELGAR, Eliza W.	Henry Howard	8 Feb 1836	
Margaret A., Miss	Charles E. Sherman	8 Aug 1837	
ELGIN, Charles F.	Hellen D. Smith	29 Jan 1863	
George	Sophia Westher*	22 Dec 1807	
James L.	Ellen Eugenia Castle	18 Nov 1886	w
Jane E.	Benjamin R. Poole	21 Dec 1858	
Mary J.	Benjamin C. Young	29 Dec 1859	
William F.	Mary E. White	18 Mar 1887	w
ELIASON, John H.	Clara C. Herbst	13 Aug 1888	w
ELKINS, John	Deborah Hood	22 Apr 1885	c
ELLAR - also see ELER, ELLER			
ELLAR, Henry	Sarah Lowe	10 Jan 1827	
ELLCORN - also see ELCORN, ALCORN			
ELLCORN, Edward	Sarah Butler	24 Aug 1865	
ELLER - also see ELER, ELLAR			
ELLER, Benjamin E.	Sarah Benson	19 Mar 1839	
Benjamin E.	Louisa A. Nolly	11 Sep 1848	
Jacob	Margaret Grimes	31 Jan 1821	
Mary R.	Luther M. Watkins	28 Jan 1893	w
Sarah E.	William Wolfe	20 Nov 1855	
William	Frances Hetchison	31 Mar 1845	
ELLICOTT, Anne Brooke	Thomas Tyson	23 Aug 1836	
ELLIOTT, Richard ****	Maria Saunders	3 May 1832	
ELLIS - also see ALLIS			
ELLIS, Easter	John Jackson	14 Dec 1798	
Elizabeth	Lewis H. Duvall	14 Jul 1806	
John	Susannah Norwood	15 Dec 1808	
Joseph	Mary Hillery	7 Jan 1818	
Kate P.	Philip C. Mase	15 Sep 1877	
Rachel	George Fletcher	28 Jul 1876	
Sarah A.	William H. Scott	8 Apr 1895	c
Thomas G.	Plantcina Ward	13 Feb 1875	
ELLISON, George W.	Mary Johnson	27 Aug 1891	c

* Part of last name from earlier reading
** Cannot read complete day; either 27 or 29
*** Day is written Mar 28, but is after Feb 26 and before Mar 4
**** Initial I or J

Name	Spouse	Date
ELLSWORTH, Katie	John Lewis	9 Aug 1881 w
ELLUMS, Joseph	Seni Howse	30 Nov 1815
ELMORE, Arthur B.	Jennie Williams	14 Nov 1877 w
Jennie	Richard A. Mackey	13 Oct 1896 w
William Thomas	Lucy Ann Shired	7 Oct 1884 w
ELMS, Jane	John Dwire	7 Mar 1835
ELSON, Ruth	Zachariah Duley	6 Mar 1806
ELVILL, Elias	Elizabeth Burrois	18 Oct 1803
EMBREY, Granville J.	Annie K. Roby	20 Dec 1890 w
Milton F.	Mary E. Caywood	19 Nov 1873
EMERSON, Edward S.	Georganna Grimes	17 Feb 1870
EMMERT, Isaac	Susan D. Hershey	8 Mar 1836
John L.	Roena B. Davis	9 Dec 1895 w
EMRICH, George W.	Lucy J. D. Mullican	16 Oct 1884 w
ENGLAND, John G.	Emiley Howard	4 May 1830
John G. Jr.	Annie L. Griffith	22 Apr 1867
ENGLE - also see INGLE		
ENGLE, Charles E.	Alice C. Hunter	5 Aug 1895 w
William	Mary Butt	19 Jan 1814
ENGLISH, Aggie C.	John T. Phebus	20 May 1884 w
Armenia	Maurice E. Phebus	1 Jun 1887 w
Catharine	William H. Grady	7 Jun 1866
David	Lydia Henderson	8 Nov 1819
James	Mary Ellen Bean	26 Dec 1837
James T.	Eva J. Collins	27 Feb 1890 w
Joseph	Elizabeth Hebern	31 Mar 1801
Joseph R.	Mary C. Thompson	15 Dec 1865
Mamie E.	Benjamin F. Vernon	1 Jun 1892 w
Mary C.	Lewis H. Metz	19 Oct 1880
Mary Prudence	James Rufus Pheabus	17 May 1869
Rebecca	Jacob Day	19 Jan 1808
Ruth	Hezekiah Metz	20 May 1873
Sarah	Martin Thompson	14 Nov 1848
Sarah H.	Andrew J. Davis	20 Aug 1862
Sarah R.	Elias J. Hill	4 Jul 1854
Thomas	Ruth Thompson	16 Jan 1819
William George	Elizabeth L. Offutt	10 Apr 1867
ENIS, John Wesley	Amelia F. Maccabee	4 Apr 1877 c
ENNIS, Barton*	Margaret Smith	20 Apr 1798
Joseph W.	Margaret Warner	23 Jun 1894 c
Mary	George Jackson	8 Apr 1811
ENSEY, Perry	Mary E. Kinsey	24 Jan 1882
ENTWISTLE, Thomas W.	Irene Bailey	5 Nov 1867
ENZLE, Marie	Frederick Eichler	15 Mar 1898 w
ERDMAN, Peter C. R.	Lee E. Brown	19 Dec 1891 w
ERHART, William	Mary E. Bartholomew	12 Mar 1892 w
ERP - also see EARP		
ERP, Cassandra	George Nelson Reid	29 Sep 1819
Catharine	John Erp	26 Jun 1862
John	Catharine Erp	26 Jun 1862
Philip	Rachel A. Ray	16 Oct 1862
Rosa	William Redmon	29 Jan 1896 w
ERTTER, Frank X.	Clara T. Graeves	24 Apr 1886 w
John F.	Mary E. Crane	13 Nov 1894 w

* His last name and her name from earlier reading

ERVIN - also see IRVIN, IRVING			
ERVIN, Hesse	Samuel Darby	29 Nov 1800	
Mary E.	Oliver Lowe	31 Jul 1894	w
Sarah	Charles Riggs	22 Aug 1798	
ESKINS, Belle	David A. Landow	3 Jan 1898	w
ESSEX, John W.	Alice R. Sonnemann	8 Nov 1881	
Josiah Jr.	Eldra D. Hilton	8 Sep 1864	
William T.	Rosa E. Kline	28 Jan 1884	
ESTEP, Alice C.	John Estep	7 Dec 1820	
Ann	William Culver	6 Jan 1807	
Eleanor	Robert Howsin	24 Jan 1815	
John	Alice C. Estep	7 Dec 1820	
ESWORTHY, Frank	Jeanette Cornwell	14 Nov 1898	w
Joseph W.	Mary E. Hickman	23 Dec 1859	
Joseph W.	Eremantha Z. Cooper	14 Apr 1863	
ESTWORTHY, Joseph W.	Charlotte Norriss	15 Sep 1884	
ETCHERSON - also see ETCHISON, ATCHERSON			
ETCHERSON, Amelia	Aquila Day	7 Jan 1805	
Carey	Daniel Aslin	30 Sep 1812	
William	Rachel Warfield	16 Apr 1812	
ETCHESON, Elijah P.	Ruth Griffith	23 Nov 1829	
John	Ann Warfield	13 Dec 1804	
Niscy	Edward Warfield	4 Dec 1805	
ETCHISON - also see ETCHERSON, ETCHESON, ATCHERSON			
ETCHISON, Annie P.	Thomas C. Crawford	23 Nov 1897	w
Caroline	James M. Etchison	17 Feb 1835	
Elias H.	Lottie Ward	11 Jan 1888	w
Elisha C., Dr.	Nettie D. Waters	18 Apr 1876	
Elizabeth Ann	Marine Duvall	1 Nov 1847	
Frederick	Christy Day	16 Nov 1807	
James M.	Caroline Etchison	17 Feb 1835	
James M.	Mary A. Williams	16 Dec 1851	
John O.	Mary V. Penn	22 May 1878	w
John W.	Flavilla Griffith	12 May 1835	
Leonidas	Hepsila Purdum	21 Mar 1865	
Louise C.	John W. Mullinix	2 Oct 1897	w
Lucinda	Henry W. Moore	12 Oct 1840	
Lucretia A.	Erasmus Clagett	16 Apr 1853	
Lydia R.	Luther W. Moore	13 Mar 1852	
Marcellus	Fannie L. King	23 Mar 1877	w
Marcellus	Blanch M. Townsend	15 Dec 1891	w
Mary C.	Joseph Spurrier	2 Feb 1855	
Mary P. J.	Horace Waters	24 Oct 1866	
Miranda	Joshua Purdom	29 Mar 1836	
Miranda E.	James W. Burdette	14 Oct 1895	w
Rhody Ann	Nathan B. Warthen	17 Mar 1847	
Samuel	Brunette Moxley	15 Mar 1815	
ETTINGER, Frank J.	Frances S. Hicks	2 Sep 1898	w
EURY, Charles	Katie Heisler	3 Aug 1895	w
EVANS, Casandra	Benjamin Leeke	30 May 1805	
D. Bargar	Mary Estelle Myers	10 Sep 1890	w
Druid H.	Phillipina Petsch	30 Aug 1890	w
Evan	Elizabeth Harrison	21 Nov 1800	
Joseph	Jane Noland	30 Nov 1869	
John H.	Mary F. Childs	10 Apr 1817	
Leah	Ro--- P. Fulkerom	10 Jun 1898	w

EVELEY - also see EVELY			
EVELEY, James E.	Margaret A. Duvall	23 Sep 1891	w
Rachel	Thomas Boswell	26 Apr 1843	
EVELIN, Ann E.	Henry W. Burgess	1 May 1850	
EVELY - also see EVELEY			
EVELY, George W.	Louisa Leizear	20 Apr 1875	
George W.	Alice Hatfield	22 Jun 1875	
Mary	William H. Duvall	10 Jul 1843	
William	Mary Cawod	23 Dec 1809	
EVERETT, Joanna C.	James Martin	31 Dec 1845	
Martha J.	M. A. Turner	18 Jan 1842	
EVERHART, Annie L.	Harvey R. Henley	30 Dec 1895	w
Daniel W.	Addie E. Henley	19 Jan 1892	w
Delia E.	Charles H. M. Peyton	13 Oct 1885	w
Ettie	Jefferson Davis Harriss	7 Oct 1885	w
Lyda M.	Louis A. Henley	6 Apr 1887	w
Thomas F.	Clara J. McCrossin	7 Nov 1894	w
EVERSFIELD, Sarah B.	Thomas L. Offutt	25 Feb 1813	
EVERSON - also see NEVERSON			
EVERSON, Eliza	William Taylor	3 Mar 1888	c
EWELL - also see YEWELL			
EWELL, Angeline	Richard H. Cashel	2 Jan 1834	
Daniel R.	Emma Walker	19 Dec 1893	c
Gustavous	Mary C. Graff	27 Feb 1838	
Polina E.	George W. Lewis	24 Jan 1839	
FAGAN, Bridget M.	Henry Clay Fowler	1 Dec 1886	w
FAHY - see FOHY			
FAIRALL - also see FERRAL			
FAIRALL, Achsah A. R.	Nathan Shaw	14 Jan 1852	
FAIRFAX, Ada S.	Allan M. Chandler	3 Oct 1892	w
Robert	Sarah Catharine Johnson	16 Feb 1885	c
FALCONER, Jeremiah	Mary Prather	29 Nov 1826	
FALL, David	Elizabeth Watts	26 Jun 1865	
Thomas	Mary Miles	30 Apr 1887	c
FALLS, Lethe	Andrew Hill	11 Jun 1892	c
FANCHER, Gilbert G.	Rosa E. Bikes	22 Mar 1897	w
FARMER, Carrie	Harry Gibbs	18 Dec 1894	w
James	Margaret Rob--*	4 Aug 1812	
Samuel	Mary Ann Preston	25 Oct 1817	
FARQUAHAR, Benjamin	Mary Dwyer	17 Aug 1805	
FARQUHAR, Charles	Cornelia H. Strain	7 May 1892	w
William J. T.	Marie W. Harvelle	24 Feb 1897	w
FARRE, Jannaro S.	Susan Sands	17 Jun 1813	
Julia Ann	William Oneale, Jr.	10 Jan 1826	
Mary Ann E.	Samuel N. Clements	7 Jan 1826	
FAUGHT, Annie D.	William R. Houtz	3 Jun 1892	w
FAW, Mary	Samuel G. Jones	6 Jun 1799	
FAWCETT - also see FOSSETT			
FAWCETT, Abram	Emma Fawcett	3 Apr 1854	
Albert C.	Sarah R. Davis	2 Feb 1869	
Annie M.	William E. Shaw	17 Jan 1866	
Benjamin	Marrian Green	4 Dec 1848	

* Remainder of name off page; looks like could be Robey

FAWCETT, Carrie	Willie T. Wheeler	13 Dec 1886	w
Edward L.	Ella J. Marlow	2 Oct 1877	w
Emma	Abram Fawcett	3 Apr 1854	
Harry C.	Marion E. Offutt	13 Nov 1862	
Mary A.	Richard Sedgwick	14 Nov 1872	
Rhoda	Joseph M. Fletcher	1 Jun 1858	
Sallie T.	John ?. Hodges	28 Nov 1883	
Sarah	Thomas E. Lloyd	9 Dec 1857	
Sarah A.	Robert Kidwell	29 May 1850	
William H.	Rebecca Snowden	6 Jan 1873	
FEARON, Ernest T.	Sarah C. Griffith	26 Oct 1897	w
FEARS, George Henry	Rosie White	5 Nov 1877	w
FEASTER - also see FEISTER, FIESTER, FISTER			
FEASTER, Jacob	Elizabeth Bennett	31 Dec 1825	
Lydia Ann	William Cecil	24 Aug 1825	
Polly	Samuel Jacobs	5 May 1825	
Sarah T.	Samuel Hebbons	23 Jul 1871	
FECHTIG, Alice	William T. Jones	4 Feb 1875	
Elizabeth H.	Horatio Trundle	29 Dec 1863	
FEDELINE, James F.	Mary C. Barns	7 Jan 1859	
FEDERLINE, Joseph A.	Anna M. Gardiner	8 May 1860	
Mary A.	Richard Case	24 Feb 1868	
Richard A.	Ann E. Sullivan	16 Oct 1860	
William E.	Sarah C. McCrossin	18 Dec 1876	
FEE. Elizabeth	Thomas Garrett	1 Feb 1799	
FEISTER - also see FEASTER			
FEISTER, Lydia	Dennis Housar	23 Sep 1823	
FELIS, Augusta	John R. Collins	19 Dec 1888	w
FELIX, Charles E.	Annie Phalen	4 Sep 1893	w
FELKA, Albert W.	Marion O. Poss	22 Sep 1894	w
FELLINGER, Emma K.	Walter G. Sparo	28 Jan 1891	
FENDLY, Janet M.	John B. Tendley	29 Jan 1817	
FENDNER, Emilia S.	Andrew H. Kessler	9 Dec 1891	w
William H.	Magdalena C. Niemeyer	26 Aug 1892	w
FENNEL, William	Bertie Jackson	31 Aug 1893	c
FENNELL, Edward	Margarett Sanders	4 Aug 1800	
FENNICAN, James P.	Elizabeth Sweeny	4 Nov 1801	
FENTON, Annie M.	James H. Caton	6 Feb 1888	w
FENWICK, Elizabeth	Thomas Barnes	22 May 1800	
Ernest S.	Frances W. Shepley	20 Jul 1892	w
James	Ann Clemens	12 May 1852	
James B.	Mary Katherine Clark	1 Oct 1890	w
Josephine R.	James H. Beall	4 Feb 1861	
FERGUSON - also see FURGERSON			
FERGUSON, Basil	Elizabeth Brashears*	8 Oct 1798	
Hamilton O.	Mary V. E. Mullican	26 Sep 1888	w
John	Elizabeth White	15 Oct 1803	
John W.	Sarah Ann Prather	16 May 1843	
FERRAL - also see FAIRALL			
FERRAL, James H.	Emily E. Jones	20 Jun 1876	
FERRALL, Ann	Christian Mosburg	28 May 1844	
John	Margaret Spates	29 Mar 1826	
FERRISS, Enola K.	John A. Herell	30 Dec 1882	w
FIDDLER, Elizabeth	Henry Nolte	13 Dec 1881	

* Part of last name from earlier reading

FIDDLER, Mary A.	Charles B. Graeves	30 Oct 1876
FIDLER, Annie D.	William Cashell	23 Feb 1892 w
Emma Maria	George Washington Marlow	27 Apr 1885 w
Frank J.	Fannie T. Barnette	19 Sep 1881 w
Lillie	Charles B. Graeves	26 Sep 1883
Rosa	Lewis B. F. Graeves	22 Apr 1884
FIELDING, Elizabeth	Solomon Bishop	13 Nov 1811
FIELDS, Ann Byrd	George W. Spates	28 Sep 1846
Cappie V.	John H. Bogley	16 Nov 1897 w
Charles W.	M. Virginia Rabbitt	23 Oct 1878 w
Delphena	Nathaniel Franklin Harriss	8 Oct 1857
Horatio H.	Mary E. Fields	4 May 1868
Jetson G.	Elizabeth A. West	14 Feb 1854
John	Mahala Grantt	7 Apr 1829
Jonathan	Margaret Case	16 May 1843
Kate R.	David H. Warfield	23 Nov 1892 w
Martha V. W.	William W. Mennis	3 Jan 1844
Mary	George Gardner	20 May 1895 w
Mary E.	Horatio H. Fields	4 May 1868
Mary Jane	George W. Pennifield	4 Nov 1851
Matthew	Rebecca G. Beckwith	30 Dec 1850
Robert	Elizabeth Granger	14 Mar 1818
Ruth	Jesse Worrell	2 Nov 1816
Verlinda	Richard Selby	8 Apr 1856
William	Margaret Ramsey	17 Dec 1812
FIESTER - also see FEASTER		
FIESTER, Joseph	Sarah Bennett	25 Nov 1834
FIFE - also see FYFFE		
FIFE, Ann	Barnett T. Norris	6 Jan 1830
John	Eleanor Hugerford	9 Dec 1800
FIGGINS, Frank B.	Fannie G. Israel	14 Mar 1893 w
FILGATE, James F.	Nellie E. Cassell	21 Aug 1894 w
FILLEY, Rosetta	Michael S. Warren	25 Jan 1882
FINACOM, Frederick A.	Laura Basten	21 Oct 1891 w
FINCH, Leroy W.	Martha H. Hunter	14 Oct 1862
FINNEY, J. Franklin	Alice A. Duvall	10 Mar 1885 w
FISH, Benjamin Robert	Susan A. Wyvill	20 Dec 1832
Bertha C.	Albert N. Mount	20 Apr 1887 w
Eleanor	James Groome	11 Sep 1802
Eleven	Mary Willett	31 Dec 1808
Elizabeth	William Shaw	16 Dec 1826
Francis	Elizabeth Green	20 Dec 1828
Francis	Elizabeth F. Hempstone	16 Jan 1834
Harriett	Edward Trail	27 Apr 1813
Hatton	Sarah Benton	18 Feb 1801
James	Susan R. Price	20 May 1837
Levin C.	Sarah E. Marlow	9 Mar 1859
Richard	Elizabeth Young	17 Dec 1800
Rosalie	John H. W. Day	18 Jan 1898 w
William	Hellen Joy	27 Dec 1808
William O.	Mollie A. McMahan	22 Jan 1877 w
FISHBACK, William	Anne Edwards	1 Jun 1809
FISHER, Alcester Ann	Julian Osmonde	23 Dec 1863
Alice	William H. Knott	24 Jul 1879 c

FISHER,	Ann E.	Samuel N. S. Williams	20 Dec 1838	
	Ann Eliza	Leonard W. Candler	30 Jan 1834	
	Anna	Henry Cephas	8 Feb 1889	c
	Anna M.	Hilleary L. Offutt	26 Oct 1855	
	Annie	William Author	27 Oct 1896	c
	Aquila	Elizabeth Clagett	17 Dec 1810	
	Artarcexes E.	Elizabeth A. Carey	15 Jul 1879	
	Artaxerxes	Mary Ann Claggett	13 Sep 1813	
	Artaxerxes	Ann M. Willson	4 Jul 1816	
	Benjamin F.	Georgie C. Hays	21 Feb 1895	c
	Charles	Ann Dove	5 Jun 1834	
	Charles T.	Jane Fisher	15 Jun 1881	w
	Constantia	Everard G. Fisher	27 Jun 1877	w
	Cornelia L.	Alex L. Bohrer	9 Dec 1847	
	Edmund E.	Mary E. Fisher	7 Jul 1868	
	Eliza E.	Alexander H. Harriss	30 Dec 1878	
	Eliza M.	Isaiah Soper	8 Dec 1852	
	Emma D.	Charles A. Case	5 Jun 1880	w
	Everard G.	Marial E. Dawes	27 Nov 1844	
	Everard G.	Mary E. West	18 Sep 1867	
	Everard G.	Constantia Fisher	27 Jun 1877	w
	Fanny	Samuel Tophouse	16 Nov 1800	
	Geary A.	Mattie M. Connelly	22 Nov 1897	w
	Harriet	George Diggs	22 Mar 1886	c
	Jane	Charles T. Fisher	15 Jun 1881	w
	John F.	Doris C. Anders	27 Dec 1893	w
	Laura V.	Ephraim G. Ayton	9 May 1881	
	Levi	Martha Thompson	6 Nov 1893	c
	Lillie	William A. Posey	3 Jun 1898	w
	Loshonius E.	Thomas M. Offutt	24 Jan 1848	
	Lydia Elizabeth	Erasmus Perry	27 Feb 1844	
	Maria M.	Henry N. Harriss	6 Apr 1861	
	Martha	Frank Magruder	11 Dec 1886	c
	Martha E.	Jonathan H. Palmer	24 Feb 1855	
	Martha E.	John Minnis	10 Dec 1873	
	Martin	Priscilla Poole Jones	6 Feb 1818	
	Mary	Thomas Peter	5 Feb 1887	c
	Mary A.	Samuel A. Riggs	9 Apr 1867	
	Mary A. C.	Thomas M. Offutt	3 Jan 1839	
	Mary C.	George W. Higgins	29 Nov 1871	
	Mary E.	James R. Norton	29 Jan 1856	
	Mary E.	Edmund E. Fisher	7 Jul 1868	
	Mary E. C.	Samuel N. S. Williams	23 Aug 1860	
	Mary V.	R. Hugh Stevens	23 May 1883	
	Mary V.	Henry T. Onley	21 Dec 1891	c
	Millard C.	Mary E. Boswell	20 May 1871	
	Nelson	Eleanor Cross	28 Jan 1825	
	Rachel A.	Joseph P. Davis	3 Jul 1876	
	Samuel	Sarah Davis	14 Mar 1885	c
	Samuel M.	Louisa Benton	27 Jan 1841	
	Samuel M.	Rosetta Benton	22 Feb 1859	
	Sarah A.	Thomas H. Poole	28 Nov 1854	
	Selah	Thomas B. Offutt	23 Mar 1808	
	Solomon	Sarah Warren	28 Sep 1881	c
	Thomas	Amy C. Offutt	28 Mar 1815	
	Thomas	Eliza Veirs	3 Feb 1829	

FISHER, William	Elizabeth Harris	9 May 1818
William	Rachel P. Marek	24 Aug 1821
William	Maria Davis	31 Jan 1824
William H. L.	Eleanor Elizabeth Claget	17 Dec 1840
William Henry	Martha Frazier	26 Oct 1868
William T.	Eliza L. Beckwith	10 Jan 1843
William T.	Susen R. Case	2 Jul 1857
William Thomas	Cassandra V. Ball	26 Jan 1854
FISTER - also see FEASTER		
FISTER, Catherine	Richard Thompson	3 Jul 1819
FITCH, James	Fanny E. Crosley	22 Oct 1857
Melien B.	Susan Wathen	22 Dec 1832
Mary W.	Nicholas W. Appleby	26 Feb 1856
Melvinia R.	James L. Trail	19 Dec 1843
FITZGERALD, Benjamin	Arra Cooper	9 Nov 1803
Edward A.	Sarah A. Johnson	13 Jan 1887 w
Eliza K.	Thomas Delihunt	20 Jan 1875
Morris	Isabel Gingell	23 Jan 1888 w
Rachel	Nicholas Bailey	23 Sep 1809
Ruth	William Burditt	16 Feb 1804
FITZGERRALD, Henry	Prissilla Cissell	10 Jan 1827
Sarah	Thomas Keith	24 Dec 1807
FITZHEW, Mary E.	John McKeney	12 Jul 1888 c
FITZHUGH, Ella	Henry Sullivan	26 May 1880
Harriet A.	Joseph A. Hill	5 Jan 1888 c
Willis	Susie Mickens	17 May 1890 c
FITZPATRICK, Owen J.	Mary T. O'Connor	29 Sep 1897 w
FIX, Maggie W.	Joseph E. Desper	25 Oct 1897 w
FLACK, Elizabeth	J. G. Killian	24 Apr 1860
Mary C.	A. Kleindienst	21 Nov 1855
Sarah	Robert Frank	13 Oct 1863
William F.	Annie M. Carr	24 May 1870
FLAGG, Martha M.	Thomas G. Flagg	9 Jun 1853
Thomas G.	Martha M. Flagg	9 Jun 1853
FLAHERTY, Ann	Patrick Lyddane	18 Mar 1822
Brian	Briget Flaherty	11 Apr 1798
Briget	Brian Flaherty	11 Apr 1798
Catharine	Peter Branham	8 Apr 1815
James O.	Sally Brannon	2 Jan 1802
John	Mary Oden	29 May 1816
Mark	Margaret Whealan	26 Dec 1801
Patrick	Mary Whealan	7 Jan 1803
FLATFORD, Amelia	Jonathan Fry	28 Aug 1799
FLEMING, Catharine	Burgess Willett	25 Jan 1814
Mary	Jesse Wade	5 Dec 1804
Rosser	Mahala A. King	27 Feb 1869
FLEMMING, John	Ann Coberth	20 Oct 1825
FLECTHALL, Anne	William White	8 Dec 1825
Arthur P.	Lulu J. Hall	5 Feb 1886 w
Daniel V.	Mary Ann Bowic	24 Sep 1823
Darky	Peter Bouic	7 Apr 1812
Elizabeth B.	William Matthews	23 Feb 1832
George Walter	Eleanor White Chiswell	12 Dec 1814
Gertie	Thomas Hoskinson	24 May 1876

FLETCHALL, James	Jane Luckett	5 Oct 1808	
Jane	William Brown	5 Sep 1838	
John T.	Mary S. Poole	29 May 1850	
Thomas	Sarah Newton Chiswell	13 Mar 1801	
Rachel Ann	William A. Chiswell	26 Jan 1846	
Sarah	William Chiswell	14 Nov 1809	
Sarah	William Matthis	11 Jan 1834	
William	Anne Trail	31 Oct 1815	
FLETCHELL, Hester W.	James Purdum	9 Feb 1844	
FLETCHER, George	Rachel Ellis	28 Jul 1876	
Joseph M.	Rhoda Fawcett	1 Jun 1858	
Peggy	William Thomas	16 Mar 1798	
FLING, James	Aggie Burriss	21 Nov 1894	w
James A.	Henrietta Trucks	22 Nov 1864	
Jane M.	John Hutchison	8 Apr 1863	
Julia E.	William H. Havener	1 Dec 1854	
Louisa C.	Morris Thompson	25 Dec 1851	
Mary Ellen	Joseph L. Carroll	10 Oct 1857	
Polly	John Barnes	8 Apr 1809	
Rebecca	James Willson	21 Jan 1828	
Rebecca Angelina	George W. Doyle	25 Mar 1845	
Susan	Charles Bunting	9 Apr 1819	
Susan	George Kemp	29 Dec 1849	
William M.	Fannie E. Sherman	29 Jan 1889	w
FLIPPEN, Flavel Philip	Alice S. Morrison	14 Dec 1886	w
FLOOD, John	Mary Andrews	13 Mar 1820	
FLOOK, Amanda C.	Benjamin F. Thompson	5 Dec 1872	
FLORANCE, Richard H.	Leila R. Osmond	24 Sep 1894	w
FLOYD, Mary E.	Silas Waits	27 Sep 1871	
FLUHART, Sarah J.	Herbert G. Miles	11 May 1883	
FLYNN, Mary E.	James R. Miles	7 Jan 1889	w
FOHY, Marty	Sarah Donnoho	6 Jan 1804	
FOLEY, Edward A.	Ida M. Reintzell	11 Jul 1885	w
FOLWELL, Charles H.	Jane Barnes	13 Mar 1873	
FONTAINE, John	America Magruder	14 Feb 1871	
FORD, Andrew	Florence G. Summers	20 Sep 1892	w
Clara J.	Thomas E. Padgett	2 Dec 1873	
Edith G.	George E. Ford	4 Aug 1897	w
Elizabeth	John Simpson	12 Jan 1803	
Ella F.	Henry Lee Miles	29 Dec 1892	w
------- M.	Mary V. Wright	* Apr 1879	
George E.	Edith G. Ford	4 Aug 1897	w
Gracie	William Lawrence	16 Aug 1893	w
James K.	Letha Jackson	6 Sep 1884	c
John A.	Rebecca Morrison	10 Jul 1844	
John A.	Mary A. Hinton	28 Oct 1848	
Lizzie A.	Bural M. Carter	10 Apr 1888	w
William	Priscilla Orme	21 Mar 1801	
William	Asena Wyvill	8 Mar 1822	
FOREMAN - also see FORMAN			
FOREMAN, Andrew	Hannah Dent	17 Aug 1802	
Eliza A.	George E. Lyles	27 Dec 1882	c
Hattie Ann	Benjamin F. Wims	25 Nov 1897	c
George T.	Sarah E. Berry	8 Feb 1872	

* Cannot read his first name or day; day between 14 and 21

FOREMAN, Mary	Clement Johnson	5 Jan 1886 c
Paul	Charlotte Hawkins	16 May 1868
Robert P.	Manzella U. Wims	17 Aug 1889 c
Robert P.	Martha E. Brown	28 Dec 1892 c
Samuel	Jennie Corn	11 Nov 1897 c
Sarah	Nathan Mason	27 Dec 1877 c
Westley	Minta Warren	26 Nov 1873
FOREST, Benjamin S.	Anna Maria Summers	18 Feb 1823
FORFLINGER, George F.	Mamie G. Leaman	9 Feb 1898
FORMAN - also see FOREMAN		
FORMAN, Martha	Charles Campbell	3 Apr 1878 c
FORNER, Caty	Ezekiel Moxley	26 May 1803
FOSIC, Arah	Richard Streiks	16 Jun 1800
FORSIDES, Mary	Thomas M. Howard	5 Feb 1813
FORSYTHE, Isaac	Ann Litten	19 Jun 1803
FOSE, Bushrod L.	Virginia L. Belt	28 Oct 1857
FOSSETT - also see FAWCETT		
FOSSETT, Hannah	Lloyd Green	30 May 1840
FOSTER, Charles E.	Adelaide Casey	25 Jun 1891 w
Thomas	Delila Lucas	13 Dec 1802
FOUCH, Nancy	William J. Weldon	4 Mar 1820
FOUKE, Edgar B.	Anna L. Harding	21 Mar 1888 w
FOWLER, Ann	Thomas Sibley	2 Apr 1833
Benjamin	Judith Scott	2 Feb 1800
Emma J.	Samuel B. Haney	6 Nov 1873
Henry Clay	Bridget M. Fagan	1 Dec 1886 w
James	Elizabeth Paxton	21 Dec 1835
James H.	Ann Ellen Bogeley	15 Nov 1864
John	Matilda Barber	26 Dec 1814
Lydia	Thomas James	29 Jan 1800
Nancy	John Douglass	10 Sep 1806
Sarah	Hugh Douglass	26 Dec 1810
William B.	Mary Krouse	14 Apr 1893 w
William C.	Alice G. Jones	24 Nov 1856
FOX, Elizabeth	Henry Paul	29 Aug 1829
Georgia A.	Thomas J. Wintermyer	4 Jul 1891 w
John	Betsey Parker	8 Sep 1821
FOY, William P.	Catharine E. Sullivan	16 Mar 1824
FRAISER - also see FRAZIER		
FRAISER, Harrison	Mary A. Bowen	21 Nov 1868
FRALEY, Ellen Othella	Alphonso M. Clagett	13 Jun 1893 w
John W.	Hinda Adamson	7 Nov 1892 w
FRANK, Robert	Sarah Flack	13 Oct 1863
FRANKLIN, Annie	John Busey	23 May 1898 c
Benjamin T.	Margarett E. Darnell	28 Jun 1834
George	Laura L. Woods	6 Oct 1887 c
Irodine	Pleasant Brown (male)	9 Dec 1890 w
James	Annie Waters	7 Jan 1891 c
John G.	Lydia Brogden	26 Aug 1891 c
Melinda	Henry Newman	3 Jun 1897 w
Nancy	Charles Powell	19 Dec 1834 c
Newton	Anna Ridout	26 Dec 1883 c
Singleton	Elizabeth Dorsey	17 Oct 1872
FRASIER, Elizabeth	Joseph Smith	4 Jul 1881 c
FRAZER, Mary	Thomas Arnold	26 Oct 1798

FRAZIER - also see FRAISER, FRASIER, FRAZER

FRAZIER,	Alfred	Rachel Peerce	8 Jan 1818
	Anna E.	Robert L. Gray	18 Feb 1893 c
	Anthony	Presha Lee	23 Oct 1823
	Basil R.	Rosa E. Willson	12 Sep 1877 c
	Betty	Charles Stewart	5 Jun 1865
	Carrie	John H. Williams	9 Oct 1889 c
	Charlotte E.	Thomas S. W. Boyd	17 May 1822
	Dorsey	Bessie McAbee	8 Jan 1897 c
	Elizabeth	Thomas Pitt Hays	24 Aug 1805
	Elizabeth	John E. Jones	8 Aug 1892 c
	Ephraim	Ginnie Copelin	4 Feb 1886 c
	Frances	Fillmore Ray	4 Nov 1891 c
	Georgana	William Thomas Long	5 Aug 1879
	George W.	Mary E. Coleman	16 Dec 1889 c
	George Wilson	Harriet Ann Frazier	10 Jun 1882 c
	Harriet A. E.	George W. Plummer	28 Apr 1897 c
	Harriet Ann	George Wilson Frazier	10 Jun 1882 c
	Hattie A.	John W. Edwards	21 Sep 1897 c
	Isaac	Jennie Warren	6 Jun 1895 c
	Isaiah M.	Leanna Frazier	27 Nov 1897 c
	John H.	Columbia Ray	11 Jan 1847
	Leanna	Isaiah M. Frazier	27 Nov 1897 c
	Lewis	Ruth Carter	14 Nov 1883 c
	Lizzie	Nacy Bowie	5 Jul 1878 c
	Martha	William Henry Fisher	26 Oct 1868
	Mary	Perry Herbert	6 Dec 1806
	Mary	John Riggs	26 Jan 1876 c
	Mary Jane	Elijah Butler	21 Mar 1870
	Nathaniel	Seanna Toogood	10 Dec 1889 c
	Ruth	Martin Rolles	28 Sep 1898 c
	William	Mariah Maccabee	8 Oct 1873
	William	Mary V. Disney	24 Dec 1894 c
	William Ednh.	Mary A. Johnson	6 Apr 1898 c
	William G.	Mary Robinson	30 Oct 1886 c
	William H.	Mary A. Prater	8 Jan 1897 c
FREDERICKS,	Jane	Samuel ?. Butler	25 Jan 1865
	Mollie	James W. Gray	4 Aug 1891 c
FREE,	Elizabeth	Jonathan Sparrow	17 Dec 1799
	John Conrad	Alliz B. D. Chaney	14 Feb 1809
	Susie	Joseph Z. Shaw	10 Jan 1882
FREELAND,	Samuel S.	Priscilla P. Douglass	25 Apr 1840
	Sarah N.	George Peter	18 Jun 1825
FREEMAN,	Adam	Mary Jones	22 Dec 1800
	Henry W.	Ella F. Brown	16 Sep 1897 c
	John T.	Annie L. Robertson	24 Sep 1895 w
	Sally	Thomas Cox	27 May 1800
FREER,	George A.	Sarah B. Hall	28 Dec 1898 w
FREIS,	Jane	Thomas Newton	27 Oct 1803
FRENCH,	William	Ann Willson	26 Apr 1825
FRERE,	Susie R.	John E. Haley	12 Feb 1898 w
FRY,	Cornelius M.	Emily C. Gray	26 Jan 1898 w
	George C.	Clara O. Ward	24 Sep 1895 w
	George H.	Maggie O. Mossburg	8 Mar 1893 w
	Hattie L.	Edward G. Ward	31 Jan 1894 w

FRY, Hattie L.	Edward G. Ward	31 Jan 1894 w
Henry M.	Marly L. Knapp	* Oct 1881 w
John H.	Wilhelmina Schlob	21 Jul 1879 w
Jonathan	Amelia Flatford	28 Aug 1799
Polly	Charles Porter	8 Apr 1803
Sarah V.	William F. Cooper	5 Apr 1889 w
FRYER, Rachel	James Northcraft	26 Jan 1802
Walter	Sarah Buxton	5 Sep 1810
FULKEROM, Ro-- P.	Leah Evans	10 Jun 1898 w
FULKS, Catharine	James Desellem	27 Dec 1805
Edgar	Gertrude E. Walker	30 Apr 1895 w
Elizabeth	Zachariah Dowden, Jr.	15 Mar 1814
Ellender	Jacob Swomley	18 Jan 1799
Rosa B.	Frank B. Severance	22 Sep 1898 w
Solomon	Juliet Dowden	28 Dec 1815
Susannah	Thomas Mullican	28 Dec 1809
Thomas I.	Fannie L. Williams	4 Aug 1897 w
FULLER, Amy M.	Ralp C. Wilton	6 Jan 1896 w
George E.	Katie Edwards	24 Nov 1885 c
Thomas	Nettie B. Lee	6 Nov 1890 c
FULTON, Florence M.	John D. Carmody	16 Oct 1897 w
FURGERSON - also see FERGUSON		
FURGERSON, John W.	Emily Duley	26 Oct 1835
FURLONG, Anna B.	Frederick J. Plant	29 Jul 1895 w
FUSS, Martha	James F. Burriss	2 Dec 1875
FYFFE - also see FIFE		
FYFFE, Eleanora	Adam Beall	20 Feb 1828
Elizabeth	Henry C. Tolle	10 Oct 1890 w
Mary G.	Benjamin F. Pope	13 Jun 1892 w
Thomas	Mollie Offutt	30 Dec 1867
Thomas H.	Elizabeth Jones	23 Apr 1838
FYHE, Mark	Beddy Noon	6 Jan 1802
GAEGLER - also see GOEGLER		
GAEGLER, Elizabeth	Louis Sadtler	13 Jan 1872
GAFFNEY, Edward	Eleanor Ryan	22 May 1826
GAGE, Harriet	George Carter	28 Dec 1875
GAINES, Charles R.	Frances C. McBride	18 Aug 1891 w
GAITHER, Agnes	William H. Williams	4 May 1892 c
Ann	Horatio Willcoxen	27 Aug 1817
Ann F.	Frederick O. Gaither	9 Dec 1850
Charles	Mary J. Thomas	13 Jun 1888 c
Daniel H. of D	Edith G. Mobley	20 Apr 1895 w
Deborah	James Ray	5 Feb 1803
Elizabeth	Elisha R. Griffith	8 Oct 1834
Elizabeth W.	William B. Magruder	7 Jun 1854
Ephraim S.	Aria Musgrove**	6 May 1819
Evelina	Moses P. Hughes	16 Jan 1837
F. O.	Mrs. Leanna Groomes	1 Jan 1867
Frances	William Henry Lee	7 Jun 1894
Frederick	Jane Gartrell	17 Jan 1800
Frederick O.	Ann F. Gaither	9 Dec 1850
George	Elizabeth E. Holland	2 Apr 1866

* Day written over; either 1 or 3
** Part of last name from earlier reading

GAITHER, George W.	Johnetta M. Graff	14 Dec 1886	w
Greenbury	Martha Gaither	26 Jan 1847	
Helen M.	John House	18 Dec 1871	
Henry C.	Eliza Worthington	28 Jan 1812	
Ida J.	James E. Rabbitt	28 Sep 1886	w
James	Catharine Dorsey	20 May 1871	
John	Annie Bond	26 Nov 1889	c
John T.	Charlotte E. Matthews	6 Feb 1891	w
Jonathan	Lucy Perry	1 Nov 1873	
Juliet	Bushrod Gartrell	17 Jun 1844	
Katie A.	William H. Rannie	6 Mar 1886	w
Mahala	James Hackett	2 Jul 1868	
Maria	Samuel R. Gaither	26 Nov 1823	
Martha	John Griffith	6 Nov 1826	
Martha	Greenbury Gaither	26 Jan 1847	
Mary	George Collins	21 Sep 1893	c
Mary C.	William H. Waters	5 Jan 1850	
Mary E.	Frank Alridge Mullican	27 Nov 1886	w
Mollie D.	John Francis Cissel	27 Nov 1883	
Paulina	Robert Ould	24 Dec 1814	
Richard	Frances Cook	31 Oct 1868	
Richard	Caroline Davis	31 May 1894	c
Samuel	Rosetta Davis	9 Oct 1890	c
Samuel R.	Maria Gaither	26 Nov 1823	
Sarah A.	Thomas D. Gaither	31 May 1847	
Susan	James Barnesly	5 Oct 1838	
Thomas	Atsie Welsh	3 Jan 1890	c
Thomas D.	Sarah A. Gaither	31 May 1847	
William R.	Mary A. D. Ricketts	9 Aug 1852	
GALER, Sarah	Walter Willson	3 Mar 1810	
GALES, Susie	Harrison Meekins	18 Apr 1881	
GALLADAY, Omer Byrd	Cora Lee Miles	4 Sep 1896	w
GALLANT, Percy E.	Lucy E. Smith	11 May 1895	w
GALLEHER, Harry E.	Bertha M. Sibley	10 Aug 1891	w
Joseph C.	Lacy Rice	3 Aug 1881	w
GALLOWAY, Joseph	Mary Bennett	27 Dec 1817	
Prissilla	James Stell	20 Feb 1811	
GALWORTH, Mary	George Haymond	30 Nov 1803	
Nancy	Laurence O'Neale	27 Aug 1806	
Rachel W.	Aquilla Hill	24 Dec 1805	
GAMBLE, Annie B.	John H. Dean	10 Oct 1870	
William	Sarah V. West	3 Dec 1872	
GAMBRIL, William G. P.	Mary C. Bowie	19 Nov 1896	c
GANDY, Harriet B.	Hiram Grady	13 Jan 1887	w
GANLEY, Catherine	John Hannan	12 Aug 1868	
James	Sarah E. Nicholls	18 Nov 1868	
Philip	Emily J. Smith	14 Feb 1873	
Philip	Florence ?. Smith	7 Jan 1890	w
John Franklin	Sophia R. McGaha	28 Nov 1876	
W. R.	Verlinda Whalan	12 Feb 1852	
GANT, George L.	Mary A. E. Charge	2 Dec 1882	c
Mary A.	Dela E. Moore	29 Jun 1865	
Rachel	John W. Peters	14 Feb 1882	c
GANTT, Albert	Kate Rivers	13 Jan 1891	c
Ann	William Moore	19 May 1874	
Charles E.	Martha E. Henderson	25 Jun 1862	

GANTT, Edward A.	Kitty Anne Anderson	2 Oct 1827	
Edward L.	Roberta E. Williams	9 Apr 1864	
Kitty Ann	Henry Allen	4 Aug 1845	
Lila V.	James S. Cole	29 Dec 1887	c
Louisa E.	John T. Hill	23 May 1862	
Margaret	Franklin Jackson	5 Apr 1883	c
Mary	George Countee	18 Mar 1879	c
GANTZ, William N.	Sarah R. Case	17 Feb 1872	
GARDENER, John	Ann V. Clements	29 Sep 1828	
GARDINER, Anna M.	Joseph A. Federline	8 May 1860	
Emma May	William E. Morgan	11 Jan 1887	w
Frances J.	James M. McDaniel	14 Nov 1894	w
Henry B.	Inez V. Bowlen	3 Dec 1888	w
Joseph	Lydia Craddick	11 Jun 1822	
Lewis G.	Mary A. Bowlen	26 Oct 1889	w
Maryann	William Thompson	3 Dec 1817	
Thomas F.	Alice V. Watkins	21 Jul 1886	w
GARDNER, Ann	Darius Darby	24 Nov 1823	
Bettie	Emmitt Marcellus Burrell	10 Nov 1886	c
Charles H.	Daisy Kerr	11 Feb 1896	w
Elizabeth	Lemuel S. Clements	9 Nov 1818	
George	Mary Fields	20 May 1895	w
Ignatius	Elizabeth Leeke	23 Dec 1808	
John	Elizabeth A. Dorsey	6 May 1828	
John	Laura E. Price	27 Sep 1898	w
Joseph	Elizabeth Chadburn	24 Dec 1802	
Lucretia	Edward B. Waters	29 Mar 1828	
Martha A.	Uriah M. Layton	30 Mar 1854	
Mary	Richard Sibley	1 Jan 1818	
Mary	Ignatius Penn	9 May 1883	
Mary J.	David L. Pugh	16 Jan 1872	
Robert	Ann Holland	18 Nov 1824	
Sarah Ann	Allen Reid	18 Dec 1827	
Susan	H. E. Hairries	11 Mar 1882	
Thomas J.	Christie A. Ray	15 Jun 1858	
William	Henrietta Simpson	23 Aug 1823	
GARLAND, William G.	Bettie L. Royer	19 Jul 1897	w
GARNER, Benjamin	Margaret Chadburn	8 Nov 1806	
George T.	Hannah C. Breen	25 Jul 1892	w
J. T.	Mary C. Clagett	17 Dec 1867	
James H.	Catharine Simpson	27 Nov 1838	
Margarett	Thomas *. Hanes	3 Apr 1827	
William A.	Mary A. Mytinger	14 May 1894	w
GARNETT, Bertie	William T. Beckwith	29 Nov 1895	c
Lawson	Mary Taney	22 Feb 1871	
Louis	Frances Packson	31 Jan 1872	
Martha	Henry Brian	7 Nov 1883	
GARRETT, Alexander	Mary D. Cecil	25 Oct 1887	w
Artemesia	George Shaw	18 Feb 1874	
Ashton	Ann Elizabeth Magruder	11 Feb 1836	
Charles E.	Annie Belle Rabbitt	27 Jan 1891	w
Edwin L.	Lilian A. Hyatt	1 Jun 1896	w
Elizabeth F.	Ignatius B. Ward	15 May 1872	

* Initial I or J

GARRETT,	Howard A.	Ella H. Carroll	16 Apr 1881
	J. Wallace	Mary J. Thompson	2 Jan 1879 w
	James E.	Mary H. Byrne	19 Apr 1884
	John	Joana Peirce	27 Aug 1804
	John H.	Alcinda Ward	5 Oct 1869
	John W.	Bertie Thrift	5 Dec 1882 w
	Kate	Miles McCanna	20 Mar 1884
	Lucinda	Hezekiah W. Moulden	10 Sep 1835
	Maggie A.	John G. Burriss	10 Aug 1867
	Serena	John Dawson	19 Feb 1829
	Susannah	John Lizear	12 Oct 1811
	Thomas	Elizabeth Fee	1 Feb 1799
	Thomas Jr.	Kitty Ann Malin	13 Aug 1835
	William	Eleanor Higgins	7 Oct 1801
	William	Frances Heeter	19 Mar 1840
GARRISON,	Thomas	Josephine Offutt	2 Apr 1896 c
	Wesley	Josephine Brewer	1 May 1885 c
GARTRELL - also see GATRELL			
GARTRELL,	Aaron	Margaret Shaw	21 Sep 1815
	Ann	James W. Higgins	24 Nov 1836
	Anna Maria	Otho Israel	26 Feb 1820
	Benjamin	Mary Gartrell	6 Jan 1804
	Bushrod	Juliet Gaither	17 Jun 1844
	Bushrod	Manelia E. Watkins	1 Jan 1864
	Jane	Frederick Gaither	17 Jan 1800
	Jane S.	Asa Clagett	22 May 1844
	John	Lurecia Beall	26 Feb 1798
	Julian	Henry Leeke	12 Dec 1827
	Mary	Benjamin Gartrell	6 Jan 1804
	Nicholas	Mary Cecilia Cross	30 Mar 1841
	Rachel	Levi Penn	30 Mar 1839
	Samuel	Peggy Dean	3 Jan 1810
	William B.	Arrana Jane Heeter	3 Apr 1834
GARY,	Evrrard	Nola Cloud	22 May 1800
	Polly	Zephaniah Lezure	10 Jan 1808
GASAWAY - also see GASSAWAY			
GASAWAY,	Ann	Joseph Hawse	2 Mar 1803
GASKINS,	Nellie G.	Benj A. Nicholson	14 Nov 1892 w
GASSAWAY - also see GASAWAY			
GASSAWAY,	Alexander A.	Elizabeth F. Miller	23 Jan 1882
	Amelia	John Thomas "ye third"	5 Sep 1822
	Betsey	William Darnes	14 Mar 1798
	Charles	Martha Holland	25 Feb 1892 c
	Elizabeth	Louis Powell	15 Feb 1898 c
	George	Elizabeth Porter	15 Apr 1817
	James	Anne Thornton	1 Aug 1872
	Jane A.	Alexander Peter	4 Nov 1857
	John	Eliza Dorsey	22 Aug 1820
	John H.	Helen Muncaster	7 Oct 1895 w
	Laura	George G. Bradley	17 Aug 1863
	Lavinia	George Peter	13 Oct 1852
	Lewis	Mary Offutt	4 Nov 1875 c
	Mary	Thomas Gibbons, Jr.	2 Jan 1818
	Mary A.	Alexander C. H. Darne	20 Oct 1846
	Mary F.	Joseph Reading	8 Dec 1897 w
	Sarah	Samuel Dawson	5 Feb 1812

GASSAWAY, Sarah C.	Walter P. Griggs	26 Nov 1894	w
GATES, Alice	Henry Clay Mullican	28 Nov 1875	
Amelia	John Gates	10 Jan 1876	
Bertha	Robert A. Linkins	30 Apr 1885	w
Charles W.	Mary Jane Walker	23 Nov 1865	
Elizabeth J.	John W. Burriss	28 Dec 1868	
Ella	William Kisner	9 Sep 1880	w
Florence M.	George W. Schellinger	13 Aug 1895	w
Frank	Agnes Croasdale	17 Dec 1887	w
G. E.	Sarah V. Robinson	9 Oct 1878	
George William	Mary M. Linton	10 Feb 1897	w
James Thomas	Mary Frances Lindsay	14 Mar 1881	
John	Amelia Gates	10 Jan 1876	
John H.	Frances Risley	1 Jan 1896	w
Margaret A.	Thomas J. Kisner	6 Feb 1866	
Mary E.	James J. Johnson	11 May 1897	w
Richard	Sarah Keisner	26 Oct 1816	
Sarah C.	William E. Allen	19 Aug 1890	w
Sarah E.	George W. Knight	11 Sep 1889	w
Thomas E.	Maggie E. Mead	7 Aug 1883	
GATEWOOD, Bertha V.	Charles F. Gill	5 Feb 1890	w
GATRELL - also see GARTRELL			
GATRELL, Richard	Anne Bowman	17 Feb 1802	
GATTON, Alethea	John Wallace	25 Sep 1810	
Anna	Edward Sanders	16 Apr 1801	
Aquila	Mary Owen	20 Dec 1804	
Benjamin	Susanah Tucker	16 Aug 1800	
Charlotte	James Reid	28 Nov 1809	
Edward W.	Rebeccah F. Harding	8 Jan 1810	
Helen	John Burgess Magruder	17 Oct 1831	
Helen	Greenbury M. Watkins	13 Jun 1842	
Kitty Ann	Greenbury M. Watkins	6 Oct 1831	
Kitty Ann	Julius A. Mounts	12 Mar 1833	
Margaret	Solomon Holland	23 Jan 1800	
Matilda	Solomon Holland	23 Mar 1815	
Samuel	Mary Jarboe	29 May 1799	
Sarah	William West	8 Feb 1831	
Thomas	Ruth Ray	22 Jan 1799	
Thomas	Essay Offutt	24 Jan 1803	
Thomas	Eleanor Meek	13 Dec 1808	
Zachariah Jr.*	Gulielma Maria Waters	14 Jan 1806	
GAUER. Adolph	Joanna Posteher	25 Apr 1863	
GEEN, Eliza	Charles A. Howard	22 Nov 1888	c
GEIGER, Washington	Lizzie Lowe	25 Mar 1890	w
GENTLE, William	Mary Thompson	6 Jan 1806	
GENTNER, Frederick C.	Louise H. Bentley	14 May 1888	w
GENUS - also see JENUS			
GENUS, Ambrose	Mary Hamilton	17 Jul 1869	
Charlotte	Frank Dorsey	9 Sep 1884	c
Charlotte	George Martin	7 Sep 1895	c
Nathaniel	Alice Thompson	25 Dec 1877	c
GEORGE, Benjamin F.	Clare B. Coffey	4 Jun 1888	w
Enoch	Mary Smith	11 Jan 1802	
John	Anna Cross	9 Feb 1824	

* His first name and her middle name from earlier reading

```
GERARD - also see GIRARD
GERARD, Estella              William C. Taylor          27 Oct 1896 w
GERHARDT, Henry              Frances E. Osmond          23 Dec 1896 w
GERHEART, Henry              Martha Bennett             14 Nov 1825
GERMAN, Mary Ann             Jacob Wildman              30 Jul 1828
GESFORD, Laura               Charles S. Barnett         31 Jul 1888 w
GETTINGER, Milton H.         Mollie Wells               24 Jun 1887 w
GETTINGS - also see GITTINGS, GIDDINGS
GETTINGS, Alice              Christopher Kisner          2 Jan 1883 w
          Emma               Madison Washington         10 Jul 1875
          Juletta            Gassaway Sellman           14 Jul 1836
          Matilda            Thomas Culver              26 Jun 1852
          Sarah              Jesse Hayden               29 May 1804
          Sarah B.           William A. Scott            5 Dec 1829
GETTY, George G.             Louise S. Burr              3 Jun 1895 w
       John                  Eleanor Carey              14 Apr 1801
GETZENDANER, Iarada A.       William Cromwell            3 Apr 1837
GETZENDANNER, Adam           Mary Dowden                 6 Feb 1810
              Addie E.       Roderick A. Barrick        10 May 1881
              Cecilia        John Candler               13 Dec 1843
              Ellen
              Christy        Alfred Spates              20 Jul 1843
              Amanda
              Daniel J.      Mary V. Schaeffer          16 Nov 1891 w
              Edward         Verlinda C. Young          22 Oct 1872
              Elizabeth      Nathan Housar               5 Nov 1807
              F. M.          Sarah E. Young             12 Mar 1873
              Joseph T.      Anna M. Trail              14 Oct 1848
              Maria S.       John L. McCulloh           24 May 1842
              Maud E.        Charles C. Waters          24 Jan 1888 w
GEW - also see GUE
GEW, George H.               Sarah E. Bowman            11 Dec 1838
     Joseph                  Elizabeth Bowman           26 Aug 1830
GHEEN, Benedict W.           Aileen M. Bridger           6 Jul 1897 w
GIBBINS, John                Eleanor Warfield            9 Jan 1804
         Sarah - see Sarah Gittins
GIBBONS, Edward Patrick      Mary E. O'Shea              * Apr 1884
         Nellie              Hezekiah Busy               2 Jun 1886 c
         Thomas Jr.          Mary Gassaway               2 Jan 1818
         Thomas G.           Mary Riley                 28 Oct 1820
GIBBS, Eliza                 Elias Thornton             26 Mar 1888 c
       Fanny L.              Benjamin C. King            8 Jan 1868
       George                Harriet A. Bowman          26 Feb 1869
       Harry                 Carrie Farmer              18 Dec 1894 w
       John H.               Sarah A. Tomes             13 Oct 1880 c
       Lloyd N.              Sallie Jackson              3 Jul 1879
       Nancy                 Burgess Powell             19 Jun 1888 c
       Nettie                Charles F. Bissett         23 Sep 1897 w
       Samuel                Ellen Dorsey                6 Sep 1873
       Samuel Jr.            Florence Green              8 Aug 1895 c
       William               Bettie Turner              13 Dec 1879 c
GIBSON, Campbell F.          Eva W. Woodward            15 Jul 1889 w
        Fannie               William H. Nicholson       17 Jul 1894 w


* No day given; between 15 and 19
```

GIBSON, George	Sydney Ann Elisabeth Riggs	30 Jul 1875	
George W.	Annie V. Hintin	22 Jan 1884	
John	Mary L. Murphy	1 Jun 1859	
John C.	Catharine Woodward	1 Mar 1889	c
John R.	Alice A. Collins	28 Sep 1891	w
John W.	Ann Eliza Peerce	22 Dec 1880	w
Lewis	Lucy Holmes	13 Sep 1881	c
Luther W.	Lucy B. Hughes	3 Sep 1888	w
Rufus	Alice V. Williams	2 Mar 1882	
Thomas A.	Carrie C. Ancarrow	25 Mar 1898	w
Vernona	William E. Lewis	5 Apr 1887	w
William E.	Ida M. Windsor	5 Nov 1879	w
GIDDINGS - also see GETTINGS, GITTINGS			
GIDDINGS, Amanda	Jesse Stewart	18 Dec 1876	
James H.	Elizabeth Greyer	28 Oct 1874	
John	Casandra Weems	11 Jun 1867	
GIFFINS, Martha	Festus M. Thompson	8 Dec 1886	w
GILBERT, Jane	Charles Black	28 Dec 1892	c
John L.	Elizabeth G. House	20 Oct 1850	
Nellie	Charles Taylor	11 Mar 1872	
Solomon	Jane A. Dempal	13 Oct 1883	c
GILCHRIST, Bernard	Eliza Lynch	24 Oct 1868	
GILL, Charles F.	Bertha V. Gatewood	5 Feb 1890	w
James P.	Anna M. Rainey	10 Nov 1869	
John C.	Bridget C. Drescher	12 Aug 1884	
Shadrack	Mary Sullivan	4 Apr 1831	
GILLILAND, Kittie H.	Abraham R. Wingate	12 Sep 1885	
GILLIS - also see GILLISS			
GILLIS, Marianne A. B.	Charles L. Hammond	7 Jun 1841	
GILLISPIE, Simon	Rachel Beall	13 Aug 1817	
GILLISS - also see GILLIS			
GILLISS, John S.	Harriet L. Ricketts	27 May 1873	
Joseph E.	Emma M. Clagett	19 Nov 1895	w
GILPIN, Anna	Samuel Willson	30 Dec 1856	
Elizabeth F.	Nathaniel B. Hogg, Jr.	29 May 1888	w
Ella	John E. Wilson	18 Oct 1865	
George E.	Elizabeth J. Adamson	5 Jul 1870	
Hannah Louisa	Edward Painter	30 Aug 1834	
Lydia S.	Edward Thomas	15 Apr 1833	
Mary	Noble Hurdle	16 Jul 1803	
Mary C.	Noah *. Willson	2 Nov 1838	
GINGELL - also see GINGLE, JINGLE, GINGLES			
GINGELL, Amelia J.	Robert C. Lester	5 Nov 1872	
Annie	Charles Lochte	4 Oct 1875	
Elizabeth I.	Robert C. Lester	24 Jun 1879	w
Frances	Richard Grissam	26 Dec 1862	
Isabel	Morris Fitzgerald	23 Jan 1888	w
John H.	Mary E. Darcey	18 Dec 1883	
Magdalene V.	John H. Hilton	25 Oct 1888	w
Mary A.	George R. Case	23 Feb 1881	
Rebecca	John W. Parsley	8 Jun 1872	
William E.	Annie Harding	21 Jul 1886	w
GINGLE, James	Mary J. Lowe	4 Feb 1861	

* Initial S or L

GINGLE, William T.	Elizabeth Parkins	16 Jan 1865	
GINGLES, James O.	Kate R. Ward	28 Nov 1870	
GIRARD - also see GERARD			
GIRARD, Mary E.	Richard H. Benson	30 Aug 1888	w
GITTINS, Sarah*	Jacob Hull	8 Nov 1800	
GITTINGS - also see GETTINGS, GIDDINGS, GITTINS			
GITTINGS, Ann Maria	Josephus Gittings	19 Nov 1856	
Annie	James R. Stewart	10 May 1888	c
Berry	Rachael Scott	25 Mar 1820	
Columbus	Margaret E. Grimes	21 Jul 1881	
Dominick	Elizabeth McDonald	26 Dec 1826	
Elizabeth	James A. Waters	11 Jan 1866	
Francis	Mary Ann Beall	4 Jul 1859	
Francis Osburn	Priscilla Kisner	16 Jan 1826	
George W.	Eleanor Walker	19 Dec 1833	
George W.	Ann Maria Magruder	** Oct 1867	
Hamilton	Jane Rabbitt	17 Oct 1854	
Hanson	Eleanora Barnes	26 Dec 1883	c
Henson	Anna Thomas	6 May 1897	c
James F.	Frances S. Bean	5 Jan 1882	
Jemima M.	Richard A. Harding	16 Oct 1828	
John H.	Mary A. C. Trucks	17 Aug 1878	
Joseph	Tabatha Beans	11 Feb 1809	
Joseph	Hallie Johnson	26 Dec 1895	c
Josephus	Ann Maria Gittings	19 Nov 1856	
Julia A.	William W. Thompson	20 Mar 1838	
Maggie	Walter Powell	22 Sep 1896	c
Mary Ann	Richard A. Clements	15 Aug 1826	
Mary Ann	Alfred Walker	23 Mar 1835	
Mary E.	Samuel F. Thompson	5 Dec 1876	
Matilda	Walter R. Case	25 Feb 1840	
Richard ***	Juliet Ann Scott	21 Apr 1825	
Serena S.	Silas Browning	4 Feb 1858	
Thomas	Christiann Perry	2 Apr 1806	
Virginia S.	William H. Hobbs	23 Nov 1885	w
William H.	Jane M. Murry	24 Mar 1798	
William H.	Elizabeth Shaw	12 Apr 1854	
GIVENS, Huldah F.	Edward T. Martin	21 Feb 1889	c
GIVLER, Myra	Charles C. Beveridge	10 Jan 1895	w
GLADMAN, Burgess K.	Eliza E. Duley	8 May 1858	
Elizabeth	Henry Nolte	30 Oct 1894	w
George C.	Kitty Ann Mansfield	14 May 1888	w
Neville (female)	George L. Dowden	26 Apr 1892	w
GLADMON, William A.	Nellie C. Lynch	23 Sep 1895	w
GLASCOTT, Bertha C.	Frederick A. Bickford	2 Aug 1895	w
GLAZE, Basil T.	Mary E. Lewis	17 Feb 1875	
Elizabeth	John G. Duvall	29 May 1827	
Hamilton	Clara B. Spates	14 Dec 1875	
Martha W.	Eburn Bird	9 Jan 1858	
William M.	Sarah E. Baker	5 May 1891	w
GLEESON, Agnes	George Robert Bowman	26 Sep 1885	w
GLISSAN, Elizabeth	John Smith	27 Nov 1827	

* Written over; could be Gibbons
** Cannot read day; either 11 or 12
*** Initial written over

GLISSAN, Harriet M.	Warner Selman	23 Feb 1825	
GLISSEN, Ellen	John Cooley	4 Feb 1834	
GLOUD, George H.	Elizabeth Boyd	27 Dec 1799	
GLOVER, Agnes C.	Levi O. Boose	5 Jan 1876	
William	Juliana J. Cashell	2 Sep 1869	
GLOYD, Ann R.	Ambrose L. Crown	26 Jan 1858	
Eden	Elizabeth Thrift	23 Apr 1835	
Elizabeth	Hezekiah Vermilian	21 Dec 1799	
Ellen Jane	Hezekiah W. Veirs	5 Jun 1847	
Eveline Matilda	James E. Leaman	7 Feb 1870	
Harriet	Allen Selby	14 Aug 1841	
Jacob A.	Mary E. Clements	10 Aug 1857	
Jacob A.	Ann Eliza Clements	4 Sep 1876	
Jane	Frederick Bowman	3 May 1823	
Jane	John G. Duvall	30 Dec 1826	
Jonathan	Kitty Limeberry	10 May 1799	
Mary A.	Joseph S. Conway	31 May 1893	w
Mary E.	Richard P. Spates	12 Feb 1872	
Rebecca Jane	John S. Leaman	3 Oct 1864	
Rose May	Charles E. Snyder	22 Nov 1887	w
Samuel	Rebecca Ann Swamley	28 Apr 1827	
William Thomas	Mrs. Elizabeth Susan Peddicord	9 Dec 1869	
GODFREY, Anne	Charles Hand	27 Dec 1800	
GODMAN, Edward*	Sarah Douglass	17 Dec 1799	
Samuel	Julia Strong	27 Dec 1866	
Samuel	Hannah Jackson	19 Oct 1874	
GODY, Walter	Charlott R. Thomas	8 Oct 1818	
GOEGLER - also see GAEGLER			
GOEGLER, Mary	Frank Hehlein	3 Sep 1868	
GOLDEN - also see GOLDING, GOULDING			
GOLDEN, Daniel	Maryann Duvall**	10 May 1819	
Frederick	Prissilla Austin	29 Nov 1810	
Henrietta	John W. Wilson	23 Mar 1869	
Margarett	Elias McDaniel	19 Nov 1800	
Sary	Nicholas Haney	13 Sep 1803	
GOLDING - also see GOLDEN			
GOLDING, Daniel	Elizabeth Harriss	12 Apr 1808	
John	Mary Ann Tuttle	30 Dec 1809	
Kitty	Isaac Shafer	27 Dec 1813	
Martha	Marshal Zep	15 May 1878	w
William	Presha Allison	9 Mar 1809	
William	Keziah Perry	12 Mar 1838	
GOLDSBOROUGH, Matilda Chase	Thomas Owen	30 Oct 1832	
GOOD, Edna C. E.	Nicholas C. Boroughs	12 Sep 1889	w
GOODE, George	Mary M. Kirby	15 Sep 1886	w
GOODEN, Samuel W.	Mary E. Dorsey	17 Apr 1872	
GOODWIN, James H.	Catharine Tree	20 Mar 1871	
GOODZEBATH, Mary	John Shaw	25 Feb 1801	
GORDON, Martha A.	John C. Cauliflower	16 Feb 1848	
Sarah	Stephen Snowden	20 Feb 1872	
Sarah Ann	William H. Dailey	13 Dec 1880	

* Names taken from earlier reading
** D all that is there; remainder from earlier reading

GORIE, John	Sarah B. Kinsey	22 Dec 1838
GORRELL, Benjamin H.	Sarah V. Hendron	11 Sep 1866
GORSUCH, Clinton B.	Daisy M. Mason	12 Nov 1894 w
GOTERT, Barbara	Conrad Heater	24 Dec 1798
GOTT, Ann Virginia	Benjamin J. Jones	6 Jan 1869
Benjamin C.	Susan Ellen Darby	17 Dec 1849
Benjamin C.	Mariel R. Cissel	13 May 1858
Benjamin N.	Anna M. Scholl	18 Apr 1883
Dora S.	John C. Carr	12 Apr 1890 w
Edward C.	Rosetta Bouic	18 May 1832
Edward C.	Mary E. Higgins	17 Nov 1859
Eleanor	James Allnutt	12 Sep 1801
Eleanor S.	John A. Chiswell	25 Oct 1876
Elizabeth	Thomas Alnutt	27 Jan 1801
George R.	Mary R. Brewer	25 Nov 1878 w
John S.	Florence Hays	31 Jan 1874
Laura R.	Thomas H. White	26 Jan 1892 w
Mary Amo	Stephen Beard	31 Jan 1879 w
Mary C.	Joseph C. White	2 Dec 1824
Mary E.	Thomas H. White	12 Dec 1855
Nathan E.	Chloe A. Warfield	2 Apr 1897 w
Richard Jr.	Mary E. Trundle	11 Nov 1833
Richard T.	Alice Poole	11 Nov 1873
Sallie E.	A. Thomas Davis	23 May 1871
Sarah E.	Elijah V. White	8 Dec 1857
Susan	Benjamin White of Benjamin	2 Dec 1831
Thomas N.	Eleanor W. Chiswell	25 Sep 1843
GOTWALD, Luther M.	Loraine L. Pyle	* Apr 1890 w
GOULD, Harriet E.	Nathan B. Clarke	7 Aug 1878 w
GOULDING - also see GOLDEN		
GOULDING, Samuel	Dolly Haney	4 Sep 1804
GOVER, Jacob F.	Ella L. Milbrook	31 Jan 1896 w
GOZLER - also see GUSZLER, GUZLER		
GOZLER, Margaret D.	John Mim--	19 Apr 1825
GRADY, Emma	William Henry Alder	26 Jul 1869
Florenc Mae	Rignald W. Beall	21 Jun 1895 w
Hiram	Martha R. Magruder	20 May 1872
Hiram	Harriet B. Gandy	13 Jan 1887 w
James	Mary Jane Leizear	18 Jun 1872
Patrick - see Patrick G. O'Grady		
William H.	Catharine English	7 Jun 1866
GRAEVES - also see GRAVES, GREAVES		
GRAEVES, Alfred G.	Effie A. Weller	27 Dec 1877 w
Charles B.	Mary A. Fiddler	30 Oct 1876
Charles B.	Lillie Fidler	26 Sep 1883
Clara T.	Frank X. Ertter	24 Apr 1886 w
Lewis B. F.	Rosa Fidler	22 Apr 1884
Louis M.	Maggie J. Bean	18 Aug 1876
GRAF, Caroline D.	George H. Culver	6 Dec 1880
GRAFF, Anna J.	Charles Cornelison	4 Mar 1865
Emily C.	David G. Lefever	12 Feb 1874
James W.	Lillie E. Trundle	30 May 1882
James W.	Caroline B. Musser	18 Dec 1893 w

* Cannot read day; before 9

Name	Spouse	Date	
GRAFF, Jessie L.	John C. Schooley	13 Oct 1891	w
Johnetta M.	George W. Gaither	14 Dec 1886	w
Mary C.	Gustavous Ewell	27 Feb 1838	
Melinda P.	Charles L. Lefevre	23 Dec 1880	
Robert T.	Sarah C. Mezger	2 Aug 1850	
GRAHAM, Bridgett	Stanislaus *. Knott	28 Sep 1850	
Isaac	Kitty Peters	19 May 1877	c
John E.	Grace H. Green	22 Jul 1880	
Maggie C.	George W. Riggs	6 Feb 1884	
Major	Florence Peters	3 May 1883	c
Margaret	Simon Johnson	3 Jun 1875	
Rachael	William Hinton	7 Dec 1863	
Sarah	Elisha Williams, Jr.	17 Nov 1812	
GRAINGER - also see GRANGER			
GRAINGER, Matilda	William Harriss	27 Dec 1809	
GRAMMER, Gotlieb C.	Matilda A. Wilms	18 Mar 1825	
GRAND, Rickey (female)	Charles L. Rice	** Jul 1882	
GRANDISON, Charles	Harriet Coleman	24 Jul 1889	w
Charlotte	Samuel Howard	13 Mar 1866	
George	Lizzie Lucas	11 Jun 1892	c
Louisa	George L. Willis	11 Jun 1892	c
GRANGER - also see GRAINGER			
GRANGER, Ann Maria	Thomas Levin Offutt	18 Apr 1870	
Anne	Madison F. Harris	1 May 1827	
Elizabeth	Robert Fields	14 Mar 1818	
Jetson	Mary R. Braddock	13 Apr 1830	
Mahela G.	Daniel Grantt	25 Jul 1822	
William	Ruth Lee	8 Aug 1839	
William	Ann M. Trundle	22 Nov 1852	
GRANSON, Eliza	William H. Dorsey	12 Feb 1890	c
GRANT - also see GRANTT			
GRANT, Hollis	Evaline Johnson	4 Oct 1898	c
Mary A.	Aloysius W. Wase	21 Jan 1853	
Rachel Ann	William E. Chambers	11 Jun 1872	
GRANTFORD, Elizabeth	William Stewart	19 Jan 1803	
GRANTT - also see GRANT			
GRANTT, Catharine	Nathan Shaw	17 Jan 1810	
Daniel	Mahela Granger	25 Jul 1822	
Elizabeth	John Doran	11 Apr 1799	
Elizabeth	James Milne	3 Aug 1835	
James	Elizabeth Madden	11 May 1809	
John	Ally Burton	6 Apr 1801	
John	Elizabeth Cooley	6 Jan 1825	
Mahala	John Fields	7 Apr 1829	
William H.	Sarah Tucker	13 May 1800	
GRAVES - also see GRAEVES			
GRAVES, Anna L.	John W. Keen	6 Jan 1871	
Benjamin	Mary Sibley	22 Dec 1800	
C. I. (male)	F. M. Kuhl	13 Jul 1878	w
GRAY - also see GREY			
GRAY, Abisha	Eleanor Miller	29 Apr 1805	
Alinda	Alfred Oden	5 Apr 1822	
Allen	Sarah Lewis	20 Dec 1892	c

* Initial L or S
** Cannot read day; between 10 and 20

GRAY, Amanda E.	Isaiah Coar	30 Aug 1871	
Ann	Henry Peters	14 Oct 1867	
Cenah	James Crawford	1 Feb 1812	
Clark H.	Sarah E. Peirce	18 Sep 1894	w
Eleanor	John M. Cox	17 Dec 1798	
Eleanor	Walter Stewart	9 Jan 1809	
Eliza A.	Albert W. Allen	1 Dec 1877	w
Elizabeth E.	William J. Bright	24 Mar 1842	
Emily C.	Cornelius M. Fry	26 Jan 1898	w
Ettie Jane	Thomas Snowden	5 Jan 1886	c
Francis	Sarah E. Ponder	10 Nov 1845	
George	Mary Welling	29 Jan 1820	
George W.	Mary Ann Morgan	22 Oct 1834	
George W.	Lilian A. Thompson	31 Mar 1897	w
James W.	Mollie Fredericks	4 Aug 1891	c
James W.	Elizabeth Mayhew	28 Aug 1895	w
John	Nancy Wivel	12 Aug 1868	
John H.	Annie L. Manning	14 Jan 1896	c
John Thomas	Elizabeth Ricketts	20 Apr 1846	
John W.	Anna S. Moxley	14 Nov 1871	
John Wesley	Annie Woodward	19 Jan 1870	
Julia Ann	Truman Winchell	11 Oct 1859	
Lizzie	Greenbury Jackson	6 Apr 1876	
Lloyd	Elizabeth Burdett	23 Oct 1832	
Martha A.	Alexander Sullivan	5 Jul 1870	
Mary A.	Joseph F. Hawkins	10 Jan 1889	c
Mary Agnes	Thomas H. Burriss	8 Feb 1883	w
Mary E.	Walter H. Henson	22 Oct 1896	c
Matilda	Thomas Kelly	16 Apr 1860	
Nettie	John W. Jones	6 Oct 1890	c
Nicholas	Mary Hean	4 Dec 1799	
Obedia	Mary Ann Beedly	1 Mar 1819	
Robert L.	Anna E. Frazier	18 Feb 1893	c
Sallie	Barton Trail	2 Jan 1872	
Samuel T.	Laura V. Offutt	24 Apr 1878	w
Sarah L.	George N. Beavers	18 Jul 1867	
Singleton H.	Frances E. Magruder	26 Dec 1895	c
Thomas	Eliza Clements	29 Oct 1890	c
Verlinda	Basil Burress	31 Dec 1832	
William	Elizabeth Been	20 Jul 1811	
William	Elizabeth Ann Stewart	6 Mar 1839	
William A.	Milinda Burris	22 Jun 1852	
William Henry	Leanna Benna	30 Dec 1897	c
William T.	Rosa V. Bowman	18 Nov 1890	w
Willis H.	Mary Lizzie Cooper	12 Jul 1884	c
GREAVES - also see GRAEVES, GRAVES			
GREAVES, James B.	Annie Israel	3 Jun 1892	w
GREEN, Albert	Emily Johnson	2 Jan 1879	c
Alethia	Patrick Dorsey	16 Feb 1881	c
Alice L.	Cornelius Davis	30 May 1884	c
Ammon	Sarah Lazenby	26 Jun 1828	
Angie	Edmund L. Amiss	28 Jan 1879	
Anna	Levin Howse	14 Jan 1812	
Anne	John Morris	19 Dec 1799	
Annie E.	Thomas E. Benson	21 Jan 1871	
Annie M.	Jesse D. Brown	27 Nov 1888	w

GREEN,	Benedict	Susan Sibley	5 Aug 1819
	Carrie	William Brewer	20 Jul 1892 c
	Cassandra	Benjamin Logan	27 Apr 1868
	Eliza	James R. Howes	22 Mar 1878
	Elizabeth	Charles Griffith	26 May 1799
	Elizabeth	Joseph Caihill	28 Sep 1801
	Elizabeth	John Clark	25 Jan 1802
	Elizabeth	Van Swearingen	21 Mar 1812
	Elizabeth	Francis Fish	20 Dec 1828
	Elizabeth	William Buxton	9 Apr 1839
	Emma M.	Ernest F. Ricks	21 Aug 1888 c
	Florence	Samuel Gibbs, Jr.	8 Aug 1895 c
	G. W.	Sylvia A. Bradley	13 Aug 1874
	George	Jane Howse	26 Apr 1814
	George A.	Carrie Neverson	19 Apr 1884
	Gillmore	Martha Nailor	27 Apr 1868
	Grace H.	John E. Graham	22 Jul 1880
	Harriet	William Devan	25 Nov 1839
	Helen	George Bonifant	22 Mar 1875
	Henry	Bridget E. Tomy	18 Feb 1858
	Henry	Clara W. Johnson	24 Jul 1890 c
	Jacob	Harriett Beall	25 Nov 1822 *
	James F.	Grace Braddock	24 Oct 1888 w
	Jane	George Rhoades	11 Mar 1839
	Jane	John Rix	27 May 1871
	Jane	Jesse Curtis	4 Jan 1872
	Jane	Elias Driver	30 May 1895 c
	Janett	James Buxton	18 Apr 1815
	John	Ida Shipley	1 Feb 1894 c
	John	Mollie Conrad	22 Dec 1897 c
	Joseph	Ellen Taylor	21 Aug 1879 c
	Joseph	Alice Brown	1? Sep 1883 c
	Joseph L.	Kate R. Weaver	3 Dec 1879 w
	Josephine	James Henry Dorsey	10 May 1876
	Laura V.	James M. Woodfield	18 Dec 1896 w
	Leonard	Susan Belmear	11 Feb 1822
	Leonidas R.	M. Addie Stonestreet	21 Apr 1880 w
	Levi	Aggie Mills	23 Mar 1895 c
	Lidella	Albert P. Mavars	4 Mar 1898 w
	Lloyd	Martha Jane Williams	23 Feb 1828
	Lloyd	Hannah Fossett	30 May 1840
	Louisa	William Dorsey	9 Nov 1874
	Lydia	Edmund C. Davis	2 Mar 1881
	Malissa J.	William F. Milburn	18 Feb 1869
	Margaret	Samuel Douglass	19 Nov 1819
	Margaret	Michael Colter	25 May 1830
	Margaret V.	Burl M. Carter	16 Dec 1880 w
	Marrian	Benjamin Fawcett	4 Dec 1848
	Mary E.	James W. Hackett	3 Sep 1890 c
	Mary Jane	William T. Norris	26 Aug 1878 w
	Melchisadec	Ann Rebecca Holt	8 Oct 1845
	Nani F.	William F. Owens	13 Dec 1894 w
	Oliver	Eliza J. Holland	1 Jun 1886 c

* Entry reads "colored and free"

GREEN, Rebecca	William Smallwood Trammell	15 Jan 1806	
Richard	Ann Ray	27 Mar 1802	
Richard	Ruth Darby	23 May 1821	
Ruth	Richard Young	28 Feb 1844	
Sukey	Joshua Chilton	2 Feb 1829	
Susan	James Williams	27 Nov 1886	c
Susanna	George W. Swailes	20 Feb 1895	c
Susannah	Charles Howard	20 May 1886	c
Susie	Moses Lewis	23 Jun 1894	c
Thomas W.	Jane Shelton	13 Mar 1829	
Vernon A.	Sadie Murray	12 May 1897	c
Wesley J.	Mira Bailer	10 Mar 1870	
William	Meriah Philips	23 Apr 1812	
William	Ann Benson	15 Mar 1821	
William	Maria Johnson	8 Oct 1874	
William E.	Maggie M. Cross	25 Jun 1891	w
William V.	Octavia Israel	9 Sep 1879	w
GREENFIELD, Ann	Perry Janes	21 Mar 1805	
Caroline	Charles H. Talbott	8 Aug 1889	w
Daniel P.	Mary E. Hamilton	23 Nov 1897	w
Delia	John Henson	10 Apr 1873	
George F.	Esther M. Pryor	14 Dec 1897	w
Levi	Gainor M. Linkins	29 May 1873	
Mary	Hardage Lane	26 Nov 1799	
Sarah	Daniel Robertson	10 Feb 1806	
Truman	Caroline Ray	4 Feb 1835	
GREENLEASE, Mary E.	John M. Adrain	6 Sep 1866	
GREENTREE, Eleanor	John Wesley Ward	13 Jan 1807	
Elizabeth	Lloyd Beall	18 Nov 1812	
Margarett	Benjamin Hinton	28 Dec 1811	
Mary	Arthur Leeman*	2 Dec 1818	
GREENWELL, Francis R.	Sarah E. Shoemaker	25 Sep 1849	
GREER, Ida S.	Samuel D. Waters	6 Sep 1898	w
Jessie F.	James F. Magee	25 Apr 1879	w
GREY - also see GRAY			
GREY, Carrie	Thomas L. Marshall	24 Apr 1893	w
GREYER, Elizabeth	James H. Giddings	28 Oct 1874	
GRIFFIN, Caleb	Ellen S. Dwyre	17 Apr 1843	
Samuel M.	Aletha A. Jenkins	17 Jun 1878	
William G.	Eva A. Brackett	19 May 1897	w
GRIFFITH, Alfred	Catharine Scholl	30 Mar 1812	
Amelia D.	Basil Macgill	22 Mar 1819	
Angelina	John D. Berry	5 Jan 1852	
Ann	Charles Holland	16 Feb 1832	
Annie L.	John G. England, Jr.	22 Apr 1867	
Artemus R.	Hattie M. Colliflower	24 Oct 1898	
Berry	Sarah Tilly	23 May 1826	
Betsey G.	Ezra Dorsey	7 Jun 1821	
Caty G.	William Benton	17 Apr 1828	
Charles	Elizabeth Green	26 May 1799	
Charles	Lina Hempstone	26 Oct 1874	
Charles H.	Hester Dorsey	20 Oct 1864	
Cleorah P.	John H. R. Wolfe	15 Oct 1889	w

* Last name not written clearly; could be Luman

GRIFFITH,	David Porter	Carrie Iona Recher	16 Sep 1897 w
	Eleanor	John Chiswell	21 May 1823
	Elisha R.	Martha J. Ober	29 Apr 1829
	Elisha R.	Elizabeth Gaither	8 Oct 1834
	Elizabeth	Thomas Griffith	31 Oct 1825
	Elizabeth	Walter W. Mobley	27 Feb 1894 w
	Ellen C.	William L. Mathews	19 Nov 1888 w
	Emily H.	Harry W. D. Waters	16 Apr 1855
	Emma C.	Walter A. Orme	27 Jul 1858
	Flavilla	John W. Etchison	12 May 1835
	Florence A.	David W. Clark	11 May 1897 w
	Frances I.	Harry G. Spurrier	25 Jan 1898 w
	Francis M.	Elizabeth Dickerson	8 Feb 1859
	Frank	Verda Griffith	8 Nov 1893 w
	Franklin	Kate Riggs	5 Jan 1869
	Georgie	Francis T. Williams	17 Jan 1882
	Henry	Lucretia T. Ober	6 Sep 1824
	Henry Jr.	Matilda Ober	16 Nov 1829
	Henry of Lyde	Eliza V. Magruder	27 May 1823
	Horatio Jr.	Rebecca H. Dorsey	26 Nov 1855
	Howard	Sarah N. Chiswell	11 Jan 1847
	Ida May	Edwin Waters	7 Nov 1881
	Isabel	William R. Griffith	1 May 1872
	James	Catherin Logan	18 Dec 1807
	Jefferson	Cordelia M. Magruder	14 Nov 1827
	Jemima Jacob	Henry Rigges	20 Nov 1804
	John	Martha Gaither	6 Nov 1826
	John H.	Elizer Scherret	30 Sep 1800
	Julia	Humphrey Cissel	26 Oct 1874
	Julia R.	Nathan S. White	8 Dec 1890 w
	Julian	Mary V. Harper	2 May 1870
	Leah	George W. Chiswell	26 Apr 1847
	Lucretia O.	Howard Heald	16 Jun 1854
	Lyde	Julia M. Snouffer	4 Dec 1894 w
	Lydia	Robert Willett	18 Dec 1821
	Maria G.	Israel G. Warfield	5 Jun 1860
	Martha J.	John F. D. Magruder	7 Nov 1865
	Mary	Barton Harriss	9 Feb 1802
	Mary	Richard Stringer	4 Dec 1811
	Mary P.	Elisha Jones	8 Oct 1829
	Mary W.	Bradley Worthington	11 Nov 1889 w
	Michael B.	Lydia Crabb	28 Aug 1823
	Milkah W.	Samuel Riggs of Reuben	2 Dec 1833
	Mordecai	Matilda Dorsey	12 Sep 1810
	Nicholas R.	Mary S. Jones	14 Dec 1850
	Orlando	Cenah Mockbee	6 Jan 1812
	Philemon	Sarah F. Riggs	22 Sep 1817
	Philemon	Harriett Thompson	31 Jan 1824
	Philemon	Sarah G. Crabb	27 Jan 1825
	Philemon	Elizabeth A. Anderson	6 Jun 1857
	Prudence J.	Harry W. D. Waters	23 Jan 1837
	Rebecca	William Davis	12 Feb 1835
	Richard H.	Mary Anne Magruder	25 Feb 1813
	Ruth	Thomas Maynard	12 Feb 1812
	Ruth	Elijah P. Etcheson	23 Nov 1829
	Samuel	Margery Buxton	15 May 1820

GRIFFITH, Sarah C.	Ernest T. Fearon	26 Oct 1897	w
Sarah M.	Zadoc M. Cooke	14 Dec 1895	w
Sarah Ridgely	Amos Brown	20 Jan 1808	
Thomas	Elizabeth Griffith	31 Oct 1825	
Thomas	Elizabeth D. Singleton	2 Mar 1869	
Ulisses	Julia Riggs	18 Apr 1838	
Ulysses Jr.	M. Blanche Linthicum	10 Jun 1868	
Uriah H.	Henrietta E. Wilcoxen	23 Nov 1846	
Uriah W.	Laura E. Waters	12 Nov 1895	w
Verda	Frank Griffith	8 Nov 1893	w
Virginia R.	Leonard C. Herr	8 Dec 1893	w
Walter	Sarah Pigman	12 Apr 1803	
Walter	Mary W. Riggs	22 Nov 1841	
William	Mary Burnsydes	9 Apr 1812	
William R.	Isabel Griffith	1 May 1872	
GRIGG, Jacob	Anne Brogden	22 Dec 1870	
GRIGGS, Annie	Aaron Pumphrey	13 Oct 1879	c
Walter P.	Sarah C. Gassaway	26 Nov 1894	w
GRIME, Catharine	John Wingfield	26 Feb 1868	c
GRIMES - also see GRYMES			
GRIMES, Angelo	Mary V. Carter	6 Aug 1889	w
Ann*	Jacob Marshberger	23 Jul 1812	
Ann Louise	Uriah M. Layton	5 Jan 1867	
Annie	William Shipley	29 Mar 1883	
Basil	Elizabeth Harvey	4 Feb 1818	
Benjamin	Sarah Lowrey	7 Mar 1807	
Benjamin F.	Martha J. Connelly	13 Oct 1863	
Clara	James R. Davis	21 Apr 1877	W
Elizabeth	William Johnson	22 Dec 1840	
Elizabeth M.	John Lisure	23 Feb 1852	
Fannie E.	William C. Duvall	12 Nov 1894	w
Franklin T.	Mary E. Hartley	30 Aug 1888	w
Georganna	Edward S. Emerson	17 Feb 1870	
George W.	Mary Ann Holland	19 Aug 1837	
Hattie L.	John B. Duley	29 Jan 1884	
James A.	Angeline Hackney	28 May 1850	
James O.	Airy E. Henley	2 Nov 1880	
John	Harriet Young	18 Jan 1839	
John	Mary Ellen Mitchell	12 Aug 1841	
John E.	Leanna Thompson	27 Jun 1895	w
Joshua	Elizabeth Doer	11 Nov 1813	
Katie M.	Zacheus Woodfield	29 Dec 1883	
Laura D.	Jacob Young	6 Aug 1874	
Laura V.	Henry C. Lawson	13 Aug 1870	
Margaret	Jacob Eller	31 Jan 1821	
Margaret E.	Columbus Gittings	21 Jul 1881	
Martha J.	Lemuel L. Miles	27 Jun 1871	
Martha V.	Lewis P. Cross	1 Sep 1877	w
Mary	Richard Whiting	22 Feb 1887	w
Mary E.	George W. Warfield	14 Nov 1892	w
Mary L.	Jetson Watkins	24 Nov 1841	
Matilda	Thomas Leizear	11 Oct 1875	
Michael	Elizabeth Sa---	28 Jun 1800	
Minnie Warren	Arthur Benson	27 Sep 1886	w

* Part of last name from earlier reading

GRIMES, Nathan	Ann Walker	9 Jan 1819	
Nettie	William H. Benson	24 Mar 1885	w
Priscilla	Thomas Parsley	23 Oct 1857	
Priscilla	Charles W. Thompson	29 Dec 1864	
Samuel T.	Annie J. Bealle*	19 Mar 1891	w
Simon	Elizabeth Lowe	30 Jul 1844	
William T.	Irene L. Ricketts	15 Oct 1888	w
GRIMMEL, Katherine G.	Charles C. Schiller	24 Aug 1895	w
GRISSAM, Richard	Frances Gingell	26 Dec 1862	
GROMES, Robert E. L.	Marion L. Groomes	9 Mar 1892	w
GROOM, Sarah	Henry Allen	21 Nov 1816	
GROOME, James	Eleanor Fish	11 Sep 1802	
GROOMES - also see GROMES, GROOM, GROOME, GROOMS			
GROOMES, Alice	John Johnson	7 Jun 1875	
Caroline	Hazel B. Cashell	28 Jan 1834	
Elizabeth E.	Thomas F. Cashell, Jr.	13 Feb 1874	
Ellen R.	William L. Cashell	23 Apr 1872	
Franklin	Mary Ann Hobbs	8 Oct 1844	
James	Saray King	4 Feb 1799	
Leanna, Mrs.	F. O. Gaither	1 Jan 1867	
Marion L.	Robert E. L. Gromes	9 Mar 1892	w
Martha Wheatly	John Fletcher Brown	16 Jan 1884	
Mary J.	James W. Allnutt	14 Jun 1870	
Thomas C.	Agnes E. Weer	10 Nov 1879	w
Thomas J.	Caroline House	24 Aug 1882	w
William E.	Delila A. Dwyer	23 Oct 1880	
GROOMS, Henson	Elizabeth Henrietta Cashel	17 Feb 1841	
Marion L.	George W. Meem	16 Jun 1896	w
Mary Ann	James W. Cashell	1 Feb 1841	
Robert	Nancy Ricketts	23 Dec 1824	
GRORUM, John H.	Ella Harper	28 Apr 1894	w
GROSHON, Charlotte C.	Elmer G. Decker	21 Aug 1897	w
GROSS, Ella	Henry C. Barnes	16 Dec 1890	c
James H.	Nannie Alexander	22 Aug 1881	c
Robert	Eliza Coates	8 Dec 1887	c
Rosa E.	Elick A. Minor	8 Jul 1897	c
GROVER, Ida M.	Samuel A. Jackson	31 Dec 1890	w
GRUBLE, Jane V.	Dr. Jacob M. Bosart	18 May 1896	w
GRYMES - also see GRIMES			
GRYMES, Elizabeth H.	George W. Wallace	25 Oct 1887	w
GU, David	Sarah Clarke	7 Dec 1807	
GUE - also see GU, GEW			
GUE, Angeline	William Thomas	11 Dec 1839	
Bessie A.	William G. Burdett	26 Oct 1895	w
Charles C.	Fannie V. Hawes	26 Mar 1895	w
Franklin E.	Ollie B. Burns	21 Jul 1891	w
George W.	Ann Burdett	7 Mar 1836	
Henry	Sarah Burdett	30 Nov 1843	
Henry	Rhoda R. Burdett	21 Dec 1866	
Hezekiah	Mary Perry	16 Nov 1829	
Horace W.	Rachel E. Moxley	24 Feb 1870	
James	Margaret L. Purdum	10 Jan 1837	
James H.	Ruth G. Young	24 Feb 1864	

* Last name could be Bealte

GUE, John J.	Sarah A. Mulligan	10 Sep 1895	w
John William Thomas	Rebecca Mobley	15 Nov 1859	
Joseph	Mary Hey	17 Dec 1798	
Keziah E.	Robert Plummer	3 Oct 1853	
Lorenzo	Carrie S. Burdett	10 Feb 1865	
Luther Thomas	Isabell Johnson	3 Dec 1868	
Maggie B.	Sandy Thomas Mullinix	1 Mar 1893	w
Martha V.	Charles W. Mobley	21 Feb 1889	w
Mary E.	Gassaway Bowman	20 Dec 1860	
Miranda	Zadok Barber	22 May 1835	
Nice	William C. Burdette	1 May 1889	w
Rhoda A.	John H. Poole	31 Aug 1892	w
Ruth	Rezin Bowman	14 Feb 1809	
Samuel	Rachel Mobley	27 Dec 1799	
Sarah A.	Richard H. Bowman	7 Apr 1863	
Sarah E.	Jacob Hager	27 Mar 1869	
Zera A.	James M. Mount	6 Jan 1897	w
GUERRY, Albert C.	Ellen G. Williams	19 Jan 1887	w
GUILLOT, Douglas J.	Lillie M. Payne	8 Apr 1897	w
GUINES, Elizabeth	John Orme	26 Dec 1798	
GUMAER, Elias D.	Sarah Ann Vinson	26 Nov 1841	
GUSZLER - also see GOZLER, GUZLER			
GUSZLER, George	Jane Davis	3 Jun 1800	
GUTH, Mary M.	Edward Brassel	22 Sep 1897	w
GUTRAY, Priscilla	Hezekiah Trail	2 Nov 1809	
GUY, Elizabeth A.	John W. Buckingham	10 Jun 1881	w
GUZLER - also see GOZLER, GUSZLER			
GUZLER, Stephen B. B.	Sarah Conner	5 Jul 1853	
HACKARK, George W.*	Henrietta Thornton	18 Apr 1881	
HACKENYOS, Della M.	James E. Waters	31 Aug 1893	w
HACKETT, Agustus	Louisa Warren	22 Dec 1870	
Belle	Henry Magruder	2 May 1889	c
Caroline	Arch Bishop	3 Dec 1874	
Charles F.	Mary E. Rives	25 Nov 1886	c
Eugene	Idella G. Onley	8 Sep 1892	c
George	Charlotte Bell	15 Oct 1874	
James	Mahala Gaither	2 Jul 1868	
James W.	Mary E. Green	3 Sep 1890	c
Joseph	Sallie Tooney	23 Jul 1890	c
Lottie	Ivorey Chandler	3 Dec 1879	c
Mamie	Alexander Swails	9 Dec 1891	c
Martha	Israel Key	16 Dec 1890	c
Mary F.	John T. Onley	22 Dec 1896	c
Susan	Beverly Thornton	24 Dec 1868	
Susan S.	John Q. A. Hood	17 Jan 1898	c
William H.	Sarah C. Spencer	7 Dec 1870	
HACKEY, Florence	William H. H. Hall	26 Jun 1889	c
HACKNEY, Angeline	James A. Grimes	28 May 1850	
Jane E.	William Low	21 Nov 1832	
Mary E.	William Whelan	31 May 1849	
HAFFNER - also see HEFFNER			
HAFFNER, Catharine	John H. Hughes	18 Dec 1823	
HAFNER, Christian	Teresa Atstere	23 Feb 1860	

* Last letters of last name difficult to read, may be incorrect

HAGAN,	Joseph A.	Katie T. McCarthy	25 Sep 1894 w
	Thomas	Rosannah Shelton	28 May 1811
HAGEN,	Laura T.	Charles O. Olsen	19 Sep 1891 w
HAGER,	Anna	Henry Nichans	21 Dec 1870
	Annie E.	Eldridge W. Beall	23 Dec 1897 w
	Lula H.	Francis E. Davis	15 May 1893 w
	Jacob	Sarah E. Gue	27 Mar 1869
HAHN,	Mary P.	George L. Okstadt	9 Mar 1895 w
HAINES - also see HANES			
HAINES,	Daniel	Rachael Israel	1 Feb 1817
	Henrietta	Charles Black	2 Jul 1881
HAIRRIES - also see HARRIS			
HAIRRIES,	H. E.	Susan Gardner	11 Mar 1882
HALBERT,	Phebe	Jeremiah Myrril	17 Feb 1801
HALE,	Reuben	Sarah Magruder	20 Mar 1893 w
	Zachariah	Sallie Davis	10 Dec 1896 c
HALEY,	John E.	Susie R. Frere	12 Feb 1898 w
HALL,	Adelaide J. A.	Samuel T. Stonestreet	13 Dec 1829
	Ann E.	Franklin Veirs	14 Dec 1846
	Annie E.	Harry L. Watkins	27 Aug 1897 w
	Bazil	Julia Riggs	13 Apr 1868
	Bertha C.	William H. Talbott	1 Sep 1885 w
	Bertha G.	Clarence E. Anderson	8 Jan 1896 w
	Caroline S.	Maj. Matthew Markland	27 May 1851
	Carrie	Howard Harrity	15 May 1890 c
	Charles	Eliza Inkinis	16 Sep 1876
	Charles	Amanda Joppey	5 Jan 1897 c
	Cyrus	Alberta Berryman	15 Apr 1889 c
	Cyrus	Ella West	29 Apr 1895 c
	Eli D.	Addie Slater	28 May 1895 c
	Elisha J.	Mary P. Brooke	3 Oct 1838
	Eleanor M.	George E. Dorsey	16 Sep 1896 w
	Elizabeth	Benjamin Jackson	26 Dec 1894 c
	Emma	George Davis	22 Oct 1885 c
	Florence	Samuel Beander	7 May 1887 c
	George	Mary Jenkins	4 May 1894 c
	George W.	Martha J. Offutt	25 Feb 1897 c
	Harriet	George Newman	30 Aug 1897 c
	Harriett	Elias H. Harding, Jr.	7 Apr 1807
	Harrison S.	Louise Towers	11 Jun 1897 w
	Henrietta	George Prater	24 Apr 1886 c
	Jacob	Florence Carter	29 Oct 1873
	James	Anne A. Moulding	29 Dec 1821
	James Jr.	Mary Snowden	27 Apr 1871
	Jane	James Tucker	22 Nov 1810
	Jane R.	David H. Bouic	12 Sep 1853
	Jesse M.	Emma Higgins	23 Jul 1863
	Jessie A.	Tudor U. Heeter	4 Jul 1892 w
	John	Amanda Magruder	14 Oct 1875
	John	Lizzie Humes	22 Jan 1887 c
	John A.	Annie E. Rice	24 Aug 1881 w
	John T. F.	Mary E. Scott	20 Sep 1893 c
	John W.	Louisa Veirs	30 Sep 1835
	Joseph	Priscilla Powell	24 Dec 1878 c
	Joseph T.	Ellen Hamilton	29 Jan 1868
	Laura F.	John W. Ridgley	10 Jun 1878 w

HALL,	Levin	Ruth E. Jones	29 May 1875
	Lizzie	Wesley Jackson	5 Sep 1889 c
	Louisa	James Smith	19 Oct 1867
	Louisa P.	George F. Nesbitt	21 Nov 1865
	Lucy	William B. Merrick	5 Feb 1856
	Lulu J.	Arthur P. Fletchall	5 Feb 1886 w
	Lydia	William Miles	21 Feb 1803
	Maria	Franklin Davis	23 Apr 1870
	Mary	William H. H. Brown	4 Mar 1875
	Mary	George Hawkins	30 Jun 1879
	Mary C.	Samuel A. Janney	10 Mar 1863
	Mary C. V.	Otho Willson	14 Jun 1825
	Mary D.	Frederick A. Thompson	15 Sep 1876
	Mary E.	Douglass H. Redmon	26 Dec 1883 w
	Mary E.	John Brown	6 Feb 1884 c
	Mary E.	William M. Robertson	3 Nov 1898 c
	Mary R.	Henry C. Burch	19 Apr 1887 w
	Nathan	Eliza Maccubbin	28 Dec 1869
	Nicodemus	Martha Robinson	13 Jun 1896 c
	Polly	Daniel Dugan	6 Oct 1814
	Quinstus C.	Rebecca M. Piles	7 Dec 1859
	Rachel	Hilliary Hebron	27 Dec 1881
	Rachel	Nathan Harper	1 Jul 1897 c
	Richard W.	Catharine Conroy	15 May 1889 w
	Robert W.	Jennie Brent	31 Jan 1895 c
	Sadie R.	Stephen N. C. Williams	4 Sep 1888 w
	Samuel	Mary Hamilton	31 May 1866
	Sarah	Jeremiah Tyler	17 Oct 1889 c
	Sarah B.	George A. Freer	28 Dec 1898 w
	Sarah Frances	Daniel W. Price	30 Dec 1884 w
	Solomon V.	Mary Jane Carey	19 May 1877 w
	Sophia	Frederick Winrod	7 Feb 1801
	Sophia M.	Lloyd F. Harding	27 Nov 1830
	Susannah	Jacob Kirkman	28 Aug 1799
	Thomas	Rebecca Piles	24 May 1824
	Thomas	Elizabeth E. Beall	30 Dec 1848
	Thomas R.	Clara Phillips	5 Jan 1860
	Victoria V.	John H. Wilson	4 Dec 1895 c
	William	Sarah Herring	2 Jan 1810
	William A.	Ida E. Lyles	2 Jun 1890 c
	William G.	Lucy Stevens	13 Aug 1889 w
	William H. H.	Florence Hackey	26 Jun 1889 c
	William J.	Mary J. Lyles	4 Mar 1890 c
	William T.	Margaret E. Powell	11 Mar 1895 c
HALLOWELL,	Eliza M.	Washington B. Chichester	21 Dec 1891 w
HALPIN,	Biddy	Martin Kyne	3 Jul 1865
	James	Margaret Culver	22 Feb 1895 w
HAMBLETON,	Ann	William Dorsey	18 Nov 1868
HAMEL - also see HAMILL			
HAMEL,	Annie	William B. Selby	7 May 1887 w
HAMELTON,	Milly*	Robert Williams	16 Jul 1875
HAMILL - also see HAMEL			
HAMILL,	Henry P.	Sallie C. Jones	26 Jul 1887 w

* This could be Hametton

HAMILTON - also see HAMELTON				
HAMILTON,	Alexander	Mary Lee	2 Nov 1870	
	Alexander	Maria Scott	9 Feb 1893	c
	Annie	Thomas Jenkins	31 Oct 1896	c
	Benjamin F.	Nancy Jane Snyder	13 Jul 1864	
	Daniel H.	Maggie E. Temple	7 Jun 1892	c
	Della	Jesse Lancaster	8 Aug 1889	c
	Dennis	Henny M. Duffen	9 Sep 1867	
	Ellen	Joseph T. Hall	29 Jan 1868	
	Harriett	Alexander Corn	20 May 1865	c
	Henry	Maria Nailor	25 Dec 1884	c
	James	Alice Bettus	5 Dec 1868	
	Julia	Levin Bell	9 Apr 1891	c
	Margaret	Robert Anderson	14 Mar 1879	c
	Mary	Samuel Hall	31 May 1866	
	Mary	Henson Plummer	3 Nov 1877	c
	Mary	Ambrose Genus	17 Jul 1869	
	Mary E.	Robert H. Harden	1 Jan 1855	
	Mary E.	Daniel P. Greenfield	23 Nov 1897	w
	Mary J.	George H. Bean	5 Dec 1893	w
	Rose Anna	Josiah Lindsay	4 Feb 1890	w
	Samuel	Elizabeth Ray	27 Dec 1808	
	William	Annie Nelson	30 May 1879	c
	William E.	Catharine Offutt	11 Apr 1893	w
	William H.	Emily Donnelly	14 Nov 1868	
	William H.	Carrie Coplin	15 Mar 1897	c
	William O.	Edith M. Sandie	13 Jul 1897	w
HAMMAN - also see HAMMOND				
HAMMAN, William		Alcinda Owone	30 Nov 1882	c
HAMMETT, William O.		Eliza S. Tabler	27 Oct 1891	w
HAMMON, Philip Gardner		Sarah Duvall	13 Mar 1807	
HAMMOND - also see HAMMAN, HAMMOND, HAYMOND				
HAMMOND,	Carrie	Philip Thomas	2 Sep 1897	w
	Charles A.	Mary A. Coleage	18 Jun 1879	c
	Charles L.	Marianne A. B. Gillis	7 Jun 1841	
	Daniel W.	Minnie W. Benson	30 Dec 1895	w
	Eleanor	Henry Duvall	10 Jan 1817	
	Elizabeth	William C. Kinsey	16 Dec 1895	w
	Henry	Emma Higgins	20 Dec 1879	c
	James E.	Mary E. Plumer	27 Oct 1887	c
	John	Mary Jane Sullivan	20 May 1846	
	Josephus	Annie V. Robinson	28 Apr 1896	c
	Josephus	Lizzie Suddon	21 Jan 1897	c
	Mary A.	James H. Scott	22 Oct 1887	c
	Mary Ann	William B. Magruder	19 Nov 1831	
	Milly	Henson Johnson	13 Jan 1870	
	Peter	Camisdella Cole	23 Dec 1865	
	Robert	Mamie Spriggs	10 Sep 1896	c
	Robert L.	Mary R. Clagett	21 Sep 1898	c
	Rosa	Lewis Harris	2 Sep 1885	w
	Sarah E.	Charles W. Johnson	20 Sep 1888	c
	William S.	Bessie Price	13 Sep 1895	w
HAMMONTREE, Anna Mary		Charles Hampton Palmer	8 Feb 1842	
HAMMONDTREE, William M.		Catharine Manley	3 Oct 1836	
HANAPHIN, Margaret		Patrick Carver	27 Feb 1871	
HAND, Charles		Anne Godfrey	27 Dec 1800	

HANDLEY, Lily	John F. Schwartzbach	5 Jan 1888 w
HANDLO, Robert	Susannah Riggs	28 Jan 1809
HANDS, Caroline	Jesse Shipley	16 Feb 1824
HANDY, Ellen	--iford Dove	25 Nov 1882 c
James	Julia Riley	18 May 1883 c
John	Louisa Campbell	15 Oct 1883 c
John	Frances Carter	25 Oct 1894 c
HANES - also see HAINES		
HANES, George W.	Gertrude Shied	3 Aug 1866
Thomas *.	Margarett Garner	3 Apr 1827
HANEY - also see HANY, HAYNIE		
HANEY, Arthur C.	Gertie M. Allnutt	17 Oct 1896 w
Charlotte	Isaiah Easton	27 Jul 1825
Dolly	Samuel Goulding	4 Sep 1804
Dolly	Jeffry Easton	20 May 1831
Eliza E.	Henry T. Whalen	31 Dec 1874
Isabella A.	William A. Bogley	21 Oct 1862
John W.	Hattie E. Ward	11 Dec 1872
Mary	Trueman Winchell	22 Jan 1823
Nicholas	Sary Golden	13 Sep 1803
Ritta C.	John H. Bogley	5 Aug 1862
Ruth	Ninian V. W. Easton	12 Sep 1834
Samuel B.	Emma J. Fowler	6 Nov 1873
Walter M.	Katie Morrison	26 Dec 1883 w
HANFMAN, Mary B. T.	Joseph D. Stang	17 Apr 1883
HANFMANN, Elizabeth C.	John A. Kunlo	9 Oct 1893 w
Joseph S. A.	Mary Augusta Hutton	16 Aug 1886 w
Josephine L.	Charles C. Cook	25 Oct 1897 w
HANNAN, John	Catherine Ganley	12 Aug 1868
HANSFORD, Lucy L.	Charles R. Wallace	5 Aug 1888 w
HANSMANN, Augusta S. H. C.	George F. Woodbury	12 Sep 1895 w
HANSON - also see HENSON		
HANSON, Reuben T.	Mahala Dorsey	8 Sep 1874
HANTZ, Elizabeth	Nathan Moore	26 Jan 1801
HANY - also see HANEY		
HANY, Benjamin	Eliza Semmes	29 Jan 1831
Elizabeth	Benjamin Thompson	25 Jan 1799
HANZSCHE, Edith	Walter W. Alleger	22 Oct 1884 w
HARDEN - also see HARDIN, HARDING		
HARDEN, Robert H.	Mary E. Hamilton	1 Jan 1855
Uriah	Caroline V. Boswell	25 Feb 1863
HARDESTY- also see HARDISTY		
HARDESTY, Ann Minerva	Wesley L. Magruder	7 Jan 1845
Jersey	Grafton Copeland	2 Nov 1882
John T.	Kate M. Lindsey	27 Feb 1883
Joseph	Julianne Peters	29 Oct 1870
Lelia A.	John P. Stone	12 Jan 1886 w
Malvine	Alfred Waters	21 Sep 1818
Mary Ann	Joseph Lewis	24 Jul 1816
Rachel	Jesse Harridy	28 Nov 1894 c
Reasen W.	Elizabeth A. Hopkins	23 Nov 1861
Samuel	Martha Maccubbin	27 Mar 1827
William M.	Martha E. Renshaw	19 Oct 1864

* Initial I or J

HARDEY - also see HARDY			
HARDEY, Nancy	James Magaha	20 Sep 1805	
HARDIN, Jackson	Julia Leizear	28 Nov 1884	w
HARDING - also see HARDEN, HARDIN			
HARDING, Alfred	Josephine Johnson	3 Sep 1886	c
Andrew J.	Maggie Myers	21 Nov 1865	
Andrew J.	Clara T. Richardson	26 Feb 1881	
Anna L.	Edgar B. Fouke	21 Mar 1888	w
Annie	William E. Gingell	21 Jul 1886	w
Arthur E.	Susie C. Leizear	23 Dec 1896	w
Benjamin F.	Mary A. Howard	26 Jan 1864	
Caroline Frances	Dade Noland	11 Jan 1816	
Catharine	Elias Moore	13 Dec 1847	
Charles F.	Ruth W. Higgins	14 Oct 1818	
Charles W.	Arabella C. Paxton	14 Nov 1879	
Edna E.	William O'Keefe	28 Sep 1897	w
Edward	Margarett Perry	21 May 1814	
Elias H. Jr.	Harriett Hall	7 Apr 1807	
Ella S.	William H. Mullican	8 Apr 1890	
Georgiana	Edward J. Penn	11 Jan 1870	
Granville J.	Kate Williams	7 Nov 1887	w
Henry	Catharine Ann Robb	2 Jun 1812	
Ida V.	James A. Baker	18 Dec 1897	w
James H.	Ada R. Moore	12 May 1892	w
Jane	Charles J. Maddox	2 Oct 1866	
John ?.	Martha Browning	15 Feb 1826	
John E.	Annie M. King	12 Dec 1894	w
John H.	Rachel Bond	10 Dec 1828	
John *.	Darcus S. Davis	23 May 1810	
John R.	Martha A. Brown	16 Mar 1863	
John S.	Christiana Boswell	8 Sep 1821	
Joseph	Sophia Young	3 Mar 1817	
Joseph	Elizabeth Moore	7 Nov 1846	
Joseph	Elizabeth Thompson	30 Jan 1856	
Joseph	Josephine G. Reynolds	11 Feb 1869	
Josiah, Dr.	Mary V. Valdinar	17 Nov 1846	
Julia	George Windeer	5 Jul 1893	c
Keturah	William H. Hays	30 Sep 1824	
Lizzie A.	Samuel Jeff. Hopkins	10 Jun 1872	
Lloyd F.	Mary Ann Knott	5 Sep 1825	
Lloyd F.	Sophia M. Hall	27 Nov 1830	
Marien S.	William W. Riley	18 May 1881	
Martha M.	Anthony Boyd Pool	26 Dec 1877	w
Mary A.	Robert W. Carter	19 Nov 1839	
Mary Ellen	Josiah Bell	16 Oct 1879	w
Minerva J.	John S. Case	18 Apr 1873	
Nicholas	Anne Belt	28 Aug 1812	
Nicholas	Mary C. Sherer	1 Jun 1893	w
Rebeccah F.	Edward W. Gatton	8 Jan 1810	
Richard	Elizabeth Anne Brown	6 Jan 1824	
Richard A.	Jemima M. Gittings	16 Oct 1828	
Sallie F.	Hiram W. Hopkins	30 May 1872	
Samuel Thomas	Martha R. Poole	8 Feb 1881	
Sarah C.	Ulysses M. Ricketts	22 May 1884	w

* Initial I or J

HARDING, Somerville	Susan Jane Tucker	31 Mar 1869	
Theresa	Alexander Jameison	6 Sep 1844	
William	Lorala Ann Brown	29 May 1840	
William H.	Hannah Cook	25 Oct 1880	c
William H.	Roberta J. Ricketts	26 Jul 1883	
HARDISTY - also see HARDESTY			
HARDISTY, Drusilla	William C. Nichols	15 Aug 1893	w
Margaret H.	Daniel L. Clark	4 Dec 1894	w
HARD?OCK, David	Anne M. Clagett	9 Mar 1829	
HARDT, Charlotte	Robert H. Allen	4 Feb 1851	
HARDY - also see HARDEY			
HARDY, Anne	Joseph Hilliard	25 Oct 1815	
Blanche A.	Clarence B. Thompson	15 Apr 1891	w
Eleanor	William S. Hays	4 Feb 1823	
Henry P.	Philomena Waring	30 Oct 1883	
James	Mahala Williams	14 Aug 1868	
Joanna Lee	Frederick W. Longley	28 Jun 1886	w
Josephus	Amanda Ball	15 Feb 1858	
Ollie L.	David J. Bready	26 Apr 1898	w
HARE, Mary	Abraham Smith	29 Nov 1824	
Jane	William Soaper	14 Sep 1825	
HARGETT, Alfred C.	Mary P. McCullough	27 Dec 1886	w
Anna R.	William E. Perrell	26 Dec 1887	w
Charles	Clara Richter	27 Sep 1887	w
Ida C.	Hama D. Mills	3 Sep 1890	w
HARING - also see HERRING			
HARING, Walter A.	Minnie Warren	12 Sep 1892	w
HARITY - also see HARRITY			
HARITY, Jesse	Mary Warfield	1 Jun 1880	
HARL, Trammell	Elizabeth Willson	10 Oct 1829	
HARMAN, Richard L.	Emma C. Best	25 Jan 1887	w
HARP - also see EARP			
HARP, Rebecca	Willson Lewis	26 Sep 1825	
HARPER, Anne	Lawson Robertson	29 Dec 1881	c
Annie E.	Robert M. Hicks	15 Nov 1869	
Charlott T.	Singleton Murphey	14 Oct 1819	
Clara E.	William F. Price	4 Feb 1896	w
Drusilla	William T. Luckett	5 Aug 1889	c
Edward	Sarah Ann Boswell	15 Apr 1800	
Edward	Elizabeth Boswell	27 Jan 1808	
Elizabeth	Francis Campbell	27 Jan 1810	
Elizabeth	John Winemiller	17 Jul 1824	
Elizabeth	Lloyd Buxton	23 Dec 1826	
Ella	John H. Grorum	28 Apr 1894	w
Ida	Jerry Jackson	24 Jan 1888	c
John	Mary Ann Doud	9 Mar 1829	
Julia	Henry Payne	22 Dec 1892	c
Luther E.	Mollie E. Davis	21 Jun 1892	w
Margarett	Philip Adams	25 Feb 1811	
Mary	Andrew Jackson	17 May 1884	c
Mary Ann	James W. Boswell	17 Oct 1843	
Mary Jane	Tilghman West	2 Feb 1829	
Mary V.	Julian Griffith	2 May 1870	
Michael	Rebecca Wheat	10 Feb 1800	
Nathan	Rachel Hall	1 Jul 1897	c
Rebecca	Lloyd Sparrow	31 Oct 1809	

HARPER,	Rhoda Ann	Joseph Browning	7 Nov 1826
	Richard	Rebecca Mackall	19 Feb 1846
	Sarah	Richard Steene	9 Sep 1807
	Sarah C.	James Only	20 May 1885 c
	Thomas	Mary Alnutt	19 Dec 1801
	Thomas	Mary Mitchell	23 Sep 1824
	Vina	Nathan T. Duffin	19 Feb 1880 c
HARR,	Edgar O.	Nettie E. Williams	13 Aug 1894 w
HARRELL - also see HERRELL			
HARRELL,	Mary E.	Flavius Claggett	24 Sep 1890 c
HARRESS - also see HARRIS			
HARRESS,	Elizabeth	Thomas Danclee	31 Dec 1805
HARRIDAY,	Eliza	Israel Key	30 Mar 1877 c
HARRIDY,	Jesse	Rachel Hardesty	28 Nov 1894 c
HARRIES - also see HARRIS			
HARRIES,	Frederick L.	Ada I. Pumphrey	21 Feb 1895 w
HARRINGTON,	Charles A.	Sarah Pennifield	13 Sep 1865
	George	Anna Crown	3 Oct 1870
HARRIS - also see HARRISS, HARRESS, HARRIES, HAIRRIES			
HARRIS,	Anna A.	Ernest M. Holland	21 Feb 1877 w
	Anne	Benjamin Harwood	16 Dec 1816
	Barton	Elizabeth Dugan	25 Feb 1817
	Charles	Hattie Bond	26 Sep 1883
	Charles	Matilda Prather	4 Aug 1896 c
	Charles R.	Estelle A. Spates	2 Dec 1878
	E. G.	Mary E. Zeigler	7 Nov 1867
	Elizabeth	William Fisher	9 May 1818
	Ephraim G.	Ida J. Zeigler	23 Jan 1877 w
	Fannie	Louis White	23 Dec 1891 c
	Florence V.	Jacob Cowan Trevey	4 May 1868
	John H.	Eliza V. Shaw	11 Mar 1875
	Joseph	Mary Harris	16 Nov 1800
	Lewis	Rosa Hammond	2 Sep 1885 w
	Loreno	William Taylor	21 Jun 1884 c
	Madison F.	Anne Granger	1 May 1827
	Madison F.	Julia Slater	14 Apr 1879
	Mary	Joseph Harris	16 Nov 1800
	Mary	Charles Williams	23 Mar 1874
	Mary Ann	Thomas B. Offutt	10 Feb 1831
	Mary Jane	Richard W. Holland	26 May 1838
	Rebeccah	Samuel Hillard	20 Aug 1810
	Richard E.	Alice E. Dwyer	15 Oct 1858
	Samuel	Emeline Smith	6 Apr 1870 c
	Sarah	James Wade	2 Oct 1817
	Sarah Ann	Henry Brown	29 Mar 1838
	Susan	Albert W. Kelley	28 Sep 1864
	Thomas	Mahala Thompson	13 Feb 1822
	Thomas D.	Citty Ann Rich	24 Jul 1889 w
HARRISON - also see HARRISSON			
HARRISON,	Alice	Arthur Meyers	26 Nov 1879 w
	Anna	Christian Wallick	15 Nov 1814
	Dennis	Lurrena Sparrow	3 Mar 1832
	Elizabeth	Evan Evans	21 Nov 1800
	Elizabeth	Henry Becks	3 Jan 1821
	Elizabeth	James E. N. Smith	20 Feb 1894 w
	Emma C.	William T. Crown	23 Nov 1887 w

HARRISON,	Harriet	Charles Offer	26 Oct 1866
	Henry C.	Mary C. Stone	7 Jan 1882
	James L.	Elizabeth Shorts	16 Oct 1889 w
	Katie V.	William W. Marquett	14 Jan 1893 w
	Loretta	Dennis Tuohey	10 Sep 1881 w
	Lucy A.	Harry Kendell	2 Apr 1877 w
	Michael W.	Bertie E. Leizear	8 Sep 1894 w
	Peggy	Thomas Hawkins	9 Jul 1805
	Rebeckah	Enoch Holland	6 Jan 1826
	Sarah H.	Levi B. Purdom	26 Feb 1818
	Virlinda	Greenbury Willson	29 Jun 1812
HARRISS - also see HARRIS			
HARRISS,	Albert U.	Ellen White	25 Jul 1895 c
	Alexander H.	Eliza E. Fisher	30 Dec 1878
	Amelia Ann	James P. Soper	23 Feb 1846
	Barton	Elizabeth Casey	25 Nov 1799
	Barton	Mary Griffith	9 Feb 1802
	Charles R.	Elizabeth Sidney	23 Dec 1897 c
	Cornelia	John Stewart	10 Jun 1867
	Dandridge	Martha E. Brown	1 Mar 1888 c
	Darcus A.	Addison White	16 Oct 1814
	Eliza	Henry Welch	21 Jun 1815
	Elizabeth	Daniel Golding	12 Apr 1808
	Elizabeth	Enoch Joy	16 Mar 1826
	Elizabeth	William Henry Trail	24 Oct 1839
	Ella	Stephen Young	19 Oct 1892 c
	Ellen	Washington Waters	3 Jan 1895 c
	Fanny	John A. Thompson	11 Mar 1862
	Harriet ?.	Aaron Craycroft	13 Oct 1838
	Henrietta	Benjamin Sharp	30 Nov 1798
	Henry	Georgianna Jones	14 Oct 1885 c
	Henry N.	Maria M. Fisher	6 Apr 1861
	Ida J.	Reverdy Dronenburg	5 Mar 1889 w
	Jane E.	Solomon Dowden	30 Jan 1849
	Jefferson Davis	Ettie Everhart	7 Oct 1885 w
	John	Elizabeth Ricketts	24 Dec 1813
	John	Henrietta Bennett	12 Nov 1825
	John F.	Clara M. Earhart	20 Oct 1886 w
	Joseph M.	Nellie Collins	13 Oct 1896 w
	Margaret V.	Richard Bean	16 May 1861
	Martha	William King	11 Sep 1890 c
	Mary	William H. Selby	5 Feb 1850
	Mary Ann	William W. Mathews	13 Aug 1826
	Mary E.	Theophilus Majors	16 Nov 1880
	Mary J.	Samuel Darby	30 Nov 1848
	Matilda	John W. Mills	30 Mar 1848
	Melinda	Thomas H. Offutt	3 Mar 1831
	Mollie	Thomas H. Stewart	12 Apr 1888 c
	N. T.	Britania C. Norris	8 Jul 1868
	Nathan T.	Cecelia E. Norris	14 Sep 1859
	Nathaniel Franklin	Delphena Fields	8 Oct 1857
	Rebecca A.	John Sellman	21 Feb 1853
	Thomas G.	Eliza Ann Craycroft	25 Oct 1836
	William	Matilda Grainger	27 Dec 1809
	William H.	Lillie Hopkins	2 Jun 1890 c

```
HARRISSON - also see HARRISON
HARRISSON, Catherine      Daniel Rose                 13 Apr 1830
HARRITY - also see HARITY
HARRITY, Annie E.         Charles E. Brown            20 Feb 1895 c
        Howard            Carrie Hall                 15 May 1890 c
HARROD, Bertha            Mitchell Hawkins             8 Feb 1892 c
        Robert            Louisa Johnson              15 Sep 1869
HARRY, Ann                William Ball                24 Dec 1816
       Eliza              John Creamer                22 Aug 1822
       Mary               John Yost                   19 Jul 1826
       Millard C.         Jessie R. Miller            24 Apr 1893 w
       Thomas             Elizabeth Wallace            6 Feb 1810
HART, Annie D.            John E. Luckett             18 Aug 1896 w
      Charles S.          Bell Yaetaman                6 Apr 1886 w
      Louisa              George Ross                 29 May 1893 c
      Priscilla           William Brown               18 Feb 1801
HARTISHELL, William A.    Tempie G. Null              13 Jul 1891 w
HARTLEY, Eleanor          Ezekiel Mobley              20 Dec 1808
         Mary E.          Franklin T. Grimes          30 Aug 1888 w
HARTSHORNE, Charles R.    Ella M. Lansdale            17 Nov 1886 w
HARVELLE - also see HARVILL
HARVELLE, Marie W.        William J. T. Farquhar      24 Feb 1897 w
HARVEY, - also see HARVY, HERVEY
HARVEY, Allin             Ruth Brashers               14 Feb 1803
        Charles           Rebecca King                11 Dec 1798
        Delilah           Snowden Anchors              9 Dec 1805
        Elizabeth         Basil Grimes                 4 Feb 1818
        Henry T.          Clara E. Armstrong           4 Feb 1889 w
        James             Anne Anchors                10 Dec 1808
        James             Elizabeth Rebecca           23 Feb 1870
                            Worrell
        John C.           Josephine Mossburg           2 Mar 1895 w
        Matilda           Artemus Sullivan             8 Apr 1834
        Priscilla         Thomas Lizear               10 Feb 1806
        Rachel A.         Hezekiah Smithson           30 Sep 1852
        Thomas P.         Martha Thomas               14 Oct 1845
        William C.        Sarah E. Brown              22 Oct 1890 w
HARVILL - also see HARVELLE
HARVILL, Daniel           Mary Jane Burris             9 Jul 1866
         Daniel           Margaret A. Pennifield      16 Jul 1874
HARVORD, Leonard          Matilda Jackson             30 Dec 1874
HARVY - also see HARVEY
HARVY, Crecilla           Alexander Beall             12 Dec 1799
HARWOOD, Anne E.          Walter Williams             18 Mar 1825
         Benjamin         Anne Harris                 16 Dec 1816
         Eleanor          James Magruder              23 Nov 1807
         Elizabeth        Walter Jones                13 Jan 1799
         Henry            Mary E. Harwood             11 Nov 1823
         Margarett        Thomas Lyles                26 Sep 1808
         Mary             Alexander Warfield           8 Feb 1807
         Mary Ann         Odle Talbott                26 Nov 1823
         Mary E.          Henry Harwood               11 Nov 1823
         Rebecca          Cardwell Breathill          26 Mar 1810
         Thomas N.        Milly Ann Plummer           27 Oct 1815
         Thomas N.        Emy Plummer                  6 Nov 1839
         William Thomas   Mary A. Butler               1 Nov 1866
```

HASKE, Maggie E.	William E. Coleman	19 May 1892	w
HASLER, Orpha	Ninian Lowe	24 Mar 1829	
HASLIN - also see ASTLIN			
HASLIN, Joseph	Mary Beard	21 Jul 1802	
HATFIELD, Alice	George W. Evely	22 Jun 1875	
HATTON, Benjamin	Jennie Thompson	16 Oct 1889	w
Susie	Joseph H. Lawrence	26 Apr 1897	w
HAUGH, Mary	Samuel B. T. Caldwell	31 Jan 1824	
HAUSLY, Hannah*	Abraham Townsend	10 Dec 1800	
HAVELL, George	Minnie Spreigel	5 Jun 1893	w
HAVENER - also see HAVNER			
HAVENER, Olivia	James A. Adrian	7 Jun 1869	
Elizabeth			
Philip A.	Minnie G. Magaha	20 Mar 1889	w
William H.	Julia E. Fling	1 Dec 1854	
HAVILAND, Marian W.	William R. Tatum	26 Sep 1893	w
HAVNER - also see HAVENER			
HAVNER, Jeremiah	Martha Hoass	26 Dec 1822	
HAWES - also see HOWES			
HAWES, Fannie V.	Charles C. Gue	26 Mar 1895	w
HAWKER, Allen	Melinda Heffner	29 Dec 1835	
Susan	James Brashear	3 May 1826	
HAWKINS, Ary James	William S. Offutt, Jr.	14 Feb 1856	
Basil William	Warnetta Lee	16 Nov 1885	
Benjamin	Attilla Cooley	14 Jan 1829	
Carrie	William H. Plummer	1 Nov 1887	c
Catharine	Nathan Pugh	27 Dec 1886	c
Charles Thomas	Julia Virginia Pope	6 Dec 1881	
Charlotte	Paul Foreman	16 May 1868	
Clara	Clement P. Martin	12 Jul 1890	c
Clinton	Henrietta Henderson	28 Jun 1895	c
Edwin D.	Fannie S. West	18 Dec 1882	
Edwin D.	Chloe E. Marlow	9 Oct 1889	w
Elizabeth	Samuel Magruder	11 Mar 1801	
Elizabeth	John H. Clagett	3 Mar 1812	
Ella M.	Albert Jenkins	20 Dec 1892	c
Ellen M.	Nathaniel Clagett	14 Aug 1847	
Emily A.	George M. Andrews	3 Jun 1889	w
George	Mary Hall	30 Jun 1879	
Gracie Ann	Luther Brown	4 Jan 1893	c
Ida	Charles Cooper	29 Apr 1897	c
James	Arah Claggett	7 Jan 1819	
James	Eliza Rhodes	20 Apr 1881	
James Jr.	Elizabeth A. Warfield	12 Feb 1851	
James H.	Sallie E. Clagett	7 Oct 1868	
James H.	Elizabeth A. Leaman	28 Nov 1892	w
John	Maggie Ricks	9 Oct 1869	
John T.	Ann E. Thompson	11 Nov 1858	
Joseph	Mary Jane Trail	15 Dec 1841	
Joseph C.	Nettie E. Duvall	16 Dec 1885	w
Joseph C.	Maggie L. Watkins	3 Dec 1888	w
Joseph F.	Mary A. Gray	10 Jan 1889	c
Joseph F.	Estella Liles	8 May 1894	c

* Hausley from earlier reading, but "au" not really readable

HAWKINS,	Katie	John Henry Randolph	1 Aug 1881 c
	Laura V.	Richard T. Pyles	2 Feb 1859
	Lizzie	Philip Washington	16 Sep 1897 c
	Louisa	John Brown	18 May 1877 c
	Mary Ellen	Samuel Thrift	10 Dec 1855
	Millie	James Crockett	25 Jan 1897 c
	Mitchell	Bertha Harrod	8 Feb 1892 c
	Mollie E.	Rezin W. Bowman	20 Dec 1872
	Nicholas	Sophia Marshall	30 Mar 1874
	Nicholas	Lydia Jenson	22 Dec 1886 c
	Peter	Elender Williams	8 Mar 1798
	Phebe	Joseph Prather	25 Apr 1867 c
	Randolph S.	Martha J. Bowman	15 Dec 1874
	Richard	Ella King	30 Oct 1890 c
	Ruthy Mary T.	Nathan T. Thompson	7 Nov 1861
	Royal A.	Gertie Lee	24 May 1887 c
	Samuel	Emily Carroll	12 Oct 1896 c
	Sarah E.	George B. Martin	14 Sep 1888 c
	Sarah J.	David H. Thompson	17 Dec 1858
	Thomas	Peggy Harrison	9 Jul 1805
	Thomas	Susan H. Clagett	30 Jan 1849
	William	Belle Macatee	31 Jul 1879
	William B.	Emma Clagett	29 Oct 1884 w
	William H.	Tersy L. C. Jackson	29 Oct 1884 c
HAWSE - also see HOWES			
HAWSE,	Ann	Phineus Stallings	5 Apr 1806
	Joseph	Ann Gasaway	2 Mar 1803
HAYDEN,	Jesse	Sarah Gettings	29 May 1804
HAYES - also see HAYS			
HAYES,	Frank	Minnie Reid	14 May 1894 w
	Leonard I. J.	Mary E. W. White	23 Oct 1888 w
HAYMOND - also see HAMMOND			
HAYMOND,	Daniel	Rachel Rhodes	12 Jun 1821
	George	Mary Galworth	30 Nov 1803
HAYNIE - also see HANEY			
HAYNIE,	John O.	Lula D. Burdett	26 Feb 1883 w
HAYS - also see HAYES			
HAYS,	Abraham S.	Elizabeth E. Tillard	23 Jan 1816
	Clara P.	George V. Davis	16 Nov 1880
	E. P.	M. E. DuFief (female)	18 Sep 1877 w
	Edward	Sarah West	28 Feb 1840
	Elizabeth E.	John A. Trundle	25 Feb 1835
	Ellen L.	William T. Poole	26 Jan 1854
	Florence	John S. Gott	31 Jan 1874
	Georgie C.	Benjamin F. Fisher	21 Feb 1895 c
	Harriet A.	Edward Baker	11 Sep 1874
	Hattie	Allen Marshall	24 Dec 1896 c
	Hattie A.	John W. Davis	15 Jan 1883
	John H. T.	Eleanor M. Jones	22 May 1837
	Leonard	Eliza Poole	24 May 1825
	Martha	Asa Dent	20 Mar 1804
	Martha M.	John T. Nicholls	4 Nov 1839
	Mary	Robert Dent	4 Apr 1801
	Mary K.	William J. Sloan	2 Jul 1866
	Mary T.	Tobias E. Bready	18 Aug 1876
	Mollie M.	John Jones, Jr.	15 Jan 1873

HAYS, Peter	Massey Collegins	23 Jun 1866	
Poulina	Nathan T. Talbott	8 Dec 1857	
Priscilla J.	Reginald Poole	1 Oct 1860	
Samuel S.	Anne Rawlings	28 Oct 1812	
Sarah	Joseph Vermelian	7 Nov 1799	
Sarah	John Candler	19 May 1804	
Thomas L.	Mary T. Pearre	12 May 1846	
Thomas Pitt	Elizabeth Frazier	24 Aug 1805	
William H.	Keturah Harding	30 Sep 1824	
William S.	Eleanor Hardy	4 Feb 1823	
HAZEN, Daniel W.	Mary E. Easton	27 Dec 1876	
James H.	Catharine Easton	18 Jul 1889	w
HAZLE, Jeremiah	Elizabeth Chambers	4 Jan 1808	
HEADLY - also see HEDLEY			
HEADLY, Miles K.	Esther Madeira	9 Jun 1827	
Rebecca	Abraham Dennis	6 Dec 1819	
HEAGY, John M.	Sedonia Pumphrey	12 Jan 1882	w
HEALD, Howard	Lucretia O. Griffith	16 Jun 1854	
HEAN, Mary	Nicholas Gray	4 Dec 1799	
HEARN, Sarah E.	Caleb H. Shreve	15 Nov 1841	
HEATER - also see HEETER			
HEATER, Conrad	Barbara Gotert	24 Dec 1798	
George	Charlotte Porter	21 Dec 1801	
John	Frances Shook	13 Feb 1806	
Kitty	Denton S. Porter	4 Mar 1806	
Mary	Edward Porter	13 Jan 1800	
HEATH, William	Volinder Boswell	30 Jan 1799	
HEATON, James D.	Cecilia M. Stribbling	10 Jan 1842	
HEBBONS, Samuel	Sarah T. Feaster	23 Jul 1871	
HEBBORN, Leonard	Emily Bruce	19 May 1877	c
HEBBUN, Patrick	Milly Coates	25 Dec 1869	
HEBBURN, Henry	Miranda Martin	15 Dec 1865	
Peter Hilleary	Harriet Isabella Jackson	3 Jan 1868	
HEBERON, Mary	Levi Holt	26 Jan 1874	
HEBERN, Elizabeth	Joseph English	31 Mar 1801	
HEBRON - also see HEBBONS, HEBBORN, HEBBUN, HEBBURN, HEBERON, HEBERN, HEPBURN			
HEBRON, Alex	Mary F. Branison	30 Aug 1898	c
Hilleary	Rachel Hall	27 Dec 1881	
Hilleary H.	Harriet A. Davis	10 Jul 1883	
James W.	Ella Douglass	11 Jul 1894	c
John T.	Eliza Taylor	28 Dec 1891	c
Lewis E.	Casey M. McPherson	16 Jul 1895	c
Maria	George Jackson	21 Oct 1893	c
Mary	Charles Dorsey	30 May 1887	c
Mary	William Dyson	20 Nov 1888	c
Nathan T.	Mallie E. Turner	29 Jan 1889	c
Richard	Susie Dwyer	14 May 1891	c
William	Caroline Blakes	27 Dec 1881	
William	Betsy Johnson	18 Apr 1892	c
William P.	Sarah E. Ricks	10 Nov 1887	c
HECKROTE, John S.	Catharine E. Brown	26 Jun 1849	
HEDDINGS, Samuel G.	Jessie J. Holladay	23 Aug 1898	w
HEDGES, Elizabeth - see Elizabeth Hodges			
Samuel	Eleanor McCoy	28 Jan 1799	

HEDLEY - also see HEADLY			
HEDLEY, Mary K.	Thomas Beall	17 Jan 1822	
HEDRICK, George P.	Mary R. Brown	3 Sep 1887	w
HEETER - also see HEATER			
HEETER, Ada Florence	Samuel T. Clagett	22 Dec 1874	
Arrana Jane	William B. Gartrell	3 Apr 1834	
Elbert	Lydia C. Offutt	4 Apr 1832	
Elizabeth M.	Samuel Connell	18 Jan 1847	
Frances	William Garrett	19 Mar 1840	
Frederick	Mary Porter	6 Feb 1811	
John	Martha A. Clagett	13 Dec 1848	
John B.	Alice C. Creamer	21 Nov 1882	w
Martha A.	James Small	18 Nov 1872	
Mary F.	William F. Small	14 Jun 1875	
Susan J.	George H. Clagett	22 May 1893	w
Tudor U.	Jessie A. Hall	4 Jul 1892	w
Vandelia	Henry C. F. Perry	3 Mar 1884	
HEFFNER - also see HAFFNER			
HEFFNER, Charlotte	James M. Windham	5 May 1840	
Daniel Stephen	Annie S. Rhodes	10 Aug 1865	
Delia L.	John R. Jones	20 Nov 1890	w
Drusilla	Leonard Howard	25 Jul 1838	
Emma J.	John William Renshaw	7 Dec 1880	
Jacob	Caroline Ransburgh	29 Nov 1837	
John T.	Martha J. Trundle	4 Apr 1862	
Lydia	Richard Stallins	31 Jan 1831	
Mary	Levin Campbell	11 Feb 1829	
Melinda	Allen Hawker	29 Dec 1835	
Samuel P.	Lucinda Crutchley	11 Dec 1850	
HEFFRON, Stephen	Rebecca J. Jenkins	24 Jan 1870	
HEGGERMAN, Mary	John E. Moroney	20 Jan 1893	w
HEHLEIN, Frank	Mary Goegler	3 Sep 1868	
HEIDER, George D.	Jennie F. Wilson	20 Mar 1878	w
HEIN, Martin F.	Ada L. Trevey	14 Nov 1894	w
HEINBACK, Henry	Sarah A. Moss	26 Oct 1885	w
HEIRONIMUS, R. S. Dean	Martha A. P. Darby	17 Nov 1857	
HEISLER, Annie	Charles Cole	26 Jun 1895	w
Bettie	John Cole	26 Feb 1898	w
John T.	Luberta Ritchie	8 Jan 1879	w
Katie	Charles Eury	3 Aug 1895	w
HEISTLER, Ferdinand	Mary E. Keith	21 Sep 1869	
HELBUSH, John William	Eleanor Sewick*	6 Sep 1800	
HELLEN, Walter	Nancy Johnson	18 Oct 1798	
HELLMUTH, Peter	Margaret Stang	1 Oct 1867	
HEMPSTONE, Ann	David Trundle, Jr.	2 Apr 1834	
Ann V.	John Spinks	1 Feb 1831	
Christian	Mary Dade	18 Dec 1839	
Christy A.	Nathan C. Dickerson	1 Dec 1834	
Eleanor	Elias Spalding	3 Jan 1801	
Eliza	Charles Spencer	3 Jan 1812	
Elizabeth F.	Francis Fish	16 Jan 1834	
Frances N.	William Trundle	30 Sep 1826	
Harriet	William Poole	30 Apr 1819	

* Last name from earlier reading, but part that is there makes this questionable

HEMPSTONE,	Henrietta L.	Frederick Jones	11 May 1872
	Lina	Charles Griffith	26 Oct 1874
	Mary Frances	E. Munroe Johnson	10 Jan 1865
	Susie	Charles W. Watts	19 Jan 1888 w
	Vernon	Ann Elizabeth Poole	11 Oct 1875
	William C.	Rebecca A. E. Sholl	2 Dec 1857
	William H.	Anne V. Trundle	9 Mar 1822
HENDERFIELD,	Ann	Isaac Brewell	12 Sep 1815
HENDERSON,	Archibald	Barbary Dawson	17 Apr 1820
	Edward	Martha Magruder	30 Dec 1892 w
	Edward W. W.	Lucy J. M. Smith	23 Dec 1897 c
	Elizabeth Jane	John P. C. Peter	1 Feb 1830
	Emzy	Theodore Hill	16 Mar 1870
	Henrietta	Clinton Hawkins	28 Jun 1895 c
	James B.	Clara S. Adamson	10 Aug 1870
	James S. H.	Rosanna J. Neel	15 Dec 1843
	John	Lydia Perry	5 May 1800
	John W.	Jessie Burriss	23 May 1890 w
	Julia	A. R. Van Nostrand	25 Jan 1853
	Lucy	Robert Lindsey	5 Dec 1860
	Lydia	David English	8 Nov 1819
	Martha E.	Charles E. Gantt	25 Jun 1862
	Mary A.	Walter F. Cashell	15 Jan 1895 w
	Nancy Ann	Levi Hill	28 Sep 1869
	Philip	Phebe Peters	18 Aug 1814
	Sarah Ann	William Musser	16 Aug 1834
	Sarah Isabella	Dr. James Edward Deets	10 Nov 1886 w
	Virginia	Benjamin T. Howard	7 Jun 1869
	William	Martha Ann Benton	3 Jan 1839
	William C.	Susan R. Dukes	11 Dec 1872
	William W.	Rachel Ann Hill	16 Mar 1843
HENDLEY - also see HENLEY			
HENDLEY,	Elizabeth*	John Pringle	2 Oct 1798
	Hester V.	Lemuel P. Burriss	21 Dec 1854
	Mary	Samuel Wheeler	12 May 1800
HENDRICKS,	Anne L.	William M. Deck	12 Nov 1885 w
HENDRON,	Sarah V.	Benjamin H. Gorrell	11 Sep 1866
HENLEY - also see HENDLEY, HENLY			
HENLEY,	Addie E.	Daniel W. Everhart	19 Jan 1892 w
	Airy E.	James O. Grimes	2 Nov 1880
	Christy	Henry A. Chapman	18 May 1869
	Edward M.	Elizabeth A. Butt	1 Feb 1866
	Elizabeth	Patrick Connelly	1 Dec 1885 w
	Emma J.	Zachariah Lowe	9 May 1881
	Harvey R.	Annie L. Everhart	30 Dec 1895 w
	James	Sarah Thorpe	22 May 1879 w
	James H.	Sarah Mobley	21 May 1874
	Jane	Washington Burriss	20 Nov 1845
	Joseph ?.	Ann E. Snyder	17 Jan 1867
	Louis A.	Lyda M. Everhart	6 Apr 1887 w
	Margaret D.	Charles R. Mobley	11 Jun 1874
	Martha E.	Joseph Mills	4 Feb 1858
	Martha E.	John William Butt	1 Feb 1866
	Mary E.	William A. Collins	8 Mar 1894 w

* Part of last name from earlier reading

HENLEY, Notley H.	Alice Jackson	8 Apr 1890	w
Patrick	Martha Day	21 Mar 1848	
Phillis	Andrew Jackson	6 May 1878	c
Robert	Sarah Mullican	20 Jan 1859	
Sarah E.	Thomas H. Burriss	8 Jun 1854	
William*	Elizabeth Judy	13 Feb 1820	
William	Elizabeth Connelly**	1 Apr 1823	
William E.	Henrietta Butt	24 Dec 1888	w
HENLY - also see HENLEY			
HENLY, Hesther Ann	Lewis Easton	7 Jul 1827	
James	Harriett Hurdle	17 Apr 1827	
Mary	Charles Kidwell	9 Jan 1819	
HENNING, James G.	Alice Ann Willson	21 Feb 1844	
HENNIS, Elizabeth	Joseph Cope	22 Apr 1799	
HENRY, Aaron	Sarah Crafford	2 Feb 1807	
Cassandra	Samuel Bonnifant	10 Jul 1818	
Elizabeth	George C. Snider	7 Mar 1810	
Emily Drennin	Lt. William Rufus Terrill	2 Mar 1858	
Emma	John Sullivan	7 Aug 1878	w
Johana	Henry Boswell	19 May 1834	
John	Rhoda Jefferson	28 Nov 1803	
Julianna	Horatio Thompson	20 Aug 1835	
Rachel	Hezekiah Weeks	13 Apr 1833	
Thomas	Catherine Snyder	29 Dec 1807	
Verlinda	Frederick Snider	27 Mar 1815	
Washington	Mary Carter	24 Jul 1875	
William Allen	Sarah Neverson	11 Oct 1869	
HENSON - also see HANSON			
HENSON, Catharine	Henry Clay	24 Dec 1896	c
James	Elizabeth Boody	22 Jan 1801	
John H.	Delia Greenfield	10 Apr 1873	
Martha	Charles G. King	28 Nov 1895	c
Walter H.	Mary E. Gray	22 Oct 1896	c
HEPBURN - also see HEBRON			
HEPBURN, John M.	Charlotte Lyday	14 Jun 1870	
HEPNER, Asa	Hettie Warfield	11 May 1880	
HERBERT, Charles	Agnes Orange	2 Jun 1870	
Elizabeth M.	Charles G. Willson	30 Nov 1882	w
Henry	Mary Smith	12 Nov 1879	c
Jesse	Catherine Pain	7 Feb 1803	
Lucretia	Henry Jackson	16 Dec 1897	c
Mary E.	Daniel A. Brown	16 Dec 1886	c
Mary F.	Edward K. Manion	12 Sep 1887	w
Perry	Mary Frazier	6 Dec 1806	
Sarah	Hilliary Williams	10 Jan 1810	
Sarah E.	James M. Soper	26 Jul 1894	w
Sarah V.	William W. Case	28 May 1891	w
HERBST, Clara C.	John H. Eliason	13 Aug 1888	w
HEREFORD, Eugene H.	Blanche C. Howell	21 Sep 1898	w
HERELL - also see HERRELL			
HERELL, John A.	Enola K. Ferriss	30 Dec 1882	w
HERR, Leonard C.	Virginia R. Griffith	8 Dec 1893	w

* Part of last name from earlier reading; initial L or S
** Part of last name from earlier reading

HERELL - also see HERRELL			
HERELL, John A.	Enola K. Ferriss	30 Dec 1882	w
HERR, Leonard C.	Virginia R. Griffith	8 Dec 1893	w
HERRELL - also see HERELL			
HERRELL, Julia M.	William E. Poole	3 Nov 1886	w
Lulie Ellen	William Jasper Waugh	17 Dec 1891	w
Mary A.	Richard L. Duvall	8 Nov 1883	
Matilda J.	Melvin L. Duvall	8 Nov 1883	
HERREN - also see HERRON			
HERREN, Margaret	William Ramsey	1 Jan 1800	
HERRING - also see HARING			
HERRING, Kitty	Benjamin Howse	5 Feb 1805	
Robert H.	Mary E. King	1 Sep 1886	c
Ruth	Charles Spates	2 Nov 1815	
Sarah	William Hall	2 Jan 1810	
HERRON - also see HERREN			
HERRON, Mary A.	Samuel Cissell	10 Feb 1874	
HERSBERGER, Hattie M.	Lawrence A. Chiswell	29 Apr 1895	w
HERSHEY, C. R.	Victoria Young	29 Nov 1873	
Susan D.	Isaac Emmert	8 Mar 1836	
HERTY, Thomas	Anne Ritchie	9 Sep 1800	
HERVEY - also see HARVEY			
HERVEY, Elizabeth	Francis Anchors	7 Jan 1807	
Elizabeth	Andrew Reed	23 Apr 1833	
HESKET, Benjamin	Lucinda Summers	2 Jun 1823	
HESSEY, Catharine	William W. Allen	31 Mar 1838	
HESSIE, William W.	Rosa E. Mobley	24 Sep 1888	w
HETCHISON, Frances	William Eller	31 Mar 1845	
HETTINGER, Annie A.	John S. Bell	17 Jan 1898	w
HEUGETTS, Nettie	George W. P. Jennett	3 Oct 1883	
HEUGHS - also see HUGHES			
HEUGHS, Hannah	James Northcroft	29 Dec 1803	
HEVERIN, John	Lucy Prater	27 Dec 1890	c
HEWEL, Henry	Rebecca Seaders	6 Dec 1799	
HEWITT, Bessee	William Cuff	29 Jul 1884	w
HEY, Mary	Joseph Gue	17 Dec 1798	
HIAT - also see HYATT			
HIAT, Elizabeth	George Davis	10 Aug 1804	
HIATT, Mimma	Richard Lansdale	10 Nov 1804	
HICKERSON, Clarence L.	Clara R. Connell	17 Jan 1882	
HICKERSON, Lucy L.	William P. Rudasill	28 Apr 1892	w
HICKEY, Laura L.	William N. Martin	10 Jan 1893	w
HICKMAN, Ann	Benjamin Cross	9 Feb 1803	
Ann	William Searsy	11 Mar 1814	
Ann	Elic L. Beeding	22 Feb 1842	
Anne	Neill Maginnis	2 Nov 1814	
Eletha	James K. Olive	7 Oct 1823	
Eliza	John Thomas	30 Dec 1818	
Elizabeth	Joseph Rose	17 Oct 1827	
George R.	Mary E. Whalan	26 Aug 1852	
Henson R. S.	Amanda Wells	24 Dec 1822	
James W.	Mary C. Cooper	7 Sep 1854	
Joshua	Elizabeth Perry	4 Feb 1817	
Lucy	Frederick Preston	17 Sep 1825	
Margarett	Henry Strider	16 Nov 1811	
Margarett	Greenberry Burk	4 Oct 1814	

HICKMAN,	Mary	Ezekiah Linthicum	26 Oct 1801
	Mary	Thomas F. W. Vinson	26 Dec 1820
	Mary	Horatio Stiles	7 Dec 1826
	Mary A.	Benjamin Burdett	26 Feb 1848
	Mary E.	Joseph W. Esworthy	23 Dec 1859
	Mary W.	Lewis Augustine Summers	26 Aug 1822
	Richard H.	Mollie B. Magaha	6 Jun 1882
	Sytha	Thomas C. Lannan	30 Dec 1822
	Thomas	Margarett Scrivener	20 Feb 1798
	Thomas	Elizabeth Sarah Vinson	3 Jan 1814
	William	Lusinda Higdon	21 Dec 1812
	William P.	Mary M. Read	17 Nov 1896 w
	William T.	Adelia M. Coberth	9 May 1838
	William T.	Ellen Cooley	25 Jan 1846
HICKS,	Frances S.	Frank J. Ettinger	2 Sep 1898 w
	Joseph	Mary Ann Shorter	28 Jan 1869
	Joseph	Clarissa Sedgwick	24 Aug 1871
	Lydia	John S. Baley	10 Sep 1832
	Nathaniel	Ella G. Washington	11 Sep 1893 c
	Robert M.	Annie E. Harper	15 Nov 1869
HIDE,	Thomas W.	Emely Wales	4 Nov 1819
HIGDON,	Carrie *.	James T. Purdum	29 Aug 1884
	Charles	Mary Williams	13 Feb 1809
	Charles L.	Susanna Lewis	30 Mar 1865
	Eleanor	Leonard Townsen	18 Jan 1803
	Ignatius	Milly Dyson	4 Jan 1806
	James	Harriet Stiles	21 Jan 1845
	John T.	Macky Case	22 Dec 1837
	Lusinda	William Hickman	21 Dec 1812
	Mary	Nathan N. Page	2 Oct 1865
	Peter	Eleanor Collyar	21 Dec 1808
	Sarah Ann	William E. Selby	30 Oct 1874
	Susannah	Jonathan Shaw	3 Mar 1806
HIGGENS,	Cornelia R.	James W. Lyddane	6 Dec 1871
	Mollie C.	Perry H. Connell	7 Jan 1884 w
HIGGINS,	Adolphus	Bettie Brown	23 Dec 1873
	Ann	John N. Roby	14 Jul 1832
	Annie	Mortimer Ambush	27 Feb 1878 c
	Annie V.	Edward T. Jeffers	20 Nov 1895 w
	Barbary E.	Lemuel C. Janes	17 Feb 1829
	Barbary Lyles	Michael R. Berry	12 Feb 1818
	Benjamin Becraft	Mary Thomas	25 Sep 1822
	Benjamin F.	Elizabeth Willson	20 Mar 1844
	Charles A. C.	Florida Prather	26 May 1856
	Charles Edwin	Mary Elizabeth Bohrer	14 Oct 1875
	Charles P.	Mary W. Warfield	24 Jan 1888 w
	Darius M.	Elizabeth L. Prather	23 Jun 1862
	Eleanor	William Garrett	7 Oct 1801
	Eleanor W. S.	Samuel S. Briggs	22 Oct 1835
	Eliza	Henry West	14 Dec 1830
	Elizabeth	James H. Turner	23 Aug 1865
	Elizabeth E.	Elisha D. Berry	3 Nov 1853
	Elizabeth L., Mrs.	Henry P. Boyd	5 Apr 1872

* Initial has blot on it

HIGGINS,	Elizabeth M.	Hamilton Crawford	5 Feb 1846	
	Emma	Jesse M. Hall	23 Jul 1863	
	Emma	Henry Hammond	20 Dec 1879	c
	Erie	Amanda Duley	18 Jan 1844	
	Ethel C.	James E. Mansfield	31 Aug 1897	w
	Francis W.	Ida E. Clagett	19 Dec 1877	w
	Franklin	Florence Connell	15 Feb 1882	
	George W.	Mary C. Fisher	29 Nov 1871	
	Henry E.	Annie M. Miller	2 Jan 1895	w
	Hilleary O.	Margaret A. Shaw	3 Apr 1854	
	Hilleary T.	Letha A. Phillips	15 Jan 1858	
	Hilleary T.	Sarah M. Williams	17 Dec 1877	w
	James B.	Mary E. Wilcoxen	10 Jun 1801	
	James B.	Mary Jane Crawford	19 Feb 1852	
	James H.	Elizabeth Pumphrey	11 Feb 1813	
	James H.	Catharine E. M. K. Lansdale	5 Oct 1837	
	James W.	Ann Gartrell	24 Nov 1836	
	Jesse T.	Margaret R. Waters	1 Aug 1837	
	John	Mary C. E. Book	5 Sep 1868	
	John J.	Laura C. Muncaster	25 Jan 1882	
	Joseph C.	Annie L. Bell	27 Apr 1885	w
	Joshua	Mamie A. Houck	23 Nov 1893	w
	Joshua C.	Mary Ann K. Edmonstone	30 Jan 1850	
	Laura J.	George W. Boswell	9 Jan 1856	
	Leanna M.	Calvin Thompson	26 Oct 1875	
	Luraner	Jonathan Becraft	10 Jun 1800	
	Luraner	George M. Knowles	29 Jun 1830	
	Martha Ann	William C. Soper	9 Nov 1840	
	Martin F.	Mary Ann Matilda Edmonstone	1 Apr 1823	
	Martin W. J.	Mary E. E. Duley	25 Jul 1833	
	Mary	Asa Clagett	31 Jan 1816	
	Mary A.	William W. White	14 Oct 1897	w
	Mary A. V.	Joseph B. Clagett	22 Dec 1852	
	Mary E.	Edward C. Gott	17 Nov 1859	
	Mary L.	D. H. Bouic	26 Oct 1875	
	Mary Lavinia	Robert P. Magruder	12 Oct 1886	w
	Matilda	Caleb Lee	8 Apr 1819	
	Rose	Joshua C. Dorsey	30 Jan 1888	w
	Ruth W.	Charles F. Harding	14 Oct 1818	
	Samuel	Matilda Crawford	20 Dec 1843	
	Sarah	Samuel W. Boswell	14 Oct 1879	
	Sarah E.	James N. Benton	14 Feb 1872	
	Statira	John Belt	15 Feb 1812	
	Thomas E.	Mary E. Osborn	24 Jan 1891	w
	Thomas L. F.	Oliva C. Orme	2 Mar 1823	
	Verlinda	Zachariah Macelfrish	9 Nov 1824	
	Viola	Bruce C. Hoskinson	15 Jun 1898	w
	Willard C.	Mary M. Moxley	6 Dec 1893	w
HILEARY - also see HILLEARY				
HILEARY,	Jane	George J. Judey	12 Aug 1822	
HILL,	Alcinda	James H. Thomas	11 Nov 1896	c
	Amanda	Herbert Dublin	26 Dec 1883	c
	Andrew	Lethe Falls	11 Jun 1892	c
	Ann	William Wheeler	25 Oct 1799	

150

HILL, Aquilla	Rachel W. Galworth	24 Dec 1805	
Augustus S.	Rosie Awkward	20 Oct 1892	c
Charles T.	Lucy V. Scott	24 Nov 1886	c
Charlotte A.	John Rounds	8 Mar 1883	c
Charlotte L.	Frederick M. Dorsey	1 Apr 1891	c
David K.	Alcinda Layton	16 May 1867	
Edmund	Annie C. Nuttle	8 Jan 1875	
Elias J.	Sarah R. English	4 Jul 1854	
Ellen	Marshall Burriss	3 Apr 1845	
Fannie	George Cook	15 Dec 1886	c
Giles	Anne Newton	4 Jan 1800	
Harriet A.	John Steele	13 Jan 1866	
Irena	Rezin T. Jones	18 Jul 1891	c
James	Eliza Thomas	15 Oct 1896	c
John	Chloe Lanham	4 Feb 1813	
John O.	Matilda M. Warring	2 May 1842	
John T.	Louisa E. Gantt	23 May 1862	
John W.	Ann M. Bowen	10 Jan 1878	c
Joseph A.	Harriet A. Fitzhugh	5 Jan 1888	c
Julia	Joseph Shehan	21 Jan 1800	
Julia Ann	James W. Howser	20 Dec 1853	
Lesir	Alvira Johnson	30 Dec 1881	c
Levi	Nancy Ann Henderson	28 Sep 1869	
Margaret	Levi B. Pennifield	18 Dec 1827	
Margery	Edward Fletch Clark	2 Dec 1880	
Martha A.	Jackson Hinton	7 Mar 1864	
Mary Jane	Thomas W. Offutt	24 Dec 1846	
Rachel A.	William Pennifield	14 Oct 1857	
Rachel Ann	William W. Henderson	16 Mar 1843	
Remus H.	Emma J. Squirrel	22 Jun 1881	c
Reuben	Rachel Martin	28 Jun 1871	
Reuben	Carrie Blair	9 Jul 1879	c
Richard	Hattie Mitchell	4 Nov 1897	c
Ruthana	George Henry Snowden	24 Oct 1878	c
Samuel T.	Mary King	4 Nov 1890	c
Sarah	Nathan Edwards	15 Nov 1876	
Sarah A.	Penock Carlile	8 Jul 1862	
Sarah E.	Horatio Keith	14 May 1844	
Susan Ann	Thomas Levin Offutt	14 Mar 1842	
Susanna	Elias Madding	19 Dec 1804	
Susanna	Henly Thompson	4 Nov 1805	
Theodore	Emzy Henderson	16 Mar 1870	
Thomas	Eleanor Wheeler	10 Apr 1799	
Vernon	Bessie Johnson	14 Aug 1894	c
William	Mary C. Wilburn	14 Apr 1857	
William	Emma Wallace	29 Apr 1865	
William M.	Mary E. Howard	26 Jan 1885	c
William Proctor	Elizabeth H. Trail	24 Mar 1897	w
HILLARD - also see HILLIARD			
HILLARD, Ann E.	James R. Stallings	22 Jan 1839	
Ann L.	George Robertson	22 Oct 1861	
Elizabeth	Elisha Nicholdson	15 Jan 1817	
James	Sarah M. Ward	22 Apr 1820	
James W.	Ann Elizabeth Measels	8 Aug 1846	
James W.	Gertrude E. V. Price	29 Dec 1892	w
Samuel	Rebeccah Harris	20 Aug 1810	

HILLARD, Thomas	Elizabeth Browning	16 Dec 1806	
Thomas B.	Hattie Miles	16 Nov 1893	w

HILLEARY - also see HILEARY, HILLIARY

HILLEARY, Aldridge G.	Lelia N. Schaeffer	19 Oct 1898	w
Mary V.	George H. Thompson	17 Sep 1861	
Sarah T. W.	Franklin Waters	3 Oct 1842	
Thomas	Sarah Wheeler	23 Nov 1803	
Walter H.	Susan Smith	6 May 1813	
HILLERY, Mary	Joseph Ellis	7 Jan 1818	

HILLIARD - also see HILLARD

HILLIARD, Joseph	Anne Hardy	25 Oct 1815	
Mary E.	Lemuel Bell	7 Dec 1860	
Solomon	Anne Kidwell	21 Jan 1819	

HILLIARY - see also see HILLEARY

HILLIARY, John H.	Mary E. Waters	13 Feb 1835	
Tilghman	Ann Worthington	31 Oct 1820	
HILTON, ---ana	Robert Calfus	15 Sep 1885	w
Ann E.	Giles W. Easton	3 Apr 1856	
Charles E.	Rachel J. E. Mullinix	11 Apr 1892	w
Clarence	Emma A. Bowen	1 Feb 1897	w
Daroth A.	Perry G. Watkins	24 Apr 1851	
Dionysius	Fannie May Bohrer	2 Apr 1895	w
Eldra D.	Josiah Essex, Jr.	8 Sep 1864	
Elizabeth	Arthur *. A. Campbell	5 Jun 1832	
Esther	William Vymeer	5 May 1825	
Fannie E.	James O. Clagett	17 Nov 1894	w
Franklin L.	Hattie L. Bohrer	15 Oct 1895	w
James	Lucy Knott	25 Dec 1817	
James R.	Florence L. Becraft	14 Nov 1887	w
Jessie I.	Luther F. Loy	20 Dec 1897	w
Jessie V.	George T. Price	11 Jun 1888	w
John H.	Annie M. Clagett	10 Apr 1878	w
John H.	Magdalene V. Gingell	25 Oct 1888	w
Joshua	Maria H. Stone	20 Dec 1820	
Juliet	Richard Sheckells	25 May 1825	
Leonard	Sarah Merryman	18 Dec 1816	
Lloyd	Rachael Watkins	4 Jan 1826	
Mary	John Stewart	26 Jun 1807	
Mary	John Burdett	9 Jan 1822	
Mary C.	Rezin G. Mullinix	30 Oct 1888	w
Mary M.	John Spalding	6 Mar 1852	
Richard W.	Louisa Jane Shipley	27 Jan 1864	
Rosa B.	Edmund W. Warfield	16 Nov 1883	
Rufus E. G.	Mary J. Appleby	20 Mar 1877	w
Samuel	Jane Piles	22 Jun 1812	
Samuel	Mary Merryman	24 Oct 1814	
Samuel	Delilah Howard	22 Apr 1816	
Sarah Ann	Nathan B. Claggett	22 Jan 1840	
Sarah E.	William Young	25 Nov 1861	
Sidonia F.	Thomas Story	4 Aug 1884	
Susanah	Charles Crockett	28 Jul 1820	
Susie R.	Edward A. Dwyer	14 Nov 1864	
William	Sarah Stewart	25 Mar 1801	
William	Anne Sedwick	31 Dec 1822	

* Initial I or J

HILTON, William T.	Frances R. Snyder	18 Nov 1850
HINES, Eleanor V.	George Forbes Prather	29 Jul 1884 w
Reuben P.	Mary E. Burriss	25 Aug 1888 w
HINSCH, George A.	Sarah H. Aaron	29 Aug 1892 w
HINTIN, Annie V.	George W. Gibson	22 Jan 1884
HINTON, Annie	John B. Watts	28 Jul 1869
Benjamin	Margarett Greentree	28 Dec 1811
Benjamin	Catherine Pennyfille	16 Feb 1828
Catharine	Henry Lowe	28 Mar 1842
Eliza Ann	Richard B. Astlin	5 May 1838
Elizabeth	Abner Tuttle	26 May 1838
Jackson	Martha A. Hill	7 Mar 1864
Mary A.	John A. Ford	28 Oct 1848
Mary M. E.	Lewis A. Johnson	29 Aug 1895 w
Nelly	Nelson Tuttle	26 Jul 1837
Rebecca	Samuel Leizear	17 Jan 1860
Walter	Margaret Lanham	29 Aug 1811
Walter	Caroline Tuttle	20 Aug 1836
William	Rachael Graham	7 Dec 1863
William	Anna Cephas	12 Dec 1872
William John	Emma F. Wiley	5 Dec 1865
HIPKINS, Crittenden C.	Carrie E. Ruble	17 Sep 1895 w
Mary A.	Henry G. Wood	4 Feb 1893 w
HIPSLEY, Evan	Kate E. Canby	5 Apr 1861
Margaret	Benjamin F. Sullivan	12 Apr 1873
HIRSH, Charles W.	Mary A. Cecil	25 Jan 1889 w
Charles W.	Mary P. Bennett	4 Nov 1895 w
HISEY, Elvin A.	Lida A. West	31 Jan 1891 w
HITCHENS, Mary Emma	Eugene Gilford Rock	5 Jul 1892 w
Willard F.	Emma L. Norris	11 Apr 1895 w
HITTLE, Mary	John Bowman	5 Jan 1799
HOARD, Joseph	Betty Jackson	8 Dec 1880 c
HOASS, Martha	Jeremiah Havner	26 Dec 1822
HOBBS, Ann E.	Benjamin F. Suddath	7 Sep 1874
Asbury	Isabel Melvin	23 Nov 1892 w
Charles	Hesther Thompson	13 Mar 1806
Clarissa	Joseph Johnson	1 Dec 1807
Eliza	Nathan Warfield	6 Dec 1819
Elizabeth	Joseph F. Robinson	4 Feb 1806
Ethel J.	William L. Purdum	3 Dec 1892 w
Hannah	Charles Sheats	1 Nov 1798
Hattie A.	John L. Walker	17 Sep 1884
Horatio	Sarah Howard	2 Jun 1806
Ida J.	Charles F. Townshend	14 Feb 1865
Jemimah R.	Fletcher A. Day	20 Oct 1896 w
Kate	George W. Cashell	15 Dec 1873
L. Adelaide	Columbus W. Day	19 Dec 1885 w
Marcy (or Marey)	John Campbell	27 Feb 1803
Martha	Henry Howser	3 Feb 1813
Mary Ann	Franklin Groomes	8 Oct 1844
Nathan M.	Joanna Worrell	2 Jun 1859
Polly	Jonathan Browning	5 Sep 1825
Priscilla	Basil Soper	9 Feb 1808
Rachel A.	William Watkins	9 Dec 1852
Rebecca	Samuel Irving	3 Oct 1849
Sarah	Evan Belt	26 Jul 1803

HOBBS, Tessy	Israel Houser	20 Nov 1798	
Thomas J.	Sarah Ann Musgrove	24 Jan 1826	
Thomas J.	Elizabeth Margaret Maria Jane Price	20 Dec 1834	
William H.	Elizabeth Purdum	19 Dec 1851	
William H.	Virginia S. Gittings	23 Nov 1885	w
HOBEN, James	Susannah Sewell	12 Jan 1799	
HODGE, John E.	Minnie Hood	10 Jun 1891	c
John M.	Elizabeth Lynn	26 May 1891	c
Nicholas	Mary Reintzel	4 Jan 1801	
HODGES, Ann	James Cook	19 May 1887	c
Anna M.	James E. Thompson	30 Oct 1893	w
Anne Ara	William Jones	12 Dec 1826	
Annie R.	Charles C. Bohrer	12 Dec 1879	w
Caleb	Catherine Cook	11 Nov 1868	
Charles C.	Rebecka White	25 Jan 1817	
Elizabeth*	Richard James	18 Oct 1805	
Emma J.	Charles R. Purdum	18 Dec 1897	w
Franklin T.	Kate G. Miller	27 May 1897	w
George T.	Mary J. Jarboe	23 Nov 1874	
James E.	Nancy Butler	4 Nov 1885	c
John	Sarah Ellen Willson	7 Jun 1837	
John ?.	Sallie T. Fawcett	28 Nov 1883	
Mary E.	Frederick Linthicum	17 Dec 1861	
Matilda A.	Alpheus Stansbury	21 Feb 1870	
Rebecca	James P. Biays	28 Oct 1867	
Sarah E.	Christopher H. Brashear	27 Sep 1852	
William	Elizabeth Windsor	6 Feb 1868	
William R.	Eva P. Bohrer	23 Oct 1882	w
HODGSON, Thomas H.	Estelle F. Smith	9 Jun 1885	
HODSON, Sarah J.	Enoch A. Parsley	27 Nov 1882	w
HOE, Moses	Harriet Lee	30 Nov 1870	
HOES - also see HOSE			
HOES, Annie	Charles Turner	24 Dec 1889	c
John H.	Nellie Diggs	9 Aug 1894	c
HOFFMAN, Annie O.	Peter J. Stang	21 Dec 1886	w
John Peter	Susannah Cole	7 Oct 1800	
HOFHEINZ, John	Henrietta S. C. S. Werner	17 Oct 1892	w
HOGAN, Charles F.	Helen J. Connell	12 Nov 1877	
Lawrence	Sarah Carlin	4 Feb 1881	
Susannah	Joseph Cox	18 Sep 1802	
HOGDON, Erasmus	Jane Douglass	26 Dec 1798	
HOGG, Nathaniel B. Jr.	Elizabeth F. Gilpin	29 May 1888	w
HOGGINS, Ann	Jonas Austin	15 Jan 1799	
HOLLADAY - also see HOLLEDAY			
HOLLADAY, Jessie J.	Samuel G. Heddings	23 Aug 1898	w
HOLLAND, Allen	Sally Brown	6 Mar 1816	
Amelia	Michael McElvane	21 Dec 1799	
Ann	Benjamin Ricketts	20 Feb 1802	
Ann	Robert Gardner	18 Nov 1824	
Ann A.	Edward Craycroft	22 Jan 1855	
Ann B.	Allen H. Bennett	13 Feb 1826	
Anna	Henry C. Bowie	1 Jan 1868	

* There is a blot on the "o"; could be Hedges

HOLLAND,	Anne	Zachariah Johnson	4 Sep 1827	
	Anne	Henry Clay Brown	12 Jan 1872	
	Annie	Robert Awkward	19 May 1890	c
	Annie L.	Samuel D. Owings	30 Nov 1896	w
	Arnold	Susanah Holland	29 Oct 1801	
	Asa	Anne Ward	5 Feb 1807	
	Augustus	Christianna Hopkins	9 May 1873	
	Benjamin	Rebecah Holland	16 Dec 1803	
	Charity	Albert Miller	19 Oct 1886	c
	Charles	Ann Griffith	16 Feb 1832	
	David S.	Mary E. Hutton	14 Oct 1868	
	Deborah	George Barnesley	3 Feb 1812	
	Eleanor	William Williams	20 Nov 1802	
	Eliza	Elemuel G. Duley	30 Jul 1825	
	Eliza J.	Oliver Green	1 Jun 1886	c
	Elizabeth	Norris Read	26 Dec 1798	
	Elizabeth E.	George Gaither	2 Apr 1866	
	Emily	Charles Powell	3 Jul 1884	c
	Enoch	Rebeckah Harrison	6 Jan 1826	
	Ercilla	Azel Waters	14 Dec 1799	
	Ernest M.	Anna A. Harris	21 Feb 1877	w
	George O.	Annie M. Nicholson	19 Jan 1897	w
	Grafton	Ellen Clagett	4 Nov 1834	
	Helen	William Irvin Brooke	31 Jan 1882	
	Isaac	Lydia Matthews	27 Mar 1821	
	James C.	Ida M. Suter	18 Oct 1866	
	John W.	Emily A. J. Trundle	22 Nov 1866	
	Laura W.	Hattersly W. Talbott	9 Feb 1874	
	Lucy ?.	John R. Warfield	* Jul 1882	
	Martha	Charles Gassaway	25 Feb 1892	c
	Martha Ann	Benjamin F. Thomas	23 Apr 1867	
	Mary	Patrick Coleman	1 Jan 1813	
	Mary	Stephen Lewis	13 Jan 1839	
	Mary Ann	George W. Grimes	19 Aug 1837	
	Mary G.	Louis W. Murphy	22 Nov 1892	w
	Massy	Sollomon Pelly	7 Aug 1799	
	Millard F.	Edith C. Rutherford	25 Jun 1886	w
	Nace	Ellen Countee	8 Jan 1867	
	Nancy	Festus Nelson	22 Dec 1894	c
	Nathan	Caroline Selby	29 Nov 1846	
	Nathan	Clara Thomas	7 Sep 1893	c
	Nathan Jr.	Martha Beall	12 Dec 1798	
	Philip	Sarah Leeke	27 Oct 1812	
	Rebecah	Benjamin Holland	16 Dec 1803	
	Rezin	Mary Ellen Powell	9 Jul 1868	
	Rhody R.	Notley Birdett	30 Jun 1836	
	Richard W.	Mary Jane Harris	26 May 1838	
	Ruth H.	William Clagett	21 Dec 1855	
	Sarah Ann	Edwin N. Darby	19 Mar 1836	
	Sarah E.	George H. Wilder	21 Sep 1866	
	Sarah T.	William Nugent	1 May 1884	
	Solomon	Margaret Gatton	23 Jan 1800	
	Solomon	Matilda Gatton	23 Mar 1815	
	Susan V.	Jonathan R. Ridgeley	6 Feb 1865	

* Cannot read day; after 6 and before 20

HOLLAND, Susanah	Arnold Holland	29 Oct 1801	
Susanna	Richard Sullivan	9 May 1815	
Thomas	Hannah J. Tucker	3 Oct 1878	c
Thomas	Susan C. Nucy	21 Sep 1892	c
Thomas Jr.	Sarah F. Ricks	28 Sep 1897	c
Virginia Lydia	Lewis Walker Steer	17 Nov 1886	w
William	Polly Waters	8 Mar 1805	
William A.	Susan Ayres	8 Nov 1867	

HOLLEDAY - also see HOLLIDAY

HOLLEDAY, David	Eleanor Riley	6 Apr 1847	

HOLLEY - also see HOLLY

HOLLEY, Belle	Jeremiah Jackson	25 Dec 1883	c
William	Caroline Davis	19 Mar 1867	

HOLLIDAY - also see HOLLADAY, HOLLEDAY

HOLLIDAY, Rachel	Solomon Williams	7 Jan 1886	c
HOLLINGSWORTH, Mary E.	James M. Wright, Jr.	1 Sep 1881	

HOLLMAN - also see HOLMAN

HOLLMAN, John H.	Mary E. Davis	28 Dec 1888	c

HOLLY - also see HOLLEY

HOLLY, Laura J.	Peter Washington	27 Dec 1897	c
William	Florence Pinket	18 Aug 1896	c

HOLMAN - also see HOLLMAN

HOLMAN, Clarence	Katie V. Brent	12 Sep 1878	c
Frances	Walter Brown	12 Aug 1876	
Henrietta	Charles Coats	27 Nov 1876	
James	Eliza E. Holmes	26 Dec 1882	c
James D.	Dora S. Mace	13 Aug 1889	w
Ralph	Emma Bowen	31 Oct 1878	c
HOLMEAD, Sarah	Jonah Milburn Speake	17 Jul 1800	
HOLMES, Ann	Lloyd Magruder	17 Mar 1807	
Eliza	Robert Howison	16 Apr 1833	
Eliza E.	James Holman	26 Dec 1882	c
Harriet A.	Augustus Boston	28 Nov 1877	c
Harriett	Warren Magruder	2 Nov 1803	
Josephine	Gilbert L. Kirby	24 Oct 1889	w
Lucy	Lewis Gibson	13 Sep 1881	c
Mary	Edward Hughes	16 Jun 1829	
Sally C.	Meshech Browning	14 Dec 1805	
Samuel M.	Della May Cooley	29 Oct 1895	w
Virginia C.	Virgil Ward	13 Nov 1883	
HOLT, Ann Rebecca	Melchisadec Green	8 Oct 1845	
Cajor G.	Mary Burton	17 Mar 1892	c
Elizabeth	Nathan Hoskinson	3 Jan 1823	
Harriet D.	John B. Edmonson	5 Oct 1870	
Laurence O.	Sarah Oden	12 Jan 1802	
Levi	Mary Heberon	26 Jan 1874	
Sarah E.	Jerry P. Awkard	29 Feb 1892	c
William	Mary D. Letton	4 May 1823	
HONERY, C. J.	George Scott	6 Feb 1868	
HOOD, Ada	Jerry Diggs	21 Dec 1898	c
Anne Elizabeth	Zadok M. Waters	6 Nov 1829	
Deborah	John Elkins	22 Apr 1885	c
Ella D.	John H. Crawford	6 Sep 1886	w
Ella V.	Franklin Jackson	3 Oct 1889	c
Eveline	Basil E. Brown	23 Apr 1895	w
Hanson	Mary E. Lynn	28 Apr 1881	

HOOD,	Harriet	Frank Johnson	15 Nov 1878
	Horace T.	Sarah C. Warren	20 Apr 1893 c
	John Q. A.	Susan S. Hackett	17 Jan 1898 c
	John W.	Angeline Dorsey	24 Jul 1875
	Martha J.	John W. Lynn	28 May 1889 c
	Mary E.	Mailin Rolls	16 Dec 1881
	Minnie	John E. Hodge	10 Jun 1891 c
	Susan	John Peters	26 Dec 1879 c
	Thomas	Susanna Boswell	9 Jul 1835
	Treasy Ellen	John Henry Dorsey	5 Apr 1898 c
HOOK,	Mary	Tiernan T. Wilds	27 Apr 1864
	Oscar B.	Martha Rearden	1 Oct 1872
HOOKER,	Elizabeth	William Cockram	9 Dec 1814
HOPEWELL,	Laura M.	William H. Clements	12 Dec 1889 c
HOPEWOOD - also see HOPWOOD			
HOPEWOOD,	Frances L.	Lewis A. Warfield	6 Oct 1885 w
	Martha E.	Alexander C. H. Thompson	16 Jun 1890 w
HOPKINS,	Absalom	Comfort M. Lynn	9 Nov 1871
	Archie M.	Eliza Awkward	9 May 1889 c
	Augustus	Elizabeth Magruder	11 Oct 1887 c
	Christianna	Augustus Holland	9 May 1873
	Eleanora	Alfred C. Bell	19 Oct 1889 c
	Eliza S.	William B. Miller	28 Apr 1874
	Elizabeth	Notley Lanham	23 Dec 1800
	Elizabeth A.	Reasen W. Hardesty	23 Nov 1861
	Eveline Ann	Julias Marlow	10 May 1844
	Francis M.	Annie M. Warfield	25 May 1893 c
	Gerard	Emily Snowden	1 Oct 1874
	Hettie	Israel Shipley	1 Jan 1881 c
	Hiram W.	Sallie F. Harding	30 May 1872
	John	Juliet Ann Jarboe	19 Jan 1825
	John A.	Mary S. Pope	25 Apr 1898 w
	John W.	Mary E. Tasco	6 Jun 1893 c
	Joseph	Eleanor Mills	16 Dec 1800
	Joseph	Mary V. Coophard	12 Jan 1866
	Joseph M.	Florence N. Degges	23 Sep 1898 w
	Lavinia	John R. Thomas	22 Apr 1867
	Levi	Emma Berry	4 May 1876 c
	Lillie	William H. Harriss	2 Jun 1890 c
	Maggie E.	George A. Jackson	27 Sep 1897 c
	Margaret	Richard Lazier	4 Feb 1802
	Mary	Charles E. Bowie	10 Jan 1889 c
	Mary A.	Joseph S. Johnson	24 Feb 1898 w
	Mary Ann	Richard Marlow	23 Mar 1846
	Mary E.	Alexander Dorsey	30 Dec 1879 c
	Mary Emma	Albert F. Carter	18 May 1898 c
	Mollie L.	John W. Delaplane	7 Jun 1881 w
	Rachel	James Anderson	2 May 1801
	Reuben	Rachel Ann Walker	14 Oct 1872
	Samuel	Mary Ann Scott	26 Dec 1831
	Samuel Jeff.	Lizzie A. Harding	10 Jun 1872
	Stephen	Catharine P. Kneas	6 Jun 1894 w
	Susan R.	George W. Myers	10 Jun 1890 c
	Thomas S.	Mary V. Bell	29 May 1895 c
	William E.	Amelia Mackall	14 Aug 1895 c

HOPKINS, William M.	Sarah R. King	17 May 1894	c
HOPWOOD - also see HOPEWOOD			
HOPWOOD, Ann	John Tucker	8 Jan 1803	
Ida V.	Edward Trail	7 Jul 1897	w
John	Heneretta Hyatt	21 Mar 1807	
Joseph	Sarah Sedgwick	26 Jan 1814	
Mary Ann	Evan Bowman	15 Jan 1839	
Matilda E.	William Bowman	5 Jan 1836	
HORAN, Maggie C.	Oscar T. Olsen	9 Oct 1891	w
HORN, John L.	Eliza Young	13 Mar 1824	
HORNER, Frank Mary E. Whitesides 5 Jun 1875			
Frank B.	Laura V. West	1 Nov 1876	
Samuel	Mary McFarland	12 Feb 1804	
Samuel	Sarah Taylor	12 Jan 1810	
HORRELL, Henry B.	Margaret Riney	19 Nov 1808	
HORSEMAN, William H.	Ella F. Webb	4 Aug 1896	w
HORTEN, R. Lee	Annie I. Armstrong	29 Jun 1898	w
HORTMAN, Margaret	George Sellman	23 Feb 1852	
HOSE -also see HOES			
HOSE, Bessie	William N. Lomax	2 Oct 1891	c
Lottie	Melville T. Jackson	4 Aug 1896	c
HOSKINS, Andrew J.	Martha J. Beckwith	26 Oct 1847	
Elisha*	Rebecca Shaw	5 Mar 1800	
George	Mary Read	24 Feb 1800	
Israel	Henrietta Dorsey	1 Jan 1870	
Mary	David Carlisle	25 Jan 1806	
HOSKINSON, Ann E.	James F. Poole	20 Dec 1853	
Bruce C.	Viola Higgins	15 Jun 1898	w
Darcus	Greenbury Browning	8 Nov 1821	
George	Jane Douglass	2 Nov 1815	
Hilleary	Maria H. Veirs	2 Sep 1836	
Hilleary	Darcus A. Veirs	23 Dec 1847	
Margaret H.	Francis Dulin	21 Jan 1824	
Mary Ellen	Richard Piles	30 Jun 1841	
Nathan	Elizabeth Holt	3 Jan 1823	
Susan R.	Benjamin F. Reid	24 Jan 1865	
Thomas	Gertie Fletchall	24 May 1876	
HOUCK, Edward H.	Ann E. Dwyer	25 Feb 1859	
Mamie A.	Joshua Higgins	23 Nov 1893	w
HOUGH, Cora May	Winfield S. Kendrick	14 Jan 1874	
Magruder	Minnie O'Doud	27 Jul 1883	
HOUSAR - also see HOWSER, HOUSER			
HOUSAR, Dennis	Lydia Feister	23 Sep 1823	
Nathan	Elizabeth Getzendanner	5 Nov 1807	
Rebecca	John Walker	5 Feb 1825	
HOUSE - also see HOWES			
HOUSE, Ann	Josias Adams	1 Sep 1810	
Anne	Benjamin Willett	19 Dec 1810	
Caroline	Thomas J. Groomes	24 Aug 1882	w
Edward	Lydia -----**	18 Oct 1820	
Elizabeth G.	John L. Gilbert	20 Oct 1850	
James G.	Rachel E. Berry	5 Apr 1838	

* Other records show him as Hoskinson
** Cannot read last name; it does not look like Fink which is in earlier reading.

HOUSE, John	Helen M. Gaither	18 Dec 1871	
Julian M.	Sidonia Allen	29 Jan 1878	w
Lawrady	Charles Davis	31 Dec 1798	
Lizzie A.	Fletcher Irvin	17 Dec 1872	
Martha E.	Benjamin Johnson	19 Apr 1837	
Mary	Charles Brown	15 Dec 1808	
Mary E.	Joseph C. Phebus	20 Oct 1881	w
Nathaniel	Eliza Berry	4 Oct 1803	
Richard Thomas	Mary M. Shipley	3 Feb 1875	
William F.	Caroline Virginia Dwyer	26 Dec 1876	
William H.	Mary A. Ricketts	12 Nov 1845	
HOUSEN, Charles L.	Antonia C. Watkins	12 Jun 1897	w
HOUSER - also see HOUSER			
HOUSER, Eleanor	John Stephens	12 Mar 1800	
Israel	Tessy Hobbs	20 Nov 1798	
James A.	Mamie M. Boroughs	23 Nov 1897	w
Lucinda	John Stallings	31 Dec 1866	
Sarah Ann	Richard Collins	17 Jul 1855	
William F.	Emma E. Scheirer	1 Jun 1897	w
HOUTZ, William R.	Annie D. Faught	3 Jun 1892	w
HOVER, Henry	Margaret A. Johnson	18 Feb 1862	
HOWARD, Addie L. G.	Lewis W. Whipp	16 Mar 1892	w
Alexander	Sarah Sheckells	18 Apr 1801	
Ann C.	Andrew Clements	13 Aug 1831	
Anne	Samuel Ayton	26 Feb 1802	
Annie E.	George C. Whipp	17 Dec 1889	w
Benjamin T.	Virginia Henderson	7 Jun 1869	
Brice W.	Kate R. Orendorff	20 Jun 1864	
Charles	Milly Doublen	4 Apr 1878	
Charles	Susannah Green	20 May 1886	c
Charles A.	Eliza Geen	22 Nov 1888	c
Clara M.	J. W. Owen	12 Apr 1880	
Cora E.	Harry E. Mulligan	20 Jan 1897	w
Daniel M.	Frances M. Thompson	2 Mar 1869	
David	Ruth S. Reid	7 Dec 1827	
Delilah	Samuel Hilton	22 Apr 1816	
Edwin	Sallie Murdock Berry	17 Dec 1883	
Eleanor	Joseph Howard	12 Sep 1801	
Elizabeth	William Plummer	14 Nov 1817	
Ellen R.	Azel Waters	9 May 1821	
Emiley	John G. England	4 May 1830	
Enoch G.	Isabella Bowie	30 Jan 1895	c
Flodoardo	Lydia Maria Robertson	10 Jun 1833	
Frank M.	Jennie M. Reynolds	12 Jul 1893	w
George	Mary A. Burkitt	9 Nov 1885	c
George R.	Mary E. Robertson	13 Mar 1861	
Greenbury	Mary Prettyman	20 Jul 1873	
Henry	Sarah Rawlings	23 Apr 1802	
Henry	Hannah Pleasants	12 Sep 1814	
Henry	Eliza W. Elgar	8 Feb 1836	
Henry	Mary F. Jones	26 Jun 1894	w
Hester Jane	Thomas J. Mitchell	22 Apr 1886	c
Jacob	Rachel Prather	8 Oct 1799	
Jacob	Priscilla Vermilion	26 Mar 1834	
Jacob P.	Linna Page	20 May 1840	
James W.	Ida V. Daffney	13 Jan 1883	

HOWARD,	Janie	Henson Brown	21 Mar 1889	c
	John A.	Louisa M. Jamison	17 Oct 1821	
	John A.	Cora S. Royer	12 Mar 1897	w
	Joseph	Eleanor Howard	12 Sep 1801	
	Joseph	Mary Thomas	14 Dec 1802	
	Josiah	Sarah E. Moore	18 Nov 1868	
	Laura V.	William J. Neel	22 Nov 1869	
	Leanna	William E. Mitchell	9 Jun 1875	
	Leonard	Drusilla Heffner	25 Jul 1838	
	Leonard W.	Laura J. Nicholson	7 May 1888	w
	Lucy Emma	James Anthony Livers	1 Oct 1835	
	Lydia	Thomas Snowden	1 Jun 1874	
	Margaret	Michael Scott	29 Jul 1893	c
	Margaret V.	Elisha Riggs	23 Feb 1869	
	Maria	John Brown	* Jul 1882	c
	Maria G.	Jacob B. Oliver	16 Jun 1885	c
	Marshall P.	Elizabeth Riggs	21 Oct 1895	w
	Martha J.	Henry Walter Clements	29 Sep 1880	
	Mary	Charles Smith	26 Aug 1869	
	Mary A.	Benjamin F. Harding	26 Jan 1864	
	Mary E.	William M. Hill	26 Jan 1885	c
	Mary E. B.	Aquila Windom	12 Aug 1815	
	Milburn	Milly Adams	29 Jul 1870	
	Rebecca	John H. Riggs	24 Jun 1800	
	Richard P.	Henrietta Mitchell	26 Oct 1893	c
	Samuel	Charlotte Grandison	13 Mar 1866	
	Sarah	Josiah T. Prather	1 Apr 1800	
	Sarah	Horatio Hobbs	2 Jun 1806	
	Sarah	Daniel Price	5 Jul 1820	
	Sarah E.	Edward T. Hurtt	22 Feb 1894	w
	Susanah	Thomas Carter	1 Dec 1869	
	Thomas	Rachel Trundle	13 Dec 1800	
	Thomas M.	Mary Forsides	5 Feb 1813	
	Thomas W.	Amey Nickson	2 Mar 1802	
	Thomas W.	Elizabeth Crabb	26 Mar 1807	
	William	Eliza Ann Bond	29 Dec 1803	
	William E.	Frances Washington	12 Sep 1888	c
	William G.	Mary Pritchard	29 Mar 1831	
	Zalphin B.	Laura M. Ricketts	19 Feb 1896	w
HOWE - also see HOWES				
HOWE,	John	Elizabeth Cross	14 Jan 1812	
HOWELL,	Blanche C.	Eugene H. Hereford	21 Sep 1898	w
	Samuel	Adele Lafitte	16 May 1857	
HOWES - also see HOWSE, HOUSE, HOWE, HAWES				
HOWES,	George R.	Mary S. Reynolds	22 Dec 1883	
	James E.	Willie A. Dwyer	30 Jan 1879	
	James R.	Eliza Green	22 Mar 1878	
	Lucrecia	Roby Penn	18 Dec 1798	
	Reubin	Anna Allnutt	5 Nov 1816	
	William E.	Lavinia Brown	6 Sep 1894	w
HOWISON,	Robert	Eliza Holmes	16 Apr 1833	
HOWSE - also see HOWES				
HOWSE,	Benjamin	Kitty Herring	7 Feb 1805	
	Jane	George Green	26 Apr 1814	

* Day too light to read; before 10

HOWSE, John	Elizabeth Smith	16 Dec 1807	
Levin	Anna Green	14 Jan 1812	
Richard	Elizabeth Willett	22 Jan 1812	
Seni	Joseph Ellums	30 Nov 1815	
HOWSER - also see HOUSAR			
HOWSER, Chloe Ann	Robert Magruder	10 Jan 1861	
Dennis M.	Rachel Ellen Carey	20 Dec 1882	
Gertrude	Thomas E. Jackson	2* Jun 1898	w
Henry	Martha Hobbs	3 Feb 1813	
James H.	Emma R. Collins	25 Feb 1863	
James W.	Julia Ann Hill	20 Dec 1853	
Levi	Elizabeth Davis	17 Nov 1868	
Margaret A.	John W. Moran	19 Oct 1858	
Pearlie J.	James T. Atwood	18 Dec 1890	w
Philip D.	Harriet E. A. Burris	21 Mar 1867	
Rachael R.	William Dove	21 May 1860	
Upton S.	Mary E. T. Darby	23 Jan 1861	
William H.	Mary Ellen Anderson	30 Nov 1876	
HOWSIN, Robert	Eleanor Estep	24 Jan 1815	
HOYLE, Ann C.	James B. Neel	8 Feb 1881	
Charity A.	Gassaway W. Linthicum	21 Sep 1847	
Cora H.	Walter H. White	23 May 1881	
David C.	Florence Eagle	2 Dec 1896	w
Eleanor	Thomas Read	21 Dec 1810	
Eliza Ann	Robert N. Spates	6 May 1833	
Elizabeth	John Coglan	23 Aug 1802	
George W.	Isabella Clark	2 Jun 1858	
George W.	Sarah F. Beall	8 Nov 1877	w
John T.	Jane A. Phillips	25 Apr 1857	
Joseph H. C.	Charlotte A. Jones	9 Feb 1855	
Mamie	William A. Waters	11 Feb 1896	w
Sarah R.	Leander Waters	12 Dec 1840	
Smith	Ella May Watkins	29 Oct 1896	w
Susan C.	James H. Beall	14 Nov 1854	
Thomas M.	Martha F. Magruder	3 Mar 1897	w
William Jason	Mattie E. Hughes	19 Oct 1898	w
HUBBARD, Byron C.	Nellie L. Hutton	4 Jun 1895	w
HUDDLESON, Ida	Charles J. Lyddane	14 Nov 1881	
George	Cordelia Ann Lansdale	30 Apr 1851	
William	Martha M. Spates	7 May 1851	
HUDDLESTON, Alice E.	Samuel H. Renshaw	15 Mar 1877	w
Harriet A.	Christopher W. Lansdale	1 Jan 1866	
Mary E.	Mahlon E. Cooper	26 Apr 1866	
HUDDLESTONE, Elizabeth	James Scrivner	8 Jan 1834	
HUDSON, Mary	William Barber	22 Oct 1817	
Richard**	Nancy Wellen	10 Feb 1798	
HUFF, Henry H.	Helen Berry	14 Nov 1878	c
John	Sarah Dorsey	1 Dec 1880	c
HUGERFORD - also see HUNGERFORD			
HUGERFORD, Eleanor	John Fife	9 Dec 1800	
HUGHES - also see HUGHS, HEUGHS			
HUGHES, Benjamin C.	Sarah V. Magruder	7 Jan 1874	
Benjamin E.	Catharine S. Young	25 Apr 1849	

* Cannot read complete day; between 21 and 29
** Part of both last names from earlier reading

HUGHES,	Bessie M.	Edwin W. Monday	15 Nov 1898 w
	Catherine E.	Joseph B. Bowers	24 Apr 1893 w
	Charles R.	Mabel G. Sanford	21 Aug 1897 w
	Edward	Eleanor E. Ayton	6 Jul 1813
	Edward	Mary Holmes	16 Jun 1829
	Fannie W.	Nathan A. Walker	21 Jan 1890 w
	Jane E.	Edwin Waters	5 Mar 1840
	John F.	Catharine M. Coberth	5 Apr 1853
	John H.	Catharine Haffner	18 Dec 1823
	Julia M.	Zachariah Beckwith	17 Dec 1878 w
	Lucy B.	Luther W. Gibson	3 Sep 1888 w
	Margaret A. D.	George N. Leapley	9 Jun 1847
	Mary C.	John W. Billups	22 Jul 1861
	Moses P.	Evelina Gaither	16 Jan 1837
	Mattie E.	William Jason Hoyle	19 Oct 1898 w
	William A.	Rose G. Bennett	31 Aug 1883
	William D.	Elizabeth Conley	15 Sep 1857
	Zachariah	Elizabeth Duvall	23 Mar 1805
HUGHS,	Easter	Basil Trundle	20 May 1799
HUGUELY,	Charles W.	Ashsah A. Cashell	10 Jan 1876
HULINGS,	Fanny J. H.	Benjamin F. Boteler	6 Sep 1876
HULINGUES,	Elizabeth	Nicholas D. Offutt, Jr.	26 Oct 1881
	Mary B.	C. Burr Vickery	3 Nov 1874
HULINS,	Joseph*	Emma J. Snyder	** Apr 1879 w
HULL,	Annie	Fenton Backhanon	31 Aug 1878 c
	Henry	Mamie Taylor	7 Jul 1894 c
	Jacob	Sarah Gittins**	8 Nov 1800
	Wilson	Frances Scott	24 May 1898 c
HUMES,	Ben	Hannah Matin	7 Feb 1898 c
	Charity Ann	Isaac J. Beckwith	27 Dec 1886 c
	Lizzie	John Hall	22 Jan 1887 c
HUNGERFORD - also see HUGERFORD			
HUNGERFORD,	Charlotte	Asher Leighton	21 Jan 1804
	Fannie B.	David Sands V. Pleasants	15 Jul 1867
HUNT,	Henrietta M. D.	Hughes Oliphant	22 Oct 1888 w
	Ross P.	Jennie A. Ryon	11 May 1898 w
HUNTER,	Alice C.	Charles E. Engle	5 Aug 1895 w
	Edward S.	Annie V. Magruder	14 Feb 1870
	Marlena	Lewis B. Burch	25 Jan 1832
	Martha H.	Leroy W. Finch	14 Oct 1862
	Mary C.	Rudolph Watkins	21 Jan 1868
	W. B.	B. Jane Willson	17 Mar 1857
HURDLE,	Harriett	James Henly	17 Apr 1827
	Leonard	Nancy Matly	24 May 1800
	James	Mary Sedgwick	19 Dec 1801
	Noble	Mary Gilpin	16 Jul 1803
	Serena	James R. Munroe	22 Apr 1830
	Washington R.	Florrie H. Knowles	26 Mar 1860
HURLEY,	Addie C.	James E. King	31 Oct 1876
	Ann	John H. Boswell	5 Jan 1842
	Eliza A.	C. T. Anderson	10 Nov 1857
	Elizabeth M.	Greenbury Magruder	13 Feb 1833

* Name very light; could be incorrect; day between 14 and 21
** Written over; could be Gibbins

HURLEY, Emma J.	Lewis B. King	6 Feb 1883	
Henry C.	Anna McCormick	11 Mar 1885	w
Ida L.	William Thomas Warthen	4 Nov 1875	
John	Milly Offutt	31 Dec 1807	
John Jr.	Sarah Offutt	16 Mar 1814	
John W.	Francis M. Richardson	13 May 1857	
Lydia M.	William E. Crutchley	22 Jun 1895	w
Mary J.	Thomas Anderson	13 Apr 1850	
Obed	Maria L. Waters	4 Oct 1856	
Sarah	Enoch Baker	17 Nov 1825	
HURLY, Rebecca	William C. Soper	20 Dec 1824	
Sarah	Hezekiah Veach	11 Sep 1809	
HURST, John W.	Grace Diggs	22 Sep 1894	w
Sarah	Joel Ketchen	11 Feb 1804	
HURTT, Edward T.	Sarah E. Howard	22 Feb 1894	w
HUTCHINSON, George L.	Elizabeth Axsha Earp	29 Oct 1889	w
Katie	Eleven Beall	24 Aug 1872	
Lee	Maggie D. Bean	25 Feb 1891	w
Rebecca	Nathan Purdom	22 Dec 1821	
Sarah M.	John R. Sullivan	3 Jan 1860	
HUTCHISON, Clara J.	John T. Schrider	26 May 1897	w
Elizabeth	James W. Sprages	14 Nov 1872	
Huldy	Nathaniel S. Oden	10 Aug 1819	
Ida E.	Thomas Johnson	27 Dec 1872	
John	Jane M. Fling	8 Apr 1863	
John T.	Mary L. Cartwright	21 Dec 1872	
Joseph	Lucinda Riggs	24 Feb 1864	
Mary E.	Vincent L. Ambler	31 Aug 1833	
Mary J.	William H. Wootton	18 Feb 1865	
Mary S.	Charles A. Scrider	10 Oct 1893	w
Samuel	Elizabeth Steele	7 Oct 1811	
Sarah	Jacob Young	8 Jan 1821	
HUTTON, Anne	Thomas Duley	15 Feb 1813	
Annie Eliza	John Adams Riggs	14 Jan 1856	
Charles C.	Mary J. Lansdale	2 Apr 1866	
Elizabeth B.	William S. Caulfield	25 Jan 1898	w
Enoch B.	Elizabeth Ann Jones	29 Jan 1834	
Lavenia C.	Richard Waters	21 Dec 1859	
Lucy W.	Joshua N. Warfield	30 Nov 1881	
Mary Augusta	Joseph S. A. Hanfmann	16 Aug 1886	w
Mary E.	David S. Holland	14 Oct 1868	
Nellie L.	Byron C. Hubbard	4 Jun 1895	w
Ulric	Mary B. Janney	9 Jan 1888	w
William R.	Mary Augusta Clopper	20 Aug 1855	
HYATT - also see HIAT			
HYATT, Annie	Philip F. Mossburg	27 Jan 1875	
Ellen A.	David A. Zeigler	12 Sep 1835	
Emily	John Alfred Umstattd	12 Nov 1849	
Heneretta	John Hopwood	21 Mar 1807	
Jesse	Mary Ellen Ball	3 Sep 1845	
Jesse T.	Ann C. Wolfe	6 Jan 1860	
Levi Thomas	Maria E. Zeigler	3 Nov 1845	
Lilian A.	Edwin L. Garrett	1 Jun 1896	w
Luther Lingon	Kate Davis Wolfe	6 Jan 1880	w
Mary Ann	Warner Welch	27 May 1843	
Mary E.	William H. Butler	28 Apr 1882	

HYATT, Mary J.	Nathan B. Warthen, Jr.	12 Feb 1879	
Meranda	Philemon M. Smith	26 Apr 1841	
Philip	Rezba Watkins	28 Jun 1822	
Towny H.	Annie B. Moxley	21 Dec 1896	w
HYDE, Clara	George P. Carroll	25 Jun 1887	w
Evelina W.	Thomas Poole	7 Nov 1846	
Maria	Benson Talbott	31 Dec 1847	
HYMES, John	Virlinder Swain	11 Jul 1799	
HYSON, Charles S.	Harriet Bowie	22 Dec 1879	c
IAGAR, Mary C.	William H. Miles	25 Feb 1895	w
IDDINGS, William A.	Fanny Peirce	14 Aug 1894	w
IDEA, Elizabeth	Allen Perry	27 Feb 1802	
IGLEHART, Ann L.	Henry W. Richardson	25 Apr 1870	
Basil B.	Amanda E. Burns	14 Mar 1865	
Catharine	Nelson Burnes	16 Jan 1837	
Elizabeth	Christopher Sipe	10 Mar 1798	
Elizabeth	Lorenzo D. Adams	9 Mar 1837	
Emily	Lewis D. Lewis	21 Dec 1837	
Emily B.	Montegue L. Richardson	26 Jan 1878	w
James L.	Isabella E. Carr	6 Jan 1876	
Jesse	Sarah Burton	5 Jan 1811	
Mamie M.	Leonard J. Wilmoth	11 Jan 1897	w
Mary E.	Richard C. Carr	20 Jul 1864	
Melvina A.	John R. Crawford	21 Dec 1865	
Sarah A.	James M. Young	7 Apr 1868	
Susannah	William Burton	13 Mar 1810	
Thomas B.	Mary C. Suddath	8 Nov 1897	w
William G.	Leah J. Watkins	30 Apr 1895	w
William R.	Sarah M. Beall	22 Apr 1873	
IMHOF, Louise K.	William L. Willis	19 Apr 1895	w
IMLAY, Laura B.	Henry J. Norris	30 Jan 1882	
Nathan T.	Annie E. Money	1 May 1882	
IMLEY, Melvin P.	Jeannie Money	22 Jun 1885	w
IMMICK, George D.	Laura Collins	20 Nov 1879	w
INCONIE -also see INKINIS			
INCONIE, Caroline	John Bacon	30 Aug 1867	
INGALLS, James F.	Lydia J. Collins	22 Sep 1881	w
Reuben A.	Janet Chick	14 Nov 1888	w
William E.	Sarah E. Collins	19 Jul 1883	w
INGLE - also see ENGLE			
INGLE, Drusilla J.	Joseph F. Day	29 Sep 1884	w
INKINIS - also see INCONIE			
INKINIS, Eliza	Charles Hall	16 Sep 1876	
INLOSE, Samuel	Elizabeth Stone	24 Nov 1800	
IRVIN - also see IRVING, ERVIN, ARVIN			
IRVIN, Fletcher	Lizzie A. House	17 Dec 1872	
Rebecca	Hutchison Brown	5 Nov 1867	
IRVING - also see IRVIN			
IRVING, Samuel	Rebecca Hobbs	3 Oct 1849	
ISEMANN, Frank	Clara E. Lee	7 Nov 1898	w
Lena	Robert L. Slagle	12 Aug 1896	w
ISHERWOOD, Robert	Martha Duley	21 Jul 1841	
Robert J.	Isabella A. Darby	6 May 1856	
ISRAEL, Annie	James B. Greaves	3 Jun 1892	w
Charles R.	Deborah J. Burdette	22 Dec 1884	w

ISRAEL,	Fannie G.	Frank B. Figgins	14 Mar 1893 w
	Octavia	William V. Green	9 Sep 1879 w
	Otho	Anna Maria Gartrell	26 Feb 1820
	Rachael	Daniel Haines	1 Feb 1817
	Roselle	Alexander Bielaski	20 Sep 1879 w
IVORY,	John	Mollie Crampton	14 Apr 1888 c
	Robert	Martha Busey	19 Aug 1880 c
	Robert	Mary A. Clagett	10 Jun 1889 c
JACKSON,	Alice	William Dunlap	22 Aug 1868
	Alice	Notley H. Henley	8 Apr 1890 w
	Amelia	John George Baker	21 Mar 1799
	Andrew	Mary Carter	3 Aug 1867
	Andrew	Sarah Brown	16 May 1868
	Andrew	Phillis Henley	6 May 1878 c
	Andrew	Sarah King	17 Oct 1882 c
	Andrew	Mary Harper	17 May 1884 c
	Andrew	Susan Taylor	1 Dec 1896 c
	Ann M.	Robert H. Warren	26 Dec 1885 c
	Athelbert	Margaret A. Smith	6 May 1880
	Basil	Stella M. Mills	19 Sep 1891 c
	Benjamin	Elizabeth Hall	26 Dec 1894 c
	Bertie	William Fennel	31 Aug 1893 c
	Bettie	James H. Russell	21 Aug 1893 c
	Betty	Joseph Hoard	8 Dec 1880 c
	Charles H.	Mary E. Thompson	27 Nov 1895 c
	Charles Henry	Eliza Lynch	28 Mar 1877 c
	Charles W.	Hester L. Carter	6 Sep 1894 c
	Charlotte	George Jackson	6 May 1870
	Daniel T.	Mary Bell Doy	14 Sep 1886 c
	David	Mary E. Kelly	18 Dec 1876
	Eleanora	Tandy Scott	16 Feb 1898 c
	Eliza E.	Alfred J. Neverson	15 May 1886 c
	Elizabeth	John H. Prather	16 Oct 1888 c
	Elizabeth	Amos Posie	9 Jun 1891 c
	Elizabeth	Augustus Cook	18 Apr 1895 c
	Ella V.	James C. Johnson	15 Jan 1887 c
	Emily	Melvin D. Brown	22 Nov 1897 w
	Frank	Katy Smith	20 Jan 1896 c
	Franklin	Margaret Gantt	5 Apr 1883 c
	Franklin	Ella V. Hood	3 Oct 1889 c
	Frederick E.	Bertha M. Parsley	9 Feb 1898 w
	George	Winay Mockbee	5 Mar 1806
	George	Mary Ennis	8 Apr 1811
	George	Charlotte Jackson	6 May 1870
	George	Salena A. Ricks	28 Dec 1877 c
	George	Maria Hebron	21 Oct 1893 c
	George A.	Maggie E. Hopkins	27 Sep 1897 c
	George William	Edith V. Neverson	19 Sep 1879 c
	Greenbury	Lizzie Gray	6 Apr 1876
	Hannah	Samuel Godman	19 Oct 1874
	Harriet Isabella	Peter Hilleary Hebburn	3 Jan 1868
	Henny	Thomas Nicholls	3 Jun 1870
	Henry	Nancy Warren	19 Sep 1874
	Henry	Lucretia Herbert	16 Dec 1897 c
	Henry H.	Barbara Clipper	15 Oct 1892 c

JACKSON,	James	Eliza Mason	18 Mar 1876
	James E.	Mary E. Daphney	5 Nov 1884 c
	James E.	Mary E. Neal	7 Dec 1896 c
	Jane	John Daphne	27 Dec 1865
	Jasper M.	Ann H. Duvall	30 Oct 1846
	Jeremiah	Belle Holley	25 Dec 1883 c
	Jerry	Ida Harper	24 Jan 1888 c
	John	Easter Ellis	14 Dec 1798
	John	Sophronia Cooper	7 Mar 1890 c
	John	Ann O. King	11 Aug 1897 c
	John	Ann Murray	4 Oct 1897 c
	John A.	Pattie Shurn	13 Jul 1898 c
	John F.	Susie A. Jackson	2 Jul 1887 c
	John W.	Emily Weldon	4 Aug 1888 c
	Joseph	Lizzie Jackson	29 Jul 1873
	Kate	William Diggs	31 Oct 1894 c
	Letha	James K. Ford	6 Sep 1884 c
	Lewis H.	Martha V. Lea	27 Feb 1889 c
	Lillie M.	William W. Spies	29 Jun 1895 w
	Lizzie	Lewis Brown	24 Sep 1870
	Lizzie	Joseph Jackson	29 Jul 1873
	Lizzie	Thomas Bowen	10 May 1894 c
	Louis	Laura V. Johnson	8 Dec 1896 c
	Lucy	Joseph Johnson	12 Jul 1877 c
	Lucy	Mortimer Ambush	15 Dec 1883
	Lucy	George W. Clipper	4 Apr 1889 c
	Maggie	John F. Branison	28 Dec 1898 c
	Margaret E.	John H. Moore	23 Dec 1878 c
	Maria	James H. Campbell	23 Jun 1866
	Maria	William Dawes	26 Dec 1876
	Maria	Samuel Washington	27 Nov 1894 c
	Martha J.	George W. W. Bowie	20 Nov 1875
	Martha J. V.	Thomas H. Johnson	12 Mar 1895 c
	Mary	Louis Primis	8 Nov 1870
	Mary	James Thomas	10 Jun 1895 c
	Mary	Thomas Lynch	13 Jul 1895 c
	Mary A.	William F. Scott	10 Feb 1892 c
	Mary E.	James F. Pearce	24 Oct 1871
	Mary E.	Alfred Bradley	25 May 1892 c
	Mary E. V.	Franklin W. Smith	26 Dec 1889 c
	Mary J.	-----y T. Johnson	11 Nov 1882 c
	Matilda	Leonard Harvord	30 Dec 1874
	Melville T.	Lottie Hose	4 Aug 1896 c
	Miley	Sarah Campbell	9 Mar 1886 c
	Millard A.	Ollie M. Woodfield	25 Jan 1897 w
	Milton	May Webster	19 Jul 1892 w
	Mollie	Richard Doy	22 Dec 1888 c
	Musco	Alcinda Ricks	29 May 1894 c
	Priscilla	Alfred Johnson	19 Oct 1876
	Rebecca	Coleman Morton	2 Apr 1879 c
	Richard	Ann Collins	17 Feb 1848
	Rosa	Walter Owens	28 Dec 1886 c
	Ruth	Thomas Wheeler	8 Oct 1798
	Sallie	Lloyd N. Gibbs	3 Jul 1879
	Samuel	Matilda St. Clair	24 Sep 1818
	Samuel	Maria E. Snowden	20 Jan 1870

JACKSON,	Samuel A.	Ida M. Grover	31 Dec 1890 w
	Sarah	George Duffin	3 Apr 1874
	Sarah	Nathan Digges	15 Sep 1874
	Sarah L.	Andrew F. Ball	8 Apr 1867
	Susie A.	John F. Jackson	2 Jul 1887 c
	Tabitha	Franklin Lee	17 Nov 1866
	Tersy L. C.	William H. Hawkins	29 Oct 1884 c
	Thomas	Margaret Prather	20 Dec 1876
	Thomas	Ginnie Proctor	31 Dec 1892 c
	Thomas A.	Lavinia Clay	26 Oct 1888 c
	Thomas E.	Gertrude Howser	2* Jun 1898 w
	Wesley	LIzzie Hall	5 Sep 1889 c
	William	Hattie Mason	27 Feb 1895 c
	William	Annie Robertson	2 Mar 1895 c
	William H.	Maggie E. Parsley	16 May 1892 w
	William W.	Ella M. Jenkins	31 May 1898 c
JACOBS,	Alverda A.	Curtis McKlee	2 Jan 1863
	Anthanet	Richard Carr	29 Jan 1828
	Dolly	Obias Easton	30 May 1807
	John	Darkey Barrett	22 Dec 1802
	Samuel	Polly Feaster	5 May 1825
JAMEISON - also see JAMISON			
JAMEISON,	Alexander	Theresa Harding	6 Sep 1844
JAMES,	Ann	Richard Boice	15 Jan 1829
	Elizabeth	Gassaway Cross	5 Feb 1806
	Henry C.	Annie L. Atwood	25 Sep 1889 w
	Horatio	Martha White	30 Sep 1824
	John B.	Ruthy Alexander	22 May 1798
	Margarett	Washington F. Boice	18 Dec 1827
	Otho	Sarah Williams	25 Dec 1809
	Thomas	Lydia Fowler	29 Jan 1800
	Richard	Elizabeth Hodges**	18 Oct 1805
JAMIESON,	Franklin	Sarah Savoy	24 Dec 1866
	John ***.	Jane E. Jones	23 Nov 1844
JAMISON - also see JAMEISON, JAMIESON			
JAMISON,	Alexander F.	Annie E. Knott	10 Apr 1882
	James	Hesther Belford	6 Apr 1813
	Jeremiah	Mary Jamison	28 Jan 1837
	Louisa M.	John A. Howard	17 Oct 1821
	Mary	Jeremiah Jamison	28 Jan 1837
	Richard	Rosella Jamison	4 Feb 1833
	Rosella	Richard Jamison	4 Feb 1833
JANES,	George	Lydia Cross	27 Nov 1832
	H--****	Eleanor M. Veirs	26 Oct 1835
	Lemuel C.	Barbary E. Higgins	17 Feb 1829
	Perry	Ann Greenfield	21 Mar 1805
	Willy	Patty Williams	8 May 1804
JANNEY,	Mary B.	Ulric Hutton	9 Jan 1888 w
	Samuel A.	Mary C. Hall	10 Mar 1863
	Sarah H.	Ernest N. Adams	27 Feb 1894 w

* Cannot read complete day; between 21 and 29
** Blot on "o"; could be Hedges
*** Initial I or J
**** There is an abbreviation which begins with H and an initial I or J

JARBOE, Ann	Benjamin Beall	7 Dec 1816	
Elizabeth	Samuel Barrett	21 Aug 1815	
Eugene E.	Mary E. Jones	16 Jan 1875	
Juliet Ann	John Hopkins	19 Jan 1825	
Mary	Samuel Gatton	29 May 1799	
Mary J.	George T. Hodges	23 Nov 1874	
Nancy	Emanuel Domini	15 Oct 1803	
Raphael T.	Elizabeth Ann Offutt	30 Apr 1869	
Raphael T.	Ellen H. Barnhouse	6 Nov 1893	w
JARBY, John W.	Laura Carter	16 Sep 1891	c
JARDINE, Edward	Catharine Craycroft	30 Dec 1872	
JARVAIS, James	Milly Willson	3 Apr 1801	
JARVIS, Harriet A.	John Robinson	15 Jan 1858	
Hilleary T.	Elizabeth Pearce	9 Jan 1833	
Mary	Levi Moulding	25 Sep 1822	
Mary E.	James W. Acres	8 Sep 1841	
Rosanna	James H. Money	1 Dec 1857	
JARVISS, James	Eliza Linch	10 Mar 1803	
JASON, Alice A.	John William Brown	6 Jul 1878	c
JEAMES, Lydia Ann*	William Jeanes	31 Jan 1839	
JEANES, Lydia	Charles T. Smith	28 Mar 1854	
William	Ann Bloice	1 Oct 1836	
William*	Lydia Ann Jeames	31 Jan 1839	
JEFFERS, Edward T.	Annie V. Higgins	20 Nov 1895	w
Jane E.	James H. Carter	21 Feb 1879	w
JEFFERSON, Hester A.	Thomas F. Cashell	4 Jun 1856	
Lydia	George Kendall	1 Dec 1873	
Rhoda	John Henry	28 Nov 1803	
JEFFRIES, Edward E.	Mary E. Neal	12 Feb 1889	c
Florence N.	Paul E. Detrick	20 Nov 1894	w
George A.	Nannie F. Brooks	3 Oct 1886	w
Lulu	Charles N. Earpe	18 Aug 1890	w
JENKINS - also see JINKINS			
JENKINS, Albert	Ella M. Hawkins	20 Dec 1892	c
Aletha A.	Samuel M. Griffin	17 Jun 1878	
Ann	Joseph Mercer	12 Feb 1831	
Anna E.	Thomas N. Kidwell	21 May 1849	
Daniel	Martha Lea	26 Dec 1870	
Eliza	James Kemp	14 Jun 1869	
Ella M.	William W. Jackson	31 May 1898	c
Enos	Sarah A. Nicholson	13 Dec 1893	w
George	Harriot Scott	22 Jan 1818	
Gertrude	Rezin Thomas Turner	8 Oct 1874	
Henry	Eleanor Smith	28 Sep 1814	
Ida	Lemuel Jones	22 Dec 1873	
James E.	Vallie Davis	24 Dec 1889	c
Jennie	Charles Sullivan	26 Apr 1897	w
John	Charlotte Sparrow	9 Feb 1808	
John	Anna Stored	22 Jul 1881	c
Lydia A.	William H. Dietz	4 Feb 1889	w
Mannie A.	James N. Davis	9 Nov 1897	c
Mary	Hezekiah Ward	20 Sep 1838	
Mary	George Hall	4 May 1894	c
Mary A.	Nathaniel B. Brown	10 Mar 1870	

* Last names as written

JENKINS, Mary F.	George R. Randolph	4 Jul 1894	c
Rebecca J.	Stephen Heffron	24 Jan 1870	
Sarah E.	William P. Layman	18 Aug 1848	
Simon	Ann Smith	9 Nov 1818	
Thomas	Sarah J. Johnson	12 Feb 1890	c
Thomas	Annie Hamilton	31 Oct 1896	c
Walter	Ruth Selby	8 Feb 1799	
JENNETT - also see JINNETT			
JENNETT, George W. P.	Nettie C. Heugetts	3 Oct 1883	
JENNIES - also see JENUS			
JENNIES, Jolina Isabella	Thomas Dorsey	14 Jan 1890	c
JENSON, Lydia	Nicholas Hawkins	22 Dec 1886	c
JENUS - also see GENUS, JENNIES			
JENUS, Emory	Harriet Diggins	8 Jan 1867	
Emory	Sallie Davis	5 Sep 1874	
JETT, Edward H.	Martha A. Ketchen	1 Oct 1881	w
Jean Krozer (male)	Marie L. Webb	* Oct 1896	w
JINGLE - also see GINGELL			
JINGLE, Jane	Hezekiah Crown	12 Apr 1834	
JINKINS - also see JENKINS			
JINKINS, Ann E.	Noah Curtis	15 Dec 1897	c
Elizabeth	Daniel Duty	20 Mar 1799	
JINNETT - also see JENNETT			
JINNETT, Francis	Elizabeth Keith	21 Nov 1821	
JOHNS, Leonard H.	Margarett Ann Williams	3 Feb 1801	
Mahala	Thomas H. Vinson	23 Dec 1818	
Marian G.	Frederick William Bause	3 Nov 1884	w
Marianna V.	Charles Martin	29 May 1877	c
Sarah	David Peter	16 Sep 1799	
JOHNSON - also see JOHNSTON, JONSTON			
JOHNSON, -----y T.	Mary J. Jackson	11 Nov 1882	c
Alexander	Mary Rawlins	1 Jun 1866	
Alexander	Rosanna Corn	18 Jun 1887	c
Alfred	Cassy Cook	7 Nov 1867	
Alfred	Priscilla Jackson	19 Oct 1876	
Alfred	Maggie Ross	12 Feb 1877	c
Alice H.	William H. Smith	30 Jan 1895	c
Alvira	Lesir Hill	30 Dec 1881	
Amey B.	William G. S. Mathews	29 Nov 1893	c
Ann E.	Cephas F. Willett	16 Oct 1855	
Annie	John F. Shryock	14 Dec 1871	
Annie	Benjamin Scales	13 Jun 1895	w
Annie L.	Henry T. Bean	10 Nov 1896	w
Asbury	Lucinda Adams	6 Apr 1885	c
Basil	Elizabeth Blowers	1 Mar 1815	
Basil	Mary Ann Blowers	7 Nov 1816	
Benjamin	Mary Northcroft	21 Jan 1803	
Benjamin	Martha E. House	19 Apr 1837	
Benjamin C. H.	Fannie Adams	13 Feb 1888	c
Bessie	Vernon Hill	14 Aug 1894	c
Betsy	William Hebron	18 Apr 1892	c
Bradley T.	Maggie P. Smith	17 Dec 1885	c
Caroline	William Brent	26 May 1881	c
Carrie E.	William L. Powell	18 Dec 1886	c

* Cannot read day; before 9

JOHNSON,	Carrie L.	Harry M. Dublin	20 Oct 1896	c
	Catharine E.	John W. Dorsey	4 Sep 1873	
	Charles	Mary Beander	19 May 1869	
	Charles	Mal Rody	3 Apr 1878	
	Charles	Ellen Beall	29 Sep 1879	c
	Charles	Elizabeth Brewer	24 Aug 1897	c
	Charles T.	Lizzie J. Watkins	21 Apr 1890	w
	Charles W.	Laura V. Owens	16 Jun 1886	c
	Charles W.	Sarah E. Hammond	20 Sep 1888	c
	Charlotte	John T. Dellehay	20 Apr 1864	
	Charlotte D.	Horace L. Murphy	30 Nov 1854	
	Clara	Charles Powell	3 Nov 1896	c
	Clara W.	Henry Green	24 Jul 1890	c
	Clement	Mary Foreman	5 Jan 1886	c
	Delia E.	Mark Davis	24 Dec 1892	c
	Della	Larkin Johnson	6 Feb 1879	c
	E. Munroe	Mary Frances Hempstone	10 Jan 1865	
	Edith	Arthur Pumphrey	3 Mar 1894	c
	Edward R.	Mary F. Mobley	24 Mar 1874	
	Effie L.	William E. Schwering	9 Feb 1891	w
	Eliza	John W. Dorsey	5 Feb 1891	c
	Elizabeth	Jacob Kron	21 Apr 1853	
	Elizabeth	Owen W. Disney	16 Apr 1870	
	Elizabeth	William Leizear	7 Dec 1870	
	Elizabeth	James H. Bolton	11 Apr 1894	w
	Elizabeth	David Turner	28 Dec 1896	c
	Ellen	John W. Lucas	27 Aug 1872	
	Ellen	Thomas Snowden	28 Jul 1876	
	Ellen	Lewis Lyles	12 Sep 1876	
	Emily	William Blincoe	27 Sep 1838	
	Emily	Thomas Crumpton	25 Dec 1878	c
	Emily	Albert Green	2 Jan 1879	c
	Emily A.	Joseph Johnson	14 Nov 1878	c
	Emma	Charles Canby	16 Aug 1873	
	Emma E.	Vernon A. Mullinix	23 Dec 1897	w
	Ephraim	Margarett Mobberly	24 Jan 1829	
	Ernest	Cora C. Magruder	14 Jan 1896	c
	Eulie	James W. N. Carroll	3 Nov 1887	c
	Eustis B.	Hattie C. Wyatt	21 Oct 1895	c
	Evaline	Hollis Grant	4 Oct 1898	c
	Flodoardo H.	Laura V. Williams	29 Sep 1896	c
	Florence	George Wright	1 May 1894	c
	Frank	Harriet Hood	15 Nov 1878	
	Frederick	Mary Peters	20 Jul 1895	c
	Frederick C.	Alice ?. Tucker	1 Aug 1884	
	George	Catherine F. Ridgeway	30 Aug 1895	w
	George	Mary Neale	14 Oct 1897	c
	George W.	Lydia E. Disney	3 Feb 1872	
	George W.	Sarah T. Benson	17 Sep 1872	
	George W.	Maria E. E. Bowen	24 Nov 1875	
	Gertie	Dennis Jordan	24 Dec 1892	c
	Greenbury	Milly Thompson	14 Mar 1821	
	Greenbury W.	Lethe Campbell	12 Mar 1885	c
	Hallie	Joseph Gittings	26 Dec 1895	c
	Harriet	Jason Pratt	7 Dec 1893	c
	Harriet E.	Isaiah Shoemaker	25 May 1866	

JOHNSON,	Harry L.	Edith Woodward	14 Sep 1897	w
	Helen	John Woodward	30 Apr 1888	c
	Henrietta	Basil Tyler	2 Apr 1879	c
	Henrietta	Henson Tyler	2 Mar 1887	c
	Henry	Fannie Brown	7 Sep 1876	
	Henry	Catharine Adams	4 May 1878	c
	Henry	------* Tyler	31 Oct 1878	c
	Henry	Catharine Neel	9 Jul 1883	
	Henry	Sarah Warren	5 May 1888	c
	Henson	Milly Hammond	13 Jan 1870	
	Henson E.	Lizzie Kelly	25 Mar 1875	
	Hezekiah	Elizabeth Tyler	4 Jun 1880	
	Horace	Priscilla Orme	15 Nov 1826	
	Horace	Lily J. Nelson	21 May 1869	
	Isaac	Eliza Dorsey	1 Sep 1865	
	Isaac	Charlotte Smith	30 May 1867	
	Isaac	Edy Williams	4 Nov 1869	
	Isaac A.	Olivia M. Myers	9 Feb 1882	
	Isabell	Luther Thomas Gue	3 Dec 1868	
	Isaiah	Annie Offutt	10 Dec 1896	c
	Jacob	Georgianna V. Lyles	22 Feb 1894	c
	Jacob I.	Beatrix V. Pope	9 Jun 1896	w
	James	Ann Riney	17 Jan 1799	
	James	Henrietta Tyler	5 Sep 1877	c
	James	Alice Toogood	14 Jun 1886	c
	James C.	Ella V. Jackson	15 Jan 1887	c
	James E.	Martha E. Lucas	18 Feb 1890	w
	James J.	Daisy Wilkinson	27 Apr 1895	w
	James J.	Mary E. Gates	11 May 1897	w
	James L.	Anna Randolph	22 Jun 1875	c
	James M.	Emma Robertson	24 Sep 1895	w
	James W.	Lizzie A. Leizear	31 Mar 1869	
	James W.	Ellen J. Leizear	1 Dec 1880	
	James W.	Emma Cole Burdette	17 May 1898	w
	Jason	Susana Cook	23 Feb 1870	
	Jeremiah	Rachel Ann Mason	12 Feb 1869	
	Joan	John Broadus	11 Jun 1867	
	John	Mary Mockbee	28 Dec 1836	
	John	Alice Groomes	7 Jun 1875	
	John	Hennie Nichols	26 May 1885	c
	John	Lena Curtis	31 Dec 1889	c
	John Edward	Emma May Pratt	29 Mar 1898	c
	John Henry	Sarah V. E. Roberson	14 May 1883	w
	John Henry	Mary Emma Neale	25 Oct 1894	c
	John T.	Mary L. Burroughs	18 Jan 1894	w
	Joseph	Clarissa Hobbs	1 Dec 1807	
	Joseph	Lucy Jackson	12 Jul 1877	c
	Joseph	Emily A. Johnson	14 Nov 1878	c
	Joseph	Fannie G. Prather	4 May 1893	c
	Joseph	Caroline Newman	27 Jan 1894	c
	Joseph S.	Mary A. Hopkins	24 Feb 1898	w
	Josephine	Alfred Harding	3 Sep 1886	c
	Joshua J.	Sarah Ann Leizear	3 Nov 1874	
	Juliet	Robert Lyles	14 Mar 1814	

* Name has blot on it

JOHNSON,	Katie	Richard Beall	22 May 1883 c
	Larkin	Della Johnson	6 Feb 1879 c
	Laura	Sandy Beckwith	26 Dec 1878 c
	Laura	George W. Smith	25 May 1885 c
	Laura	Henry Dorsey	2 Jun 1887 c
	Laura V.	Louis Jackson	8 Dec 1896 c
	Lavinia	Daniel J. Brooks	16 Dec 1880 c
	Lavinia	Lloyd Magruder	30 Dec 1874
	Lewis A.	Mary M. E. Hinton	29 Aug 1895 w
	Lizzie	George Thompson	24 Dec 1895 c
	Louisa	Robert Harrod	15 Sep 1869
	Lucinda	William Matthews	19 Nov 1885 c
	Lucy	Philip Stephenson	5 Nov 1874
	Magaret	Alexander Watson	15 Jul 1898 c
	Margaret	William Lee	3 Feb 1871
	Margaret	Henson Scott	30 Dec 1884 c
	Margaret	Charles Laurence	26 Jul 1894 w
	Margaret A.	Henry Hover	18 Feb 1862
	Margaret A.	Nicholas E. Musgrove	5 May 1868
	Margarett	Isaac Walker	25 Dec 1818
	Maria	William Green	8 Oct 1874
	Marion	John H. Smith	5 Jan 1893 c
	Martha	John Nicholson	10 Mar 1869
	Martha	Edward Lews	24 Dec 1874
	Martha	George Dorsey	27 Dec 1883 c
	Martha A.	Marshall Easton	18 Dec 1883
	Martha A.	George S. Adams	3 Mar 1886 c
	Martha A. M.	John Clipper	17 Jun 1895 c
	Mary	William Bath	11 Apr 1804
	Mary	John Thompson	30 Jan 1869
	Mary	Nicholas Lee	16 Dec 1875
	Mary	Augustus Brogden	11 Sep 1879 c
	Mary	Dennis W. Lee	28 Dec 1886 c
	Mary	George W. Ellison	27 Aug 1891 c
	Mary	James Vinson	16 Feb 1895 c
	Mary A.	Asbury Williams	28 Dec 1896 c
	Mary A.	William Ednh. Frazier	6 Apr 1898 c
	Mary Ann	William Jones	28 Oct 1835
	Mary Ann	Joseph P. Brown	1 Oct 1870
	Mary E.	Aaron Doublin	27 Mar 1873
	Mary E.	William N. Scales	12 Nov 1895 c
	Mary J.	Francis T. Leizear	9 Jan 1867
	Mary L.	John Lethbridge	26 Jul 1870
	Mary R.	John W. Nichollson	28 Jan 1851
	Mary V.	Tilghman E. Dove	10 Oct 1894 c
	Matilda	George Tucker	9 Jan 1866
	Matilda	Reuben A. Talliaferro	5 May 1867
	Melinda	Wesley Boyd	1 Apr 1879 c
	Millie L.	Oliver Johnson	16 May 1894 c
	Mollie	John H. Baker	29 Oct 1891 c
	Nancy	Walter Hellen	18 Oct 1798
	Nathan	Mary Dorsey	4 Jun 1881 c
	Nelson	Mary J. Saunders	17 Apr 1871
	Oliver	Lucinda Lancaster	5 Jun 1883
	Oliver	Millie L. Johnson	16 May 1894 c
	Oliver G.	Ida J. Kuster	29 Mar 1892 w

JOHNSON,	Philip	Rachel Beander	26 Sep 1877 c
	Priscilla	Benjamin Cross	9 Mar 1801
	Rachel	Albert Segalls	6 Sep 1873
	Rachel A.	------ J. Chambers	* Nov 1882 c
	Rebecca	Isaiah F. Marshall	9 Jun 1886 c
	Reuben	Eliza Proctor	9 Jul 1896 c
	Rhoda	Baker W. Nicholson	19 Oct 1857
	Richard B.	Cinderella Dustin	18 Oct 1879 w
	Robert	Rebecca Cephas	15 May 1875
	Rosa	Edward Perry	18 Oct 1888 c
	Rose A.	John Williams	3 Dec 1890 c
	Rosie E.	James J. Peters	8 Dec 1885 w
	Sadie	James Warner	4 Jun 1896 c
	Sallie M.	Octavius O. Baker	14 Oct 1880
	Sally	William Offut	27 Mar 1871
	Samuel	Lizzie Warren	20 Feb 1875
	Samuel	Martha A. Ricks	24 Jul 1879
	Samuel	Carrie Dorsey	16 May 1893 c
	Samuel H.	Anna Carter	30 Dec 1889 c
	Samuel K.	Annie C. Schooly	28 Jan 1873
	Samuel T.	Henrietta Chambers	28 Oct 1880 c
	Sarah	John Murphey	24 Feb 1818
	Sarah	Benjamin Wilburn	28 Mar 1820
	Sarah	Edward A. Fitzgerald	13 Jan 1887 w
	Sarah	Charles Combash	27 Nov 1890 c
	Sarah Catharine	Robert Fairfax	16 Feb 1885 c
	Sarah E.	Tasker Carter	29 Jul 1880
	Sarah E.	Charles H. Butler	16 Dec 1891 c
	Sarah J.	Thomas N. Kidwell	23 Dec 1843
	Sarah J.	Thomas Jenkins	12 Feb 1890 c
	Sidney (female)	James Arnold	29 Dec 1870
	Simon	Margaret Graham	3 Jun 1875
	Sophia	Edward Laird	23 Jul 1883 c
	Susan	J. N. Butler	21 Dec 1881
	Tabitha	Moses Walker	31 Dec 1800
	Thomas	Catherine Stewart	13 Mar 1868
	Thomas	Ida E. Hutchison	27 Dec 1872
	Thomas B.	Alethy Reid	28 Feb 1816
	Thomas H.	Martha J. V. Jackson	12 Mar 1895 c
	Thomas R.	Isabel Tucker	6 Dec 1887 w
	Thomas W.	Henrietta Davis	20 Dec 1893 c
	William	Mary White	11 Jul 1820
	William	Maria A. Dasey	13 Sep 1822
	William	Elizabeth Grimes	22 Dec 1840
	William	Elizabeth Stewart	5 Aug 1869 c
	William	Maggie Offutt	29 Dec 1875
	William	Alcinda Bowie	27 Jun 1878 c
	William	Sarah T. Reid	30 Sep 1884 w
	William	Louisa Chambers	3 May 1886 c .
	William E.	Emeline Cook	21 Oct 1896 c
	William H.	Eliza Davis	19 Apr 1866 c
	William S.	Ruth A. Snowden	24 Dec 1892 w
	Wilson	Mary E. Davis	7 Sep 1893 c
	Wilson G.	Lizzie V. Keiler	9 May 1892 w

* First name and day too light to read; day between 14 and 20

JOHNSON, Zachariah	Anne Holland	4 Sep 1827	
JOHNSTON - also see JOHNSON			
JOHNSTON, Alfred	Jane Stephenson	14 May 1879	c
Eulalie	Nicholas King	20 Nov 1865	
Helen A.	D. Cameron Morrison	14 Nov 1864	
Lydia F.	E. Barrett Prettyman	6 Jun 1855	
Margaret	O. C. Badger	27 Oct 1852	
Mary W.	Cooke D. Luckett	8 Nov 1869	
JONES, -----* T.	Martha E. Taylor	18 Dec 1860	
Alexander	Mary Waner	7 Nov 1798	
Alexander	Laura Turner	14 Apr 1898	c
Alice G.	William Fowler	24 Nov 1856	
Amanda	Thomas Davis	21 Jan 1889	c
Amy	James Proctor	23 Feb 1875	
Andrew J.	Sarah J. Cissel	5 Dec 1859	
Ann E.	Charles W. Shreeve	18 Oct 1859	
Ann M.	William Mannake	8 Feb 1849	
Ann M.	Franklin Cummins	1 Apr 1850	
Ann Mary	Columbus Dade	16 Jan 1856	
Anne	William Shanks	4 Feb 1804	
Anne	William Roberts	10 Nov 1818	
Annie Kate	George W. Parsley, Jr.	19 Sep 1887	w
Ben	Rosa Morton	23 May 1892	w
Benajmin	Anna Riney	7 Apr 1806	
Benjamin J.	Ann Virginia Gott	6 Jan 1869	
Benjamin W.	Margaret Willson	7 Jan 1802	
Brooke	Trecy Knott	3 Jan 1809	
C. P.	Mary Maud Parkinson	30 Sep 1871	
Caroline	William Douglass	28 Oct 1856	
Carrie Lee	Joseph A. Raum	26 May 1891	w
Catherine	Allen Peddicoart	18 Dec 1810	
Catharine S.	John L. T. Jones	24 Dec 1847	
Charles	Ruth Ducker	31 Jan 1803	
Charles	Sarah E. Trail	12 Oct 1896	w
Charles B.	Jane Clements	1 Oct 1836	
Charles B.	Valetta Clements	3 Nov 1841	
Charles B.	Mary Vance	22 Nov 1853	
Charles B.	Lavinia Lyddane	31 Jan 1883	w
Charles O.	Matilda Offutt	26 Feb 1812	
Charles Offutt	Rebecca Offutt	22 Jan 1799	
Charles Scott	Belle Brown	29 Nov 1893	w
Charlotte	John Beall	28 Dec 1807	
Charlotte A.	Joseph H. C. Hoyle	9 Feb 1855	
Clara R.	James R. Wallace	3 May 1888	c
Cora ?.	James R. Proctor	13 Apr 1892	c
Daniel T.	Mary Sellman	9 Jan 1836	
David T.	Mary Ann Dawson	20 Jan 1840	
Dennis	Mary Campbell	16 Mar 1824	
Dennis	Mollie Peter	31 May 1879	c
Eleanor	Rebal W. Nally	15 Jan 1802	
Eleanor M.	John H. T. Hays	22 May 1837	
Elilah	Matthew Read	10 Sep 1818	
Elisha	Mary P. Griffith	8 Oct 1829	
Eliza	Robert Chambers	11 Feb 1871	

* First name is written over

JONES, Eliza V.	James W. Kinney	12 Jan 1892	w
Elizabeth	Carlton Belt, Jr.	25 Feb 1799	
Elizabeth	William Edmonston	2 Mar 1802	
Elizabeth	Samuel Willett Cox	2 Oct 1826	
Elizabeth	Thomas H. Fyffe	23 Apr 1838	
Elizabeth Ann	Enoch B. Hutton	29 Jan 1834	
Elizabeth H.	Charles W. Owen	27 Oct 1896	w
Emily Ann	Hezekiah W. Trundle	25 Apr 1835	
Emily E.	James H. Ferral	20 Jun 1876	
Emily J.	George H. Clements	17 Nov 1876	
Erasmus	Charlotte Lyles	14 Jun 1869	
Evan	Sarah West	18 Feb 1808	
Evan A.	Rachel G. Riggs	4 Jan 1856	
Franklin	Ruth Plummer	24 Dec 1877	c
Frederick	Henrietta L. Hempstone	14 May 1872	
George A.	Harriet Scott	17 Dec 1896	c
George D.	Evie W. Allnutt	12 Dec 1891	
Georgianna	Henry Harriss	14 Oct 1885	c
Gustavus	Elizabeth A. Plummer	27 May 1851	
Hannah N.*	Charles P. Pollard	2 May 1821	
Harriet N.	John A. T. Kilgour	6 Feb 1849	
Henry	Eleanor Trundle	24 Dec 1807	
Henry	Mary Oneal	27 Jan 1820	
Henry	Maria E. Peters	26 Dec 1877	c
Henry	Lelita Campbell	7 Jan 1885	c
Henry C.	Sarah Walter	3 Oct 1816	
Henry R.	Mary Eloise Scholl	7 Jan 1876	
Horatio	Susanna Ricketts	2 Sep 1806	
Ignatius	Viney Jones	28 Mar 1799	
Isaac	Sarah Poole	12 Dec 1833	
Isaac T.	Mary L. Beall	26 Mar 1863	
J. Walter	Mollie J. Walters	23 Apr 1867	
Jane E.	John **. Jamieson	23 Nov 1844	
Jemima	Edward Buttler	2 Dec 1805	
John	Sarah Stewart	6 Nov 1798	
John	Anne Upton	16 Dec 1811	
John	Elizabeth Darnall	18 Jan 1830	
John	Susan Smith	13 Sep 1884	c
John Jr.	Mollie M. Hays	15 Jan 1873	
John of Evan	Ann S. Waters	25 Feb 1820	
John of Nathan	Christiana C. Offutt	4 Nov 1817	
John A.	Judy Streaks	21 Dec 1820	
John A.	Rose M. Darby	3 Jan 1866	
John E.	Elizabeth Frazier	8 Aug 1892	c
John L. T.	Catharine S. Jones	24 Dec 1847	
John R.	Delia L. Heffner	20 Nov 1890	w
John W.	Nettie Gray	6 Oct 1890	c
Joseph	Deborah Welsh	16 Nov 1822	
Joseph H.	Elizabeth Clagett	16 Jan 1821	
Joseph Isaac	Elizabeth Duvall	22 Nov 1805	
Joseph James Wilkerson	Ann Newton Chiswell	22 Dec 1806	
Josiah W.	Mary E. Barnsley	30 May 1864	

* Part of last name from earlier reading
** Initial I or J

JONES, Judy	Joshua Carr	11 Apr 1826	
Laura	William W. Darby	27 Aug 1882	
Lemuel	Ida Jenkins	22 Dec 1873	
Leonidas	Elizabeth J. King	25 Feb 1853	
Levi	Lucy Saylor	19 Aug 1878	
Levi T.	Mary A. Carter	21 Sep 1895	c
Lizzie R.	William T. Jones	9 Dec 1867	
Lloyd S.	Teresa Ann Beall	25 Jan 1836	
Lucinda	Michael Connelly	22 Apr 1830	
Lucy	Lawson Clarke	3 Aug 1802	
Lucy	George Braxton	11 May 1877	
Margaret	James Wilson Perry	17 Jan 1799	
Margaret B.	Thomas Lyddane	27 Nov 1848	
Margaret C.	Patrick H. McLeod	27 May 1839	
Margaret E.	Daniel T. Shreve	22 Nov 1852	
Maria	David Joshua Scott	12 Mar 1869	
Marian Elizabeth	Lee R. Martin	15 Feb 1898	w
Marian H.	George F. Burdette	20 Jul 1886	w
Martha	Jacob Aldridge	5 Feb 1805	
Martha A.	James W. Mallonee	1 Feb 1897	w
Martha V.	John F. Keenan	8 May 1855	
Mary	Adam Freeman	22 Dec 1800	
Mary	Leonard Piles	11 Apr 1814	
Mary	Winfield S. McAbee	10 Sep 1875	
Mary	Dorsey McKimer	10 Oct 1896	c
Mary E.	Thomas F. Chiswell	13 Feb 1833	
Mary E.	Thomas Trundle	11 Jan 1848	
Mary E.	Eugene E. Jarboe	16 Jan 1875	
Mary F.	Henry Howard	26 Jun 1894	w
Mary Grace	Uriah Snyder	23 Feb 1876	
Mary I.	Richard E. Sellman	3 Apr 1889	w
Mary Jane	Nicholas X. Wade	27 Oct 1851	
Mary S.	Nicholas R. Griffith	14 Dec 1850	
Monnica C.	Thomas Bowen	11 Oct 1810	
Moses W.	Sarah Brown	15 Jan 1803	
Nancy H.	Joshua *. Brown	12 Dec 1816	
Nathan	Anna Buxton	18 Jan 1800	
Notley	Viletta Lanham	22 Jan 1805	
Priscilla Poole	Martin Fisher	6 Feb 1818	
Rachel	Zepheniah Cissell	27 Nov 1809	
Rebecca P.	John Piles	25 Oct 1824	
Rezin T.	Irena Hill	18 Jul 1891	c
Richard A.	Elizabeth Ann Offutt	11 Apr 1844	
Richard E.	Anna E. Mayer	18 Nov 1895	w
Richard H.	Emeline B. Beall	16 Jun 1833	
Robert	Eleanor Beall	18 Aug 1812	
Robert	Cornelia Lowe	23 Mar 1897	c
Ruth	James Archy	28 Dec 1803	
Ruth E.	Levin Hall	29 May 1875	
Sabrey	William Lanham	23 Dec 1805	
Sallie C.	Henry P. Hamill	26 Jul 1887	w
Samuel	Cecilia S. Kilgour	27 Oct 1863	
Samuel	Eliza J. Cook	6 Oct 1870	
Samuel	Elizabeth Smith	12 Nov 1883	

* Initial I or J

JONES, Samuel G.	Mary Faw	6 Jun 1799	
Sarah	Truman Jones	19 Dec 1801	
Sarah	Samuel Soaper	30 Nov 1812	
Sarah	Benoni Dawson	14 Jul 1827	
Sarah	Reuben Mannakee	15 Feb 1848	
Sarah	Thomas L. Jones	18 Sep 1852	
Sarah	John Young	30 Mar 1812	
Sarah E.	John H. Dade	25 Mar 1851	
Sarah E.	Benjamin White	16 Jan 1868	
Sarah E.	James F. Byrne	19 Nov 1892	w
Sarah Ellen	Frederick Keys	13 May 1884	c
Spencer C.	Ellen Brewer	21 Dec 1871	
Susa G.	George T. Barnsley	10 Jun 1890	w
Susan E.	William H. Magruder	22 Nov 1853	
Susannah	Benjamin Barnes	17 Apr 1802	
Sylvester C.	Caroline Noland	5 Sep 1868	
Thomas L.	Mary T. Poole	20 Feb 1840	
Thomas L.	Sarah Jones	18 Sep 1852	
Tracy Anne	Zedekiah Cooke	3 Feb 1806	
Truman	Sarah Jones	19 Dec 1801	
Viney	Ignatius Jones	28 Mar 1799	
W. H.	M. Ellen Parsley	22 Jan 1872	
Walter	Elizabeth Harwood	13 Jan 1799	
William	Margaret Selby	11 Jun 1810	
William	Anne Ara Hodges	12 Dec 1826	
William	Mary Ann Johnson	28 Oct 1835	
William Jr.	Fannie Anderson	20 Nov 1871	
William L.	Annie M. Miles	10 Oct 1892	w
William M.	Leanah Downes	10 Apr 1819	
William R.	Eliza L. Richards	31 Dec 1801	
William T.	Lizzie R. Jones	9 Dec 1867	
William T.	Alice Fechtig	4 Feb 1875	
William W.	Annie P. Ayler	16 Apr 1889	w
Zephaniah	Sarah C. Cissell	9 Mar 1840	
Zephaniah N.	Cassandra West	30 Nov 1852	
JONSTON - also see JOHNSTON			
JONSTON, Marian J.	William Bond	22 Nov 1870	
JOPPEY, Amanda	Charles Hall	5 Jan 1897	c
JOPPIE, Annie	Henry Offutt	25 Nov 1868	
JOPPY, Amos	Charlotte Ellen Debter	8 Oct 1868	
JORDAN - also see JOURDAN			
JORDAN, Dennis	Gertie Johnson	24 Dec 1892	c
Eleanor	Zachariah Musgrove	10 Dec 1802	
Elizabeth	Richard Dudley	16 Jan 1807	
William	Martha Thompson	18 Oct 1817	
JOSEPH, Gustav	Sidonie Cartrysse	16 Sep 1895	w
JOURDAN - also see JORDAN			
JOURDAN, Anne	Basil Beall	13 Dec 1801	
JOY, Elizabeth	Patrick Busey	13 Jul 1829	
Enoch	Ann O'Neale	15 Jan 1807	
Enoch	Elizabeth Harriss	16 Mar 1826	
Hellen	William Fish	27 Dec 1808	
Johanna A.	George F. Barnes	6 Jun 1896	w
JOYCE, Sarah M.	Jerome B. Weller	8 Jan 1867	
JUDEY, George H.	Ann Juliett Clements	18 Mar 1823	
George J.	Jane Hileary	12 Aug 1822	

JUDY, Elizabeth	William *. Henley	13 Feb 1820
Henry W.	Ann Whitter	29 Oct 1813
Mary	William Morrison	1 Jan 1810
KABLE, John Jr.	Sarah E. R. Leeke	6 Sep 1853
KANE - also see CAIN, KEAN		
KANE, Josephine L.	John Robert Cleveland	10 Jun 1892 w
KARN, Franklin H.	Annie L. Dudrow	21 Jun 1892 w
KAZLE, Joseph	Julia A. Neurath	9 Apr 1894 w
KEAFAUVER, Jacob L.	Mary L. Morrison	7 Mar 1872
KEAN - also see KANE		
KEAN, Joseph	Sarah Purdom	25 Oct 1811
Joshua V.	Anne D. Purdum	9 Jan 1810
KEARN, Kitty	John Mackenall	19 Oct 1807
KEAST, David N.	Sophia F. Stonestreet	15 Apr 1891 w
KEBBY, Mary	Alben Luxtin	13 Jun 1801
KEEBLEY, William E.	Dallas Trail	13 Nov 1867
KEEFER, Christian M.	Sally Leanian	4 Dec 1862
KEELING, Hettie J.	Arthur J. Cooper	8 Oct 1894 w
KEEN - also see KEENE		
KEEN, John W.	Anna L. Graves	6 Jan 1871
KEENAN, John F.	Martha V. Jones	8 May 1855
KEENE - also see KEEN		
KEENE, Amanda E.	Charles H. Lefever	23 Apr 1877
John	Ketura Lane	3 Dec 1803
Newton	Elizabeth Dulin	18 Feb 1824
Rosa H.	George D. Stewart	25 Jul 1896 w
KEESE, Charles W.	Mary S. LeNoir	18 May 1875
Mary	Louis Behrens	26 Mar 1860
KEESEE, Mary B.	John H. Sprouse	20 Oct 1891 w
KEETH - also see KEITH		
KEETH, Caleb	Priscilla Bennett	28 Jul 1834
KEILER, Eliza	Farnham Brian	7 May 1886 w
Joseph T.	Hannah E. Black	25 May 1885
Lizzie V.	Wilson G. Johnson	9 May 1892 w
KEIRAN, Richard	Mary Whelan	7 Feb 1825
KEISER - also see KEYSER		
KEISER, Cleon Leroy	Pinkie Corila Rhine	5 Jun 1896 w
Lewis	Henrietta Petty	19 Nov 1885 w
KEISNER, Sarah	Richard Gates	26 Oct 1816
KEITH - also see KEETH, KEYTH		
KEITH, Andrew J.	Matilda Cramlet	7 Dec 1863
Ann	Jetson Boswell	10 Apr 1838
Bessie M.	John A. Dillehay	18 Feb 1896 w
Caroline R.	Samuel C. Andrews	26 Aug 1858
Edward Thomas	Margaret E. Andrews	20 Jan 1869
Eleanor	Matthew Reed	2 Mar 1803
Elizabeth	Francis Jinnett	21 Nov 1821
Henrietta	Thomas W. Moore	10 Mar 1863
Horatio	Sarah E. Hill	14 May 1844
James Nathan	Laura Jane Nicholson	14 Oct 1869
John	Emma Ladingham	26 May 1870
Mary E.	Ferdinand Heistler	21 Sep 1869
Prissilla	Hezekiah Beall	18 Nov 1811

* Part of last name from earlier reading; initial L or S

KEITH, Sarah F.	William Moore	2 Jun 1863	
Thomas	Sarah Fitzgerrald	24 Dec 1807	
KELCHNER, Annie V.	John R. Boarman	27 Jun 1892	w
Daisy L.	Edward V. Robey	19 Jun 1895	w
KELLER, Ada May	James E. Mobley	13 Jan 1896	w
Florence V.	Joseph A. Selby	1 Oct 1883	
KELLEY - also see KELLY			
KELLEY, Albert W.	Susan Harris	28 Sep 1864	
Benjamin H.	Emma E. Miller	29 Apr 1885	w
Daniel B.	Mary Wootten	5 Apr 1866	
Henry	Madeline Watts	1 Dec 1879	
James E.	Josie M. Collis	26 Oct 1892	w
John N.	Mary A. Mulleague	4 Mar 1886	w
John W.	Sarah E. Duvall	19 Jan 1878	w
Lillie	Clarence A. Chapman	2 Jun 1897	w
Martha	Lewis Lee	18 Sep 1890	c
Matilda	John H. Tasco	9 May 1873	
Michael C.	Nora C. Broderick	3 Aug 1895	w
Nellie	Millard L. Rice	16 Sep 1890	w
Rachel M.	William H. Thomas	29 Dec 1887	c
Susan D.	William Nelson	19 Jun 1895	w
William B.	Mary A. McCarthy	10 Nov 1888	w
William H.	Anna Dent	15 Apr 1890	c
KELLOGG, Edith S.	Alexander F. B. Prescott	16 Sep 1889	w
Henry	Lucretia W. Poole	2 Sep 1857	
KELLY - also see KELLEY			
KELLY, Annie G.	Bernard W. McCrossin	17 May 1886	w
Benjamin of Thomas	Elizabeth Moore	22 Dec 1800	
Catharine E.	Thomas O. Duvall	23 Nov 1880	
Eliza	William Case	22 Dec 1798	
Georgianna B.	Henry T. Bean	21 Dec 1888	w
Janie	Edward T. Schwartzback	31 Oct 1891	w
Lizzie	Henson E. Johnson	25 Mar 1875	
Mary C.	Ernest Ricketts	19 May 1886	w
Mary C.	George F. Bean	9 Nov 1892	w
Mary E.	David Jackson	18 Dec 1876	
Mary E.	John Lynch	8 Apr 1884	
Nelson	Salena Taylor	24 Nov 1881	c
Thomas	Matilda Gray	16 Apr 1860	
William J.	Margaret M. Ray	21 Jan 1860	
KEMP, Alexander	Ellen E. Ecker	16 Dec 1886	w
Eliza	William J. Rabbitt	8 Feb 1844	
Eliza	William A. Shreve	1 Mar 1881	
Emma E.	Rufus E. Baker	17 Dec 1889	w
David	Matilda Lashley	30 Mar 1836	
George	Susan Fling	29 Dec 1849	
Henry	Amanda Trail	3 Nov 1828	
J. C. W.	Florence E. Adams	19 Nov 1870	
Jacob	Ann Rabbitt	5 Apr 1842	
Jacob J.	Annie A. Baker	5 Dec 1882	w
James	Eliza Jenkins	14 Jun 1869	
James M.	Bessie E. Duvall	24 May 1897	w
John Peter	Laura Thompson	6 Mar 1871	
Katie	William Schwartzel	20 Sep 1894	w
Louisa V.	William Valdenar	13 Feb 1868	

KEMP, Mary	Jacob Kisner	14 Jan 1813	
Mary V.	James F. Turner	24 Apr 1871	
Samuel	Elizabeth G. Welsh	24 Feb 1886	w
KENDALL - also see KINDALL			
KENDALL, George	Lydia Jefferson	1 Dec 1873	
Josephine	James W. Daymude	20 Aug 1879	
Julia	James William Sullivan	13 Sep 1876	
Louisa	John A. Sullivan	5 Mar 1878	w
Margaret W.	Napoleon B. Vincent	11 Sep 1843	
KENDELL, Harry	Lucy A. Harrison	2 Apr 1877	w
KENDRICK, Winfield S.	Cora May Hough	14 Jan 1874	
KENGLA, Charles Robert	Mary J. Lyddane	27 Jan 1875	
Joseph T.	Clara A. Clagett	24 Oct 1870	
KENNEDY, Thomas	Rosamond H. Thomas	23 Oct 1798	
KENNILL, George	Martha Ann Cole	17 Jun 1895	w
KENT, Henry	Anne Riggs	29 Jan 1822	
KENTZ, Anna	Lee Miller	21 Dec 1896	c
KERNS, Joseph W.	Amanda R. Pasco	13 Jul 1898	w
KERR, Daisy	Charles H. Gardner	11 Feb 1896	w
James K. Jr.	Susie E. Davis	23 Dec 1896	w
KERSHNER, Hannah	John Davis	28 May 1816	
KESSLER, Andrew H.	Emilia S. Fendner	9 Dec 1891	w
Clara	Frederick Sinyard	9 Jan 1895	w
Z. Windsor	E. Victoria Ayton	6 Feb 1866	
KETCHEN, Joel	Sarah Hurst	11 Feb 1804	
Martha A.	Edward H. Jett	1 Oct 1881	w
KETTNER, James D.	Mary C. Schlosser	19 Jul 1893	w
KEY, Eliza M.	John Scott	10 Jul 1816	
Israel	Eliza Harriday	30 Mar 1877	c
Israel	Martha Hackett	16 Dec 1890	c
John	Anne Thompson	2 Feb 1801	
Lloyd	Anne Campbell	10 Sep 1823	
Rachel	Thomas McDonough	28 Dec 1865	
KEYS, Chandler	Angelina Edmonstone	11 Nov 1834	
Edward	Cora Thomas	13 Dec 1892	c
Florence M.	Charles F. Randall	9 Jun 1891	w
Frederick	Sarah Ellen Jones	13 May 1884	c
James E.	Mollie Steward	2 Nov 1898	c
John W.	Josephine Riley	28 Mar 1866	
KEYSER - also see KEISER			
KEYSER, Peter	Sarah Merson	14 Aug 1866	
KEYTH - also see KEITH			
KEYTH, George	Sally Walker	24 Apr 1822	
KICHNERT, Charles J.	Margaret C. Scott	7 Oct 1878	w
KIDWELL, Ann	William Easton	26 Dec 1838	
Ann	Samuel McAtee	25 Jun 1839	
Ann Elizabeth	Charles L. Cunningham	11 Oct 1865	
Anne	Solomon Hilliard	21 Jan 1819	
Charles	Mary Henly	9 Jan 1819	
Eleanor W.	Samuel Smith	8 Jan 1833	
Elizabeth	Thomas Easton	25 Sep 1855	
Francis	Anne Lansdale	3 Jun 1813	
Harry F.	Lena M. Ogle	3 Dec 1894	w
John H.	Ida E. Knowles	14 Apr 1868	
Mollie	William A. Offutt	11 Jan 1888	w
Phebe	George A. Selby	15 May 1896	w

KIDWELL,	Robert	Sarah A. Fawcett	29 May 1850
	Sarah A.	Julius West	10 Dec 1844
	Thomas N.	Sarah J. Johnson	23 Dec 1843
	Thomas N.	Anna E. Jenkins	21 May 1849
KIERNAN,	Hugh	Eleanor Richards	23 Apr 1822
	James	Christianna Richards	27 Jun 1819
KIGER,	Mary E.	Laurence A. Dawson	16 Jan 1844
KILGOUR,	Cecilia S.	Samuel Jones	27 Oct 1863
	Charlotte E.	Benjamin F. White	22 Dec 1874
	John A. T.	Harriet N. Jones	6 Feb 1849
	Martha M.	A. W. Chilton	21 Feb 1865
	Rosetta	Lewis Shots	13 Aug 1839
	Virginia	Charles O. Vandevanter	19 Oct 1875
	William	Rose Queen	27 Oct 1858
KILLIAN,	J. G.	Elizabeth Flack	24 Apr 1860
KIMBLE,	Jennie M.	Jesse P. King	3 Dec 1888 w
	William	Rebecca Weeks	27 Jan 1862
KINCHEN,	John	Margaret Brown	13 Nov 1799
KINDALL - also see KENDALL, KENDELL, KINDLE			
KINDALL,	Elizabeth	John *. Mobley	8 Feb 1827
KINDER,	Amelia	Philemon G. Watkins	7 May 1886 w
	Catharine	Benjamin Oden	30 Dec 1812
	George W.	Katie A. Curlett	16 Nov 1887 w
	John	Nancy Read	25 Jan 1806
	John	Kitty Nicholdson	24 Dec 1810
	John R.	Ann E. Dove	29 Jan 1862
	Sarah A.	David H. King	18 Nov 1868
KINDLE - also see KINDALL			
KINDLE,	Annie	Charles Carter	1 Sep 1890 w
	Azariah	Amelia Nicholson	3 Dec 1802
	Catharine	Singleton Self	6 Nov 1812
	Mary Ann	Robert Bronough	16 Dec 1828
KING,	Albert	Annie Clagett	24 Jul 1890 c
	Amos	Jane King	5 Jun 1867
	Ann M.	Ely Duvall	1 Nov 1810
	Ann O.	John Jackson	11 Aug 1897 c
	Annie	Isaac S. Coplin	21 Jul 1897 c
	Annie G.	Reuben M. Brown	10 Dec 1872
	Annie M.	John E. Harding	12 Dec 1894 w
	Beda C.	Willie H. Burdette	9 Aug 1897 w
	Benjamin	Nackey Penn	1 Dec 1804
	Benjamin C.	Fanny L. Gibbs	8 Jan 1868
	Bradley T.	Sarah W. Dowden	14 Jun 1892 w
	Calvin H.	Mary E. Pryor	9 Oct 1869
	Charity	Thomas Watkins	30 Apr 1803
	Charles	Agnes Beall	10 May 1826
	Charles C.	Elizabeth Watkins	15 Oct 1866
	Charles G.	Martha Henson	28 Nov 1895 c
	Charles H.	Margaret William	4 Apr 1882 c
	Charles Lewis	Virginia E. Wallace	22 Jan 1869
	Clarinda	Nimrod Davis	3 Jan 1827
	Cora I.	John J. Burdette	27 Dec 1897 w
	Crittenden	Maggie F. Watkins	24 Apr 1882
	David	Highley Crow	26 Aug 1816

* Initial I or J

KING, David H.	Sarah A. Kinder	18 Nov 1868	
David H.	Cordelia Drudge	12 Jul 1895	w
Delany	Mary Sybell Ward	3 Sep 1896	w
Edward C.	Harriet M. Dutrow	26 Jan 1895	w
Elias	Elizabeth Thompson	4 Jan 1819	
Elias V.	Lizzie Purdum	2 Apr 1892	w
Eliza	Levi Moulding	27 Dec 1829	
Elizabeth	John E. Burdett	6 Jun 1871	
Elizabeth ?.	Joshua D. Piles	20 Aug 1867	
Elizabeth J.	Leonidas Jones	25 Feb 1853	
Elizabeth R.	Hamilton Burdett	25 Feb 1833	
Ella	Richard Hawkins	30 Oct 1890	c
Emma	Luther Snowden	15 Jan 1880	c
Emma E.	James E. Norris	25 Sep 1876	
Ernest	Lola May Lawson	30 Nov 1897	w
Evie L.	John O. T. Watkins	19 Mar 1883	w
Fannie L.	Marcellus Etchison	23 Mar 1877	w
Frances E.	James E. Ayton	11 Nov 1870	
Franklin M.	Avondale M. Watkins	8 Jun 1898	w
Franklin S.	Lizzie Williams	16 Oct 1876	
Frederick	Anna E. Shrider	10 Sep 1891	w
George E.	Julia A. Burdett	30 Dec 1861	
Georgie W.	Lincoln Burdette	23 Feb 1886	w
Hannah	Charles Simes	29 Nov 1897	c
Harriet	Willson King	10 Nov 1876	
Harry Clay	Ida J. Bright	23 Dec 1884	c
Harry J.	Manovia E. Watkins	14 Apr 1896	w
Hary C.	Lizzie A. Allen	8 Aug 1872	
Hetty W.	Thompson Williams	25 Apr 1883	
Horace	Mary Owens	4 Sep 1878	
Ida S.	Thomas F. Monday	20 Nov 1888	w
Isaac N.	Nancy O. Prather	9 May 1842	
James	Kitty Caton	17 Feb 1801	
James E.	Addie C. Hurley	31 Oct 1876	
James R.	Della W. Woodfield	26 Dec 1896	w
Jane	Amos King	5 Jun 1867	
Jemimah P.	Reuben Brown	30 Jan 1850	
Jesse	Lydia Walker	24 Dec 1817	
Jesse P.	Jennie M. Kimble	3 Dec 1888	w
John	Jemima Miles	16 Dec 1800	
John	Susan Ray	29 Aug 1829	
John A.	Hannah Norwood	20 Dec 1873	
John B.	Lillie M. Burns	1 Oct 1881	w
John D.	Lucinda A. Watkins	21 Feb 1862	
John M.	Amy C. Brewer	16 Sep 1853	
John M.	Mary K. Waters	17 Feb 1875	
Lewis B.	Emma J. Hurley	6 Feb 1883	w
Lorena	John Lee	9 May 1873	
Lucy	Uriah Wallace	7 Jan 1875	c
Luther N.	Ida F. Burdett	14 May 1884	w
Maggie	William Clements	26 Oct 1871	
Maggie	Elijah Lancaster	12 Nov 1890	c
Maggie M.	John D. Burdette	14 Jan 1896	w
Mahala A.	Rosser Fleming	27 Feb 1869	
Margaret A.	John T. Norris	24 Mar 1860	
Martha R.	Maurice Watkins	2 Jan 1894	w

KING, Mary	Henry Smith	31 May 1849	
Mary	Samuel T. Hill	4 Nov 1890	c
Mary Ann T.	Edward Lewis	24 Mar 1831	
Mary E.	George Webster	15 Feb 1852	
Mary E.	William E. Riggs	3 Dec 1862	
Mary E.	Robert H. Herring	1 Sep 1886	c
Mary J.	Charles H. Tilley	6 May 1886	c
Mary L.	Samuel B. Talbert	19 Mar 1861	
Mayer M.	Abbie Cohen	18 Oct 1887	w
Middleton	Mahala Summers	17 May 1822	
Middleton N.	Frances R. Waters	4 Jan 1886	w
Nicholas	Eulalie Johnston	20 Nov 1865	
Rebecca	Charles Harvey	11 Dec 1798	
Rosie B.	Titus W. Day	2 Mar 1886	w
Ruthy	Basil Poole	9 Jan 1800	
Sallie	Obediah Layton	25 Mar 1852	
Sarah	Andrew Jackson	17 Oct 1882	c
Sarah Catharine	Selas B. Duvall	16 Dec 1865	
Sarah R.	Horace Warfield	1 Dec 1843	
Sarah R.	William M. Hopkins	17 May 1894	c
Sarah Thomas	Lewin T. Benson	13 Nov 1844	
Saray	James Groomes	4 Feb 1799	
Sena S.	Caleb Lewis	16 Dec 1842	
Singleton	Jane Rebecca Lewis	9 Jan 1834	
Susan	Benjamin Schrider	6 May 1862	
Thomas	Elizabeth Snowden	3 Mar 1877	
Thomas O.	Ida E. Burns	1* Nov 1888	w
Thomas Peter	Elvira London**	6 Dec 1867	
Upton	Polly Bates	13 Dec 1817	
Warren	Ann Belt	21 Dec 1824	
Washington	Anne Mitchell	1 Jul 1876	
William	Delilah Miles	4 Aug 1804	
William	Anna Bowen	15 Nov 1884	c
William	Martha Harriss	11 Sep 1890	c
William H.	Elizabeth Butler	2 Jan 1890	c
Willson	Harriet King	10 Nov 1876	
Zadok S.	Joanna Sibley	7 May 1861	
Zadok S.	Mary E. Lewis	20 Sep 1872	
KINGSBURRY, Charles T.	Mary E. Reid	10 Jan 1876	
KINGSBURY, Albert T.	Rosie I. Walter	27 Dec 1890	w
Charles T.	Alice C. Reid	5 May 1891	w
KINNA, Luella	Joseph H. Price	22 Dec 1893	w
Maggie E.	William W. Cecil	11 Aug 1893	w
Nathan	Jane R. Pickens	1 Jan 1870	
KINNARD, Anna T.	Edward Porter	8 Jun 1853	
KINNEY, James W.	Eliza V. Jones	12 Jan 1892	w
Susan W.	William Z. Leaman	13 Mar 1871	
William	Sarah E. Phelps	18 May 1836	
KINNIEL, Charles D.	Nellie Carter	11 Jan 1889	w
KINSEY, Benjamin	Rebecca Bond	7 Mar 1827	
Ella	James Reed	6 Aug 1891	w
Letitia	William Starkey	11 Dec 1822	
Levi R.	Columbia Rabbitt	7 Jun 1870	

* Cannot read complete day; between 14 and 18
** This could be Loudon

KINSEY, Mary E.	Perry Ensey	24 Jan 1882	
Sarah B.	John Gorie	22 Dec 1838	
William C.	Elizabeth Hammond	16 Dec 1895	w
KIRBY, Gilbert L.	Josephine Holmes	24 Oct 1889	w
John W.	Emily E. Whitehouse	30 Apr 1867	
John W.	Mary M. Turner	24 Jul 1883	
Laura F.	Samuel T. Atwell	9 May 1889	w
Margaret E.	George M. Stadtler	23 Jan 1892	w
Mary M.	George Goode	15 Sep 1886	w
KIRK, George A.	Minnie G. Bender	10 May 1894	w
KIRKMAN, Jacob	Susannah Hall	28 Aug 1799	
KIRKPATRICK, Elizabeth	Alfred Spates	31 Mar 1832	
KIRKWOOD, Columbus	Lola V. Brumidi	23 Jul 1891	w
Peter	Sarah Allen	5 Jun 1806	
KISNER, Christopher	Eveline Walker	11 Jan 1836	
Christopher	Alice Gettings	2 Jan 1883	w
Curtis W.	Sarah E. Dean	12 Nov 1873	
Elizabeth	Ignatius Mullican	16 Jul 1863	
Hannah	Ignatius Burriss	12 Mar 1877	w
Jacob	Mary Kemp	14 Jan 1813	
Martha	George W. Riley	10 Sep 1855	
Martha C.	Isaiah Mullican	31 May 1870	
Mary	Walter L. Case	9 Jan 1813	
Mary F.	John T. Case	25 Feb 1862	
Nettie	Arthur L. Mullican	15 Apr 1897	w
Priscilla	Francis Osburn Gittings	16 Jan 1826	
Tabitha	Jackson Ellsworth Dorsey	21 May 1885	w
Thomas J.	Margaret A. Gates	6 Feb 1866	
Verlinda	James Willson	13 Dec 1817	
William	Lethea Bean	19 Feb 1827	
William	Ella Gates	9 Sep 1880	w
KITE, Mary A.	W. Simon	15 Sep 1857	
KLAY - also see CLAY			
KLAY, Adam	Sabina Summers	22 Dec 1802	
KLEINDENST, Emma E. V.	William H. Carr	4 May 1878	w
KLEINDIENST, A.	Mary C. Flack	21 Nov 1855	
Frank S.	Lillie E. Campbell	29 Oct 1878	
KLINE - also see CLINE			
KLINE, Catharine	Frank Morrow	28 Aug 1889	w
Rosa E.	William T. Essex	28 Jan 1884	
KLUG, Mary B.	Frank S. Baxter	7 May 1895	w
KNAPP, Marly, L.	Henry M. Fry	1 Oct 1881	w
KNEAS, Catharine P.	Stephen Hopkins	6 Jun 1894	w
KNIGHT, David	Lucinda Burriss	16 Sep 1886	w
Edward	Martha Burriss	8 Jan 1886	w
Franklin L.	Lavinia H. Dorsey	11 Aug 1851	
George W.	Sarah E. Gates	11 Sep 1889	w
William Henry	Margaret Ann Burris	23 May 1883	
KNOBEL - also see NOBLE			
KNOBEL, Charles J.	Mary Thomas	29 Oct 1891	w
KNOCH, Carrie E.	Edward F. Stearns	17 Oct 1892	w
Emilie E.	Albert N. Scott	5 Dec 1892	w
KNODE, Joseph R.	Eliza V. Dwyer	2 Jan 1843	
Mary J.	Benjamin F. Edmonds	14 Jul 1858	
KNORLEINE, George	Mary E. Windham	1 May 1882	

KNOTT - also see NOT

KNOTT, Alexander B.	Elizabeth Allnutt	22 Dec 1846
Annie E.	Alexander F. Jamison	10 Apr 1882
Charlotte	Joseph Anderson	22 Jan 1845
Elizabeth	Nelson Thompson	6 Jan 1845
Francis	Mary J. Cissell	2 Jun 1862
Hetty	John H. Austin	22 Nov 1827
John B.	Ann Campbell	25 Jan 1825
Joseph H.	Mary A. Knott	17 Aug 1865
Julian	William Edelen	20 Jan 1829
Lawrence A.	Mary C. Smith	21 Oct 1853
Leonard	Lucy Burgess Offutt	31 Jan 1804
Lewis	Lucy Sprigg	24 Dec 1801
Lewis	Elizabeth Beard	6 Jan 1806
Louisa	John H. Austin	21 Sep 1840
Lucy	James Hilton	25 Dec 1817
Maria	John Carlin	4 Feb 1836
Mary	Solomon Plummer	21 May 1840
Mary A.	Joseph H. Knott	17 Aug 1865
Mary Ann	Lloyd F. Harding	5 Sep 1825
Mary E.	John G. Clark	29 Oct 1895 w
Matilda	Silas Ward	13 Feb 1827
Stanislaus *.	Bridgett Graham	28 Sep 1850
Susan	Richard Edelin	19 Sep 1843
Trecy	Brooke Jones	3 Jan 1809
William D.	Annie B. Carlin	23 Dec 1893 w
William H.	Alice Fisher	24 Jul 1879 c
Willie H.	Emma Trail	31 Oct 1877 w
KNOWLES, Alma R.	Jerry S. Ashburn	6 Sep 1892 w
Columbia	John N. Darby	22 Oct 1853
Florrie H.	Washington R. Hurdle	26 Mar 1860
George M.	Luraner Higgins	29 Jun 1830
Georgianna	William H. Mannakee	26 Jun 1866
Ida E.	John H. Kidwell	14 Apr 1868
Mary E.	Archibald White	1 Jun 1853
William G.	Martha Ann Warfield	21 Oct 1835
KNOX, Anna O.	Con Marrast Perkins	5 Oct 1883
Mary Ellen	Matthew McIntyre	6 Nov 1882
William	Susanah Drudge	7 Sep 1800
KOEHLER, John	Julia Sullivan	4 May 1894 w
KORN - also see CORN		
KORN, Emma M.	William E. Pairo	14 Jul 1891 w
KOSS, Caty	Zachariah Tucker	3 Sep 1801
KRAFT, John G.	Alice A. Metzger	24 Apr 1871
KRAMER - also see CRAMER, CREAMER		
KRAMER, Catharine	Frank Schroth	23 Jan 1884
James T.	Johnnie Trundle	2 Jun 1884 w
Joshua	Rebecca Rhine	1 Dec 1883
Mary	Earl Disbro	17 Jan 1894 w
KRANTZ, Walter B.	Mettie W. Doll	16 Oct 1878 w
KREGEL, Frederick L.	Mary Augusta Clark	30 May 1853
KREESPARK, Eva	Christian Larmann	29 Nov 1842
KRON, Jacob	Elizabeth Johnson	21 Apr 1853
KROON, Elizabeth E.	Nathaniel P. Moore	23 Feb 1869

* Initial L or S

KROUSE - also see CROUSE			
KROUSE, Mary	William B. Fowler	14 Apr 1893	w
KRUSEN - see CRUSEN			
KUHL, F. M. (female)	C. I. Graves	13 Jul 1878	w
KUHN, Anthony	Frances Spates	22 Dec 1841	
KUMMER - also see COMER			
KUMMER, Charles E.	Lettitia G. Chandlee	17 Jul 1860	
KUNLO, John A.	Elizabeth C. Hanfmann	9 Oct 1893	w
KUSTER - also see CUSTER			
KUSTER, Frederick W.	Isabelle C. Nicholson	21 Jun 1886	w
Ida J.	Oliver G. Johnson	29 Mar 1892	w
KYNE, Martin	Biddy Halpin	3 Jul 1865	
LACEY, John	Emily M. Lodge	17 Apr 1817	
Robert A.	Maria Darne	13 Aug 1830	
William ?.	Isabel L. Smith	* Oct 1896	c
LACKLAND, Catharine	Ignatius Davis	22 Nov 1806	
James C.	Matild Crabb	23 Dec 1817	
Jane Lynn	Robert Read	21 Oct 1817	
Rosetta L.	Craven V. Beeding	27 May 1816	
LADINGHAM, Emma	John Keith	26 May 1870	
LaDOMUS, George S.	Sarah E. Webster	23 Mar 1878	w
LAFITTE, Adele	Samuel Howell	16 May 1857	
LAHY, Rachel Jackson	Richard Lewis Ball	20 Feb 1850	
Mary	Philip Varnum	11 Nov 1871	
LAIR, Moses	Fannie Welsh	10 Jul 1883	
LAIRD, Edward	Sophia Johnson	23 Jul 1883	c
Philip D.	Ella G. Magruder	1 Dec 1885	w
William	Helen Dunlop	7 Oct 1822	
William	Arianna F. Dunlop	22 Jul 1834	
LAMAR, George H.	Edith May Stonestreet	18 Apr 1894	w
Hilleary	Ellen Bowie	25 Oct 1886	c
Hilleary	Sarah Bowie	8 Dec 1888	c
LAMB, Roscoe G.	Annie W. Weller	4 Jan 1893	w
LAMBATH, Alonzo E.	Susie S. Quinter	13 May 1893	w
LAMBILEN, Lula M.	Henry F. Snoots	22 Mar 1898	w
LANCASTER - also see LANCESTER			
LANCASTER, Elijah	Susan E. Brown	5 Jun 1879	c
Elijah	Maggie King	12 Nov 1890	c
Harriet A. R.	George A. Adams	7 Apr 1888	c
Isaac	Anne Thomas	13 Jul 1871	
Jesse	Della Hamilton	8 Aug 1889	c
John W.	Laura R. Newman	28 Dec 1896	c
Lucinda	Oliver Johnson	5 Jun 1883	
Maggie	William T. Luckett	6 Jun 1881	c
Maggie E.	Frank Davis	31 Dec 1889	c
Rosie	Howard Prather	3 Jun 1896	c
William	Mary C. Bowie	27 Aug 1894	c
LANCESTER, Abraham	Isadora Taylor	14 Dec 1876	
LANDON, William Riley	Virginia Magruder	19 Nov 1872	
LANDOW, David A.	Belle Eskins	3 Jan 1898	w
LANDRUM, Annie	Mark D. Cline	20 Dec 1888	w
LANDSDALE - also see LANSDALE			
LANDSDALE, Christopher W.	Harriet A. Huddleston	1 Jan 1866	

* Cannot read day; before 9

LANE, Elvira		Ninian Edwards	20 Feb 1803
	Hardage	Mary Greenfield	26 Nov 1799
	Jessie B.	Hynes E. Terry	29 Dec 1896 w
	Ketura	John Keene	3 Dec 1803
	Rebecca	David O'Neale	15 Oct 1798
LANEHART, George		Hannah Shoemaker	14 Nov 1853
LANEY, Alice D.		John W. Stewart	9 Nov 1876
LANG, Charles A.		Mollie Totten	9 Jun 1890 w
	Claibron	Maria Batson	13 Aug 1828
LANGDON, Thomas W.		Catharine Campbell	23 Nov 1824
LANGFORD, Ann		Nathaniel Boreham	25 May 1805
	Richard	Amelia Soper	22 May 1801
LANGSTER, Emma		Otho Beall	8 Dec 1876
LANGVILL, William		Nancy Current	7 Jan 1805
LANHAM - also see LANNOM			
LANHAM, Chloe		John Hill	4 Feb 1813
	Clarissa Ann	Israel Trammell	21 Mar 1842
	Eleatha	Charles A. Burnett	18 Jul 1805
	John	Lucy Ray	14 Jan 1800
	Levi	Ruth Musgrove	15 Dec 1813
	Lloyd	Anne Butt	16 Mar 1810
	Margaret	Walter Hinton	29 Aug 1811
	Margarett	Henry Beall	2 Oct 1815
	Notley	Elizabeth Hopkins	23 Dec 1800
	Notley Wheat	Sarah Bond	30 Dec 1807
	Susannah	Joshua Dial	16 Jan 1807
	Thomas	Charity Beall	10 Jan 1803
	Thomas	Susanna Willson	26 Jan 1821
	Verlinda	Solomon Barnett	6 Nov 1812
	Viletta	Notley Jones	22 Jan 1805
	William	Sabrey Jones	23 Dec 1805
LANNAN, Thomas C.		Sytha Hickman	30 Dec 1822
LANNE----, Agnes*		Thomas E. Cowling	30 Oct 1878
LANNOM - also see LANHAM			
LANNOM, Elizabeth		Edward Warren	30 Sep 1880
LANSDALE - also see LANDSDALE			
LANSDALE, Abigal		John Culpepper	26 May 1828
	Anne	Francis Kidwell	3 Jun 1813
	Catharine E. M. K.	James H. Higgins	5 Oct 1837
	Charles G.	Catherine Elenor Mackelfish King Pumphrey	9 Dec 1819
	Cordelia Ann	George Huddleson	30 Apr 1851
	Eleanor	Samuel Shum	6 Apr 1817
	Eleanor	Basil Berry	18 Sep 1821
	Ella M.	Charles R. Hartshorne	17 Nov 1886 w
	Henry	Mary Busson	5 May 1808
	John	Mary Pumphrey	7 Dec 1809
	Margaret	Greenby Belt	25 Feb 1808
	Mary	James Reynolds	18 Jun 1812
	Mary	Henry Busey	16 Jan 1827
	Mary J.	Charles C. Hutton	2 Apr 1866
	Rebecca	Samuel Magruder	8 Apr 1815
	Richard	Mimma Hiatt	10 Nov 1804

* Remainder of last name has a blot on it

LANSDALE, Sally	John Padgett	2 Dec 1823	
Thomas F.	Eliza W. Strain	29 Jan 1880	
LANSEY, Rachell	Elias Spriggs	5 Oct 1870	
LAPORTE, Delia	John O. Cantwell	14 Oct 1889	w
LARMAN, James Mortimer	Elizabeth M. Thompson	* Jan 1883	
Matilda	Alfred Bassford	29 May 1818	
Sarah E.	Leonard E. Ogle	19 Jan 1886	w
William E.	Catherine R. Thompson	16 Jan 1893	w
LARMANN, Christian	Eva Kreespark	29 Nov 1842	
LARNER, Katharine	John Clancey	31 Jan 1801	
Mary	Michael Lyddan	13 Oct 1808	
LASHEARE - also see LEIZEAR			
LASHEARE, Ruth	John Collins	9 Jan 1802	
LASHLEY, Arnold	Elizabeth Lee	22 Dec 1800	
Matilda	David Kemp	30 Mar 1836	
LATTON - also see LAYTON			
LATTON, Mary E.	John D. White	23 Jan 1865	
LAURENCE - also see LAWRENCE			
LAURENCE, Charles	Margaret Johnson	26 Jul 1894	w
Richard	Charlotte Warfield	3 Sep 1824	
LAURENS, Mary	Thomas Edwards	29 Jul 1831	
LAUXMANN, Michael G.	Annie G. Scroggins	6 Aug 1890	w
Nettie H.	Albert W. Barron	20 Aug 1885	w
LAVALLEY, Rosie A.	Edward L. Brown	2 Jan 1895	w
LAVENDER, Rosa A.	Henry Yost	10 May 1887	w
LAWMAN, James	Julia Cooley	12 Dec 1840	
LAWRENCE - also see LAURENCE			
LAWRENCE, David	Margaret H. Sebastian	3 Jan 1865	
Joseph H.	Susie Hatton	26 Apr 1897	w
Louisa A.	William T. Cummings	5 Jun 1888	w
William	Gracie Ford	16 Aug 1893	w
LAWSON, Bettie	William Murphey	12 May 1886	c
Henry C.	Laura V. Grimes	13 Aug 1870	
John H.	Lethe Layton	14 Jan 1823	
John H.	Isabella Snowden	17 Oct 1878	c
Lola May	Ernest King	30 Nov 1897	w
Mark	Mary P. Snowden	3 Jul 1880	c
Nancy H.	Jeromone Lidderd	26 Dec 1849	
Nora D.	Jesse E. Mullinix	19 Dec 1893	w
Rachel	Albert Whiting	19 Oct 1867	
Susie E.	John W. Ashton	17 Mar 1884	w
LAY, J. C.	Mary A. Batchelor	5 Feb 1868	
LAYMAN, William P.	Sarah E. Jenkins	18 Aug 1848	
LAYTON - also see LATTON, LEIGHTON			
LAYTON, Alcinda	David K. Hill	16 May 1867	
Alvertra A.	John W. Clagett	1 Jan 1867	
Annetta K.	John W. Sharer	9 May 1868	
Asher Sr.	Rachel Browning	20 Nov 1824	
John R.	Eliza Ann Miles	9 Nov 1830	
Lethe	John H. Lawson	14 Jan 1823	
Louiza H.	Archibald Nicholls	9 Jul 1842	
Mary E.	Richard T. West	26 Nov 1867	
Obediah	Sallie King	25 Mar 1852	
Sarah	John Thomas Soper	15 Dec 1832	

* Cannot read day; between 2 and 9

LAYTON, Sarah C.	John E. Ward	5 Jun 1836
Sarah E.	John H. Thompson	7 Jun 1843
Uriah M.	Martha A. Gardner	30 Mar 1854
Uriah M.	Ann Louise Grimes	5 Jan 1867
LAZENBY, Ann	Zachariah Duley	1 Jun 1798
Catharine	Joseph Soper	27 Mar 1847
Cephas	Mary Beall	21 Jun 1803
James	Margary Beall	18 Jan 1808
James T.	Eliza Shaw	21 Jan 1830
Julia A.	John H. Barker	7 Dec 1863
Ruth	John Beggarly	17 Nov 1806
Sarah	Ammon Green	26 Jun 1828
William F.	Laura Baker	24 Feb 1868
LAZIER - also see LEIZEAR		
LAZIER, Matilda	Jacob Beard	21 Oct 1813
Richard	Margaret Hopkins	4 Feb 1802
LEA - also see LEE		
LEA, Fannie J.	Edward C. Dickenson	30 Oct 1874
George T.	Bettie Cobbin	20 Jul 1887 c
Jarret	Caroline Dorsey	24 May 1888 c
Martha	Daniel Jenkins	26 Dec 1870
Martha V.	Lewis H. Jackson	27 Feb 1889 c
Richard I.	Annie R. Brown	22 Dec 1888 w
Sophronia	Washington Ryon	5 Dec 1862
Thomas J.	Anna G. Wilson	13 Jul 1885 w
Walter	Lucy Snowden	21 Oct 1887 w
William	Sarah Braxton	5 Dec 1894
LEACH - also see LEATCH		
LEACH, Ann W.	Llewellyn Phipps Davis	3 Jan 1837
Eliza L.	Nathan Brown	14 Apr 1818
Jesse	Sarah Willett	20 Jan 1807
Mary	Arthur Prather	5 Jun 1876
LEADBEATER, Edward T.	Clara L. Chandlee	7 Oct 1861
LEADINGHAM, Isabella	Nicholas Ray	26 Dec 1861
Jane	Bazilla F. Mullican	4 Mar 1861
Mary E.	Thomas J. Ray	12 May 1862
LEAKE - also see LEEKE		
LEAKE, John	Rose Nokes	19 Oct 1874
Sarah	William Brown	2 Apr 1821
LEAMAN - see also LEAMON, LEEMAN, LEMMON		
LEAMAN, Christian T.	Martha W. Young	11 Mar 1863
Daniel R.	Catharine J. Smith	16 Jan 1866
Daniel R.	Henrietta E. Williams	5 Nov 1874
Elizabeth A.	James H. Hawkins	28 Nov 1892 w
Hattie C.	Percial T. Lewis	14 Nov 1892 w
Hezekiah	Virginia Dowden	11 Nov 1861
James E.	Eveline Matilda Gloyd	7 Feb 1870
John	Mary Appleby	21 Oct 1818
John Franklin	Jane Eversfield Young	10 Jan 1868
John S.	Rebecca Jane Gloyd	3 Oct 1864
Joseph	Charlotte McDade	21 May 1828
Laura E.	Joseph H. Miller	9 Oct 1871
M. Agnes	Edward L. Magruder	27 Nov 1895 w
Maggie E.	James B. Appleby	29 Oct 1877 w
Mamie G.	George F. Forflinger	9 Feb 1898
Maria J.	Richard T. Mitchell	26 Nov 1856

LEAMAN, Mary A.	Andrew J. D. Cooley	6 Sep 1886	w
Mary L.	James E. Divine	29 Jul 1893	w
Rebecca J.	Frederick C. Chorley	14 Oct 1896	w
Richard A.	Eleanor H. Young	27 Sep 1865	
Richard T.	Florence E. McLane	17 Oct 1888	w
Susanna R.	James C. Appleby	31 Jan 1850	
William R.	Susan McF. Smith	2 May 1867	
William Z.	Susan W. Kinney	13 Mar 1871	
LEAMON - also see LEAMAN			
LEAMON, Alice E.	Jacob M. Corbett	2 Mar 1891	w
Elizabeth A. R.	John C. H. Richter	21 Jan 1860	
Flora V.	Willie Windsor	12 Nov 1895	w
George W.	Martha E. Metts	27 May 1867	
John S.	Elizabeth A. Watkins	29 Oct 1868	
Richard A.	Harriet Sibley	23 Dec 1848	
Robert H.	Susen M. Appleby	28 Mar 1860	
Susie D.	Thomas M. C. Metz	12 Mar 1872	
LEANIAN, Sally	Christian Keefer	4 Dec 1862	
LEAPLY, George N.	Margaret A. D. Hughes	9 Jun 1847	
LEARRICK, Jacob B.	Mary Ann Scaggs	13 Nov 1851	
LEASURE - also see LEIZEAR			
LEASURE, Drusilla	James Bayley	11 Aug 1806	
LEATCH - also see LEACH			
LEATCH, Jessee	Mary Letton	18 Apr 1799	
Sarah	William Slater	18 Dec 1798	
LEAVENWORTH, Abel E.	Lucy E. Wardsworth	12 Aug 1889	w
LECHLIDER, Joseph R.	Mamie V. Valdenar	22 Dec 1896	w
LEE - also see LEA			
LEE, Ann	Nathan Nailor	2 Dec 1868	
Ann B.	Aaron R. Saunders	6 Sep 1831	
Caleb	Matilda Higgins	8 Apr 1819	
Catharine	Tilghman Bachers	30 Nov 1870	
Charles H.	Mary Uncles	4 Nov 1891	c
Clara E.	Frank Isemann	7 Nov 1898	w
Deborah	James Wallace	8 Jan 1806	
Dennis W.	Mary Johnson	28 Dec 1886	c
Dennis W.	James Anna Awkard	16 Oct 1894	c
Elizabeth	Arnold Lashley	22 Dec 1800	
Elizabeth	Beverly Thornton	4 Dec 1878	
Emily	John H. Weems	18 Feb 1874	
Emily	John R. Busey	24 Dec 1875	
Emily	William Carter	21 Jul 1881	c
Franklin	Tabitha Jackson	17 Nov 1866	
Gertie	Royal A. Hawkins	24 May 1887	c
Harriet	Moses Hoe	30 Nov 1870	
Henry	Amanda Walker	2 Jun 1868	
Ida E.	Millard F. Doy	10 Jun 1885	c
Idella	William Busey	5 Apr 1876	
James	Alethea Trundle	23 Mar 1815	
James	Sarah Robertson	14 Nov 1883	c
James H.	Martha Owens	19 Oct 1886	c
Jane	James H. Beckwood	20 Feb 1873	
John	Frances Warfield	26 Apr 1869	
John	Lorena King	9 May 1873	
John	Susannah Bond	2 Jan 1896	c
Julia Ann	Richard Mercer	8 Jul 1872	

LEE, Josephine	Samuel C. Watkins	24 Sep 1898	w
Leantha J. V.	Uriah W. Young	11 Sep 1897	c
Lewis	Martha Kelley	18 Sep 1890	c
Malinda	Charles Henry Warren	23 Nov 1895	c
Mamie M.	George A. Brown	15 Jun 1896	c
Margaret	Benjamin Dyan	17 May 1817	
Maria	William R. Doy	30 May 1879	c
Martha	Lemuel B. Mitchell	7 Jun 1883	
Mary	Alexander Hamilton	2 Nov 1870	
Mary	Charles Segler	3 Apr 1871	
Mary Christian	Tench Ringold	15 Apr 1799	
Mary J.	William Henry Williams	14 Aug 1879	
Mary Jane	Edward Brogden	2 Jan 1877	
Minnie L.	Francis Braxton	30 Apr 1894	c
Miranda	William Dunley	6 Jun 1881	c
Matilda Jane	William H. Lee	17 Feb 1881	c
Nettie B.	Thomas Fuller	6 Nov 1890	c
Nicholas	Mary Johnson	16 Dec 1875	
Noah	Elizabeth Diggings	19 Sep 1883	c
Patrick H.	Lillie Williams	20 Dec 1887	c
Presha	Anthony Frazier	23 Oct 1823	
Richard	Warnetta Brandenson	21 Dec 1867	
Ruth	William Granger	8 Aug 1839	
Sadie	Charles C. Swan	30 Mar 1893	c
Samuel	Martha Beander	18 Sep 1878	c
Wallace	Sarah Tyler	22 May 1880	
Warnetta	Basil William Hawkins	16 Nov 1885	
Washington	Maria Combash	7 Apr 1877	c
William	Jane Beander	23 Dec 1865	
William	Margaret Johnson	3 Feb 1871	
William	Emma Stewart	2 Sep 1875	
William A.	Ida B. Wells	6 Oct 1898	w
William H.	Matilda Jane Lee	17 Feb 1881	c
William Henry	Frances Gaither	7 Jun 1894	
LEEK - also see LEEKE			
LEEK, Harriet M.	William Washington Duffin	21 Aug 1885	c
Henry	Ann S. Powel	1 Dec 1885	c
Nancy	James Brown	18 Jan 1803	
Obed	Betsey Burdett	28 Oct 1801	
LEEKE - also see LEAKE, LEEK			
LEEKE, Anne	William Owen	12 Jan 1801	
Benjamin	Casandra Evans	30 May 1805	
Elizabeth	Fielder Thompson	29 Jan 1805	
Elizabeth	Ignatius Gardner	23 Dec 1808	
Elizabeth	Zachariah Burdit	16 Dec 1825	
Henry	Julian Gartrell	12 Dec 1827	
Jesse	Elizabeth Douglass	31 Oct 1820	
Philip W.	Elizabeth H. Dennis	10 Dec 1822	
Samuel	Rebecca Candler	27 Mar 1818	
Sarah	Philip Holland	27 Oct 1812	
Sarah E. R.	John Kable, Jr.	6 Sep 1853	
LEEMAN - also see LEAMAN			
LEEMAN, Arthur*	Mary Greentree	2 Dec 1818	

* Last name not written clearly; could be Luman

LEFEVER, Charles H.	Amanda E. Keene	23 Apr 1877	
David G.	Emily C. Graff	12 Feb 1874	
LEFEVRE, Charles L.	Melinda P. Graff	23 Dec 1880	
LEIGHTON - also see LAYTON			
LEIGHTON, Asher	Charlotte Hungerford	21 Jan 1804	
Mary	Charles Miles	24 Dec 1803	
LEISHEAR - also see LEIZEAR			
LEISHEAR, Fannie E.	James F. Anderson	25 Mar 1867	
LEISHIEAR, Elizabeth Ann	Lewis W. Odell	30 Apr 1846	
LEISURE - also see LEIZEAR			
LEISURE, Elias	Mary Sullivan	25 Sep 1805	
John T.	Sarah A. Thompson	15 Dec 1846	
LEITER, Margaret H.	Robert R. Wallach	29 Mar 1897	w
LEIZEAR - also see LASHEARE, LAZIER, LEASURE, LEISHEAR, LEISHIEAR, LEISURE, LEZURE, LISHARE, LISHEAR, LISURE, LIZEAR, LIZIER, LIZURE, LYSHEAR			
LEIZEAR, Bertie E.	Michael W. Harrison	8 Sep 1894	w
Elijah	Sarah E. White	20 Jan 1880	w
Elizabeth	Levi Shaw	15 Mar 1869	
Elizabeth Ann	William G. W. Leizear	7 Nov 1870	
Ellen J.	James W. Johnson	1 Dec 1880	
Emeline	Horace Thompson	12 Nov 1873	
Eugene W.	Maggie Leizear	11 Sep 1878	w
Francis T.	Mary J. Johnson	9 Jan 1867	
George W.	Rebecca Leizear	9 May 1876	
Harriet A.	John S. Leizear	15 Dec 1875	
Henry H.	Dora E. VanHorn	7 Dec 1896	w
Jane	Caleb Calvert	23 Feb 1832	
John S.	Harriet A. Leizear	15 Dec 1875	
Joseph	Catharine Calvite	15 Oct 1872	
Julia	Jackson Hardin	28 Nov 1884	w
Lewis M.	Emily J. Easton	2 Mar 1893	w
Lewis M. D.	Rachel A. Leizear	24 Dec 1878	
Lizzie A.	James W. Johnson	31 Mar 1869	
Louisa	George W. Evely	20 Apr 1875	
Maggie	Eugene W. Leizear	11 Sep 1878	w
Margaret	William M. Porter	11 Jan 1831	
Margaret	Charles F. Phair	17 Jan 1884	w
Martha	William H. Bukoffskey	1 May 1866	
Martha E.	John Smith	29 Oct 1872	
Mary Jane	James Grady	18 Jun 1872	
Mary V.	James A. Bryan	20 May 1881	
Rachel A.	Lewis M. D. Leizear	24 Dec 1878	
Rebecca	George W. Leizear	9 May 1876	
Robert F.	Mary L. O'Brien	8 Nov 1893	w
Richard T.	Margaret Rook	14 Feb 1888	w
Samuel	Rebecca Hinton	17 Jan 1860	
Samuel J.	Sarah I. Sullivan	4 Jan 1881	
Sarah	Joseph B. Beckwith	13 Jan 1877	
Sarah Ann	Joshua J. Johnson	3 Nov 1874	
Stella	Edgar Merson	15 Jun 1897	w
Susie C.	Arthur E. Harding	23 Dec 1896	w
Thomas	Matilda Grimes	11 Oct 1875	
William	Elizabeth Johnson	7 Dec 1870	
William G. W.	Elizabeth Ann Leizear	7 Nov 1870	
William H.	Margaret J. Ricketts	18 Jan 1898	w

LEIZEAR, William P.	Ida J. Brown	29 Nov 1877	w
LEIZIER - also see LEIZEAR			
LEIZIER, Samuel	Eleanor Sullivan	5 Dec 1807	
LEKITES, Isaac W.	Susan A. Thompson	9 Feb 1865	
LEMBRICK, John A.	Josephine Burdett	23 Oct 1874	
LEMMON - also see LEAMAN			
LEMMON, Daniel	Jane Sibley	14 Aug 1821	
Elizabeth	Samuel Appleby	12 Dec 1821	
Mary	Amos Saffell	24 Nov 1813	
LEMON, Solomon	Eleanor Maran	29 Mar 1826	
LeNOIR, Mary S.	Charles W. Keese	18 May 1875	
LEONARD, John A. B.	Susan H. Peter	19 Dec 1839	
LESTER, Robert C.	Amelia J. Gingell	5 Nov 1872	
Robert C.	Elizabeth J. Gingell	24 Jun 1879	w
LETCHER, Martha	Robert H. Taylor	19 May 1866	
Rebecca	Alexander Robertson	8 Feb 1867	
LETHBRIDGE, John	Mary L. Johnson	26 Jul 1870	
LETT, Ruth	Charles Small	15 Apr 1885	w
lETTON - also see LITTON			
LETTON, Anna Maria	John W. Spates	3 Sep 1850	
John W.	Mary George Riley	27 Nov 1834	
Mary	Jessee Leatch	18 Apr 1799	
Mary D.	William Holt	4 May 1823	
Michael H.	Mary Sands	16 Apr 1840	
LEVELLE, Joseph	Sarah Edmonstone	2 Feb 1803	
LEVENTON, John	Mary Ann Magruder	20 Apr 1820	
LEVERING, William	Susana White	17 Nov 1799	
LEVIUS, Mary Frances	Jesse Quakenbush	5 Aug 1882	w
LEVY, William E. B.	Agnes Murphey	25 Jun 1881	w
LEWIS, Alice H.	J. Wellington Boyer	28 Jan 1844	
Ann B.	Horatio Thompson	21 Dec 1829	
Annie E.	J. Latimer Warfield	26 Mar 1884	w
Arnold T.	Sarah R. Watkins	12 Dec 1834	
Benjamin	Louisa Williams	20 Nov 1891	c
Caleb	Sena S. King	16 Dec 1842	
Catharine	Vinson Brewer	1 May 1827	
Catherine	Charles W. Caldwell	5 Oct 1842	
Charles H.	Edna G. Warfield	26 Jul 1892	
Charlotte	Mercer Brown	14 Feb 1825	
Charlotte	Thomas H. Young	21 Dec 1830	
David	Rebecca M. Clagett	13 Feb 1829	
Ditha Ann	Joshua Riggs	18 Dec 1835	
Drusilla	Jeremiah Browning	31 Dec 1808	
Edward	Mary Ann T. King	24 Mar 1831	
Edward D.	Margaret E. Perrell	18 Nov 1887	w
Eleanor	Francis Mattingly	2 Jul 1833	
Elizabeth	Edward Phelps	9 Jan 1812	
Elizabeth	James Chambers	28 Mar 1814	
Elizabeth	Benjamin Pritchard	10 Oct 1815	
Emma	Thomas F. Purdum	3 Jan 1876	
George S.	Emma J. Lyle	11 Jul 1881	
George W.	Nancy Walker	26 Nov 1822	
George W.	Polina E. Ewell	24 Jan 1839	
Hannah Ann	Philip H. Butcher	12 Nov 1838	
Henry A.	Hattie E. Bruce	18 Apr 1891	w
Ida M.	Greenbury W. Burdette	12 Apr 1887	w

LEWIS, James R.	Margarett Baker	20 Dec 1827	
Jane	Zadok Windsor	20 Dec 1803	
Jane Rebecca	Singleton King	9 Jan 1834	
Jeremiah	Mary Windsor	13 Dec 1805	
Jeremiah	Valinda C. Burdette	26 May 1892	w
John	Lucinda Pennifield	14 Feb 1824	
John	Edna Murphey	17 Oct 1825	
John	Katie Ellsworth	9 Aug 1881	w
John A.	Julia A. Shaw	21 Nov 1856	
John B.	Cassander Austin	5 Feb 1821	
John H.	Annie Webster	17 Oct 1898	w
John L.	Carrie D. Waters	13 Jul 1894	w
Jonathan	Elizabeth Watkins	20 Dec 1807	
Jordan	Alvina Matthews	21 Mar 1866	
Joseph	Elizabeth Burton	27 Apr 1805	
Joseph	Elizabeth Robey	17 Nov 1814	
Joseph	Mary Ann Hardesty	24 Jul 1816	
Joseph H.	Almeda Miles	26 Jan 1849	
Joseph Henry	Rachel Ann Matthews	30 Aug 1880	
Joshua	Nancy Burgess*	18 Dec 1817	
Julia	John Wran	6 Jul 1893	c
Laura W.	Richard T. Burdette	17 Jan 1880	w
Lethe Ann	Elisha Beall	12 Dec 1823	
Levi	Rebecca Winsor**	18 Dec 1798	
Lewis D.	Emily Iglehart	21 Dec 1837	
Louisa	John Chunn	14 Jun 1892	c
Lucinda	Martin Thompson	20 Apr 1849	
Mahlon T.	Georgie Moriarty	8 Dec 1876	
Mary	Ephraim Murphey	21 Jan 1800	
Mary	John M. Williams	28 Mar 1825	
Mary Ann	William Stiles	18 Dec 1819	
Mary E.	Zadok S. King	20 Sep 1872	
Mary E.	Basil T. Glaze	17 Feb 1875	
Mary M.	John W. Bean	11 Aug 1887	w
Milton B.	Mary J. Adams	22 Sep 1890	c
Moses	Susie Green	23 Jun 1894	c
Percial T.	Hattie C. Leaman	14 Nov 1892	w
Priscilla	William Williams	17 Feb 1841	
Richard	Elizabeth Beall	1 Feb 1799	
Rosalie H.	John M. Baker	27 Oct 1897	w
S. Edith	James H. Purdum	5 Apr 1884	
Sallie E.	James C. Bean	2 Mar 1891	w
Samuel	Tamsan Markward*	20 Aug 1800	
Sarah	Michael Murphey	6 Nov 1805	
Sarah	Andrew Biggs	16 Dec 1817	
Sarah	Allen Gray	20 Dec 1892	c
Sarah E.	W. J. Dronenburg	10 Jan 1865	
Stephen	Mary Holland	13 Jan 1839	
Susan	John William Wellin	27 Oct 1834	
Susan	George Parsley	22 Jan 1845	
Susanna	Charles L. Higdon	30 Mar 1865	
Susannah	Jeremiah Spriggs	22 Dec 1886	c

* Last name from earlier reading
** Earlier readings have Winn; court records show Winsor to be correct

LEWIS, Thomas	Sarah Lizear	28 Oct 1813	
Thomas H.	Lydia E. Purdom	9 Dec 1834	
Thornton	Rose Williams	26 Mar 1890	c
Washington	Caroline Davis	26 May 1836	
William	Rachel Ann Stalling	22 Feb 1840	
William	Mary Awkward	8 Aug 1866	
William E.	Vernona Gibson	5 Apr 1887	w
William J.	May Belle Watkins	20 Nov 1882	
William L.	Margaret Darby	15 Nov 1894	w
William T.	Jane Truman	16 Feb 1850	
Willson	Rebecca Harp	26 Sep 1825	
LEWS, Edward	Martha Johnson	24 Dec 1874	
LEZURE - also see LEIZEAR			
LEZURE, Zephaniah	Polly Gary	10 Jan 1808	
LIDDAN - also see LYDDANE			
LIDDAN, Biddy	Michael Connely	25 Jan 1813	
Mary	Evan Price	16 Feb 1813	
LIDDERD - also see LYDDARD			
LIDDERD, Jerome	Nancy H. Lawson	26 Dec 1849	
LIFFORD, Isaac	Sarah Melton	15 Jan 1818	
LIGHTER, Clarence F.	Jane D. Phillips	13 Sep 1888	w
LILES - also see LYLES			
LILES, Caroline	Fenton Taylor	12 Jun 1877	c
Estella	Joseph F. Hawkins	8 May 1894	c
LILLEY, Henry B. W.	Lucinda R. Lodge	26 May 1825	
LIMEBERRY, Kitty	Jonathan Gloyd	10 May 1799	
LIN - also see LYNN			
LIN, Amelia*	Beal Duvall	30 Jan 1818	
LINCH - also see LYNCH			
LINCH, Eliza	James Jarviss	10 Mar 1803	
George T.	Lucind Wilson	22 Dec 1876	
LINCOLN, John	Eliza Powell	5 Dec 1878	
Mary	George Offutt	21 Feb 1889	c
Sarah C.	Evan C. Nugent	30 Jul 1878	c
LINDIG, Henry M.	Sarah E. Norris	27 Oct 1891	w
Lizzie A.	Charles E. Morningstar	16 Dec 1885	w
LINDSAY - also see LINDSEY, LINSEY			
LINDSAY, George H.	Martha E. Murphy	12 Jan 1874	
Josiah	Rose Anna Hamilton	4 Feb 1890	w
Kitty	Benjamin Wilburn	23 Apr 1821	
Mary Frances	James Thomas Gates	14 Mar 1881	
Martha	George D. Price	31 Aug 1897	w
Sarah J.	William Tucker	5 Jan 1893	w
LINDSEY, Anna E.	Lewis Miller	2 May 1873	
Kate M.	John T. Hardesty	27 Feb 1883	
Lottie	Charles Tyler	8 Apr 1895	c
Robert	Lucy Henderson	5 Dec 1860	
LINE - also see LYNE			
LINE, Edwin T.	Nettie C. Reynolds	3 Jun 1896	w
LINKENS, Ann C.	Seneca Vanhorne	1 Sep 1863	
LINKIN, Martha	Robert Simpson	9 Jan 1883	c
LINKINS, Gainor M.	Levi Greenfield	29 May 1873	
James A.	Lucy A. Dwyer	6 Jun 1870	
Robert A.	Bertha Gates	30 Apr 1885	w

* Part of last name from earlier reading

LINKINS, Thomas B.	Gainor M. Barnes	14 Nov 1866
LINKUM, Alfred	Leana Nelson	6 Apr 1876 c
LINN - also see LYNN		
LINN, Caroline	Columbus Campbell	4 Feb 1868
Martha	Samuel Scott	4 May 1875
Mary	Henry Matthews	16 May 1878 c
Sarah	Alex Askins	24 Aug 1871
LINSEY - also see LINDSAY		
LINSEY, Lucy A.	Patrick O'Donnell	16 Oct 1872
LINSTID, Anna Maria	William Willson	17 Apr 1817
Thomas	Anna Mariah Summers	27 Oct 1803
LINTHICUM, Charles G.	Ann S. Pearre	10 Jun 1850
Charles G.	Alice B. Purdum	27 Feb 1888 w
Elizabeth	James Magruder	9 Dec 1799
Elizabeth B.	Jeremiah McKnew	11 Oct 1836
Ezekiah	Mary Hickman	26 Oct 1801
Florence O.	Dr. D. C. Owings	21 Nov 1877 w
Frederick	Rachel Macklefresh	28 Nov 1801
Frederick	Mary E. Hodges	17 Dec 1861
Gassaway W.	Charity A. Hoyle	21 Sep 1847
George F.	Emma N. Thompson	13 Jun 1882
George F.	Martha E. Best	5 Apr 1887 w
Hattie B.	John Miller	24 Mar 1885 w
Herbert W.	Laura C. Vinson	10 Nov 1898 w
Joseph H.	Margaret J. R. Walker	23 Dec 1889
Julia	Noah Watkins	21 Nov 1871
Laura V.	Columbus O. Woodward	23 Nov 1869
M. Blanche	Ulysses Griffith, Jr.	10 Jun 1868
Mary	John Magruder	4 Nov 1799
Mary G.	Mercer Brown	12 Dec 1831
Miel E.	Mary L. Purdum	25 Apr 1887
Otis Mills	Ella M. Stonestreet	24 Oct 1894 w
Sarah	Samuel Carr	15 Jan 1834
Zachariah	Ann Clagett	31 Oct 1803
LINTON, Mary M.	George William Gates	10 Feb 1897 w
LISHARE - also see LEIZEAR, LISHEAR		
LISHARE, John	Nancy Warren*	26 Jun 1800
LISHEAR, Kezanna	Gabriel Deselm	20 Apr 1805
Thomas G.	Priscilla L. Miller	31 Jul 1844
LISURE, John	Elizabeth M. Grimes	23 Feb 1852
LITTLETON, James	Sarah Moffit	15 Jan 1833
LITTEN - also see LETTON		
LITTEN, Ann	Isaac Forsythe	19 Jun 1803
LITTON, Brice	Harriott Moore	23 Sep 1803
Sary	Richard B. Smith	10 Sep 1803
LITZSINGER, Minnie L.	Richard L. Boeman	10 Nov 1891 w
LIVER, Anthony	Sarah Allgood	23 Aug 1800
LIVERS, Emily	John Clements	29 Sep 1835
James Anthony	Lucy Emma Howard	1 Oct 1835
Lydia Ann	Thomas N. Clements	29 Oct 1825
Rebecca	Henry Avey	6 Jun 1832
LIZEAR - also see LEIZEAR		
LIZEAR, Elias	Mary Ann Thompson	11 Jan 1838
Henry	Martha Beall	26 Apr 1815

* Part of last name from earlier reading

LIZEAR, John	Susannah Garrett	12 Oct 1811	
John S.	Annie Padgett	28 May 1878	w
Sarah	Thomas Lewis	28 Oct 1813	
Thomas	Priscilla Harvey	10 Feb 1806	
LIZIER, Sarah A.	Levi T. Appleby	10 Jan 1857	
Susannah	Zachariah Bailey	1 Mar 1808	
LIZURE, Rachell	Philip Cissell	21 Jan 1800	
LLOYD, L. L.	Becca Rhodes	2 Oct 1877	w
Thomas E.	Sarah Fawcett	9 Dec 1857	
LOCHTE - also see LOCK, LOCKE			
LOCHTE, Agnes	George Miller	4 Oct 1875	
Charles	Annie Gingell	4 Oct 1875	
Harriet	Joseph Moran	9 May 1894	w
LOCK - also see LOCHTE			
LOCK, Laura	Joseph Braddock	6 Feb 1839	
LOCKE - also see LOCHTE			
LOCKE, Elizabeth	William Perry Braddock	15 Jun 1843	
Sarah Ann	John Braddock	27 Jul 1839	
LOCKWAD, Levi*	Mary R. Wallace	12 Apr 1898	c
LOCKWOOD, Elise Smith	Raymond B. Potter	4 Apr 1898	w
Julia G.	Richard H. Cockrell	4 Apr 1898	w
LODGE, Caroline	William Phillips	28 Jun 1825	
Emily M.	John Lacey	17 Apr 1817	
Harriet P.	Ranney Thomas	15 Jun 1819	
James L.	Alice V. Warfield	25 Nov 1864	
Juliann P.	John C. Owens	10 Dec 1822	
Keren S.	James W. Marshall	16 Oct 1850	
Lucinda R.	Henry B. W. Lilley	26 May 1825	
Lee Davis	Lelia Ella White	31 Aug 1887	w
LOGAN, Benjamin	Cassandra Green	27 Apr 1868	
Catherin	James Griffith	18 Dec 1807	
George William	Ann Drudge	14 Jan 1803	
LOMAN - also see LOWMAN			
LOMAN, William S.	Clara B. Moore	23 Sep 1890	w
LOMAX, Dangerfield	Florence Norris	24 Oct 1894	c
Edward	Susan Clarence	30 Dec 1886	c
George	Elizabeth Crawley	11 Jul 1893	c
Grace	James Allen	13 Sep 1897	c
Thomas	Martha E. Magruder	18 Dec 1867	
William	Ara Thompson	28 May 1835	
William	Elizabeth Simms	14 Aug 1890	c
William N.	Bessie Hose	2 Oct 1891	c
LONDON, Elvira**	Thomas Peter King	6 Dec 1867	
LONG, Ella F.	Bernard Monday, Jr.	18 Sep 1896	w
Emma	William H. Barnett	12 May 1896	w
Horace J.	Augusta W. Thomas	2 Feb 1894	w
James	Margaret Sanford	21 Jun 1798	
Mollie	Gideon Miller	8 Feb 1896	c
Nicholas	Mary Ann Powell	24 Sep 1873	
Rosie Sarah	Stephen Robertson	29 Jun 1891	w
Sallie	Thomas Walker	28 Dec 1882	c
William Thomas	Georgana Frazier	5 Aug 1879	
LONGLEY, Frederick W.	Joanna Lee Hardy	28 Jun 1886	w

* Last name difficult to read; could be Locknead
** Last name could be Loudon

LOVE, John	E. Marian West	24 Jan 1861
LOVEJOY - also see LOVJOY		
LOVEJOY, Ann	Thomas Owens	16 Feb 1815
Margarete	Hammond Duvall	14 Jan 1806
Mary	Philip Duvall	27 Feb 1802
Samuel	Sarah Shipley	29 Apr 1826
LOVELESS, George A.	Maggie Soper	29 Jul 1889 w
LOVELL, Rosa M.	John B. Bowman	24 Sep 1895 w
William A.	Dorothy A. Burriss	4 Nov 1889 w
LOVJOY - also see LOVEJOY		
LOVJOY, Susan	Hezekiah Owens	17 Feb 1818
LOW, Benedict	Sarah Walker	9 Jan 1819
Louisa	John Easton	1 Oct 1856
William	Jane E. Hackney	21 Nov 1832
LOWE, Anne	Alexander Offutt	20 Feb 1798
Catherine Ann	John Morrisson	9 Jan 1833
Claraphine G.	Armistead Matthews	1 Jan 1889 w
Cornelia	Robert Jones	23 Mar 1897 c
Elizabeth	Andrew Marrs*	3 Oct 1811
Elizabeth	Ozwald Clements	12 Jan 1817
Elizabeth	Simon Grimes	30 Jul 1844
Emily S.	Michael T. Whelan	2 Jan 1889 w
Henry	Anne Dillehay	8 Oct 1823
Henry	Catharine Hinton	28 Mar 1842
Ida M.	Maurice W. Bray	1 Jul 1893 w
James	Sarah C. Benson	19 Jun 1860
James R.	Mary E. Dove	22 Dec 1884 w
James W.	Mary A. Lowe	25 Sep 1884 w
James Walter	Janett Ritchie	17 Oct 1888 w
Joseph S.	Annie M. Bolton	12 Jun 1894 w
Lawrence	Cora Rebecca Selby	15 Apr 1884
Lizzie	Washington Geiger	25 Mar 1890 w
Margaret A.	Henry J. Norris	15 Sep 1862
Mary	William Butler	18 Dec 1810
Mary A.	James W. Lowe	25 Sep 1884 w
Mary A.	James N. Selby	15 Jun 1885
Mary E.	William H. Carlin	18 Dec 1868
Mary J.	James Gingle	4 Feb 1861
Matilda	Allen Miles	31 Oct 1857
Nathan	Elizabeth Easton	28 Jul 1830
Nettie E.	Allen H. Oden	11 Oct 1892 w
Ninian	Orpha Hasler	24 Mar 1829
Ninian	Eleanor Tuttle	27 Mar 1847
Oliver	Mary E. Ervin	31 Jul 1894 w
Perry W.	C. C. Clements	10 Jan 1867
Richard	Catharine Easton	12 Jun 1855
Richard H.	Sarah E. Astlin	22 Dec 1865
Richard T.	Louisa McCrossin	6 May 1880
Richard T.	George Emma Miles	7 Aug 1883
Sarah	Henry Ellar	10 Jan 1827
Sarah C.	James C. Norris	12 Jun 1867
Sarah Elizabeth	Giles Washington Easton	10 Nov 1886 w
Teresia A.	James W. Smith	24 Oct 1851
William M.	Elizabeth Jane Campbell	3 Feb 1826

* Last name from earlier reading

LOWE, William T.	Clora E. Dove	11 Feb 1885	w
Zachariah	Miranda Bloyce	10 Mar 1849	
Zachariah	Emma J. Henley	9 May 1881	
LOWERY - also see LOWREY			
LOWERY, George	Annie V. McCrossin	6 Nov 1895	w
LOWMAN - also see LOMAN			
LOWMAN, Amelia J.	Cephas H. Sheckles	27 Jan 1853	
John	Anne Mills	24 Aug 1815	
LOWREY - also see LOWERY			
LOWREY, Sarah	Benjamin Grimes	7 Mar 1807	
LOWRY, Brice	Sarah Appleby	28 Jan 1799	
Helen O.	Robert B. Peter	13 Oct 1896	w
Henry	Grace M. Dykes	10 Feb 1883	w
LOY, Luther F.	Jessie I. Hilton	20 Dec 1897	w
Richard F.	Lydia R. Best	29 Mar 1876	
Zachariah	Julia Plummer	15 Oct 1873	
LUARD, Ellenor L.	Harold Bird	15 Dec 1887	w
LUCAS, Bettie	Benjamin Smith	13 Feb 1883	c
Carrie C.	Clifford A. Lucas	11 Jan 1898	w
Clifford A.	Carrie C. Lucas	11 Jan 1898	w
Delila	Thomas Foster	13 Dec 1802	
Eleanor	Alfred Weeden	17 Jan 1807	
Henry	Louisa Proctor	6 Sep 1877	c
John	Precious Chambers	14 Dec 1801	
John W.	Ellen Johnson	27 Aug 1872	
Lizzie	George Grandison	11 Jun 1892	c
Maggie E.	Clifton F. Nicholson	27 Nov 1894	w
Maria	William Tapsico	19 May 1894	c
Martha E.	James E. Johnson	18 Feb 1890	w
Mary	William Nelson	9 Jul 1892	c
Sarah L.	John R. Nicholson	17 Dec 1895	w
William T.	Mary I. Terry	9 Aug 1890	c
LUCKET, Airy	Laurence Braxton	18 Jul 1877	c
Thomas	Emma J. Doy	28 Nov 1878	c
LUCKETT, Catherine L.	Luther Young	15 Oct 1891	c
Cooke D.	Mary W. Johnston	8 Nov 1869	
Jane	James Fletchall	5 Oct 1808	
John	Amanda Nelson	12 Sep 1895	c
John E.	Annie D. Hart	18 Aug 1896	w
Juliet	James Simpson	3 Nov 1803	
William	Lizzie Williams	13 Sep 1894	c
William T.	Maggie Lancaster	6 Jun 1881	c
William T.	Drusilla Harper	3 Aug 1889	c
LUFFBOROUGH, Nathan	Harriet Margaret Thomas	30 Jan 1844	
LUHN, Charles A.	Sarah C. C. McLain	10 Nov 1877	
George C.	Alice McLane	28 May 1881	w
George W.	Amelia M. Reid	23 May 1888	w
Mary R.	Charles W. Miles	10 Apr 1873	
Mary Rebecca	Robert T. Cooley, Jr.	17 Aug 1872	
Randolph	Sarah E. Price	8 Oct 1878	w
LUISY, Patsy	William Olliver	17 May 1819	
LUMAN, Arthur - see Arthur Leeman			
LUMSDEN, Elizabeth R.	Beverly W. Bond	8 Nov 1876	
LUMSDON, William Otis	Rachel Pottinger Magruder	7 May 1833	
LUNSFORD, Lafayette	Ann Archer	24 Jan 1883	w

LUPTON, Eliza	Thomas J. Dewar	20 Feb 1826	
LUSBY, Louise E.	Selig C. Wallach	17 Mar 1893	w
Mary	Henry Parker	10 Sep 1885	c
Sadie	Hubert Swann	21 Apr 1896	w
LUSKEY, Annie M.	Harry Warner	5 Mar 1894	w
Ida C.	Horace E. Van Tassell	5 Sep 1890	w
LUTTON, Robert C.	Mary C. Davis	19 Aug 1889	w
LUXTIN, Alben	Mary Kebby	13 Jun 1801	
LYDARD - also see LYDDARD			
LYDARD, Matilda W.	Samuel P. Reed	8 Feb 1882	
Jerome	Antonia Nicholson	25 Aug 1885	w
LYDAY, Charlotte	John M. Hepburn	14 Jun 1870	
Henry	Charlotte Allen	29 Oct 1861	
LYDDAN, James	Ann Adams	19 Mar 1812	
Laurence	Mary Anne Oden	18 May 1816	
Lawrence	Mary Whealan*	10 Oct 1799	
Michael	Mary Larner	13 Oct 1808	
Nancy	Stephen Connelly	22 Aug 1803	
LYDDANE - also see LIDDAN			
LYDDANE, Bridget	Patrick Whalan	10 Jul 1822	
Charles J.	Ida Huddleson	14 Nov 1881	
Francis L.	Eliza A. Willson	30 Jan 1861	
Grace	Charles H. Quigley	26 Oct 1876	
James W.	Cornelia R. Higgens	6 Dec 1871	
Kate	Thomas N. Bailey	17 Jan 1895	w
Lavinia	Charles B. Jones	31 Jan 1883	
Mary J.	Charles Robert Kengla	27 Jan 1875	
Nicholas	Mary Ann Barrett	7 Feb 1831	
Patrick	Ann Flaherty	18 Mar 1822	
Rosie	Charles Veirs	25 Jan 1887	w
Stephen M.	Sarah H. Smith	8 Aug 1848	
Thomas	Margaret B. Jones	27 Nov 1848	
LYDDANNE, James E.	Harriet H. Magruder	21 Nov 1837	
LYDDARD - also see LYDARD, LIDDERD			
LYDDARD, Louisa E.	Filmore C. Watkins	11 May 1876	
LYLE, Emma J.	George S. Lewis	11 Jul 1881	
LYLES - also see LILES			
LYLES, Amanda	William Warren	5 Mar 1875	
Anna	Joseph Cooper	2 May 1895	c
Charlotte	Erasmus Jones	14 Jul 1869	
Christina	Moses Prather	5 Mar 1875	
Elizabeth A.	Lyles R. Robinson	6 Sep 1831	
George E.	Eliza A. Foreman	27 Dec 1882	c
George W.	Mary F. Robertson	29 Jan 1892	c
Georgianna V.	Jacob Johnson	22 Feb 1894	c
Harrad	Ellen Nailor	14 Jun 1867	
Harriet	John Beard	2 Feb 1815	
Ida E.	William A. Hall	2 Jun 1890	c
James W.	Sarah E. Bruce	16 Sep 1880	c
John	Margaret Douglass	31 Dec 1873	
Kitty	Isaac Breathed	31 Dec 1811	
Lair	James Albert Proctor	13 Jun 1882	c
Lewis	Ellen Johnson	12 Sep 1876	
Lizzie	Robert Thomas	28 Dec 1882	c

* Last name from earlier reading

LYLES,	Maggie	William H. Thomas Smith	24 Dec 1879
	Maggie A.	Charles Curtis	11 Aug 1881 c
	Mary	Archibald Oden	16 Dec 1830
	Mary A.	Ellsworth Potts	20 Jul 1893 c
	Mary J.	William J. Hall	4 Mar 1890 c
	Priscilla	John Williams	22 Dec 1813
	Robert	Juliet Johnson	14 Mar 1814
	Robert	Mary E. Washington	27 Dec 1871
	Teresa	Hilleary Magruder	5 Sep 1878 c
	Thomas	Margarett Harwood	26 Sep 1808
	William	Elizabeth Neal	9 Dec 1891 c
	William	Mary O. Brown	20 Jul 1893 c
LYMAN,	Henry H.	Louisa F. Davis	12 Oct 1894 w
LYNCH - also see LINCH			
LYNCH,	Eliza	Bernard Gilchrist	24 Oct 1868
	Eliza	Charles Henry Jackson	28 Mar 1877 c
	Gilmore	Hensy Duffin	3 Sep 1869
	Harriet	Peter Mitchell	14 Apr 1882 c
	John	Mary E. Kelly	8 Apr 1884
	John H.	Maria C. Smith	3 Jan 1871
	John T.	Sarah Cooley	22 Mar 1828
	Maggie V.	Lewis E. Morgal	11 Apr 1882
	Margaret A.	John Thomas	9 May 1881
	Martha A.	James N. Mills	23 May 1873
	Martin	Susan Clara Davis	8 Jul 1871
	Nellie C.	William A. Gladmon	23 Sep 1895 w
	Robert	Mary Norman	24 Jun 1889 c
	Thomas	Mary Jackson	13 Jul 1895 c
	Thomas H.	Oregeri V. Bailey	27 Oct 1869
	William	Linney Spates	24 Mar 1825
	William T.	Mary Agnes Tarmon	12 Nov 1860
LYNE - also see LINE			
LYNE,	Elizabeth	James E. Edwards	30 Dec 1829
LYNN - also see LIN, LINN			
LYNN,	Comfort M.	Absalom Hopkins	9 Nov 1871
	Elizabeth	John M. Hodge	25 May 1891 c
	Ethel R.	Carl Sherwood	14 Oct 1896 w
	George	Susan Dublin	2* Apr 1887 c
	John W.	Martha J. Hood	28 May 1889 c
	Joseph	Norah Mitchell	13 May 1875
	Mary E.	Hanson Hood	28 Apr 1881
LYON,	Amanda A.	Samuel G. Paxton	12 Nov 1860
	Benjamin	Rachel Davis	27 Aug 1803
	Benjamin	Margaret Willcoxen	22 Aug 1810
	Benjamin	Sarah Warfield	13 Jan 1845
LYONS,	John	Sarah Welch	20 Nov 1799
	Lulu H.	William G. Chiswell	9 Nov 1880
LYSHEAR - also see LEIZEAR			
LYSHEAR,	Gassaway	Matilda Watkins	15 Mar 1809
MACABEE,	Amelia	Jacob Neal	4 Dec 1878 c
McABEE - also see MACABEE, MACKABEE, MACABY, MOCKBEE			
McABEE,	Bessie	Dorsey Frazier	8 Jan 1897 c
	John	Hester Ellen Smith	15 Sep 1846

* Cannot read complete day; between 25 and 28

McABEE, Winfield S.	Mary Jones	10 Sep 1875
MACABY, Maggie	James Thomas Speak	27 May 1873
McALLISTER, Annie	James Burgess	26 Aug 1896 c
MACATEE - also see McATEE		
MACATEE, Belle	William Hawkins	31 Jul 1879
McATEE - also see MACATEE, McATTEE		
McATEE, Elizabeth	Joseph Morgan	23 Aug 1806
George	Mary Poole	10 Mar 1808
James	Elizabeth Elder	18 May 1814
James U.	Laura V. White	1 Jan 1877
James W.	Henrietta E. Williams	10 Jan 1843
John S.	Ann L. Umstadtt	28 Mar 1842
Massa	William Owens	22 Jan 1807
Samuel	Ann Kidwell	25 Jun 1839
William	Lucy Sprigg	3 Aug 1805
Zachariah W.	Virginia Purdum	1 Jan 1873
McATTEE, Martha E.	William R. Beall	20 Jul 1839
McBEE - also see MOCKBEE		
McBEE, Eleanor	Robert D. Brannan	23 Nov 1824
McBRIDE, Frances C.	Charles R. Gaines	18 Aug 1891 w
McCABE, Edward L.	Annie M. Trott	26 Dec 1894 w
MACCABEE - also see McBEE		
MACCABEE, Amelia F.	John Wesley Enis	4 Apr 1877 c
Jane	Nelson Tyler	29 Oct 1874
Mariah	William Frazier	8 Oct 1873
McCALL, Orson G.	Edith G. Mitchel	18 Jan 1896 w
McCALLASTER, Charles	Ella Braxter	22 May 1889 w
McCANN, John	Eleanor Burgess	6 Apr 1808
McCANNA, Miles	Kate Garrett	20 Mar 1884
McCARDELL, Rosanna	Michael Nowlan	9 Feb 1829
McCARTHY, Katie T.	Joseph A. Hagan	25 Sep 1894 w
Mary A.	William B. Kelley	10 Nov 1888 w
McCARTY, Harriet	Anderson T. Dennis	9 Feb 1835
McCAULEY, Oscar F.	Margaret Bowie	10 Nov 1857
McCENEY, George B.	Maggie Childs	2 Feb 1886 w
Henry C.	Anna Stephen	23 Dec 1850
Rosa	William H. Childs	13 Dec 1886 w
MACCHALL - also see MACKALL		
MACCHALL, R. L.	Mary V. Suter	2 Oct 1869
McCIMES, Augustus	Elizabeth Turner	10 Apr 1865
McCOOLY, Josephine	Odo W. Woodley	17 Feb 1883
McCORMICK, Ann E.	Robert L. Brockett	11 Jun 1842
Anna	Henry C. Hurley	11 Mar 1885 w
George	Maria Belt*	24 Oct 1799
Margaret	James Welsh	10 Aug 1857
William T.	Ann Braddock	1 Nov 1841
McCOY, Eleanor	Samuel Hedges	28 Jan 1799
James	Margaret Chaney	11 Jan 1823
Rachel	William W. Austin	11 Jan 1823
McCROSSEN, William H.	Florence E. V. Case	16 Oct 1888 w
McCROSSIN, Annie V.	George Lowery	6 Nov 1895 w
Bernard W.	Annie G. Kelly	17 May 1886 w
Catherine	Samuel F. Vance	7 Apr 1874
Clara J.	Thomas F. Everhart	7 Nov 1894 w

* This could be Bell

McCROSSIN,	Laura H.	Edward T. Brown	15 Jan 1883 w
	Mary A.	Charles H. Thrift	7 Apr 1874
	(Mary) Maggie (M.)	Charles (H.) W. Pennifield*	18 Nov 1884
	Sarah C.	William E. Federline	18 Dec 1876
McCROSSON,	Louisa	Richard T. Lowe	6 May 1880
MACCUBBIN,	Eliza	Nathan Hall	28 Dec 1869
	Hellen	John Burgess	19 Mar 1800
	John	Ruth Williams	14 Mar 1804
	M. V.	William H. Sterling	26 Dec 1863
	Martha	Samuel Hardesty	27 Mar 1827
McCUBBIN,	Ann	Daniel Carroll	10 Jan 1799
McCULLOH,	John L.	Maria S. Getzendanner	24 May 1842
McCULLOUGH,	Mary P.	Alfred C. Hargett	27 Dec 1886 w
McCULLY,	Matthew	Josephine Rupli	14 Jul 1891 w
McDADE,	Charlotte	Joseph Leaman	21 May 1828
	Margarett	David J. Carlyle	12 Feb 1819
McDANIEL,	Elias	Margarett Golden	19 Nov 1800
	James M.	Frances J. Gardiner	14 Nov 1894 w
McDANIELS,	Madeline	Alexander Stevens	26 Oct 1880
McDAVITT,	Catharine	Levi Sibley	19 Dec 1828
	Margaret	Nelson Digges	19 Dec 1828
	Tabitha	John Mockabee	8 Feb 1811
McDEVITT,	Elizabeth	John Mockbee	6 Apr 1835
McDONALD,	Anna	William A. Davis	12 May 1870
	Catherine	Ely Mobly	20 Jun 1811
	Elizabeth	Dominick Gittings	26 Dec 1826
	Henry	Lycinda Mason	3 Mar 1882 c
	James W.	Frances ?. Poole	** Jan 1880
	John	Mary Benton	7 May 1863
	Katharine F.	George M. Bradley, Jr.	8 Dec 1897 w
	Mary	James H. Cross	11 Feb 1810
	Mary L.	Arthur Branson	30 Sep 1893 c
	William T.	Ellen B. Dill	1 Oct 1894 w
McDONAUGH,	Eliza	James M. Windham	19 Jun 1848
McDONNOUGH,	Thomas	Malinda Arnold	27 Feb 1860
McDONOUGH,	Carrie T.	Samuel P. Miles	27 Feb 1888 w
	Luther C.	Mary E. Remick	6 Dec 1892 w
	Thomas	Rachel Key	28 Dec 1865
McDOWELL,	Isaac	Nancy Selby	31 May 1817
MACE,	Dora S.	James D. Holman	13 Aug 1889 w
	Franklin	Fanny R. Riley	7 Feb 1854
MACELFRESH - also see MACKELFRESH			
MACELFRESH,	Zachariah	Verlinda Higgins	9 Nov 1824
McELVANE - also see MACKLEVAIN			
McELVANE,	Michael	Amelia Holland	21 Dec 1799
McENERY,	Sarah	Timothy McEnery	25 Mar 1897 w
	Timothy	Sarah McEnery	25 Mar 1897 w
McFARLAND,	Charlotte	Joseph McKinstry	17 Mar 1817
	Julietta	Abraham Palmer	8 Mar 1832
	Margaret	George Bowlen	18 Dec 1809
	Mary	Samuel Horner	12 Feb 1804
McFEE,	John	Sarah Scrivner	6 Aug 1814

* Parts in () are in a different handwriting from rest of entry
** Cannot read complete day; between 20 and 29

McGAHA - also see MAGAHA
McGAHA, Sophia R.   John Franklin Ganly   28 Nov 1876
McGEE - also see MAGEE
McGEE, James   Kitty Doyle   27 Aug 1806
MACGILL, Amelia J.   William E. Wood   16 Jun 1896 w
        Basil   Amelia D. Griffith   22 Mar 1819
MacGILL, Basil   Elizabeth Dorsey   6 Feb 1826
MACGILL, Henrietta D.   Michael L. Peugh   5 Nov 1849
        Lloyd T.   Mary Riggs   8 Nov 1856
        Marion G.   James Andrews   7 Oct 1845
McGINNIS - also see MAGINNIS
McGINNIS, Rodolph   Barbara Mackall   13 Mar 1805
        William R.   Julia Snyder   18 Aug 1884 w
McGLAUGHLIN - also see McLAUGHLAN
McGLAUGHLIN, Ellen   Baker Nicholson   5 Nov 1828
McGREGOR, Charles   Mary E. Burdette   19 May 1886 w
McINTIRE - also see McINTYRE
McINTIRE, William   Attelia ?. Oliver   12 Feb 1879 w
MACINTOSH, Allin   Eleanor Robey   23 Aug 1798
McINTOSH, Charles   Annie M. Moulden   20 Apr 1882
        George W.   Mollie C. Mossburg   10 Mar 1868
        William   Sarah E. Colliflower   24 Oct 1867
McINTYRE - also McINTIRE
McINTYRE, Matthew   Mary Ellen Knox   6 Nov 1882
MACK---, Eliza A.*   Bryant Brown   22 Feb 1867
MACKABEE - also see McABEE
MACKABEE, Hattie   Samuel Brown   30 Jan 1879 c
McKAIG, Joseph   Hester Thompson   11 Aug 1886 c
MACKALL - also see MACCHALL
MACKALL, Amelia   William E. Hopkins   14 Aug 1895 c
        Anne   John Wells   27 Apr 1832
        Barbara   Rodolph McGinnis   13 Mar 1805
        Benjamin   Anne Darby   29 Dec 1813
        Jeremiah   Sarah Brown   27 Dec 1883 c
        Joseph A.   Rachel A. Powell   24 Feb 1880 c
        Lewellen   Hannah Brown   23 Sep 1870
        Rebecca   James Wells   14 May 1806
        Rebecca   Richard Harper   19 Feb 1846
        Susannah   Dathan Darby   19 Dec 1808
MACKATEE - also see McATEE
MACKATEE, Chloe Ellen   George W. Darby, Jr.   23 Oct 1837
McKAY, James Duff   Elizabeth Anderson   16 Jun 1890 w
McKEE - also see MACKEY
McKEE, Joseph   Margarett Bowland   13 Nov 1813
MACKELFRESH - also see MACKLEFRESH, MACELFRESH
MACKELFRESH, John   Ann Becraft   4 Sep 1817
MACKENALL - also see MACKNALL
MACKENALL, John   Kitty Kearn   19 Oct 1807
McKENEY, John   Mary E. Fitzhew   12 Jul 1888 c
McKENNEY - also see McKINNEY
McKENNEY, Margaret E.   Samuel Mansfield   18 Jun 1863
        Martha   Thomas H. Carroll   11 Apr 1887 c
        Mary J.   Charles F. Ault   17 Mar 1871
        Susan A.   John W. Ault   18 Jun 1863

* Remainder of last name written over

McKENZIE, William	Alice P. Trice	29 Apr 1897 w
MACKEY - also see McKEE		
MACKEY, James	Sarah Case	28 Dec 1811
Priscilla*	Thomas C. Nicholls	14 Apr 1800
Richard A.	Jennie Elmore	13 Oct 1896 w
McKIMER, Dorsey	Mary Jones	10 Oct 1896 c
McKINNEY - also see McKENNEY		
McKINNEY, James A.	Jessie A. Swain	19 Oct 1898 w
McKINSTRY, Joseph	Charlotte McFarland	17 Mar 1817
McKLEE, Curtis	Alverda A. Jacobs	2 Jan 1863
MACKLEFRESH - also see MACKELFRESH		
MACKLEFRESH, Charles	Elizabeth S. Chiswell	5 Feb 1800
Rachel	Frederick Linthicum	28 Nov 1801
MACKLEVAIN - also see McELVANE		
MACKLEVAIN, Elizabeth	William Orr	17 Dec 1801
MACKLIN, Littleton	Edith Browning	4 Jan 1833
MACKNALL - also see MACKENALL		
MACKNALL, John	Rosy Downy	21 Apr 1815
McKNEW - also see McNEW, MACMEW		
McKNEW, Jeremiah	Elizabeth B. Linthicum	11 Oct 1836
MACKNEW, Nathan	Jennett Prather	10 Feb 1806
McKNIGHT, Mary Jane	George W. Conner	18 Jan 1869
McLAIN, Sarah C. C.	Charles A. Luhn	10 Nov 1877
McLANE, Alice	George C. Luhn	28 May 1881 w
Florence E.	Richard T. Leaman	17 Oct 1888 w
McLAUGHLAN - also see McGLAUGHLIN		
McLAUGHLAN, John	Tomsey Poole	15 Sep 1824
McLAUGHLIN, Mary Ann	Joseph T. Crosby	19 Feb 1833
McLEOD, Patrick H.	Margaret C. Jones	27 May 1839
McMAHAN - also see McMAHON		
McMAHAN, Mollie A.	William O. Fish	22 Jan 1877 w
McMAHEN, John	Honora Barrett	7 Aug 1883
McMAHEW, Dennis	Mary R. Burgess	5 Apr 1858
McMAHON - also see McMAHAN		
McMAHON, Edward	Valeria D. Peugh	7 Sep 1871
Patrick	Laura Bryant	5 Dec 1891 w
McMANNUS, George R.	Addie E. Bailey	10 Jun 1890 w
MACMEW - also see McKNEW		
MACMEW, Basil	Sarah Walker	28 Mar 1798
McNAUGHTON, Charles H.	Ada Beall	4 Apr 1865
McNEAL, Henry W.	Myrtie V. Reese	2 Nov 1891 w
McNEW - also see McKNEW		
McNEW, Eliza M.	Basil E. Williams	7 Jan 1852
Jeremiah	Henrietta Ray	13 Jan 1811
McPHERSON, Casey M.	Lewis E. Hebron	16 Jul 1895 c
Elizabeth V.	Allen Thomas	1 Oct 1897 c
Jennie	Henry S. Williams	8 Jan 1880 c
Sarah	James Threcker	13 Aug 1800
McREYNOLDS, Frederick W.	Jessie B. Stabler	6 Oct 1894 w
McROY, Bessie V.	William E. Daphney	8 Nov 1898 c
James	Nannie Beckwith	10 Jan 1872
James H.	Maria F. Daphney	28 Jul 1897 c
McWHIRT, Eva	Benjamin B. Alsop	28 Apr 1891 w
MADDEN, Elizabeth	James Grantt	11 May 1809

* Last name from earlier reading

MADDEN, Joseph	Susannah Sparrow	18 Nov 1801
Susannah	Newman Bacon	26 Jan 1824
Walter	Elizabeth Mudd	2 Sep 1802
MADDING, Elias	Susanna Hill	19 Dec 1804
MADDOX, Charles J.	Jane Harding	2 Oct 1866
MADIERA, Esther	Miles K. Headly	9 Jun 1827
MADIGAN, James	Annie E. Easton	18 Nov 1890 w
MAGAHA - also see McGAHA		
MAGAHA, Ida M.	George W. Shoemaker	16 Oct 1890 w
James	Nancy Hardey	20 Sep 1805
John W.	Manzella Smith	20 Nov 1882
Minnie G.	Philip A. Havener	20 Mar 1889 w
Mollie B.	Richard H. Hickman	6 Jun 1882
MAGEE - also see McGEE		
MAGEE, Elizabeth	Richard Ross	30 Mar 1819
James F.	Jessie F. Greer	25 Apr 1879 w
MAHAGAN, Mattie P.	Samuel S. Daughton	20 Jun 1892 w
MAGINIS - also see McGINNIS		
MAGINIS, Amos W.	Susan Copeland	26 Dec 1835
MAGINNIS, Neill	Anne Hickman	2 Nov 1814
MAGINNISS, Mary Ann	Thomas Benson	22 Nov 1821
MAGR-----, Eleanor*	Edward Douglass	5 Dec 1799
MAGRUDER, A. William	Mollie Wilson	9 Jan 1882
Airy A.	Aaron Turner	20 Mar 1886 c
Alexander	Louisa Powers	7 Jan 1886 c
Amanda	John Hall	14 Oct 1875
America	John Fontaine	14 Feb 1871
Ann Maria	George W. Gittings	** Oct 1867
Ann Elizabeth	Ashton Garrett	11 Feb 1836
Ann P.	Basil Waters	18 Mar 1799
Annie V.	Edward S. Hunter	14 Feb 1870
Archibald S.	Narcissa Adamson	19 Jan 1844
Artamesia	Daniel M. Darne	23 Apr 1829
Betsey Lynn	John Wootton	17 Jun 1806
Carlton	Catherine Wells	17 Nov 1818
Caroline	Edward Talbott	11 Mar 1819
Caroline	Enoch Morland	1 Feb 1842
Catharine***	Thomas Watkins	24 Apr 1798
Columbia J.	Edward H. Waters	21 Jun 1869
Cora C.	Ernest Johnson	14 Jan 1896 c
Cordelia M.	Jefferson Griffith	14 Nov 1827
Dennis	Helen Peters	27 Dec 1881
Edith M.	Harry J. Burroughs	11 Sep 1896 w
Edward	Laura Wilson	6 Feb 1851
Edward L.	M. Agnes Leaman	27 Nov 1895 w
Eliza	William Talbott	2 Sep 1812
Eliza A.	Zephaniah Cissel	7 Sep 1831
Eliza Ann	John Henry Winemiller	4 Dec 1832
Eliza V.	Henry Griffith of Lyde	27 May 1823
Elizabeth	Lloyd Magruder	20 Feb 1803
Elizabeth	Benjamin Perry	1 Feb 1804
Elizabeth	Nathan Cook	17 Nov 1825

* See note at Edward Douglass
** Cannot read complete day; 11 or 12
** Last name from earlier reading

MAGRUDER,	Elizabeth	Augustus Hopkins	11 Oct 1887 c
	Elizabeth H.	Zachariah D. Waters	3 May 1856
	Ella	Winfield S. Magruder	23 Nov 1874
	Ella G.	Philip D. Laird	1 Dec 1885 w
	Elma E.	Juliette S. Donnelly	3 Sep 1889 w
	Eugene B.	Mattie Renshaw	4 Jan 1898 w
	Fielder	Matild Magruder	12 May 1806
	Frances E.	Singleton H. Gray	26 Dec 1895 c
	Frank	Martha Fisher	11 Dec 1886 c
	George	Anne Turner	30 Mar 1801
	George D.	Currie Neverson	26 Dec 1895 c
	Georgiana	William H. Adams	4 Jul 1888 c
	Grace	Emanuel Main	9 Nov 1826
	Greenbury	Elizabeth M. Hurley	13 Feb 1833
	H. Bradley	Laura Beatty	8 Dec 1869
	Hannah S.	William E. Muncaster	14 Oct 1867
	Harriet E.	Otho Z. Muncaster	5 Apr 1849
	Harriet H.	James E. Lyddanne	21 Nov 1837
	Harriett	Zachariah Muncaster	24 Sep 1804
	Henry	Jane Woods	29 Apr 1868
	Henry	Belle Hackett	2 May 1889 c
	Hezekiah R.	Ella V. Whittington	19 Jul 1876
	Hilleary	Teresa Lyles	5 Sep 1878 c
	James	Elizabeth Linthicum	9 Dec 1799
	James	Eleanor Harwood	23 Nov 1807
	James	Hester Turner	13 Oct 1893 c
	James Jr.	Elizabeth A. T. Riggs	30 Nov 1830
	James L.	Mary C. Mullican	8 Nov 1880
	James L.	Frances Ann Mullican	29 Mar 1887 w
	Jennie	James W. Boswell	24 Jul 1894 w
	John	Mary Linthicum	4 Nov 1799
	John	Deborah Willcoxen	18 Dec 1810
	John B.	Mary Beall	20 Dec 1803
	John Burgess	Helen Gatton	17 Oct 1831
	John F. D.	Martha J. Griffith	7 Nov 1865
	John W.	Caroline M. Bradley	3 Dec 1833
	Jonathan	Sophronia J. Bean	7 Sep 1880
	Joseph	Elizabeth Shelton	3 Sep 1817
	Julia Ann	Peyton W. Taylor	5 Apr 1827
	Julia B.	Thomas D. Singleton	21 Apr 1869
	Julian	Willietta Beall	23 Nov 1895 w
	Lavinia	S. H. Coleman	2 Oct 1871
	Lewis	Susan Willson	30 Jun 1845
	Lloyd	Elizabeth Magruder	20 Feb 1803
	Lloyd	Ann Holmes	17 Mar 1807
	Lloyd	Lavinia Johnson	30 Dec 1874
	Martha	John Willett	24 Dec 1811
	Martha	Edward Henderson	30 Dec 1892 w
	Martha A.	Charles A. Togood	27 Jul 1889 w
	Martha Alberta	Alexander West	8 Dec 1875
	Martha E.	Thomas Lomax	18 Dec 1867
	Martha F.	Thomas M. Hoyle	3 Mar 1897 w
	Martha R.	Hiram Grady	20 May 1872
	Martha W.	Basil Barry	25 Oct 1830
	Mary	Thomas Watkins	30 Jan 1812
	Mary	Wilson B. Tschiffely	6 May 1876

MAGRUDER, Mary ?.	James H. Crockett	30 Jun 1898	c
Mary Ann	John Leventon	20 Apr 1820	
Mary Anne	Thomas C. Magruder	22 Apr 1812	
Mary Anne	Richard H. Griffith	25 Feb 1813	
Mary C.	Simon Stewart	30 May 1887	c
Mary Catherine Holmes	John A. Carter	11 May 1830	
Mary E.	John L. Dorsey	10 Apr 1889	c
Mary Emma	Thomas W. Waters	16 Nov 1871	
Matilda	Fielder Magruder	12 May 1806	
Matilda N.	Henry Stoffer	8 Jan 1844	
Mira C.	John W. Anderson	15 Feb 1831	
Olivia Dunbar	Philip Stone	11 Oct 1842	
Rachel	Baker Waters	26 Jun 1838	
Rachel A.	Samuel W. Magruder, Jr.	18 Oct 1877	w
Rachel Pottinger	William Otis Magruder	7 May 1833	
Rebecca	William Willson	10 Jan 1801	
Rebecca	Elbert Perry	3 Feb 1806	
Rebecca	Alexander Winsor	5 Nov 1821	
Rebecca D.	Zadok M. Cooke	27 Nov 1821	
Rebecca G.	Robert J. Davidson	24 Oct 1879	w
Robert	Catharine Offutt	1 Mar 1809	
Robert	Chloe Ann Howser	10 Jan 1861	
Robert A.	Lavenia C. Ball	1 Mar 1858	
Robert P.	Mary Lavinia Higgins	12 Oct 1886	w
Rufus K.	America Pritchard	18 Oct 1850	
Samuel	Elizabeth Hawkins	11 Mar 1801	
Samuel	Eleanor Wallace	16 Dec 1806	
Samuel	Harriett Becraft	22 Feb 1814	
Samuel	Rebecca Lansdale	8 Apr 1815	
Samuel	Eleanor Childs	23 Nov 1820	
Samuel B.	Eleanor Warren	21 Mar 1808	
Samuel T.	Elizabeth Worthington	11 Jan 1844	
Samuel W.	Martha Riley	23 Nov 1841	
Samuel W. Jr.	Rachel A. Magruder	18 Oct 1877	w
Sara	Pierre Christie Stevens	6 Oct 1885	w
Sarah	Reuben Hale	20 Mar 1893	w
Sarah A.	George P. Castleman	12 Jul 1888	w
Sarah V.	Zachariah M. Waters	18 May 1858	
Sarah V.	Benjamin C. Hughes	7 Jan 1874	
Thomas C.	Mary Anne Magruder	22 Apr 1812	
Thomas L.	Martha V. Offutt	25 Sep 1884	w
Vandalia	Thomas J. Owen	17 Nov 1869	
Virginia	William Riley Landon	19 Nov 1872	
Walter	Mary Childs	6 Dec 1823	
Walter	Eliza A. White	3 Jul 1866	
Walter	Minnie Quackenbush	16 Feb 1887	w
Warren	Harriett Holmes	2 Nov 1803	
Warren V.	Annie Renshaw	14 Nov 1893	w
Wesley L.	Ann Minerva Hardesty	7 Jan 1845	
William	Lucy Williams*	15 Feb 1798	
William	Isabella Cooke	31 Oct 1872	
William B.	Mary Ann Hammond	19 Nov 1831	

* Part of last name from earlier reading

MAGRUDER, William B.	Elizabeth W. Gaither	7 Jun 1854	
William E.	Margaret H. Brooke	21 May 1864	
William H.	Susan E. Jones	22 Nov 1853	
William M.	Mary M. Stewart	16 Nov 1875	
William W.	Catherine E. Baker	1 Mar 1860	
William Walter	Leanna Benton	4 Jun 1833	
Winfield S.	Ella Magruder	23 Nov 1874	
Zachariah L.	Alice E. Duvall	30 Apr 1866	
Zachariah L.	Belle Warfield	22 Dec 1873	
Zadok	Rachael Cook	28 Nov 1822	
MAGUIRE, John	Mary Nolte	20 Oct 1894	w
MAHN, Elizabeth	Harry C. Voght	1 Feb 1887	w
MAIN, Emanuel	Grace Magruder	9 Nov 1826	
MAJORS, John T.	Mary Robertson	20 Feb 1843	
Theophilus	Mary E. Harriss	16 Nov 1880	
Uriah	Lucinda Arnold	22 Dec 1879	w
MALEN, William	Catharine Sands	31 Aug 1816	
MALIN, Kitty Ann	Thomas Garrett, Jr.	13 Aug 1835	
MALLONEE - also see MALONE			
MALLONEE, James W.	Martha A. Jones	1 Feb 1897	w
MALLORY, James S.	Sophie B. Abert	8 Nov 1878	
M. A., Mrs.	Adrian R. Wadsworth	24 Aug 1869	
MALONE - also see MALLONEE			
MALONE, Elizabeth	Solomon Mobley	20 Jan 1808	
MANAKEE - also see MANNAKE			
MANAKEE, A. M.	William Oneale, Jr.	17 Sep 1855	
Mary	Joseph G. Alcorn	5 Oct 1869	
Octavia J.	I. Overton Williams	20 Feb 1860	
William	Mary Crown	30 Mar 1820	
William	Mary Elizabeth Coale	28 Mar 1850	
MANDEL, Zachariah	Ann Carlyle	28 Jan 1813	
MANGUN, John	Sarah Ray	9 Sep 1816	
Thomas	Ann Read	10 Nov 1819	
MANION, Edward K.	Mary F. Herbert	12 Sep 1887	w
MANLEY - also see MENNLY			
MANLEY, Elizabeth R.	Zedekiah Swann	5 Sep 1809	
MANLY, Ann Willett	Benjamin Poole	21 Dec 1814	
Catharine	William M. Hammondtree	3 Oct 1836	
MANNAKE - also see MANAKEE			
MANNAKE, Caroline	Owen J. Edmonstone	29 Jun 1843	
William	Ann M. Jones	8 Feb 1849	
MANNAKEE, Eliza R.	Charles R. Murphey	4 Mar 1851	
John S.	Elizabeth A. Orme	3 May 1823	
Mary E.	Charles Nicholls	10 Oct 1854	
Reuben	Sarah Jones	15 Feb 1848	
William H.	Georgianna Knowles	26 Jun 1866	
MANNAR, Claiborne H. Jr.	Angeline R. Beall	10 Feb 1892	w
MANNING, Annie L.	John H. Gray	14 Jan 1896	c
MANSFIELD, Adeline	Truman Hesekiah Smallwood	21 Apr 1892	w
Charles	Mary Ellen Whalan	17 Oct 1842	
Charles	Julia A. Norris	18 Jun 1861	
Charles Americus	Ida R. Mullican	1 Dec 1897	w
David A.	Mollie F. Mullican	12 Apr 1894	w
Emma	Hezekiah E. Perrell	23 Oct 1889	w

MANSFIELD, James E.	Ethel C. Higgins	31 Aug 1897	w
Kitty Ann	George C. Gladman	14 May 1888	w
Samuel	Margaret E. McKenney	18 Jun 1863	
MANYPENNY, Burnham W.	Lizzie R. Crum	8 Feb 1896	w
MARAN - also see MORAN			
MARAN, Eleanor	Solomon Lemon	29 Mar 1826	
MARBLE, Frederick J.	Louise M. Milligan	5 Sep 1891	w
MARBRY, Robert	Matilda Davis	3 May 1898	c
MAREK - also see MERRICK			
MAREK, Rachel P.	William Fisher	24 Aug 1821	
MARIOTT - also MARRIOTT			
MARIOTT, Anna	Richard Addison	22 Dec 1873	
MARK, Matilda	Basil Beall	20 Feb 1819	
MARKER, Catharine	Brice Selby	8 Oct 1801	
MARKHAM, John	Susanna Brooke Bank*	14 Jan 1804	
MARKLAND, Matthew, Maj.	Caroline S. Hall	27 May 1851	
MARKWALDER, John	Honora Curtin	25 Feb 1873	
MARKWARD, George H.	Sadie R. Squires	17 Feb 1898	w
Tamsan*	Samuel Lewis	20 Aug 1800	
MARLOW, Alice G.	John D. Wormwood	5 Nov 1894	w
Anna M.	John B. Allnutt	3 Nov 1863	
Annie M.	Charles E. Benson	18 May 1891	w
Benjamin T.	Hester A. Pope	13 Sep 1863	
Chloe E.	Edwin D. Hawkins	9 Oct 1889	w
Cornelia	Henry C. Barnes	8 Feb 1881	
Elias P.	Emma V. Clark	26 Nov 1878	
Eliza	George Campbell	14 Aug 1882	c
Ella J.	Edward L. Fawcett	2 Oct 1877	w
George Washington	Emma Maria Fidler	27 Apr 1885	w
Hallie R.	Franklin M. Turner	9 Sep 1875	
Harriet E.	Joshua Thomas Robey	22 Feb 1871	
India	Charles B. Ager	24 Nov 1885	w
James	Elizabeth S. Cole	27 Nov 1845	
Julias	Evaline Ann Hopkins	10 May 1844	
Mary	Washington Waters	30 Apr 1879	c
Ozborn	Sarah Wheeler	24 Jan 1809	
Richard	Mary Ann Hopkins	23 Mar 1846	
Sarah E.	Levin C. Fish	9 Mar 1859	
Sarah E. A.	Thomas P. Soper	17 May 1852	
Thomas R.	Florence V. Thompson	8 Feb 1889	w
William E.	Mary A. Duvall	13 Apr 1896	w
William M.	Martha S. Stewart	10 Oct 1862	
MARLOWE, Winafred	John Myers	10 Oct 1809	
MARQUETT, William W.	Katie V. Harrison	14 Jan 1893	w
MARRIOTT - also see MARIOTT			
MARRIOTT, Benjamin F.	Christiana Budd	30 May 1889	c
Maria	Levi Webb	4 Mar 1828	
Matilda	Henry Brown	4 Oct 1854	
Thomas	Mary Ellen Price	22 Dec 1835	
MARRS, Andrew**	Elizabeth Lowe	3 Oct 1811	
MARSHALL, Allen	Hattie Hays	24 Dec 1896	c
Blanche	William G. Cary	1 Apr 1889	w
Isaiah	Sarah A. Randell	24 May 1875	

* Part of last name from earlier reading
** Last name from earlier reading

MARSHALL,	Isaiah F.	Rebecca Johnson	9 Jun 1886 c
	James F.	Lydia A. Baker	17 Jun 1885 c
	James H.	Leanna Thomas	3 Jan 1889 c
	James W.	Keren S. Lodge	16 Oct 1850
	L. Anna	Franklin T. Bishop	13 Sep 1866
	Louisa G.	Horton G. Thompson	11 Apr 1888 w
	Robert E.	Martha E. Tyson	26 Sep 1892 w
	Samuel H.	Lorena L. Wynkoop	19 Sep 1895 w
	Sophia	Nicholas Hawkins	30 Mar 1874
	Thomas H.	Sarah L. Pyfer	5 Jul 1882
	Thomas L.	Carrie Grey	24 Apr 1893 w
MARSHBERGER,	Jacob	Annastatia Dyall	17 Dec 1819
	Jacob	Ann Grimes*	23 Jul 1812
MARTIN,	Agatha	Henson Carroll	18 Oct 1866
	Ann M. W.	Samuel B. Childs	16 Oct 1857
	Asbury R.	Annie M. Stewart	16 Dec 1875
	Bertha	Charles Meekins	12 Nov 1896 c
	Betsy	Robert Thompson	16 Oct 1829
	Bretania R.	Joseph O. Tindley	13 Aug 1884 w
	Carrie	Benjamin T. Simms	31 Oct 1889 c
	Charles	Marianna V. Johns	29 May 1877 c
	Clement P.	Clara Hawkins	12 Jul 1890 c
	David	Rachael A. Sands	28 Sep 1826
	Edward T.	Huldah F. Givens	21 Feb 1889 c
	Eliza	John Strode	15 Feb 1814
	Eliza A.	George Patterson	29 Nov 1866
	Eulie	Charles Nichols	11 Sep 1890 c
	Eva	William H. Prather	19 Aug 1889 c
	George	Charlotte Genus	7 Sep 1895 c
	George B.	Sarah E. Hawkins	14 Sep 1888 c
	Hattie	Edward Miles	27 Feb 1896 c
	Helen L.	George W. Dallas	12 Apr 1876
	Henson	Lucy Carter	13 May 1893 c
	James	Joanna C. Everett	31 Dec 1845
	James R.	Georgiana Thomas	16 Jul 1887 c
	Joseph	Margaret A. Musgrove	14 Aug 1878
	Kate H.	George W. Smoot, Jr.	4 Jan 1893 w
	Lee R.	Marian Elizabath Jones	15 Feb 1898 w
	Lenox	Anne M. Shields	28 Jan 1828
	Liza	Charles Douglass	24 Mar 1874
	Lizzie	Martin Broadnix	24 Dec 1867
	Lizzie Blair	William Alberts Mills	27 Sep 1881 w
	Louisa	John Morsell	26 Nov 1879 c
	Louisa	Henry Snowden	28 Oct 1880 c
	Mary	Horatio Clagett	16 Feb 1824
	Mary	Elmore E. Boyd	19 Jan 1888 c
	Mary L.	Elias Driver	24 Dec 1891 c
	Miranda	Henry Hebburn	15 Dec 1865
	Rachel	Reuben Hill	28 Jun 1871
	Samuel Sr.	Ellen Cole	26 Dec 1828
	Sophia	Thomas John Clagett	3 Dec 1811
	William H.	Anne M. Offutt	26 Dec 1881 c
	William H. H.	Josephine R. Norris	21 Mar 1864
	William N.	Laura L. Hickey	10 Jan 1893 w

* Part of last name from earlier reading

MARVIN, William	Eleanor Chiswell	22 Jan 1844	
MASE, Philip C.	Kate P. Ellis	15 Sep 1877	
MASSI - also see MASSEY			
MASI, Walter C.	Agnes C. Steele	3 Oct 1877	w
MASON, Ann	Hubert Nelson	22 Jun 1867	
Ann Maria	John H. Swailes	7 Mar 1876	
Annie	Charles W. Warner	1 Sep 1890	w
Augustus	Georggie Conrad	18 Apr 1881	
Basil	Eleanor Somerville	29 Sep 1891	c
Benjamin F.	Annie L. Nichols	20 Dec 1895	c
Carlton	Sallie Swales	2 Apr 1872	
Charles W.	Sedonia Wims	4 Jan 1898	c
Clara	Tilghman Brown	10 Dec 1885	c
Clara	Samuel Cooper, Jr.	2 Dec 1891	c
Cora L.	Paul T. Perkins	13 Jun 1894	w
Daisy M.	Clinton B. Gorsuch	12 Nov 1894	w
Dolly	Frank Newman	15 May 1880	c
Eliza	James Jackson	18 Mar 1876	
Emily	George Dorsey	28 Sep 1876	
Frances	Jeremiah Awkward	22 Oct 1855	
Franklin	Martha Beckett	6 Jun 1881	c
George	Henrietta Coats	22 Jan 1869	
Hattie	William Jackson	27 Feb 1895	c
Hattie	James Brown	20 Mar 1895	c
Henrietta	Lewis Barber	29 Jun 1878	
Henrietta	Elijah Beander	24 Dec 1879	w
Henrietta	Samuel Dove	2 Apr 1892	c
James	Laura Smith	18 Feb 1892	c
James E.	Amelia E. Thompson	22 Dec 1886	c
James P.	Anna M. Taylor	5 Jan 1892	c
Jerry	Idella Somerville	23 Jul 1896	c
John	Harriet Brown	29 May 1882	c
Katie	Samuel D. Stearn	29 Dec 1887	w
Levi	Aletha Beckwith	31 Oct 1895	c
Lycinda	Henry McDonald	3 Mar 1882	c
Mary L.	Edward Adams	2 Jan 1890	c
Nathan	Sarah Foreman	27 Dec 1877	c
Rachel Ann	Albert Miles	26 Apr 1866	
Rachel Ann	Jeremiah Johnson	12 Feb 1869	
Robert H.	Ida E. Warfield	18 Nov 1886	c
Samuel	Maggie Conrad	30 Apr 1887	c
Susan E.	William H. Ransel	9 Apr 1887	c
Susan E.	Lloyd J. Coates, Jr.	3 Feb 1897	c
Susan T.	Lewis Watson	14 Jun 1897	w
Westard T.	Ann Noland	20 Jan 1806	
MASSEY - also see MASI			
MASSEY, J. L.	Emily Thomas	29 Jul 1872	
MASTIN, Galveston	Rosa Bell Wright	16 Jul 1890	w
Julia T.	William Alfred Streeks	25 Nov 1884	
MATHERS, Rosa L.	Walter W. Watkins	10 Nov 1891	w
MATHEWS - also see MATTHEWS			
MATHEWS, James B.	Harriet Stewart	4 Jan 1887	c
John E.	Annie S. Mossburg	23 May 1881	
Richard	Kattie Sprigg	12 Jan 1882	c
William G. S.	Amey B. Johnson	29 Nov 1893	c
William L.	Ellen C. Griffith	19 Nov 1888	w

MATHEWS, William W.	Mary Ann Harriss	13 Aug 1826	
MATHEWSON, Jessie E.	William W. Russell	5 May 1891	w
MATHIAS, Jesse O.	Tresey J. Belt	24 Jul 1894	w
MATIN, Hannah	Ben Humes	7 Feb 1898	c
MATHIS - also see MATTHIS			
MATHIS, Mary	Thomas Wiggins	3 Feb 1841	
MATLOCK, Samuel A.	Anna E. Davis	16 Feb 1857	
MATLY, Nancy	Leonard Hurdle	24 May 1800	
MATTHEW, Rachel	John Butler	14 Dec 1869	
MATTHEWS - also see MATHEWS			
MATTHEWS, Alvina	Jordan Lewis	21 Mar 1866	
Ann	Archibald Mullican	23 Apr 1805	
Armistead	Claraphine G. Lowe	1 Jan 1889	w
Carrie Ann	Joseph W. Beavers	27 Dec 1866	
Charles H.	Lydia E. Perry	11 Sep 1888	w
Charlotte E.	John T. Gaither	6 Feb 1891	w
Ella F.	Benjamin R. White	11 Nov 1873	
George W.	Sarah C. Trail	2 May 1868	
George W.	Clarie E. Norris	10 Dec 1879	w
Hannah R.	Henry C. Wheatley	30 Jul 1889	w
Henry	Mary Linn	16 May 1878	c
James E.	Mary Anna Dorsey	29 Dec 1890	c
James M.	Sarah A. Suit	16 Dec 1893	w
Jennie	William Raddy	14 Oct 1880	c
John William	Mary Ellen Bennett	16 Nov 1886	w
Joseph	Christie Smith	23 Aug 1884	c
Liza	Moses Clark	13 Jun 1889	c
Lucinda	Henry Wakes	14 Aug 1889	c
Lydia	Isaac Holland	27 Mar 1821	
Margaret	George Mayhew	30 Sep 1868	
Mary Mildred	George R. Astlin	* Apr 1879	
Rachel Ann	Joseph Henry Lewis	30 Aug 1880	
Sarah Ann	David S. Waters	23 Jan 1816	
Sylvester	Susan Williams	20 Jun 1883	
Tobias	Sarah Ann Boose	7 Sep 1810	
Walter	Lucy Powell	10 Jan 1889	c
William	Elizabeth B. Fletchall	23 Feb 1832	
William	Lucinda Johnson	19 Nov 1885	c
William H.	Mary L. Pratt	27 Oct 1886	c
MATTHIS - also see MATHIS			
MATTHIS, William	Sarah Fletchall	11 Jan 1834	
MATTINGLY, Francis	Eleanor Lewis	2 Jul 1833	
Joseph W.	Ella Squiers	9 Oct 1882	
MAUGHT, Conrad	Mirah Willson	16 Oct 1847	
MAUS - also see MOSS			
MAUS, Lillie B.	James F. Allen	28 Aug 1888	w
Mary E.	Hiram Spencer	17 Feb 1863	
Oliver S.	Ellen E. Case	26 Apr 1871	
MAVARS, Albert P.	Lidella Green	4 Mar 1898	w
MAYER, Anna E.	Richard E. Jones	18 Nov 1895	w
MAYHEW, Elizabeth	James W. Gray	28 Aug 1895	w
George	Margaret Matthews	30 Sep 1868	
William	Lizzie Mobley	12 Jun 1895	w

* Cannot read day; between 14 and 21

MAYNARD, James H., Dr.	Harriet E. Myers	31 May 1870
Nathan	Jemima E. Chiswell	27 Nov 1854
Thomas	Ruth Griffith	12 Feb 1812
MEAD, Maggie E.	Thomas E. Gates	7 Aug 1883
MEASELS, Ann Elizabeth	James W. Hillard	8 Aug 1846
George L.	Martha Mobley	15 Apr 1862
MEBANE, Samuel S.	Anna Belle Coleman	28 Mar 1878 c
MEDLEY, Delyla	John Ball	9 Feb 1828
Elijah	Maryann Thompson	19 Jan 1828
Elizabeth	Asa M. Williams	17 Jan 1832
Ellen Maria	James A. S. Nicholson	30 Mar 1840
John T.	Jane Rebecca Nichollson	2 Dec 1840
Ruth	Walter Nichollson	26 Mar 1834
William	Della Brown	2 May 1891 c
MEEK, Eleanor	Thomas Gatton	13 Dec 1808
MEEKINS - also see MICKINS		
MEEKINS, Charles	Bertha Martin	12 Nov 1896 c
Harrison	Susie Gales	18 Apr 1881
MEEKS, Nellie E.	George W. Trammell	7 Oct 1897 w
MEEM, Georgie I.	Frederick R. Merryman	28 Jan 1889 w
George W.	Marion L. Grooms	16 Jun 1896 w
Mary E.	George T. Edwards	3 Jun 1887 w
Otto C.	Ella E. Beall	21 Feb 1876
MELTEN - also see MILTON, MELTON		
MELTEN, Raphael	Sarah Mitchell	16 May 1816
MELTON, Lewis	Rebecca Ridgley	10 May 1876
Sarah	Isaac Lifford	15 Jan 1818
MELVIN, Isabel	Asbury Hobbs	23 Nov 1892 w
MENNIS - also see MINES		
MENNIS, William W.	Martha V. W. Fields	3 Jan 1844
MENNLY - also see MANLEY		
MENNLY, Washington H.	Maria Sparrow	1 Mar 1830
MERCER, Joseph	Ann Jenkins	12 Feb 1831
Richard	Julia Ann Lee	8 Jul 1872
MERCHANT, James T.	Sarah A. Morrison	23 Dec 1858
Jessy	Elizabeth Dunn	20 Nov 1799
John	Mary J. Mockbee	5 Jun 1851
John O.	Margaret E. Mullican	18 Dec 1856
Mary E.	Jackson Moulden	22 Nov 1850
MERCIER, Richard C.	Emma D. Oxley	27 Sep 1892 w
MERIDIS, Major	Margaret Newman	26 Dec 1881 c
MERRICK - also see MAREK		
MERRICK, Amanda	Greenbury Penn	21 Apr 1834
Amelia Ann	Otho Saffell	7 Mar 1826
Catharine	Jacob B. Merrick	16 Jan 1837
Debby	Nicholas Benson	23 Feb 1838
Henrietta	Thomas Read	1 Aug 1818
Jacob B.	Catharine Merrick	16 Jan 1837
Michael	Virlender Bowman	21 May 1800
William B.	Lucy Hall	5 Feb 1856
MERRITT, James A. E.	Mary Browning	7 Sep 1836
MERRYMAN, Frederick R.	Georgie I. Meem	28 Jan 1889 w
Mary	Samuel Hilton	24 Oct 1814
Sarah	Leonard Hilton	18 Dec 1816
Zachariah	Mary Moore	24 Dec 1811

MERSON, Alice V.	Joshua R. Burns	19 Dec 1883	
Edgar	Stella Leizear	15 Jun 1897	w
George A.	Mary E. Dutrow	26 Dec 1893	w
Harry G.	Mamie B. Easton	1 Sep 1897	w
Henry R.	Lizzie Dumhart	27 Sep 1890	w
Martha E.	William E. Beall	12 Oct 1895	w
Sarah	Peter Keyser	14 Aug 1866	
METTS, Martha E.	George W. Leamon	27 May 1867	
METZ, Catharine	James Whitehouse	4 Jan 1847	
Enoch G.	Fannie Snyder	27 Apr 1874	
Geneva M.	Nathaniel Waters	14 Sep 1896	w
Hezekiah	Mary Elizabeth Baker	15 Dec 1841	
Hezekiah	Ruth English	20 May 1873	
John W.	Mary E. Parsley	4 Oct 1869	
Lewis H.	Mary C. English	19 Oct 1880	
Thomas M. C.	Susie D. Leamon	12 Mar 1872	
METZGAR - also see MEZGER			
METZGAR, Fanny	Andrew J. Baxter	4 Jan 1863	
Gayhart	Elizabeth Ann Young	18 Sep 1838	
William W.	Amanda Cashell	24 Oct 1876	
METZGER, Alice A.	John G. Kraft	24 Apr 1871	
William	Harriet M. Trail	11 Dec 1829	
MEWSHAW, Charles A.	Maggie E. Ricketts	24 Apr 1890	w
MEZGER - also see METZGAR			
MEZGER, Sarah C.	Robert T. Graff	2 Aug 1850	
MICHAELS, Andrew	Martha Pearce	12 May 1843	
MICKINS - also see MEEKINS			
MICKINS, Susie	Willis Fitzhugh	17 May 1890	c
MIDDLETON, Alpheus	Frances E. Duvall	17 Dec 1858	
Benjamin F.	Elizabeth Connelly	9 Dec 1833	
Elizabeth	William Burkhead	31 Mar 1814	
Erasmus J.	Jane Noblitt	12 Sep 1842	
Matilda	Isaac Riley	10 Dec 1818	
Richard	Sarah Simpson	1 May 1806	
Samuel	Anne Culver	4 May 1809	
MILBRICK, Daniel A.	Mary H. Shotwell	11 Jul 1893	w
MILBROOK, Ella L.	Jacob F. Gover	31 Jan 1896	w
MILBURN, Lewis C.	Jessie M. Milstead	23 Sep 1890	w
William F.	Malissa J. Green	18 Feb 1869	
MILES - also see MYLES			
MILES, Albert	Rachel Ann Mason	26 Apr 1866	
Albert	Elizabeth Moore	19 Nov 1897	w
Alice V.	Edward E. Ward	12 Feb 1887	w
Allen	Mary L. Trail	28 Jun 1824	
Allen	Matilda Lowe	31 Oct 1857	
Almeda	Joseph H. Lewis	26 Jan 1849	
Almetia M.	Charles W. Nicholson	21 Nov 1882	w
Amon R.	Catharine J. Watkins	19 Nov 1861	
Andrew J.	Ruthie E. Shipley	1 Mar 1892	w
Annie E.	James B. Soper	18 Dec 1883	
Annie E.	John E. Crampton	10 Apr 1890	w
Annie M.	William L. Jones	10 Oct 1892	w
Cassandra	William L. Trail	23 Feb 1825	
Cedalia M.	Franklin M. Bright	27 Apr 1898	w
Charles	Mary Leighton	24 Dec 1803	
Charles	Catharine Sim	18 Feb 1815	

MILES, Charles W.	Mary R. Luhn	10 Apr 1873	
Cora Lee	Omer Byrd Galladay	4 Sep 1896	w
Delilah	William King	4 Aug 1804	
Edward	Hattie Martin	27 Feb 1896	c
Eliza Ann	John R. Layton	9 Nov 1830	
Elizabeth	Basil Mobley	13 May 1815	
Elizabeth	Samuel P. Bowman	2* Feb 1879	c
Elizabeth E.	Miller Parker	16 Oct 1897	w
Ella S.	George E. Walker	31 Oct 1876	
Emma Florence	John William Benson	1 Feb 1879	w
George	Ella V. Beall	17 Oct 1877	w
George	Fannie M. Beall	10 Jan 1882	
George Emma	Richard T. Lowe	7 Aug 1883	
Greenberry L.	Kitty Williams	3 Jan 1854	
Hannah E.	William Henry Poole	21 Dec 1847	
Hattie	Thomas B. Hillard	16 Nov 1893	w
Henry	Lydia Davis	12 Feb 1894	c
Henry Lee	Ella F. Ford	29 Dec 1892	w
Herbert G.	Sarah J. Fluhart	11 May 1883	
James	Mary Stewart	26 Mar 1885	c
James H.	Ellvira M. Beall	30 Dec 1830	
James R.	Sarah L. Mossburg	4 Aug 1865	
James R.	Mary E. Flynn	7 Jan 1889	w
Jemima	John King	16 Dec 1800	
John	Matilda Poole	10 Aug 1816	
Julia	James E. Washington	4 Dec 1893	c
Lemuel L.	Martha J. Grimes	27 Jun 1871	
Marietta	William L. Williams	15 Nov 1859	
Mary	Thomas Fall	30 Apr 1887	c
Mary Ann	Zachariah J. H. W. Burdett	20 Jan 1846	
Mary C.	John Baker	3 Apr 1852	
Mary E.	Allen S. Orme	23 Dec 1893	w
Nathan	Susan Thompson	3 Feb 1815	
Nathan E.	Eliza Robertson	31 May 1847	
Nathan E.	Laura J. Pyles	7 Oct 1874	
Nathen	Susannah Thompson	26 Dec 1809	
Ollie	William B. White	20 Dec 1892	w
Pattie	James Copeland	24 Oct 1883	c
Rebecca	Samuel T. Baken	5 Nov 1896	c
Rebecca R.	Wilson E. I. Poole	10 Feb 1851	
Remus H.	Sarah Frances Moore	7 Oct 1884	w
Samuel	Mary E. Riggs	30 Dec 1823	
Samuel P.	Carrie T. McDonough	27 Feb 1888	w
Susan R.	Isaac J. Moore	6 Dec 1887	w
Susie E.	Henry L. Peirce	13 Feb 1894	w
Uriah	Sarah A. Benson	12 Feb 1853	
Virginia Ann	Jacob Umstadtt	9 Apr 1851	
William	Lydia Hall	21 Feb 1803	
William	Eleanor Connoway	17 Feb 1817	
William H.	Annie E. Athey	2 Sep 1886	w
William H.	Mary C. Iagar	25 Feb 1895	w
MILFORD, Thomas	Cleland Veirs	25 Jun 1849	

* Day has blot on it; either 25 or 26

MILLARD, Mary*		Alexander Robertson	23 Apr 1800
MILLER, Ada A.		Lem A. Warfield	10 Dec 1852
	Adolph W.	Florence M. Ober	16 Jul 1886 w
	Albert	Charity Holland	19 Oct 1886 c
	Annie Bruce	James H. Zeigler	26 Oct 1875
	Annie M.	Henry E. Higgins	2 Jan 1895 w
	Charles G.	Agnes N. Beedle	25 Nov 1891 w
	Christopher	Margaret Mills	22 Oct 1840
	Daniel	Mary Boose	14 Apr 1810
	Edward E.	Ida J. Byrne	29 Sep 1890 w
	Eleanor	Abisha Gray	29 Apr 1805
	Elizabeth	Thomas Chambers	5 Dec 1878 c
	Elizabeth Ann	John Allnutt	1 Nov 1837
	Elizabeth F.	Alexander A. Gassaway	23 Jan 1882
	Elizabeth P.	William T. Thom	9 Oct 1888 w
	Emma E.	Benjamin H. Kelley	29 Apr 1885 w
	Emmeline	William R. Selby	2 Feb 1886 w
	Frank M.	Emma C. Brashears	24 Apr 1883
	George	Agnes Lochte	4 Oct 1875
	George M.	Gertrude M. Brown	9 Apr 1898 w
	Gideon	Mollie Long	8 Feb 1896 c
	Hattie A.	James J. Beall	28 Nov 1888 w
	Isaac	Elce Duer	10 Sep 1812
	J. Hite	Nannie L. Offutt	14 Aug 1883
	Jacob	Nancy Ricketts	30 Dec 1806
	Jacob	Ann Wallick	10 Jul 1823
	Jacob	Mary Bennett	17 Oct 1843
	Jacob	Emily M. Cashell	11 Feb 1874
	Jennie	James F. Dawson	3 Jun 1864
	Jessie R.	Millard C. Harry	24 Apr 1893 w
	John	Eleanor Barnett**	14 Apr 1798
	John	Hattie B. Linthicum	24 Mar 1885 w
	John	Virginia Dorsey	24 Dec 1886 c
	John R.	Elizabeth Braddock	24 Feb 1838
	Joseph H.	Laura E. Leaman	9 Oct 1871
	Kate G.	Franklin T. Hodges	27 May 1897 w
	Leathan	Columbus Boyer	2 Apr 1884
	Lee	Anna Kentz	21 Dec 1896 c
	Lewis	Anna E. Lindsey	2 May 1873
	Marshall	Margaret E. Ashby	31 Jan 1889 w
	Martha V.	Theodore C. Bell	26 Aug 1886 w
	Mary Ann	Evan Burdett	13 Nov 1828
	Patty	John Reed	9 Jan 1805
	Priscilla L.	Thomas G. Lishear	31 Jul 1844
	Rebecca	Zachariah Dowden	6 Feb 1852
	Rebecca	William Waters	29 May 1867
	Sarah	William H. Bowman	20 Dec 1841
	Sarah	Benjamin F. Thomas	28 Apr 1874
	Savilla	Richard H. Bennett	20 Apr 1850
	Velinda C.	James W. Selby	22 Dec 1862
	William	Rebecca Watkins	9 Dec 1852
	William B.	Eliza S. Hopkins	28 Apr 1874

* Last name from earlier reading
** Last name could be Barrett

MILLES, James*	Susanna Selby	23 Jun 1818	
MILLIGAN, Louise M.	Frederick J. Marble	5 Sep 1891	w
MILLS - also see MILLES			
MILLS, Aggie	Levi Green	23 Mar 1895	c
Anne	John Lowman	24 Aug 1815	
Charles Richard	Mary E. Day	5 Nov 1879	
Eleanor	Joseph Hopkins	16 Dec 1800	
Elizabeth	William D. Belt	3 Jan 1810	
Elizabeth	Isaac Ricketts	11 Jun 1861	
Elizabeth	Nathan R. Snyder	14 Dec 1881	
Hama D.	Ida C. Hargett	3 Sep 1890	w
Horace F.	Susie A. Carter	15 May 1883	
James A.	Mary E. Mills	30 Oct 1876	
James N.	Martha A. Lynch	23 May 1873	
James S.	Sarah A. Cooley	30 Mar 1886	w
John L.	Ida V. Butt	16 Dec 1889	w
John R.	Ruth A. Swailes	4 Jul 1896	c
John W.	Matilda Harriss	30 Mar 1848	
John W.	Ida A. Ward	9 Nov 1892	w
Joseph	Martha E. Henley	4 Feb 1858	
Maggie B.	Hezekiah Day	10 Apr 1896	w
Margaret	Christopher Miller	22 Oct 1840	
Martha R.	Thomas F. Shannon	15 Sep 1888	w
Mary	John O. Crown	21 May 1895	w
Mary Ann	John Oden	8 Jun 1840	
Mary E.	James A. Mills	30 Oct 1876	
Nathaniel	Deborah Ann Burdett	11 Dec 1845	
Rebecca	William B. Ober	14 Apr 1808	
Richard	Mary S. Saffell	8 Feb 1849	
Samuel	Ellen Oden	1 Mar 1874	
Stella M.	Basil Jackson	19 Sep 1891	c
Susan R.	Jacob Day, Jr.	24 Dec 1846	
Thomas	Ann Brown	16 Nov 1840	
Thomas	Susan Day	14 Aug 1877	w
Thomas H.	Linney Willson	18 Jun 1817	
Virginia	John Burns	27 Feb 1871	
William	Mary Eveline Caho	29 Dec 1836	
William Alberts	Lizzie Blair Martin	27 Sep 1881	w
MILNE, Andrew	Mollie Walter	1 Apr 1892	w
James	Elizabeth Grantt	3 Aug 1835	
MILSTEAD, Annie	John A. Bennett	21 Jan 1864	
Jessie M.	Lewis C. Milburn	23 Sep 1890	w
Thomas L.	Martha E. Thompson	30 Jan 1893	w
MILTON - also see MELTON			
MILTON, Viny	Vernon Combash	13 Jan 1898	c
MIM--, John	Margaret D. Gozler	19 Apr 1825	
MINES, John	Eliza Beall	26 Mar 1822	
John	Mary Dunlop	1 Feb 1842	
John L. B.	Martha R. Willson	2 Jun 1849	
Martha T.	John I. Campbell	2 Jun 1836	
MINNIS, Elizabeth	Erasmus West	23 Jul 1872	
John	Martha E. Fisher	10 Dec 1873	
Mary Frances	John A. Thrift	12 Sep 1866	
Richard M.	Sarah M. Davis	22 Oct 1872	

* Name as written; other records show Joseph Mills to be coreect

MINOR, Elick A.	Rosa E. Gross	8 Jul 1897	c
MIRE, Martha A.	James A. Biggs	24 Sep 1839	
MITCHEL, Edith G.	Orson G. McCall	18 Jan 1896	w
MITCHELL, Anne*	Thomas A. Cooley	28 Feb 1811	
Anne	Washington King	1 Jul 1876	
Cassy	Thomas Quinn	27 Nov 1875	
Elizabeth A.	Amos J. Cooley	9 Jun 1857	
Elizabeth M.	Hezekiah Williams	9 Sep 1867	
Hattie	Richard Hill	4 Nov 1897	c
Henrietta	Richard P. Howard	26 Oct 1893	c
Horace T.	Caroline H. Dorsey	7 Feb 1871	
James	Lydia Brown	1 Sep 1891	c
Jeremiah	Verlinda Brown	26 Dec 1811	
John	Ann Phelps	5 Apr 1836	
Laura	Henry Warfield	5 Apr 1871	
Lemuel B.	Martha Lee	7 Jun 1883	c
Mary	Thomas Harper	23 Sep 1824	
Mary Ellen	John Grimes	12 Aug 1841	
Norah	Joseph Lynn	13 May 1875	
Peter	Harriet Lynch	14 Apr 1882	c
R. T.	Sarah C. White	15 Nov 1858	
Richard T.	Maria J. Leaman	26 Nov 1856	
Sarah	Raphael Melten	16 May 1816	
Susanna	Solomon Veirs	9 Feb 1805	
Thomas J.	Jemima Bond	9 Apr 1868	
Thomas J.	Hester Jane Howard	22 Apr 1886	c
William E.	Leanna Howard	9 Jun 1875	
Zadoc	Delia Cooper	25 May 1866	
MOBBERLY, Margarett	Ephraim Johnson	24 Jan 1829	
MOBBLEY, Malvinia	James Page	17 Jan 1846	
MOBLEY, Andrew J.	Hattie A. Selby	17 Dec 1889	w
Basil	Catharine Winsor	11 May 1815	
Basil	Elizabeth Miles	13 May 1815	
Charles R.	Margaret D. Henley	11 Jun 1874	
Charles R.	Lillie H. Oden	19 Jun 1883	
Charles W.	Martha V. Gue	21 Feb 1889	w
Edith G.	Daniel H. Gaither of D	20 Apr 1895	w
Eleanor	Michael Sipe	27 Dec 1802	
Elizabeth	Richard Price, Jr.	9 Feb 1802	
Elizabeth	David Thompson	3 Jan 1809	
Elizabeth	Thomas Willburn	11 Sep 1820	
Elizabeth H.	Benjamin L. Burgess	3 Jan 1832	
Ezekiel	Eleanor Hartley	20 Dec 1808	
G. W.	Mary F. Bell	23 Oct 1876	
George W.	Amanda Taylor	31 Jan 1898	w
Henry	Sarah C. Nicholson	29 Jan 1862	
James E.	Ada May Keller	13 Jan 1896	w
James W.	Mary E. Waer	18 Jun 1897	w
John **.	Elizabeth Kindall	8 Feb 1827	
John W.	Mary G. Selby	22 Aug 1891	w
Lewis	Jemima Thompson	3 Dec 1807	
Lizzie	William Mayhew	12 Jun 1895	w
Mahlon F.	Laura Cole	8 Nov 1882	w

* Part of last name from earlier reading
** Initial I or J

MOBLEY, Martha	George L. Measels	15 Apr 1862	
Mary E.	William H. Mobley	3 Mar 1890	w
Mary F.	Edward R. Johnson	24 Mar 1874	
Rebecca	John William Thomas Gue	15 Nov 1859	
Rosa E.	William W. Hessie	24 Sep 1888	w
Samuel T.	Julia Arnold	18 Aug 1853	
Sarah	James H. Henley	21 May 1874	
Solomon	Elizabeth Malone	20 Jan 1808	
Walter W.	Elizabeth Griffith	27 Feb 1894	w
William H.	Mary E. Mobley	3 Mar 1890	w
MOBLY, Ely	Catherine McDonald	20 Jun 1811	
Rachel	Samuel Gue	27 Dec 1799	
MOCKABEE - see also McBEE, McABEE, MOCKBEE			
MOCKABEE, Ann	John Prather	22 Sep 1868	
John	Tabitha McDavitt	8 Feb 1811	
MOCKBEE, Anthony	Anne Robertson	2 Jan 1811	
Basil	Rachel B. Crafford	23 Mar 1804	
Cenah	Orlando Griffith	6 Jan 1812	
Elizabeth Ann	Isaac P. Sinclair	25 Aug 1834	
John	Elizabeth McDevitt	6 Apr 1835	
Mary	Jacob Umstaddt	7 Jan 1811	
Mary	John Johnson	28 Dec 1836	
Mary	Franklin Duvall	15 Nov 1866	
Mary J.	John Merchant	5 Jun 1851	
Patsy	William Tomlinson	9 Jan 1813	
Pricey	Henry Chambers	14 Dec 1803	
Sally	Ambrus Wingate	15 Oct 1808	
Sarah	Thomas Collins	20 Feb 1810	
Tabitha	Washington Appleby	7 Nov 1827	
Winay	George Jackson	5 Mar 1806	
MOFFIT, Sarah	James Littleton	15 Jan 1833	
MOLAN, John B.	Dorcas Roberts	13 Jan 1817	
MOLAND, Joseph	Margaret Welsh	2 Oct 1806	
Margaret	Erasmus Earp	29 Dec 1824	
Thomas	Elizabeth Ogden	26 Feb 1805	
MOLESWORTH, Amelia C.	Job M. C. Bennett	28 Feb 1887	
Anne	Erwin Bowman	7 Aug 1829	
Annie C.	Titus W. Warfield	12 Nov 1885	w
Ella V.	Holland Pearre	2 Jul 1888	w
Joshua	Harriet C. Warfield	20 Aug 1889	w
Mary E.	John E. Warfield	28 Apr 1887	w
MONDAY, Bernard	Catharine A. Dove	12 May 1852	
Bernard	Mary O. Bevan	6 Jun 1861	
Bernard Jr.	Ella F. Long	18 Sep 1896	w
Clara O.	Augustus C. Ward	27 Dec 1886	w
Edwin W.	Bessie M. Hughes	15 Nov 1898	w
Emma	Edward G. Ward	30 Dec 1889	w
Marian	Milton Mundy	5 Oct 1882	
Thomas F.	Ida S. King	20 Nov 1888	w
MONEY, Annie E.	Nathan T. Imlay	1 May 1882	
James H.	Rosanna Jarvis	1 Dec 1857	
Jeannie	Melvin P. Imley	22 Jun 1885	w
Mary F.	Charles V. Morrison	16 Jul 1891	w
MONRED, John E.	Maggie M. Davis	13 Jan 1894	w

MONROE - also see MUNRO

MONROE, A. E.*	Joseph Broders	13 Nov 1856	
MONTGOMERY, Charles W.	Mary L. Davis	24 Jan 1894	w
MOON, Homer C.	Mary G. Ward	28 Apr 1894	w
MOORE, Ada R.	James H. Harding	12 May 1892	w
Albert G.	Sallie Wiley	4 Mar 1886	w
Amonadshanddai	Mary Brewer	31 Dec 1832	
Ann	Archibald Whips	15 May 1817	
Basil	Anna Reindertz	14 Dec 1799	
Cassandra	James Sullivan	4 Jan 1808	
Clara B.	William S. Loman	23 Sep 1890	w
Dela E.	Mary A. Gant	29 Jun 1865	
Edgar W.	Annie D. Wheatley	7 Jun 1893	w
Elias	Catharine Harding	13 Dec 1847	
Elias	Sarah F. Moore	9 Dec 1879	w
Elizabeth	Benjamin Kelly of Thomas	22 Dec 1800	
Elizabeth**	Hezekiah Wheat	17 Apr 1804	
Elizabeth	Thomas Burditt	21 May 1811	
Elizabeth	Joseph Harding	7 Nov 1846	
Elizabeth	Albert Miles	19 Nov 1897	w
Hamilton	Eveline Smallwood	2 Apr 1828	
Harriott	Brice Litton	23 Sep 1803	
Henry L.	Ann Burdict	19 Jun 1817	
Henry W.	Lucinda Etchison	12 Oct 1840	
Isaac J.	Susan R. Miles	6 Dec 1887	w
James	Elizabeth Bradburn	31 Dec 1803	
John	Margaret Sidney	15 Sep 1897	c
John H.	Margaret E. Jackson	23 Dec 1878	c
John William	Elleanora Perry	13 Aug 1895	w
Joseph P.	Lacey Townsend	27 Feb 1877	w
Julia Ellen	John W. Dorsey	19 Dec 1893	c
Lilly C.	Frank P. Stone	20 Dec 1892	w
Lucy	Thomas Reid	12 Nov 1825	
Luther James	Lyddia E. Warfield	17 Dec 1880	
Luther W.	Lydia R. Etchison	13 Mar 1852	
Mahala	George K. Redman	6 Mar 1834	
Margaret	Walter Welsh	10 Sep 1810	
Mary	Jeremiah Saffell	18 Dec 1802	
Mary	Zachariah Merryman	24 Dec 1811	
Minnie A.	Ernest T. Walker	28 Mar 1894	w
Nancy	Benjamin Burch	16 May 1816	
Nathan	Elizabeth Hantz	26 Jan 1801	
Nathaniel	Anne Wheeler	20 Jan 1819	
Nathaniel P.	Elizabeth E. Kroon	23 Feb 1869	
Nathaniel P.	Fannie D. Williams	28 Jun 1892	w
Philemon	Margarett Ann Redman	18 Dec 1826	
Robert B.	Mary W. Cooke	16 Apr 1895	w
Robert Rowland	Margaret G. Tyson	14 Jul 1886	w
Robert S.	Atlantic Butler	10 Jul 1884	c
Romulus L.	Mary T. Bentley	1 Sep 1834	
Sarah Ann	Jacob Vanhorn	9 May 1865	
Sarah E.	Josiah Howard	18 Nov 1868	

* In brackets after names is "Alex. Co., Va."
** Last name partially covered by a line; looks like Moore

MOORE, Sarah F.	Elias Moore	9 Dec 1879	w
Sarah Frances	Remus H. Miles	7 Oct 1884	w
Sophia	Charles Bevin	20 Dec 1799	
Sophia	James Roston	19 Feb 1816	
Thomas W.	Henrietta Keith	10 Mar 1863	
William	Sarah F. Keith	2 Jun 1863	
William	Ann Gantt	19 May 1874	
William H. T.	Jane Carter	8 Nov 1866	
MOR---, Albert F.*	Mary F. Peacock	* Oct 1867	

MORAN - also see MARAN

MORAN, Frances	Harmon T. Moran	9 Oct 1868	
Harmon T.	Frances Moran	9 Oct 1868	
Hezekiah	Rachel Musgrove	22 Jul 1815	
John W.	Margaret A. Howser	19 Oct 1858	
Joseph	Harriet Lochte	9 May 1894	w
Peter	Rebecca Selby	20 Nov 1812	
Rebecca	John Reed	23 Sep 1814	

MORELAND - also see MORLAND

MORELAND, Rachel	Allison Nailor	23 Apr 1835	
MORELEY, Rebecca	John Troop	26 Dec 1798	
MORGAL, Lewis E.	Maggie V. Lynch	11 Apr 1882	
Phares L.	Carrie V. Simpson	12 Apr 1898	w
MORGAN, Elizabeth	Thomas Benson	18 Jan 1811	
Joel	Jane C. Coleman	15 Mar 1819	
Joseph	Elizabeth McAtee	23 Aug 1806	
Joseph T.	Lucretia V. Burton	10 Dec 1863	
Mary Ann	George W. Gray	22 Oct 1834	
Mordecai	Mary Josephine Davis	16 Jan 1856	
Susan D.	John Nuse	2 Oct 1895	w
William E.	Emma May Gardiner	11 Jan 1887	w
MORIARTY, Georgie	Mahlon T. Lewis	8 Dec 1876	

MORLAND - also see MORELAND

MORLAND, Enoch	Caroline Magruder	1 Feb 1842	
MORNINGSTAR, Charles E.	Lizzie A. Lindig	16 Dec 1885	w
Rosie	David S. Ward	19 Jul 1897	w
MORONEY, John E.	Mary Heggerman	20 Jan 1893	w

MORRIS - also see MORRISS

MORRIS, Ida J.	Frank Rhodes	20 Jul 1895	c
John	Anne Green	19 Dec 1799	
Mary C.	James E. Bumbrey	28 May 1897	c
Robert	Leanna Oneale	26 Dec 1842	

MORRISON - also see MORRISSON

MORRISON, Alice S.	Flavel Philip Flippen	14 Dec 1886	w
Anne	William Brashears	1 Jan 1810	
Catharine V.	James M. Beall	23 Dec 1873	
Charles V.	Mary F. Money	16 Jul 1891	w
D. Cameron	Helen A. Johnston	14 Nov 1864	
Henrietta	Benjamin H. Warthen	10 Jun 1851	
James	Nannie Bogley	26 Dec 1883	w
Katie	Walter M. Haney	26 Dec 1883	w
Mary L.	Jacob L. Keafauver	7 Mar 1872	
Rebecca	John A. Ford	10 Jul 1844	
Sarah A.	James T. Merchant	23 Dec 1858	
William	Mary Judy	1 Jan 1810	

* Remainder of last name has blot on it; day if either 11 or 12

MORRISS - also see MORRIS
MORRISS, Thomas　　　　　　Mary Cookendaffer　　　　26 Mar 1800
MORRISSON - also see MORRISON
MORRISSON, John　　　　　　Catherine Ann Lowe　　　　9 Jan 1833
MORROW, Frank　　　　　　　Catharine Kline　　　　　28 Aug 1889 w
MORSELL, Arthur L.　　　　　Sallie P. Wilson　　　　　9 Sep 1892 w
　　　　　Elizabeth　　　　　Henry Willson　　　　　　 1 Jul 1803
　　　　　John　　　　　　　　Louisa Martin　　　　　　26 Nov 1879 c
MORTIMER, John T.　　　　　 Deborah A. Bennett　　　　16 Feb 1861
MORTON, Coleman　　　　　　 Rebecca Jackson　　　　　 2 Apr 1879 c
　　　　　Martha　　　　　　　William B. Simms　　　　 24 Jul 1875
　　　　　Rosa　　　　　　　　Ben Jones　　　　　　　　23 May 1892 w
MOSBURG - also see MOSSBURG
MOSBURG, Christian　　　　　Ann Ferrall　　　　　　　28 May 1844
　　　　　Daniel　　　　　　　Sarah Riggs　　　　　　　13 Jun 1815
MOSELEY, John W.　　　　　　Margaret D. Peter　　　　12 Feb 1861
MOSS - also see MAUS
MOSS, Emma J.　　　　　　　 George M. Bennett　　　　22 May 1865
　　　　　Sarah A.　　　　　 Henry Heinback　　　　　 26 Oct 1885 w
MOSSBURG - also see MOSBURG
MOSSBURG, Annie S.　　　　　John E. Mathews　　　　　23 May 1881
　　　　　Benjamin A.　　　　Fannie C. Burdette　　　24 Dec 1890 w
　　　　　Catherine　　　　　James R. Walker　　　　 21 Dec 1858
　　　　　Charles M.　　　　 Mary A. Trail　　　　　　3 Oct 1894 w
　　　　　Henry W.　　　　　 Ann Eliza Benson　　　　 19 May 1845
　　　　　Isabel E.　　　　　Thomas F. Darne　　　　　10 Sep 1895 w
　　　　　Josephine　　　　　John C. Harvey　　　　　 2 Mar 1895 w
　　　　　Katie　　　　　　　Thomas Carson　　　　　　* Jan 1883
　　　　　Maggie O.　　　　　George H. Fry　　　　　　8 Mar 1893 w
　　　　　Mollie C.　　　　　George W. McIntosh　　　10 Mar 1868
　　　　　Philip F.　　　　　Annie Hyatt　　　　　　　27 Jan 1875
　　　　　Rosalpha　　　　　 Frederick C. Stang　　　10 Oct 1870
　　　　　Sarah L.　　　　　 James R. Miles　　　　　 4 Aug 1865
　　　　　Susie　　　　　　　Alexander Small　　　　　2 Mar 1895 w
　　　　　William C.　　　　 Mary Burche　　　　　　　4 Aug 1879 w
　　　　　William C.　　　　 Bertie C. Stevens　　　 16 Jun 1884 w
　　　　　William H.　　　　 Alice V. Nicholson　　　31 Oct 1883
MOULDEN - also see MOULDIN, MOULDING
MOULDEN, Annie M.　　　　　 Charles McIntosh　　　　 20 Apr 1882
　　　　　Catharine　　　　　William O. Conner　　　 19 Sep 1827
　　　　　Cora V.　　　　　　Albert T. Clayton　　　 27 Jun 1892 w
　　　　　Dennis　　　　　　 Sarah Ann Oneale　　　　 8 Mar 1826
　　　　　Eli　　　　　　　　Martha E. Riggs　　　　 10 Mar 1868
　　　　　Elias　　　　　　　Eliza E. Thompson　　　 16 Feb 1841
　　　　　Elias N.　　　　　 Mary E. Smith　　　　　　18 Jun 1849
　　　　　Eliza　　　　　　　James Payne　　　　　　　2 Nov 1829
　　　　　Elizabeth　　　　　Erasmus Earp　　　　　　28 Jan 1837
　　　　　Hezekiah W.　　　　Lucinda Garrett　　　　 10 Sep 1835
　　　　　Jackson　　　　　　Mary E. Merchant　　　　22 Nov 1850
　　　　　Jesse　　　　　　　Eleanor Wellen　　　　　 6 Mar 1818
　　　　　Joseph O.　　　　　Anna A. Thompson　　　　 8 Dec 1887 w
　　　　　Margaret S.　　　　Samuel H. Cator　　　　 13 Dec 1881
　　　　　Melissa　　　　　　Winfield S. Beall　　　 26 Oct 1875
　　　　　Rachel Ann　　　　 Nicholas Whelan, Jr.　　17 Apr 1847

* Cannot read day; before 9

MOULDEN, Samuel J.	Jane R. Thompson	26 Dec 1848
Verlinder	Franklin A. Oden	17 Jul 1850
MOULDIN, Mertimer	Mary L. Thompson	28 Dec 1852
MOULDING, Anne A.	James Hall	29 Dec 1821
Julia Ann	William H. Trail	1 May 1837
Levi	Mary Jarvis	25 Sep 1822
Levi	Eliza King	27 Dec 1829
Rachel	Robert Ricketts	30 Mar 1826
Susannah	William Campbell	24 Dec 1806
MOUNT, Albert N.	Bertha C. Fish	20 Apr 1887 w
Emma V.	Jacob J. Souder	22 Apr 1884
Ethel W.	Titus J. Day	27 Jan 1894 w
Fannie G.	Richard H. Stanley	21 Dec 1886 w
James M.	Zera A. Gue	6 Jan 1897 w
Sarah Frances	George W. Anderson	19 Oct 1846
William	Sarah Baker	3 Aug 1831
MOUNTS, Julius A.	Kitty Ann Gatton	12 Mar 1833
MOURRER, William H.	Lydia Oden	1 Mar 1858
MOWYER - also see MOYER		
MOWYER, Ransel	Ruth Burress	26 Jan 1830
MOXLEY, Anna S.	John W. Gray	14 Nov 1871
Annie B.	Towny H. Hyatt	21 Dec 1896 w
Brunette	Samuel Etchison	15 Mar 1815
Caleb	Elizabeth Wolf	22 Jan 1821
Daisy V.	Walter A. Cline	21 Dec 1897 w
Della M.	James O. Moxley	19 Dec 1893 w
Ezekiel	Caty Forner	26 May 1803
Ezekiel	Hattie V. Thompson	9 Nov 1874
Garrison	Martha A. Bellison	17 Dec 1895 w
Gustavus	Alice V. Thompson	24 Nov 1891 w
Hattie V.	Edward L. Bellison	7 Nov 1887 w
James A.	Hattie V. Easton	23 Oct 1895 w
James O.	Della M. Moxley	19 Dec 1893 w
Juliet	John T. Sheckles	6 Feb 1852
Laura C.	Louis B. Easton	5 Dec 1893 w
Laura V.	Joshua W. Brown	19 Dec 1891 w
Mary E.	Enoch S. Watkins	14 Feb 1893 w
Mary M.	Willard C. Higgins	6 Dec 1893 w
Rachel E.	Horace W. Gue	24 Feb 1870
William	Lethea Watkins	8 Jan 1821
Willie B.	Minnie J. Bellison	17 Jan 1888 w
MOYER - also see MOWYER		
MOYER, Mary C.	William Renshaw	3 Oct 1890 w
MOZIER, Theodore	Mary Brent	22 Dec 1845
MUDD, Elizabeth	Walter Madden	2 Sep 1802
MUIR, Andrew Jr.	Fannie P. Purdum	22 May 1875
James	Belle N. Purdom	8 Oct 1873
William S.	Lydia W. Chichester	1 Jun 1894 w
MULCAHY, John	Eliza Jane Sullivan	6 Jan 1869
Patrick F.	Margaret M. Santman	16 Oct 1895 w
MULLEAGUE, Mary A.	John N. Kelley	4 Mar 1886 w
MULLEN, Charles William	Susie A. Runalds	5 Nov 1879 c
MULLER, Bernhard Reinhold	Katie Weisser	15 Dec 1897 w
MULLICAN, Annie B.	James T. Creamer	28 Sep 1886 w
Archibald	Ann Matthews	23 Apr 1805
Archibald	Mary F. Thrift	11 Sep 1871

MULLICAN,	Arthur L.	Nettie Kisner	15 Apr 1897	w
	Basil	Tabitha Walker	10 Apr 1822	
	Bazilla F.	Jane Leadingham	4 Mar 1861	
	Benjamin	Matilda Clagett	17 Jan 1816	
	Bertha	Charles C. Ricketts	31 May 1892	w
	Christina	William O. Parsly	26 Jan 1885	w
	Clara	William R. VanHorn	8 Jan 1886	w
	Clara V.	Charles W. Simonson	17 Dec 1879	w
	Effie	Columbus G. Bean	23 Feb 1897	w
	Elizabeth	Thomas Walker	15 Dec 1825	
	Elizabeth A.	John Francis Blundon	16 Nov 1880	
	Emma L.	Wallace E. Ricketts	14 Oct 1891	w
	Frances Ann	James L. Magruder	29 Mar 1887	w
	Frank Alridge	Mary E. Gaither	27 Nov 1886	w
	George D.	Mary Clark	4 Jan 1875	
	George W.	Minnie E. West	20 Apr 1898	w
	Harriet	Jonathan Sibley	13 Jan 1819	
	Henrietta	John A. Selby	20 Jan 1898	w
	Henry	Carilla Walker	3 Mar 1829	
	Henry	Susan S. Crown	15 Mar 1859	
	Henry Clay	Alice Gates	28 Nov 1875	
	Ida R.	Charles Americus Mansfield	1 Dec 1897	w
	Ignatius	Elizabeth Kisner	16 Jul 1863	
	Isaiah	Martha C. Kisner	31 May 1870	
	James	Mary Smith	29 Dec 1817	
	John	Lucinda Dowden	18 Nov 1818	
	John	Harriet Beans	27 Dec 1818	
	John	Nelly Murphey	31 Dec 1825	
	John	Elizabeth F. Ricketts	26 Dec 1854	
	Juliet S.	William G. Burriss	12 Oct 1848	
	Kattie	John S. West	1 Sep 1879	
	Lucy J. D.	George W. Emrich	16 Oct 1884	w
	Margaret A.	Reuben Burriss	1 Mar 1855	
	Margaret E.	John O. Merchant	18 Dec 1856	
	Mary C.	James L. Magruder	8 Nov 1880	
	Mary Minerva	John C. Power	1 Jan 1877	
	Mary V. E.	Hamilton O. Ferguson	26 Sep 1888	w
	Mollie F.	David A. Mansfield	12 Apr 1894	w
	Nathan B.	Martha Baker	27 Jan 1841	
	Nicholas	Eleanor Brown	28 Dec 1822	
	Reuben T.	Mary Rabbitt	23 Dec 1847	
	Salathiel T.	Harriet J. Ward	10 Dec 1861	
	Sarah	Robert Henley	20 Jan 1859	
	Sarah E.	Oliver T. Vanhorne	10 Apr 1861	
	Thomas	Susannah Fulks	23 Dec 1809	
	Thomas	Mary Price	20 Dec 1843	
	Thomas T.	Gertie B. Butt	25 Apr 1895	w
	William	Elizabeth Douden	29 Dec 1800	
	William	Elizabeth Piles	31 Dec 1803	
	William	Eliza Ann Creamer	13 Oct 1857	
	William G.	Florence L. VanHorn	18 Feb 1895	w
	William H.	Martha J. Boswell	26 Feb 1850	
	William H.	Ella S. Harding	8 Apr 1890	
MULLIGAN,	George W.	Ella J. Young	25 Oct 1897	w
	Florence	George M. Best	10 Jun 1890	w

MULLIGAN, Harry E.	Cora E. Howard	20 Jan 1897	w
Sarah A.	John J. Gue	10 Sep 1895	w
MULLINEAUX, James R.	Emily J. Darby	6 Jul 1889	w
MULLINIX, Alice F.	Basil T. Warfield	28 Dec 1886	w
Cerita M.	John N. Broadhurst	1 May 1896	w
Cordelia B.	Edward E. Watkins	7 Dec 1888	w
Jesse E.	Nora D. Lawson	19 Dec 1893	w
John W.	Louise C. Etchison	2 Oct 1897	w
Mary E.	James E. Day	1 Mar 1886	w
Mary R.	James T. Bean	16 Dec 1889	w
Rachel J. E.	Charles E. Hilton	11 Apr 1892	w
Rezin G.	Mary C. Hilton	30 Oct 1888	w
Richard A.	Fannie Z. Watkins	1 Apr 1889	w
Sandy Thomas	Maggie B. Gue	1 Mar 1893	w
Vernon A.	Emma E. Johnson	23 Dec 1897	w
Vertie K.	Edward D. Warfield	11 Jan 1894	w
MUNCASTER, Edwin M.	Rachel Robertson	24 May 1836	
Harriet M.	Walter M. Talbott	9 Nov 1857	
Helen	John H. Gassaway	7 Oct 1895	w
Laura C.	John J. Higgins	25 Jan 1882	
Luther M.	Mary S. Willson	20 Jan 1896	w
Otho Z.	Harriet E. Magruder	5 Apr 1849	
William E.	Hannah S. Magruder	14 Oct 1867	
Zachariah	Harriett Magruder	24 Sep 1804	
MUNDY, Milton	Marian Monday	5 Oct 1882	
MUNRO - also see MONROE			
MUNRO, Charlotte Louise	Josiah Loring Whittington	6 Oct 1884	w
George A.	Elizabeth H. Thompson	6 Nov 1858	
MUNROE, James R.	Serena Hurdle	22 Apr 1830	
Jonathan	Nancey Beeding	23 Mar 1801	
MURDICT, Sally L.	Luthur M. Purdum	27 Mar 1894	w
MURDOCK, George W.	Annie L. Norris	29 May 1893	w
Wallace	Mildred A. Peck	25 Aug 1896	w
MURPHEY, Agnes	William E. B. Levy	25 Jun 1881	w
Alexandra	Samina L. Richardson	29 Nov 1825	
Benjamin	Mary Nicholls	17 Oct 1825	
Charles R.	Eliza R. Mannakee	4 Mar 1851	
Edna	John Lewis	17 Oct 1825	
Elizabeth T.	Richard R. Brown	11 May 1846	
Ephraim	Mary Lewis	21 Jan 1800	
Erasmus	Nancy Parker	28 Jan 1805	
Greenbury	Susanna Warfield	11 Jan 1806	
Henrietta	Robert Darnale	12 Jun 1815	
Horace L.	Charlotte D. Johnson	30 Nov 1854	
Jemima	Tilghman Cross	28 May 1832	
John	Sarah Johnson	24 Feb 1818	
John	Mary Wheeler	30 Dec 1824	
Mary	Isaiah Cross	6 Nov 1832	
Michael	Sarah Lewis	6 Nov 1805	
Nelly	John Mullican	31 Dec 1825	
Reuben	Lydia Thompson	15 Sep 1836	
Sarah	William Shaw	24 Aug 1841	
Sarah A.	Levi Shaw	16 Nov 1859	
Singleton	Charlott T. Harper	14 Oct 1819	
William	Bettie Lawson	12 May 1886	c

MURPHEY, William E.	Julia Ann Vermillion	4 Feb 1834	
MURPHY, Ann E.	William R. Windsor	15 Aug 1861	
Bridget	James E. Murray	15 Apr 1881	
Carrie M.	William W. Darby	17 Feb 1885	w
Charles H.	Mary E. Richardson	12 Dec 1854	
Elizabeth B.	Richard J. Benson	21 Dec 1897	w
Franklin W.	Georgiana Bacon	3 Feb 1890	c
Gladys	David T. Poore	25 Nov 1884	w
Helen	Jacob B. Richards	11 Jul 1892	w
Kate V.	Charles M. Pool	2* Sep 1886	w
Kitty	Hilleary Easton	7 Feb 1821	
Louis W.	Mary G. Holland	22 Nov 1892	w
Maggie	Benjamin Reid	5 Oct 1875	
Margaret A.	John Thompson	1 Jun 1857	
Maria M.	Samuel Ward	3 Jul 1882	
Martha E.	George H. Lindsay	12 Jan 1874	
Mary	James A. Bowie	2 Mar 1889	c
Mary L.	John Gibson	1 Jun 1859	
Michael J.	Lizzie Riggs	29 Jan 1880	
Minnie M.	William H. Dutrow	23 Nov 1892	w
Nettie	John W. Coplin	31 Dec 1885	c
Rachel	Geveneur Davis	5 Sep 1868	
Susan	Benjamin C. Tucker	11 Dec 1873	
William J.	Katie Sourvier	7 Aug 1888	w
Winfield J.	Celea A. Cuff	19 Jan 1880	w
MURRAY, Ann	John Jackson	4 Oct 1897	c
Columbus	Hattie Stewart	19 May 1896	c
Emma	John Clipper	1 Aug 1891	c
James E.	Bridget Murphy	15 Apr 1881	
Margaret A.	Amos Skinner	15 Mar 1825	
Mary A.	Howard K. Bane	24 Jun 1896	w
Richard	Dorathy Aldridge	1 Feb 1802	
Robert	Mary Nelson	19 May 1897	c
Sadie	Vernon A. Green	12 May 1897	c
Sarah	Zachariah Yates	9 Dec 1817	
Sarah E.	William Wheatly	2 Mar 1824	
MURREY, Brittey	Charles C. Sickels	23 Sep 1897	c
MURRY, Jane	William H. Gittings	24 Mar 1798	
MUSE, Charles H.	Florence N. Spencer	25 Aug 1898	w
Thomas	Alice Conrad	8 Oct 1898	c
Thomas W.	Nancy E. Peacock	25 Jul 1851	
MUSGROVE, Amelia	James Stutzson	14 Jan 1823	
Anne Rebecca	Perry Bowman	4 Dec 1830	
Anthony	Mary Ann Simpson	5 Nov 1800	
Aria**	Ephraim S. Gaither	6 May 1819	
Caleb	Jane E. Adams	18 Nov 1845	
Charles W.	Susan A. Thompson	10 Dec 1868	
Eliza	Alexander Duvall	15 Mar 1819	
Eliza F.	Andrew E. Easton	26 Dec 1889	w
Fanny	William Scott	8 Mar 1811	
Francis B.	Clara E. Briggs	21 Dec 1891	w
Lilie	Lewis L. Burroughs	24 Dec 1887	w
Margaret A.	Joseph Martin	14 Aug 1878	

* Cannot read complete day; before 27
** Part of last name from earlier reading

MUSGROVE, Mary	Collin Cordell	10 Nov 1808	
Nancy	William Wilkinson	21 Aug 1821	
Nicholas E.	Margaret A. Johnson	5 May 1868	
Rachel	Orlando White	29 Dec 1809	
Rachel	Hezekiah Moran	22 Jul 1815	
Ruth	Levi Lanham	15 Dec 1813	
Sallie A.	John A. Ray	24 May 1892	w
Sarah Ann	Thomas J. Hobbs	24 Jan 1826	
Zachariah	Eleanor Jordan	10 Dec 1802	
MUSSER, Caroline B.	James W. Graff	18 Dec 1893	w
H. M.	Mary E. Burdette	20 Oct 1882	
William	Sarah Ann Henderson	16 Aug 1834	
William	Maria C. Cromwell	5 Mar 1857	
MYERS, Anne	John Ray	11 Oct 1815	
Arthur	Alice Harrison	26 Nov 1879	w
George W.	Susan R. Hopkins	10 Jun 1890	c
Harriet E.	Dr. James H. Maynard	31 May 1870	
Jennie F.	Charles W. Craver	19 Dec 1892	w
John	Winafred Marlowe	10 Oct 1809	
John C.	Martha J. Duley	30 Nov 1848	
Lavinia	George R. Bell	17 Jun 1885	
Magdalene	John Bessant	9 Aug 1815	
Maggie	Andrew J. Harding	21 Nov 1865	
Mary Estelle	D. Bargar Evans	10 Sep 1890	w
Olivia M.	Isaac A. Johnson	9 Feb 1882	
Ruth V.	William Henry Snowden	20 Dec 1865	
Sarah	Robert Stevenson	16 May 1821	
MYLES - also see MILES			
MYLES, George B.	Lucy B. Ramey	19 Jul 1897	w
MYRRIL, Jeremiah	Phebe Halbert	17 Feb 1801	
MYTINGER, Mary A.	William A. Garner	14 May 1894	w
NAILOR - also see NAYLOR			
NAILOR, Achsah	Townsend Coates	5 Apr 1879	c
Allison	Rachel Moreland	23 Apr 1835	
Ellen	Harrad Lyles	14 Jun 1867	
Henry	Teresa E. Dorsey	29 Dec 1896	c
Maria	Charles Peter	24 Jan 1872	
Maria	Henry Hamilton	25 Dec 1884	c
Martha	Gillmore Green	27 Apr 1868	
Nathan	Ann Lee	2 Dec 1868	
NALLY - also see NOLLY			
NALLY, Rebal W.	Eleanor Jones	15 Jan 1802	
NASBY, Frederick	Isabella Simpson	19 Mar 1878	c
NAYLOR - also see NAILOR			
NAYLOR, Nathan S. T.	Hepy E. Betler	30 Jun 1884	c
NEAL - also see NEALE, NEEL, NEELE			
NEAL, Anne	Ignatius Butler	2 Nov 1885	c
Elizabeth	William Lyles	9 Dec 1891	c
Jacob	Amelia Macabee	4 Dec 1878	c
John T.	Martha White	30 Dec 1896	c
Lizzie	Leroy Williams	10 Dec 1868	
Louisa	Reuben Robinson	1 May 1873	
Mary E.	Edward E. Jeffries	12 Feb 1889	c
Mary E.	James E. Jackson	7 Dec 1896	c
Thomas	Isabella Davis	19 Mar 1891	w

NEALE,	Barbara	Bernard O'Neill	25 May 1809
	Charles Henry	Cora Virginia Tyler	16 Nov 1886 c
	Mary	George Johnson	14 Oct 1897 c
	Mary Emma	John Henry Johnson	25 Oct 1894 c
	Miles	Caroline Semmes	21 May 1833
NEEDHAM,	Mary Ann	Patrick O'Conner	31 Jan 1816
NEEL - also see NEAL, NEALE, NEELE			
NEEL,	Catharine	Henry Johnson	9 Jul 1883
	Eliza	Charles Brooks	20 Jan 1873
	James B.	Ann C. Hoyle	8 Feb 1881
	Laura H.	Samuel Riggs	15 May 1876
	Mary	William A. Waters	26 Jan 1863
	Rosanna J.	James S. H. Henderson	15 Dec 1843
	Sarah I.	Alonza Sellman	12 Jul 1870
	Thomas	Mary Offutt	* Feb 1884 c
	William J.	Laura V. Howard	22 Nov 1869
NEELE,	Thomas	Mary Willson	13 Mar 1843
NEFF,	Annie H.	Edward C. Ebert	17 Feb 1891 w
NEHOUSE,	Florence S.	Joshua B. Dill	12 Nov 1896 w
	Francis W.	Maggie A. Duvall	9 Apr 1895 w
NELSON,	Alice	Robert Brown	21 Jan 1884 c
	Amanda	John Luckett	12 Sep 1895 c
	Anna	George W. Cooper	4 Jul 1891 c
	Annie	William Hamilton	30 May 1879 c
	Charles	Rebecca Warfield	19 Jan 1886 c
	David T.	Martha Braxton	8 Dec 1890 c
	Dennis	Henrietta Williams	25 May 1868
	Emeline	Nelson Scales	14 Nov 1868
	Festus	Nancy Holland	22 Dec 1894 c
	Frances N.	Richard S. Worthington	20 Jun 1889 w
	Hubert	Ann Mason	22 Jun 1867
	Hugh	Katharine G. Peter	5 Nov 1890 w
	Lavinia	Alexander Brown	25 Aug 1875
	Leana	Alfred Linkum	6 Apr 1876 c
	Lily J.	Horace Johnson	21 May 1869
	Lucinda	Julius Brawner	24 Dec 1872
	Maranda	Luther Owings	17 Apr 1815
	Mary	Robert Murray	19 May 1897 c
	Mary A.	Hamilton Wallace	14 Feb 1883
	Orlando	Annie E. Plummer	27 May 1863
	Robert E.	Rosa B. Crawford	25 Jun 1890 w
	Rosa	Thomas H. Cooper	13 Jul 1895 c
	William	Mary Lucas	9 Jul 1892 c
	William	Susan D. Kelley	19 Jun 1895 w
	William	Lillie Blair	9 Jul 1895 c
	Willie A.	William A. Braxton	13 Jul 1896 c
NERVESON - also see NEVERSON			
NERVESON,	Matilda	Silas Waits	3 Feb 1866
NESBIT,	Anne	Abraham Becraft	24 Nov 1803
	Frederick	Sarah Budd	10 Apr 1871
NESBITT,	George F.	Louisa P. Hall	21 Nov 1865
NEUCY - also see NUCEY, NEWCY			
NEUCY,	Robert	Mary E. Brogden	19 Nov 1870
	Robert	Helen Shedrick	31 Jul 1889 c

* Cannot read day; either 2 or 3

```
NEUMANN - also see NEWMAN
NEUMANN, William          Lucy M. P. Reigle          16 Dec 1878 w
NEURATH, Julia A.         Joseph Kazle                9 Apr 1894 w
NEVERSON - also see NERVESON, EVERSON
NEVERSON, Alfred J.       A. Virginia Swailes        26 Dec 1883 c
          Alfred J.       Eliza E. Jackson           15 May 1886 c
          Carrie          George A. Green            19 Apr 1884
          Currie          George D. Magruder         26 Dec 1895 c
          Edith V.        George William Jackson     19 Sep 1879 c
          Samuel E.       Clara Riggs                22 Oct 1873
          Samuel E.       Annie Swailes              25 Feb 1896 c
          Sarah           William Allen Henry        11 Oct 1869
NEVITT, James             Sarah Stephens             14 Oct 1800
        Joseph            Mary E. Tarman             29 Dec 1847
        Sarah             John Williams              25 Dec 1806
NEWCY - also see NUCEY
NEWCY, Lizzie             Walter Budd                 5 May 1892 c
NEWMAN - also see NEUMANN
NEWMAN. Alfred            Margaret Nolan             21 Oct 1874
        Caroline          Joseph Johnson             27 Jan 1894 c
        Charles           Janie Collings             25 Nov 1879 w
        Charles W.        Lucy J. Clagett            19 Feb 1889 c
        Frank             Dolly Mason                15 May 1880 c
        George            Harriet Hall               30 Aug 1897 c
        Henry             Melinda Franklin            3 Jun 1897 c
        Ida F.            William M. Beall           13 Apr 1887 w
        Laura R.          John W. Lancaster          28 Dec 1896 c
        Margaret          Major Meridis              26 Dec 1881 c
        Mary              William Turner             21 Jan 1891 c
        Morton M.         Agnes Palmer               16 Dec 1885 c
        Tasker            Louisa Wood                16 Jun 1870
        William M.        Mary G. Andrews            12 Mar 1896 w
NEWTON, Alosius           Verlinda Pearce             3 Feb 1822
        Anne              Giles Hill                  4 Jan 1800
        Harriet           Massum Tuttle              22 Jan 1834
        Martha T.         Edward E. Thompson         31 Mar 1875
        Thomas            Jane Freis                 27 Oct 1803
NICHANS - also see NICKENS
NICHANS, Henry            Anna Hager                 21 Dec 1870
NICHOLAS, Philip          Rachel Chaney              22 Aug 1815
NICHOLDSON - also see NICHOLSON
NICHOLDSON, Elisha        Elizabeth Hillard          15 Jan 1817
            Kitty         John Kinder                24 Dec 1810
NICHOLES - also see NICHOLLS
NICHOLES, Priscilla       John Swink                 16 Dec 1817
NICHOLLS - also see NICHOLES, NICHOLS
NICHOLLS, Archibald       Louiza H. Layton            9 Jul 1842
          Belle           Joseph H. Cooley           30 Oct 1883
          Camden R.       Lucy C. Wade               22 Dec 1856
          Charles         Mary E. Mannakee           10 Oct 1854
          Columbia V.     Thomas Broome              23 Feb 1875
          Edward          Anne Vinson                23 Dec 1811
          Elizabeth       Thomas Birdwhistle          1 Jan 1806
          Elizabeth       Edmond G. Duley            23 Apr 1835
          Elizabeth E.    Lawson Day                  8 Sep 1884 w
          Evan            Rebeccah Quary             29 Feb 1808
```

NICHOLLS,	George T.	Courtney Burdett	29 Jan 1879	w
	George W.	Louisa Nicholls	22 Oct 1851	
	Harriet A.	James P. Wade	4 Nov 1847	
	Henry	Anne Catharine Connelly	9 Jun 1842	
	John T.	Martha M. Hays	4 Nov 1839	
	Louisa	George W. Nicholls	22 Oct 1851	
	Margaret	Lawson Day	25 Dec 1849	
	Mary	Benjamin Murphey	17 Oct 1825	
	Mary Elizabeth	Hezekiah Lewis Trundle	22 Apr 1839	
	Mary Isabell	C. W. Thompson	4 Mar 1868	
	Naomi	William Swink	15 Jan 1829	
	Nicholas	Elizabeth Prather	20 Mar 1811	
	Peggy	Amos Skinner	23 Apr 1812	
	Polly	Thomas Stonestreet	18 Dec 1799	
	Samuel Thomas	Sarah Oneale	24 Feb 1825	
	Sarah E.	Benjamin S. White	24 Feb 1851	
	Sarah E.	Dathan Broome	4 Mar 1868	
	Sarah E.	James Ganley	17 Nov 1868	
	Susanah	Laurence Pearen	4 Oct 1814	
	Thomas	Henny Jackson	3 Jun 1870	
	Thomas C.	Priscilla Mackey*	14 Apr 1800	
	Thomas S.	Sarah Ellen Anderson	29 Jul 1846	
	William	Angeline Wade	4 Nov 1847	
NICHOLLSON - also see NICHOLSON				
NICHOLLSON,	Baker	Mary Ann Croply	21 Jan 1842	
	Delia	Edward Drudge	21 Jan 1847	
	James A. S.	Lydia E. Andrews	10 Jan 1848	
	Jane Rebecca	John T. Medley	2 Dec 1840	
	John W.	Mary R. Johnson	28 Jan 1851	
	Lloyd H.	Ann M. Purdy	16 Feb 1847	
	Walter	Ruth Medley	26 Mar 1834	
NICHOLS - also see NICHOLLS				
NICHOLS,	Annie L.	Benjamin F. Mason	20 Dec 1895	c
	Camden R.	Emily T. Walters	** Apr 1879	
	Charles	Eulie Martin	11 Sep 1890	c
	Charles K.	Ida S. Bowman	7 Mar 1893	w
	Edith J.	James A. Boxall	26 Sep 1898	w
	Edward	Anna V. Trundle	9 Nov 1854	
	Elbert	Gertrude Cashell	10 Oct 1894	w
	Emily M.	William T. White	28 May 1897	w
	Hennie	John Johnson	26 May 1885	c
	Jenny R.	Henry Cooley	13 Jun 1853	
	Laura F.	Charles L. Young	18 Feb 1892	w
	Lillian L.	William H. Clough	29 Jul 1889	w
	Lizzie	George Taylor	11 Apr 1887	c
	Louisa Ann	Jonas B. Snepp	15 Sep 1855	
	Mary A.	William R. Austin	14 Jan 1879	w
	Mary P.	Earnest H. Richter	1 Dec 1863	
	William	Ann E. Taylor	7 Oct 1842	
	William C.	Drusilla Hardisty	15 Aug 1893	w
NICHOLSON - also see NICHOLDSON, NICHOLLSON				
NICHOLSON,	Alice V.	William H. Mossburg	31 Oct 1883	
	Amelia	Azariah Kindle	3 Dec 1802	

* Last name from earlier reading
** Cannot read day; between 14 and 21

NICHOLSON, Ann M.	Samuel Cissell	26 Mar 1864	
Annie M.	George O. Holland	19 Jan 1897	w
Antonia	Jerome Lydard	25 Aug 1885	w
Asa	Cordeny Basford	9 Sep 1813	
Baker	Ellen McGlaughlin	5 Nov 1828	
Baker	Julia A. Nicholson	30 Aug 1850	
Baker W.	Rhoda Johnson	19 Oct 1857	
Barbara E.	George D. Custer	22 Nov 1881	
Benjamin A.	Nellie G. Gaskins	14 Nov 1892	w
Cassandra	John Peters	15 Oct 1839	
Charles W.	Almetia M. Miles	21 Nov 1882	w
Clifton F.	Maggie E. Lucas	27 Nov 1894	w
Eleanor N.	Lewis W. Poole	18 Jun 1895	w
Ellen A.	Henry L. Clements	2 Dec 1881	w
Elizabeth*	Michael Whealan	17 Feb 1798	
Elizabeth	Zachariah Oden	21 Dec 1844	
Emily J.	George W. Norwood	21 Dec 1880	
Frank S.	Annie M. Dillehay	3 Mar 1890	w
George E.	Mary E. Custer	7 Feb 1888	w
Henrietta C.	Charles Reely	6 Sep 1862	
Isabella C.	Frederick W. Kuster	21 Jun 1886	w
James M.	Bessie V. Price	17 Dec 1895	w
James A. S.	Ellen Maria Medley	30 Mar 1840	
James S.	Caroline Ward	6 Jun 1861	
Jennie	George Washington Damude	27 Dec 1876	
Joanna	Lafayette M. Dwyer	13 Aug 1874	
John	Tabitha Oden	11 Apr 1799	
John	Martha Johnson	10 Mar 1869	
John T.	Mary E. Pickens	19 Dec 1856	
John H.	Merab Sexton	12 Nov 1896	w
John R.	Sarah L. Lucas	17 Dec 1895	w
John T.	Julia A. Danewood	21 Nov 1895	w
Joseph	Jennie Action	3 Feb 1879	
Julia A.	Baker Nicholson	30 Aug 1850	
Laura J.	Leonard W. Howard	7 May 1888	w
Laura Jane	James Nathan Keith	14 Oct 1869	
Margaret Z.	Thomas C. Nicholson	4 Aug 1879	
Martha	William Taylor	9 May 1870	
Mary C.	Franklin Cooley	6 Dec 1865	
Richard C.	Susan R. Reed	14 Jan 1875	
Richard H.	Isabella C. Bennett	29 Dec 1870	
Sarah A.	Enos Jenkins	13 Dec 1893	w
Sarah C.	Henry Mobley	29 Jan 1862	
Savillia B.	Andrew J. Daley	25 Oct 1881	w
Susannah	Benjamin Sedgwick	2 Jan 1799	
Thomas	Charlotte Warfield	16 Oct 1820	
Thomas C.	Margaret Z. Nicholson	4 Aug 1879	
Vernon H.	Martha S. Young	12 Dec 1883	
Walter	A. Rosetta Thompson	24 Feb 1865	
William H.	Carrie H. Young	19 Nov 1883	
William H.	Fannie Gibson	17 Jul 1894	w
NICKENS - also see NICHANS			
NICKENS, Emma	Turner S. Adams	14 May 1898	c

* Part of last name from earlier reading

NICKSON - also see NIXON			
NICKSON, Amey	Thomas W. Howard	2 Mar 1802	
NIEMEYER, Magdalena C.	William H. Fendner	26 Aug 1892	w
NIPLE, Annie M.	Enoch S. Creamer	12 Jan 1898	w
Minnie D.	Marvin B. Stevens	4 Jul 1898	w
NOBBS, James B.	Ellen Ross	30 May 1839	
NOBLE - also see KNOBEL			
NOBLE, George W.	Bettie White	12 Dec 1883	
NOBLITT, Jane	Erasmus J. Middleton	12 Sep 1842	
NOKES, Richard F.	Olivia R. Peters	18 May 1888	c
Rose	John Leake	19 Oct 1874	
NOLAN, Lucy	Henry Turner	14 Nov 1874	
Margaret	Alfred Newman	21 Oct 1874	
NOLAND - also see NOLAN, NOLEN, NOWLAN			
NOLAND, Ann	Westard T. Mason	20 Jan 1806	
Caroline	Sylvester C. Jones	5 Sep 1868	
Charles K.	Fannie Frazier Cooley	11 May 1894	c
Dade	Caroline Frances Harding	11 Jan 1816	
David	Josaphine Offutt	14 Jan 1865	
Elizabeth	Perry Chase	15 May 1869	
Jane	Joseph Evans	30 Nov 1869	
Jane L.	Joseph T. Bailey	21 Feb 1843	
Mary Ann	Stephen Anderson	24 Dec 1824	
Mary M.	Noah H. Sedgwick	19 Dec 1881	
Sarah A.	Isaac T. Davis	12 Nov 1887	c
Thomas	Louisa Campbell	14 Feb 1890	c
NOLEN, Elizabeth	Giles Easton	2 Apr 1799	
NOLLY - also see NALLY			
NOLLY, Louisa A.	Benjamin E. Eller	11 Sep 1848	
NOLTE, Henry	Elizabeth Fiddler	13 Dec 1881	
Henry	Elizabeth Gladman	30 Oct 1894	w
Mary	John Maguire	20 Oct 1894	w
NOON, Beddy	Mark Fyhe	6 Jan 1802	
NORMAN, James D.	Catharine J. Beeding	7 Dec 1836	
Mary	Robert Lynch	24 Jun 1889	c
Sarah	George Rivers	4 Jun 1881	c
NORRIS - also see NORRISS			
NORRIS, Alice V.	Richard S. Cornwell	7 Nov 1887	w
Annie L.	George W. Murdock	29 May 1893	w
Barnett T.	Ann Fife	6 Jan 1830	
Britania C.	N. T. Harriss	8 Jul 1868	
Cecelia E.	Nathan T. Harriss	14 Sep 1859	
Charles E.	Mamie Trail	18 Dec 1894	w
Clara V.	Zadok Ricketts	15 Jan 1890	w
Clarie E.	George W. Matthews	10 Dec 1879	w
Eleanor	Henry Winemiller	1 Mar 1806	
Ella	Millard Price	20 May 1893	w
Emma L.	Willard F. Hitchens	11 Apr 1895	w
Florence	Dangerfield Lomax	24 Oct 1894	c
Henrietta	Richard H. Arnold	10 Jan 1866	
Henry J.	Margaret A. Lowe	15 Sep 1862	
Henry J.	Laura B. Imlay	30 Jan 1882	
Henry J.	Lilly Ashby	1 Mar 1898	w
James C.	Sarah C. Lowe	12 Jun 1867	
James E.	Emma E. King	25 Sep 1876	

NORRIS,	James H.	Nonie E. Dutrow	30 Dec 1884	w
	John T.	Margaret A. King	24 Mar 1860	
	Josephine R.	William H. H. Martin	21 Mar 1864	
	Julia A.	Charles Mansfield	18 Jun 1861	
	Lizzie	Charles Sedgwick	25 Sep 1879	c
	Mary	John Yates	22 Feb 1816	
	Rebecca	George B. McClellan Athey	11 Jun 1884	w
	Rebecca	William Brown	26 Jun 1895	c
	Sarah E.	Henry M. Lindig	27 Oct 1891	w
	Thomas	Elizabeth Draper	19 Feb 1869	
	William T.	Mary Jane Green	26 Aug 1878	w
NORRISS - also see NORRIS				
NORRISS,	Charlotte	Joseph W. Estworthy	15 Sep 1884	
	Harriet	Thomas J. Reed	24 Dec 1878	w
	Rebecca	William Boyer*	23 Feb 1822	
NORTEN - also see NORTON				
NORTEN,	Isabel C.	Charles A. Walden	22 Aug 1891	w
NORTHCRAFT,	Catharine	Francis Buxton	2 Apr 1809	
	Elizabeth	Thomas W. Riggs	26 Oct 1826	
	James	Rachel Fryer	26 Jan 1802	
NORTHCROFT,	Anne America	Charles Riggs	5 Feb 1833	
	James	Hannah Heughs	29 Dec 1803	
	Mary	Benjamin Johnson	21 Jan 1803	
NORTON - also see NORTEN				
NORTON,	Chloe Ann	Charles Stewart	19 May 1798	
	James R.	Mary E. Fisher	29 Jan 1856	
NORWOOD,	Bradley J.	Margaretta Trail	4 Feb 1887	w
	George W.	Emily J. Nicholson	21 Dec 1880	
	Gilbert D.	Hattie E. Beall	12 Jan 1892	w
	Hannah	John A. King	20 Dec 1873	
	Jacob C.	Effy I. Beall	12 Jan 1892	w
	John H.	Frances Dent	** Jul 1882	
	Susannah	John Ellis	15 Dec 1808	
NOT - also see KNOTT				
NOT,	Catharine	Rezin B. Offutt	8 Feb 1801	
NOURSE,	Charles H.	Maria Robertson	14 Oct 1841	
	Charles H.	Elizabeth J. Peter	3 Mar 1849	
	Charles H. Jr.	Alice Darby	14 Jun 1871	
	Henry D.	Sarah A. Peter	23 Aug 1889	w
NOWLAN - also see NOLAND				
NOWLAN,	Michael	Rosanna McCardell	9 Feb 1829	
NOYES,	Marie L.	Arthur E. Dowell	5 Apr 1892	w
NUCEY - also see NEUCY, NEWCY				
NUCEY,	Susie C.	Robert Askins	21 Feb 1895	c
NUCY,	Susan C.	Thomas Holland	21 Sep 1892	c
NUGENT,	Annie	Isaiah Taylor	10 Jun 1896	c
	Emma	Stephen Waters	4 Mar 1897	c
	Evan C.	Sarah C. Lincoln	30 Jul 1878	c
	John H.	Ruth A. Snowden	10 Jun 1878	c
	Joseph A.	Ella J. Davis	29 Sep 1887	c
	Susan A.	Benjamin T. Charge	13 Jan 1887	c
	William	Sarah T. Holland	1 May 1884	

* Blot on last two letters of last name; Boyer may be incorrect
** Cannot read day; after 10

NULL, Tempie G.	William A. Hartishell	13 Jul 1891	w
NUSE, John	Susan D. Morgan	2 Oct 1895	w
NUSZ, Frederick	Ann Saffell	29 Dec 1830	
NUTTLE, Annie C.	Edmund Hill	8 Jan 1875	
OBER, Florence M.	Adolph W. Miller	16 Jul 1886	w
Lucretia T.	Henry Griffith	6 Sep 1824	
Martha J.	Elisha R. Griffith	29 Apr 1829	
Matilda	Henry Griffith, Jr.	16 Nov 1829	
William B.	Rebecca Mills	14 Apr 1808	
OBERMANN, Henrietta D. E.	Frank Schmid	9 Apr 1891	w
O'BRIAN, Tabathy	Amos Beall	14 Dec 1802	
O'BRIEN, Joanna E.	Patrick Ward	2 Oct 1871	
Mary L.	Robert F. Leizear	8 Nov 1893	w
Matthew	Eliza Sterne	15 Jul 1879	
O'CONNER, Patrick	Mary Ann Needham	31 Jan 1816	
William O'Neale	Mary Thompson	5 Feb 1819	
O'CONNOR, Mary T.	Owen J. Fitzpatrick	29 Sep 1897	w
ODELL, Lewis W.	Elizabeth Ann Leishiear	30 Apr 1846	
ODEN - also see OWDEN			
ODEN, Alfred	Alinda Gray	5 Apr 1822	
Alfred	Rachel Sedwick	23 Apr 1835	
Alfred J.	Eleanor S. Wyvell	13 Apr 1850	
Alfred N.	Elizabeth M. Richardson	13 Sep 1855	
Allen H.	Nettie E. Lowe	11 Oct 1892	w
Almira	Martin A. Stang	18 Jun 1872	
Archibald	Mary Lyles	16 Dec 1830	
Benjamin	Catharine Kinder	30 Dec 1812	
Elizabeth	Henry Arnold	11 Nov 1826	
Ellen	Samuel Mills	1 Mar 1874	
Florence	Charles C. Page	3 Dec 1885	w
Franklin A.	Verlinder Moulden	17 Jul 1850	
George W.	Elizabeth H. Arnold	3 Jan 1852	
Ida	Lewis E. Bolton	19 May 1877	w
John	Mary Ann Mills	8 Jun 1840	
John Thomas	Mary Jane Carter	2 Jul 1883	
John W.	Martha C. Peters	3 Dec 1866	
Kesiah F.	Thomas H. Butcher	13 Dec 1859	
Lillie H.	Charles R. Mobley	19 Jun 1883	
Lydia	William Pelly	26 Nov 1800	
Lydia	William H. Mourrer	1 Mar 1858	
Mary	John Flaherty	29 May 1816	
Mary Anne	Laurence Lyddan	18 May 1816	
Mary E.	James Henry Bolton	11 Jul 1872	
Nathaniel S.	Huldy Hutchison	10 Aug 1819	
Priscilla	John Campbell	24 Dec 1798	
Richard B.	Susanna Oden	25 Nov 1864	
Richard H.	Susan E. Cooley	7 Aug 1878	
Sarah*	Laurence O. Holt	12 Jan 1802	
Susanna	Richard B. Oden	25 Nov 1864	
Tabitha	John Nicholson	11 Apr 1799	
Thomas	Caroline Carter	8 Mar 1881	w
William	Kesiah V. Becraft	21 Sep 1881	
Zachariah	Elizabeth Nicholson	21 Dec 1844	

* Written O.Den in record

ODEN, Zacharias	Tabitha Reed	28 Apr 1824	
ODLE, Cassandra	John Austin	13 Feb 1799	
Jane	Archibald Offutt	1 Jan 1803	
Sally	David Claggett	16 Feb 1801	
ODONNELL, Agnes	Rezin Thomas Sullivan	19 Aug 1868	
O'DONNELL, James	Mary E. Ray	25 Sep 1862	
Patrick	Lucy A. Linsey	16 Oct 1872	
O'DOUD, Minnie	Magruder Hough	27 Jul 1883	
OFFER, Charles	Harriet Harrison	26 Oct 1866	
OFFUT, William	Sally Johnson	27 Mar 1871	
OFFUTT - also see OFFUT			
OFFUTT, Aaron	Anne Robertson	24 Dec 1812	
Alexander	Anne Lowe	20 Feb 1798	
Alice M.	George W. Diederick	1 Jan 1878	w
Amelia	William Warren	10 Jun 1878	c
Amy C.	Thomas Fisher	28 Mar 1815	
Andrew	Elizabeth Warfield	19 Apr 1802	
Anne M.	William H. Martin	26 Dec 1881	c
Annie	Isaiah Johnson	10 Dec 1896	c
Archibald	Jane Odle	1 Jan 1803	
Asbury	Ann Saunders	19 Apr 1871	
Barruch	Verlinda Offutt	25 Feb 1799	
Basil	Eleanor H. Clagett	13 Nov 1805	
Bettie E.	Nathaniel Clagett	17 Feb 1862	
Cassandra	Washington Offutt	4 Mar 1801	
Catharine	Robert Magruder	1 Mar 1809	
Catharine	Cephas F. Willett	4 Jan 1847	
Catharine	William E. Hamilton	11 Apr 1893	w
Charlotte Ann	John Offutt	18 Dec 1841	
Christiana C.	John Jones of Nathan	4 Nov 1817	
Clara C.	William Theodore Stauffer	12 May 1873	
Clarisa	Warren Offutt	13 Aug 1810	
Clarissa Ann	David H. Trundle	2 Jun 1835	
Colmore	Mary Ann Offutt	14 Jan 1809	
Colmore	Elizabeth Ann Poole	8 Feb 1847	
Elizabeth	Thomas W. Offutt	12 Mar 1811	
Elizabeth Ann	Richard A. Jones	11 Apr 1844	
Elizabeth Ann	Raphael T. Jarboe	30 Apr 1869	
Elizabeth L.	William George English	10 Apr 1867	
Emily A.	John W. Creamer	25 Oct 1880	
Essay	Thomas Gatton	24 Jan 1803	
Evelina	Horatio Beall	2 Jun 1825	
Frank	Matilda J. Brown	12 Nov 1868	
George	Mary Lincoln	21 Feb 1889	c
George McC.	Amy F. Bruner	28 Dec 1896	w
George W.	Sarah Scott	25 Jul 1821	
Harriet	John Offutt	1 Jun 1825	
Harriott	William Offutt	16 Feb 1802	
Henry	Annie Joppie	25 Nov 1868	
Henry	Henny Thomas	11 Jun 1879	
Henry W.	Lucy L. Saunders	7 Jan 1889	w
Hilleary L.	Anna M. Fisher	26 Oct 1855	
Hilleary L.	Kate N. Peter	15 Nov 1887	w
James	Roanna Eleanor Candler	18 Jan 1826	
James	Mary Ann White	20 Mar 1849	

OFFUTT,	Jane	Absalom Thrift	21 Dec 1803	
	John	Harriet Offutt	1 Jun 1825	
	John	Charlotte Ann Offutt	18 Dec 1841	
	Josaphine	David Noland	14 Jan 1865	
	Joseph C.	Eletha Clagett	27 Nov 1834	
	Joseph W. C.	Sarah R. Veirs	22 Mar 1880	w
	Josephine	Thomas Garrison	2 Apr 1896	c
	Joshua W.	Rachel J. Offutt	27 Jan 1846	
	Julia A.	William G. Counselman	15 Feb 1864	
	Laura V.	Samuel T. Gray	24 Apr 1878	w
	Lavinia E.	Richard S. Creamer	5 Feb 1884	
	Lee	Mary E. Clements	20 Nov 1888	w
	Lois Eunice	John L. Collins	7 Apr 1868	
	Lucretia	Mordica Offutt	15 Feb 1836	
	Lucy Burgess	Leonard Knott	31 Jan 1804	
	Lydia C.	Elbert Heeter	4 Apr 1832	
	Maggie	William Johnson	29 Dec 1875	
	Maggie	Ambrose Proctor	27 Dec 1888	c
	Marion E.	Harry C. Fawcett	13 Nov 1862	
	Martha J.	George W. Hall	25 Feb 1897	c
	Martha V.	Thomas L. Magruder	25 Sep 1884	w
	Mary	James Clingan	6 Mar 1810	
	Mary	Lewis Gassaway	4 Nov 1875	c
	Mary	Thomas Neel	* Feb 1884	c
	Mary A.	William E. Perry	5 Dec 1872	
	Mary Ann	Colmore Offutt	14 Jan 1809	
	Mary Louisa	Robert Hamilton Campbell	27 Aug 1892	w
	Mary O.	William T. Campbell	15 Jul 1891	c
	Matilda	Charles O. Jones	26 Feb 1812	
	Matilda	John L. Butt	19 Jun 1856	
	Milly	John Hurley	31 Dec 1807	
	Mollie	Thomas Fyffe	30 Dec 1867	
	Mordica	Lucretia Offutt	15 Feb 1836	
	Nancy	William West	6 Feb 1799	
	Nannie L.	J. Hite Miller	14 Aug 1883	
	Nicholas D.	Rachel H. Offutt	22 Jan 1856	
	Nicholas D.	Mary Louisa Anderson	24 Sep 1867	
	Nicholas D. Jr.	Elizabeth Hulingues	26 Oct 1881	
	Polly	Thomas B. Scott	16 Nov 1815	
	Priscilla	Thomas H. L. Offutt	3 Mar 1800	
	Rachel H.	Nicholas D. Offutt	22 Jan 1856	
	Rachel J.	Joshua W. Offutt	27 Jan 1846	
	Rachell	Thomas Clagett	12 Jan 1802	
	Rebecca	Charles Offutt Jones	22 Jan 1799	
	Rebecca	Perry Wade	21 Nov 1820	
	Rezin	Jane Dunley	27 Nov 1875	
	Rezin B.	Catharine Not	8 Feb 1801	
	Richard	Mary E. Selby	2 Apr 1883	w
	Rose B.	Guy B. Bradley	14 Dec 1896	w
	Sarah	John Cartenhour	27 Dec 1806	
	Sarah	John Hurley, Jr.	16 Mar 1814	
	Sarah	Samuel West	10 Mar 1825	
	Sarah A.	Nathan S. White, Jr.	15 Dec 1874	

* Cannot read day; 2 or 3

OFFUTT, Sarah W.	Gerard Van Buren	20 Sep 1813	
Thomas B.	Selah Fisher	23 Mar 1808	
Thomas B.	Mary Ann Harris	10 Feb 1831	
Thomas H.	Melinda Harriss	3 Mar 1831	
Thomas H.	Mary Conroy	1 Feb 1880	
Thomas H. L.	Priscilla Offutt	3 Mar 1800	
Thomas L.	Sarah B. Eversfield	25 Feb 1813	
Thomas L.	Rachel A. Selby	11 May 1852	
Thomas Levin	Susan Ann Hill	14 Mar 1842	
Thomas Levin	Ann Maria Granger	18 Apr 1870	
Thomas M.	Mary A. C. Fisher	3 Jan 1839	
Thomas M.	Loshonius E. Fisher	24 Jan 1848	
Thomas Odle	Charity Benton	16 Jul 1800	
Thomas W.	Elizabeth Offutt	12 Mar 1811	
Thomas W.	Mary Jane Hill	24 Dec 1846	
Thomas W.	Rachel E. Ricketts	31 Mar 1868	
Verlinda	Burruch Offutt	25 Feb 1799	
Virlinder	Charles Beatty	13 Apr 1799	
Warren	Clarisa Offutt	13 Aug 1810	
Washington	Cassandra Offutt	4 Mar 1801	
William	Harriott Offutt	16 Feb 1802	
William	Flora Somerville	9 Jun 1896	c
William A.	Mollie Kidwell	11 Jan 1888	w
William Edward	Amanda Wood	7 Oct 1880	c
William G.	Bettie Williams	24 Jul 1879	
William H.	Catharine L. Scott	22 Jan 1824	
William S. Jr.	Ary James Hawkins	14 Feb 1856	
Winfield	Mary E. Stern	22 Aug 1877	
Zadok of William	Elizabeth L. Scott	2 Jan 1816	
OGDEN, Elizabeth	Thomas Moland	26 Feb 1805	
William	Virginia Robertson	14 Feb 1889	w
OGLE, E. Leonard	Sarah E. Larman	19 Jan 1886	w
Lena M.	Harry F. Kidwell	3 Dec 1894	w
O'GRADY, Patrick G.*	Rebecca A. Warren	28 Apr 1880	w
Rebecca A.	William A. Roberts	25 Sep 1894	w
O'HARE, Christopher S.	Anne E. Shreve	15 Nov 1841	
O'KEEFE, William	Edna E. Harding	28 Sep 1897	w
OKSTADT, George L.	Mary P. Hahn	9 Mar 1895	w
OLDFIELD, Ruth Ann	William H. Bell	28 Dec 1869	
William A.	Lillie M. Curtis	** Mar 1890	w
OLDS, Edson B.	Mabel Bradford	1 Oct 1895	w
OLIPHANT, Hughes	Henrietta M. D. Hunt	22 Oct 1888	w
OLIVE, James K.	Eletha Hickman	7 Oct 1823	
Virginia A. F.	Thomas W. Winchester	2 May 1846	
OLIVER, Attelia ?.	William McIntire	12 Feb 1879	w
Jacob B.	Maria G. Howard	16 Jun 1885	c
Samuel	Ara E. Clagett	25 Nov 1851	
Thomas W.	Eva B. Thomas	14 May 1889	w
OLLIVER, William	Rebecca Wilburn	6 Jul 1799	
William	Patsy Luisy	17 May 1819	
OLSEN, Charles O.	Laura T. Hagen	19 Sep 1891	w
Oscar T.	Maggie C. Horan	9 Oct 1891	w

* This may be Patrick G. O. Grady
** Cannot read day; either 1 or 2

O'NEAL - also see O'NEALE			
O'NEAL, Clara E.	Daniel Collins	6 Nov 1883	
Horatio G.	Annie B. Cassidy	2 Jun 1894	w
ONEAL, Mary	Henry Jones	27 Jan 1820	
O'NEALE - also see O'NEAL, ONEAL, ONEALE, O'NEILL			
O'NEALE, Ann	Enoch Joy	15 Jan 1807	
Anne	Samuel Spates	31 Jul 1817	
David	Rebecca Lane	15 Oct 1798	
Elizabeth	William O. West	8 Mar 1821	
Hester E.	Horatio C. Allison	22 Oct 1890	w
Isaac	Mary Wise	16 Dec 1853	
Laurence	Nancy Galworth	27 Aug 1806	
William	Anne Ball	6 May 1804	
ONEALE, Betsey	John Smith	22 Apr 1823	
Eleanor E.	James M. Cutts	16 Dec 1833	
Eliza J.	Edward J. Denison	28 Oct 1842	
Elizabeth	Edward Digges	27 Apr 1809	
Emeline	John Ricketts	18 Jan 1838	
Joana*	Allen B. Peddicord	16 Apr 1820	
Leanna	Robert Morris	26 Dec 1842	
Sarah	Samuel Thomas Nicholls	24 Feb 1825	
Sarah Ann	Dennis Moulden	8 Mar 1826	
Susanna H.	James Peter	8 Jan 1830	
William Jr.	Julia Ann Farre	10 Jan 1826	
William Jr.	A. M. Manakee	17 Sep 1855	
O'NEILL - also see O'NEALE			
O'NEILL, Bernard	Barbara Neale	25 May 1809	
ONEILL, Nelly	George Richards	30 Nov 1823	
ONLEY, Henry T.	Mary V. Fisher	21 Dec 1891	c
Idella G.	Eugene Hackett	8 Sep 1892	c
John T.	Mary F. Hackett	22 Dec 1896	c
Mary Jane	Charles H. Brown	23 Dec 1869	
William E.	Maud A. Busey	6 Apr 1896	c
ONLY, James	Sarah C. Harper	20 May 1885	c
Mary V.	John H. Owens	16 Apr 1889	c
ORAM - also see ORME			
ORAM, Edward W.	Altonia Davis	30 Sep 1886	c
Mimie	William H. Smith	29 Dec 1896	c
Nathan	Betsy Clarke	24 May 1800	
ORANGE, Agnes	Charles Herbert	2 Jun 1870	
OREM - also see ORME			
OREM, William L.	Harriet May Simpson	6 Mar 1891	w
ORENDORFF - also see ORNDORFF			
ORENFORFF, Kate R.	Brice W. Howard	20 Jun 1864	
Sarah E.	Lemuel P. Townsend	10 Feb 1859	
O'RILEY, Henry	Elizabeth Se-----**	6 Jun 1798	
ORME - also see ORAM, OREM			
ORME, Allen S.	Mary E. Miles	23 Dec 1893	w
Ann	Josiah W. Redman	5 Jul 1809	
Anne	Charles T. E. Penn	18 Nov 1829	
Charles H.	Debora H. Pleasants	7 Feb 1841	
Deborah	Brooke Edmonston	7 Mar 1799	

* Name very light; could be Jennie
** Cannot read remainder of last name; earlier readings have Sewart and Sewal

ORME, Eleanor	John Peter	19 Feb 1798	
Elizabeth	Elijah Edmonston	30 Mar 1807	
Elizabeth	Greenbury Penn	15 Jan 1827	
Elizabeth	Jacob Barry	2 Apr 1828	
Elizabeth A.	John S. Mannakee	3 May 1823	
Harriet Ann	Benjamin J. Perry	9 Apr 1829	
James	Mary E. P. Belt	16 Jan 1854	
John	Elizabeth Guines	26 Dec 1798	
Mary	Hosea Edmonston	4 Jun 1808	
Nancy	Basil Belt	28 Jan 1808	
Nathan	Polly Beall	21 Jan 1800	
Oliva C.	Thomas L. F. Higgins	2 Mar 1823	
Patrick	Mary Sewall	19 Dec 1801	
Priscilla	William Ford	21 Mar 1801	
Priscilla	Horace Johnson	15 Nov 1826	
Rebecca	Solomon Sibley	25 Apr 1831	
Richard J.	Ann Crabb	18 Nov 1800	
Sarah	Charles Beall	2 Feb 1816	
Walter A.	Emma C. Griffith	27 Jul 1858	
ORMSTEAD - also see ARMSTEAD			
ORMSTEAD, Addison	Annie Adams	17 Aug 1887	c
ORNDORFF - also see ORENDORFF			
ORNDORFF, William O.	Mary J. Dove	9 Nov 1874	
ORR, William	Elizabeth Macklevain	17 Dec 1801	
OSBORN - also see OZBURN			
OSBORN, Margaret	Sabret Cecil	20 Dec 1828	
Mary	Thomas Duley	15 Nov 1823	
Mary E.	Thomas E. Higgins	24 Jan 1891	w
OSBORNE, Henry T.	Annie L. Shoemaker	29 Nov 1897	w
O'SHEA, Mary E.	Edward Patrick Gibbons	* Apr 1884	
OSMOND, Evadna A.	James S. Cahill	11 Mar 1895	w
Frances E.	Henry Gerhardt	23 Dec 1896	w
Julian E.	Clara E. Dwyer	25 Jan 1890	w
Leila R.	Richard H. Florance	24 Sep 1894	w
Vina D.	David G. Cleland	8 Nov 1897	w
OSMONDE, Julian	Alcester Ann Fisher	23 Dec 1863	
OULD, Robert	Paulina Gaither	24 Dec 1814	
OVERS, Mary	Mortimer Ambush	16 Feb 1897	c
OWDEN - also see ODEN			
OWDEN, Richard H.	Mary E. Case	18 Jun 1887	w
OWEN, Anne	James Smith	5 Jun 1810	
Catherine G.	Thomas J. Beall	4 Jan 1858	
Charles W.	Elizabeth H. Jones	27 Oct 1896	w
Edward W.	Elizabeth Ann Clagett	25 Oct 1830	
Elizabeth	Cornelius Sullivan	16 Jan 1805	
J. W.	Clara M. Howard	12 Apr 1880	
Mary	Aquila Gatton	20 Dec 1804	
Mary	John A. Brightwell	12 Nov 1834	
Octava (female)	Ely Beall	5 Jun 1802	
Octavia B.	William H. Childs	5 Oct 1874	
Thomas	Matilda Chase Goldsborough	30 Oct 1832	
Thomas J.	Vandalia Magruder	17 Nov 1869	
Washington	Ruthy Berry	7 Jan 1806	

* No day given; between 15 and 19

OWEN, Washington W.	Angelina G. Robinson	9 Nov 1836	
William	Anne Leeke	12 Jan 1801	
William Brook	Margaret Pope	22 Mar 1806	
OWENS - also see OWINGS			
OWENS, Ceney	Hale Wyvell	18 Jul 1809	
D. F. (Dr.)	Elizabeth M. Wells	14 May 1879	w
Dennis	Mary E. Dorsey	8 Jul 1890	c
Emma E.	Joseph F. Rhine	27 Nov 1872	
Hezekiah	Susan Lovjoy	17 Feb 1818	
John C.	Juliann P. Lodge	10 Dec 1822	
John C.	Ida C. Beall	8 Jan 1895	c
John H.	Mary V. Only	16 Apr 1889	c
Joseph	Rachel Boyd	12 Feb 1805	
Laura V.	Charles W. Johnson	16 Jun 1886	c
Louisa E.	Jesse Diggins	6 Apr 1892	c
Margaret	Gustavus W. Dorsey	26 Nov 1866	
Martha	John G. Duffin	9 Apr 1883	c
Martha	James H. Lee	19 Oct 1886	c
Martha J.	Charles H. Coburn	28 Apr 1869	
Mary	Horace King	4 Sep 1878	
Mary A.	James Rounds	30 Aug 1874	
Mary E.	Jonathan D. Barnsley	16 May 1864	
Nancy	William Cissell	21 Dec 1802	
Rebeccah	William Stewart	4 Dec 1809	
Rhoda Ann	Jonathan Stewart	2 Feb 1844	
Rosannah	Samuel White	9 Jul 1818	
Sarah Ellen	George W. Rhine	28 Jun 1875	
Sarah T.	William T. Duffin	11 Feb 1878	c
Solomon	Sallie Davis	29 Jun 1897	c
Thomas	Ann Lovejoy	16 Feb 1815	
Thomas	Rachel A. Adams	27 Jul 1874	
Walter	Rosa Jackson	28 Dec 1886	c
William	Massa McAtee	22 Jan 1807	
William T.	Nani F. Green	13 Dec 1894	w
Wilson	Blanche Clagett	16 Jul 1894	c
OWINGS - also see OWENS			
OWINGS, Christopher	Rebecca M. Turnbull	11 Feb 1823	
D. C., Dr.	Florence O. Linthicum	21 Nov 1877	w
Lewis	Elizabeth Duvall	1 Jan 1817	
Luther	Maranda Nelson	17 Apr 1815	
Samuel C.	Mary Y. Willis	27 Oct 1814	
Samuel D.	Annie L. Holland	30 Nov 1896	w
OWONE, Alcinda	William Hamman	30 Nov 1882	c
OXLEY, Emma D.	Richard C. Mercier	27 Sep 1892	w
OZBURN - also see OSBORN			
OZBURN, Leonard Pile	Sarah Thrasher	5 Aug 1799	
PACE, William Hamilton	Arietta J. Childs	13 Oct 1877	w
PACKSON - also see PAXTON			
PACKSON, Frances	Louis Garnett	31 Jan 1872	
PADGETT, Anna C.	John W. Collier	18 Jan 1878	w
Annie	John S. Lizear	28 May 1878	w
Arthur J.	Fannie M. Stephens	20 Dec 1881	
Bettie M.	John H. Allnutt	21 Aug 1895	w
Eliza B.	Benjamin Sparrow	22 Feb 1842	
Isabel	Robert Stephens	31 Jan 1882	

PADGETT,	James	Rachel A. Whalen	18 May 1854	
	John	Sally Lansdale	2 Dec 1823	
	John	Ann V. Reintzell	31 Dec 1879	w
	Julia Ann	William Duley	8 Jul 1849	
	Mary	Shadrack B. Case	13 Nov 1855	
	Mary E.	Henry C. Ashley	29 May 1878	w
	Moses	Offy Acton	23 Dec 1817	
	Thomas E.	Clara J. Ford	2 Dec 1873	
	Trecey Ann	George Carey	10 Apr 1830	
PAGE,	Adele E.	Franklin C. Betts	17 Dec 1890	w
	Alice M.	Charles E. Thompson	28 Jan 1896	w
	Charles C.	Florence Oden	3 Dec 1885	w
	George W.	Rebecca Williams	17 Dec 1840	
	James	Malvinia Mobbley	17 Jan 1846	
	Lillie	William E. Perrell	29 Feb 1892	w
	Linna	Jacob P. Howard	20 May 1840	
	Nathan N.	Mary Higdon	2 Oct 1865	
	Thomas	Elizabeth Willson	18 Jan 1811	
	Thomas	Isabella Purdy	24 Nov 1855	
	William H. B.	Louisa W. Smith	26 Sep 1871	
PAIN - also see PAYNE				
PAIN,	Catherine	Jesse Herbert	7 Feb 1803	
	Margaret	Archibald Summers	30 Mar 1803	
PAINTER,	Edward	Hannah Louisa Gilpin	30 Aug 1834	
PAIRO,	William E.	Emma M. Korn	14 Jul 1891	w
PALMER - also see PALMORE, PARMER				
PALMER,	Abraham	Julietta McFarland	8 Mar 1832	
	Agnes	Morton M. Newman	16 Dec 1885	c
	Charles Hampton	Anna Mary Hammontree	8 Feb 1842	
	Eliza	John T. Towers	27 Oct 1854	
	Elizabeth Ann	Richard H. Presgraves	2 Jan 1838	
	Florence	Wesley Brooks	28 Jul 1897	c
	Jonathan H.	Martha E. Fisher	24 Feb 1855	
	Mary	William Riley	23 Jun 1809	
	William P.	Cleora Duvall	14 May 1831	
PALMORE - also see PALMER				
PALMORE,	Eleanor	Nehemiah Beall	2 Mar 1810	
	Martha	Frederick Adamson	28 Feb 1809	
PANGLE,	Annie E.	Melvin N. Steele	18 May 1894	w
PARDEW,	Jeremiah R.	Maria E. Waters	23 May 1892	w
PARKER,	Anna	Robert Dodson	21 Sep 1881	c
	Annie	John Thorn	5 Nov 1887	c
	Betsey	John Fox	8 Sep 1821	
	Charles H.	Mary L. Sewall	22 Nov 1879	c
	Emma	Robert E. Talley	20 May 1893	c
	George	Mary Ratrie	29 Nov 1826	
	Henrietta	Camden Duffin	7 Nov 1894	c
	Henry	Mary Lusby	10 Sep 1885	c
	J. Thomas	Laura Clarke	18 Jun 1867	
	James A.	Ann Maria Trucks	11 Jan 1868	
	John C.	Anna E. Curtis	17 Nov 1855	
	Jonathan	Anne Davis	14 Oct 1800	
	Lewis B.	Elizabeth A. Shoemaker	26 Nov 1855	
	Lonie	Frank Stewart	15 Jun 1898	c
	Miller	Elizabeth E. Miles	16 Oct 1897	w
	Nancy	Erasmus Murphey	28 Jan 1805	

PARKER, Thomas *.	Julia Buxton	23 Dec 1824
William J.	Anna M. Bentley	11 Nov 1872
PARKINS, Elizabeth	William T. Gingle	16 Jan 1865
PARKINSON, Mary Maud	C. P. Jones	30 Sep 1871
PARMER - also see PALMER		
PARMER, Mary	John Boyd	10 Mar 1798
PARRIE - also see PEARRE, PERRY		
PARRIE, Carrie V.	Fletcher R. Veitch	29 Nov 1864
PARSLEY, Bertha M.	Frederick E. Jackson	9 Feb 1898 w
Edgar M.	Annie E. Wilson	29 Sep 1898 w
Elizabeth	William Baker	25 Apr 1800
Elizabeth A.	Peter Colletan	26 Dec 1859
Enoch A.	Sarah J. Hodson	27 Nov 1882 w
George	Susan Lewis	22 Jan 1845
George W. Jr.	Annie Kate Jones	19 Sep 1887 w
James	Margarett Anderson	28 Sep 1808
James L.	Elizabeth A. Ridgley	1 Jul 1835
James R.	Estelle Ray	22 Sep 1898 w
James W.	Sarah U. Boswell	5 Dec 1882 w
John H.	Cordelia A. Search	3 Feb 1885 w
John W.	Rebecca Gingell	8 Jun 1872
Jonas	Eleanor Clayton	30 Nov 1799
M. Ellen	W. H. Jones	22 Jan 1872
Maggie E.	William H. Jackson	16 May 1892 w
Mary E.	John W. Metz	4 Oct 1869
Richard	Martha V. Baker	25 Apr 1844
Richard	Elizabeth Easton	12 Feb 1862
Richard H.	Sarah C. Sheaffer	25 Dec 1866
Thomas	Mahala Ann Walker	6 Dec 1832
Thomas	Priscilla Grimes	23 Oct 1857
Thomas	Mary Ward	24 Feb 1877 w
William Henry	Margaret Ann Ray	19 Dec 1833
PARSLY, William O.	Christina Mullican	26 Jan 1885 w
PASCO, Amanda R.	Joseph W. Kerns	13 Jul 1898 w
PATRICK, Elizabeth	Elisha Chambers	23 Jan 1811
PATTERSON, George	Eliza A. Martin	29 Nov 1866
George C.	Prudence A. Bean	18 Jul 1848
Lancelot H.	Mary F. Daly	30 Nov 1882 w
Margarett St. Claire	Abraham Barnes	28 Nov 1831
PAUL, Henry	Eleanor Adams	28 Jan 1801
Henry	Elizabeth Fox	29 Aug 1829
PAXTON - also see PACKSON		
PAXTON, Arabella	Charles W. Harding	14 Nov 1879
Elizabeth	James Fowler	21 Dec 1835
PAXTON, Louis M.	Ellen D. Carroll	3 Jul 1883 w
Samuel G.	Amanda A. Lyon	12 Nov 1860
Sarah R.	James B. Williams	9 Feb 1870
William E.	Annie C. Bean	30 Apr 1872
PAY, Rachel	Samuel Weemes	26 Feb 1867
PAYNE - also see PAIN		
PAYNE, Henry	Julia Harper	22 Dec 1892 c
James	Eliza Moulden	2 Nov 1829
Lillie	William Thrift	28 Sep 1896 w

* Initial I or J

PAYNE, Lillie M.	Douglas J. Guillot	8 Apr 1897	w
Thomas H.	Minerva Ann Shryock	10 Oct 1836	
PAYTON - also see PEYTON			
PAYTON, Ann S.	Jonathan Buckman	21 Feb 1833	
PEACK, Harriet E.	William H. Snider	20 Feb 1852	
PEACOCK, Heator B.	Elizabeth Coe	26 Nov 1844	
Mary F.	Albert F. Mor---*	* Oct 1867	
Mary J.	William C. Damron	21 Nov 1889	w
Nancy E.	Thomas W. Muse	25 Jul 1851	
PEAKE, Ellen	Jesse Young	3 Jun 1879	c
PEARCE - also see PEIRCE			
PEARCE, Elizabeth	Hilleary T. Jarvis	9 Jan 1833	
Henry	Eliza Shaw	26 Jun 1851	
James	Prissilla Mariah Perry	4 Jun 1818	
James F.	Mary E. Jackson	24 Oct 1871	
Martha	Andrew Michaels	12 May 1843	
Powel C.	Elizabeth Tucker	15 Oct 1851	
Verlinda	Alosius Newton	3 Feb 1822	
William C.	Louisa Valdaner	19 Apr 1829	
PEAREN, Laurence	Susanah Nicholls	4 Oct 1814	
PEARRE - also see PERRY, PARRIE			
PEARRE. Ann S.	Charles G. Linthicum	10 Jun 1850	
George C.	Sallie M. Thompson	25 Aug 1887	w
Holland	Ella V. Molesworth	2 Jul 1888	w
Mary T.	Thomas L. Hays	12 May 1846	
PEARSON, Priscilla	John Dyson	24 Feb 1832	
PECK, James	Elizabeth Yardley	8 Jun 1802	
Mildred A.	Wallace Murdock	23 Aug 1896	w
Nathan T.	Mary Dowden	3 Jan 1802	
Ophelia	Edward L. Dawkins	2 Jul 1894	c
PEDDICOART, Allen	Catherine Jones	18 Dec 1810	
Cynthia	Nacy Thompson	22 Dec 1812	
Sary	Levi Chambers	15 Nov 1802	
PEDDICORD, Allen B.	Joana Oneale**	16 Apr 1820	
Amanda M. M.	Francis L. Beall	13 Sep 1850	
Elizabeth Susan, Mrs.	William Thomas Gloyd	9 Dec 1869	
Florence	Herbert T. Weeks	21 Apr 1896	w
Jeremiah E.	Emma J. Veirs	20 Jan 1870	
Mary J. R.	Napoleon B. Pryor	12 Feb 1851	
Sarah C.	John Wesley Ward	17 May 1866	
Thomas E.	Elizabeth S. Clagett	2 Feb 1861	
Thomas E.	Mary E. Briggs	20 May 1889	w
Thomas J.	Ara R. Clagett	27 Oct 1860	
PEDDICORT, Rebecca	Richard Thompson	21 Dec 1810	
PEERCE - also see PEIRCE, PEARCE			
PEERCE, Ann Eliza	John W. Gibson	22 Dec 1880	w
Rachel	Alfred Frazier	8 Jan 1818	
PEIRCE - also see PEARCE			
PEIRCE, Fanny	William A. Iddings	14 Aug 1894	w
Henry L.	Susie E. Miles	13 Feb 1894	w
Joana	John Garrett	27 Aug 1804	
Sarah E.	Clark H. Gray	18 Sep 1894	w

* Remainder of last name has blot on it; day 11 or 12
** Name very light; could be Jennie

PELLY, Sollomon	Massy Holland	7 Aug 1799	
William	Lydia Oden	26 Nov 1800	
PELTON, Elizabeth	Samuel Scott	6 Oct 1888	c
PENDLETON, Selina D.	John C. Wilson	11 Aug 1863	
PENN, Alice E.	James E. Duvall	27 Jan 1862	
Ann	Caleb R. Penn	11 Oct 1817	
Augusta	Joseph Duvall	21 Dec 1881	
Betsey	Basil Davis	2 Feb 1805	
Caleb R.	Ann Penn	11 Oct 1817	
Caleb R.	Elizabeth D. Purdom	11 Dec 1839	
Charles T. E.	Anne Orme	18 Nov 1829	
Edward J.	Georgiana Harding	11 Jan 1870	
Elberta	Oliver N. Briggs	20 Nov 1894	w
Elizabeth	James Archbold	18 Apr 1817	
Elizabeth	Nathan Edmonstone	10 Feb 1823	
Elizabeth	Asa Crawford	25 Mar 1829	
Elizabeth	Eleazar O. Earnest	10 Mar 1862	
Erastus V.	Mary P. Young	27 Dec 1854	
George W.	Margaret Duvall	25 Mar 1841	
Grace	William A. Bogley	9 Oct 1895	w
Greenbury	Elizabeth Orme	15 Jan 1827	
Greenbury	Amanda Merrick	21 Apr 1834	
Higgerson B.	Josephine Warfield	* Jan 1880	w
Ignatius	Mary Gardner	9 May 1883	
Jerusha A.	John G. Duvall	15 Jun 1863	
John	Selah Ann Crawford	15 Jan 1822	
Keziah	Jonathan Baker	14 Dec 1858	
Levi	Rachel Gartrell	30 Mar 1839	
Mary	Rezin Duvall	27 Jul 1875	
Mary Ellen	James C. Brown	6 Jan 1827	
Mary V.	John O. Etchison	22 May 1878	w
Nackey	Benjamin King	1 Dec 1804	
Owen	Emeline Reid	16 Aug 1841	
Reuben	Anne Record	16 Jan 1833	
Rezin	Aletha Thompson	20 Oct 1820	
Roby	Lucrecia Howes	18 Dec 1798	
Sarah	Walter Darby	2 Mar 1814	
Susan A.	Emanuel Maddison Duvall	5 Mar 1839	
Stephen	Elender Scrivner	26 Oct 1798	
Thomas G.	Mary F. Duvall	13 Apr 1883	w
William	Sarah Pitts	17 Apr 1811	
William	Emma J. Sparrow	23 Jan 1867	
William	Emma Shaw	27 Dec 1886	w
PENNELL, Minerva E.	Anthony T. Crowley	14 Sep 1897	w
PENNEYFILLE - also see PENNYFIELD			
PENNEYFILLE, Catherine	Benjamin Hinton	16 Feb 1828	
PENNIFIELD - also see PENNYFIELD, PENNEYFILLE, PENNIFILL			
PENNIFIELD, Ara	Upton West	28 Dec 1837	
Charles	(Mary) Maggie (M.)	18 Nov 1884	
(H.) W.**	McCrossin		
Eleanor	William Henry Case	31 Dec 1839	
Elizabeth	William Priestly	21 Mar 1878	w
George W.	Mary Jane Fields	4 Nov 1851	

* Cannot read day; either 20 or 21
** Parts in () are in a different handwriting from rest of entry

PENNIFIELD, Isabella R.	William T. Redden	26 Oct 1876
Levi B.	Margaret Hill	18 Dec 1827
Lucinda	John Lewis	14 Feb 1824
Margaret A.	Daniel Harvill	16 Jul 1874
Patsy	Walter Case	9 Jan 1822
Sarah	Charles A. Harrington	13 Sep 1865
William	Rachel A. Hill	14 Oct 1857
PENNIFILL, Joseph C.	Jennie Burriss	2 Sep 1869
PENNYFIELD, Thomas	Maria Williams	23 Jun 1822
PERHAM, Sidney H.	Elizabeth B. Webster	28 May 1897 w
PERKINS, Con Marrast	Anna O. Knox	5 Oct 1883
Daniel M.	Lucretia Wheeler	28 Oct 1818
Emma E.	James T. Watlington	4 Jul 1894 w
Minnie	James T. Andrews	19 Apr 1888 w
Paul T.	Cora L. Mason	13 Jun 1894 w
Sylvia	John Atcherson	16 Jan 1800
PERNA, Frank	Mary A. Dean	18 Dec 1893 w
PERRELL, Hezekiah E.	Emma Mansfield	23 Oct 1889 w
Margaret E.	Edward D. Lewis	18 Nov 1887 w
William E.	Anna R. Hargett	26 Dec 1887 w
William E.	Lillie Page	29 Feb 1892 w
PERRIL, Agnes	William F. Rinehart	27 Jan 1892 w
PERRY - also see PEARRE, PARRIE		
PERRY, Allen	Elizabeth Idea	27 Feb 1802
Amanda	Peyton D. Vinson	15 Nov 1883 w
Basil M.	Delilah Elizabeth Waters	10 Feb 1801
Benjamin	Elizabeth Magruder	1 Feb 1804
Benjamin J.	Harriet Ann Orme	9 Apr 1829
Catherine	Charles A. Beall	9 May 1864
Christiann	Thomas Gittings	2 Apr 1806
Cora	John L. Ball	15 Nov 1898 w
Delila E.	John R. Bussard	15 Jan 1810
Edgar R.	Bertha L. Ball	27 Apr 1891 w
Edward	Rosa Johnson	18 Oct 1888 c
Elbert	Rebecca Magruder	3 Feb 1806
Elbert	Elizabeth R. Clagett	23 Feb 1848
Elbert	Lillie Clagett	17 Mar 1891 w
Eleanora C.	Charles Counselman	25 Apr 1846
Elias	Aquelina Waters	14 Dec 1803
Eliza Ann	Washington Duvall	11 Dec 1824
Elizabeth	Joshua Hickman	4 Feb 1817
Elleanora	John William Moore	13 Aug 1895 w
Erasmus	Lydia Elizabeth Fisher	27 Feb 1844
Gassaway	Sarah Beall	9 Jan 1817
Henry C. F.	Vandelia Heeter	3 Mar 1884
James Wilson	Margaret Jones	17 Jan 1799
John	Jane Alnutt	18 Dec 1799
John	Catharine V. Wailes	14 May 1833
John H.	Anna M. Senter	14 Dec 1859
John S.	Fanny M. Wallace	5 Oct 1809
Keziah	William Golding	12 Mar 1838
Laura	Authur *. Taylor	22 Mar 1898 w
Lucy	Hezekiah Dison	23 Feb 1799

* Initial N or W

PERRY,	Lucy	Jonathan Gaither	1 Nov 1873	
	Lydia	John Henderson	5 May 1800	
	Lydia E.	Charles H. Matthews	11 Sep 1888	w
	Margaret	Jacob L. Bohrer	6 Dec 1855	
	Margarett	Edward Harding	21 May 1814	
	Marion A.	Thomas Sullivan	8 May 1895	w
	Marshal B.	Sarah Ann Spates	23 Jan 1827	
	Mary	Hezekiah Gue	16 Nov 1829	
	Mary Ann	William Tomlinson	24 Mar 1840	
	Matilda	Eden Beall	19 Jan 1813	
	Matilda	John Counselman	5 Apr 1836	
	Ninian M.	Hannah A. Daily	12 Feb 1877	w
	Phebe R.	Jacob Wilbert	27 Dec 1882	
	Priscilla Mariah	James Pearce	4 Jun 1818	
	Racheal A.	Henry Polkinhorn	3 Jan 1859	
	Rachel	Becra Ashton	23 Nov 1798	
	Rebecca	Benjamin B. Dawes	18 Jun 1827	
	Richard H.	Margaret Waters	17 Oct 1870	
	Ruth	William Worthington	9 Mar 1798	
	Sallie E.	William Shoemaker	8 Oct 1889	w
	Samuel	Drady Warman	6 Mar 1806	
	Samuel	Catharine Cecil	21 Feb 1824	
	Sarah*	Isaac Williams	5 Aug 1819	
	William	Alvina Davis	18 Nov 1875	
	William E.	Mary A. Offutt	5 Dec 1872	
PETER - also see PETERS				
PETER,	Alexander	Jane A. Gassaway	4 Nov 1857	
	Barbara U.	George E. Burroughs	27 Dec 1888	w
	Charles	Maria Nailor	24 Jan 1872	
	David	Sarah Johns	16 Sep 1799	
	David F.	Lavinia R. Williams	24 Jun 1891	w
	Edward C.	Mary G. Vinson	26 Jun 1888	w
	Elizabeth	Thomas Peter	28 Nov 1856	
	Elizabeth J.	Charles H. Nourse	3 Mar 1849	
	George	Sarah N. Freeland	18 Jun 1825	
	George	Lavinia Gassaway	13 Oct 1852	
	George H.	Maggie Ann Watson	14 May 1866	
	Henry	Rachel Stewart	24 Jul 1886	c
	James	Susanna H. Oneale	8 Jan 1830	
	Jennie	James J. Beall	5 Oct 1885	w
	John	Eleanor Orme	19 Feb 1798	
	John P. C.	Elizabeth Jane Henderson	1 Feb 1830	
	Katharine G.	Hugh Nelson	5 Nov 1890	w
	Kate N.	Hilleary L. Offutt	15 Nov 1887	w
	Margaret	Thomas Dick	3 Dec 1798	
	Margaret D.	John W. Moseley	12 Feb 1861	
	Mary A.	Thomas Dawson	3 Jan 1889	w
	Mary E.	Walter M. Burroughs	29 Dec 1896	w
	Mollie	Dennis Jones	31 May 1879	c
	Robert B.	Helen O. Lowry	13 Oct 1896	w
	Sarah A.	Henry D. Nourse	23 Aug 1889	w
	Sarah F.	John E. Slaymaker	5 Jan 1893	w
	Sarah L.	William L. Dunlop	30 Nov 1878	w
	Susan H.	John A. B. Leonard	19 Dec 1839	

* Smeared; could be Berry

PETER, Thomas		Elizabeth Peter	28 Nov 1856
Thomas		Mary Fisher	5 Feb 1887 c
PETERS - also see PETER			
PETERS, Alice		Noah Curtise	29 Apr 1876
Anna		Jacob Bettis	15 Jul 1875
Catharine D.		David A. Wetzel	26 Jan 1898 w
Charles		Amey Cecill	8 Mar 1803
Ellen		John Mullen	30 May 1833
Florence		Major Graham	3 May 1883
Helen		Dennis Magruder	27 Dec 1881
Henry		Ann Gray	14 Oct 1867
James J.		Sallie Drudge	18 Oct 1882 w
James J.		Rosie E. Johnson	8 Dec 1885 w
John		Eleanor Bassford	2 Aug 1813
John		Cassandra Nicholson	15 Oct 1839
John		Susan Hood	26 Dec 1879 c
John R.		Treacy Thompson	11 Nov 1879 c
John W.		Rachel Gant	14 Feb 1882 c
Julianne		Joseph Hardesty	29 Oct 1870
Kitty		Isaac Graham	19 May 1877 c
Lucy J.		Zachariah Pumphrey	11 Apr 1892 w
Maria E.		Henry Jones	26 Dec 1877 c
Martha C.		John W. Oden	3 Dec 1866
Mary		Frederick Johnson	20 Jul 1895 c
Mary A.		Charles W. Thomson	23 Sep 1880 c
Olivia R.		Richard F. Nokes	18 May 1888 c
Phebe		Philip Henderson	18 Aug 1814
Ruthy		Richard Phelps	25 Mar 1809
Travilla E.		Flora Windsor	31 Dec 1883
Verlinda		William Andrews	25 Feb 1813
PETSCH, Phillipina		Druid H. Evans	30 Aug 1890 w
PETTY, Henrietta		Lewis Keiser	19 Nov 1885 w
James S.		Achsah D. Waters	23 Nov 1889 w
PEUGH - also see PUGH			
PEUGH, David L.		Ellen R. Ayton	10 Dec 1844
Mamie E.		Willie H. Burdette	20 Nov 1895 w
Michael L.		Henrietta D. Macgill	5 Nov 1849
Uriah H.		Mary Ellen Duvall	26 Jun 1849
Valeria D.		Edward McMahon	7 Sep 1871
PEYTON - also see PAYTON			
PEYTON, Charles H. M.		Delia E. Everhart	13 Oct 1885 w
PHAIR, Charles F.		Margaret Leizear	17 Jan 1884 w
William H.		Lizzie Soper	5 Feb 1892 w
PHALEN - also see PHEALEN, PHELAN			
PHALEN, Annie		Charles E. Felix	4 Sep 1893 w
PHEABUS - also see PHEBUS			
PHEABUS, James Rufus		Mary Prudence English	17 May 1869
PHEALEN - also see PHALEN			
PHEALEN, Hannah		William Webb	20 Apr 1826
PHEBUS - also see PHEABUS, PHOEBUS			
PHEBUS, George A.		Josephine Catharine Burriss	12 Jun 1876
John T.		Aggie C. English	20 May 1884 w
Joseph C.		Mary E. House	20 Oct 1881 w
Mamie M.		David F. Verts	15 Sep 1896 w
Maurice E.		Armenia English	1 Jun 1887 w

PHEBUS, Olie M.	Ferris Bowen (male)	28 Sep 1896	w
PHELAN - also see PHALEN			
PHELAN, Mary	John Robertson	18 Jun 1812	
PHELPS, Ann	John Mitchell	5 Apr 1836	
Charlotte	Benjamin Cissell	10 Feb 1836	
Comfort	Philip H. Duvall	30 Apr 1822	
Edward	Sarah Andrews	25 Apr 1807	
Edward	Elizabeth Lewis	9 Jan 1812	
Elijah	Elizabeth Staley	16 Feb 1828	
Isaiah	Elizabeth Andrews	10 May 1800	
James H.	Lydia Staley	4 Sep 1829	
Jutson W.	Mary E. Briscoe	21 Mar 1846	
Leatha Ann	Thomas Reed	13 Oct 1835	
Milton T.	Adella Soper	7 May 1887	w
Richard	Ruthy Peters	25 Mar 1809	
Sarah E.	William Kinney	18 May 1836	
Walter	Sarah Williams	21 Dec 1842	
PHENIX, Beverly	Mary Tabitha Snowden	10 Nov 1874	
Thomas	Rebecca M. Smith	9 Mar 1852	
PHILIPS, Elizabeth	Alexander Reid	23 Feb 1804	
Meriah	William Green	23 Apr 1812	
PHILLIPS, Clara	Thomas R. Hall	5 Jan 1860	
Howard	Ann Read	3 Feb 1815	
Israel K.	Martha E. Brown	18 Jul 1889	w
James E.	Susan White	24 Jun 1875	
James S.	Anna L. Chapline	27 Mar 1883	
Jane A.	John T. Hoyle	25 Apr 1857	
Jane D.	Clarence F. Lighter	13 Sep 1888	w
Letha A.	Hilleary T. Higgins	15 Jan 1858	
Mollie C.	Richard D. Clagett	4 Oct 1887	w
Nancy	Basil Cohoo	17 Dec 1798	
Sallie	Owen C. Brown	4 Jan 1888	w
Samuel	Mary Catharine Arnold	27 Feb 1860	
Sarah A.	George Z. Warner	6 Nov 1873	
Sarah R.	John A. Chiswell	21 Nov 1851	
Thomas L.	Harriet A. Appleby	19 Jan 1859	
William	Caroline Lodge	28 Jun 1825	
PHOEBUS - also see PHEBUS			
PHOEBUS, Anna M.	Edward B. Brown	15 Jan 1883	
PICKENS, Jacob	Mary P. Andrews	19 Apr 1865	
Jane R.	Nathan Kinna	1 Jan 1870	
Mary E.	John T. Nicholson	19 Dec 1856	
PICKINS, Jacob	Louisana Thompson	31 Mar 1836	
Judy Ann	Sylvester Thompson	27 Oct 1862	
PICKETT, Charles F.	Annie Duvall	11 Sep 1876	
PIERCE- also see PEARCE, PEIRCE			
PIERCE, Ann*	George Thompson	25 Mar 1895	c
Mary S.	William E. Carlin	7 May 1890	w
PIGMAN, Sarah	Walter Griffith	12 Apr 1803	
PILES - also see PYLES			
PILES, Benjamin F.	Sallie R. Dade	25 Jan 1873	
Catharine J.	Benjamin F. Dyson	8 Apr 1863	
Elizabeth	William Mullican	31 Dec 1803	
Francis	Ann Poole	10 Feb 1798	

* This could be Prince

PILES, Francis	Sarah Poole	15 Apr 1813	
Hilleary	Matilda Bruner	22 Dec 1827	
Huldah A.	Richard G. White	3 Jan 1853	
Jane	Samuel Hilton	22 Jun 1812	
John	Rebecca P. Jones	25 Oct 1824	
Joshua D.	Elizabeth ? King	20 Aug 1867	
Leonard	Mary Jones	11 Apr 1814	
Margaret	Emory M. Beall	9 Jan 1832	
Mary Louisa	Bushrod Washington Reed	21 Jan 1842	
Nancy	Edwin Clarke	20 Jan 1841	
Rebecca	Thomas Hall	24 May 1824	
Rebecca M.	Quinstus C. Hall	7 Dec 1859	
Richard	Eleanor Reed	19 Mar 1803	
Richard	Mary Ellen Hoskinson	30 Jun 1841	
William F.	Ruth Elizabeth Beall	11 Jun 1845	
William H.	Eliza Ann Dalzell	28 Sep 1846	
William W.	Emeline Price	8 Mar 1859	
PILLSBURY, Mary A.	William H. Benson	2 Sep 1897	w
PINDELL, Richard C.	Sarah F. Benson	11 Jan 1875	
PINKET, Florence	William Holly	18 Aug 1896	c
PINKETT, Benjamin F.	Mary F. C. Adams	25 Aug 1891	w
PIPKINS, Charles E.	Margaret Smith	4 Jun 1868	
PIQETT, Alfred C.	Lizzie T. Beall	22 Jan 1884	w
PITTS, Sarah	William Penn	17 Apr 1811	
PLANT, Frederick J.	Anna B. Furlong	29 Jul 1895	w
James	Ellen Daly	25 Jul 1885	w
PLATER, Jane	Elisha W. Williams	16 Jan 1826	
Jane	Frank Wallace	16 Sep 1897	c
Maria	John J. Stull	23 Oct 1827	
PLEASANT, Anna	John T. Stewart	13 May 1890	c
PLEASANTS, David Sands V.	Fannie B. Hungerford	15 Jul 1867	
Debora H.	Charles H. Orme	7 Feb 1841	
Hannah	Henry Howard	12 Sep 1814	
James Snowden	Jane Plater Williams	19 Nov 1858	
Sarah E.	Alban Brooke	2 Jan 1878	w
William H.	Mary C. Vinson	15 Sep 1847	
PLUMB, Charles F.	Flora W. Conover	* Aug 1898	w
PLUMER, Mary E.	James E. Hammond	27 Oct 1887	c
PLUMMER, Aletha	William Somerville	22 May 1888	c
Ann	George N. Reed	4 Jan 1854	
Annie E.	Orlando Nelson	27 May 1863	
Caroline	Edward Blake	12 Oct 1871	c
Elizabeth	Richard Thompson	23 Dec 1816	
Elizabeth A.	Gustavus Jones	27 May 1851	
Emily Catharine	Henson Weldon	15 Mar 1869	
Emy	Thomas N. Harwood	6 Feb 1839	
Eveanner	George E. Price	29 Jun 1866	
George W.	Harriet A. E. Frazier	28 Apr 1897	c
Hannah	James George Terry	7 Sep 1888	c
Hanson	Clara Burriss	9 Nov 1871	
Harriet Ann	Horace Thompson	16 Dec 1853	
Henry	Luginia Redman	29 Jun 1872	
Henson	Mary Hamilton	3 Nov 1877	c
Howard A.	Ida R. Crawford	15 Dec 1890	w

* Cannot read day; before 5

PLUMMER, Joseph	Verlinda ?. Veatch	21 Jan 1812	
Joseph H.	Mary J. Swailes	28 Dec 1885	c
Joshua Dorsey	Alice Victorine Ward	17 Nov 1886	w
Julia	Zachariah Loy	15 Oct 1873	
Laura	Clarence Davis	2 Jul 1889	c
Lucetta	Joshua W. Dorsey	21 Mar 1804	
Martha E.	John A. Trundle	17 Aug 1857	
Martha E.	Rezin T. Snowden	24 Dec 1886	c
Marvin E.	Alice V. Clagett	8 Jun 1881	
Matilda J.	Jacob Washington	16 Dec 1874	
Milly Ann	Thomas N. Harwood	27 Oct 1815	
Nancy S.	George T. Williams	8 Nov 1879	c
Richard	Ann Virginia Burns	1 Jan 1866	
Robert	Keziah E. Gue	3 Oct 1853	
Ruth	Franklin Jones	24 Dec 1877	c
Samuel N.	Mary A. Sibley	28 Jan 1890	w
Samuel R.	Ellen R. Pope	14 Dec 1876	
Solomon	Cordelia Thompson	3 Mar 1824	
Solomon	Mary Knott	21 May 1840	
William	Elizabeth Howard	14 Nov 1817	
William C.	Mary Bruce	21 Dec 1877	c
William H.	Carrie Hawkins	1 Nov 1887	c
POINTER, Alexander	Sarah Ann Bowen	26 Nov 1867	
POLEY, Bessie E.	Alan A'Dale	18 Nov 1890	w
POLKINHORN, Henry	Racheal A. Perry	3 Jan 1859	
POLLARD, Charles P.	Hannah N. Jones*	2 May 1821	
Priscilla J.	Archibald O. Douglass	4 Sep 1821	
POLLOCK, George F.	Cora L. Williams	15 Oct 1889	w
PONDER, Jesse	Sophia West	17 Oct 1822	
Sarah E.	Francis Gray	10 Nov 1845	
Sarah E.	John War	15 Jan 1850	
Sophia	Jacob Crampfield	28 Dec 1864	
POOL, Anthony Boyd	Martha M. Harding	26 Dec 1877	
Charles M.	Kate V. Murphy	** Sep 1886	w
Mahlin A.	Susannah Brown	11 May 1857	
POOLE, Aaron	Hessa Browning	11 Dec 1798	
Algernon	Mamie W. Waters	17 May 1886	w
Alice	Richard T. Gott	11 Nov 1873	
Ann	Francis Piles	10 Feb 1798	
Ann Elizabeth	Vernon Hempstone	11 Oct 1875	
Ann P.	William Selman	26 Nov 1838	
Annie E.	David L. Blakemore	3 Mar 1890	w
Annie M.	Thomas Berry	4 Feb 1879	
Annie M.	Robert T. Cooley	6 Feb 1879	
Basil	Ruthy King	9 Jan 1800	
Benjamin	Ann Willett Manly	21 Dec 1814	
Benjamin R.	Jane E. Elgin	21 Dec 1858	
Caleb	Caroline Adams	23 Dec 1874	
Charles A.	Sarah E. Best	16 Oct 1897	w
Charles I.	Sarah A. Beall	8 Jan 1895	w
Eli	Patience Barnes	5 Mar 1825	
Eliza	Leonard Hays	24 May 1825	
Elizabeth	John H. Duvall	2 Feb 1814	

* Part of last name from earlier reading
** Cannot read day; between 20 and 27

POOLE,	Elizabeth Ann	Colmore Offutt	8 Feb 1847
	Emily W.	Byron W. Walling	23 Jan 1883 w
	Eugene A.	Ella C. Towles	5 Jan 1880 w
	Florence P.	Richard Poole	22 Nov 1869
	Frances ?.	James W. McDonald	2* Jan 1880 w
	Frederick S.	Mary T. D. Williams	12 Aug 1833
	Greenbury C.	Ida B. Brown	21 Sep 1881 w
	Harriet A. R.	Rinaldo P. Snyder	12 Jan 1875
	Henrietta	John A. Young	5 Jun 1893 w
	Imogene	Edward T. Beall	9 Nov 1897 w
	Isaac R.	Mary Ellen Dawson	10 Mar 1842
	James F.	Ann E. Hoskinson	20 Dec 1853
	John	Sally Dickerson	19 Jun 1826
	John H.	Rhoda A. Gue	31 Aug 1892 w
	John W.	Susan E. Cooley	20 Feb 1849
	John W.	Mary M. Stiles	6 Feb 1857
	John W.	Mary Effie Allnutt	3 Mar 1884
	Julia Ann	Rezin E. Sheckles	22 May 1895 w
	Lewis W.	Eleanor N. Nicholson	18 Jun 1895 w
	Lorenzo D.	Sallie M. Divine	4 Dec 1878
	Lucretia W.	Henry Kellogg	2 Sep 1857
	Martha R.	Samuel Thomas Harding	8 Feb 1881
	Mary	George McAtee	10 Mar 1808
	Mary	Jacob Apsey	24 Jan 1835
	Mary E.	William C. Bowman	15 Jan 1867
	Mary S.	John T. Fletchall	29 May 1850
	Mary T.	Thomas L. Jones	20 Feb 1840
	Matilda	John Miles	10 Aug 1816
	Minerva	Reuben Brown	9 Nov 1840
	Minnie W.	Alfred Wilson	21 Jun 1892 w
	Philip N.	Margaret L. V. Watkins	15 May 1878 w
	Prissilla	Samuel H. Clagett	18 Dec 1809
	Rebecca	John Young	27 Dec 1817
	Reginald	Priscilla J. Hays	1 Oct 1860
	Reuben N.	Hepsie G. Purdum	19 Feb 1894 w
	Richard	Florence P. Poole	22 Nov 1869
	Rosalie	Rev. Henry Thomas	23 Nov 1885 w
	Sallie D.	W. F. Bevan	2 Jun 1885
	Sarah	Francis Piles	15 Apr 1813
	Sarah	Isaac Jones	12 Dec 1833
	Sarah E.	William A. Cady	1 May 1855
	Thomas	Sarah A. E. Willson	14 May 1832
	Thomas	Evelina W. Hyde	7 Nov 1846
	Thomas H.	Sarah A. Fisher	28 Nov 1854
	Tomsey	John McLaughlan	15 Sep 1824
	Warner	Eleanor Wyvell	2 Feb 1813
	William	Harriet Hempstone	30 Apr 1819
	William D.	Rebecca Dickerson	11 Apr 1831
	William E.	Julia M. Herrell	3 Nov 1886 w
	William E.	Essie H. Sheckells	27 Sep 1898 w
	William Henry	Hannah E. Miles	21 Dec 1847
	William T.	Ellen L. Hays	26 Jan 1854
	William Wallace	Avilda A. Allnutt	23 Aug 1855
	Wilson E. I.	Rebecca R. Miles	10 Feb 1851

* Cannot read complete day; between 20 and 29

POORE, David T.	Gladys Murphy	25 Nov 1884	w
POOSE, Catherine	Horatio Trundle	15 Jan 1802	
POPE, Beatrix V.	Jacob I. Johnson	9 Jun 1896	w
Benjamin F.	Mary G. Fyffe	13 Jun 1892	w
Cloe E.	William Thompson of Richard	10 Feb 1836	
Eleanor	Henry Roberts	2 Jan 1822	
Ellen R.	Samuel R. Plummer	14 Dec 1876	
Emeline	John M. Stewart	14 Aug 1834	
George T.	Lucy M. Stewart	22 Dec 1834	
Hester A.	Benjamin T. Marlow	13 Sep 1863	
James	Eliza Ann Bonnifant	11 Aug 1830	
Joseph M.	Matilda A. Thompson	6 Jun 1870	
Julia Virginia	Charles Thomas Hawkins	6 Dec 1881	
Lilian A.	Clinton Bowman	28 Dec 1896	w
Margaret	William Brook Owen	22 Mar 1806	
Margaret	Zachariah Read	4 Jan 1816	
Margarett	Zachariah Reed	31 Oct 1812	
Mary S.	John A. Hopkins	25 Apr 1898	w
Thomas	Elizabeth Case	12 Aug 1817	
Thomas H.	Annie V. Stevens	26 Feb 1896	w
PORTER, Catharine A.	Micajah Rogers	24 Nov 1835	
Charles	Polly Fry	8 Apr 1803	
Charles G.	Jane Thomas	6 Oct 1842	
Charlotte	George Heater	21 Dec 1801	
David A.	Mary Ray	15 Dec 1800	
Denton S.	Kitty Heater	4 Mar 1806	
Edward	Mary Heater	13 Jan 1800	
Edward	Ann T. Kinnard	8 Jun 1853	
Elizabeth	George Gassaway	15 Apr 1817	
Elizabeth G.	Samuel P. Thomas	24 Sep 1845	
Isaiah	Hannah Braddock	2 Jun 1812	
John E.	Altie M. Butler	26 Jan 1885	c
Mary	Frederick Heeter	6 Feb 1811	
Mary D.	H. Bradley Davidson	2 Jan 1890	w
Rebecca M.	William J. Thomas	18 Oct 1837	
Sarah	Reuben Rowzee	21 Feb 1857	
William	Estelle Posey	11 Jun 1891	w
William M.	Margaret Leizear	11 Jan 1831	
POSEY - also see POSIE			
POSEY, Catharine A. M.	Samuel C. Busey	1 May 1849	
Elizabeth	George Weems	15 Nov 1864	
Estelle	William Porter	11 Jun 1891	w
John H.	Sarah Boyd	11 Sep 1878	w
Joseph	Ella Thompson	9 Oct 1889	w
Mary E.	John W. Burroughs	3 Apr 1852	
Mary J.	Isaac Bettis	26 Dec 1883	c
William A.	Lillie Fisher	3 Jun 1898	w
POSIE, Amos	Elizabeth Jackson	9 Jun 1891	c
POSS, Marion O.	Albert W. Felka	22 Sep 1894	w
POSTEHER, Joanna	Adolph Gauer	25 Apr 1863	
POSTER, Ann M. C.	Frederick J. Schwatzpeck	4 Jun 1856	
POTTER, Albert I.	Cecelia M. Ulrich	18 Jun 1894	w
Raymond B.	Elise Smith Lockwood	4 Apr 1898	w
POTTS, Amanda	Nathan Waters	14 Jun 1892	c
Ellsworth	Mary A. Lyles	20 Jul 1893	c

POTTS, Hattie Ellen	Washington M. Bowie	28 Feb 1872	
Melinda*	Marsham Tuttle	1 Feb 1829	
Reuben H.	Ella Warren	26 Dec 1883	c
POWEL, Ann S.	Henry Leek	1 Dec 1885	c
POWELL, Adam	Flora Ross	9 Feb 1882	
Burgess	Nancy Gibbs	19 Jun 1888	c
Charles	Nancy Franklin	19 Dec 1834	c
Charles	Emily Holland	3 Jul 1884	c
Charles	Clara Johnson	3 Nov 1896	c
Edward	Elizabeth Sewell	11 Sep 1886	c
Eli	Margaret Wright	23 Sep 1896	c
Eliza	John Lincoln	5 Dec 1878	
Elizabeth O.	William H. Davis	14 Dec 1891	c
Ella	John Pumphrey	16 Jun 1881	c
Emma	Ignatius Dimes	2 Oct 1886	c
Grafton N.	Margaret Ann Scrivener	15 Mar 1827	
Henry	Margie Weeden	27 Jul 1882	w
Henry	Carrie E. Bowen	1 May 1894	c
Hilleary	Mary M. Warren	4 Aug 1896	c
James H.	H. Elizabeth Dodson	16 Feb 1870	
John	Eleanor Steel	24 Dec 1798	
John S.	Mary E. Budd	4 Oct 1887	c
Louis	Elizabeth Gassaway	15 Feb 1898	c
Lucy	Walter Matthews	10 Jan 1889	c
Margaret E.	William T. Hall	11 Mar 1895	c
Mary Ann	Nicholas Long	24 Sep 1873	
Mary Ellen	Washington Spencer	20 May 1833	
Mary Ellen	Rezin Holland	9 Jul 1868	
Nancy	William Storred	18 May 1898	c
Pattie	Edward Simms	24 May 1898	c
Priscilla	Joseph Hall	24 Dec 1878	c
Rachel	William H. Cole	6 Sep 1888	c
Rachel A.	Joseph A. Mackall	24 Feb 1880	c
Richard	Mary Warfield	23 Dec 1896	c
Sarah R.	George A. W. Edwards	25 Jun 1891	c
Sophia	James R. Blair	28 Mar 1889	c
Thomas	Alverta Smith	4 Apr 1895	c
Walter	Maggie Gittings	22 Sep 1896	c
William L.	Carrie E. Johnson	18 Dec 1886	c
William O.	Mary C. Dorsey	25 Jul 1888	c
William S.	Hallie S. Roberts	6 Dec 1882	w
Wilson H.	Lulie Young	14 Dec 1882	c
POWER, Elenora	Zachariah T. Briggs	6 Sep 1898	w
Elias	Mary Brown	16 Nov 1810	
Fannie	George V. Crouse	16 Apr 1895	w
John C.	Mary Minerva Mullican	1 Jan 1877	
Luisa	Joseph P. Smith	4 Feb 1819	
Richard	Anne Drudge	12 Jan 1810	
POWERS, Isaac N.	Elizabeth Winemiller	31 Dec 1828	
Louisa	Alexander Magruder	7 Jan 1886	c
Mary	William H. Sylvester	23 Dec 1891	w
PRAITER - also see PRATER			
PRAITER, Charles W.	Laura Bolden	23 May 1885	c

* Part of last name from earlier reading

PRAITHER - also see PRATHER			
PRAITHER, Rezin	Elizabeth Brown	10 Jun 1886	c
PRATER - also see PRATOR, PRAITER			
PRATER, Bertha	George Carroll	21 May 1893	c
George	Henrietta Hall	24 Apr 1886	c
Lucy	John Heverin	27 Dec 1890	c
Mary A.	William H. Frazier	8 Jan 1897	c
Theresa	Henry Williams	1 May 1891	c
PRATHER - also see PRAITHER			
PRATHER, Anne O.	Benedict H. Duley	20 Jun 1816	
Arthur	Mary Leach	5 Jun 1876	
Baruch	Casandra Swearingen	11 Dec 1799	
Deborah	Willson Walker	8 Oct 1801	
Edward H.	Mary V. Davis	27 Oct 1887	c
Eliza	Benedict H. Duley	7 Oct 1821	
Elizabeth	Nicholas Nicholls	20 Mar 1811	
Elizabeth L.	Darius M. Higgins	23 Jun 1862	
Emeline	William Boyd	17 Oct 1836	
Fannie G.	Joseph Johnson	4 May 1893	c
Florida	Charles A. C. Higgins	26 May 1856	
George	Martha Dorsey	23 Dec 1872	
George Forbes	Eleanor V. Hines	29 Jul 1884	w
Helen	Basil Ray	11 Jun 1874	
Henry	Elizabeth Ratliff	29 Nov 1826	
Howard	Rosie Lancaster	3 Jun 1896	c
Ida J.	James W. Bell	4 Feb 1891	c
Isaiah T.	Mary C. Thompson	24 Oct 1895	c
Jennett	Nathan Macknew	10 Feb 1806	
John	Ann Mockabee	22 Sep 1868	
John	Rachel Williams	12 May 1894	c
John H.	Elizabeth Jackson	16 Oct 1888	c
Joesph	Phebe Hawkins	25 Apr 1867	c
Josiah T.	Sarah Howard	1 Apr 1800	
Louisa	Lewis Wallis	28 May 1867	
Lucretia	James Clagett	13 Aug 1889	c
Lucy	Sykes Beckwith	14 Jun 1820	
Margaret	Thomas Jackson	20 Dec 1876	
Marshall	Amanda Bowie	1 Jan 1870	
Mary	Jeremiah Falconer	29 Nov 1826	
Mary	Horace W. Storred	29 Dec 1897	c
Matilda	Charles Harris	4 Aug 1896	c
Moses	Christina Lyles	5 Mar 1875	
Nancy O.	Isaac N. King	9 May 1842	
Nelly	Benjamin Cracroft	8 Dec 1798	
Rachel	Jacob Howard	8 Oct 1799	
Rezin	Albina Riggs	4 Mar 1867	
Rezin	Annie Simpson	13 Aug 1889	c
Sarah	Thomas H. Wilxocen	20 Apr 1798	
Sarah Ann	John W. Ferguson	16 May 1843	
Thomas	Jenny Beall	22 Feb 1800	
William	Elizabeth Adamson	2 Jun 1798	
William	Rachel Ann Smith	3 May 1842	
William	Martha Sellers	20 May 1895	c
William H.	Melvina Beall	23 Oct 1879	
William H.	Eva Martin	19 Aug 1889	c

PRATOR - also see PRATER			
PRATOR, Henry	Millie Brooks	8 Feb 1872	
PRATT, Albin	Mary Isabella Cooke	3 Feb 1874	
Amanda M.	Isaiah Squirrel	30 Oct 1879	c
Charles E., Dr.	Mary E. White	13 Dec 1878	w
Clem	Florence Thorn	5 Dec 1896	c
Eliza	William H. Pratt	22 Mar 1894	c
Emma May	John Edward Johnson	29 Mar 1898	c
Jason	Mary E. Dorsey	8 May 1889	c
Jason	Harriet Johnson	7 Dec 1893	c
Lewis	Sylvana Waters	9 May 1872	
Mary A.	Brandon Cook	27 Jan 1868	
Mary E.	William H. Turner	18 Aug 1898	c
Mary L.	William H. Matthews	27 Oct 1886	c
William H.	Helen Cook	14 Sep 1878	c
William H.	Eliza Pratt	22 Mar 1894	c
William T.	Mary E. Clagett	24 Oct 1893	w
PRESCOTT, Alexander F. B.	Edith S. Kellogg	16 Sep 1889	w
Charles C.	Caroline A. Shedd	22 Feb 1898	w
Lillian J.	Edward H. Abbe	16 Sep 1889	w
PRESGRAVES, Richard H.	Elizabeth Ann Palmer	2 Jan 1838	
PRESTON, Anna Eliza	Wesley Bennett	1 Oct 1828	
Frederick	Lucy Hickman	17 Sep 1825	
Mary Ann	Samuel Farmer	25 Oct 1817	
PRETTYMAN, Charles W.	Rosa V. Bouic	7 Dec 1881	
E. Barrett	Lydia F. Johnston	6 Jun 1855	
Forrest J.	Elizabeth R. Stonestreet	17 Oct 1888	w
Henry	Laura Bowman	28 Sep 1870	
Josephine	Samuel Bacon	5 Nov 1879	c
Mary	Greenbury Howard	20 Jul 1873	
Miriam	Albert J. Almoney	10 Dec 1884	
PRICE. Bertha E.	Willaim Q. Stouffer	23 Feb 1891	w
Bessie	William S. Hammond	13 Sep 1895	w
Bessie V.	James M. Nicholson	17 Dec 1895	w
Clifford E.	Gertrude V. Brown	29 Feb 1892	w
Cora D.	Franklin Day	22 Mar 1893	w
Daisy V.	Richard Bagby	2 Jun 1896	w
Daniel	Sarah Howard	5 Jul 1820	
Daniel W.	Sarah Frances Hall	30 Dec 1884	w
Elizabeth	Martin Whelan	20 Nov 1828	
Elizabeth	Nelson Conner	11 Jun 1844	
Elizabeth Margaret Maria Jane	Thomas J. Hobbs	20 Dec 1834	
Emeline	William W. Piles	8 Mar 1859	
Evan	Mary Liddan	16 Feb 1813	
Franklin W.	Laura Bready	23 Mar 1855	
George D.	Martha Lindsay	31 Aug 1897	w
George E.	Eveanner Plummer	29 Jun 1866	
George T.	Jessie V. Hilton	11 Jun 1888	w
Gertrude E. V.	James W. Hillard	29 Dec 1892	w
Henry	Elizabeth Redman	8 Dec 1804	
Ida	Samuel Cartwright	9 May 1891	c
Jane M.	John P. Craycroft	2* Nov 1844	

* Cannot read day; either 20 or 21

PRICE, John	Elizabeth Reid	17 Jul 1820	
John	Lizzie Day	3 Aug 1874	
John	Kitty Baker	1 Nov 1879	c
John T.	Molly Washington	17 Jun 1895	c
Joseph H.	Luella Kinna	22 Dec 1893	w
Juliet A.	John J. Barnesley	22 Feb 1843	
Laura E.	John Gardner	27 Sep 1898	w
Mary	James Dwyer	17 Aug 1805	
Mary	Thomas Mullican	20 Dec 1843	
Mary	Francis Chase	17 Apr 1867	
Mary E.	John H. Thompson	28 Oct 1843	
Mary Ellen	Thomas Marriott	22 Dec 1835	
Millard	Ella Norris	20 May 1893	w
Minnie B.	Walter G. Smith	12 Sep 1892	w
Montgomery	Sallie R. Pyles	7 Nov 1881	
Mortimer L.	Sarah Annie Brown	27 Oct 1886	w
Richard Jr.	Elizabeth Mobley	9 Feb 1802	
Samuel	Catharine Crowley*	19 Nov 1816	
Sarah A.	Henry S. Dove	28 Jun 1871	
Sarah E.	Randolph Luhn	8 Oct 1878	w
Sarah J.	Louis Dean	19 Dec 1895	c
Susan R.	James Fish	20 May 1837	
Wallace B.	Harriet A. M. Bowen	12 Apr 1880	
William	Ammy Summers	20 Dec 1807	
William F.	Clara E. Harper	4 Feb 1896	w
William T.	Algerine R. Turner	16 Aug 1881	
PRIESTLY, William	Cordelia A. Radcliffe	24 Oct 1867	
William	Elizabeth Pennifield	21 Mar 1878	w
PRIMIS, Louis	Mary Jackson	8 Nov 1870	
PRINCE, Ann - see Ann Pierce			
William	Everline Dorsey	20 Aug 1818	
PRINGLE, John	Elizabeth Hendley*	2 Oct 1798	
PRITCHARD, America	Rufus K. Magruder	18 Oct 1850	
Benjamin	Elizabeth Lewis	10 Oct 1815	
Elizabeth	Lucien S. Cummings	17 Oct 1831	
Mary	William G. Howard	29 Mar 1831	
Sabina	John Waggoner	26 Nov 1832	
PRITCHETT, Hanson	Elizabeth Smith	12 Jan 1803	
PROCTER - also see PROCTOR			
PROCTER, Richard	Rachel A. Ditter	10 Mar 1868	
PROCTON, Lewis G.	Flora Rozier	9 Aug 1893	c
PROCTOR - also see PROCTER			
PROCTOR, Airy	John Boswell	22 Aug 1876	
Ambrose	Rachel Williams	26 Oct 1874	
Ambrose	Maggie Offutt	27 Dec 1888	c
Ann L.	Frank Veny	16 May 1882	c
Eliza	Reuben Johnson	9 Jul 1896	c
Frederick	Mary Debtor	3 Nov 1866	
Frederick	Dinah Smith	6 Jun 1876	
Ginnie	Thomas Jackson	31 Dec 1892	c
James	Amy Jones	23 Feb 1875	
James Albert	Lair Lyles	13 Jun 1882	c
James R.	Cora ?. Jones	13 Apr 1892	c
Lewis	Sarah Robertson	10 Jan 1871	

* Part of last name from earlier reading

PROCTOR, Louisa	Henry Lucas	6 Sep 1877	c
Louisa	Jesse Wise	20 Oct 1898	c
Luella M.	Dominique B. Constantine	21 Mar 1898	w
Martha	Alfred Dorsey	1 Feb 1867	
Martha	----- Sewall*	** Apr 1879	c
Martha	Robert Warren	16 Feb 1889	
Mary Virginia	Daniel Braxton	24 Oct 1883	
William F.	Rachel V. Bowie	1 Oct 1888	c
PROUT, Fanny R.	John T. Vinsen	28 Aug 1861	
PRYOR, Esther M.	George F. Greenfield	14 Dec 1897	w
George E.	Elizabeth Ann Willson	5 Mar 1825	
Mary E.	Calvin H. King	9 Oct 1869	
Napoleon B.	Mary J. R. Peddicord	12 Feb 1851	
PUGH - also see PEUGH			
PUGH, David L.	Mary J. Gardner	16 Jan 1872	
Nathan	Catharine Hawkins	27 Dec 1886	c
Samuel T.	Emily J. Purdum	23 Jan 1875	
PUMPHERY, Richard	Louisa C. Snowden	27 Aug 1885	c
PUMPHREY - also see PUMPHERY, PUMPHRY			
PUMPHREY, Aaron	Annie Griggs	13 Oct 1879	c
Ada A.	Byron Trevey	9 Oct 1895	w
Ada I.	Frederick L. Harries	21 Feb 1895	w
Ann	Robert Connell	12 Feb 1816	
Anne E.	Isaac V. Warner	20 Dec 1866	
Annie	Asbury Williams	2 Jun 1894	c
Arthur	Edith Johnson	3 Mar 1894	c
Caleb	Laura R. Bowen	7 Sep 1897	c
Catherine	Charles G. Lansdale	9 Dec 1819	
Elenor Mackelfish King			
Elizabeth	James H. Higgins	11 Feb 1813	
Elizabeth C.	Samuel Connell	2 Feb 1841	
Henry A.	Rebecca Connell	23 Jan 1845	
Horace T.	Martha Bacon	8 Apr 1880	
James	Martha Stewart	15 Mar 1883	c
John	Ella Powell	16 Jun 1881	c
Mary	John Lansdale	7 Dec 1809	
Mary J.	Philip J. Connell	15 Feb 1853	
Mary Lavinia	Israel P. Warner	10 Nov 1870	
Samuel	Rachel Cecill	23 Mar 1816	
Samuel	Mary Campbell	25 Mar 1828	
Sedonia	John M. Heagy	12 Jan 1882	w
Sophia	Thomas Sills	10 Jun 1880	c
Vallie	Joshua Dorsey	26 Nov 1872	
William F.	Alice V. Snyder	19 Mar 1890	w
William Reuben	Hattie A. Shekell	13 Apr 1882	
Zachariah	Lucy J. Peters	11 Apr 1892	w
PUMPHRY, Caleb	Anna J. Bowen	3 May 1869	
William E.	Elizabeth Ann Connell	17 Nov 1840	
PURCEL, Anna Mariah	Charles T. Queen	19 Jan 1818	
PURDOM - also see PURDUM			
PURDOM, Belle N.	James Muir	8 Oct 1873	
Cassandra	James W. Burdett	14 Apr 1840	

* Cannot read his first name and the last name is questionable; day between 5 and 25

PURDOM, Charles R.	Mary Shaw	24 Jan 1829	
Elizabeth D.	Caleb R. Penn	11 Dec 1839	
Henrietta Maria	William Watkins	24 Jan 1829	
John	Eleanor Rigges	19 Apr 1805	
John R.	Mary S. Watkins	17 Dec 1850	
Joshua	Miranda Etchison	29 Mar 1836	
Keziah	John U. Riggs	11 Dec 1841	
Levi B.	Sarah H. Harrison	26 Feb 1818	
Lydia E.	Thomas H. Lewis	9 Dec 1834	
Martha Ann	Howard Young	19 Dec 1834	
Nathan	Rebecca Hutchinson	22 Dec 1821	
Sarah	Joseph Kean	25 Oct 1811	
Zadock	Matilda White	23 Jan 1813	
PURDUM - also see PURDOM			
PURDUM, Alice B.	Charles G. Linthicum	27 Feb 1888	w
Anne D.	Joshua V. Kean	9 Jan 1810	
Charles R.	Emma J. Hodges	18 Dec 1897	w
Elizabeth	William H. Hobbs	19 Dec 1851	
Ellen F.	William H. Broome	30 Jan 1877	w
Emily J.	Samuel T. Pugh	23 Jan 1875	
Fannie P.	Andrew Muir, Jr.	22 May 1875	
Harriet E.	William F. Duvall	10 Dec 1875	
Hattie A.	Joseph M. Burdette	18 Dec 1882	
Henrietta M.	William E. Ward	15 Jan 1879	w
Hepsie G.	Reuben N. Poole	19 Feb 1894	w
Hepsila	Leonidas Etchison	21 Mar 1865	
James	Hester W. Fletchell	9 Feb 1844	
James H.	S. Edith Lewis	5 Apr 1884	
James M.	Emma A. Davis	15 Oct 1895	w
James T.	Carrie ?. Higdon	29 Aug 1884	
Joseph J.	Laura May Davis	12 Apr 1897	w
Lizzie	Elias V. King	2 Apr 1892	w
Luther M.	Sally L. Murdict	27 Mar 1894	w
Maggie E.	Charles E. Thompson	28 Feb 1883	
Margaret	Robert A. Suddath	23 Jan 1867	
Margaret L.	James Gue	10 Jan 1837	
Mary L.	Miel E. Linthicum	25 Apr 1887	
Mollie	William V. Beall	27 Nov 1878	
Rosa B.	Samuel H. W. Browning	21 Dec 1896	
Sarah E. A.	Reverdy Browning	29 Jan 1884	
Thomas F.	Emma Lewis	3 Jan 1876	
Virginia	Zachariah W. McAtee	1 Jan 1873	
William L.	Ethel J. Hobbs	3 Dec 1892	w
PURDY, Ann M.	Lloyd H. Nichollson	16 Feb 1847	
Isabella	Thomas Page	24 Nov 1855	
Richard	Martha Bennett	25 May 1827	
PYFER, Sarah L.	Thomas H. Marshall	5 Jul 1882	
PYLE, Loraine L.	Luther M. Gotwald	* Apr 1890	w
PYLES - also see PILES			
PYLES, Annie E.	Edward E. Crockett	23 Jul 1884	
Ida	Elias Beall	9 Nov 1880	
Laura J.	Nathan E. Miles	7 Oct 1874	
Marbra J.	Isaac N. Shipley	9 Jun 1863	
Michael T.	Mary F. Williams	14 Nov 1893	w

* Cannot read day; before 9

PYLES, Nannie E.	Thomas O. White	30 Nov 1883	
Richard	Susan Benson	25 Feb 1847	
Richard	Laura V. Stacks	18 Apr 1887	w
Richard T.	Laura V. Hawkins	2 Feb 1859	
Sallie R.	Montgomery Price	7 Nov 1881	
Thomas M.	Bettie Williams	24 Nov 1873	
QUACKENBUSH, Jesse	Mary Frances Levius	5 Aug 1882	w
Minnie	Walter Magruder	16 Feb 1887	w
QUARY - also QUERY			
QUARY, Hannah	David Spohn	10 Jun 1812	
Rebeccah	Evan Nicholls	29 Feb 1808	
Sally	John Wood	11 Nov 1804	
QUEEN, Annie	Nicholas E. Ray	4 Oct 1892	w
Charles T.	Anna Mariah Purcel	19 Jan 1818	
Rose	William Kilgour	27 Oct 1858	
QUERY - also see QUARY			
QUERY, Betsey	Lewald Young	2 Jun 1828	
Charlotte	William Counselman	2 Mar 1826	
QUIGLEY, Charles H.	Grace Lyddane	26 Oct 1876	
QUINN, Thomas	Cassy Mitchell	27 Nov 1875	
QUINTER, Susie S.	Alonzo E. Lambath	13 May 1893	w
QUIRK, Mary Ellen	Charles F. Trill	11 Oct 1880	w
RABBETT, Edward	Elizabeth Swearingen	8 Oct 1814	
Henry	Anne Wilburn	6 Jun 1805	
Jenny	William Wilburn	21 Feb 1803	
John	Rebecca Barrett	5 Jan 1808	
RABBITT, Albert F.	Alice M. Bready	23 Feb 1878	w
Alexander	Lelia C. Venable	20 Apr 1897	w
Ann	Jacob Kemp	5 Apr 1842	
Anne L.	Samuel K. Bready	25 Nov 1873	
Annie Belle	Charles E. Garrett	27 Jan 1891	w
Catherine	William Carlyle	12 Feb 1831	
Catherine E.	Joseph L. Carroll	11 Jan 1866	
Columbia	Levi R. Kinsey	7 Jun 1870	
Eleanor	George A. Snyder	12 Mar 1886	w
Eliza V.	John Thompson	6 Mar 1872	
Georgie	Benjamin H. Thompson	10 Jan 1878	w
Ietta A.	Edward E. Welsh	6 Apr 1874	
James E.	Ida J. Gaither	28 Sep 1886	w
Jane	Hamilton Gittings	17 Oct 1854	
Jeratia Ann	John H. Austin	23 Aug 1846	
Joseph R.	Rosa Campbell	3 Nov 1875	
Lizzie	James Edward Thompson	29 Nov 1878	
M. Virginia	Charles W. Fields	23 Oct 1878	w
Mary	Charles Beckwith	21 Jul 1819	
Mary	Reuben T. Mullican	23 Dec 1847	
Mary E.	William L. Baker	3 Sep 1872	
Rachel A.	William Baker	7 Aug 1855	
Rebecca	John E. Baker	29 Jul 1847	
Rebecca	Edward Craycroft	3 Jan 1871	
Rebecca J.	Alfred C. Warthen	31 Oct 1887	w
Samuel	Victoria C. Adamson	12 Dec 1855	
Samuel E.	Emeline Robertson	15 Jan 1896	w
Thomas	Elizabeth A. Baker	19 Nov 1846	

RABBITT, Thomas H.	Mary Catherine Ball	15 Apr 1841
Thomas T.	Teresa E. Crown	12 Feb 1866
William H.	L. Jane Davis	4 Jun 1867
William J.	Eliza Kemp	8 Feb 1844
RACHE, Florence M.	Wallie T. Drake	16 Aug 1898 w
RADCLIFF - also see RATCLIFF		
RADCLIFF, John W.	Margaret Ann Barrett	18 Mar 1846
RADCLIFFE, Cordelia A.	William Priestly	24 Oct 1867
RADDY, William	Jennie Matthews	14 Oct 1880 c
RAGAN, Basil	Harriett Adams	11 Nov 1813
RAINER, John	Caroline Adams	28 Aug 1838
RAINEY - also see RANNEY, RANEY, RANNIE		
RAINEY, Anna M.	James P. Gill	10 Nov 1869
RAMEY, John	Rachel Browning	8 Dec 1830
Lucy B.	George B. Myles	19 Jul 1897 w
RAMSAY, Elizabeth	Joseph Alvey	16 Jan 1821
RAMSEY, Margaret	William Fields	17 Dec 1812
William	Margaret Herren	1 Jan 1800
RANDALL, Charles F.	Florence M. Keys	9 Jun 1891 w
RANDELL, Sarah A.	Isaiah Marshall	24 May 1875
RANDOLPH, Anna	James L. Johnson	22 Jun 1875 c
George R.	Mary F. Jenkins	4 Jul 1894 c
John Henry	Katie Hawkins	1 Aug 1881 c
Lewis	Mary E. Ridgeley	4 Aug 1866
Robert	Daphne A. Corn	23 Aug 1881 c
Robert H.	Margaret A. Bowie	21 Mar 1895 c
RANEY - also see RAINEY		
RANEY, James P.	Mary A. Curtin	18 Sep 1880 w
Mary M.	Charles F. Divine	17 Feb 1890 w
RANKINS, Nancy	Thomas Willson	24 Sep 1798
RANNEBERGER, Sarah	David H. Bouic	5 Jul 1864
RANNEY - also see RAINEY, RANEY		
RANNEY, Grace E.	John B. Diamond	6 Nov 1877 w
RANNIE, James	Mary J. Weer	29 Jun 1881 w
Martha E.	William C. Dwyer	5 Dec 1868
William H.	Katie A. Gaither	6 Mar 1886 w
RANSBURGH - also see REMSBURG		
RANSBURGH, Caroline	Jacob Heffner	29 Nov 1837
RANSEL, William H.	Susan E. Mason	9 Apr 1887 c
RANSON, Thomas	Louisa Young	1 Jan 1870
RAPLEY, Mary Florence	Charles G. Stone	4 Jun 1883
William H.	Lizzie L. Batchelor	9 Nov 1885
RATCLIFF - also see RADCLIFF		
RATCLIFF, John Martin	Sarah Clements	26 Jan 1819
RATLIFF, Anne Tracy	Ignatius Dyal	22 Dec 1809
Elizabeth	Henry Prather	29 Nov 1826
Francis	Tabitha Thompson	4 Feb 1807
Mary	James Alexander Shaw	22 Nov 1800
RATRIE, Mary	George Parker	29 Nov 1826
RAUM, Joseph A.	Carrie Lee Jones	26 May 1891 w
RAWLINGS, Anne	Samuel S. Hays	28 Oct 1812
Eliza	Elbert Shaw	20 Nov 1837
James	Elizabeth Adams	1 Jun 1840
James H.	Sarah A. Richardson	16 Jun 1804
Mary	William Valdenar	8 Feb 1833
Polly	Edward Berry	1 Feb 1802

RAWLINGS, Sarah	Henry Howard	23 Apr 1802
RAWLINS, Elizabeth	James Brown	16 Feb 1828
Lizzie	M. H. Austin	10 Nov 1864
Mary	Alexander Johnson	1 Jun 1866
Rachel E.	Rush L. Wright	29 Dec 1896 w
RAY, Addison N.	Mary C. Burris	26 Jan 1876
Amelia	John H. Ricketts	9 Feb 1847
Ann	Richard Green	27 Mar 1802
Anne	Camden Riley	16 Jan 1800
Anne	William Thorn	2 Feb 1810
Annie I.	John P. Ray	14 Sep 1898 w
Basil	Eleanor Reynolds	2 Mar 1810
Basil	Helen Prather	11 Jun 1874
Caroline	Truman Greenfield	4 Feb 1835
Christie A.	Thomas J. Gardner	15 Jun 1858
Clara A.	James F. Wilson	31 May 1892 w
Columbia	John H. Frazier	11 Jan 1847
David A.	Rhoda A. Ward	15 Jun 1854
Eleazar	Eliza Earp	24 Aug 1865
Elizabeth	William Beall	12 Nov 1800
Elizabeth	Samuel Hamilton	27 Dec 1808
Elizabeth	Thomas H. Burriss	19 Oct 1854
Estelle	James R. Parsley	22 Sep 1898 w
Fillmore	Frances Frazier	4 Nov 1891 c
George	Sarah Robertson	5 Mar 1807
George F.	Alice V. Bogley	23 Sep 1885 w
Harriet E.	Philip J. Case	8 Nov 1877
Harriet R.	Joshua Thompson	30 Nov 1848
Henrietta	Jeremiah McNew	13 Jan 1811
Hester J.	Tobias R. Elcorn	12 May 1898 c
Icidean	Clarence E. Burriss	19 Sep 1893 w
James	Deborah Gaither	5 Feb 1803
Jared	Eliza Ann Thompson	15 Apr 1829
John	Anne Myers	11 Oct 1815
John	Polly Anderson	30 Jan 1822
John A.	Sallie A. Musgrove	24 May 1892 w
John Henry	Mary Jane Carter	14 Jun 1898 w
John P.	Leanna W. Ward	25 Oct 1870
John P.	Annie I. Ray	14 Sep 1898 w
Joseph	Harriet Ann Ward	29 Jan 1844
Lancelot Wilson	Airah Brown	28 Mar 1811
Lucy	John Lanham	14 Jan 1800
Margaret Ann	William Henry Parsley	19 Dec 1833
Margaret M.	William J. Kelly	21 Jan 1860
Maria V.	Owen S. Duvall	16 Jun 1869
Martha J.	John T. Ricketts	8 Jan 1856
Mary	David A. Porter	15 Dec 1800
Mary	William J. Earp	17 Sep 1874
Mary E.	James O'Donnell	25 Sep 1862
Mary E.	Granville T. Thornton	1 Nov 1898 c
Mary Elizabeth	Ignatius H. Ward	5 Jan 1841
Mary J. D.	William C. Crawford	30 Dec 1878
Nancy	Horace W. Ward	13 Jan 1842
Nathaniel	Louisa Dutch	23 Dec 1867
Nicholas	Verlinda Cooke	5 Jan 1820
Nicholas	Isabella Leadingham	26 Dec 1861

RAY, Nicholas E.	Annie Queen	4 Oct 1892	w
Philip H.	Virginia J. Riggs	8 Dec 1886	w
Rachel A.	Philip Erp	16 Oct 1862	
Rebeccah	William Candler	27 Jun 1803	
Richard T.	Mary Rebecca Cashel	25 Jan 1875	
Ruth	Thomas Gatton	22 Jan 1799	
Sarah	John Mangun	9 Sep 1816	
Susan	John King	29 Aug 1829	
Susan E.	John T. Thompson	6 Feb 1854	
Susan R.	Nathan R. Selby	4 Feb 1847	
Thomas J.	Mary E. Leadingham	12 May 1862	
William H.	Virginia De la Fayette Ward	17 Feb 1842	
William T.	Mary S. Sheaffer	16 Nov 1871	
REA, Nellie	Charles Nial Saxton	25 Jan 1894	w
READ - also see REED, REID			
READ, Alexander	Minty Bradock	26 Oct 1801	
Ann	Howard Phillips	3 Feb 1815	
Ann	Thomas Mangun	10 Nov 1819	
Elizabeth	Washington Busey	4 Oct 1809	
Ignatius D.	Martha E. Cook	27 Dec 1847	
James	Elizabeth Cochrane	23 Sep 1809	
John	Priscilla Summers	14 Jan 1804	
John M.	Delilah Riney	24 Apr 1813	
Martha E.	Howard M. Selby	23 Aug 1882	w
Mary	George Hoskins	24 Feb 1800	
Mary	Meshech Tucker	28 Dec 1809	
Mary M.	William P. Hickman	17 Nov 1896	w
Matthew	Elilah Jones	10 Sep 1818	
Nancy	John Kinder	25 Jan 1806	
Norris	Elizabeth Holland	26 Dec 1798	
Robert	Jane Lynn Lackland	21 Oct 1817	
Robert	Francis Davis (female)	12 Nov 1822	
Rosetta	Thomas J. Thompson	6 Jan 1837	
Susan	Alexander Suter	20 Apr 1815	
Thomas	Eleanor Hoyle	21 Dec 1810	
Thomas	Henrietta Merrick	1 Aug 1818	
Thomas	Rachel Colliar	28 Dec 1824	
Zachariah	Margaret Pope	4 Jan 1816	
READING - also see REDDEN, REDING			
READING, Joseph	Mary F. Gassaway	8 Dec 1897	w
REAMEY, Richard H.	Mamie C. Booth	26 Nov 1896	w
REARDEN - also see RIORDAN			
REARDEN, Martha	Oscar B. Hook	1 Oct 1872	
REBER, George F.	Mary R. Dowden	15 Oct 1886	w
RECHER, Carrie Iona	David Griffith Porter	16 Sep 1897	w
RECORD, Anne	Reuben Penn	16 Jan 1833	
REDDEN - also see READING			
REDDEN, William T.	Isabella R. Pennifield	26 Oct 1876	
REDDICK, Louisa	Robert D. Williams	18 May 1893	c
REDING - also see READING			
REDING, Harrett	Ignatius Drury	4 Dec 1799	
REDMAN, Ann	George Ward	17 Dec 1798	
Daniel F.	Rachel Ann Burgess	1 Apr 1886	c
Eleanor	Beale Ayton	20 Jun 1803	
Elizabeth	Henry Price	8 Dec 1804	

REDMAN, George K.	Mahala Moore	6 Mar 1834	
James H.	Julia Brady	29 Mar 1875	
John	Harriet Ward	25 Jan 1800	
Josiah W.	Ann Orme	5 Jul 1809	
Levi	Catherine Coho	17 Oct 1804	
Luginia	Henry Plummer	29 Jun 1872	
Lulie	Turner Carter	20 Apr 1896	w
Margarett Ann	Philemon Moore	18 Dec 1826	
Martha	Richard Barrett	22 Oct 1840	
REDMON, Douglass H.	Mary E. Hall	26 Dec 1883	w
Joseph	Octavia J. Redmon	6 Dec 1880	
Mollie Ann	Jackson M. Cooper	11 Oct 1886	w
Octavia J.	Joseph Redmon	6 Dec 1880	
William	Rosa Erp	29 Jan 1896	w
REDMOND, Sarah	Joseph Steel	16 Dec 1889	w
REED- also see READ, REID			
REED, Alfred	Elizabeth Ann Case*	18 Dec 1826	
Allen	Susan R. Baldwin	10 Sep 1869	
Andrew	Elizabeth Hervey	23 Apr 1833	
Bushrod Washington	Mary Louisa Piles	21 Jan 1842	
Cassandra	Nelson W. Earp	8 Aug 1853	
Charlotte H.	Jason P. Warthen	19 Oct 1882	w
Edward P.	Rebecca H. Davis	29 Oct 1867	
Eleanor	Richard Piles	19 Mar 1803	
Eleanor	Richard F. Stallings	8 Apr 1870	
Eliza Jane	Roszell Woodward	19 Sep 1867	
Fidelia E.	Darius F. Watkins	10 Jul 1886	w
George N.	Ann Plummer	4 Jan 1854	
George W.	Harriet Selby	16 Feb 1883	
Harriet L.	James P. Walter	27 Jul 1863	
James	Ella Kinsey	6 Aug 1891	w
James	Agnes Bean	6 Jan 1897	w
Joanna	George W. Day	30 Jan 1879	w
John	Patty Miller	9 Jan 1805	
John	Rebecca Moran	23 Sep 1814	
John	Laura Day	** Feb 1878	w
Lewis	Mattie Thompson	19 Dec 1895	w
Matthew	Eleanor Keith	2 Mar 1803	
Ninian	Matilda Ann Thompson	1 Feb 1832	
Olive A.	William E. Warthen	8 Jun 1881	w
Ruth	Peter Smith	8 Jan 1852	
Samuel P.	Matilda W. Lydard	8 Feb 1882	
Tabitha	Zacharias Oden	28 Apr 1824	
Thomas	Leatha Ann Phelps	13 Oct 1835	
Thomas J.	Harriet Norriss	24 Dec 1878	w
Virginia	Franklin Willson	12 Jan 1863	
Zachariah	Margarett Pope	31 Oct 1812	
REEDER, Emma	George M. Burdett	6 Nov 1888	w
REELY - also see RILEY			
REELY, Charles	Henrietta C. Nicholson	6 Sep 1862	
REESE, Myrtie V.	Henry W. McNeal	2 Nov 1891	w
REEVES, Robert B.	Lily Bageot	13 Aug 1890	w
REICHENBACH, William F.	Clara E. Suter	24 Aug 1881	c

* Middle name written over; looks like Ann
** No day given; 11 or before

REICHER - see RECHER
REID - also see READ, REED

REID,			
Airah	Stephan Robertson	15 Jan 1816	
Alethy	Thomas B. Johnson	28 Feb 1816	
Alexander	Elizabeth Philips	23 Feb 1804	
Alice A.	Wallace S. Shipley	9 Apr 1888	w
Alice C.	Charles T. Kingsbury	5 May 1891	w
Allen	Sarah Ann Gardner	18 Dec 1827	
Amelia M.	George W. Luhn	23 May 1888	w
Benjamin	Ann Waters	19 Dec 1814	
Benjamin	Maggie Murphy	5 Oct 1875	
Benjamin F.	Susan R. Hoskinson	24 Jan 1865	
Cassy	John Crawford	17 Mar 1865	
Eleanor	John Thomas Veirs	10 Sep 1825	
Eletha	Thomas Coclyn	12 Apr 1828	
Eleven	Martha Ann Boice	9 Mar 1829	
Elizabeth	John Price	17 Jul 1820	
Emeline	Owen Penn	16 Aug 1841	
George	Elizabeth Smith	31 May 1826	
George Nelson	Cassandra Erp	29 Sep 1819	
Henry	Mary Ann Dillehay	21 Nov 1835	
Henson	Martha Smallwood	11 Apr 1820	
Hiram	Elizabeth Dillehay	15 Dec 1828	
James	Charlotte Gatton	28 Nov 1809	
James C.	Annie Mary Brown	29 May 1893	w
John M.	Mary Ann Clark	8 Nov 1802	
John T.	Annie R. Cooley	18 Apr 1893	w
Lucy Ann	Ignatius Warren	2 Jun 1870	
Mary E.	Charles T. Kingsbury	10 Jan 1876	
Minnie	Frank Hayes	14 May 1894	w
Philip	Catherine J. Thompson	13 Dec 1882	w
Ruth S.	David Howard	7 Dec 1827	
Sarah T.	William Johnson	30 Sep 1884	w
Sophia J.	John T. Buxton	15 Jan 1872	
Stephen A.	Mary R. Carlin	20 Dec 1895	w
Susan R.	Richard C. Nicholson	14 Jan 1875	
Sylvester	Nellie F. Burke	9 Feb 1887	w
Thomas	Lucy Moore	12 Nov 1825	
Verlinda	Richard B. Turner	4 Oct 1850	
William	Elizabeth Barthlow	28 Dec 1808	
William	Martha Case	21 Oct 1828	
William	Sarah Ann Thompson	13 Sep 1847	
William S.	Alice E. Browning	23 Apr 1894	w
REIDY, Nora	John D. Coughlan	26 Nov 1897	w
REIGLE, Lucy M. P.	William Neumann	16 Dec 1878	w
REINDERTZ, Anna	Basil Moore	14 Dec 1799	

REINHART - also see RHINEHART RINEHART

REINHART, David J.	Annie M. Williams	8 Oct 1877	w
Louis E.	Anntonie Sheckells	5 Apr 1897	w
REINTZEL, Daniel	Ann Robertson	20 Dec 1800	
Mary	Nicholas Hodge	4 Jan 1801	
REINTZELL, Ann V.	John Padgett	31 Dec 1879	w
Ida M.	Edward A. Foley	11 Jul 1885	w
REMICK, Mary E.	Luther C. McDonough	6 Dec 1892	w
REMMETON, Elizabeth	Richard Stewart	23 Dec 1799	

REMSBURG - also see RAMSBURGH			
REMSBURG, Daniel T.	Mary E. Young	11 Apr 1856	
RENSHAW, Annie	Warren V. Magruder	14 Nov 1893	w
Eliza Ellen	John M. Clayton Williams	4 Apr 1887	w
Elizabeth	John G. Bohrer	15 Oct 1850	
Henry	Mary S. Spates	3 Dec 1850	
Henry	Eliza E. Spates	7 Nov 1865	
John William	Emma J. Heffner	7 Dec 1880	
Martha E.	William M. Hardesty	19 Oct 1864	
Mattie	Eugene B. Magruder	4 Jan 1898	w
Samuel H.	Alice E. Huddleston	15 Mar 1877	w
Thomas	Anna Maria Spates	29 Jan 1862	
William	Mary C. Moyer	3 Oct 1890	w
REPP, Eva B.	Harry S. Ridgely	19 Oct 1898	w
Lottie H.	David Caldwell	24 Apr 1897	w
REX, John	Mary A. Duvall	10 Mar 1853	
REYNOLD, Ann	John Bean	1 Jan 1839	
REYNOLDS, Alexander	Fannie Wilburn	25 Jan 1881	
Edwin C.	Julia V. Solyom de Antalf--*	26 Dec 1896	w
Eleanor	Basil Ray	2 Mar 1810	
Elizabeth	James Collinson Battey	26 Sep 1846	
Elley	Mary Upton	19 Dec 1803	
Henry L.	Jane E. B. Williams	17 Jul 1893	w
James	Mary Lansdale	18 Jun 1812	
Jennie M.	Frank M. Howard	12 Jul 1893	w
Josephine G.	Joseph Harding	11 Feb 1869	
Mary S.	George R. Howes	22 Dec 1883	
Nettie C.	Edwin T. Line	3 Jun 1896	w
RHINE - also see RINE			
RHINE, Augustus W.	Helen Beckwith	21 Sep 1871	
George W.	Sarah Ellen Owens	28 Jun 1875	
Joseph F.	Emma E. Owens	27 Nov 1872	
Maggie	Thomas Beckwith	13 Jun 1871	
Pinkie Corila	Cleon Leroy Keiser	5 Jun 1896	w
Rebecca	Joshua Kramer	1 Dec 1883	
W. H. (male)	M. A. T. Vanhorn	2 Dec 1867	
RHINEHART - also see REINHART, RINEHART			
RHINEHART, Laurence	Rebecca Richter	10 Aug 1859	
Rebecca	John Rosendoff	2 Jan 1878	w
RHOADES, George	Jane Green	11 Mar 1839	
RHODES, Annie R.	Daniel Stephen Heffner	10 Aug 1865	
Becca	L. L. Lloyd	2 Oct 1877	w
Eliza	James Hawkins	20 Apr 1881	
Frank	Ida J. Morris	20 Jul 1895	c
George	Rose Lee Roland	1 Oct 1891	c
John	Ann Busey	13 Dec 1816	
Margaret A.	William J. Dronenburg	9 Jan 1849	
Rachel	Daniel Haymond	12 Jun 1821	
Sarah	James Baker	2 Nov 1875	
Thomas	Eliza Dyson	24 Mar 1875	
RICE, Annie E.	John A. Hall	24 Aug 1881	w

* Cannot make out last 2 or 3 letters

RICE, Charles L.	Rickey Grand	* Jul 1882	
George R.	Bertie M. Tschiffely	30 Dec 1865	
Jane A. L.	Elgar L. Tscheffely	12 Nov 1866	
Jesse William	Mary M. Smith	10 Feb 1874	
Lacey B.	Clifton L. Tschiffely	26 Sep 1898	w
Lacy	Joseph C. Galleher	3 Aug 1881	w
Lydia	Thomas R. Bowen	1 Mar 1889	c
Mary V.	Edgar D. Vinson	25 Feb 1873	
Millard L.	Nellie Kelley	16 Sep 1890	w
Mollie	John Tillett	22 Jun 1875	
RICH, Ann R.	Barton S. Robey	30 Jan 1867	
Citty Ann	Thomas D. Harris	24 Jul 1889	w
Idie E.	William S. Duvall	26 Nov 1877	w
RICHARD - also see RICHERD			
RICHARD, Sarah	Harrison Cleveland	8 Dec 1798	
RICHARDS, Catherine	Bennedict Adams	27 Jan 1807	
Christianna	James Kiernan	27 Jun 1819	
Eleanor	Hugh Kiernan	23 Apr 1833	
Eliza L.	William R. Jones	31 Dec 1801	
Elizabeth	Osborn S. Willson	4 Jan 1813	
George	Nelly Oneill	30 Nov 1823	
Harry B.	Grace B. Allen	17 Mar 1898	w
Jacob B.	Helen Murphy	11 Jul 1892	w
Mary	George Riley	18 Oct 1810	
Mary Ann	Turner Willson	25 Jan 1817	
Sarah Ann	Richard Butt	21 Dec 1814	
Sary	Hazel Butt	31 Dec 1803	
Tabitha	T. James Suter	17 May 1810	
Tabitha	Joseph M. Semmes	22 Feb 1813	
RICHARDSON, Ann D.	James Burside	3 Nov 1835	
Clara T.	Andrew J. Harding	26 Feb 1881	
Elizabeth M.	Alfred N. Oden	13 Sep 1855	
Francis M.	John W. Hurley (male)	13 May 1857	
George H.	Sarah J. Thomspon	22 Nov 1897	w
Henry W.	Ann L. Iglehart	25 Apr 1870	
James F.	Mary E. Cosgrave	31 Oct 1896	w
Mary E.	Charles H. Murphy	12 Dec 1854	
Montegue L.	Emily B. Iglehart	26 Jan 1878	w
Robert J. T.	Alice V. VanHorn	26 Feb 1889	w
Rosetta	Daniel Diggins	28 Dec 1896	c
Samina L.	Alexandra Murphey (male)	29 Nov 1825	
Sarah A.	James H. Rawlings	16 Jun 1804	
RICHERD - also see RICHARD			
RICHERD, John	Maria Appleby	30 Mar 1835	
RICHEY - also see RITCHIE			
RICHEY, Stephen O.	Sarah R. White	7 Nov 1878	w
RICHTER, Christianna	John Snyder	21 Aug 1861	
Clara	Charles Hargett	27 Sep 1887	w
Earnest H.	Mary P. Nichols	1 Dec 1863	
Joanna F.	Jacob F. Snider	11 Jan 1853	
John C. H.	Elizabeth A. R. Leamon	21 Jan 1860	
Rebecca	Laurence Rhinehart	10 Aug 1859	

* Cannot read day; between 10 and 20

RICKETTS,	Albert H.	Ida E. Trail	28 Apr 1897 w
	Alice A.	Samuel L. Robertson	24 Dec 1880
	Alice E.	Charles F. Ricketts	15 Jan 1880 w
	Ann Maria	Richard Clagett	5 Nov 1860
	Ardella M.	John Thomas Davis	29 Sep 1880
	Benjamin	Ann Holland	20 Feb 1802
	Benjamin	Elizabeth R. Trail	31 Dec 1828
	Caroline A.	George Bean	22 Mar 1860
	Charles C.	Bertha Mullican	31 May 1892 w
	Charles F.	Alice E. Ricketts	15 Jan 1880 w
	Charles F.	Carrie V. Bennett	22 Feb 1898 w
	Delilah	Allen Selby	9 Jun 1815
	Drusilla	Levin Easton	27 Feb 1801
	Edward T.	Leanna Baker	30 Mar 1875
	Eliza Ann	John A. Beckwith	10 Mar 1834
	Elizabeth	Jane Harriss	24 Dec 1813
	Elizabeth	John W. Baker	8 Jan 1824
	Elizabeth	Elijah Thompson	13 Apr 1825
	Elizabeth	John Thomas Gray	20 Apr 1846
	Elizabeth F.	John Mullican	26 Dec 1854
	Elizabeth R.	Nathaniel W. Ricketts	29 Dec 1847
	Ella J.	Thomas Berry	23 Jul 1889 w
	Emily C.	John H. Clagett	7 Nov 1848
	Ernest	Mary C. Kelly	19 May 1886 w
	George H.	Ida E. Bean	27 Apr 1882
	Harriet L.	John S. Gilliss	27 May 1873
	Helen L.	Julian F. Walters	10 Jun 1895 w
	Henry T.	Martha E. Storay	2 Oct 1879
	Henson R.	Martha A. Carlyle	2 Feb 1858
	Irene L.	William T. Grimes	15 Oct 1888 w
	Isaac	Nancy Bean	2 Feb 1837
	Isaac	Elizabeth Mills	11 Jul 1861
	Jacob	Charlotte Bean	14 Nov 1840
	James W.	Rosella V. Collins*	5 Sep 1871
	John	Sarah Ricketts	6 Apr 1811
	John	Emeline Oneale	18 Jan 1838
	John H.	Amelia Ray	9 Feb 1847
	John T.	Harriet A. Day	11 Jun 1851
	John T.	Martha J. Ray	8 Jan 1856
	Laura M.	Zalphin B. Howard	19 Feb 1896 w
	Laura S.	James N. Suddath	18 Mar 1879 w
	Laura V.	Henry C. Ward	26 Dec 1859
	Laura V.	William W. Ricketts	8 Mar 1883
	Laura Virginia	George F. Crown	2 Jan 1869
	Leonidas	Mary G. Ricketts	6 Aug 1878 w
	Maggie E.	Charles A. Mewshaw	24 Apr 1890 w
	Margaret J.	William H. Leizear	18 Jan 1898 w
	Martha A.	Samuel E. Selby	14 Sep 1857
	Martha O.	Samuel H. Dyott	20 Mar 1894 w
	Mary A.	William H. House	12 Nov 1845
	Mary A.	Basil T. Bean	6 Jan 1852
	Mary A. D.	William R. Gaither	9 Aug 1852
	Mary G.	Leonidas Ricketts	6 Aug 1878 w
	Mary R.	Nelson H. Robertson	2 Sep 1876

* This could be Rosetta

RICKETTS,	Mary S.	William A. Ricketts	9 Feb 1888	w
	Matilda J.	Richard H. Ricketts	17 Oct 1854	
	Merchant	Guliel Mariah Trail	12 Feb 1817	
	Minerva	Henry E. Selby	4 Sep 1879	
	Nancy	Jacob Miller	30 Dec 1806	
	Nancy	Robert Grooms	23 Dec 1824	
	Nathaniel W.	Elizabeth R. Ricketts	29 Dec 1847	
	Nicholas	Rachel Trail	15 Apr 1811	
	Rachel	James W. Day	6 Aug 1878	w
	Rachel E.	Thomas W. Offutt	31 Mar 1868	
	Rebecca	Robert McKendry Butt	26 Jan 1869	
	Richard	Julia Ann Connell	10 Oct 1839	
	Richard E.	Christian Trail	3 Dec 1850	
	Richard H.	Matilda J. Ricketts	17 Oct 1854	
	Robert	Rachel Moulding	30 Mar 1826	
	Robert	Letha Burress	26 Dec 1839	
	Roberta J.	William H. Harding	26 Jul 1883	
	Roberta J.	John C. Riley	22 Apr 1890	w
	Sarah	John Ricketts	6 Apr 1811	
	Singleton	Sally Barclay	22 Aug 1805	
	Susan	William R. Selby	19 Jan 1846	
	Susanna	Horatio Jones	2 Sep 1806	
	U. Magruder	Ella Davis	9 Aug 1880	
	Ulysses M.	Sarah C. Harding	22 May 1884	w
	Uriah	Emma Burroughs	15 Dec 1880	w
	Verlinda	Notley Trail	19 Mar 1817	
	Wallace E.	Emma L. Mullican	14 Oct 1891	w
	William	Fanny Trail	18 Dec 1822	
	William A.	Mary S. Ricketts	9 Feb 1888	w
	William Henry	Susanna Trail	10 Dec 1857	
	William Thomas	Delila Selby	8 Dec 1846	
	William W.	Laura V. Ricketts	8 Mar 1883	
	Zadok	Serena A. Bean	21 Jan 1862	
	Zadok	Clara V. Norris	15 Jan 1890	w
RICKS,	Alcinda	Musco Jackson	29 May 1894	c
	Ernest F.	Emma M. Green	21 Aug 1888	c
	James	Kitty Ricks	28 Jul 1876	
	Jetta	George W. Ball	14 Nov 1876	
	John F.	Ann Elizabeth Scott	13 Jul 1878	c
	John F.	Hannah Snowden	27 Sep 1893	c
	John M.	Ida V. Bargus	15 Dec 1897	c
	Kitty	James Ricks	28 Jul 1876	
	Maggie	John Hawkins	9 Oct 1869	
	Martha A.	Samuel Johnson	24 Jul 1879	
	Monroe	Amanda Dorsey	8 Sep 1868	
	Salena A.	George Jackson	28 Dec 1877	c
	Sarah E.	William P. Hebron	10 Nov 1887	c
	Sarah F.	Thomas Holland, Jr.	28 Sep 1897	c
RIDDLE,	James	Ariana Steuart	6 May 1800	
RIDGELEY - also see RIDGELY, RIDGLEY				
RIDGELEY,	Henry	Rachel Ann Selby	16 Sep 1866	
	Jonathan R.	Susan V. Holland	6 Feb 1865	
	Maria	John Bruce	31 Jan 1874	
	Nicholas	Mary Dells	6 Dec 1805	
	Mary E.	Lewis Randolph	4 Aug 1866	
RIDGELY,	Ann	Alfred Henry Dashiel	25 Oct 1815	

RIDGELY, Elizabeth	John T. Case	21 Dec 1860	
Elizabeth D.	Samuel L. Thompson	17 Feb 1873	
Fanny	William H. Beard	12 Aug 1895	c
Georgiana	Charles W. W. Washington	10 Oct 1898	
Harry S.	Eva B. Repp	19 Oct 1898	w
Irwin Oliver	Florence Brown	27 Mar 1894	w
John T.	Margaret E. Brown	22 Nov 1877	w
John W.	Matilda Brown	18 Feb 1884	w
Lucy S.	John Stone	17 Oct 1821	
Susanna	John Thompson	14 Oct 1805	
RIDGEWAY, Catherine F.	George Johnson	30 Aug 1895	w
Justice	Anne Artist	7 Aug 1798	
RIDGLEY - also see RIDGELEY			
RIDGLEY, Charles F.	Daisie F. Wachter	26 Oct 1897	w
Elizabeth A.	James L. Parsley	1 Jul 1835	
Henry	Fanny Williams	21 Dec 1880	
Jasper	Mary Brown	19 Sep 1867	
John W.	Laura F. Hall	10 Jun 1878	w
Rebecca	Lewis Melton	10 May 1876	
William T.	Carrie Dwyer	17 Oct 1894	w
RIDOUT, Anna	Newton Franklin	26 Dec 1883	c
Mary E.	William A. Wood	17 Nov 1891	c
Rachel	Vachel Duffin	17 Jul 1868	
RIEL, Ella	William Wright	12 Oct 1874	
RIFFLE, George	Mary Conner*	17 Apr 1819	
RIGGES - also see RIGGS			
RIGGES, Eleanor	John Purdom	19 Apr 1805	
George W.	Eliza Robertson	18 Jan 1803	
Henry	Jemima Jacob Griffith	20 Nov 1804	
RIGGLER, Julia	Milton Stewart	26 Sep 1895	c
RIGGS - also see RIGGES			
RIGGS, Albina	Rezin Prather	4 Mar 1867	
Amon Jr.	Isabella Willett	19 Dec 1801	
Anna H.	LeDoux E. Riggs	2 Jun 1894	w
Anne	Henry Kent	29 Jan 1822	
Asenath R.	Richard Young	3 Mar 1847	
Benjamin W.	Asenath R. Brewer	14 Feb 1844	
Bradly J.	Ida C. Watkins	14 Dec 1889	w
Caroline E.	Caleb Dorsey	11 Jan 1834	
Charles	Sarah Ervin	22 Aug 1798	
Charles	Anne America Northcroft	5 Feb 1833	
Clara	Samuel E. Neverson	22 Oct 1873	
Edmond	Jane Willson	21 May 1799	
Eletha	John S. Ball	15 Feb 1831	
Elisha	Margaret V. Howard	23 Feb 1869	
Elizabeth	Marshall P. Howard	21 Oct 1895	w
Elizabeth A.	Sylvester Burns	16 Mar 1856	
Elizabeth A. T.	James Magruder, Jr.	30 Nov 1830	
George W.	Maggie C. Graham	6 Feb 1884	
Henry	Mary L. Wood	18 Oct 1879	
Isaac	Anne Sanders	27 Sep 1800	
James	Senor Tracey	18 Dec 1805	
Jane T.	Remus Dorsey	8 Feb 1826	

* Part of last name from earlier reading

RIGGS,	John	Mary Frazier	26 Jan 1876	c
	John Adams	Annie Eliza Hutton	14 Jan 1856	
	John H.	Rebecca Howard	24 Jun 1800	
	John T.	Catharine Dorsey	13 Oct 1897	c
	John U.	Keziah Purdom	11 Dec 1841	
	Joshua	Ditha Ann Lewis	18 Dec 1835	
	Joshua L.	Mary M. Beall	7 Jan 1889	w
	Julia	Ulisses Griffith	18 Apr 1838	
	Julia	Bazil Hall	13 Apr 1868	
	Julia	John H. Shaw	29 Sep 1881	w
	Kate	Franklin Griffith	5 Jan 1869	
	Kezia	Joseph Woodfield	21 Mar 1849	
	LeDoux E.	Anna H. Riggs	2 Jun 1894	w
	Lizzie	Michael J. Murphy	29 Jan 1880	
	Lucinda	Joseph Hutchison	24 Feb 1864	
	Martha E.	Eli Moulden	10 Mar 1868	
	Mary	George W. Darby	13 Dec 1809	
	Mary	Lloyd T. Macgill	8 Nov 1856	
	Mary E.	Samuel Miles	30 Dec 1823	
	Mary W.	Walter Griffith	22 Nov 1841	
	Matilda	Hilleary Ball	7 May 1822	
	Matilda	Richard Young	14 Jan 1826	
	Melissa D.	Francis A. Bowman	13 Dec 1864	
	Perry	Harriet Davis	29 Jul 1874	
	Rachel G.	Evan A. Jones	4 Jan 1856	
	Rebecca	Robert Spriggs	16 Dec 1873	
	Reuben H.	Laura M. Young	28 Aug 1883	
	Reubin	Mary Willson Thomas	6 Feb 1805	
	Samuel	Laura H. Neel	15 May 1876	
	Samuel of R	Elizabeth H. Worthington	26 Oct 1875	
	Samuel of Reuben	Milkah W. Griffith	2 Dec 1833	
	Samuel A.	Mary A. Fisher	9 Apr 1867	
	Sarah	Aza Darbey	20 Sep 1808	
	Sarah	Daniel Mosburg	13 Jun 1815	
	Sarah F.	Philemon Griffith	22 Sep 1817	
	Shadrack	Mary E. Snowden	22 Nov 1880	
	Susannah	Robert Handlo	28 Jan 1809	
	Sydney Ann Elizabeth	George Gibson	30 Jul 1875	
	Thomas W.	Elizabeth Northcraft	26 Oct 1826	
	Virginia J.	Philip H. Ray	8 Dec 1886	w
	William	Maria Stanton	18 Jul 1893	c
	William E.	Mary E. King	3 Dec 1862	
RILEY - also see REELY				
RILEY,	Camden	Anne Ray	16 Jan 1800	
	Camden	Harriett Windham	7 Feb 1824	
	Eleanor	David Holleday	6 Apr 1847	
	Elizabeth B.	William H. Taylor	26 Oct 1868	
	Fanny R.	Franklin Mace	7 Feb 1854	
	Frederick	Elizabeth Sedgwick	20 Dec 1806	
	George	Mary Richards	18 Oct 1810	
	George W.	Martha Kisner	10 Sep 1855	
	Harry	Rosie B. Bean	5 Jul 1897	w
	Isaac	Matilda Middleton	10 Dec 1818	
	Jerry D.	Mattie E. Brooks	3 Feb 1897	c

RILEY, John C.	Roberta J. Ricketts	22 Apr 1890	w
Josephine	John W. Keys	28 Mar 1866	
Julia	James Handy	18 May 1883	c
Lizzie	Samuel M. Byroad	14 Aug 1877	w
Marion M.	Emily Carter	18 Nov 1889	w
Martha	Samuel W. Magruder	23 Nov 1841	
Mary	Arnold T. Winsor	18 Aug 1818	
Mary	Thomas G. Gibbons	28 Oct 1820	
Mary	James Windham	2 Mar 1826	
Mary George	John W. Letton	27 Nov 1834	
Rachel	Christopher Taylor	25 Nov 1843	
Sarah A.	Edward M. Veirs	25 Nov 1845	
William	Mary Palmer	23 Jun 1809	
William F.	Ann Sedgwick	27 Oct 1802	
William W.	Marien S. Harding	18 May 1881	
RINE - also see RHINE			
RINE, Catharine	John W. Beall	9 Sep 1831	
RINEHART - also see RHINEHART			
RINEHART, Henry	Emma Williams	25 Feb 1880	
William F.	Agnes Perril	27 Jan 1892	w
RINEY, Ann	James Johnson	17 Jan 1799	
Anna	Benjamin Jones	7 Apr 1806	
Delilah	John M. Read	24 Apr 1813	
Margaret	Henry B. Horrell	19 Nov 1808	
Thomas	Catharine Chaney	25 Sep 1815	
RINGOLD, Richard	Eliza Smith	2 Mar 1801	
Tench	Mary Christian Lee	15 Apr 1799	
RIORDAN - also see REARDEN			
RIORDAN, Johanna	John Rush	27 Nov 1880	w
RISLEY, Frances	John H. Gates	1 Jan 1896	w
RITCHIE - also see RICHEY			
RITCHIE, Anne	Thomas Herty	9 Sep 1800	
Janett	James Walter Lowe	17 Oct 1888	w
Luberta	John T. Heisler	8 Jan 1879	w
RITENOUR, Kate	John T. Benson	1 Jun 1865	
RITTENOUR, A. B.	Maggie E. Buxton	18 Aug 1873	
RITTER, Charles N.	Carrie E. Birch	14 Jan 1896	w
Helen	John F. Brown	4 Sep 1896	w
RIVERS, Geroge	Sarah Norman	4 Jun 1881	c
Kate	Albert Gantt	13 Jan 1891	c
RIVES, Mary E.	Charles F. Hackett	25 Nov 1886	c
RIX, John	Jane Green	27 May 1871	
John F.	Maria Brown	24 Dec 1869	
ROACH - also see ROCHE			
ROACH, Dora	Ernest Saunders	5 Jan 1898	w
Mahlon	Elizabeth Young	4 Jan 1810	
ROBB, Catharine Ann	Henry Harding	2 Jun 1812	
Jane N.	Upton Beall	6 Dec 1810	
ROBERSON - also see ROBERTSON			
ROBERSON, Alcinda	Frank S. Wheatley	20 Jun 1895	c
Lucy C.	Daniel G. Barnes	19 May 1896	c
Sarah V. E.	John Henry Johnson	14 May 1883	
ROBERTS, Dorcas	John B. Molan	13 Jan 1817	
Drury	Lameck Saffle	21 Feb 1807	
Hallie S.	William S. Powell	6 Dec 1882	w
Henry	Eleanor Pope	2 Jan 1822	

ROBERTS, Mary	Lilburn Brashears	15 Jan 1803	
William	Susan P. Cloud	29 Apr 1814	
William	Anne Jones	10 Nov 1818	
William A.	Rebecca A. O'Grady	25 Sep 1894	w
William H.	Sarah E. Robertson	1 Jun 1897	w
ROBERTSON - also see ROBERSON			
ROBERTSON, Alexander	Mary Millard*	23 Apr 1800	
Alexander	Rebecca Letcher	8 Feb 1867	
Ann	Daniel Reintzel	20 Dec 1800	
Anne	Anthony Mockbee	2 Jan 1811	
Anne	Aaron Offutt	24 Dec 1812	
Annie	William Jackson	2 Mar 1895	c
Annie L.	John T. Freeman	24 Sep 1895	w
Daniel	Sarah Greenfield	10 Feb 1806	
Eliza	George W. Rigges	18 Jan 1803	
Eliza	Thomas Chayney	11 Jul 1805	
Eliza	Nathan E. Miles	31 May 1847	
Elizabeth	William Baker	28 Feb 1824	
Emeline	Samuel E. Rabbitt	15 Jan 1896	w
Emma	James M. Johnson	24 Sep 1895	w
George	Ann L. Hillard	22 Oct 1861	
George	Amanda D. Cromwell	14 May 1883	c
George J.	Mary E. Whalen	20 Oct 1880	
Grace	Jesse C. Bowen	24 Oct 1898	w
Jane	Luther Snowden	14 Sep 1870	
John	Mary Phelan	18 Jun 1812	
Lawson	Anne Harper	29 Dec 1881	c
Lelia A.	George W. Thompson	24 Sep 1887	w
Lydia Maria	Flodoardo Howard	10 Jun 1833	
Maria	Charles H. Nourse	14 Oct 1841	
Mary	John T. Majors	20 Feb 1843	
Mary	Lewis Clifton	30 Aug 1890	c
Mary E.	George R. Howard	13 Mar 1861	
Mary F.	George W. Lyles	29 Jan 1892	c
Mary G.	Richard B. Bean	10 May 1882	w
Minora	Henry Clements	3 Mar 1887	c
Nelson H.	Mary R. Ricketts	2 Sep 1876	
Nelson R.	Ann S. C. Veirs	27 Dec 1837	
Phebe	Samuel Wright	2 Jun 1800	
Rachel	Edwin M. Muncaster	24 May 1836	
Rena	Albert Wallace	6 Feb 1895	c
Robert	Lucy Ward	1 Nov 1868	
Samuel L.	Alice A. Ricketts	24 Dec 1880	
Sarah	George Ray	5 Mar 1807	
Sarah	Lewis Proctor	10 Jan 1871	
Sarah	James Lee	14 Nov 1883	c
Sarah E.	William H. Roberts	1 Jun 1897	w
Stephan	Airah Reid	15 Jan 1816	
Stephen	Rosie Sarah Long	29 Jun 1891	w
Susan R.	William **. Dorsey	31 Oct 1825	
Virginia	William Ogden	14 Feb 1889	w
William	Harriett Cook	30 Sep 1813	
William M.	Mary E. Hall	3 Nov 1898	c

* Last name from earlier reading
** Initial I or J

```
ROB--, Margaret*             James Farmer              4 Aug 1812
ROBEY - also see ROBY
ROBEY, Alice                 John C. Truxton          24 Apr 1872
       Barbara N.            John Willcoxen           25 Nov 1830
       Berry                 Margarett Brown          19 May 1828
       Berry Jr.             Lucretia Burton          19 Aug 1801
       Barton S.             Ann R. Rich              30 Jan 1867
       Edward V.             Daisy L. Kelchner        19 Jun 1895 w
       Eleanor               Allin Macintosh          23 Aug 1798
       Elizabeth             Joseph Lewis             17 Nov 1814
       Jemima                Lewis Barrett            25 Sep 1869
       John                  Elizabeth A. Woodjett     6 Jan 1815
       Joshua Thomas         Hariet E. Marlow         22 Feb 1871
       Wilton                Susie E. Barrett         17 Dec 1878 w
ROBINSON, Angelina G.        Washington W. Owen        9 Nov 1836
          Annie V.           Josephus Hammond         28 Apr 1896 c
          Eliza Ann          Aaron Turner             14 Jun 1865
          Ellen              Lewis H. Ball            21 Mar 1840
          John T.            Harriet A. Jarvis        15 Jan 1858
          Joseph F.          Elizabeth Hobbs           4 Feb 1806
          Kate J.            James R. Aylmer          11 Jul 1885
          Lyles R.           Elizabeth A. Lyles        6 Sep 1831
          Mamie E.           Walter Carter            29 Nov 1897 c
          Martha             Nicodemus Hall           13 Jun 1896 c
          Mary               William G. Frazier       30 Oct 1886 c
          Mary Ann           George F. Wise           19 May 1873
          Reuben             Louisa Neal               1 May 1873
          Sarah V.           G. E. Gates               9 Oct 1878
ROBY - also see ROBEY
ROBY, Annie K.               Granville J. Embrey      20 Dec 1890 w
      Basil                  Deborah Beall            13 Dec 1832
      Berry                  Dorcas Browning           6 Aug 1833
      Henry                  Elizabeth Browning       22 Dec 1800
      John N.                Ann Higgins              14 Jul 1832
      Margaret E.            Thomas B. Burton         21 Jan 1861
      Mary Ann               Middleton Davis          13 Sep 1821
      William B.             Margarett Soper          18 Dec 1830
ROCHE - also see ROACH
ROCHE, Elizabeth**           Hiram Beall              26 Jan 1824
ROCK, Eugene Gilford         Mary Emma Hitchens        5 Jul 1892 w
RODY, Mal                    Charles Johnson           3 Apr 1878
ROGERS, Claude               Eugenia Crawford         28 Jul 1894 w
        Micajah              Catharine A. Porter      24 Nov 1835
ROLAND, Rose Lee             George Rhodes             1 Oct 1891 c
ROLINSON - also see ROLLISON
ROLINSON, Henry              Leana Crummer            15 Mar 1880 c
ROLISON, William             Sarah R. Chiswell         2 Jan 1865
ROLLES - also see ROLLS
ROLLES, Martin               Ruth Frazier             28 Sep 1898 c
ROLLINS - also see RAWLINS
ROLLINS, Florence            Perry Tyler              *** Jul 1882
```

* Remainder of name off page; looks like could be Robey
** Insert in a different handwriting has been made after Hiram
   and another before Elizabeth; not clear enough to read
*** Cannot read day; between 10 and 20

ROLLINS, Isaac W.	M. Bess Thompson	18 Sep 1866	
Mary F.	Washington Spence	14 Mar 1893	c
William C.	Sarah A. Thompson	24 May 1858	
ROLLISON - also see ROLINSON, ROLISON			
ROLLISON, John C.	Annie M. Savage	14 Aug 1898	w
ROLLS - also see ROLLES			
ROLLS, Mailin	Mary E. Hood	16 Dec 1881	
ROOK, Margaret	Richard T. Leizear	14 Feb 1888	w
ROOT, Jacob	Eliza Ann Zeigler	2 May 1835	
ROSE, Daniel	Catherine Harrisson	13 Apr 1830	
Joseph	Elizabeth Hickman	17 Oct 1827	
Maria	William H. Warren	9 May 1885	c
ROSENDOFF, John	Rebecca Rhinehart	2 Jan 1878	w
ROSS, Alfred	Rachel Stewart	8 Jul 1886	c
Cordelia	Isaac E. M. Warren	12 Nov 1885	
Ellen	James B. Nobbs	30 May 1839	
Flora	Adam Powell	9 Feb 1882	
George	Louisa Hart	29 May 1893	c
Ginnie	Thomas Blackston	17 May 1893	c
Harriet Ann	Henry Clagett	3 Jan 1898	c
John T.	Mary V. Stewart	31 Dec 1895	w
Maggie	Alfred Johnson	12 Feb 1877	c
Richard	Elizabeth Magee	30 Mar 1819	
ROSTON, James	Sophia Moore	19 Feb 1816	
ROUNDS, James	Mary A. Owens	30 Aug 1874	
John	Charlotte A. Hill	8 Mar 1883	c
Mary A.	John H. Budd	28 Oct 1885	c
ROWAN, Mary R.	Godtlieb S. Stadtler	22 Aug 1891	w
ROWZEE - also see ROZER			
ROWZEE, Reuben	Sarah Porter	21 Feb 1857	
ROYER, Adam	Cordelia Baker	1 Jan 1812	
Bettie L.	William G. Garland	19 Jul 1897	w
Cora S.	John A. Howard	12 Mar 1897	w
Lizzie Z.	James B. Schroder	10 Nov 1894	w
ROZER - also see ROWZEE, ROZIER			
ROZER, Charles B.	Mary E. Anderson	29 Dec 1882	w
Francis W.	F. Virginia Anderson	19 Sep 1860	
ROZIER, Flora	Lewis G. Procton	9 Aug 1893	c
John	Frances Battis	26 Dec 1873	
Martha J.	Thomas J. Birch	26 Jun 1890	c
RUBLE, Carrie E.	Crittenden C. Hipkins	17 Sep 1895	w
RUDASILL, William P.	Lucy L. Hickerson	28 Apr 1892	w
RUDD, Linnie	William H. Schaefer	29 Jul 1890	w
RUNALDS, Susie A.	Charles William Mullen	5 Nov 1879	c
RUPLI, Josephine	Matthew McCully	14 Jul 1891	w
RUSE, Lavinia	Edgar D. Vinson	5 Aug 1895	w
RUSH, John	Johanna Riordan	27 Nov 1880	w
RUSK, Samuel	Mariya Dennis	27 Sep 1825	
RUSSEL, George Washington	Deborah Bond	20 Aug 1885	c
RUSSELL, Annie	John Washington	11 Oct 1877	c
Bettie	Andrew Shafer	22 Dec 1871	
Carrie	Carlo F.L.Z. Caracristi	3 Oct 1891	w
George W.	Lizzie Budd	12 Jul 1877	c
James H.	Bettie Jackson	21 Aug 1893	c
John T.	Katherine Wendehuth	6 Jun 1895	w
Matilda P.	William Brewer	12 Feb 1878	w

RUSSELL, Mary H.	William P. Bradley	6 Jan 1875
Perry	Maggie Campbell	21 Mar 1898 c
Robert G.	Susan H. Worthington	31 Aug 1818
Virginia	John B. Brewer	6 Oct 1874
William W.	Jessie E. Mathewson	5 May 1891 w
RUST, Sallie J.	William M. Canby	8 Jan 1884
RUTHERFORD, Edith C.	Millard F. Holland	25 Jun 1886 w
RYAN - also see RYON		
RYAN, Eleanor	Edward Gaffney	22 May 1826
Mary	John Bean	4 Dec 1828
Pocahontas	Charles E. Bishop	26 Jun 1889 w
Rebecca J.	James W. Simons	20 Aug 1878 w
RYE, Edwin A.*	Julia I. N. Williams	20 Nov 1876
RYON - also see RYAN		
RYON, Jennie A.	Ross P. Hunt	11 May 1898 w
Samuel E.	Rebecca ?. Burgess	1 Jul 1867
Washington	Sophronia Lea	5 Dec 1862
RYS - see note at Edwin A. RYE		
SA----, Elizabeth**	Michael Grimes	28 Jun 1800
SADTLER, Louis	Elizabeth Gaegler	13 Jan 1872
SAFFELL - also see SAFFLE		
SAFFELL, Airy M.	John T. Selby	8 Nov 1882 w
Amos	Mary Lemmon	24 Nov 1813
Ann	Frederick Nusz	29 Dec 1830
Cassandra	Hezekiah Selby	16 Nov 1814
Charles Jr.	Elizabeth M. Thompson	3 Jan 1828
Deborah	Orlando Saffell	11 Oct 1813
Hezekiah	Lydda Davis	8 Sep 1804
Jeremiah	Mary Moore	18 Dec 1802
Lydia	Reubin Saffell	24 Nov 1814
Mary	Lewis Barber	16 Feb 1831
Mary S.	Richard Mills	8 Feb 1849
Orlando	Deborah Saffell	11 Oct 1813
Otho	Amelia Ann Merick	7 Mar 1826
Reubin	Lydia Saffell	24 Nov 1814
Sarah	Benjamin Easton	21 Dec 1826
Sarah V.	John A. Stewart	10 Apr 1855
Thomas W.	Mary Caroline Stewart	4 Apr 1834
Thomas W.	Teresa Ann Stewart	16 Jan 1837
William Orlando	Ruth Ann Dunhardt	19 Nov 1879
SAFFLE, Lameck	Drury Roberts	21 Feb 1807
SAGE, Charles W.	Mary Ellen Warfield	21 Sep 1880
Harriet R.	Henry Dwyer	17 May 1880
ST. CLAIR, Matilda	Samuel Jackson	24 Sep 1818
SANDERS - also see SAUNDERS		
SANDERS, Ann	Ashford Trail	28 Dec 1803
Anne	Isaac Riggs	27 Sep 1800
Edward	Anna Gatton	16 Apr 1801
Margarett	Edward Fennell	4 Aug 1800
SANDIE, Edith M.	William O. Hamilton	13 Jul 1897 w
SANDS, Catharine	William Malen	31 Aug 1816
Elizabeth	Jesse Severns	8 Mar 1826

* This could be Rye
** Page torn; remainder of last name missing

SANDS, Elizabeth Ann	John Duley	2 Dec 1841
Harriet Ann	John W. Spates	22 Jan 1845
Mary	George Culp	16 Feb 1803
Mary	Michael H. Letton	16 Apr 1840
Rachael A.	David Martin	28 Sep 1826
Susan	Jannaro S. Farre	17 Jun 1813
William	Peona Cool	14 Nov 1814
SANFORD, Mabel G.	Charles R. Hughes	21 Aug 1897 w
Margaret	James Long	21 Jun 1798
SANTEE, Michael J. Jr.*	Elizabeth Whitton	8 Jan 1898 w
SANTMAN, Margaret M.	Patrick F. Mulcahy	16 Oct 1895 w
Willoughby	Lula M. Appleby	12 Sep 1895 w
SAULSMAN, George H.	Ida White	12 Nov 1895 w
SAUMENIG, Samuel S.	Rosa A. Easton	7 Mar 1889 w
SAUNDERS - also see SANDERS		
SAUNDERS, Aaron R.	Ann B. Lee	6 Sep 1831
Ann	Asbury Offutt	19 Apr 1871
Annie A.	Robert G. Davidson	18 Jan 1853
Caroline	Brice Selby	23 Sep 1817
Ernest	Dora Roach	5 Jan 1898 w
John	Emily C. W. White	15 Nov 1852
Lucy L.	Henry W. Offutt	7 Jan 1889 w
Maria	Richard **. Elliott	3 May 1832
Mary J.	Nelson Johnson	17 Apr 1871
Nathan W.	Addie Clagett	24 Dec 1879 w
SAVAGE, Annie M.	John C. Rollison	14 Aug 1898 w
William P.	Ann E. Waters	26 Nov 1888 w
SAVOY, Nanny	John White	1 Dec 1868
Sarah	Franklin Jamieson	24 Nov 1866
SAXTON - also see SEXTON		
SAXTON, Charles Nial	Nellie Rea	25 Jan 1894 w
Samuel S.	Carrie B. Burnett	13 Jun 1891 w
SAYER, Elizabeth	John Wise	22 Feb 1816
SAYLOR, Eliza B.	Wallace B. Daniel	20 Feb 1826
Lucy	Levi Jones	19 Aug 1878
SCAGGS, Mary Ann	Jacob B. Learrick	13 Nov 1851
SCALES, Benjamin	Annie Johnson	13 Jun 1895 w
Nelson	Emeline Nelson	14 Nov 1868
William N.	Mary E. Johnson	12 Nov 1895 c
SCANLON, Charles	Mary A. Walker	27 Mar 1894 w
SCHAB, Frederick S.	Margaret M. Dutton	19 Jul 1888 w
SCHAEFER - also see SHAEFFER		
SCHAEFER, Elizabeth A.	John W. Boggess	1 Sep 1891 w
William H.	Linnie Rudd	29 Jul 1890 w
SCHAEFFER, Elizabeth A.	William J. Williams	26 Nov 1883
Lelia N.	Aldridge G. Hilleary	19 Oct 1898 w
Mary V.	Daniel J. Getzendanner	16 Nov 1891 w
SCHAFFER, Thomas H.	Elizabeth Young	14 Feb 1867
SCHARER - also see SCHERRER, SCHEIRER, SHERER,		
SHEARER, SHERRER, SHAERER		
SCHARER, Charles	Ellen Cragin	22 Jan 1879 w
SCHEARER, Caroline	Henry Schrieder	22 Mar 1870
SCHEELE, Mabel A.	Alfred M. Vaux	16 Mar 1892 w

* Could be Sauter, Santer, Sautee; also could be Whitter
** Initial I or J

SCHEIRER - also see SCHARER			
SCHEIRER, Emma E.	William F. Houser	1 Jun 1897	w
SCHELLINGER, George W.	Florence M. Gates	13 Aug 1895	w
SCHERIN, Eleanor	John Corn	25 Aug 1800	
SCHERRER - also see SCHARER			
SCHERRER, William	Katie Curtin	14 Feb 1893	w
SCHERRET, Elizer	John H. Griffith	30 Sep 1800	
SCHILLER, Annie L.	James R. Ball	26 Oct 1896	w
Charles C.	Katherine G. Grimmel	24 Aug 1895	w
SCHISSEL - also see CISSEL			
SCHISSEL, Samuel	Margaret D. Beall	20 Jan 1825	
SCHLADT, Peter A.	Annie Alvorth	18 Nov 1892	w
SCHLENTHER, John A.	Catharina M. Barnes	28 Oct 1895	w
SCHLOB, Wilhelmina	John F. Fry	21 Jul 1879	w
SCHLOSSER, Mary C.	James D. Kettner	19 Jul 1893	w
SCHMID, Frank	Henriette D.E. Obermann	9 Apr 1891	w
SCHOLL - also see SHOLL			
SCHOLL, Anna M.	Benjamin N. Gott	18 Apr 1883	
Caroline V.	Frank P. Clark	8 Jul 1887	w
Catharine	Alfred Griffith	30 Mar 1812	
Margaret	Samuel Willson	25 Mar 1824	
Mary Eloise	Henry R. Jones	7 Jan 1876	
SCHOOLEY, John C.	Jessie L. Graff	13 Oct 1891	w
SCHOOLY, Annie C.	Samuel K. Johnson	28 Jan 1873	
SCHRIDER - also see SCRIDER			
SCHRIDER, Anna E.	Frederick King	10 Sep 1891	w
Benjamin	Susan King	6 May 1862	
John T.	Clara J. Hutchison	26 May 1897	w
SCHRIEDER, Henry	Caroline Schearer	22 Mar 1870	
SCHRODER, James B.	Lizzie Z. Royer	10 Nov 1894	w
SCHROEDER, Henry A. A.	Lelia S. Brett	6 May 1898	w
SCHROTH, Frank	Catharine Kramer	23 Jan 1884	
SCHWAB, Rose	George W. Byron	21 Nov 1896	w
SCHWARTZBACH - also see SWARTZBACK, SCHWATZPECK			
SCHWARTZBACH, John F.	Lily Handley	5 Jan 1888	w
SCHWARTZBACK, Edward T.	Janie Kelly	31 Oct 1891	w
SCHWARTZBECK, Louis A.	Hattie S. Baughman	1 Jul 1893	w
SCHWARTZEL, William	Katie Kemp	20 Sep 1894	w
SCHWATZPECK, Frederick J.	Ann M. C. Poster	4 Jun 1856	
SCHWERING, William E.	Effie L. Johnson	9 Feb 1891	w
SCISSEL - also see CISSEL			
SCISSEL, Rebecca	John Belt	5 Nov 1806	
SCOTT, Albert N.	Emilie E. Knoch	5 Dec 1892	w
Alfred	Sarah Blacklock	17 Oct 1868	
Amos	Anne West	11 Sep 1798	
Ann Elizabeth	John F. Ricks	13 Jul 1878	c
Catharine L.	William H. Offutt	22 Jan 1824	
Cecilia B.	John W. Anderson	19 Oct 1896	w
Charlotte	Robert Brown	1 Feb 1894	c
David Joshua	Maria Jones	12 Mar 1869	
Elizabeth	John Joseph Benton	23 Feb 1815	
Elizabeth L.	Zadok Offutt of William	2 Jan 1816	
Elizabeth Margaret	Patrick D. Cavenaugh	29 Dec 1840	
Emma F.	James C. Chesaldine	3 Sep 1896	w
Frances	Samuel Carter	1 Jun 1893	c
Frances	Wilson Hull	24 May 1898	c

SCOTT, Frances V.	John T. Stetson	25 Oct 1869	
George	C. J. Honery	6 Feb 1868	
Harriet	George A. Jones	17 Dec 1896	c
Harriot	George Jenkins	22 Jan 1818	
Harry R.	Alta M. Winfree	24 Sep 1896	w
Henry	Mary Turley	21 May 1885	c
Henson	Margaret Johnson	30 Dec 1884	c
James H.	Mary A. Hammond	22 Oct 1887	c
Jane R.	Tilghman E. Dove	1 Aug 1889	c
John	Eliza M. Key	10 Jul 1816	
John D.	Mary E. Browning	14 Nov 1848	
Judith	Benjamin Fowler	2 Feb 1800	
Juliet Ann	Richard ?. Gittings	21 Apr 1825	
Lucy V.	Charles T. Hill	24 Nov 1886	c
Margaret C.	Charles J. Kichnert	7 Oct 1878	w
Margaret E.	Oratio Clagett	28 Feb 1832	
Maria	Alexander Hamilton	9 Feb 1893	c
Mary	John Bacon	27 Dec 1883	c
Mary Ann	Samuel Hopkins	26 Dec 1831	
Mary D.	Henry Carter	17 May 1878	c
Mary E.	John T. F. Hall	20 Sep 1893	c
Michael	Margaret Howard	29 Jul 1893	c
Rachael	Berry Gittings	25 Mar 1820	
Rachel	William Young	17 Sep 1844	
Rachel Ann	William Charity	24 Apr 1884	c
Robert E. L.	Minnie Bray	5 Aug 1891	w
Samuel	Martha Linn	4 May 1875	
Samuel	Elizabeth Pelton	6 Oct 1888	c
Sarah	George W. Offutt	25 Jul 1821	
Sarah	David Williams	17 Aug 1888	c
Tandy	Eleanora Jackson	16 Feb 1898	c
Thomas	Annie Bowen	5 Sep 1868	
Thomas Jr.	Margarett Williams	8 Aug 1814	
Thomas B.	Polly Offutt	16 Nov 1815	
Thomas B.	Elizabeth Briggs	1 Jan 1824	
William	Fanny Musgrove	8 Mar 1811	
William A.	Sarah B. Gettings	5 Dec 1829	
William F.	Mary A. Jackson	10 Feb 1892	c
William H.	Sarah A. Ellis	8 Apr 1895	c
SCRIDER - also see SCHRIDER			
SCRIDER, Charles A.	Mary S. Hutchison	10 Oct 1893	w
SCRIVENER, Allen	Martha Thompson	20 Oct 1853	
Margaret Ann	Grafton N. Powell	15 Mar 1827	
Margarett	Thomas Hickman	20 Feb 1798	
SCRIVNER, Elender	Stephen Penn	26 Oct 1798	
James	Elizabeth Huddlestone	8 Jan 1834	
Rezin	Mary Sears	3 Feb 1813	
Sarah	John McFee	6 Aug 1814	
Sarah	Leonard Williams	17 Dec 1814	
SCROGGINS, Annie G.	Michael G. Lauxmann	6 Aug 1890	w
SEADERS - also see SEEDERS			
SEADERS, Rebecca	Henry Hewel	6 Dec 1799	
SEAL, Alley	William Burgess	16 Jun 1801	
SEALS, Ferdinand	Hattie Weldon	20 Sep 1889	c
SEAR, William	Sarah Duley	27 Dec 1814	
SEARCH, Cordelia A.	John H. Parsley	3 Feb 1885	w

SEARES, Lethana*	Turner Ball	12 Jan 1818	
SEARS, Catharine	Levy Baker	30 Mar 1815	
Mary	Rezin Scrivner	3 Feb 1813	
William	Rachel Ann Duvall	15 Nov 1842	
SEARSY, William	Ann Hickman	11 Mar 1814	
SEATON, John	Marcy Ann Wise	4 Jan 1800	
SEBASTIAN, Margaret H.	David Lawrence	3 Jan 1865	
SEDGEWICK - also see SEDWICK			
SEDGEWICK, Mary	Alexander Callico	4 Jan 1800	
SEDGWICK, Ann	William F. Riley	27 Oct 1802	
Benjamin	Susannah Nicholson	2 Jan 1799	
Caroline	Samuel T. Dickerson	8 Nov 1866	
Catharine A.	William H. Budd	** Jan 1880	
Charles	Lizzie Norriss	25 Sep 1879	c
Clarissa	Joseph Hicks	24 Aug 1871	
Elizabeth	Alexander Davis	6 Feb 1802	
Elizabeth	Frederick Riley	20 Dec 1806	
Harry	Bessie Smith	4 Feb 1898	c
Horace	Emma Cook	22 Dec 1887	c
Jane	Jonas B. Snap	24 Dec 1841	
Joshua	Ella Bowen	6 Apr 1883	c
Julianna	Thomas Bond	20 Mar 1867	
Keziah	Aden Bowman	3 Jan 1809	
Mary	James Hurdle	19 Dec 1801	
Noah H.	Mary M. Noland	19 Dec 1881	
Richard	Mary A. Fawcett	14 Nov 1872	
Samuel	Marcellena Wright	13 Dec 1866	
Sarah	Joseph Hopwood	26 Jan 1814	
Thomas	Ann Atcherson	20 Feb 1799	
Thomas	Massie Williams	8 Apr 1868	
William	Ann Bowman	5 Dec 1811	
SEDWICK - also see SEDGEWICK			
SEDWICK, Anne	William Hilton	31 Dec 1822	
Rachel	Alfred Oden	23 Apr 1835	
SEEDERS - also SEADERS			
SEEDERS, Anne	John Yewell	3 Apr 1804	
SEEK, Margaret A.	William ***. Carroll	24 May 1893	w
SEGALLS, Albert	Rachel Johnson	6 Sep 1873	
SEGLER, Charles	Mary Lee	3 Apr 1871	
SELBEY, Mary	John Wright	31 Dec 1806	
SELBY - also see SELBEY, SILBY			
SELBY, Alice A.	Francis T. Douglass	22 Jan 1870	
Allen	Sarah Davis	9 Jan 1810	
Allen	Delilah Ricketts	9 Jun 1815	
Allen	Harriet Gloyd	14 Aug 1841	
Bessie J.	George T. Beavers	29 Dec 1896	w
Brice	Catharine Marker	8 Oct 1801	
Brice	Caroline Saunders	23 Sep 1817	
Caroline	Nathan Holland	29 Nov 1846	
Cora Rebecca	Lawrence Lowe	15 Apr 1884	
Delila	William Thomas Ricketts	8 Dec 1846	
Elizabeth V.	John W. Bean	3 Jun 1875	

* Both last names from earlier reading
** Cannot read day; between 21 and 29
*** Blot on initial

SELBY,	George A.	Phebe Kidwell	15 May 1896	w
	Harriet	Georg W. Reed	16 Feb 1883	
	Hattie A.	Andrew J. Mobley	17 Dec 1889	w
	Henry E.	Minerva Ricketts	4 Sep 1879	
	Hezekiah	Cassandra Saffell	16 Nov 1814	
	Howard M.	Martha E. Read	23 Aug 1882	w
	James N.	Mary A. Lowe	15 Jun 1885	
	James W.	Velinda C. Miller	22 Dec 1862	
	John	Elizabeth Berry	15 Nov 1806	
	John A.	Henrietta Mullican	20 Jan 1898	w
	John E.	Margaret Beall	18 May 1820	
	John T.	Margaret Ann Bowman	10 Jan 1861	
	John T.	Airy M. Saffell	8 Nov 1882	w
	Joseph A.	Florence V. Keller	1 Oct 1883	
	Margaret	William Jones	11 Jun 1810	
	Mary A.	Frederick T. Case	18 Jun 1861	
	Mary Ann	William E. Baker	21 Jul 1848	
	Mary E.	Richard Offutt	2 Apr 1883	w
	Mary G.	John W. Mobley	22 Aug 1891	w
	Nancy	Isaac McDowell	31 May 1817	
	Nancy	John C. L. Creamer	2 Feb 1851	
	Nathan R.	Susan R. Ray	4 Feb 1847	
	Nicholas E.	Teresa J. Arnold	24 Apr 1897	w
	Rachel A.	Thomas L. Offutt	11 May 1852	
	Rachel Ann	Henry Ridgeley	16 Sep 1866	
	Rebecca	Elijah Collins	9 Sep 1800	
	Rebecca	Peter Moran	20 Nov 1812	
	Rhoda	Otho H. Duvall	22 Dec 1849	
	Richard	Verlinda Fields	8 Apr 1856	
	Rose Anna	James M. Elder	18 May 1879	w
	Ruth	Walter Jenkins	8 Feb 1799	
	Samuel E.	Martha A. Ricketts	14 Sep 1857	
	Sarah	Stephen Willson	5 Feb 1812	
	Sarah Ann	Evan Bowman	25 Jan 1871	
	Susanna	James Milles*	23 Jun 1818	
	Thomas	Rebeccah Burgess	7 Aug 1810	
	William B.	Annie Hamel	7 May 1887	w
	William E.	Sarah Ann Higdon	30 Oct 1874	
	William H.	Mary Harriss	5 Feb 1850	
	William R.	Susan Ricketts	19 Jan 1846	
	William R.	Emmeline Miller	2 Feb 1886	w
SELF,	Singleton	Catharine Kindle	6 Nov 1812	
SELLERS,	Martha	William Prather	20 May 1895	c
SELLMAN,	Alonza	Sarah I. Neel	12 Jul 1870	
	Gassaway	Juletta Gettings	14 Jul 1836	
	Gassaway	Sarah E. Berry	27 Apr 1882	
	George	Ann Tuttle	31 Aug 1850	
	George	Margaret Hortman	23 Feb 1852	
	Georgie A.	William E. Dill	4 Apr 1888	w
	John	Rebecca A. Harriss	21 Feb 1853	
	John P.	Elizabeth Young	31 Oct 1898	w
	Mary	Daniel T. Jones	9 Jan 1836	
	Mary A.	Coonrod P. Weaver	26 Jan 1856	
	Nancy E.	George N. Walter	20 Mar 1888	w

* Name as written; other records show Joseph Mills to be correct

SHAW, William	Sarah Murphey	24 Aug 1841
William E.	Annie M. Fawcett	17 Jan 1866
SHEA, Mary Lee	Harry L. Burdette	26 May 1886 w
SHEAFFER - also see SCHAEFER		
SHEAFFER, Sarah C.	Richard H. Parsley	25 Dec 1866
SHEARER - also see SCHARER		
SHEARER, Bertie S.	Robert L. Clabaugh	30 Nov 1896 w
Mollie	Joseph Ambrose Dove	6 Oct 1885 w
SHEARRER, John	Mary A. Dwyer	19 Dec 1868
SHEATS, Charles	Hannah Hobbs	1 Nov 1798
SHECKELLS - also see SHEKELLS, SHECKELS, SHECKLES		
SHECKELLS, Anntonie	Louis E. Reinhart	5 Apr 1897 w
Essie H.	William E. Poole	27 Sep 1898 w
Harriet	Grafton Duvall	26 Feb 1834
Richard	Juliet Hilton	25 May 1825
Sarah	Alexander Howard	18 Apr 1801
SHECKELS, Sarah Rebecca	Charles W. Souder	17 Nov 1886 w
SHECKLES, Asa	Rebecca Boone	5 Apr 1811
SHECKLES, Cephas H.	Amelia J. Lowman	27 Jan 1853
John T.	Juliet Moxley	6 Feb 1852
Nathan E.	Edith B. Bowen	5 Oct 1893 w
Rezin E.	Julia Ann Poole	22 May 1895 w
William S.	Rachel A. Barber	20 Feb 1866
SHEDD, Caroline A.	Charles C. Prescott	22 Feb 1898 w
Mary L.	Frank H. Buechler	31 Aug 1897 w
SHEDRICK, Helen	Robert Neucy	31 Jul 1889 c
Lizzie	Nathan Anderson	16 May 1893 c
SHEERWOOD - also see SHERWOOD		
SHEERWOOD, Gerrard	Sarah Weeks	16 Dec 1800
SHEHAN, Joseph	Julia Hill	21 Jan 1800
SHEKELL, Hattie A.	William Reuben Pumphrey	13 Apr 1882
SHEKELLS - also see SHECKELLS		
SHEKELLS, Abraham	Harriett Thompson	6 Oct 1823
Elender	Robert Wilson	29 Oct 1798
SHELLEY, Aaron	Henrietta Swailes	2 Jun 1886 c
SHELTON - also see CHILTON		
SHELTON, Elizabeth	Joseph Magruder	3 Sep 1817
Henry	Maggie Wood	1 Nov 1898 c
Jane	Thomas W. Green	13 Mar 1829
John	Agnes Cooke	14 Feb 1893 c
Joshua	Elizabeth Dyur	22 Feb 1810
Martha	Josias Douglass	5 Feb 1806
Rosannah	Thomas Hagan	28 May 1811
SHEPHERD, Thomas	Bersheba Swann	13 Jan 1830
SHEPLEY, Frances W.	Ernest S. Fenwick	20 Jul 1892 w
SHERER - also see SCHARER		
SHERER, Mary C.	Nicholas Harding	1 Jun 1893 w
SHERIDAN, Palma	Henry M. Black	3 Sep 1895 w
SHERMAN, Charles E.	Miss Margaret A. Elgar	8 Aug 1837
Fannie E.	William M. Fling	29 Jan 1889 w
Matilda	Hanson Willson	28 May 1828
SHERN - also see SHURN		
SHERN, Charles W.	Mary F. Adams	20 Nov 1890 c
William H.	Admenia E. Wallace	27 Feb 1894 c
SHERRER - also see SCHARER		
SHERRER, Franklin P.	Elizabeth A. Wood	4 Dec 1894 w

SHAW, Anna R.	Simon H. Williams	3 Mar 1887	c
Annie E.	William L. Beall	19 Dec 1871	
Annie L.	Thomas F. Thompson	9 Aug 1883	
Catherine	Thomas Hilleary Burriss	25 Oct 1841	
Daniel	Mary Ann Bowen	21 Jun 1872	
Daniel	Emeline Brown	13 May 1876	
Edward	Virginia Sullivan	1 Jul 1878	
Elbert	Eliza Rawlings	20 Nov 1837	
Eliza	James T. Lazenby	21 Jan 1830	
Eliza	Henry Pearce	26 Jun 1851	
Eliza V.	John H. Harris	11 Mar 1875	
Elizabeth	Charles Williams	22 Feb 1800	
Elizabeth	Edward H. Williams	23 Nov 1829	
Elizabeth	William H. Gittings	12 Apr 1854	
Elizabeth E.	Walter B. Ealy	21 Dec 1897	w
Emma	William Penn	27 Dec 1886	w
George	Artemesia Garrett	18 Feb 1874	
George W.	Martha E. Case	25 Mar 1847	
Isaiah	Ann H. Cashell	7 Dec 1852	
James Alexander	Mary Ratliff	22 Nov 1800	
James L.	Eliza Thompson	29 Nov 1830	
James W.	Mary L. Souder	21 May 1896	w
John	Mary Goodzebath	25 Feb 1801	
John	Deborah Snider	11 Jan 1840	
John H.	Julia Riggs	29 Sep 1881	w
John W.	Sarah M. Case	16 Jan 1838	
Jonathan	Susannah Higdon	3 Mar 1806	
Jonathan R.	Elizabeth Jane Williams	12 Dec 1833	
Joseph Z.	Susie Free	10 Jan 1882	
Julia A.	John A. Lewis	21 Nov 1856	
Laura M.	James H. Bond	4 May 1881	
Leonard D.	Ann H. Bennett	23 Mar 1832	
Levi	Sarah A. Murphey	16 Nov 1859	
Levi	Elizabeth Leizear	15 Mar 1869	
Lucretia M.	Harrison D. Darby	19 Nov 1864	
Lucy	James Bolton	23 Nov 1799	
Margaret	Aaron Gartrell	21 Sep 1815	
Margaret A.	Hilleary O. Higgins	3 Apr 1854	
Martha F.	Julian M. Brunett	27 Dec 1893	w
Martha R.	John G. Trundle	6 Feb 1867	
Mary	Charles R. Purdom	24 Jan 1829	
Mary E.	John W. Brown	22 Nov 1852	
Mary E.	Henry M. Clagett	14 Jan 1873	
Mary E.	Clarence Lee Bennett	7 Sep 1898	w
Mary E. A.	Mortimer T. Young	23 Sep 1867	
Mary Jane	Zachariah J. Davis	17 Aug 1843	
Nathan	Catharine Grantt	17 Jan 1810	
Nathan	Achsah A. R. Fairall	14 Jan 1852	
Rebecca	Elisha Hoskins	5 Mar 1800	
Rezin	Anna Crim	31 Jan 1799	
Sarah	Francis Beall	25 Nov 1806	
Sarah	G. Francis Cashell	8 Mar 1865	
Sarah Ann	Theophilus L. Benton	6 Mar 1843	
Susan	Reuben Baker	31 Dec 1839	
Susannah	William Thompson	14 Dec 1836	
William	Elizabeth Fish	16 Dec 1826	

SHAW, William	Sarah Murphey	24 Aug 1841
William E.	Annie M. Fawcett	17 Jan 1866
SHEA, Mary Lee	Harry L. Burdette	26 May 1886 w
SHEAFFER - also see SCHAEFER		
SHEAFFER, Sarah C.	Richard H. Parsley	25 Dec 1866
SHEARER - also see SCHARER		
SHEARER, Bertie S.	Robert L. Clabaugh	30 Nov 1896 w
Mollie	Joseph Ambrose Dove	6 Oct 1885 w
SHEARRER, John	Mary A. Dwyer	19 Dec 1868
SHEATS, Charles	Hannah Hobbs	1 Nov 1798
SHECKELLS - also see SHEKELLS, SHECKELS, SHECKLES		
SHECKELLS, Anntonie	Louis E. Reinhart	5 Apr 1897 w
Essie H.	William E. Poole	27 Sep 1898 w
Harriet	Grafton Duvall	26 Feb 1834
Richard	Juliet Hilton	25 May 1825
Sarah	Alexander Howard	18 Apr 1801
SHECKELS, Sarah Rebecca	Charles W. Souder	17 Nov 1886 w
SHECKLES, Asa	Rebecca Boone	5 Apr 1811
SHECKLES, Cephas H.	Amelia J. Lowman	27 Jan 1853
John T.	Juliet Moxley	6 Feb 1852
Nathan E.	Edith B. Bowen	5 Oct 1893 w
Rezin E.	Julia Ann Poole	22 May 1895 w
William S.	Rachel A. Barber	20 Feb 1866
SHEDD, Caroline A.	Charles C. Prescott	22 Feb 1898 w
Mary L.	Frank H. Buechler	31 Aug 1897 w
SHEDRICK, Helen	Robert Neucy	31 Jul 1889 c
Lizzie	Nathan Anderson	16 May 1893 c
SHEERWOOD - also see SHERWOOD		
SHEERWOOD, Gerrard	Sarah Weeks	16 Dec 1800
SHEHAN, Joseph	Julia Hill	21 Jan 1800
SHEKELL, Hattie A.	William Reuben Pumphrey	13 Apr 1882
SHEKELLS - also see SHECKELLS		
SHEKELLS, Abraham	Harriett Thompson	6 Oct 1823
Elender	Robert Wilson	29 Oct 1798
SHELLEY, Aaron	Henrietta Swailes	2 Jun 1886 c
SHELTON - also see CHILTON		
SHELTON, Elizabeth	Joseph Magruder	3 Sep 1817
Henry	Maggie Wood	1 Nov 1898 c
Jane	Thomas W. Green	13 Mar 1829
John	Agnes Cooke	14 Feb 1893 c
Joshua	Elizabeth Dyur	22 Feb 1810
Martha	Josias Douglass	5 Feb 1806
Rosannah	Thomas Hagan	28 May 1811
SHEPHERD, Thomas	Bersheba Swann	13 Jan 1830
SHEPLEY, Frances W.	Ernest S. Fenwick	20 Jul 1892 w
SHERER - also see SCHARER		
SHERER, Mary C.	Nicholas Harding	1 Jun 1893 w
SHERIDAN, Palma	Henry M. Black	3 Sep 1895 w
SHERMAN, Charles E.	Miss Margaret A. Elgar	8 Aug 1837
Fannie E.	William M. Fling	29 Jan 1889 w
Matilda	Hanson Willson	28 May 1828
SHERN - also see SHURN		
SHERN, Charles W.	Mary F. Adams	20 Nov 1890 c
William H.	Admenia E. Wallace	27 Feb 1894 c
SHERRER - also see SCHARER		
SHERRER, Franklin P.	Elizabeth A. Wood	4 Dec 1894 w

SHERWOOD - also see SHEERWOOD
SHERWOOD,	Albert T.	Maggie Conner	24 Jun 1884
	Carl	Ethel R. Lynn	14 Oct 1896 w
	Emma J.	Randolph L. Warren	4 Jun 1889 w
	Maybell R.	George A. Blackman	3 Jul 1894 c
SHEVES,	Richard F.	Charles W. Smoot (male)	11 Dec 1888 w
SHIED,	Gertrude	George W. Hanes	3 Aug 1866
SHIELDS,	Anne M.	Lenox Martin	28 Jan 1828
	William	Ruth Duvall	5 Mar 1803
SHIPLEY,	Ellen	James Andrews	16 Sep 1847
	Ida	John Green	1 Feb 1894 c
	Isaac N.	Marbra J. Pyles	9 Jun 1863
	Israel	Hettie Hopkins	1 Jan 1881 c
	Hattie	Edward Alcorn	19 Nov 1891 c
	Jesse	Caroline Hands	16 Feb 1824
	Kitty	Rezin Duvall	19 Feb 1828
	Larkin	Eliza Bertton	4 May 1829
	Louisa Jane	Richard W. Hilton	27 Jan 1864
	Martha A.	William M. Burdett	13 Mar 1856
	Mary E.	Nathan R. Edelin	7 Apr 1849
	Mary M.	Richard Thomas House	3 Feb 1875
	Rachel A.	Hanson C. Anderson	1 Nov 1847
	Rebecca	Samuel P. Browning	12 Jan 1807
	Richard	Elizabeth Benton	1 Jan 1825
	Ruth	William Benton	16 Dec 1835
	Ruthie E.	Andrew J. Miles	1 Mar 1892 w
	Samuel	Courtney Barber	22 Jan 1814
	Sarah	Samuel Lovejoy	29 Apr 1826
	Smith	Mary Wren	30 Apr 1891 c
	Thomas N.	Emily J. Duley	9 May 1871
	Upton W. D.	Elizabeth A. Smith	9 Oct 1848
	W. C. R.	Margaret L. Bennett	24 Dec 1851
	Wallace S.	Alice A. Reid	9 Apr 1888 w
	William	Annie Grimes	29 Mar 1883
SHIRCLIFF,	William H.	Nellie E. Wilson	16 Apr 1890 w
SHIRED,	Lucy Ann	William Thomas Elmore	7 Oct 1884 w
SHOEMAKER,	Annie L.	Henry T. Osborne	29 Nov 1897 w
	David	Louisa Tomlinson	11 Jan 1830
	Edith	William Counselman	30 Nov 1829
	Edward	Mary E. Vermillion	20 Feb 1860
	Elizabeth A.	Lewis B. Parker	26 Nov 1855
	George W.	Ida M. Magaha	16 Oct 1890 w
	Hannah	George Lanehart	14 Nov 1853
	Isaiah	Harriet E. Johnson	25 May 1866
	Lewis E.	Mary E. Eld	13 Nov 1862
	Mary E.	Thomas C. Tallman	30 Dec 1865
	Rachel	John Thomas Dean	31 Oct 1843
	Sarah E.	Francis R. Greenwell	25 Sep 1849
	William	Martha L. Bohrer	6 Dec 1887 w
	William	Sallie E. Perry	8 Oct 1889 w
SHOEMATE,	Walker D.	Sarah Williams	26 Jul 1830

SHOLL - also see SCHOLL
SHOLL,	Rebecca A. E.	William C. Hempstone	2 Dec 1857

SHOOK - also see SHUCK
SHOOK,	Charles	Priscilla Ball	27 Feb 1805
	Frances	John Heater	13 Feb 1806

SHORTER, Mary Ann	Joseph Hicks	28 Jan 1869	
SHORTS, Annie A.	Arthur E. Burriss	16 Jan 1896	w
Elizabeth	James L. Harrison	16 Oct 1889	w
Fannie	William Bowman	12 Jul 1871	
Henrietta A.	Artemas Sullivan	20 May 1872	
John H.	Nancy E. Thompson	4 Aug 1896	w
SHOTS, Lewis	Rosetta Kilgour	13 Aug 1839	
SHOTWELL, Mary H.	Daniel A. Milbrick	11 Jul 1893	w
SHREEVE - also see SHREVE			
SHREEVE, Benjamin Jr.	Mary E. Trundle	29 Nov 1828	
Charles W.	Ann E. Jones	18 Oct 1859	
SHREEVES, James	Susan Ann Brown	6 Sep 1832	
John	Amanda Bright	24 Dec 1870	
SHREVE - also see SHREEVE			
SHREVE, Anne E.	Christopher S. O'Hare	15 Nov 1841	
Caleb H.	Sarah E. Hearn	15 Nov 1841	
Daniel T.	Margaret E. Jones	22 Nov 1852	
Samuel	Mary A. Culver	10 Feb 1851	
William A.	Eliza Kemp	1 Mar 1881	
SHRINER, Anthoney	Cassandra Smith*	27 Jun 1800	
Cornelia Elizabeth	William H. Benson	26 Aug 1875	
SHRYOCK, John F.	Annie Johnson	14 Dec 1871	
Minerva Ann	Thomas H. Payne	10 Oct 1836	
SHUCK - also see SHOOK			
SHUCK, Lydia	John West	4 Apr 1801	
SHUM, Eleanor	Littleton Waters	26 Dec 1826	
Samuel	Eleanor Lansdale	6 Apr 1817	
SHURN - also see SHERN			
SHURN, Pattie	John A. Jackson	13 Jul 1898	c
SIBLEY, Bertha M.	Harry E. Galleher	10 Aug 1891	w
Harriet	Richard A. Leamon	23 Dec 1848	
James E. L.	Lillie May Watkins	10 Dec 1894	w
Jane	Daniel Lemmon	14 Aug 1821	
Joanna	Zadock S. King	7 May 1861	
Jonathan	Harriet Mullican	13 Jan 1819	
Joseph	Harriet A. Benson	7 Jan 1863	
Joshua	Alcinda J. Dowden	20 Dec 1859	
Levi	Catharine McDavitt	19 Dec 1828	
Levi	Sarah Willson	7 Mar 1832	
Mary	Benjamin Graves	22 Dec 1800	
Mary A.	Samuel N. Plummer	28 Jan 1890	w
Mattie S.	Frederick F. Bowman	22 Mar 1893	w
Solomon	Rebecca Orme	25 Apr 1831	
Susan	Benedict Green	5 Aug 1819	
Thomas	Nancy Williams	23 Feb 1820	
Thomas	Ann Fowler	2 Apr 1833	
Elizabeth	Walter Wilburne	6 Jan 1818	
Richard	Mary Gardner	1 Jan 1818	
SICKELS, Charles C.	Brittey Murrey	23 Sep 1897	c
SIDNEY, Elizabeth	Charles R. Harriss	23 Dec 1897	c
Margaret	John Moore	15 Sep 1897	c
SILBY - also see SELBY			
SILBY, Sarah	John A. Burford	18 Sep 1813	

* Last name from earlier reading

Name	Spouse	Date	
SILENCE, William	Susan Creamer	30 Apr 1851	
SILLS, Thomas	Sophia Pumphrey	10 Jun 1880	c
SIM, Catharine	Charles Miles	18 Feb 1815	
SIMES - also see SIMMS			
SIMES, Charles	Hannah King	29 Nov 1897	c
SIMMES, Cecilia	John Spalding	3 Apr 1809	
SIMMONDS - also see SIMONS			
SIMMONDS, James H.	Mollie J. West	15 Jun 1869	
SIMMONS, Eleanor	Zachariah Williams	21 Feb 1805	
Ellsworth	Henrietta Brooke	8 Mar 1896	c
Mary W.	Henry Winsor	17 Nov 1818	
SIMMS - also see SEMMES, SIM, SIMS, SIMES, SIMMES			
SIMMS, Benjamin T.	Carrie Martin	31 Oct 1889	c
Catharine	Elisha Adamson	2 May 1833	
Christie	Moses Tibbs	9 Feb 1893	c
Edward	Pattie Powell	24 May 1898	c
Elizabeth	William Lomax	14 Aug 1890	c
Frederick D.	Mary Arthur	8 Oct 1898	c
Hilleary	Mary E. Williams	26 Dec 1895	c
John	Ara Thomas	17 Jan 1867	
John F.	Mary E. Bond	25 Sep 1878	c
Luretta	Andrew J. Barrett	3 Jan 1840	
Nathan	Sophia Watkins	9 Sep 1875	
Susie	Mortimer Sewell	3 Sep 1891	c
Thomas	Lucy Warren	23 Jul 1873	
Walter	Florence Thompson	26 Oct 1891	c
William	Annie R. Dorsey	6 Dec 1890	c
William B.	Martha Morton	24 Jul 1875	
SIMON, W.	Mary A. Kite	15 Sep 1857	
SIMONS - also see SIMMONDS			
SIMONS, James W.	Rebecca J. Ryan	20 Aug 1878	w
SIMONSON, Charles W.	Clara V. Mullican	17 Dec 1879	w
SIMPSON, Allen	Sarah Benson	12 May 1802	
Annie	Rezin Prather	13 Aug 1889	c
Carrie V.	Phares L. Morgal	12 Apr 1898	w
Catharine	James H. Garner	27 Nov 1838	
Elizabeth	Elisha Atcheson	15 Dec 1801	
Frances	George Thomas	15 Sep 1891	c
Harriet May	William L. Orem	6 Mar 1891	w
Henrietta	William Gardner	23 Aug 1823	
Henry C.	Angeline Weller	3 Oct 1866	
Isabella	Frederick Nasby	19 Mar 1878	c
James	Juliet Luckett	3 Nov 1803	
John	Elizabeth Ford	12 Jan 1803	
John D.	Mary V. Bogley	30 Dec 1885	w
Joseph	Martha Corn	15 Jun 1866	
Joseph M.	Isabella Davis	28 Aug 1893	c
Mary Ann	Anthony Musgrove	5 Nov 1800	
Parmelia*	Thomas Warbough	25 Oct 1799	
Robert	Martha Linkin	9 Jan 1883	c
Ruth	Ephraim Atchison	11 Sep 1800	
Sarah	Richard Middleton	1 May 1806	
William	Mary Willson	22 May 1800	

* Part of last name from earlier reading

SIMS - also see SIMMS

SIMS, Edward	Emma Adams	8 Dec 1898	c
SINCLAIR, Isaac P.	Elizabeth Ann Mockbee	25 Aug 1834	
John	Mildred Dishman	2 May 1831	
SINGLETON, Elizabeth D.	Thomas Griffith	2 Mar 1869	
Thomas D.	Julia B. Magruder	21 Apr 1869	
SINYARD, Frederick	Clara Kessler	9 Jan 1895	w
SIPE, Christopher	Elizabeth Iglehart	10 Mar 1798	
John	Mary Bloom	24 Aug 1804	
Michael	Eleanor Mobley	27 Dec 1802	
SISSON, Margaret V.	William J. Ayres	15 Dec 1893	w
SKILES, Thomas D.	Kate E. Watkins	15 Nov 1869	
SKINNER, Amos	Peggy Nicholls	23 Apr 1812	
Amos	Margaret A. Murray	15 Mar 1825	
SLAGLE, Robert L.	Lena Isemann	12 Aug 1896	w
SLATER, Addie	Eli D. Hall	28 May 1895	c
Ida B.	Charles T. Stearn	10 Jul 1889	w
Julia	Madison F. Harris	14 Apr 1879	
Mary	Joseph Crown	26 Nov 1798	
Minnie M.	Millard S. Boroughs	27 Feb 1888	w
Rachel*	Benjamin Dillaha	14 Oct 1799	
Reuben	Mary F. Abel	14 Feb 1853	
William	Sarah Leatch	18 Dec 1798	
SLAYMAKER, John E.	Sarah F. Peter	5 Jan 1893	w
SLEMMER, Charles	Mary N. Willson	7 Aug 1850	
SLOAN, William J.	Mary K. Hays	2 Jul 1866	
SMACKUM, Jesse	Mary Beckett	19 Dec 1870	
SMALL, Alexander	Susie Mossburg	2 Mar 1895	w
Arthur C.	Adele T. Archer	14 Sep 1898	w
Charles	Ruth Lett	15 Apr 1885	w
James	Martha A. Heeter	18 Nov 1872	
Robert	Martha E. Dwyer	25 Nov 1881	w
William F.	Mary F. Heeter	14 Jun 1875	
SMALLWOOD, Anne	John Downs	2 Jul 1832	
Eveline	Hamilton Moore	2 Apr 1828	
Henry	Theresa Williams	8 Dec 1809	
Jane S.	Remus G. Carter	19 Apr 1832	
Martha	Henson Reid	11 Apr 1820	
Philip	Martha Burdest	26 Mar 1831	
Rebecca	Edward Cole	12 Apr 1819	
Susanah	Abner Cloud	9 Feb 1799	
Truman	Adeline Mansfield	21 Apr 1892	w
Hesekiah			
SMITH, Abraham	Mary Hare	29 Nov 1824	
Aleckiah	Airana Streeks	27 Dec 1832	
Alverta	Thomas Powell	4 Apr 1895	c
Angelina	John W. Spates	21 Jan 1833	
Ann	Simon Jenkins	9 Nov 1818	
Anna	Mortimer Campbell	26 Dec 1888	c
Anna E.	Charles H. Dyson	22 Mar 1887	c
Arundel	Margaret Wootton	24 Jul 1832	
Benjamin	Jane Smith	1 Apr 1875	
Benjamin	Bettie Lucas	13 Feb 1883	c
Bessie	Harry Sedgwick	4 Feb 1898	c

* Last name from earlier reading

SMITH, Budd F.	Josephine Cartwright	4 Jun 1886	c
Cassandra*	Anthony Shriner	27 Jun 1800	
Catharine	Jesse Taylor	3 Apr 1811	
Catharine	John Adams	14 Oct 1869	
Catharine J.	Daniel R. Leaman	16 Jan 1866	
Charles	Mary Ann Young	17 Apr 1827	
Charles	Sarah H. Braddock	8 May 1845	
Charles	Mary Howard	26 Aug 1869	
Charles F.	Maggie A. Corbett	20 Feb 1889	w
Charles H.	Laura J. Streeks	1 Oct 1884	w
Charles T.	Lydia Jeanes	28 Mar 1854	
Charlotte	Isaac Johnson	30 May 1867	
Christie	Joseph Matthews	23 Aug 1884	c
Deborah	George Bowman	29 Jun 1805	
Dennis	Agatha Carroll	16 Sep 1880	c
Dinah	Frederick Proctor	6 Jun 1876	
Edward	Parthenia Cockeral	21 Aug 1803	
Effie	William Thomas	9 Dec 1895	c
Eleanor	Henry Jenkins	28 Sep 1814	
Eleanor	Alfred Basford	12 Feb 1824	
Eliza	Richard Ringold	2 Mar 1801	
Elizabeth	James Baggerly	17 Oct 1798	
Elizabeth	George Reid	31 May 1826	
Elizabeth	Hanson Pritchett	12 Jan 1803	
Elizabeth	John Howse	16 Dec 1807	
Elizabeth	Samuel Jones	12 Nov 1883	
Elizabeth A.	Upton W. D. Shipley	9 Oct 1848	
Emeline	Samuel Harris	6 Apr 1870	c
Emily	Peter M. Dorsey	7 Apr 1890	c
Emily J.	Philip Ganley	14 Feb 1873	
Estelle F.	Thomas H. Hodgson	9 Jun 1885	
Florence ?.	Philip Ganley	7 Jan 1890	w
Franklin W.	Mary E. V. Jackson	26 Dec 1889	c
Franklin W.	Mary F. Tyler	18 Oct 1894	c
George	Bettie Cartwright	7 Aug 1895	c
George W.	Laura Johnson	25 May 1885	c
Green Berry	Josephine Thornton	1 Feb 1883	c
Harriet Ann	James Cook	23 Oct 1873	
Hellen D.	Charles F. Elgin	29 Jan 1863	
Henrietta	Dorey Benton	14 Nov 1809	
Henry	Mary King	31 May 1849	
Henry S.	Maria L. Somervell	7 Dec 1891	w
Hester Ellen	John McAbee	15 Sep 1846	
Hettie W.	John W. Brewer	14 Aug 1890	w
Isabel L.	William ?. Lacey	** Oct 1896	c
Jacob A.	Mary Millie Williams	23 Mar 1898	c
James	Anne Owen	5 Jun 1810	
James	Tabitha Windsor	2 Sep 1812	
James	Louisa Hall	19 Oct 1867	
James E. N.	Elizabeth Harrison	20 Feb 1894	w
James W.	Teresia A. Lowe	24 Oct 1851	
Jane	Lloyd Adamson	7 Jan 1813	
Jane	Benjamin Smith	1 Apr 1875	

* Last name from earlier reading
** Cannot read day; before 9

SMITH, John	Ann Corcoran	13 May 1815	
John	Betsey Oneale	22 Apr 1823	
John	Elizabeth Glissan	27 Nov 1827	
John	Maria Vermillion	6 Mar 1844	
John	Martha E. Leizear	29 Oct 1872	
John H.	Marion Johnson	5 Jan 1893	c
John J.	Martha C. Burriss	29 Aug 1893	w
John M.	Salva Edelen	22 Dec 1884	w
Joseph	Elizabeth Frasier	4 Jul 1881	c
Joseph P.	Luisa Power	4 Feb 1819	
Josephine	John H. Crumbaugh	31 Dec 1868	
Katie L.	Charles W. Coleman	15 Apr 1896	c
Katy	Frank Jackson	20 Jan 1896	c
Laura	James Mason	18 Feb 1892	c
Lizzie	Edwin R. Aldrich	29 Sep 1885	w
Louisa H.	William H. B. Page	26 Sep 1871	
Lucy E.	Percy E. Gallant	11 May 1895	w
Lucy J. M.	Edward W. W. Henderson	23 Dec 1897	c
Maggie	Robert Twine	2 Nov 1882	
Maggie P.	Bradley T. Johnson	17 Dec 1885	c
Manzella	John W. Magaha	20 Nov 1882	
Margaret*	Barton Ennis	20 Apr 1798	
Margaret	Charles E. Pipkins	4 Jun 1868	
Margaret	George Gustavus Bowman	4 Jun 1868	
Margaret A.	Athelbert Jackson	6 May 1880	
Maria C.	John H. Lynch	3 Jan 1871	
Mary	Enoch George	11 Jan 1802	
Mary	James Browning	23 Sep 1802	
Mary	David Carlysle	10 Nov 1817	
Mary	James Mullican	29 Dec 1817	
Mary	Henry Herbert	12 Nov 1879	c
Mary C.	Lawrence A. Knott	21 Oct 1853	
Mary E.	Elias N. Moulden	18 Jun 1849	
Mary E.	Washington Day	17 Feb 1855	
Mary E.	Julian Wade	15 Feb 1871	
Mary E.	Silas Waits	13 Nov 1884	c
Mary L.	William H. Taggart	12 May 1897	w
Mary Lusette C.	Sidney Barnhouse	23 Dec 1864	
Mary M.	Jesse William Rice	10 Feb 1874	
Mary M.	Thomas R. Wheeler	9 Mar 1876	
Matilda	John Cox	1 Sep 1800	
Miles	Nelly Warfield	19 May 1876	
Nacey W.	Anna M. Anderson	26 May 1846	
Nancy	William H. Cook	28 Feb 1865	
Octavia	Richard Wootton	11 Mar 1835	
Peter	Juliann Thompson	30 Dec 1840	
Peter	Ruth Reed	8 Jan 1852	
Philemon M.	Meranda Hyatt	26 Apr 1841	
Philemon M.	Helen R. Conner	23 Jan 1897	w
Rachel Ann	William Prather	3 May 1842	
Rebecca M.	Thomas Phenix	9 Mar 1852	
Rena H.	Charles M. Towson	29 May 1897	w
Richard B.	Sary Litton	10 Sep 1803	
Robert E. L.	Fannie Tschiffelly	28 Dec 1891	w

* His last name and her name from earlier reading

SMITH, Ruth A.	William J. Squirrel	31 May 1877	c
Samuel	Matilda Boyer*	19 Oct 1821	
Samuel	Eleanor W. Kidwell	8 Jan 1833	
Sarah F.	Mahlon Browning	24 May 1858	
Sarah H.	Stephen M. Lyddane	8 Aug 1848	
Sarah M.	Andrew J. Arnold	2 Aug 1856	
Solomon	Jane Cockrane	22 Jan 1812	
Susan	Walter H. Hilleary	6 May 1813	
Susan	John Jones	13 Sep 1884	c
Susan	Brook Doy	28 Oct 1897	c
Susan McF.	William R. Leaman	2 May 1867	
Susannah	Shadrack Bowman	24 Dec 1810	
Thomas O.	Laura V. Anderson	18 Jan 1847	
Victorine	Rufus H. Davis	18 Jan 1876	
Virginia	Adam Washington	24 Oct 1888	c
Walter G.	Minnie B. Price	12 Sep 1892	w
Warrington G.	Margaret B. Chichester	23 Jan 1890	w
Wesley	Virginia Carroll	21 Dec 1865	
William	Mary Beavin	3 Nov 1801	
William	Elizabeth Whalen	9 Jan 1836	
William	Susan Thompson	14 Dec 1887	c
William H.	Alice H. Johnson	30 Jan 1895	c
William H.	Mimie Oram	29 Dec 1896	c
William H. Thomas	Maggie Lyles	24 Dec 1879	
SMITHSON, Hezekiah	Rachel A. Harvey	30 Sep 1852	
SMITZEN, Jane	William D. Vermillion	6 Oct 1840	
SMIZER, George	Martha A. Willson	11 Aug 1847	
George	Virginia Willson	21 Dec 1857	
SMOOT, Charles W. (male)	Richard F. Sheves	11 Dec 1888	w
George W. Jr.	Kate H. Martin	4 Jan 1893	w
Joseph	Ann E. Darne	8 May 1844	
May M.	William H. Edwards	29 Sep 1897	w
Robert W.	Margaret A. White	18 Feb 1850	
Stephen W.	Cecelia Vinson	12 Dec 1884	
SNAP - also see SNEPP			
SNAP, Jonas B.	Jane Sedgwick	24 Dec 1841	
SNELL, Martha	Thomas Caton	12 Jan 1801	
SNEPP - also see SNAP			
SNEPP, Jonas B.	Louisa Ann Nichols	15 Sep 1855	
SNIDER - also see SNYDER			
SNYDER, Caroline	Perry Bowman	8 Nov 1827	
Deborah	John Shaw	11 Jan 1840	
Frederick	Verlinda Henry	27 Mar 1815	
George C.	Elizabeth Henry	7 Mar 1810	
Jacob F.	Joanna F. Richter	11 Jan 1853	
Joseph	Jane Whitesides	22 Dec 1838	
Moses	Deborah Burdett	5 Mar 1824	
Samuel	Kitty Coogle	27 May 1822	
William H.	Harriet E. Peack	20 Feb 1852	
SNOOTS, Harry F.	Lula M. Lambilen	22 Mar 1898	w
SNOUFFER, Elizabeth M.	Harry B. Cramer	21 Nov 1889	w
Julia M.	Lyde Griffith	4 Dec 1894	w
SNOWDEN, Achsa L.	Alonzo E. Snowden	1 Jul 1895	c
Agnes S.	John Brown	9 Oct 1883	c

* Last name very light; earlier reading has Bryer

SNOWDEN,	Alonzo E.	Achsa L. Snowden	1 Jul 1895 c
	Angeline	Nathan Bowie	17 Nov 1879
	Antonia	Charles E. Clagett	26 Sep 1895 c
	Charles Agustus	Elijah Ann Thomas	3 Mar 1885 c
	Charlie H.	Carrie E. Campbell	6 May 1896 c
	David L.	Harriet B. Bowie	12 Feb 1868
	Elizabeth	Thomas King	3 Mar 1877
	Emily	Gerard Hopkins	1 Oct 1874
	George	Martha L. Brooks	8 Apr 1873
	George	Fanny Dorsey	11 Jun 1883
	George Henry	Ruthana Hill	24 Oct 1878 c
	Hannah	John F. Ricks	27 Sep 1893 c
	Henry	Louisa Martin	28 Oct 1880 c
	Isabella	John H. Lawson	17 Oct 1878 c
	John	Mary Waters	19 Apr 1869
	John W.	Addie Burton	23 Nov 1878 c
	Laura B.	Richard T. Budd	24 Nov 1883
	Louisa C.	Richard Pumphery	27 Aug 1885 c
	Lucy	Walter Lea	21 Oct 1887 w
	Luther	Jane Robertson	14 Sep 1870
	Luther	Emma King	15 Jan 1880 c
	Maria E.	Samuel Jackson	20 Jan 1870
	Mary	James Hall, Jr.	27 Apr 1871
	Mary	Samuel Clagett	28 May 1896 c
	Mary E.	Shadrack Riggs	22 Nov 1880
	Mary P.	Robert Doy	11 Jul 1877 c
	Mary P.	Mark Lawson	3 Jul 1880 c
	Mary Tabitha	Beverly Phenix	10 Nov 1874
	Nicholas B.	Phoebe A. Waters	29 Sep 1885 c
	Rachel A.	William Henry Thomas	30 Nov 1866
	Rebecca	William H. Fawcett	6 Jan 1873
	Rebecca	Robert Diggs	* Sep 1883
	Rezin T.	Martha E. Plummer	24 Dec 1886 c
	Richard	Virginia Thomas	28 Nov 1878
	Richard N.	Elizabeth R. Warfield	26 Dec 1834
	Ruth A.	John H. Nugent	10 Jun 1878 c
	Ruth A.	William S. Johnson	24 Dec 1892 w
	Sarah	George Stevenson	30 Jun 1896 c
	Stephen	Sarah Gordon	20 Feb 1872
	Susan	Charles Aslun	18 Mar 1869
	Thomas	Lydia Howard	1 Jun 1874
	Thomas	Ellen Johnson	28 Jul 1876
	Thomas	Ettie Jane Gray	5 Jan 1886 c
	Vachel	Mary Butler	12 Oct 1875 c
	William Henry	Ruth V. Myers	20 Dec 1865
	Willis T.	Rosie M. Chase	25 Jun 1891 c
SNYDER - also see SNIDER			
SNYDER,	Alice V.	William F. Pumphrey	19 Mar 1890 w
	Ann E.	Joseph **. Henley	17 Jan 1867
	Annie	William Waters	16 Feb 1898 w
	C. W. (female)	J. B. Stewart	17 Jun 1872
	Catherine	Thomas Henry	29 Dec 1807
	Charles E.	Rose May Gloyd	22 Nov 1887 w

* Cannot read day; before 19
** Initial has blot on it

SNYDER, Drusilla	James M. W. Briggs	8 Jan 1868	
Emma J.	Joseph Hulins*	* Apr 1879	w
Fannie	Enoch G. Metz	27 Apr 1874	
Frances R.	William T. Hilton	18 Nov 1850	
George A.	Eleanor Rabbitt	12 Mar 1886	w
George W.	Mary S. Snyder	29 Dec 1865	
Greenbury	Mary Snyder	6 Nov 1837	
Iona M.	James F. Burdette	20 Feb 1897	w
James T.	Sarah E. Duvall	14 Jul 1873	
John	Christianna Richter	21 Aug 1861	
Julia	William R. McGinnis	18 Aug 1884	w
Kate	Winfield S. Wallich	12 Feb 1873	
Leannah	Robert B. Briggs	9 Jun 1862	
Mary	Greenbury Snyder	6 Nov 1837	
Mary Grace	Barton Trail	21 May 1884	w
Mary S.	George W. Snyder	29 Dec 1865	
Nancy Jane	Benjamin F. Hamilton	13 Jul 1864	
Nathan R.	Elizabeth Mills	14 Dec 1881	
Rachel P.	Elonzo M. Briggs	4 Dec 1872	
Rinaldo P.	Harriet A. R. Poole	12 Jan 1875	
Romulus	Sarah Ann Trail	15 Oct 1839	
Uriah	Mary Grace Jones	23 Feb 1876	
Virginia	William Walter	17 Mar 1873	
William	Nancy Trail	17 Apr 1845	
SOAPER - also see SOPER			
SOAPER, Charles	Elizabeth Aldridge	13 Jan 1801	
Samuel	Sarah Jones	30 Nov 1812	
William	Jane Hare	14 Sep 1825	
SOLYOM De ANTALF--, Julia V.**	Edwin C. Reynolds	26 Dec 1896	w
SOMERVELL, Maria L.	Henry S. Smith	7 Dec 1891	w
SOMERVELLE, Amelia H.	John L. Dawson	7 Sep 1871	
SOMERVILLE, Abraham	Virginia Williams	17 Mar 1892	c
Eleanor	Basil Mason	29 Sep 1891	c
Flora	William Offutt	9 Jun 1896	c
Idella	Jerry Mason	23 Jul 1896	c
William	Aletha Plummer	22 May 1888	c
SONNEMANN, Alice R.	John W. Essex	8 Nov 1881	
SOPER - also see SOAPER			
SOPER, Adella	Milton T. Phelps	7 May 1887	w
Alexander E.	Mary Beard	20 Sep 1841	
Alexander E.	Rebecca Williams	5 Jan 1844	
Alexander S.	Roberta Chick	9 Mar 1883	w
Amelia	Richard Langford	22 May 1801	
Barton	Mary Burton	29 Dec 1812	
Basil	Priscilla Hobbs	9 Feb 1808	
Eleanor	William Bryan	4 Apr 1817	
Elias P.	Mary E. Baker	12 Apr 1859	
Elizabeth Anne	John White	3 May 1817	
Henry E.	Mary P. White	10 Jan 1893	w
Isaiah	Eliza M. Fisher	8 Dec 1852	
James B.	Annie E. Miles	18 Dec 1883	
James M.	Sarah E. Herbert	26 Jul 1894	w

* Name very light; could be incorrect; day between 14 and 21
** Cannot make out last 2 or 3 letters

SOPER, James P.	Amelia Ann Harriss	23 Feb 1846	
John	Ruth Barnes	10 Jun 1800	
John Thomas	Sarah Layton	15 Dec 1832	
Joseph	Eleanor Tucker	28 Dec 1803	
Joseph	Catharine Lazenby	27 Mar 1847	
Lizzie	William H. Phair	5 Feb 1892	w
Lizzie A.	George A. Darby	23 Mar 1871	
Maggie	George A. Loveless	29 Jul 1889	w
Margarett	William B. Roby	18 Dec 1830	
Mary	Charles Delarn	28 Mar 1812	
Mary V.	James Doyle	11 Mar 1896	w
Nathan	Ann Bozwell	3 Nov 1807	
Rebeccah	Benjamin Cross	20 May 1812	
Robert	Chloe Campbell	20 Jun 1807	
Sary	Thomas Cross	25 Jan 1804	
Susannah	Stephen Tuttle	10 Feb 1809	
Thomas P.	Sarah E. A. Marlow	17 May 1852	
Vandelia R.	Zachariah A. Williams	25 Oct 1882	
William C.	Rebecca Hurly	20 Dec 1824	
William C.	Martha Ann Higgins	9 Nov 1840	
SOTHORON, Henry G.	Ann Clarke	13 Jan 1823	
SOUDER, Charles W.	Sarah Rebecca Sheckels	17 Nov 1886	w
Emma V.	Edward Webster	14 Apr 1888	w
Jacob J.	Emma V. Mount	22 Apr 1884	
Mary L.	James W. Shaw	21 May 1896	w
Philip B.	Mary E. Warthen	12 Jan 1883	
SOUDERS, John	Sarah Dove	8 Mar 1881	
SOURVIER, Katie	William J. Murphy	7 Aug 1888	w
SOUTHERLAND - also see SUTHERLAND			
SOUTHERLAND, Snowden	Gertrude A. Barkes	5 Jul 1898	w
SPALDING, Christy A.	James A. Carlyle	24 Feb 1840	
Elias	Eleanor Hempstone	3 Jan 1801	
John	Cecilia Simmes	3 Apr 1809	
John	Mary M. Hilton	6 Mar 1852	
SPARO, Walter G.	Emma K. Fellinger	28 Jan 1891	
SPARROW, Alfred	Martha Sparrow	23 Feb 1825	
Benjamin	Milly Duley	27 Dec 1805	
Benjamin	Eliza B. Padgett	22 Feb 1842	
Charlotte	John Jenkins	9 Feb 1808	
Elie	Ann Dial	22 Oct 1816	
Elizabeth	Joseph Collins	9 Nov 1816	
Emma J.	William Penn	23 Jan 1867	
George W.	Mary E. Crown	21 May 1874	
Hezekiah	Elizabeth Chambers	4 Mar 1815	
Ida V.	Gideon D. Briggs	3 Dec 1873	
James W.	Mary S. Case	22 Aug 1872	
Jonathan	Elizabeth Free	17 Dec 1799	
Laura F.	William F. Trail	21 Feb 1876	
Lloyd	Rebecca Harper	31 Oct 1809	
Lurrena	Dennis Harrison	3 Mar 1832	
Maria	Daniel Collins	21 Jan 1826	
Maria	Washington H. Mennly	1 Mar 1830	
Mary C.	J. W. Briggs	14 Nov 1872	
Martha	Alfred Sparrow	23 Feb 1825	
Samuel V.	Mary A. Crown	30 Dec 1890	w
Sarah	Thomas Sparrow	30 Jan 1805	

Name	Spouse	Date	
SPARROW, Susannah	Joseph Madden	18 Nov 1801	
Thomas	Sarah Sparrow	30 Jan 1805	
William	Eliza Campbell	20 Mar 1802	
SPARSHOTT, Lizzie M.	Frank B. Cogswell	11 Jul 1894	w
SPATES, Alfred	Elizabeth Kirkpatrick	31 Mar 1832	
Alfred	Christy Amanda Getzendanner	20 Jul 1843	
Ann Maria	E. Gilmore Duley	28 Sep 1869	
Anna Maria	Thomas Renshaw	29 Jan 1862	
Cassandra	Laurence Ball	5 May 1814	
Charles	Ruth Herring	2 Nov 1815	
Clara B.	Hamilton Glaze	14 Dec 1875	
Eliza E.	Henry Renshaw	7 Nov 1865	
Estelle A.	Charles R. Harris	2 Dec 1878	
Fannie T.	Charles M. Butler	4 Jan 1867	
Frances	Anthony Kuhn	22 Dec 1841	
George W.	Ann Byrd Fields	28 Sep 1846	
John W.	Angelina Smith	21 Jan 1833	
John W.	Harriet Ann Sands	22 Jan 1845	
John W.	Anna Maria Letton	3 Sep 1850	
Lavinia	Joshua Davis	30 Dec 1824	
Linney	William Lynch	24 Mar 1825	
Margaret	John Ferrall	29 Mar 1826	
Martha M.	William Huddleson	7 May 1851	
Mary S.	Henry Renshaw	3 Dec 1850	
Richard P.	Milly Brashears	20 Dec 1814	
Richard P.	Jane E. Benton	11 Feb 1857	
Richard P.	Mary E. Gloyd	12 Feb 1872	
Robert N.	Eliza Ann Hoyle	6 May 1833	
Samuel	Anne O'Neale	31 Jul 1817	
Sarah Ann	Marshal B. Perry	23 Jan 1827	
SPAYTS, Matilda	John A. Williams	7 Nov 1815	
SPEAK, James Thomas	Maggie Macaby	27 May 1873	
SPEAKE, Jonah Milburn	Sarah Holmead	17 Jul 1800	
Rufus H.	Eliza W. Vinson	29 Dec 1829	
SPEARS, Mary	Laurence White	23 Mar 1814	
SPENCE, Washington	Mary F. Rollins	14 Mar 1893	c
SPENCER, Charles	Eliza Hempstone	3 Jan 1812	
Edna A.	James B. Dulin	29 Apr 1896	w
Enoch	Alice Bush	31 Dec 1874	
Elizabeth	Frank Woodward	13 Dec 1887	w
Florence N.	Charles H. Muse	25 Aug 1898	w
Hiram	Mary E. Maus	17 Feb 1863	
James	Henrietta H. Curtis	21 Oct 1872	
Sarah C.	William H. Hackett	7 Dec 1870	
Washington	Mary Ellen Powell	20 May 1833	
SPIES, William W.	Lillie M. Jackson	29 Jun 1895	w
SPINKS, John	Ann V. Hempstone	1 Feb 1831	
SPOHN, David	Hannah Quary	10 Jun 1812	
SPRAGES, James W.	Elizabeth Hutchison	14 Nov 1872	
SPREADBROUGH, Mrs. Elizabeth	John T. Burroughs	29 Dec 1884	w
SPREIGEL, Minnie	George Havell	5 Jun 1893	w
SPRIGG, Ann V.	Joseph Anderson	28 Nov 1867	
Debora Jane	Edward A. Wyvill	6 Oct 1879	
Eleanor	Hammond Duvall	21 May 1834	

SPRIGG, Elizabeth	Edward Wyvill	21 Jul 1830	
Kattie	Richard Mathews	12 Jan 1882	c
Lucy	Lewis Knott	24 Dec 1801	
Lucy	William McAtee	3 Aug 1805	
Rebecca	Henry Butler	11 Nov 1880	c
SPRIGGS, Elias	Rachell Lansey	5 Oct 1870	
Fannie	Samuel Cole	16 Sep 1872	
Jeremiah	Susannah Lewis	22 Dec 1886	c
Mamie	Robert Hammond	10 Sep 1896	c
Mary	Thomas Turner	19 Nov 1874	
Robert	Rebecca Riggs	16 Dec 1873	
Sarah	Perry Campbell	7 Apr 1891	c
SPROUSE, John H.	Mary B. Keesee	20 Oct 1891	w
SPURRIER, Harry G.	Frances I. Griffith	25 Jan 1898	w
Joseph	Mary C. Etchison	2 Feb 1855	
Joshua	Harriet Baker	19 Feb 1799	
SQUIERS, Ella	Joseph W. Mattingly	9 Oct 1882	
SQUIRES, Sadie R.	George H. Markward	17 Feb 1898	w
SQUIRREL, Emma J.	Remus H. Hill	22 Jun 1881	c
Harriet A.	Samuel Budd	12 Nov 1866	
Isaiah	Amanda M. Pratt	30 Oct 1879	c
Martha	Charles Cole	1 Dec 1881	
William J.	Ruth A. Smith	31 May 1877	c
STABLER, Frederick	Martha R. Brooke	5 Nov 1866	
James P.	Allice Brooke	18 Nov 1870	
Jessie B.	Frederick W. McReynolds	6 Oct 1894	w
STACKS, Laura V.	Richard Pyles	18 Apr 1887	w
Mary E.	George N. Darcey	2 Oct 1877	w
STADTLER, George M.	Margaret E. Kirby	23 Jan 1892	w
Godtlieb S.	Mary R. Rowan	22 Aug 1891	w
STAFFORD, John	Ann Wright	3 Nov 1810	
STALEY, Elizabeth	Elijah Phelps	16 Feb 1828	
Lydia	James H. Phelps	4 Sep 1829	
STALLING, Rachel Ann	William Lewis	22 Feb 1840	
STALLINGS, James R.	Ann E. Hillard	22 Jan 1839	
John	Lucinda Houser	31 Dec 1866	
Phineus	Anne Hawse	5 Apr 1806	
Richard F.	Eleanor Reed	8 Apr 1870	
Sarah A.	Richard H. Burdett	15 Dec 1863	
STALLINS, Richard	Lydia Heffner	31 Jan 1831	
STALLIONS, Rebecca	Thomas Whalan	18 Aug 1800	
STANDIFORD, William H.	Bessie M. Abell	21 Feb 1891	w
STANG, Frederick C.	Rosalpha Mossburg	10 Oct 1870	
Joseph D.	Mary B. T. Hanfman	17 Apr 1883	
Josephine E.	William H. Cook	16 Feb 1869	
Margaret	Peter Hellmuth	1 Oct 1867	
Martin	Cornelia Carter	3 Oct 1882	
Martin A.	Almira Oden	18 Jun 1872	
Peter J.	Annie O. Hoffman	21 Dec 1886	w
STANLEY, Charles A.	Mary A. Adams	31 Oct 1863	
Richard H.	Fannie G. Mount	21 Dec 1886	w
STANSBURY, Alpheus	Matilda A. Hodges	21 Feb 1870	
STANTON, Maria	William Riggs	18 Jul 1893	c
Mollie J.	Frederick J. Wiley	26 Jun 1871	
STARKEY, William	Letitia Kinsey	11 Dec 1822	
STARKS, Paul	Mary E. Beckett	15 Oct 1892	c

STARNELL, Edward W.	Rosa Lee Byrne	14 Feb 1890 w
STATIA, William	Mary Ann Taylor	29 Nov 1800
STAUB, Isaac N.	Mollie A. Bruner	5 Sep 1879 w
Jenia E.	C. W. Thomas	23 Mar 1880 w
STAUFFER - also see STOUFFER, STOFFER		
STAUFFER, William Theodore	Clara C. Offutt	12 May 1873
STEARN - also see STERN		
STEARN, Charles T.	Ida B. Slater	10 Jul 1889 w
John W.	Sallie F. Baugher	12 Jan 1887 w
Marion E.	William H. Case	27 Oct 1886 w
Samuel D.	Katie Mason	29 Dec 1887 w
STEARNS, Edward F.	Carrie E. Knoch	17 Oct 1892 w
STEDMAN, James W.	Margaret R. Cooper	27 Nov 1864
STEEL, Eleanor	John Powell	24 Dec 1798
Gerrard	Linny Biggs	27 Dec 1819
Joseph	Sarah Redmond	16 Dec 1889 w
Samuel	Lucy Edmonston	19 Oct 1808
STEELE, Agnes C.	Walter C. Masi	3 Oct 1877 w
Elizabeth	Samuel Hutchison	7 Oct 1811
Hamlin	Grace Denney	11 Jun 1877 c
James	Patty Welsh	7 Jun 1802
John	Harriet A. Hill	13 Jan 1866
Melvin N.	Annie E. Pangle	18 May 1894 w
William	Elizabeth Bradburn	15 Oct 1817
STEENE, Richard	Sarah Harper	9 Sep 1807
STEER, Lewis Walker	Virginia Lydia Holland	17 Nov 1886 w
STEERS, William W.	Rosella Whitmer	26 Jun 1895 w
STELL, James	Prissilla Galloway	20 Feb 1811
STEPHEN, Anna	Henry C. McCeney	23 Dec 1850
STEPHENS - also see STEVENS		
STEPHENS, Fannie M.	Arthur J. Padgett	20 Dec 1881
John	Eleanor Houser	12 Mar 1800
Mary Ann	Augustus Brown	18 Nov 1835
Robert	Isabel Padgett	31 Jan 1882
Sarah	James Nevitt	14 Oct 1800
STEPHENSON - also see STEVENSON		
STEPHENSON, Andrew M.	Minerva Becraft	21 Apr 1841
James	Elizabeth C. Beall	4 May 1835
Jane	Alfred Johnston	14 May 1879 c
Philip	Lucy Johnson	5 Nov 1874
STERLING, William H.	M. V. Maccubbin	26 Dec 1863
STERN - also see STEARN		
STERN, Mary E.	Winfield Offutt	22 Aug 1877
STERNE, Eliza	Matthew O'Brien	15 Jul 1879
STETSON, John T.	Frances V. Scott	25 Oct 1869
STEUART - also see STEWART		
STEUART, Arianna	James Riddle	6 May 1800
STEVENS - also see STEPHENS		
STEVENS, Alexander	Madeline McDaniels	26 Oct 1880
Annie A.	Henry C. Crown	5 Oct 1882
Annie V.	Thomas H. Pope	26 Feb 1896 w
Bertie C.	William C. Mossburg	16 Jun 1884 w
Isabelle E.	Edward W. O. Young	3 Apr 1895 c
Lizzie E.	Lemuel Buckingham	30 Dec 1876
Lucy	William G. Hall	13 Aug 1889 w

STEVENS, Marvin B.	Minnie D. Niple	4 Jul 1898	w
Pierre Christie	Sara Magruder	6 Oct 1885	w
R. Hugh	Mary V. Fisher	23 May 1883	
STEVENSON - also see STEPHENSON			
STEVENSON, Edward	Cassy Wallace	5 Jan 1874	
George	Sarah Snowden	30 Jun 1896	c
John T.	Rachel Woodward	27 May 1885	
Matilda	Freeborn Garretson Waters	18 Jun 1816	
Robert	Sarah Myers	16 May 1821	
STEWARD - also see STEWART			
STEWARD, Margaret	John Clemons	15 Jul 1896	c
Mary	Moses Wilson	8 Dec 1879	c
Mollie	James E. Keys	2 Nov 1898	c
Richard	Harriet Clagett	24 Dec 1867	
Thomas	Elizabeth Edmonston	12 Nov 1883	
STEWART - also see STUART, STEUART, STEWARD			
STEWART, Anna Maria	John W. Belt	24 Feb 1834	
Annie	William G. Washington	2 Jan 1888	c
Annie M.	Asbury R. Martin	16 Dec 1875	
Catharine Ann	Eli Burriss	16 Jan 1837	
Catherine	Thomas Johnson	13 Mar 1868	
Charles	Chloe Ann Norton	19 May 1798	
Charles	Betty Frazier	5 Jun 1865	
Charles	Jane Bean	28 Sep 1869	
Charles B.	Annie Wilson	26 May 1892	c
Charlotte	Alexander White	2 May 1885	c
David H.	Ellen R. Davis	22 Aug 1889	c
Edward	Sophie Washington	12 Dec 1892	c
Elizabeth	William Johnson	5 Aug 1869	c
Elizabeth Ann	William Gray	6 Mar 1839	
Emma	William Lee	2 Sep 1875	
Fanny	James H. Colley	20 Apr 1891	c
Frank	Lonie Parker	15 Jun 1898	c
George D.	Rosa H. Keene	25 Jul 1896	w
Harriet	James B. Mathews	4 Jan 1887	c
Hattie	Columbus Murray	19 May 1896	c
J. B. (male)	C. W. Snyder	17 Jun 1872	
James R.	Annie Gittings	10 May 1888	c
Jesse	Amanda Giddings	18 Dec 1876	
John	Mary Hilton	26 Jun 1807	
John	Cornelia Harriss	10 Jun 1867	
John A.	Sarah V. Saffell	10 Apr 1855	
John M.	Emeline Pope	14 Aug 1834	
John T.	Anna Pleasant	13 May 1890	c
John W.	Alice D. Laney	9 Nov 1876	
Jonathan	Rhoda Ann Owens	2 Feb 1844	
Jonathan	Willy E. Watkins	3 Feb 1860	
Josephine	Robert Cooper	18 Jan 1879	
Joshua	Clarissa Belt	24 Jun 1806	
Louisa	Samuel Contee	8 Aug 1878	c
Lucinda	George A. Crockett	16 Aug 1892	c
Lucy M.	George T. Pope	22 Dec 1834	
Martha	Charles Duvall	11 Jun 1867	
Martha	James Pumphrey	15 Mar 1883	
Martha S.	William M. Marlow	10 Oct 1862	

STEWART, Mary	James Miles	26 Mar 1885	c
Mary Caroline	Thomas W. Saffell	4 Apr 1834	
Mary E.	William T. Belt	29 Feb 1848	
Mary M.	William M. Magruder	16 Nov 1875	
Mary V.	John T. Ross	31 Dec 1895	w
Mat	Martha Detter	13 May 1875	
Matthew	Eliza E. Budd	7 Oct 1890	c
Milly Ann	John Cecill	22 May 1801	
Milton	Julia Riggler	26 Sep 1895	c
Rachel	Alfred Ross	8 Jul 1886	c
Rachel	Henry Peter	24 Jul 1886	c
Richard	Elizabeth Remmeton	23 Dec 1799	
Richard	Elizabeth Chaney	24 Jan 1821	
Richard W.	Eliza Duvall	9 Apr 1891	c
Rosie	William Thompson	4 Feb 1892	c
Samuel	Margaret Thrasher	2 May 1811	
Sarah	John Jones	6 Nov 1798	
Sarah	William Hilton	25 Mar 1801	
Simon	Mary C. Magruder	30 May 1887	c
Teresa Ann	Thomas W. Saffell	16 Jan 1837	
Thomas	Mary E. Beanman	4 Nov 1892	c
Thomas H.	Mollie Harriss	12 Apr 1888	c
Walter	Eleanor Gray	9 Jan 1809	
William	Hellen Beall	22 May 1798	
William	Elizabeth Grantford	19 Jan 1803	
William	Rebeccah Owens	4 Dec 1809	
William	Darkey Case	6 Nov 1820	
William	Maria Isabella Baker	18 May 1892	c
William Henry	Mary J. Baker	6 Jun 1876	
STILES, Harriet	James Higdon	21 Jan 1845	
Horatio	Mary Hickman	7 Dec 1826	
Lethea	Stephen Tuttle	12 Nov 1817	
Mary M.	John W. Poole	6 Feb 1857	
William	Mary Ann Lewis	18 Dec 1819	
William	Henrietta E. Woltz	8 Jun 1825	
STOCKER, George A.	Mary J. Coy	22 Dec 1891	w
STODDART, Isaac	Mary Busey	31 Dec 1874	
STOFFER - also see STAUFFER			
STOFFER, Henry	Matilda N. Magruder	8 Jan 1844	
STONE, Anne E.	Edward H. Brown	31 Oct 1863	
Anna Maria	Francis G. Blackford	14 Jan 1830	
Charles G.	Mary Florence Rapley	4 Jun 1883	
Elizabeth	Samuel Inlose	24 Nov 1800	
Elizabeth Frances	Joseph Henry Bodine	7 Sep 1861	
Frank P.	Lilly C. Moore	20 Dec 1892	w
Ida	Montgomery Clagett	25 Jan 1870	
James	Ruthy Benson	23 Dec 1816	
John	Lucy S. Ridgely	17 Oct 1821	
John G.	Margaret E. Clagett	4 Feb 1881	
John P.	Lelia A. Hardesty	12 Jan 1886	w
Maria H.	Joshua Hilton	20 Dec 1820	
Mary C.	Henry C. Harrison	7 Jan 1882	
Philip	Olivia Dunbar Magruder	11 Oct 1842	
Philip	Kate Tschiffely	17 Feb 1885	w
Sarah	John Williams	26 Dec 1799	
Sarah Ann	Avory C. Beall	21 Jun 1841	

STONE, Thomas		Margaret Jane Beall	10 Apr 1844
STONESTREET, Caroline H.		Frank B. Thomas	24 Jan 1894 w
	Edith May	George H. Lamar	18 Apr 1894 w
	Edward E.	Martha R. Berry	14 Oct 1852
	Elizabeth R.	Forrest J. Prettyman	17 Oct 1888 w
	Ella M.	Otis Mills Linthicum	24 Oct 1894 w
	M. Addie	Leonidas R. Green	21 Apr 1880 w
	Martha W.	Charles Abert, Jr.	12 Jan 1880 w
	Samuel T.	Adelaide J. A. Hall	13 Dec 1829
	Sarah	Walter Dorsett	22 Dec 1819
	Sophia F.	David N. Keast	15 Apr 1891 w
	Thomas	Polly Nicholls	18 Dec 1799
STORAY - also see STORY			
STORAY, Martha E.		Henry T. Ricketts	2 Oct 1879
STORED - also see STORRED, STORRIED			
STORED, Anna		John Jenkins	22 Jul 1881 c
	Horace	Virginia Turley	28 Dec 1885 c
STORRAGE - also see STORRIDGE			
STORRAGE, John		Estella Butler	9 Nov 1896 c
STORRED - also see STORED			
STORRED, Horace W.		Mary Prather	29 Dec 1897 c
	William	Nancy Powell	18 May 1898 c
STORRID, Alice B.		Basil T. Dorsey	13 Jul 1891 c
	Mary C.	William T. Dixon	14 Aug 1897 c
STORRIDGE - also see STORRAGE			
STORRIDGE, Henrietta		Alexander Barnes	13 Jan 1877
STORRIED - also see STORED			
STORRIED, Annie V.		Stephen N. Warren	10 May 1898 c
STORY - also see STORAY			
STORY, Ephraim		Eliza Jane Thompson	12 Nov 1850
	Thomas	Sidonia F. Hilton	4 Aug 1884
STOUFFER - also see STAUFFER			
STOUFFER, William Q.		Bertha E. Price	23 Feb 1891 w
STOUT, Robert W.		Mamie F. Willard	3 Dec 1892 w
STRAIGHNEY, Ada		John F. Branson	31 Jul 1889 c
STRAIN, Cornelia H.		Charles Farquhar	7 May 1892 w
	Eliza W.	Thomas F. Lansdale	29 Jan 1880
STRAITNER, Charles		Agnes Dorsey	3 Aug 1895 c
STRAUS, Harry		Susie B. Yeatman	17 Apr 1895 w
STREAKS, Judy		John A. Jones	21 Dec 1820
STREEKS, Ariana		Aleckiah Smith	27 Dec 1832
	Laura J.	Charles H. Smith	1 Oct 1884 w
	William Alfred	Julia T. Mastin	25 Nov 1884
STREIKS, Richard		Arah Fosic	16 Jun 1800
STRIBBLING, Cecilia M.		James D. Heaton	10 Jan 1842
STRIDER, Henry		Margarett Hickman	16 Nov 1811
STRINGER, Richard		Mary Griffith	4 Dec 1811
STRODE, John		Eliza Martin	15 Feb 1814
STRONG, Julia		Samuel Godman	27 Dec 1866
STROW, Helen A.		James E. Beatty	10 Aug 1896 w
STUART - also see STEWART			
STUART, George R.		Lillie M. Briggs	9 Feb 1897 w
STUBBS, Amy		Turner Willson	14 Nov 1864
	Mary A.	Oliver B. Clark	* Jan 1883 w

* Cannot read day; either 10 or 11

STUBINGER, Sophia A.	George W. Butler	9 Mar 1886	w
STULL, John J.	Maria Plater	23 Oct 1827	
STUTZSON, James	Amelia Musgrove	14 Jan 1823	
SUDDATH, Benjamin F.	Ann E. Hobbs	7 Sep 1874	
James N.	Laura S. Ricketts	18 Mar 1879	w
Mary C.	Thomas B. Iglehart	8 Nov 1897	w
Robert A.	Margaret Purdum	23 Jan 1867	
SUDDON, Lizzie	Josephus Hammond	21 Jan 1897	c
SUGARS, Joseph	Louisa V. Vermillion	4 Jan 1825	
SUIT, Sarah A.	James M. Matthews	16 Dec 1893	w
SULLIVAN, Alexander	Martha A. Gray	5 Jul 1870	
Ann E.	Richard A. Federline	16 Oct 1860	
Ann E.	George H. Zeigler	15 Feb 1871	
Artemas	Henrietta A. Shorts	20 May 1872	
Artemus	Matilda Harvey	8 Apr 1834	
Arthur M.	Mary R. Donaldson	7 Oct 1891	w
Basil James	Susan R. Ward	12 Mar 1866	
Benjamin F.	Margaret A. Hipsley	12 Apr 1873	
Benjamin Franklin	Sarah Ann Bowman	14 Jun 1858	
Catharine	Abner Brelsford	30 Mar 1813	
Catharine E.	William P. Foy	16 Mar 1824	
Charles	Jennie Jenkins	26 Apr 1897	w
Cornelius	Elizabeth Owen	16 Jan 1805	
Edith	Tyson B. Baker	7 Sep 1881	w
Eleanor	Samuel Leizier	5 Dec 1807	
Eliza Jane	John Mulcahy	6 Jan 1869	
Florence M.	Sameul B. Wetherald	26 Jun 1882	
Henry	Ella Fitzhugh	26 May 1880	
James	Cassandra Moore	4 Jan 1808	
James William	Julia Kendall	13 Sep 1876	
John	Emma Henry	7 Aug 1878	w
John ?.	Daisy V. Bran----on*	* Oct 1896	
John A.	Louisa Kendall	5 Mar 1878	w
John R.	Sarah M. Hutchinson	3 Jan 1860	
Julia	John Koehler	4 May 1894	w
Lizzie T.	Curtis J. Dangler	14 Oct 1896	w
Mary	Elias Leisure	25 Sep 1805	
Mary	William Davis	10 Feb 1809	
Mary	Shadrack Gill	4 Apr 1831	
Mary E.	Benjamin H. Thompson	13 Nov 1890	w
Mary J.	Shadrack A. Bowman	28 Dec 1889	w
Mary Jane	John Hammond	20 May 1846	
Perry	Catharine Thompson	4 Jan 1858	
Rezin Thomas	Agnes Odonnell	10 Aug 1868	
Richard	Susanna Holland	9 May 1815	
Robert	Eleanor Butler	24 Dec 1800	
Sarah	Amos Brelsford	21 Apr 1814	
Sarah I.	Samuel J. Leizear	4 Jan 1881	
Thomas	Marion A. Perry	8 May 1895	w
Virginia	Edward Shaw	1 Jul 1878	
William	Nancy Crockett	21 Dec 1835	
SUMMERS, A. H.	Virginia Veirs	17 Nov 1852	
Ammy	William Price	20 Dec 1807	

* Entire entry is blurred; day is before 9

SUMMERS,	Ann E.	Samuel F. Bennett	14 Feb 1873
	Anna Maria	Benjamin S. Forest	18 Feb 1823
	Anna Mariah	Thomas Linstid	27 Oct 1803
	Archibald	Margaret Pain	30 Mar 1803
	Benjamin	Virlinda Beckwith*	11 Oct 1798
	Denton	Mary Anne Thompson	25 Dec 1811
	Elizabeth	Jeremiah Browning	30 Apr 1803
	Florence G.	Andrew Ford	20 Sep 1892 w
	James	Sarah Boyd	15 Oct 1801
	Jamima	Lewis Barber	19 Jun 1821
	Leah	Horace Willson	7 Apr 1818
	Lethy	John Walker	7 Sep 1805
	Lewis Augustine	Mary W. Hickman	26 Aug 1822
	Lucinda	Benjamin Hesket	2 Jun 1823
	Mahala	Middleton King	17 May 1822
	Mary L.	Charles H. Crabb	28 Nov 1811
	Priscilla	John Read	14 Jan 1804
	Sabina	Adam Klay	22 Dec 1802
	Sarah	Frederick Adamson	25 Jan 1803
	Sarah	Samuel Beckwith	22 Mar 1826
	Thomas	Ann Bogess	22 Dec 1802
	Walter W.	Sarah Swearingen	23 Apr 1805
	Zadock	Jennie Earp	22 Oct 1868
SUNNIONS,	Ann	William Birdwhistele	1 Apr 1820
SUTER,	Alexander	Susan Read	20 Apr 1815
	Clara E.	William R. Reichenbach	24 Aug 1881
	Ida M.	James C. Holland	18 Oct 1866
	Mary V.	R. L. Macchall	2 Oct 1869
	Minnie S.	Wilson D. Buck	23 Jun 1884 w
	T. James	Tabitha Richards	17 May 1810
SUTHERLAND - also see SOUTHERLAND			
SUTHERLAND,	Charles	Elizabeth W. Brewer	2 Nov 1869
SUTTON,	James A.	Mollie V. Bell	24 Sep 1890 w
SWAILES - also see SWALES, SWAILS			
SWAILES,	A. Virginia	Alfred J. Neverson	26 Dec 1883 c
	Anne Y.	Josiah Willcoxen	17 Dec 1810
	Annie	Samuel E. Neverson	25 Feb 1896 c
	George W.	Susanna Green	20 Feb 1895 c
	Henrietta	Aaron Shelley	2 Jun 1886 c
	John T.	Anna L. Williams	31 May 1889 c
	John H.	Ann Maria Mason	7 Mar 1876
	Margaret	John Burress	1 Jan 1811
	Mary	Lewis Bond	23 Dec 1896 c
	Mary J.	Joseph H. Plummer	28 Dec 1885 c
	Ruth A.	John R. Mills	4 Jul 1896 c
SWAILS,	Alexander	Mamie Hackett	9 Dec 1891 c
SWAIN,	Jessie A.	James A. McKinney	19 Oct 1898 w
	Virlinder	John Hymes	11 Jul 1799
	William	Eliza Ann Burress	19 Dec 1828
SWALES - also see SWAILES			
SWALES,	Martha A.	John B. J. Bowen	26 Dec 1881 c
	Sallie	Carlton Mason	2 Apr 1872
SWAMLEY - also see SWOMLEY			
SWAMLEY,	Rebecca Ann	Samuel Gloyd	28 Apr 1827

* Part of last name and day from earlier reading

SWAN, Charles C.	Sadie Lee	30 Mar 1893	c
Edward	Maria Louisa Thrift	12 Nov 1844	
Rebecca	Thomas Veatch	21 Dec 1816	
SWANN, Ann C. D.	George Apsey	17 Feb 1829	
Bersheba	Thomas Shepherd	13 Jan 1830	
Cassandra	Benedict Darnale	6 May 1815	
Hubert	Sadie Lusby	21 Apr 1896	w
Mary J.	George Apsey	15 Oct 1832	
Rosa M.	Bradley Brown	8 Sep 1896	c
William	Mary Barrett	19 Apr 1815	
Zedekiah	Elizabeth R. Manley	5 Sep 1809	
SWART, Addie O.	John A. Talbott	2 Aug 1881	
Alphonso M.	Caroline E. Thompson	24 May 1893	w
SWARTZBACK - also see SCHWARTZBACH			
SWARTZBACK, John W.	Mary E. Bottomy	15 Apr 1874	
SWEARINGEN, Casandra	Baruch Prather	11 Dec 1799	
Cassie	Thomas S. Davis	29 Nov 1806	
Eleanor	William Elson Willson	12 Nov 1807	
Elizabeth	Edward Rabbett	8 Oct 1814	
Ruth	Thomas Bridget	26 Sep 1814	
Sarah	Walter W. Summers	23 Apr 1805	
Susan	James E. Willcoxen	29 Jan 1810	
Van	Milley Davis	27 May 1806	
Van	Elizabeth Green	21 Mar 1812	
SWEENY, Elizabeth	James P. Fennican	4 Nov 1801	
Ella A.	James W. Anawalt	27 Jul 1893	w
Mary	John Cross	19 Mar 1810	
SWICK, James E.	Charlotte Broughton	22 Jul 1895	w
SWIFT, Elisha W.	Susanna Darby	23 Feb 1835	
SWIGER, Michael H.	Sarah Y. Easton	1 Jun 1837	
SWINK, John	Priscilla Nicholes	16 Dec 1817	
William	Naomi Nicholls	15 Jan 1829	
SWOMLEY - also see SWAMLEY			
SWOMLEY, Jacob	Ellender Fulks	18 Jan 1799	
SYLVESTER, William H.	Mary Powers	23 Dec 1891	w
TABLER, Eliza S.	William O. Hammett	27 Oct 1891	w
Mary*	John M. Caffery	7 Jul 1871	
TAGGART, William H.	Mary L. Smith	12 May 1897	w
TALBERT, Mary R.	Adam B. Dolly	23 Feb 1858	
Samuel B.	Mary L. King	19 Mar 1861	
William F.	Matilda C. Darby	24 Mar 1862	
Zadok	Henrietta Benson	22 Apr 1839	
TALBOT - also see TALBERT			
TALBOT, Henry	Sarah Benson	18 Jul 1812	
TALBOTT, Ann Maria	John T. Williams	11 Jun 1841	
Benson	Maria Hyde	31 Dec 1847	
Charles H.	Caroline Greenfield	8 Aug 1889	w
Edward	Caroline Magruder	11 Mar 1819	
Eliza M.	Isaac H. Davis	12 Sep 1888	w
Emmeline M.	O. L. Bradford	1 Nov 1844	
Hattersly W.	Laura W. Holland	9 Feb 1874	
John A.	Addie O. Swart	2 Aug 1881	
Mary	Collin Williamson	4 Jun 1798	

* Last name very light; could be incorrect

TALBOTT, Mary Ann	Joseph Anderson	10 Mar 1823	
Nathan T.	Poulina Hays	8 Dec 1857	
Odle	Mary Ann Harwood	26 Nov 1823	
Theophilus	Virgnia Austin	27 Apr 1875	
Walter M.	Harriet M. Muncaster	9 Nov 1857	
William	Eliza Magruder	2 Sep 1812	
William H.	Bertha C. Hall	1 Sep 1885	w
TALLEY - also see TELLEY			
TALLEY, Robert E.	Emma Parker	20 May 1893	c
TALLIAFERRO, Reuben A.	Matilda Johnson	5 May 1867	
TALLMAN, Thomas C.	Mary E. Shoemaker	30 Dec 1865	
TANEY, Ann S.	Thomas C. Willcox	18 Nov 1890	w
Catharine H.	James M. Willcox	16 Oct 1883	
Joseph	Christina Craig	1 Mar 1874	
Mary	Lawson Garnett	22 Feb 1871	
Nelly Ann	Toliver Wallace	7 Aug 1873	
William	Columbia Willson	10 Mar 1845	
TANNIHILL, Mary	John Turnbull	11 Jul 1801	
TAPSICO, William	Maria Lucas	19 May 1894	c
TARELL - also see TERRILL			
TARELL, Ann	Patrick Carroll	25 Jun 1798	
TARMAN, Asa	Eleanor R. Burriss	12 May 1829	
Harriet A.	John G. Burris	7 Sep 1852	
Mary E.	Joseph Nevitt	29 Dec 1847	
Samuel	Eleanor Ball	15 Dec 1829	
Thomas L.	Emily A. Shanks	1 Jun 1859	
TARMON, Mary Agnes	William T. Lynch	12 Nov 1860	
TASCO, John H.	Matilda Kelley	9 May 1873	
Mary E.	John W. Hopkins	6 Jun 1893	c
TATUM, William R.	Marian W. Haviland	26 Sep 1893	w
TAYLOR, Amanda	George W. Mobley	31 Jan 1898	w
Ann E.	William Nichols	7 Oct 1842	
Anna M.	James P. Mason	5 Jan 1892	c
Arthur *.	Laura Perry	22 Mar 1898	w
Basil	Eliza Tyler	27 Dec 1870	
Basil	Sarah Taylor	1 Sep 1880	
Charles	Nellie Gilbert	11 Mar 1872	
Christopher	Rachel Riley	25 Nov 1843	
Eliza	John T. Hebron	28 Dec 1891	c
Ella J.	Albert Young	18 Dec 1895	w
Ellen	Joseph Green	21 Aug 1879	c
Fenton	Caroline Liles	12 Jun 1877	
George	Rebecca Colson	2 Aug 1860	
George	Lizzie Nichols	11 Apr 1887	c
Harry C.	Maria A. Deitz	14 Dec 1887	w
Henson	Tony Ann Davis	4 Aug 1887	c
Isadora	Abraham Lancester	14 Dec 1876	
Isaiah	Annie Nugent	10 Jun 1896	c
Jacquelin P.	Katharine Wall	10 Jun 1895	w
Jesse	Catharine Smith	3 Apr 1811	
John R.	Susie J. Boswell	4 Feb 1884	w
John T.	Louisa Brogden	26 Oct 1887	c
Mamie	Henry Hull	7 Jul 1894	c
Maria	William Beckwith	29 Oct 1879	c

* Initial N or W

TAYLOR, Martha E.	------ T. Jones*	18 Dec 1860	
Mary Ann	William Statia	29 Nov 1800	
Mary Ann	Charles Batchelor	28 Feb 1859	
Mary Jane	James Brashears	27 Feb 1843	
Mary M.	James W. Dillehay	13 Jan 1877	w
Peyton W.	Julia Ann Magruder	5 Apr 1827	
Richard Thomas	Mary Daymude	5 Aug 1879	
Robert	Nettie Arnold	1 Mar 1893	w
Robert H.	Martha Letcher	19 May 1866	
Salena	Nelson Kelly	24 Nov 1881	c
Sarah	Samuel Horner	12 Jan 1810	
Sarah	Basil Taylor	1 Sep 1880	
Susan	Andrew Jackson	1 Dec 1896	c
William	Martha Nicholson	9 May 1870	
William	Catharine Williams	** Sep 1883	c
William	Loreno Harris	21 Jun 1884	c
William	Eliza Everson	3 Mar 1888	c
William C.	Estella Gerard	27 Oct 1896	w
William H.	Elizabeth B. Riley	26 Oct 1868	
Winnie	Charles Woodley	18 Nov 1874	
TELLEY - also see TALLEY			
TELLEY, Sarah	Wallace H. Brown	11 May 1898	c
TEMPLE, Maggie E.	Daniel H. Hamilton	7 Jun 1892	c
TENDLEY - also see TINDLEY			
TENDLEY, John B.	Janet M. Fendly	29 Jan 1817	
TENNENT, John G.	Kate H. Allen	2 Sep 1898	w
TENNEY, Mary	Ignatius Drury	26 Apr 1800	
TERRILL - also see TARELL			
TERRILL, William Rufus, Lt.	Emily Drennen Henry	2 Mar 1858	
TERRY, Annie	Lloyd Coates	18 Nov 1890	c
Hynes E.	Jessie B. Lane	29 Dec 1896	w
James	Matilda Carroll	9 Sep 1870	
James George	Hannah Plummer	7 Sep 1888	c
John A.	Mary E. Thatcher	23 Apr 1889	w
Martha	Samuel William Henry Dobbins	31 Dec 1896	c
Mary I.	William T. Lucas	9 Aug 1890	c
THATCHER, Lidia	Peter Valet	7 Feb 1801	
Mary E.	John A. Terry	23 Apr 1889	w
THOM, William T.	Elizabeth P. Miller	9 Oct 1888	w
THOMAS, Allen	Elizabeth V. McPherson	1 Oct 1897	c
Alverda	William E. Barnard	16 Nov 1887	w
Almira C.	David C. Y. Bolinger	17 Sep 1880	w
Anna	Henson Gittings	6 May 1897	c
Anne	Isaac Lancaster	13 Jul 1871	
Ara	John Simms	17 Jan 1867	
Augusta W.	Horace J. Long	2 Feb 1894	w
Benjamin F.	Martha Ann Holland	23 Apr 1867	
Benjamin F.	Sarah Miller	28 Apr 1874	
C. W.	Jenia E. Staub	23 Mar 1880	w
Catherine	George W. Dorsey	22 Aug 1894	c
Caroline	Robert Awkward	2 Nov 1858	

* First name is written over
** Cannot read day; before 19

THOMAS,	Charles	Susie A. America	5 Aug 1897 w
	Charles E.	Martha E. Carter	25 Sep 1890 c
	Charlott R.	Walter Gody	8 Oct 1818
	Clara	Nathan Holland	7 Sep 1893 c
	Cora	Edward Keys	13 Dec 1892 c
	Edward	Lydia S. Gilpin	15 Apr 1833
	Elijah Ann	Charles Agustus Snowden	3 Mar 1885 c
	Eliza	John Alexander Veatch	21 Jun 1822
	Eliza	James Hill	15 Oct 1896 c
	Eliza M.	Joseph H. Bradley, Jr.	22 Nov 1856
	Elizabeth	David W. Thompson	4 Aug 1892 c
	Emily	J. L. Massey	29 Jul 1872
	Eva B.	Thomas W. Oliver	14 May 1889 w
	Frank B.	Caroline H. Stonestreet	24 Jan 1894 w
	Frank M.	Mary H. Beaton	9 Oct 1894 w
	George	Frances Simpson	15 Sep 1891 c
	Georgiana	James R. Martin	16 Jul 1887 c
	Harriet	Howard Woods	5 May 1880
	Harriet Margaret	Nathan Luffborough	30 Jan 1844
	Harry	Henrietta Brown	27 Dec 1883 c
	Henny	Henry Offutt	11 Jun 1879
	Henrietta E.	William H. Briggs	4 May 1836
	Henry, Rev.	Rosalie Poole	23 Nov 1885 w
	Henry M.	Mary R. Young	13 Oct 1888 c
	Isabella	John William Diggs	23 Nov 1884 c
	James	Mary Jackson	10 Jun 1895 c
	James H.	Alcinda Hill	11 Nov 1896 c
	Jane	Charles G. Porter	6 Oct 1842
	Jennie	Oliver Watts	2 Jan 1879 c
	John	Nancy Berry	19 Nov 1798
	John	Eliza Hickman	30 Dec 1818
	John "ye third"	Amelia Gassaway	5 Sep 1822
	John	Harriet V. Brent	28 May 1872
	John	Eliza Chase	3 Jun 1873
	John	Margaret A. Lynch	9 May 1881
	John M.	Harriet Margaret Dunlop	15 Nov 1832
	John R.	Lavinia Hopkins	22 Apr 1867
	Josephine	Michael S. Warren	18 Sep 1889 c
	Kitty	James W. Walker	8 Oct 1825
	Laura	John Thomas Watts	20 Dec 1883 c
	Leanna	James H. Marshall	3 Jan 1889 c
	Maggie L.	Edward F. Chappell	3 Feb 1894 w
	Marshall	Winnie White	27 Feb 1890 c
	Martha	Thomas P. Harvey	14 Oct 1845
	Martha	Julius Curtis	10 Sep 1895 c
	Mary	Joseph Howard	14 Dec 1802
	Mary	Benjamin Becraft Higgins	25 Sep 1822
	Mary	Hilleary Washington	28 Dec 1882
	Mary	Charles J. Knobel	29 Oct 1891 w
	Mary A.	James W. Brogden	4 Oct 1895 c
	Mary F.	Michael S. Warren	*30 Jan 1879 c
	Mary J.	Charles Gaither	13 Jun 1888 c
	Mary Willson	Reubin Riggs	6 Feb 1805

* Out of order in book; entered in with Nov 1880 licenses

THOMAS,	Philip	Carrie Hammond	2 Sep 1897 w
	Ranney	Harriet P. Lodge	15 Jun 1819
	Robert	Betsey West	8 Jun 1866
	Robert	Lizzie Lyles	28 Dec 1882 c
	Rosamond H.	Thomas Kennedy	23 Oct 1798
	Samuel P.	Elizabeth G. Porter	24 Sep 1845
	Sarah E.	Charles A. Adams	4 Apr 1888 c
	Virginia	Richard Snowden	28 Nov 1878
	William	Peggy Fletcher	16 Mar 1798
	William	Angeline Gue	11 Dec 1839
	William	Mary E. Beander	17 May 1877 c
	William	Effie Smith	9 Dec 1895 c
	William Eli	Lucy Budd	28 Sep 1898 c
	William H.	Martha Jane Budd	17 Jan 1871
	William H.	Susie Carter	3 May 1883 c
	William H.	Rachel M. Kelley	29 Dec 1887 c
	William Henry	Rachel A. Snowden	30 Nov 1866
	William J.	Rebecca M. Porter	18 Oct 1837
	William J.	Exzeal Williams	3 Oct 1886 c
THOMPSON - also see THOMSON			
THOMPSON,	A. Rosetta	Walter Nicholson	24 Feb 1865
	Acka	Charles Andrews	13 Sep 1824
	Airy M.	James N. Benton	12 Mar 1868
	Albert B.	Sarah L. Bowman	15 Apr 1856
	Alcinda L.	John S. Duvall	1 Jun 1858
	Aletha	Rezin Penn	20 Oct 1820
	Alexander C. H.	Martha E. Hopewood	16 Jun 1890 w
	Alice	Nathaniel Genus	25 Dec 1877 c
	Alice V.	Gustavus Moxley	24 Nov 1891 w
	Amanda C.	John W. Walker	21 Feb 1870
	Amanda J.	Thomas G. Ward	22 Dec 1866
	Amelia	Aaaron Bland	15 Apr 1891 c
	Amelia E.	James E. Mason	22 Dec 1886 c
	Annabelle V.	Patrick H. Coonry	26 Oct 1855
	Ann E.	John T. Hawkins	11 Nov 1858
	Ann Rebecca	William Doyle	1 Aug 1842
	Anna A.	Joseph O. Moulden	8 Dec 1887 w
	Anne	John Key	3 Feb 1801
	Annie E.	Rufus M. Belt	22 Dec 1873
	Ara	William Lomax	28 May 1835
	Benjamin	Elizabeth Hany	25 Jan 1799
	Benjamin	Ann E. Atwood	7 Jan 1833
	Benjamin F.	Amanda C. Flook	5 Dec 1872
	Benjamin H.	Georgie Rabbitt	10 Jan 1878 w
	Benjamin H.	Mary E. Sullivan	13 Nov 1890 w
	C. W.	Mary Isabell Nicholls	4 Mar 1868
	Calvin	Leanna M. Higgins	26 Oct 1875
	Caroline E.	Alphonso M. Swart	24 May 1893 w
	Caroline Elizabeth	James Hanson Crawford	25 Dec 1832
	Cassandra	Leonard Bean	1 Oct 1816
	Catharine	Jacob Day	25 Nov 1817
	Catharine	Washington Earp	4 Aug 1824
	Catherine	Perry Sullivan	4 Jan 1858
	Catherine J.	Philip Reid	13 Dec 1882 w
	Catherine R.	William E. Larman	16 Jan 1893 w

THOMPSON, Cena   Francis Walker   19 Feb 1811
         Charles   Laura Williams   23 Feb 1892 c
         Charles A.   Ellen S. Belt   5 Dec 1877 w
         Charles E.   Maggie E. Purdum   28 Feb 1883 w
         Charles E.   Alice M. Page   28 Jan 1896 w
         Charles W.   Priscilla Grimes   29 Dec 1864
         Clara B.   Charles R. Walters   28 Oct 1891 w
         Clarence B.   Blanche A. Hardy   15 Apr 1891 w
         Cordelia   Solomon Plummer   3 Mar 1824
         David   Elizabeth Mobley   3 Jan 1809
         David H.   Sarah J. Hawkins   17 Dec 1858
         David W.   Elizabeth Thomas   4 Aug 1892 c
         Deborah   M. W. Belt   27 Feb 1877 w
         Drusilla J.   Enoch George Ward   29 Jan 1835
         E. Columbus   Sarah Ann Burns   12 Dec 1854
         Edgar A.   Annie M. Clagett   21 Dec 1881
         Edward E.   Martha T. Newton   31 Mar 1875
         Eleanor   Nicholas Boswell   3 Mar 1810
         Eleanora   Joseph D. Thompson   24 Dec 1889 w
         Elijah   Elizabeth Ricketts   13 Apr 1825
         Eliza   James L. Shaw   29 Nov 1830
         Eliza Ann   Jared Ray   15 Apr 1829
         Eliza E.   Elias Moulden   16 Feb 1841
         Eliza Jane   Ephraim Story   12 Nov 1850
         Elizabeth   Robert Windsor   6 May 1805
         Elizabeth   Jeremiah Brown   8 Jan 1816
         Elizabeth   John Burgess   10 Jan 1818
         Elizabeth   Elias King   4 Jan 1819
         Elizabeth   Joseph Harding   30 Jan 1856
         Elizabeth   Willson L. Earp   28 Jan 1863
         Elizabeth   Ambrose Welling   24 Feb 1866
         Elizabeth H.   George A. Munro   6 Nov 1858
         Elizabeth M.   Charles Saffell, Jr.   3 Jan 1828
         Elizabeth M.   James Mortimer Larman   * Jan 1883
         Ella   Joseph Posey   9 Oct 1889 w
         Emma N.   George F. Linthicum   13 Jun 1882
         Evan   Elizabeth Anderson   27 Dec 1813
         Festus M.   Martha Giffins   8 Dec 1886 w
         Fielder   Elizabeth Leeke   29 Jan 1805
         Florence   Walter Simms   26 Oct 1891 c
         Florence V.   Thomas R. Marlow   8 Feb 1889 w
         Frances M.   Daniel M. Howard   2 Mar 1869
         Frances V.   Samuel H. Easton   13 Apr 1868
         Frederick A.   Mary D. Hall   15 Sep 1876
         George   Ann Pierce**   25 Mar 1895 c
         George   Lizzie Johnson   24 Dec 1895 c
         George H.   Mary V. Hilleary   17 Sep 1861
         George W.   Mahala Blowers   23 Feb 1835
         George W.   Lelia A. Robertson   24 Sep 1887 w
         Grace E.   Windsor L. Bean   2 Feb 1898 w
         Harriet A.   Rezin Duvall   21 Feb 1849
         Harriett   Abraham Shekells   6 Oct 1823
         Harriett   Philemon Griffith   31 Jan 1824

* Cannot read day; between 2 and 9
** This could be Prince

THOMPSON,	Hattie V.	Ezekiel Moxley	9 Nov 1874
	Henly	Susanna Hill	4 Nov 1805
	Henry	Sarah Boswell	30 Mar 1809
	Henry	Lydia Calwight	31 Oct 1812
	Henry S.	Sarah E. Williams	4 Feb 1874
	Hessy	Ignatius Ward	30 Apr 1811
	Hester	Joseph McKaig	11 Aug 1886 c
	Hesther	Charles Hobbs	13 Mar 1806
	Hezekiah	Eliza Bennett	18 Aug 1817
	Horace	Harriet Ann Plummer	16 Dec 1853
	Horace	Emeline Leizear	12 Nov 1873
	Horatio	Ann B. Lewis	21 Dec 1829
	Horatio	Julianna Henry	20 Aug 1835
	Horton G.	Louisa G. Marshall	11 Apr 1888 w
	Ida M.	John C. Cole	15 Jan 1889 w
	Isabella	Charles H. Coopard	6 Feb 1871
	James	Elizabeth Clagett	16 Feb 1837
	James A.	Martha A. Thompson	12 Aug 1869
	James A.	Eliza E. Baker	18 Jul 1878 w
	James E.	Anna M. Hodges	30 Oct 1893 w
	James Edward	Lizzie Rabbitt	29 Nov 1878
	Jane R.	Samuel J. Moulden	26 Dec 1848
	Jemima	Lewis Mobley	3 Dec 1807
	Jennie	James Chambers	17 Mar 1883 c
	Jennie	Benjamin Hatton	16 Oct 1889 w
	John	Susanna Ridgely	14 Oct 1805
	John	Margaret A. Murphy	1 Jun 1857
	John	Mary Johnson	30 Jan 1869
	John	Eliza V. Rabbitt	6 Mar 1872
	John	Emeline Brown	11 Dec 1878 c
	John A.	Fanny Harriss	11 Mar 1862
	John H.	Mary Burnes	3 Mar 1832
	John H.	Sarah E. Layton	7 Jun 1843
	John H.	Mary E. Price	28 Oct 1843
	John H.	Caroline Allnutt	6 Oct 1845
	John T.	Susan E. Ray	6 Feb 1854
	Joseph D.	Eleanora Thompson	24 Dec 1889 w
	Joseph M.	Lulie B. Beamer	10 Aug 1895 w
	Joshua	Harriet R. Ray	30 Nov 1848
	Judson	Cenah Boswell	22 Jan 1811
	Julia Ann	Benjamin Walker	31 Oct 1825
	Julia M.	Everett H. Cecil	3 Jul 1880
	Juliann	Peter Smith	30 Dec 1840
	Katie V.	Clarence B. Allnutt	8 Nov 1893 w
	Keziah	Benoni Belt	16 Jan 1813
	Laura	John Peter Kemp	6 Mar 1871
	Leanna	John E. Grimes	27 Jun 1895 w
	Lewis F.	Jennetter Boswell	5 Apr 1881
	Lilian A.	George W. Gray	31 Mar 1897 w
	Louisana	Jacob Pickins	31 Mar 1836
	Lucinda	Cornelius M. Bean	17 Nov 1861
	Lucretia J.	Addison F. Dodd	19 Jul 1877 w
	Lydia	Reuben Murphey	15 Sep 1837
	M. Bess	Isaac W. Rollins	18 Sep 1866
	M. Velinda	Leonard S. Chapman	12 Sep 1864
	Mahala	Thomas Harris	13 Feb 1822

THOMPSON,	Margaret	David Anderson	5 Feb 1799
	Margaret	Stacey Crawford	2 Jun 1825
	Marion W.	Cornelia J. Williams	30 Jul 1883
	Martha	William Jordan	18 Oct 1817
	Martha	Allen Scrivener	20 Oct 1853
	Martha	Martin Cuff	26 Jun 1879
	Martha	Levi Fisher	6 Nov 1893 c
	Martha A.	James A. Thompson	12 Aug 1869
	Martha C.	Robert Brown	13 Sep 1847
	Martha C.	Milford Warren	13 Dec 1888 c
	Martha E.	Thomas L. Milstead	30 Jan 1893 w
	Martha R.	Maurice E. ?. Duvall	11 Jun 1883
	Martin	Sarah English	14 Nov 1848
	Martin	Lucinda Lewis	20 Apr 1849
	Mary	William Gentle	6 Jan 1806
	Mary	William O'Neale O'Conner	5 Feb 1819
	Mary Ann	George Boswell	8 Mar 1820
	Mary Ann	Elias Lizear	11 Jan 1838
	Mary Anne	Denton Summers	25 Dec 1811
	Mary C.	Joseph R. English	15 Dec 1865
	Mary C.	Isaiah T. Prather	24 Oct 1895 c
	Mary E.	Charles H. Jackson	27 Nov 1895 c
	Mary J.	J. Wallace Garrett	2 Jan 1879 w
	Mary L.	Mertimer Mouldin	28 Dec 1852
	Mary L.	George William Woodfield	* Jan 1880
	Maryann	Elijah Medley	19 Jan 1828
	Massy A.	John Crawford	27 Oct 1821
	Matilda	John H. Burnes	21 Apr 1829
	Matilda	Samuel C. Thompson	8 Oct 1844
	Matilda A.	Joseph M. Pope	6 Jun 1870
	Matilda Ann	Ninian Reed	1 Feb 1832
	Mattie	Lewis Reed	19 Dec 1895 w
	Middleton	Mary Clarke	15 Dec 1805
	Mildred	Joseph Anderson	10 Mar 1814
	Milly	Greenberry Johnson	14 Mar 1821
	Mollie	George W. Burriss	11 Sep 1891 w
	Mollie V.	Alphonzo N. Clagetts	26 Jul 1877 w
	Morris	Louisa C. Fling	25 Dec 1851
	Mortimer	Marian Willson	2 Jan 1857
	Nacy	Cynthia Peddicoart	22 Dec 1812
	Nancy	Wesley Clements	29 Mar 1843
	Nancy E.	John H. Shorts	4 Aug 1896 w
	Nannie	Washington Thompson	16 Apr 1889 w
	Nathan	Ann Cooper	24 Dec 1814
	Nathan T.	Ruthy Mary T. Hawkins	7 Nov 1861
	Nellie A.	Allen H. Burdette	19 Feb 1884
	Nelson	Elizabeth Knott	6 Jan 1845
	Oliver W.	Laura L. Clagett	20 Feb 1883 w
	Otho ?.	Mary E. Beckard	20 Aug 1884 c
	Polly	John Boswell	5 Mar 1800
	Richard	Rebecca Peddicort	21 Dec 1810
	Richard	Elizabeth Plummer	23 Dec 1816

* Cannot read day; either 20 or 21

THOMPSON,	Richard	Catherine Fister	3 Jul 1819	
	Richard H.	Anna Blowers	6 Feb 1835	
	Robert	Sophia Culp	28 Mar 1821	
	Robert	Betsy Martin	16 Oct 1829	
	Ruth	Thomas English	16 Jan 1819	
	Ruth E.	Charles A. Crawford	21 Nov 1850	
	Sallie M.	George C. Pearre	25 Aug 1887	w
	Samuel C.	Matilda Thompson	8 Oct 1844	
	Samuel F.	Mary E. Gittings	5 Dec 1876	
	Samuel L.	Elizabeth D. Ridgely	17 Feb 1873	
	Sarah A.	John T. Leisure	15 Dec 1846	
	Sarah A.	William C. Rollins	24 May 1858	
	Sarah Ann	William Reid	13 Sep 1847	
	Sarah Ann	Edward Woodfield	11 Jun 1873	
	Sarah C.	Samuel F. Bennett	23 Feb 1846	
	Sarah E.	Hamilton Crawford	22 Nov 1866	
	Sarah J.	George H. Richardson	22 Nov 1897	w
	Sidonia L.	Edgar Dodd	19 Jul 1877	w
	Susan	Nathan Miles	3 Feb 1815	
	Susan	William Smith	14 Dec 1887	c
	Susan A.	Isaac W. Lekites	9 Feb 1865	
	Susan A.	Charles W. Musgrove	10 Dec 1868	
	Susanna	William Thompson	17 Dec 1813	
	Susannah	Nathen Miles	26 Dec 1809	
	Susie Axia	John J. Bottlemay	1 Oct 1880	w
	Sylvester	Judy Ann Pickins	27 Oct 1862	
	Sylvester	Mary C. Beavers	30 Jan 1866	
	Tabitha	Francis Ratliff	4 Feb 1807	
	Theodore C.	Effie Duvall	26 Dec 1888	w
	Thomas	Rhoda Darby	5 Apr 1814	
	Thomas	Drusilla Darby	6 Oct 1828	
	Thomas F.	Annie L. Shaw	9 Aug 1883	
	Thomas J.	Rosetta Read	6 Jan 1837	
	Treacy	John R. Peters	11 Nov 1879	c
	Washington	Nannie Thompson	16 Apr 1889	w
	William	Ann Brashears	19 Dec 1803	
	William	Mary Walden	4 Feb 1804	
	William	Susanna Thompson	17 Dec 1813	
	William	Maryann Gardiner	3 Dec 1817	
	William	Anne Burns	19 Apr 1832	
	William	Susannah Shaw	14 Dec 1836	
	William	Rosie Stewart	4 Feb 1892	c
	William of Richard	Cloe E. Pope	10 Feb 1836	
	William H.	Alice Brook	28 May 1884	c
	William Jefferson	Catharine V. Bennett	16 Jan 1872	
	William T.	Florence M. Appleby	* Feb 1879	w
	William W.	Julia A. Gittings	20 Mar 1838	
	Zaccheus C.	Ellen V. Crawford	24 Jan 1874	
	Zach	Mary Anderson	12 Sep 1822	
	Zach	Susan Duvall	10 Jan 1848	
	Zachariah	Sally Wyvell	17 Jan 1827	
	Zachariah	Margaret A. V. Carroll	17 Feb 1893	w

* Day has blot on it; either 25 or 26

THOMSON - also see THOMPSON		
THOMSON, Charles W.	Mary A. Peters	23 Sep 1880 c
THORN, Florence	Clem Pratt	5 Dec 1896 c
John	Annie Parker	5 Nov 1887 c
William	Anne Ray	2 Feb 1810
THORNTON, Anne	James Gassaway	1 Aug 1872
Belle	Charles Dyson	2 Sep 1890 c
Beverly	Susan Hackett	24 Dec 1868
Beverly	Elizabeth Lee	4 Dec 1878
Elias	Eliza Gibbs	26 Mar 1888 c
Frances	Edward W. Waters	3 Oct 1886 c
Granville T.	Mary E. Ray	1 Nov 1898 c
Henrietta	George W. HackARK*	18 Apr 1881
John	Martha Bond	16 Dec 1887 c
John T.	Sarah Dent	21 Feb 1896 c
Josephine	Green Berry Smith	1 Feb 1883 c
Perry	Mary E. Cole	8 Feb 1894 c
THORPE, Sarah	James Henley	22 May 1879 w
THRASHER - also see THRESHER		
THRASHER, Margaret	Samuel Stewart	2 May 1811
Sarah	Leonard Pile Ozburn	5 Aug 1799
THRECKER, James	Sarah McPherson	13 Aug 1800
THRESHER - also see THRASHER		
THRESHER, Elezabeth	Benjamin Davis	16 Feb 1798
THRIFT, Absalom	Jane Offutt	21 Dec 1803
Ann M. M.	Harrison G. Ward	25 Nov 1879 w
Bertie	John W. Garrett	5 Dec 1882 w
Charles H.	Mary A. McCrossin	7 Apr 1874
Elizabeth	Eden Gloyd	23 Apr 1835
Elizabeth J.	George W. Case	30 Dec 1850
James M.	Charity D. Waters	27 Jun 1825
John A.	Mary Frances Minnis	12 Sep 1866
Laura R.	John W. Carroll	16 May 1863
Maria Louisa	Edward Swan	12 Nov 1844
Mary	James H. Claggett	24 Dec 1838
Mary F.	Archibald Mullican	11 Sep 1871
Samuel	Ara M. S. Clagett	24 Jan 1839
Samuel	Mary Ellen Hawkins	10 Dec 1855
William	Lillie Payne	28 Sep 1896 w
TIBBS, Moses	Christie Simms	9 Feb 1893 c
TILLARD, Elizabeth E.	Abraham S. Hays	23 Jan 1816
TILLETT, John	Mollie Rice	22 Jun 1875
TILLEY - also see TILLY		
TILLEY, Albert H.	Alice V. Clark	21 Mar 1896 c
Charles H.	Mary J. King	6 May 1886 c
Laura J.	Joseph R. Adams	27 Apr 1882 c
Samuel	Mary Washington	5 Oct 1891 c
TILLING, John Henry	Dellia Wyville	2 Apr 1877 w
TILLY - also see TILLEY		
TILLY, Sally	Berry Griffith	23 May 1826
TINDLEY - also see TENDLEY		
TINDLEY, Joseph O.	Bretania R. Martin	13 Aug 1884 w
TINSON, John	Harriet Walker	21 Dec 1878 c
TIPPETT, Edward D.	Sarah Ann Williams	1 Feb 1810

* Last letters of last name difficult to read; may be incorrect

Name	Spouse	Date	
TITLOW, Samuel L.	Ida J. Trail	7 May 1888	w
Thomas R.	Jennie M. Weer	11 May 1872	
TOBTAN, Washington*	Annie M. Clark	14 Oct 1884	w
TODD, Anna	Henry Bussard	8 Oct 1817	
Rachel	Lewis Carroll	17 Nov 1879	
TOGOOD - also see TOOGOOD			
TOGOOD, Charles A.	Martha A. Magruder	27 Jul 1889	w
TOLLE, Henry C.	Elizabeth Fyffe	10 Oct 1890	w
TOMES, Sarah A.	John H. Gibbs	13 Oct 1880	c
TOMLINSON, Louisa	David Shoemaker	11 Jan 1830	
William	Patsy Mockbee	9 Jan 1813	
William	Mary Ann Perry	24 Mar 1840	
TOMY, Bridget E.	Henry Green	18 Feb 1858	
TOOGOOD - also see TOGOOD			
TOOGOOD, Alice	James Johnson	14 Jun 1886	c
Elizabeth	Samuel Cambash	30 May 1887	c
Maggie	William Combash	23 Dec 1879	c
Margaret	Washington Tyler	12 Apr 1882	
Martha	Charles Anderson	19 May 1866	
Seanna	Nathaniel Frazier	10 Dec 1889	c
TOONEY, Sallie	Joseph Hackett	23 Jul 1890	c
TOPHOUSE, Samuel	Fanny Fisher	16 Nov 1800	
TORPIN - also see TURPIN			
TORPIN, Richard Jr.	Ellen T. Banrsley	15 Feb 1897	w
TOTTEN, James E.	Elizabeth Carroll	9 Jun 1890	w
Mollie	Charles A. Lang	9 Jun 1890	w
TOUELL, Philip	Mary Whealan	22 Feb 1800	
TOWERS, John T.	Eliza Palmer	27 Oct 1854	
Louise	Harrison S. Hall	11 Jun 1897	w
TOWLES, Ella C.	Eugene A. Poole	5 Jan 1880	w
Joseph M.	Fannie A. Upton	25 Jun 1897	w
TOWNSEN, Leonard	Eleanor Higdon	18 Jan 1803	
TOWNSEND, Abraham	Hannah Hausly**	10 Dec 1800	
Blanche M.	Marcellus Etchison	15 Dec 1891	w
Elizabeth	Basil D. Beall	14 Oct 1806	
Florence	Harry O. Dorsey	31 Oct 1887	w
Jesse	Mahala Duley	29 Sep 1814	
Lacey	Joseph P. Moore	27 Feb 1877	w
Lemuel P.	Sarah E. Orendorff	10 Feb 1859	
TOWNSHEND, Charles F.	Ida J. Hobbs	14 Feb 1865	
TOWSON, Charles M.	Rena H. Smith	29 May 1897	w
TRACEY, Senor	James Riggs	18 Dec 1805	
TRAIL, Amanda	Henry Kemp	3 Nov 1828	
Ann	John Burkhead	30 Nov 1813	
Anna M.	Joseph T. Getzendanner	14 Oct 1848	
Anne	William Fletchall	31 Oct 1815	
Ashford	Ann Sanders	28 Dec 1803	
Barton	Sallie Gray	2 Jan 1872	
Barton	Mary Grace Snyder	21 May 1884	w
Catharine E.	Charles E. Davis	5 Sep 1867	
Christian	Richard E. Ricketts	3 Dec 1850	
Dallas	William E. Keebley	13 Nov 1867	
Edward	Harriett Fish	27 Apr 1813	

* As Written; other records show Topham to be correct
** Hausley from earlier reading, but "au" not really readable

TRAIL, Edward	Ida V. Hopwood	7 Jul 1897	w
Eleanor	Wilfred Young	20 Jan 1824	
Elizabeth H.	William Proctor Hill	24 Mar 1897	w
Elizabeth R.	Benjamin Ricketts	31 Dec 1828	
Emma	Willie H. Knotts	31 Oct 1877	w
Fanny	William Ricketts	18 Dec 1822	
Guliel Mariah	Merchant Ricketts	12 Feb 1817	
Harriet M.	William Metzger	11 Dec 1829	
Hezekiah	Priscilla Gutray	2 Nov 1809	
Hezekiah	Catherine Bray	28 Dec 1811	
Hezekiah	Sarah Ann Baker	14 Dec 1841	
Ida E.	Albert H. Ricketts	28 Apr 1897	w
Ida J.	Samuel L. Titlow	7 May 1888	w
Isabel	Francis T. Cahill	20 Dec 1877	w
James	Mary Buxton	11 May 1811	
James L.	Melvinia R. Fitch	19 Dec 1843	
James T.	Mollie E. Benson	20 Dec 1870	
Jane	William H. Benson	5 Feb 1842	
Julia A.	Robert A. Davis	11 Apr 1861	
Leonard W.	Delia S. Wailes	10 Dec 1832	
Mamie	Charles E. Norris	18 Dec 1894	w
Margaretta	Bradley J. Norwood	4 Feb 1887	w
Mary A.	Charles M. Mossburg	3 Oct 1894	w
Mary Ann	George Buxton	4 Dec 1802	
Mary Jane	Joseph Hawkins	15 Dec 1841	
Mary L.	Allen Miles	28 Jun 1824	
Mattie A.	Richard H. Bennett	4 May 1881	
Nancy	William Snyder	17 Apr 1845	
Nathan	Susanna Buxton	19 Dec 1801	
Nathan L.	Harriet Beard	13 Dec 1843	
Nelson J.	Susan C. Carter	7 Mar 1872	
Notley	Verlinda Ricketts	19 Mar 1817	
Perry	Mary Ann Bean	17 Nov 1846	
Rachel	William Buxton	11 Apr 1806	
Rachel	Nicholas Ricketts	15 Apr 1811	
Richard L.	Mary P. Ward	1 Jan 1873	
Sarah Ann	Romulus Snyder	15 Oct 1839	
Sarah C.	George W. Matthews	2 May 1868	
Sarah E.	Charles Jones	12 Oct 1896	w
Susanna	William Henry Ricketts	10 Dec 1857	
Susannah	Clement Boswell	24 Dec 1821	
William	Ann Belt	30 Mar 1807	
William F.	Laura F. Sparrow	21 Feb 1876	
William H.	Julia Ann Moulding	1 May 1837	
William H.	Mary E. Cahill	24 Jan 1898	w
William Henry	Elizabeth Harriss	24 Oct 1839	
William L.	Cassandra Miles	23 Feb 1825	
TRAMMELL, George	Mary A. Dove	1 Jan 1870	
George W.	Nellie E. Meeks	7 Oct 1897	w
Israel	Clarissa Ann Lanham	21 Mar 1842	
Jane R.	Nicholas T. W. Ward	10 Oct 1871	
Susan P.	Horace Benton	26 Oct 1837	
William Smallwood	Rebecca Green	15 Jan 1806	
TRAVERS, Boyd	Margaret Adams	22 Jan 1817	
TRAVERSE, Sally Maria	Thomas Cook	2 Jan 1800	

TREE, Catharine	James H. Goodwin	20 Mar 1871	
TREVEY, Ada L.	Martin F. Hein	14 Nov 1894	w
Byron	Ada A. Pumphrey	9 Oct 1895	w
Jacob Cowan	Florence V. Harris	4 May 1868	
TREVY, Lelia E.	Charles O. Bean	7 Mar 1888	w
TRICE, Alice P.	William McKenzie	29 Apr 1897	w
TRILL, Charles F.	Mary Ellen Quirk	11 Oct 1880	w
TRIPLETT, William H.	Kitty Alexander	3 Mar 1806	
TRIPPE, Edward	Catherine D. Bowie	29 Nov 1841	
TROOP, John	Rebecca Moreley	26 Dec 1798	
TROTT, Annie M.	Edward L. McCabe	26 Dec 1894	w
TROUT, Charles H.	Bettie E. Bowen	8 May 1896	w
Valentine Tobias	Margaret Ellen Becraft	6 Oct 1869	
TRUCKS - also see TRUX			
TRUCKS, Ann Maria	James A. Parker	11 Jan 1868	
Henrietta	James A. Fling	22 Nov 1864	
John E.	Elizabeth J. White	7 Feb 1859	
Martha E.	John T. Barns	19 Jan 1855	
Mary A. C.	John H. Gittings	17 Aug 1878	
TRUMAN, Elizabeth	John H. Boswell	10 Feb 1853	
Jane	William T. Lewis	16 Feb 1850	
John	Ann Biggs	30 Dec 1859	
TRUNDLE, Alethea	James Lee	23 Mar 1815	
Ann	Stephen White	12 Dec 1823	
Ann M.	William Granger	22 Nov 1852	
Anna V.	Edward Nichols	9 Nov 1854	
Anne V.	William H. Hempstone	9 Mar 1822	
Basil	Easter Hughs	20 May 1799	
Charlott	Alfred Belt	18 Dec 1809	
Clarissa A.	David Trundle	22 May 1851	
Daniel	Esther Belt	18 Nov 1802	
David	Clarissa A. Trundle	22 May 1851	
David Jr.	Ann Hempstone	2 Apr 1834	
David H.	Clarissa Ann Offutt	2 Jun 1835	
Delilah	Andrew Barneclow	21 Jan 1807	
Eleanor	Henry Jones	24 Dec 1807	
Eleanor A.	James O. Trundle	5 Nov 1859	
Emily A. J.	John W. Holland	22 Nov 1866	
Harriet	Samuel Craven	30 Nov 1831	
Henrietta J.	William D. Brooke	25 Sep 1860	
Hezekiah Lewis	Mary Elizabeth Nicholls	22 Apr 1839	
Hezekiah W.	Emily Ann Jones	25 Apr 1835	
Horatio	Catherine Poose	15 Jan 1802	
Horatio	Elizabeth H. Fechtig	29 Dec 1863	
Isaih	Casander V. Burriss	* Oct 1844	
James E.	Katie D. Bowie	10 Jun 1890	w
James O.	Eleanor A. Trundle	5 Nov 1859	
James Otho	Ann Eliza Dorsey	15 Feb 1864	
James T.	Lizzie E. Chiswell	14 Jan 1867	
John	Elizabeth Wells	29 Jan 1799	
John	Mary Veatch	25 Feb 1799	
John A.	Elizabeth E. Hays	25 Feb 1835	
John A.	Martha E. Plummer	17 Aug 1857	
John G.	Martha R. Shaw	6 Feb 1867	

* Cannot read day; either 24 or 25

TRUNDLE, Johnnie	James T. Kramer (male)	2 Jun 1884	w
Lethe	Levy Wilcoxen	3 Nov 1801	
Lillie E.	James W. Graff	30 May 1882	
Martha J.	John T. Heffner	4 Apr 1862	
Mary E.	Benjamin Shreeve	29 Nov 1828	
Mary E.	Richard Gott, Jr.	11 Nov 1833	
Otho	Elizabeth Burns	20 Jan 1804	
Otho W.	Sarah White	18 Dec 1838	
Perry L.	Barbaray E. Dawson	17 Dec 1838	
Rachel	Thomas Howard	13 Dec 1800	
Robertus	Margaret E. Butler	10 Feb 1871	
Sarah H.	Peter A. Bowic	14 Jan 1824	
Thomas	Mary E. Jones	11 Jan 1848	
Thomas W.	Henny Adams	18 Mar 1823	
William	Frances N. Hempstone	30 Sep 1826	
TRUX - also see TRUCKS			
TRUX, Mary	Samuel White	3 Feb 1812	
TRUXTON, John C.	Alice Robey	24 Apr 1872	
TSCHEFFELEY, Elgar L.	Jane A. Rice	12 Nov 1866	
TSCHIFFELLY, Fannie	Robert E. L. Smith	28 Dec 1891	w
TSCHIFFELY, Bertie M.	Thomas R. Rice	30 Dec 1865	
Clifton L.	Lacey B. Rice	26 Sep 1898	w
Frederick L.	Ella V. Watkins	27 Mar 1893	w
Kate	Philip Stone	17 Feb 1885	w
Wilson B.	Mary Magruder	6 May 1876	
TUCKER, Alice ?.	Frederick C. Johnson	1 Aug 1884	
Annie E.	John N. Vanhorn	25 Sep 1889	w
Benjamin C.	Susan Murphy	11 Dec 1873	
Charlotte	Erasmus Wise	16 Oct 1809	
Clara	Tilghman Crummer	12 Oct 1874	
Eleanor	Joseph Soper	28 Dec 1803	
Elizabeth	Powel C. Pearce	15 Oct 1851	
George	Matilda Johnson	9 Jan 1866	
Hannah J.	Thomas Holland	3 Oct 1878	c
Isabel	Thomas R. Johnson	6 Dec 1887	w
James	Jane Hall	22 Nov 1810	
John	Ann Hopwood	8 Jan 1803	
Levi	Susannah Collins	23 Mar 1799	
Louisa	Landon Worthington	17 Feb 1829	
Mary V.	Bailey E. Datcher	31 Dec 1890	c
Meshech	Mary Read	28 Dec 1809	
Ruth M.	J. Randolph Weer	30 Jan 1883	w
Sarah	George Warren	12 Jun 1799	
Sarah	William H. Grantt	13 May 1800	
Susan Jane	Somerville Harding	31 Mar 1869	
Susanah	Benjamin Gatton	16 Aug 1800	
William	Nancy Burress	18 Jan 1821	
William	Sarah J. Lindsay	5 Jan 1893	w
Zachariah	Caty Koss	3 Sep 1801	
TUNIA, James R.	Florence Campbell	3 Nov 1891	c
TUNNELY, Monarchy*	Joseph Compton	13 Nov 1799	
TUOHEY, Dennis	Loretta Harrison	10 Sep 1881	w
TURLEY, Martha	Henry Dorsey	28 Dec 1885	c

* Part of last name from earlier reading

TURLEY, Mary	Henry Scott	21 May 1885	c
Samuel	Verdie Beall	25 Dec 1882	c
Virginia	Horace Stored	28 Dec 1885	c
TURNBULL, Elizabeth	John Dickerson	18 Sep 1806	
James	Rebecca Belt	9 Jan 1812	
John	Mary Tannihill	11 Jul 1801	
Margaret	Nathan Dickerson	6 Dec 1801	
Rebecca M.	Christopher Owings	11 Feb 1823	
William	Harriet Dorsey	12 Dec 1826	
TURNER, Aaron	Eliza Ann Robinson	14 Jun 1865	
Aaron	Airy A. Magruder	20 Mar 1886	c
Algerine R.	William T. Price	16 Aug 1881	
Anna	Malcolm Barks	30 Oct 1878	
Anne	George Magruder	30 Mar 1801	
Bettie	William Gibbs	13 Dec 1879	c
Carrie V.	Clarence F. Carroll	17 Dec 1895	w
Charles	Annie Hoes	24 Dec 1889	c
David	Elizabeth Johnson	28 Dec 1896	c
Elizabeth	Augustus McCimea	10 Apr 1865	
Ella F.	John F. Burdett	20 Feb 1883	
Franklin M.	Hallie R. Marlow	9 Sep 1875	
George H.	Edna Ward	12 Apr 1895	c
George W. B.	Ida E. Andrews	21 Jan 1890	w
Harry	Mary J. Elbert	11 Oct 1894	w
Henry	Lucy Nolan	14 Nov 1874	
Hester	James Magruder	13 Oct 1893	c
James F.	Mary V. Kemp	24 Apr 1871	
James H.	Elizabeth Higgins	23 Aug 1865	
John	Augusta Clarke	13 Oct 1864	
Laura	Alexander Jones	14 Apr 1898	c
Louisa	Ephraim Willson Brown	4 Nov 1830	
M. A.	Martha J. Everett	18 Jan 1842	
Mallie E.	Nathan T. Hebron	29 Jan 1889	c
Mary C.	Elijah Brown	22 Nov 1886	c
Mary E.	John Wheeler	24 Dec 1888	c
Mary J.	Richardson Wilcox	8 Nov 1880	
Mary M.	John W. Kirby	24 Jul 1883	
Rezin Thomas	Gertrude Jenkins	8 Oct 1874	
Richard	Elizabeth Beall	10 Jan 1799	
Richard B.	Verlinda Reid	4 Oct 1850	
Richard H.	Susan H. Calvert	3 Jun 1867	
Samuel	Amanda M. Williams	16 Apr 1822	
Sarah	Enoch Edmonston	2 Jan 1809	
Thomas	Mary Spriggs	19 Nov 1874	
William	Ruth Blackburn	27 Jan 1804	
William	Mary Newman	21 Jan 1891	c
William H.	Mary E. Pratt	18 Aug 1898	c
TURPIN - also see TORPIN			
TURPIN, Ollie	Robert F. Worsham	5 Jul 1897	w
TUTTEL, Ann	James H. Welling	29 Jan 1828	
TUTTLE, Abner	Elizabeth Hinton	26 May 1838	
Addison	Mary A. Douglass	9 Oct 1822	
Ann	George Sellman	31 Aug 1850	
Caroline	Walter Hinton	20 Aug 1836	
Eleanor	Ninian Lowe	27 Mar 1847	

TUTTLE,	Marsham	Melinda Potts*	1 Feb 1829
	Mary Ann	John Golding	30 Dec 1809
	Massum	Harriet Newton	22 Jan 1834
	Nelson	Nelly Hinton	26 Jul 1837
	Samuel	Rachel Collier	13 Apr 1808
	Stephen	Susannah Soper	10 Feb 1809
	Stephen	Lethea Stiles	12 Nov 1817
TWINE,	Robert	Maggie Smith	2 Nov 1882
TYLER,	-----**	Henry Johnson	31 Oct 1878
	Basil	Henrietta Johnson	2 Apr 1879 c
	Bertie	Alexander Backet	24 Apr 1894 c
	Charles	Lottie Lindsey	8 Apr 1895 c
	Cora Virginia	Charles Henry Neale	16 Nov 1886 c
	Eliza	Basil Taylor	27 Dec 1870
	Elizabeth	Hezekiah Johnson	4 Jun 1880
	Ella	George Daniels	9 Jun 1892 c
	Hattie	William H. Warfield	24 Mar 1892 c
	Henrietta	James Johnson	5 Sep 1877 c
	Henry	Margaret Brown	3 Jan 1874
	Henson	Mary Duvall	9 Jun 1881 c
	Henson	Henrietta Johnson	2 Mar 1887 c
	Jeremiah	Sarah Hall	17 Oct 1889 c
	John C.	Martha Bettus	4 Jun 1881 c
	John H.	Mary Brown	7 Feb 1888 c
	Littie	Mount V. Duff	27 Dec 1888 c
	Martha E.	Elijah Broun	14 Oct 1875
	Mary F.	Franklin W. Smith	18 Oct 1894 c
	Nelson	Jane Maccabee	29 Oct 1874
	Perry	Florence Rollins	*** Jul 1882 c
	Samuel	Cora Bowens	6 Aug 1892 c
	Sarah	Wallace Lee	22 May 1880
	Washington	Margaret Toogood	12 Apr 1882
	Washington	Martha Duvall	21 Dec 1896 c
TYMAN,	Drucilla	John Henry Diggs	2 Jun 1881 c
TYSEY,	John Carter	Rebecca Warren	18 Sep 1867
TYSON,	Margaret G.	Robert Rowland Moore	14 Jul 1886 w
	Martha E.	Robert E. Marshall	26 Sep 1892 w
	Thomas	Ann Brooke Ellicott	23 Aug 1836
ULRICH,	Cecelia M.	Albert I. Potter	18 Jun 1894 w
UMBERGER,	John W.	Lillie M. Burdette	22 Oct 1898 w
UMPSTALLD,	Benjamin	Virlinda Cawood	30 Jan 1805
UMSTADDT,	Jacob	Mary Mockbee	7 Jan 1811
UMSTADTT,	Ann L.	John S. McAtee	28 Mar 1842
	Jacob	Virginia Ann Miles	9 Apr 1851
UMSTATTD,	John Alfred	Emily Hyatt	12 Nov 1849
UMSTEAD,	Elizabeth R.	William Z. T. Umstead	31 Jan 1873
	Emma W.	Theodore E. Childs	13 Nov 1882 w
	Georgia A.	Jonathan C. Williams	14 Nov 1882 w
	Laura	Samuel G. Barnsley	16 Oct 1877 w
	Mary E.	John H. Worthmiller	22 Jan 1889 w
	William Z. T.	Elizabeth R. Umstead	31 Jan 1873

* Part of last name from earlier reading
** Name has blot on it
*** Cannot read day; between 10 and 20

UNCLES, Mary	Charles H. Lee	4 Nov 1891	c
UNDERHILL, Irving	Margaret Willson	13 Aug 1887	w
UNGLESBEE, Beall G. W.	Minnie W. Bohrer	29 Mar 1893	w
Edward L.	Lillie V. Duvall	7 Sep 1892	w
Tony T.	Carrie B. Easton	17 Jul 1893	w
Willie	Mina Burns	30 Apr 1888	w
UPTON, Anne	John Jones	16 Dec 1811	
Fannie A.	Joseph M. Towles	25 Jun 1897	w
Jemima	William S. Willson	27 Dec 1825	
Leah	Henry Willson	21 Dec 1815	
Mary	Elley Reynolds	19 Dec 1803	
Mary	George Virmillian	11 Oct 1819	
VALDANER, Louisa	William C. Pearce	19 Apr 1829	
VALDENAR Mamie V.	Joseph R. Lechlider	22 Dec 1896	w
Martha	Wesley Browning	22 Oct 1833	
William	Mary Rawlings	8 Feb 1833	
William	Louisa V. Kemp	13 Feb 1868	
VALDENARE, Francis	Elizabeth Culver	28 Mar 1821	
VALDINAR, Mary V.	Dr. Josiah Harding	17 Nov 1846	
VALET, Peter	Lidia Thatcher	7 Feb 1801	
VanBUREN, Gerard	Sarah W. Offutt	20 Sep 1813	
VANCE, Mary	Charles B. Jones	22 Nov 1853	
Samuel F.	Catherine McCrossin	7 Apr 1874	
VANCOSE, Susannah	Daniel Collins	8 Dec 1802	
VANDEVANTER, Charles O.	Virginia Kilgour	19 Oct 1875	
VANFOSSEN, Amos	Margaret Ann Burnsides	6 Aug 1823	
VanHORN, Alice V.	Robert J. T. Richardson	26 Feb 1889	w
Charles A.	Harriet L. Easton	20 Apr 1886	w
Dora E.	Henry H. Leizear	7 Dec 1896	w
Florence L.	William G. Mullican	18 Feb 1895	w
William R.	Clara Mullican	8 Jan 1886	w
VANHORN, Gabriel G.	Jane Ayton	23 Jul 1803	
Jacob	Sarah Ann Moore	9 May 1865	
John N.	Annie E. Tucker	25 Sep 1889	w
M. A. T.	W. H. Rhine (male)	2 Dec 1867	
VANHORNE, Oliver T.	Sarah E. Mullican	10 Apr 1961	
Seneca	Ann C. Linkens	1 Sep 1863	
VanNOSTRAND, A. R.	Julia Henderson	25 Jan 1853	
VanTASSELL, Horace E.	Ida C. Luskey	5 Sep 1890	w
VANTERS, Ann M.	James F. Walden	5 Aug 1841	
VARNUM, Philip	Mary Lahy	11 Nov 1817	
VAUX, Alfred M.	Mabel A. Scheele	16 Mar 1892	w
VEACH - also see VEATCH, VEITCH			
VEACH, Hezekiah	Sarah Hurly	11 Sep 1809	
VEATCH, Caroline M.	Halkiah W. Willson	25 Apr 1821	
John Alexander	Eliza Thomas	21 Jun 1822	
Mary	John Trundle	25 Feb 1799	
Sarah	Joseph Browning	18 Jan 1817	
Thomas	Rebecca Swan	21 Dec 1816	
Verlinda ?.	Joseph Plummer	21 Jan 1812	
VEIRS, Ann E.	Lee M. Dade	21 Jan 1836	
Ann S. C.	Nelson R. Robertson	27 Dec 1837	
Charles	Rosie Lyddane	25 Jan 1887	w
Cleland	Thomas Milford	25 Jun 1849	
Cordelia	Jesse Darby	1 Mar 1852	

VEIRS, Daniel	Mary Darnale	19 Jan 1813	
Darcus A.	Hilleary Hoskinson	23 Dec 1847	
Edward M.	Sarah A. Riley	25 Nov 1845	
Eleanor M.	H---- Janes*	26 Oct 1835	
Eliza	Thomas Fisher	3 Feb 1829	
Elizabeth	Dentin Darby	11 Apr 1810	
Emma J.	Jeremiah E. Peddicord	20 Jan 1870	
Emma C.	William Dawson	5 Dec 1882	w
Franklin	Ann E. Hall	14 Dec 1846	
Hezekiah W.	Ellen Jane Gloyd	5 Jun 1847	
Ida	James Frank Brown	8 Sep 1886	w
Jane	Samual Darby	24 Dec 1817	
Jane B.	Stephen C. Cromwell	7 Feb 1893	w
Jesse	Sophia Veirs	3 Feb 1829	
John Thomas	Eleanor Reid	10 Sep 1825	
Josephine	H. Clinton Allnutt	23 Oct 1877	w
Julianna	Edward O. Edmonston	12 Mar 1857	
Kate M.	W. Kenon Whiting	29 Mar 1880	
Levi	Sarah Whittaker	1 Jan 1811	
Louisa	John W. Hall	30 Sep 1835	
Maria H.	Hilleary Hoskinson	2 Sep 1836	
Mary	Stephen M. White	2 Dec 1824	
Mary	Samuel C. Young	23 Nov 1831	
Mary A. M.	William V. Bouic	2 Jan 1844	
Sally T.	John B. Byrd	4 Aug 1862	
Samuel E.	Valeria W. Allnutt	25 Jan 1886	w
Sarah R.	Joseph W. C. Offutt	22 Mar 1880	w
Scott	Lydia Dyson	17 Aug 1839	
Solomon	Susanna Mitchell	9 Feb 1805	
Sophia	Jesse Veirs	3 Feb 1829	
Susan	Thomas B. Benson	10 Mar 1841	
Susan Ann	William T. Aud	31 Jul 1862	
Tafa	Jeremiah Dyson	29 Dec 1806	
Virginia	A. H. Summers	17 Nov 1852	
William C. W.	Elizabeth Belmear	30 Jan 1816	
William F.	Emeline Cooley	10 Mar 1841	
VEITCH - also see VEATCH			
VEITCH, Fletcher R.	Carrie V. Parrie	29 Nov 1864	
Mary V.	Downs M. Woodward	20 Aug 1889	w
VENABLE, Hallie	Lewis D. Williams	4 Aug 1883	
Lelia C.	Alexander Rabbitt	20 Apr 1897	w
McDowell R.	Alice J. Watkins	22 Jul 1872	
VENY, Frank	Ann L. Proctor	16 May 1882	c
VERMELIAN - also see VIRMILLIAN			
VERMELIAN, Joseph	Sarah Hays	7 Nov 1799	
VERMILIAN, Hezekiah	Elizabeth Gloyd	21 Dec 1799	
VERMILION, Priscilla	Jacob Howard	26 Mar 1834	
VERMILLION, Benjamin	Maria Ann Boice	18 Dec 1827	
James	Elizur Burgiss	15 Oct 1821	
Julia Ann	William E. Murphey	4 Feb 1834	
Louisa V.	Joseph Sugars	4 Jan 1825	
Maria	John Smith	6 Mar 1844	
Mary E.	Edward Shoemaker	20 Feb 1860	

* There is an abbreviation which begins with H and an initial I or J

VERMILLION, William D.	Jane Smitzen	6 Oct 1840	
VERNON, Benjamin F.	Mamie E. English	1 Jun 1892	w
VERTS, Daivd F.	Mamie M. Phebus	15 Sep 1896	w
VICKERY, C. Burr	Mary B. Hulingues	3 Nov 1874	
VINCENT, Brooke	Grace Clagett	31 Aug 1897	w
William	Frances E. Chiswell	3 Mar 1804	
VINSEN, John T.	Fanny R. Prout	28 Aug 1861	
William T.	Susen A. Willig	23 Nov 1863	
VINSON, Ann Mary	John P. Wheeler	17 Oct 1843	
Anna E.	Thomas W. Vinson	6 Jun 1868	
Anne	John Vinson	29 Apr 1805	
Anne	Edward Nicholls	23 Dec 1811	
Benjamin T.	Eliza W. Vinson	* Sep 1882	w
Cecelia	Stephen W. Smoot	12 Dec 1884	
Charles H.	Cecilia E. Beall	21 Apr 1865	
Edgar D.	Mary V. Rice	25 Feb 1873	
Edgar D.	Lavinia Ruse	5 Aug 1895	w
Eliza W.	Rufus H. Speake	29 Dec 1829	
Eliza W.	Benjamin T. Vinson	* Sep 1882	w
Elizabeth A.	William Comley	2 Dec 1862	
Elizabeth Sarah	Thomas Hickman	3 Jan 1814	
Fillmore	Nettie Vinson	2 Jan 1877	
Harriet E.	Thomas H. Barwise	29 Nov 1856	
Harriett	John Wallace	10 Jan 1816	
James	Mary Johnson	16 Feb 1895	c
John	Anne Vinson	29 Apr 1805	
Laura C.	Herbert W. Linthicum	10 Nov 1898	w
Mary C.	William H. Pleasants	15 Sep 1847	
Mary G.	Edward C. Peter	26 Jun 1888	w
Napoleon B.	Margaret W. Kendall	11 Sep 1843	
Nettie	Fillmore Vinson	2 Jan 1877	
Peyton D.	Amanda Perry	15 Nov 1883	w
Sarah Ann	Elias D. Gumaer	26 Nov 1841	
Thomas F. W.	Mary Hickman	26 Dec 1820	
Thomas H.	Mahala Johns	23 Dec 1818	
Thomas W.	Anna E. Vinson	6 Jun 1868	
William H.	Elizabeth C. Beall	14 Sep 1848	
VIRMILLIAN - also see VERMELIAN			
VIRMILLIAN, George	Mary Upton	11 Oct 1819	
VOGHT, Harry C.	Elizabeth Mahn	1 Feb 1887	w
VOLEUTYN, David S.**	Martha Dean	6 Apr 1891	w
VOWELL, H. N. (female)	W. F. Creighton	4 Apr 1862	
Thomas	Charlotte Douglass	3 Apr 1806	
VYMEER, William	Esther Hilton	5 May 1825	
WACHTER, Daisie F.	Charles F. Ridgley	26 Oct 1897	w
WADE, Angeline	William Nicholls	4 Nov 1847	
Dorcas	Robert B. Wade	28 Oct 1807	
Emma A.	Andrew B. Arnold	28 Dec 1891	w
J. Julian	Mary E. Smith	15 Feb 1871	
James	Sarah Harris	2 Oct 1817	
James P.	Harriet A. Nicholls	4 Nov 1847	
Jesse	Mary Fleming	5 Dec 1804	

* Cannot read day; either 17 or 19
** This could be Volentyn

WADE, John	Anne West	3 Jan 1811	
Lucy A.	Robert L. Young	2 Jun 1888	w
Lucy C.	Camden R. Nicholls	22 Dec 1856	
Mary E.	Stephen R. Austin	22 Jan 1878	w
Nicholas X.	Mary Jane Jones	27 Oct 1851	
Perry	Rebecca Offutt	21 Nov 1820	
Philip	Lydia Ann Dorsey	21 Aug 1882	c
Robert B.	Dorcas Wade	28 Oct 1807	
Sophia B.	William J. Dronenburg	31 Dec 1877	w
WADSWORTH, Adrian R.	Mrs. M. A. Mallory	24 Aug 1869	
WAER, Mary E.	James W. Mobley	18 Jun 1897	w
WAGGONER, John	Sabina Pritchard	26 Nov 1832	
WAILES - also see WALES			
WAILES, Catharine V.	John Perry	14 May 1833	
Delia S.	Leonard W. Trail	10 Dec 1832	
Sarah A.	Horatio Willcoxen	30 Jul 1832	
WAITS, Silas	Matilda Nerveson	3 Feb 1866	
Silas	Mary E. Floyd	27 Sep 1871	
Silas	Mary E. Smith	13 Nov 1884	c
WAKES, Henry	Lucinda Matthews	14 Aug 1889	c
WALDEN, Charles A.	Isabel C. Norten	22 Aug 1891	w
James F.	Ann M. Vanters	5 Aug 1841	
Mary	William Thompson	4 Feb 1804	
WALES - also see WAILES			
WALES, Emely	Thomas W. Hide	4 Nov 1819	
Eveline	Nathan S. White	3 Oct 1823	
WALKER, Alfred	Mary Ann Gittings	23 Mar 1835	
Amanda	Henry Lee	2 Jun 1868	
Amanda E.	Nathan H. Darby	26 Nov 1878	
Ann	Nathan Grimes	9 Jan 1819	
Annie	Charles Crumpton	15 Jul 1885	c
Benjamin	Julia Ann Thompson	31 Oct 1825	
Carilla	Henry Mullican	3 Mar 1829	
Clara	John Cuff	8 Nov 1886	w
Crittenden H.	Rebecca V. Coomes	22 Jan 1884	
Eleanor	Stephen Artis	15 Dec 1829	
Eleanor	George W. Gittings	19 Dec 1833	
Elisha	Mary Walker	2 Nov 1803	
Emma	Daniel R. Ewell	19 Dec 1893	c
Ernest T.	Minnie A. Moore	28 Mar 1894	w
Eveline	Christopher Kisner	11 Jan 1836	
Eveline R.	Cornelius H. Browning	25 Nov 1890	w
Francis	Cena Thompson	19 Feb 1811	
George E.	Ella S. Miles	31 Oct 1876	
Gertrude E.	Edgar Fulks	30 Apr 1895	w
Harriet	John Tinson	21 Dec 1878	c
Henry	Elizabeth Wathen	12 Jan 1829	
Isaac	Margarett Johnson	25 Dec 1818	
James K.	Emma Waters	18 Mar 1879	w
James R.	Catherine Mossburg	21 Dec 1858	
James W.	Kitty Thomas	8 Oct 1825	
John	Lethy Summers	7 Sep 1805	
John L.	Hattie A. Hobbs	17 Sep 1884	
John W.	Amanda C. Thompson	21 Feb 1870	
Joseph	Rose Debtor	14 Sep 1869	
Laura	Thomas Willcoxen	28 Mar 1860	

WALKER,	Laura C.	John H. Boswell	6 Jan 1859
	Lula B.	Willis B. Burdette	6 Jun 1896 w
	Lydia	Jesse King	24 Dec 1817
	Mahala Ann	Thomas Parsley	6 Dec 1832
	Mamie	William M. Carlisle	19 Nov 1889 w
	Margaret J. R.	Joseph H. Linthicum	23 Dec 1889
	Margarett	Benjamin Cross	12 Sep 1798
	Mary	Elisha Walker	2 Nov 1803
	Mary A.	Charles Scanlon	27 Mar 1894 w
	Mary Jane	Charles W. Gates	23 Nov 1865
	Moses	Tabitha Johnson	31 Dec 1800
	Nancy	George W. Lewis	26 Nov 1822
	Nathan	Ann Beck	20 Jul 1798
	Nathan A.	Fannie W. Hughes	21 Jan 1890 w
	Rachel Ann	Reuben Hopkins	14 Oct 1872
	Rosie	Charles Bacon	14 May 1885 c
	Sally	George Keyth	24 Apr 1822
	Sarah	Basil Macmew	28 Mar 1798
	Sarah	Benedict Low	9 Jan 1819
	Tabitha	Basil Mullican	10 Apr 1822
	Thomas	Elizabeth Mullican	15 Dec 1825
	Thomas	Sallie Long	28 Dec 1882 c
	Thomas	Mary Bond	19 Apr 1888 c
	William Alfred B.	Laura A. Day	22 Dec 1890 w
	Willson	Deborah Prather	8 Oct 1801
WALL,	Katharine	Jacquelin P. Taylor	10 Jun 1895 w
WALLACE - also see WALLACH, WALLICH, WALLICK			
WALLACE,	Admenia E.	William H. Shern	27 Feb 1894 c
	Albert	Rena Robertson	6 Feb 1895 c
	Ann R.	William C. Bowman	24 Dec 1861
	Benedict	Annie E. Dowden	27 Sep 1871
	Cassy	Edward Stevenson	5 Jan 1874
	Charles R.	Lucy L. Hansford	5 Aug 1888 w
	Columbus	Sarah Conley	28 Sep 1858
	Eleanor	Charles Young	13 Nov 1806
	Eleanor	Samuel Magruder	16 Dec 1806
	Elizabeth	Thomas Harry	6 Feb 1810
	Emma	William Hill	29 Apr 1865
	Emma B.	Elisha O. Williams	5 Jun 1854
	Fanny M.	John S. Perry	5 Oct 1809
	Frank	Jane Plater	16 Sep 1897 c
	George W.	Elizabeth H. Grymes	25 Oct 1887 w
	Hamilton	Susan Caster	10 Feb 1879 c
	Hamilton	Mary A. Nelson	14 Feb 1883
	Hamilton	Hannah Davis	28 Dec 1893 c
	Ida	Gustavus Williams	6 Oct 1883 c
	James	Deborah Lee	8 Jan 1806
	James R.	Clara R. Jones	3 May 1888 c
	Jemima	David Digges	31 Dec 1874
	John	Ann Wheeler	3 Dec 1800
	John	Alethea Gatton	25 Sep 1810
	John	Harriett Vinson	10 Jan 1816
	John	Carrie Webster	9 May 1878 c
	Larkin	Hannah E. Dorsey	23 Jan 1890 w
	Laura	Hilleary Young	18 May 1870

WALLACE,	Leanna	Marshall Clagett	* Jun 1877 c
	Mary	Roy Coleman	29 Mar 1875
	Mary	William ?. Chambers	** Jul 1882
	Mary R.	Levi Lockwad***	12 Apr 1898 c
	Michael	Alice B. Benson	20 Sep 1875
	Robert	Mary Key Watts	3 Oct 1816
	Toliver	Nelly Ann Taney	7 Aug 1873
	Uriah	Lucy King	7 Jan 1875 c
	Virginia E.	Charles Lewis King	22 Jan 1869
	William	Martha Brooke	28 Dec 1800
WALLACH - also see WALLACE			
WALLACH,	Selig C.	Louise E. Lusby	17 Mar 1893 w
	Robert R.	Margaret H. Leiter	29 Mar 1897 w
WALLICH,	J. W.	Warnetta A. Ayton	25 Sep 1877 w
	James E.	Annie R. Bennett	28 Nov 1875
	Winfield S.	Kate Snyder	12 Feb 1873
WALLICK,	Ann	Jacob Miller	10 Jul 1823
	Christian	Anna Harrison	15 Nov 1814
	James E.	Marcella A. Bowman	19 Dec 1867
WALLING,	Byron W.	Emily W. Poole	23 Jan 1883 w
WALLIS,	Lewis	Louisa Prather	28 May 1867
WALLS,	Watkins	Octavia O. Wootton	19 Oct 1846
WALSTON,	Lorenzo	Sophia Cole	25 Oct 1893 c
WALTER,	George N.	Nancy E. Sellman	20 Mar 1888 w
	Irene C.	Ira E. Biser	7 Jul 1898 w
	James P.	Harriet L. Reed	27 Jul 1863
	John	Rebecca Housar	5 Feb 1825
	John E.	Eliza J. Butts	25 May 1881 w
	Lizzie	Arthur E. Wells	23 Mar 1890 w
	Mollie	Andrew Milne	1 Apr 1892 w
	Nettie W.	Jonathan Barnes	13 Nov 1894 w
	Rosie I.	Albert T. Kingsbury	27 Dec 1890 w
	Sarah	Henry C. Jones	3 Oct 1816
	Thomas	Elizabeth Barton	16 Jul 1828
	William	Virginia Snyder	17 Mar 1873
WALTERS,	Anne	Allen M. Benson	27 Aug 1879 w
	Charles R.	Clara B. Thompson	28 Oct 1891 w
	Emily T.	Camden R. Nichols	**** Apr 1879
	Julian F.	Helen L. Ricketts	10 Jun 1895 w
	Mollie J.	J. Walter Jones	23 Apr 1867
WANER,	Mary	Alexander Jones	7 Nov 1798
WAR,	John	Sarah E. Ponder	15 Jan 1850
WARBOUGH,	Thomas	Parmelia Simpson*****	25 Oct 1799
WARD,	Alcinda	John H. Garrett	5 Oct 1869
	Alice Victorine	Joshua Dorsey Plummer	17 Nov 1886 w
	Anne	Asa Holland	5 Feb 1807
	Augustus C.	Clara O. Monday	27 Dec 1886 w
	Caroline	James S. Nicholson	6 Jun 1861
	Carrie B.	William C. Watkins	17 Oct 1893 w
	Carson	Kate M. Coomes	29 Apr 1890 w

* Day has blot on it; between 12 and 27
** Cannot read day; before 10
*** Last name difficult to read; could be Locknead
**** Cannot read day; between 14 and 21
***** Part of last name from earlier reading

WARD,	Charles W.	Hattie L. Duvall	1 Sep 1887	w
	Clara O.	George C. Fry	24 Sep 1895	w
	David L.	Cedalia V. Woodfield	4 Jan 1898	w
	David S.	Rosie Morningstar	19 Jul 1897	w
	Edna	George H. Turner	12 Apr 1895	c
	Edward E.	Alice V. Miles	12 Feb 1887	w
	Edward G.	Emma Monday	30 Dec 1889	w
	Edward G.	Hattie L. Fry	31 Jan 1894	w
	Enoch G.	Elizabeth Crawford	1 Sep 1851	
	Enoch George	Drusilla J. Thompson	29 Jan 1835	
	George	Ann Redman	20 Dec 1798	
	George	Cassandra Willson	26 Feb 1802	
	Harriet	John Redman	25 Jan 1800	
	Harriet Ann	Joseph Ray	29 Jan 1844	
	Harriet J.	Salathiel T. Mullican	10 Dec 1861	
	Harrison G.	Ann M. M. Thrift	25 Nov 1879	w
	Hattie E.	John W. Haney	11 Dec 1872	
	Henrietta R.	Franklin E. Burdette	13 Jan 1898	w
	Henry	FLora Dorsey	29 Jan 1869	
	Henry C.	Laura V. Ricketts	26 Dec 1859	
	Hezekiah	Mary Jenkins	20 Sep 1838	
	Horace W.	Nancy Ray	13 Jan 1842	
	Ida A.	John W. Mills	9 Nov 1892	w
	Ignatius	Hessy Thompson	30 Apr 1811	
	Ignatius B.	Elizabeth F. Garrett	15 May 1872	
	Ignatius H.	Mary Elizabeth Ray	5 Jan 1841	
	Ignatius H.	Alverta Davis	1 Aug 1894	w
	James	Anne Darby	20 Apr 1812	
	John E.	Sarah C. Layton	5 Jun 1836	
	John Wesley	Eleanor Greentree	13 Jan 1807	
	John Wesley	Sarah C. Peddicord	17 May 1866	
	Kate R.	James O. Gingles	28 Nov 1870	
	Leanna W.	John P. Ray	25 Oct 1870	
	Lillie S.	Leonard C. Burns	18 May 1887	w
	Lottie	Elias H. Etchison	11 Jan 1888	w
	Lucy	Robert Robertson	1 Nov 1868	
	Maggie M.	William H. Dunawin	11 Dec 1893	w
	Marian L.	Zachariah T. Duvall	11 Nov 1889	w
	Martha E.	Greenbury W. Burdett	25 Nov 1840	
	Mary	Thomas Parsley	24 Feb 1877	w
	Mary G.	Homer C. Moon	28 Apr 1894	w
	Mary L.	Henry T. Earnest	3 Feb 1868	
	Mary P.	Richard L. Trail	1 Jan 1873	
	Plantcina	Thomas G. Ellis	13 Feb 1875	
	Mary Sybell	Delany King	3 Sep 1896	w
	Nicholas T. W.	Jane R. Trammell	10 Oct 1871	
	Otho C.	Eliza E. Whalen	29 Mar 1887	w
	Patrick	Joanna E. O'Brien	2 Oct 1871	
	Rhoda A.	David A. Ray	15 Jun 1854	
	Samuel	Maria M. Murphy	3 Jul 1882	
	Sarah	John Boswell	24 Dec 1823	
	Sarah M.	James Hillard	22 Apr 1820	
	Silas	Matilda Knott	13 Feb 1827	
	Susan R.	Basil James Sullivan	12 Mar 1866	
	Thomas G.	Amanda J. Thompson	22 Dec 1866	
	Thomas G.	Martha Whalen	19 Oct 1886	w

WARD,	Verlinda	Franklin Duvall	14 Jan 1868
	Virgil	Virginia C. Holmes	13 Nov 1883
	Virginia De la Fayette	William H. Ray	17 Feb 1842
	William E.	Josephine Burris	1 Jan 1873
	William E.	Henrietta M. Purdum	15 Jan 1879 w
	William E.	Isidora Bogley	23 Jan 1889 w
	William H.	Verlinna Beall	28 Nov 1833
WARDSWORTH,	Lucy E.	Abel E. Leavenworth	12 Aug 1889 w
WARFIELD,	Albert G.	Margaret G. Watkins	13 Aug 1842
	Alexander	Mary Harwood	8 Feb 1807
	Alice V.	James L. Lodge	25 Nov 1864
	Allen	Mary Dugan	26 Jul 1808
	Andrew	Jane Dorsey	26 Aug 1882 c
	Ann	John Etcheson	13 Dec 1804
	Anna	Robert Warfield	3 Sep 1812
	Anne	Thomas Brown	23 Jan 1883 c
	Annie	Isaac White	19 Aug 1880 w
	Annie M.	Francis M. Hopkins	25 May 1893 c
	Arnold	Margaret Browning	21 Mar 1798
	Axia	Daniel Browning	7 Feb 1801
	Basil	Ann Ceicill	16 Feb 1803
	Basil T.	Alice F. Mullinix	28 Dec 1886 w
	Belle	Zachariah L. Magruder	22 Dec 1873
	Charlotte	Thomas Nicholson	16 Oct 1820
	Charlotte	Richard Laurence	3 Sep 1824
	Chloe A.	Nathan E. Gott	2 Apr 1897 w
	David H.	Kate R. Fields	23 Nov 1892 w
	Deborah J.	Alexander N. Crowder	10 Dec 1860
	Della	William D. Bell	8 Nov 1887 w
	Edmund W.	Rosa B. Hilton	16 Nov 1883
	Edna G.	Charles H. Lewis	26 Jul 1892
	Edward	Niscy Etcheson	4 Dec 1805
	Edward D.	Vertie K. Mullinix	11 Jan 1894 w
	Edwin	Sarah Ann Darby	4 Jan 1847
	Eleanor	John Gibbins	9 Jan 1804
	Elizabeth	Andrew Offutt	19 Apr 1802
	Elizabeth A.	James Hawkins, Jr.	12 Feb 1851
	Elizabeth Ann	Walter W. Waters	2 Jan 1826
	Elizabeth J.	Basil E. Boyer	30 Dec 1882 w
	Elizabeth R.	Richard N. Snowden	26 Dec 1834
	Exerline	Jacob M. Allnutt	22 Feb 1881 w
	Frances	John Lee	26 Apr 1869
	George E.	Susie Clagett	7 Feb 1896 c
	George W.	Sarah Bentley	21 Oct 1835
	George W.	Mary E. Grimes	14 Nov 1892 w
	Greenbury	Elizabeth Alder	13 Mar 1817
	Harriet C.	Joshua Molesworth	20 Aug 1889 w
	Helen E.	Hanson Bond	20 Sep 1872
	Henry	Laura Mitchell	5 Apr 1871
	Hettie	Asa Hepner	11 May 1880
	Horace	Sarah R. King	1 Dec 1843
	Ida E.	Robert H. Mason	18 Nov 1886 c
	Israel G.	Maria G. Griffith	5 Jun 1860
	Israel G. Jr.	Katie L. Church	3 Nov 1897 w
	J. Latimer	Annie E. Lewis	26 Mar 1884 w

WARFIELD,	James A.	Mary Bowie	1 Dec 1881	
	Jeffrey	Martha Bond	22 Jul 1878	c
	John E.	Mary E. Molesworth	28 Apr 1887	w
	John G.	Drusy Ann Warthen	20 Dec 1853	
	John R.	Lucy ?. Holland	* Jul 1882	
	John T.	Rachel V. Dorsey	1 Nov 1862	
	John W.	Lucy Dunley	3 Jan 1889	c
	Josephine	Higgerson B. Penn	** Jan 1880	
	Joshua D.	Delilah H. Duvall	17 Jan 1849	
	Joshua N.	Lucy W. Hutton	30 Nov 1881	
	Juliet	Alpheus Williams	9 Sep 1805	
	Larkin	Lethea Blackburn	14 Mar 1827	
	Laura A.	Charles G. Davis	21 Nov 1882	
	Laura L.	John Cooper	3 Feb 1876	c
	Lem A.	Ada A. Miller	10 Dec 1852	
	Lena M.	Dr. Vernon H. Dyson	25 Oct 1898	w
	Lewis A.	Frances L. Hopwood	6 Oct 1885	w
	Lizzie W.	Clarence F. Webb	14 Jul 1890	w
	Lyddia E.	Luther James Moore	17 Dec 1880	
	Martha Ann	William G. Knowles	21 Oct 1835	
	Mary	Rezin Darbey	3 Dec 1799	
	Mary	Jesse Harity	1 Jun 1880	
	Mary	Richard Powell	23 Dec 1896	c
	Mary Ann	Rezin Welch	19 Sep 1807	
	Mary E.	John W. Boyer	12 Sep 1896	w
	Mary Ellen	Charles W. Sage	21 Sep 1880	
	Mary W.	Charles P. Higgins	24 Jan 1888	w
	Mollie L.	Alexander Broome	2 Dec 1878	
	Nathan	Eliza Hobbs	6 Dec 1819	
	Nelly	Miles Smith	19 May 1876	
	Nora V.	Lot B. Duvall	9 Jul 1895	c
	Philip	Sarah Davis	28 Apr 1801	
	Rachel	William Etcherson	16 Apr 1812	
	Rebecca	Charles Nelson	19 Jan 1886	c
	Robert	Anna Warfield	3 Sep 1812	
	Sarah	Jacob Young	24 Sep 1833	
	Sarah	Benjamin Lyon	13 Jan 1845	
	Sarah A.	Zachariah T. Clagett	10 Jan 1861	
	Sarah T.	Isiah Dent	10 Jul 1867	
	Susanna	Greenbury Murphey	11 Jan 1806	
	Thomas O.	Ruth L. Clark	24 Nov 1897	w
	Titus W.	Annie C. Molesworth	12 Nov 1885	w
	William	Martha Bye	12 Apr 1803	
	William H.	Emma C. Burdette	22 Dec 1890	w
	William H.	Hattie Tyler	24 Mar 1892	c
	Zadock	Rachael Chambers	23 Dec 1801	
WARING - also see WARRING				
WARING,	Philomena	Henry P. Hardy	30 Oct 1883	
WARLICK,	Margarett	Adamson Waters	29 Nov 1814	
WARMAN,	Drady	Samuel Perry	6 Mar 1806	
WARNER,	Charles W.	Annie Mason	1 Sep 1890	w
	George Z.	Sarah A. Phillips	6 Nov 1873	
	Harry	Annie M. Luskey	5 Mar 1894	w

* Cannot read day; between 6 and 20
** Cannot read day; either 20 or 21

WARNER,	Isaac V.	Anne E. Pumphrey	20 Dec 1866
	Israel P.	Mary Lavinia Pumphrey	10 Nov 1870
	James	Sadie Johnson	4 Jun 1896 c
	Margaret	Joseph W. Ennis	23 Jun 1894 c
WARREN,	Ann	George Washington	5 Sep 1878 c
	Basil	Mary Ann Adams	13 Oct 1827
	Charles Henry	Malinda Lee	23 Nov 1895 c
	Edward	Elizabeth Lannom	30 Sep 1880
	Eleanor	Samuel B. Magruder	21 Mar 1808
	Eliza	Charles Bouie	26 Dec 1892 c
	Eliza Ann	John Henry Clarence	3 Jan 1868
	Ella	Reuben H. Potts	26 Dec 1883 c
	George	Sarah Tucker	12 Jun 1799
	Isaac E. M.	Cordelia Ross	12 Nov 1885
	Ignatius	Lucy Ann Reid	2 Jun 1870
	James Z. W.	Eliza E. E. Washington	11 Apr 1889 c
	Jennie	Charles A. Weber	26 Dec 1881
	Jennie	Isaac Frazier	6 Jun 1895 c
	John	Catharine R. Duvall	29 Oct 1885 c
	Lela	Hilleary Young	30 Sep 1886 c
	Lizzie	Samuel Johnson	20 Feb 1875
	Louisa	Augustus Hackett	22 Dec 1870
	Lucy	Thomas Simms	23 Jul 1873
	Margaret A.	William E. Brown	5 Nov 1896 c
	Mary M.	Hilleary Powell	4 Aug 1896 c
	Mattie	John Duffin	18 May 1893 c
	Michael S.	Mary F. Thomas	*30 Jan 1879 c
	Michael S.	Rosetta Filley	25 Jan 1882
	Michael S.	Josephine Thomas	18 Sep 1889 c
	Milford	Martha C. Thompson	13 Dec 1888 c
	Minnie	Walter A. Haring	12 Sep 1892 w
	Minta	Westley Foreman	26 Nov 1873
	Nancy**	John Lishare	26 Jun 1800
	Nancy	Henry Jackson	19 Sep 1874
	Patrick	Ellen Lews	1 Aug 1876
	Randolph L.	Emma J. Sherwood	4 Jun 1889 w
	Rebecca	John Carter Tysey	18 Sep 1867
	Rebecca A.	Patrick G. O'Grady	28 Apr 1880 w
	Robert	Martha Proctor	16 Feb 1889 c
	Robert H.	Ann M. Jackson	26 Dec 1885 c
	Rose Annie	Nelson Dorsey	3 Mar 1876
	Sarah	Solomon Fisher	28 Sep 1881 c
	Sarah	Henry Johnson	5 May 1888 c
	Sarah C.	Horace T. Hood	20 Apr 1893 c
	Savanna	Alexander Brown	1 Mar 1897 c
	Sophia	Josiah Brogden	29 Jun 1866
	Stephen N.	Annie V. Storried	10 May 1898 c
	Vernon	Leila Carroll	30 Apr 1891 c
	William	Amanda Lyles	5 Mar 1875
	William	Amelia Offutt	10 Jun 1878 c
	William H.	Maria Rose	9 May 1885 c
WARRING - also see WARING			
WARRING,	Henry Jr.	Anna B. Clopper	31 Dec 1868

* Out of order in book; entered in with Nov 1880 licenses
** Part of last name from earlier reading

WARRING, Matilda M.		John O. Hill	2 May 1842
WARTHAN - also see WATHAN			
WARTHAN, L. T.		Martha Darby	8 Oct 1856
	Sarah E.	Julius A. Crockett	31 Dec 1856
WARTHEN, Alfred C.		Rebecca J. Rabbitt	31 Oct 1887 w
	Annie L.	Horace E. Young	4 Jan 1881
	Benjamin H.	Henrietta A. Morrison	10 Jun 1851
	Drusy Ann	John G. Warfield	20 Dec 1853
	Jason P.	Charlotte H. Reed	19 Oct 1882 w
	Mary E.	Philip B. Souder	12 Jan 1883
	Nathan B.	Rhody Ann Etchison	17 Mar 1847
	Nathan B.	Emma A. Adams	15 Sep 1870
	Nathan B. Jr.	Mary J. Hyatt	12 Feb 1879
	William E.	Olive A. Reed	8 Jun 1881 w
	William Thomas	Ida L. Hurley	4 Nov 1875
WASBURN, William W.		Sarah J. Arnold	26 Mar 1867
WASE, Aloysius W.		Mary A. Grant	21 Jan 1853
WASHINGTON, Adam		Virginia Smith	24 Oct 1888 c
	Anna Laura	William Davis	* Sep 1882 c
	Blanche A.	Thomas N. Wire	27 Jul 1892 w
	Charles W. W.	Georgiana Ridgely	10 Oct 1898
	Daniel W.	Sarah Ann Countee	27 Dec 1870
	Eliza E. E.	James Z. W. Warren	11 Apr 1889 c
	Ella	Albert Brown	31 Dec 1879 c
	Ella G.	Nathaniel Hicks	11 Sep 1893 c
	Emma	William H. Bell	9 May 1887 c
	Florence	William Diggs	6 Dec 1897 c
	Frances	William E. Howard	12 Sep 1888 c
	George	Ann Warren	5 Sep 1878 c
	George	Mary S. Young	8 Oct 1883 c
	Harriet A.	Joseph Boyd	** May 1883
	Hezekiah	Caroline Willson	25 May 1866
	Hilleary	Mary Thomas	28 Dec 1882
	Jacob	Matilda J. Plummer	16 Dec 1874
	James E.	Julia Miles	4 Dec 1893 c
	John	Annie Russell	11 Oct 1877 c
	John	Kate Brent	10 Sep 1884 c
	Lucinda	William Williams	8 Aug 1893 c
	Madison	Emma Gettings	10 Jul 1875
	Mary	Samuel Tilley	5 Oct 1891 c
	Mary E.	Robert Lyles	27 Dec 1871
	Mary E.	William E. Duvall	3 Oct 1895 c
	Molly	John T. Price	17 Jun 1895 c
	Peter	Laura J. Holly	27 Dec 1897 c
	Philip	Lizzie Hawkins	16 Sep 1897 c
	Richard	Louisa Bright	19 Aug 1875
	Samuel	Maria Jackson	27 Nov 1894 c
	Somerset	Elizabeth Boyd	22 Dec 1881
	Sophie	Edward Stewart	12 Dec 1892 c
	William G.	Annie Stewart	2 Jan 1888 c
WATERS, Achsah D.		James S. Petty	23 Nov 1889 w
	Adamson	Margarett Warlick	29 Nov 1814
	Alfred	Malvine Hardesty	21 Sep 1818

* Cannot read day; either 2 or 4
** Cannot read day; between 16 and 19

WATERS, Andrew J.	Keturah A. Windsor	18 Dec 1857	
Ann	Benjamin Reid	19 Dec 1814	
Ann	William Allison	28 Sep 1819	
Ann E.	William P. Savage	26 Nov 1888	w
Ann S.	John Jones of Evan	25 Feb 1820	
Annie	James Franklin	7 Jan 1891	c
Aquelina	Elias Perry	14 Dec 1803	
Azel	Ercilla Holland	14 Dec 1799	
Azel	Cassandra Williams	14 Oct 1805	
Azel	Ellen R. Howard	9 May 1821	
Baker	Rachel Magruder	26 Jun 1838	
Basil	Ann P. Magruder	18 Mar 1799	
Benjamin Jr.	Dorithy Edmonston	25 Apr 1812	
Carrie D.	John L. Lewis	13 Jul 1894	w
Casandra	Solomon Waters	1 Oct 1800	
Catherine	Joshua W. Dorsey	13 Feb 1833	
Charity D.	James M. Thrift	27 Jun 1825	
Charles C.	Maud E. Getzendanner	24 Jan 1888	w
David S.	Sarah Ann Matthews	23 Jan 1816	
Delilah Elizabeth	Basil M. Perry	10 Feb 1801	
Edward B.	Lucretia Gardner	29 Mar 1828	
Edward H.	Columbia J. Magruder	21 Jun 1869	
Edward W.	Frances Thornton	3 Oct 1886	c
Edwin	Jane E. Hughes	5 Mar 1840	
Edwin	Ida May Griffith	7 Nov 1881	
Eliza	Zachariah Waters	29 May 1838	
Elizabeth	William Belt	22 Feb 1804	
Elizabeth	Robert Edmonston	17 Sep 1816	
Elizabeth	Thomas Davis	11 Aug 1892	c
Ellen M.	Washington Waters	21 Aug 1867	
Emma	James K. Walker	18 Mar 1879	w
Florence E.	Ollie C. Baker	15 Jun 1896	w
Frances R.	Middleton N. King	4 Jan 1886	w
Franklin	Sarah T. W. Hilleary	3 Oct 1842	
Freeborn Garretson	Matilda Stevenson	18 Jun 1816	
George W.	Sarah Jane Chaney	14 Nov 1853	
Gulielma Maria*	Zachariah Gatton, Jr.	14 Jan 1806	
Harriet A.	Nathan Cook	14 Dec 1863	
Harriet Anne	Percy H. Willson	15 Mar 1897	w
Harry W. D.	Prudence J. Griffith	23 Jan 1837	
Harry W. D.	Emily H. Griffith	16 Apr 1855	
Horace	Charity D. Boyd	10 May 1815	
Horace	Mary J. Dorsey	24 Jan 1850	
Horace	Mary P. J. Etchison	24 Oct 1866	
Horace D.	Valeria Dorsey	7 Oct 1878	w
James A.	Elizabeth Gittings	11 Jan 1866	
James E.	Della M. Hackenyos	31 Aug 1893	w
John	Sarah White	9 Oct 1811	
John	Dolly Edmonstone	18 Nov 1820	
Laura E.	Uriah W. Griffith	12 Nov 1895	w
Laura S.	James M. Woodfield	19 Sep 1885	w
Leander	Sarah R. Hoyle	12 Dec 1840	
Littleton	Eleanor Shum	26 Dec 1826	

* His first name and her middle name from earlier reading

WATERS, Lucretia	Eden Edmonston	31 May 1809	
Mamie W.	Algernon Poole	17 May 1886	w
Margaret	Richard H. Perry	17 Oct 1870	
Margaret R.	Jesse T. Higgins	1 Aug 1837	
Maria E.	Jeremiah R. Pardew	23 May 1892	w
Maria L.	Obed Hurley	4 Oct 1856	
Mary	Samuel Waters	10 Jan 1833	
Mary	John Snowden	19 Apr 1869	
Mary E.	John H. Hilliary	13 Feb 1835	
Mary E.	Harry N. Burns	17 Oct 1889	w
Mary E.	James C. Davis	27 Oct 1893	w
Mary Eliza	Richard Thomas White	1 Jan 1858	
Mary K.	John M. King	17 Feb 1875	
Mary M.	Washington Waters	28 Nov 1848	
Minnie	Edward G. Cissel	24 Apr 1889	w
Nacey	Harriett White	8 Feb 1825	
Nathan	Amanda Potts	14 Jun 1892	c
Nathaniel	Achsah Dorsey	22 Jun 1809	
Nathaniel	Geneva M. Metz	14 Sep 1896	w
Nettie D.	Dr. Elisha C. Etchison	18 Apr 1876	
Phoebe A.	Nicholas B. Snowden	29 Sep 1885	c
Polly	Robert Edmonstone	25 Nov 1804	
Polly	William Holland	8 Mar 1805	
Rachael	John Bean	5 Dec 1820	
Reuben	Marianne Dunly	25 Mar 1869	
Richard	Lavenia C. Hutton	21 Dec 1859	
Richard D.	Lucinda Willson	12 Feb 1818	
Samuel	Mary Waters	10 Jan 1833	
Samuel D.	Ida S. Greer	6 Sep 1898	w
Samuel D. Jr.	Ella M. Bond	11 Dec 1871	
Sarah Ann	Henry W. Dorsey, Jr.	27 May 1829	
Solomon	Casandra Waters	1 Oct 1800	
Stephen	Emma Nugent	4 Mar 1897	c
Susan	John Braxton	30 Aug 1897	c
Susan M.	Harry W. Dorsey	9 Apr 1844	
Sylvana	Lewis Pratt	9 May 1872	
Thomas	Martha M. Dawson	5 Dec 1864	
Thomas W.	Mary Emma Magruder	16 Nov 1871	
Walter W.	Elizabeth Ann Warfield	2 Jan 1826	
Washington	Anne Williams	5 Jun 1829	
Washington	Mary M. Waters	28 Nov 1848	
Washington	Ellen M. Waters	21 Aug 1867	
Washington	Mary Marlow	30 Apr 1879	c
Washington	Ellen Harriss	3 Jan 1895	c
William	Rebecca Miller	29 May 1867	
William	Annie Snyder	16 Feb 1898	w
William A.	Mary Neel	26 Jan 1863	
William A.	Mamie Hoyle	11 Feb 1896	w
William A.	Maria E. L. Willson	17 Sep 1896	w
William H.	Mary C. Gaither	5 Jan 1850	
William P.	Carrie B. Childs	21 Oct 1874	
Zachariah	Eliza Waters	29 May 1838	
Zachariah D.	Elizabeth H. Magruder	3 May 1856	
Zachariah M.	Sarah V. Magruder	18 May 1858	
Zachariah McC.	Susie A. Davis	26 Oct 1897	w
Zadok M.	Anne Elizabeth Hood	6 Nov 1829	

WATHAN - also see WARTHAN
WATHAN,	Eleanor	Thomas Atwell	24 May 1800
	Leonard	Mary Clagett	27 Oct 1821
WATHEN,	Elizabeth	Henry Walker	12 Jan 1829
	Henry	Mary A. Wathen	2 Jan 1833
	Mary A.	Henry Wathen	2 Jan 1833
	Susan	Melien B. Fitch	22 Dec 1836
WATHING,	Mary	Thomas Dunn	23 Oct 1800
WATKINS,	Alice	McDowell R. Venable	22 Jul 1872
	Alice V.	Thomas F. Gardiner	21 Jul 1886 w
	Alonzo C.	Mary L. Boyer	26 Jul 1893 w
	Annie E.	Philip Elfrey	5 Oct 1895 w
	Antonia C.	Charles L. Housen	12 Jun 1897 w
	Arey	Jeremiah Watkins	7 Aug 1855
	Avondale M.	Franklin M. King	8 Jun 1898 w
	Benjamin F.	Sarah J. Benson	11 Nov 1868
	Bradley	Rebecca Z. Burdette	9 Oct 1896 w
	Carrie E.	Jesse D. Boyer	9 Jan 1894 w
	Carrie G.	Andrew J. Brandenburg	4 Nov 1889 w
	Catharine J.	Amon R. Miles	19 Nov 1861
	Darius F.	Fidelia E. Reed	10 Jul 1886 w
	Deborah	Walter Appleby	10 Mar 1827
	Edgar P.	Lucretia Batchelor	22 Apr 1878 w
	Edith M.	William H. Wright	13 Mar 1890 w
	Edward E.	Cordelia B. Mullinix	7 Dec 1888 w
	Elizabeth	Jonathan Lewis	20 Dec 1807
	Elizabeth	Charles C. King	15 Oct 1866
	Elizabeth A.	John S. Leamon	29 Oct 1868
	Ella May	Smith Hoyle	29 Oct 1896 w
	Ella V.	Frederick L. Tschiffely	27 Mar 1893 w
	Enoch S.	Mary E. Moxley	14 Feb 1893 w
	Eudolphia	Reuben E. Watkins	12 Feb 1889 w
	Fannie Z.	Richard A. Mullinix	1 Apr 1889 w
	Fillmore C.	Louisa E. Lyddard	11 May 1876
	Florida B.	Vachel H. Davis	26 Feb 1895 w
	Francis W.	Florence P. Davis	23 Aug 1897 w
	Gassaway	Catherine Willett	20 Apr 1826
	Greenbury M.	Kitty Ann Gatton	6 Oct 1831
	Greenbury M.	Helen Gatton	13 Jun 1842
	Harry L.	Annie E. Hall	27 Aug 1897 w
	Ida Belle	Robert E. Clagett	3 Jul 1894 w
	Ida C.	Bradley J. Riggs	14 Dec 1889 w
	Ida M.	Henry C. Edwards	10 Jul 1884 w
	James H.	Mary E. Burdett	22 Nov 1892 w
	James W.	Charlotte J. Williams	11 Dec 1872
	Jeremiah	Arey Watkins	7 Aug 1855
	Jetson	Mary L. Grimes	24 Nov 1841
	John O. T.	Evie L. King	19 Mar 1883 w
	Joseph D.	Ida V. Day	15 Nov 1893 w
	Joseph G.	Nettie F. Beall	17 Feb 1893 w
	Julia A.	John H. Bellison	8 Dec 1891 w
	Kate E.	Thomas D. Skiles	15 Nov 1869
	Laura D.	Titus G. Day	16 Oct 1885 w
	Laura V.	Richard T. Burdett	11 Jun 1875
	Leah J.	William G. Iglehart	30 Apr 1895 w
	Lethea	William Moxley	8 Jan 1821

WATKINS,	Levi L.	Elizabeth J. Burton*	20 Dec 1864	
	Lillie May	James E. L. Sibley	10 Dec 1894	w
	Lucinda A.	John D. King	21 Feb 1862	
	Luther M.	Martha T. Watkins	8 Oct 1857	
	Luther M.	Kate Darby	18 Dec 1878	w
	Luther M.	Mary R. Eller	28 Jan 1893	w
	Maggie F.	Crittenden King	24 Apr 1882	
	Maggie L.	Joseph C. Hawkins	3 Dec 1888	w
	Manelia E.	Bushrod Gartrell	1 Jan 1864	
	Manovia E.	Harry J. King	14 Apr 1896	w
	Margaret G.	Albert G. Warfield	13 Aug 1842	
	Margaret L. V.	Philip N. Poole	15 May 1878	w
	Marshall C.	Olivia J. Brown	29 May 1884	
	Marshall C.	Mary E. Watkins	2 Dec 1897	w
	Martha T.	Luther M. Watkins	8 Oct 1857	
	Mary E.	Marshall C. Watkins	2 Dec 1897	w
	Mary J.	Charles T. Johnson	21 Apr 1890	w
	Mary S.	John R. Purdom	17 Dec 1850	
	Matilda	Gassaway Lyshear	15 Mar 1809	
	Maurice	Martha R. King	2 Jan 1894	w
	May Belle	William J. Lewis	20 Nov 1882	
	Minnie E.	William B. Brandenburg	31 Jan 1893	w
	Noah	Julia Linthicum	21 Nov 1871	
	Nora	Charles H. Barber	6 Apr 1898	w
	Oliver T.	Eleanor J. Brewer	23 Dec 1851	
	Perry G.	Daroth A. Hilton	24 Apr 1851	
	Philemon G.	Amelia Kinder	7 May 1886	w
	Rachael	Lloyd Hilton	4 Jan 1826	
	Rebecca	William Miller	9 Dec 1852	
	Reuben E.	Eudolphia Watkins	12 Feb 1889	w
	Rezba	Philip Hyatt	28 Jun 1822	
	Richard	Elizabeth Beddo	8 Mar 1800	
	Rudolph	Mary C. Hunter	21 Jan 1868	
	Samuel C.	Josephine Lee	24 Sep 1898	w
	Sarah R.	Arnold T. Lewis	12 Dec 1834	
	Sophia	Nathan Simms	9 Sep 1875	
	Spencer	Maria W. Brooke	14 Jun 1870	
	Thomas	Catharine Magruder**	24 Apr 1798	
	Thomas	Charity King	30 Apr 1803	
	Thomas	Mary Magruder	30 Jan 1812	
	Thomas	Mary Willson	9 Jan 1818	
	Uriah T.	Margaret A. Brown	26 Nov 1884	w
	W. Maurice	Madora H. Cecil	15 Nov 1887	w
	Walter W.	Rosa L. Mathers	10 Nov 1891	w
	William	Henrietta Maria Purdom	24 Jan 1829	
	William	Rachel A. Hobbs	9 Dec 1852	
	William C.	Carrie B. Ward	17 Oct 1893	w
	Willy E.	Jonathan Stewart	3 Feb 1860	
WATLINGTON,	James T.	Emma E. Perkins	4 Jul 1894	w
WATSON,	Alexander	Magaret Johnson	15 Jul 1898	c
	Lewis	Susan T. Mason	14 Jun 1897	w
	Lucy	William Clarkson	3 Jan 1807	
	Maggie Ann	George H. Peter	14 May 1866	

* Entry reads Burton; family researcher says should be Buxton
** Last name from earlier reading

WATTS, Charles W.	Susie Hempstone	19 Jan 1888	w
Elizabeth	David Fall	26 Jun 1865	
John B.	Annie Hinton	28 Jul 1869	
John Thomas	Laura Thomas	20 Dec 1883	c
Julia	Robert Blackwell	5 Sep 1881	
Madeline	Henry Kelley	1 Dec 1879	
Mary Key	Robert Wallace	3 Oct 1816	
Nathaniel	Sarah Ann Delzell	19 Sep 1855	
Nelson	Anna Douglass	29 Jul 1868	
Oliver	Jennie Thomas	2 Jan 1879	c
Richard	Jane Chase	21 Aug 1867	
Wesley	Nellie Alexander	28 Nov 1872	
WAUGH, Julia Ann	Ephraim Brown	5 Nov 1873	
William Jasper	Lulie Ellen Herrell	17 Dec 1891	w
WAYMAN, Maria	William Davis	30 Jan 1869	
WEABER, Mary V.	Charles J. Brandenburg	7 Nov 1892	w
WEADON - also see WEEDEN			
WEADON, Francis M.	Sarah Jane Briscoe	6 Nov 1837	
WEAVER, Bettie	Charles Clagett	15 Jan 1889	c
Coonrod P.	Mary A. Sellman	26 Jan 1856	
Eliza S.	Jeremiah B. Wilbur	15 Aug 1883	
Kate R.	Joseph L. Green	3 Dec 1879	w
Remus G.	Emma F. Burdett	8 Aug 1887	w
Sarah E.	James W. Beavers	11 Dec 1895	w
WEBB, Clarence F.	Lizzie W. Warfield	14 Jul 1890	w
Elizabeth C.	George H. Sharp	3 Jan 1822	
Ella F.	William H. Horseman	4 Aug 1896	w
Henrietta	Christopher Andrews	12 Apr 1814	
Levi	Maria Marriott	4 Mar 1828	
Marie L.	Jean Krozer Jett	* Oct 1896	w
Susan	George Baltzer	28 Dec 1808	
William	Hannah Phealen	20 Apr 1826	
WEBER, Charles A.	Jennie Warren	26 Dec 1881	w
Robert L.	Rose Bagon	19 Jan 1897	w
WEBSTER, Alice V.	Amos Whipp	11 Aug 1892	w
Annie	John H. Lewis	17 Oct 1898	w
Carrie	John Wallace	9 May 1878	c
Charles	Jennie Diggins	17 Jul 1868	
Charles I.	Mary C. Bartelmes	2 Mar 1895	w
Edward	Emma V. Souder	14 Apr 1888	w
Elizabeth B.	Sidney H. Perham	28 May 1897	w
George	Mary E. King	15 Feb 1852	
George **.	Annie V. White	21 Nov 1889	c
Georgie A.	William N. Bean	25 Mar 1878	w
Glendora	John T. Beander	13 Jan 1891	c
Josias	Rosa Cook	27 Feb 1879	c
May	Milton Jackson	19 Jul 1892	w
Sarah E.	George S. LaDomus	23 Mar 1878	w
WEEDEN - also see WEADON			
WEEDEN, Alfred	Eleanor Lucas	17 Jan 1807	
Margie	Henry Powell	27 Jun 1882	w
WEEKS, Herbert T.	Florence Peddicord	21 Apr 1896	w
Hezekiah	Rachel Henry	13 Apr 1833	

* Cannot read day; before 9
** Initial L or S

WEEKS, Magge E.	Frank Dwyer	19 Mar 1892	w
Rebecca	William Kimble	27 Jan 1862	
Sarah	Gerrard Sheerwood	16 Dec 1800	
WEEMES - also see WIMS			
WEEMES, Samuel	Rachel Pay	26 Feb 1867	
WEEMS, Casandra	John Giddings	11 Jun 1867	
George	Elizabeth Posey	15 Nov 1864	
John H.	Emily Lee	18 Feb 1874	
John Thomas	Maria E. Windeer	19 Sep 1894	c
Mary Jane	Richard Duvall	9 Sep 1867	
Warner	Maria E. Duffin	31 Dec 1878	
WEER, Agnes E.	Thomas C. Groomes	10 Nov 1879	w
J. Randolph	Ruth M. Tucker	30 Jan 1883	w
Jennie M.	Thomas R. Titlow	11 May 1872	
Mary J.	James Rannie	29 Jun 1881	w
WEISSER, Katie	Bernhard Reinhold Muller	15 Dec 1897	w
WELCH - also see WELSH			
WELCH, Henry	Eliza Harriss	21 Jun 1815	
Mary	Nicholas Whalan	21 Feb 1814	
Rezin	Mary Ann Warfield	19 Sep 1807	
Sarah	John Lyons	20 Nov 1799	
Warner	Mary Ann Hyatt	27 May 1843	
WELDON, Catharine	Robert Davis	3 Mar 1886	c
Emily	John W. Jackson	4 Aug 1888	c
Hattie	Ferdinand Seals	20 Sep 1889	c
Henry	Virginia Williams	13 Jun 1878	c
Henson	Emily Catharine Plummer	15 Mar 1869	
William J.	Nancy Fouch	4 Mar 1820	
WELLEN - also see WELLIN			
WELLEN, Eleanor	Jesse Moulden	6 Mar 1818	
Nancy*	Richard Hudson	10 Feb 1798	
WELLER, Angeline	Henry C. Simpson	3 Oct 1866	
Annie W.	Roscoe G. Lamb	4 Jan 1893	w
Effie A.	Alfred G. Graeves	27 Dec 1877	w
Jerome B.	Sarah M. Joyce	8 Jan 1867	
Marie C.	Edgar H. Cashell	6 Apr 1896	w
Mary G.	Alexander E. Wessell	29 Oct 1889	w
Maurice J.	Lizzie W. Cissell	8 Jan 1867	
WELLIN - also see WELLEN			
WELLIN, John William	Susan Lewis	27 Oct 1834	
WELLING, Ambrose	Elizabeth Thompson	24 Feb 1866	
Betsey	Elijah Biggs	28 Dec 1818	
Christanna	James Chadwell	15 Jun 1875	
James H.	Ann Tuttel	29 Jan 1828	
James H.	Martha Bolton	26 May 1874	
Jane	John Basford	4 Apr 1827	
Mary	George Gray	29 Jan 1820	
Mary A. L.	John W. Bennett	17 Mar 1869	
Mary E.	Thomas W. Dorsey	17 Feb 1862	
William D.	Martha Andrews	6 May 1871	
William W.	Mary Ellen Dorsey	19 Apr 1859	
WELLMORE, Zachariah	Sarah Beddo	22 Dec 1806	

* Part of last names from earlier reading

WELLS, Albert H.	Sarah Elizabeth Adamson	2 Jan 1836	
Amanda	Henson R. S. Hickman	24 Dec 1822	
Arthur E.	Lizzie Walter	23 Mar 1890	w
Barbara	John T. Connelly	29 Dec 1841	
Benjamin	Matilda Jane Belt	21 Dec 1832	
Catherine	Carlton Magruder	17 Nov 1818	
Elizabeth	John Trundle	29 Jan 1799	
Elizabeth Ann	James Carey	21 Dec 1829	
Elizabeth M.	Dr. D. F. Owens	14 May 1879	w
Ida B.	William A. Lee	6 Oct 1898	w
James	Rebecca Mackall	14 May 1806	
John	Anne Mackall	27 Apr 1832	
Mary Ann	John D. Willson	7 Jan 1829	
Mollie	Milton H. Gettinger	24 Jun 1887	w
Richard	Anne Belt	10 Sep 1799	
WELSH - also see WELCH			
WELSH, Atsie	Thomas Gaither	3 Jan 1890	c
Deborah	Joseph Jones	16 Nov 1822	
Edward	Katie E. Burke	25 May 1895	w
Edward E.	Ietta A. Rabbitt	6 Apr 1874	
Elizabeth G.	Samuel Kemp	24 Feb 1886	w
Fannie	Moses Lair	10 Jul 1883	
James	Anne Dugan	3 Mar 1813	
James	Margaret McCormick	10 Aug 1857	
Maggie	Patrick Cuff, Jr.	12 Dec 1883	
Margaret	Joseph Moland	2 Oct 1806	
Patty	James Steele	7 Jun 1802	
Philip	Polly Dillorder	8 Dec 1806	
Sarah	John Connelly	11 Feb 1801	
Walter	Margaret Moore	10 Sep 1810	
WELTBERGER, John W.	Mary Elizabeth Bohrer	20 Nov 1843	
WENDEHUTH, Katherine	John T. Russell	6 Jun 1895	w
WERNER, Henrietta S.C.S.	John Hofheinz	17 Oct 1892	w
WESSELL, Alexander E.	Mary G. Weller	29 Oct 1889	w
WEST, Alexander	Martha Alberta Magruder	8 Dec 1875	
Amos	Ella F. Connell	23 Feb 1891	w
Ann	Erasmus West	1 Jan 1829	
Anne	Amos Scott	11 Sep 1798	
Anne	John Wade	3 Jan 1811	
Betsey	Robert Thomas	8 Jun 1866	
Cassandra	Zephaniah N. Jones	30 Nov 1852	
E. Marian	John Love	24 Jan 1861	
Edwin M.	Olivia A. Bogley	6 Jun 1894	w
Eleanor	James H. Dowden	5 Aug 1846	
Eliza C.	William R. Beall	25 Jan 1860	
Elizabeth A.	Jetson G. Fields	14 Feb 1854	
Ella	Cyrus Hall	29 Apr 1895	c
Erasmus	Ann West	1 Jan 1829	
Erasmus	Elizabeth Minnis	23 Jul 1872	
Fannie S.	Edwin D. Hawkins	18 Dec 1882	
Henry	Eliza Higgins	14 Dec 1830	
James L.	Margaret E. T. Baker	21 Jun 1855	
John	Lydia Shuck	4 Apr 1801	
John S.	Kattie Mullican	1 Sep 1879	
Julius	Sarah A. Kidwell	10 Dec 1844	
Laura V.	Frank B. Horner	1 Nov 1876	

WEST, Leona S.	Richard H. Barnitz	11 Aug 1884	
Lida A.	Elvin A. Hisey	31 Jan 1891	w
Margarett	James M. Austin	15 Feb 1831	
Mary	Charles Conners	13 Aug 1888	w
Mary E.	Everard G. Fisher	18 Sep 1867	
Minnie E.	George W. Mullican	20 Apr 1898	w
Mollie J.	James H. Simmonds	15 Jun 1869	
Richard T.	Rachel R. Cross	16 Nov 1846	
Richard T.	Mary E. Layton	26 Nov 1867	
Samuel	Sarah Offutt	10 Mar 1825	
Sarah	Evan Jones	18 Feb 1808	
Sarah	Edward Hays	28 Feb 1840	
Sarah V.	William Gamble	3 Dec 1872	
Sophia	Jesse Ponder	17 Oct 1822	
Tilghman	Mary Jane Harper	2 Feb 1829	
Upton	Ara Pennifield	28 Dec 1837	
William	Nancy Offutt	6 Feb 1799	
William	Sarah Gatton	8 Feb 1831	
William A.	Mary E. Campbell	18 Feb 1879	w
William O.	Elizabeth O'Neale	8 Mar 1821	
WESTHER, Sophia*	George Elgin	22 Dec 1807	
WETHERALD, Samuel B.	Florence M. Sullivan	26 Jun 1882	
WETZEL - also see WHETZEL			
WETZEL, David A.	Catharine D. Peters	26 Jan 1898	w
WHALAN - also see WHALEN, WHALIN, WHEALAN, WHELAN			
WHALAN, Mary E.	George R. Hickman	26 Aug 1852	
Mary E.	Americus Biggs	28 Feb 1870	
Mary Ellen	Charles Mansfield	17 Oct 1842	
Patrick	Bridgett Lyddane	10 Jul 1822	
Nicholas	Mary Welch	21 Feb 1814	
Peter	Sally Connelly	14 Oct 1800	
Thomas	Rebecca Stallions	18 Aug 1800	
Thomas	Mary Ball	17 Oct 1816	
Verlinda	W. R. Ganley	12 Feb 1852	
WHALEN, Columbia	Charles W. Wood	16 May 1859	
Eliza E.	Otho C. Ward	29 Mar 1887	w
Elizabath	William Smith	9 Jan 1836	
Henry T.	Eliza E. Haney	31 Dec 1874	
James E.	Emma J. Bagin	2 Jan 1879	w
John C.	Fannie Collier	10 Feb 1876	
Martha	Thomas G. Ward	19 Oct 1886	w
Mary E.	George J. Robertson	20 Oct 1880	
Mary Ellen	George William Dove	18 Dec 1861	
Michael	Susan E. Chambers	23 Dec 1848	
Michael	Alice Day	13 Nov 1879	
Norah J.	William H. Berry	2 Dec 1860	
Rachel A.	James Padgett	18 May 1854	
Thomas	Mary Connelley	15 Nov 1807	
Thomas	Nora J. Carlisle	22 Feb 1854	
William S.	Mary E. Willson	2 Mar 1854	
WHALEY, Mary	Ishmael Dove	19 Feb 1840	
WHALIN - also see WHALAN			
WHALIN, Thomas	Ellender Carey	19 Jan 1799	
WHEALAN, Margaret	Mark Flaherty	26 Dec 1801	

* Part of last name from earlier reading

WHEALAN, Mary*	Lawrence Lyddan	10 Oct 1799	
Mary	Philip Touell	22 Feb 1800	
Mary	Patrick Flaherty	7 Jan 1803	
Michael	Elizabeth Nicholson*	17 Feb 1798	
Nicholas	Anne Connelly	3 Feb 1812	
WHEAT, Hezekiah	Elizabeth Moore**	17 Apr 1804	
John M.	Miriam Berry	8 Nov 1826	
Mary	Arthur Dillaha	18 Nov 1805	
Rebecca	Michael Harper	10 Feb 1800	
WHEATLEY, Annie D.	Edgar W. Moore	7 Jun 1893	w
Frank S.	Alcinda Roberson	20 Jun 1895	c
Helen G.	Harry K. Corrick	12 Nov 1889	w
Henry C.	Hannah R. Matthews	30 Jul 1889	w
Irene	John Campbell	26 Dec 1891	c
James E.	Cora L. Bissett	28 Jul 1896	w
Laura V.	William E. Dulin	27 Oct 1896	w
WHEATLY, William	Mary Cashell	8 Jun 1804	
William	Sarah E. Murray	2 Mar 1824	
WHEELER, ---ewell	Grace Jane Bell	13 Feb 1890	w
Ann	John Wallace	3 Dec 1800	
Anne	Nathaniel Moore	20 Jan 1819	
Eleanor	Thomas Hill	10 Apr 1799	
Frances E.	Simon Cheny	14 Dec 1869	
John	Mary E. Turner	24 Dec 1888	c
John P.	Ann Mary Vinson	17 Oct 1843	
Katie M.	Andrew F. Burgess	21 Oct 1897	w
Lucretia	Daniel M. Perkins	28 Oct 1818	
Mary	John Murphey	30 Dec 1824	
Richard	Ann H. Burdett	13 Feb 1849	
Samuel	Mary Hendley	12 May 1800	
Sarah	Thomas Hilleary	23 Nov 1803	
Sarah	Ozborn Marlow	24 Jan 1809	
Thomas	Ruth Jackson***	8 Oct 1798	
Thomas R.	Mary M. Smith	9 Mar 1876	
William	Ann Hill	25 Oct 1799	
Willie T.	Carrie Fawcett	13 Dec 1886	w
WHELAN - also see WHALAN			
WHELAN, Linny	Zachariah Collins	13 Aug 1823	
Martin	Elizabeth Price	20 Nov 1828	
Mary	Richard Keiran	7 Feb 1825	
Michael T.	Emily S. Lowe	2 Jan 1889	w
Nicholas Jr.	Rachel Ann Moulden	17 Apr 1847	
Patrick	Bridget Conner	15 Apr 1816	
William	Mary Davis	16 Dec 1824	
William	Mary E. Hackney	31 May 1849	
WHETZEL - also see WETZEL			
WHETZEL, Nancy	James Collins	12 Jan 1799	
WHIMS - also see WIMS			
WHIMS, Sarah Ellen	Archibald Beander	18 Jul 1866	
WHIPP, Amos	Alice V. Webster	11 Aug 1892	w
George C.	Annie E. Howard	17 Dec 1889	w
George W. V.	Annie C. Davis	17 Dec 1895	w

* Last name from earlier reading
** Last name partially covered by a line; looks like Moore
*** Part of last name from earlier reading

WHIPP, Lewis W.	Addie L. G. Howard	16 Mar 1892 w
WHIPS, Archibald	Ann Moore	15 May 1817
WHIRL, Hiram	Rebecca Duvall	19 Dec 1825
WHISNER, Peter H.	Virginia L. Childs	13 Apr 1874
WHITAKER - also see WHITTAKER		
WHITAKER, Eleanor W.	Benjamin G. Cissell	23 May 1833
WHITE, Addison	Darcas A. Harriss	16 Oct 1814
Alexander	Charlotte Stewart	2 May 1885 c
Amanda	Walter Adams	5 Aug 1898 c
Ann	Joseph White	17 Dec 1846
Anne	Stephen Dawson	29 Sep 1815
Annie	Robert Coates	24 Oct 1878 c
Annie V.	George *. Webster	21 Nov 1889 c
Archibald	Mary E. Knowles	1 Jun 1853
Benjamin	Rachel Chiswell	4 Dec 1815
Benjamin	Rebecca Darby	16 Mar 1820
Benjamin	Sarah E. Jones	16 Jan 1868
Benjamin of Benjamin	Susan Gott	2 Dec 1831
Benjamin F.	Margaret A. Allnutt	19 Dec 1851
Benjamin F.	Charlotte E. Kilgour	22 Dec 1874
Benjamin R.	Ella F. Matthews	11 Nov 1873
Benjamin S.	Sarah E. Nicholls	24 Feb 1851
Bettie	George W. Noble	12 Dec 1883
Charlott	Charles Beall	10 Oct 1818
Eleanor	Lawrence Allnutt	7 Dec 1825
Eleanor	Joseph N. Chiswell	20 Nov 1840
Elijah V.	Sarah E. Gott	8 Dec 1857
Eliza A.	Walter Magruder	3 Jul 1866
Elizabeth	Benedict Beckwith	28 Jan 1800
Elizabeth	John Ferguson	15 Oct 1803
Elizabeth J.	John E. Trucks	7 Feb 1859
Ellen	Albert U. Harriss	25 Jul 1895 c
Emily C. W.	John Saunders	15 Nov 1852
Emma G.	Josiah H. Clark	12 Mar 1884
George W.	Martha Ann Crown	10 Mar 1873
George W.	Margaret E. Case	16 Oct 1879 w
Harriett	Thomas Clagett	28 Nov 1812
Harriett	Nacey Waters	8 Feb 1825
Harry B.	Sarah E. Bowman	21 Dec 1897 w
Harvey Jones	Ida Dyson	28 Nov 1893 w
Henson	Martha Copelin	24 Oct 1876
Hester C.	Richard W. Williams	29 Oct 1863
Ida	George H. Saulsman	12 Nov 1895 w
Isaac	Eliza Jane Bruce	15 Nov 1865
Isaac	Annie Warfield	19 Aug 1880 c
James	Deborah Dillon	18 Oct 1823
John	Sarah Windom	6 Feb 1817
John	Elizabeth Anne Soper	3 May 1817
John	Sarah A. White	14 Dec 1842
John	Nanny Savoy	1 Dec 1868
John	Aletha Wright	25 May 1871
John	Sofie Bacon	13 Nov 1878
John D.	Mary E. Latton	23 Jan 1865

* Initial L or S

WHITE, Joseph	Ann White	17 Dec 1846	
Joseph C.	Mary C. Gott	2 Dec 1824	
Joseph T.	Sallie E. Brunner	25 Nov 1889	w
Laura V.	James U. McAtee	1 Jan 1877	
Laurence	Mary Spears	23 Mar 1814	
Lelia Ella	Lee Davis Lodge	31 Aug 1887	w
Louis	Fannie Harris	23 Dec 1891	c
Margaret A.	Robert W. Smoot	18 Feb 1850	
Margaret E.	Nathan W. Allnutt	23 Dec 1850	
Maria L.	James W. Clagett	19 Feb 1853	
Martha	Horatio James	30 Sep 1824	
Martha	John T. Neal	30 Dec 1896	c
Mary	William Johnson	11 Jul 1820	
Mary Ann	James Offutt	20 Mar 1849	
Mary D.	James H. Drane	12 Jan 1813	
Mary E.	Dr. Charles E. Pratt	13 Dec 1878	w
Mary E.	William F. Elgin	18 Mar 1887	w
Mary E.	Honore M. Claggett	26 Aug 1889	w
Mary E. W.	Leonard I. J. Hayes	23 Oct 1888	w
Mary N.	Edward E. Burton	12 Mar 1895	w
Mary P.	Henry E. Soper	10 Jan 1893	w
Matilda	Zadock Purdom	23 Jan 1813	
Nathan S.	Eveline Wales	3 Oct 1823	
Nathan S.	Ella C. Bouic	19 Oct 1882	w
Nathan S.	Julia R. Griffith	8 Dec 1890	w
Nathan S. Jr.	Sarah A. Offutt	15 Dec 1874	
Nellie Smith	Harry McGill Williams	11 Nov 1890	w
Orlando	Rachel Musgrove	29 Dec 1809	
Rachel	John Busey	13 Jun 1827	
Rachel	Benjamin W. Allnutt	10 Jan 1866	
Rebecka	Charles C. Hodges	25 Jan 1817	
Richard G.	Huldah A. Piles	3 Jan 1853	
Richard Thomas	Mary Eliza Waters	1 Jan 1858	
Rosie	George Henry Fears	5 Nov 1877	w
Sallie	Charles T. Young	21 Feb 1884	
Samuel	Mary Trux	3 Feb 1812	
Samuel	Rosannah Owens	9 Jul 1818	
Samuel C.	Maggie Chiswell	22 Jan 1874	
Samuel R.	Sarah E. Bouic	10 Nov 1862	
Sarah	John Waters	9 Oct 1811	
Sarah	Otho W. Trundle	18 Dec 1838	
Sarah A.	John White	14 Dec 1842	
Sarah C.	R. T. Mitchell	15 Nov 1858	
Sarah E.	Elijah Leizear	20 Jan 1880	w
Sarah R.	Stephen O. Richey	7 Nov 1878	w
Stephen	Ann Trundle	12 Dec 1823	
Stephen M.	Mary Veirs	2 Dec 1824	
Stephen N. C.	Elizabeth Chiswell	4 Jul 1837	
Susan	James E. Phillips	24 Jun 1875	
Susan Ann	Alexander Dade	7 Jan 1850	
Susana	William Levering	17 Nov 1799	
Thomas H.	Mary E. Gott	12 Dec 1855	
Thomas H.	Laura R. Gott	26 Jan 1892	w
Thomas O.	Nannie E. Pyles	30 Nov 1883	
Virginia	Joseph N. Chiswell	16 Aug 1869	
Walter H.	Cora H. Hoyle	23 May 1881	

WHITE, William	Anne Fletchall	8 Dec 1825	
William	Frances Brogden	30 Nov 1882	c
William B.	Ollie Miles	20 Dec 1892	w
William T.	Emily M. Nichols	28 May 1897	w
William W.	Mary A. Higgins	14 Oct 1897	w
Winnie	Marshall Thomas	27 Feb 1890	c
WHITEHOUSE, Emily E.	John W. Kirby	30 Apr 1867	
James	Catharine Metz	4 Jan 1847	
WHITER - also see WHITTER			
WHITER, Mary Elizabeth	John Thomas Beall	7 Sep 1868	
WHITESIDE, Mary Ann	William R. Duvall	30 Oct 1842	
WHITESIDES, Jane	Joseph Snider	22 Dec 1838	
Mary E.	Frank Horner	5 Jun 1875	
WHITING, Albert	Rachel Lawson	19 Oct 1867	
D. W.	Alberda J. Clagett	5 May 1860	
Richard	Mary Grimes	22 Feb 1887	w
Sarah	Thomas Copland	20 Apr 1886	c
W. Kenon	Kate M. Veirs	29 Mar 1880	
WHITMER, Rosella	William W. Steers	26 Jun 1895	w
WHITTAKER - also see WHITAKER			
WHITTAKER, Henry Robert	Mary Edwards*	19 Sep 1798	
Robert Alexander	Elizabeth Byrn	6 Jan 1817	
Sarah	Levi Veirs	1 Jan 1811	
WHITTER - also see WHITER			
WHITTER, Ann	Henry W. Judy	29 Oct 1813	
WHITTINGTON, Ella V.	Hezekiah R. Magruder	19 Jul 1876	
Josiah Loring	Charlotte Louise Munro	6 Oct 1884	w
Martin E.	Elizabeth M. Cusiak	23 Jan 1895	w
WHITTON, Elizabeth**	Michael J. Santee, Jr.	8 Jan 1898	w
WIGGINS, Thomas	Mary Mathis	3 Feb 1841	
WIGHT, Otis C.	Mary J. Buchanan	28 Jul 1847	
WIGTON, Ann M.	John S. Brown	26 Dec 1817	
WILBERT, Jacob	Phebe R. Perry	27 Dec 1882	
WILBUR, Jeremiah B.	Eliza S. Weaver	15 Aug 1883	
WILBURN - also see WILLBURN			
WILBURN, Anne	Henry Rabbett	6 Jun 1805	
Anne E.	Isaac H. Baker	25 Sep 1871	
Benjamin	Kitty Lindsay	23 Apr 1821	
Fannie	Alexander Reynolds	25 Jan 1881	
Mary C.	William Hill	14 Apr 1857	
Rebecca	William Olliver	6 Jul 1799	
Rezin	Dolly Bradburn	24 Jan 1807	
William	Jenny Rabbett	21 Feb 1803	
WILBURNE, Walter	Elizabeth Sibly	6 Jan 1818	
WILCOX - also see WILLCOX			
WILCOX, Richardson	Mary J. Turner	8 Nov 1880	
WILCOXEN - also see WILLCOXEN			
WILCOXEN, Henrietta E.	Uriah H. Griffith	23 Nov 1846	
Levy	Lethe Trundle	3 Nov 1801	
Mary E.	James B. Higgins	10 Jun 1801	
Theophilus	Mary A. Dwyer	10 Feb 1872	

* Part of last name from earlier reading
** Could be Sauter, Santer, Sautee; also could be Whitter

WILCOXEN, Thomas H.	Sarah Prather	20 Apr 1798	
William	Anne Cleland	10 Jun 1801	
WILDER, George H.	Sarah E. Holland	21 Sep 1866	
WILDMAN, Jacob	Mary Ann German	30 Jul 1828	
Joseph	Emma Cole	30 Oct 1895	w
WILDS, Tiernan T.	Mary Hook	27 Apr 1864	
WILEY - also see WYLIE			
WILEY, Catherine S.	Walter H. Aikens	5 Dec 1871	
Emma F.	William John Hinton	5 Dec 1865	
Frederick J.	Mollie J. Stanton	26 Jun 1871	
James	Mahala Arundell	16 Jan 1840	
Sallie	Albert G. Moore	4 Mar 1886	w
Samuel H.	Jane Ann Confrey	28 Dec 1870	
Thomas J. C.	Mollie F. Chaney	30 Mar 1875	
William Harrison	Ann E. Cashell	16 Oct 1861	
WILKERSON, Jennie	Samuel J. Argent	25 May 1892	w
WILKINSON, Bennett R.	Octavia B. Cashell	24 Oct 1893	w
Daisy	James J. Johnson	27 Apr 1895	w
Daniel	Dorcas Ann Dawson	7 Apr 1827	
John T.	Anna C. Young	30 Nov 1887	w
William	Nancy Musgrove	21 Aug 1821	
WILLARD, Mamie F.	Robert W. Stout	3 Dec 1892	w
Sallie W.	William H. Curtis	3 Sep 1887	w
WILLBURN - also see WILBURN			
WILLBURN, Benjamin	Sarah Johnson	28 Mar 1820	
Thomas	Elizabeth Mobley	11 Sep 1820	
WILLCOX - also see WILCOX			
WILLCOX, James M.	Catharine H. Taney	16 Oct 1883	
Thomas C.	Ann S. Taney	18 Nov 1890	w
WILLCOXEN - also see WILCOXEN			
WILLCOXEN, Amos	Cassandra Chambers	28 may 1800	
Anne	Elijah Chambers	21 Nov 1806	
Deborah	John Magruder	18 Dec 1810	
Drusilla L. T.	Samuel Young	1 Feb 1825	
Horatio	Ann Gaither	27 Aug 1817	
Horatio	Catharine Amelia Williams	19 Feb 1827	
Horatio	Sarah A. Wailes	30 Jul 1832	
James E.	Susan Swearingen	29 Jan 1810	
John	Barbara N. Robey	25 Nov 1830	
Josiah	Anne Y. Swailes	17 Dec 1810	
Margaret	Benjamin Lyon	22 Aug 1810	
Peggy Ann	Nathaniel Clagett	14 Dec 1807	
Rezin	Margaret Chambers	22 Dec 1800	
Thomas	Laura Walker	28 Mar 1860	
WILLETT, Ann	Robert Case	10 Apr 1816	
Benjamin	Anne House	19 Dec 1810	
Burgess	Catharine Fleming	25 Jan 1814	
Catherine	Gassaway Watkins	20 Apr 1826	
Cephas F.	Catharine Offutt	4 Jan 1847	
Cephas F.	Ann E. Johnson	16 Oct 1855	
Edward	Ann Barber	28 Oct 1813	
Elizabeth	Richard Howse	22 Jan 1812	
Isabella	Amon Riggs, Jr.	19 Dec 1801	
John	Martha Magruder	24 Dec 1811	
Mary	Ninian T. Willett	1 Mar 1808	

WILLETT,	Mary	Eleven Fish	31 Dec 1808	
	Meredith R.	Honor M. Darby	12 May 1845	
	Ninian T.	Mary Willett	1 Mar 1808	
	Robert	Lydia Griffith	18 Dec 1821	
	Sarah	Jesse Leach	20 Jan 1807	
WILLIAM,	Margaret	Charles H. King	4 Apr 1882	c
WILLIAMS,	Alice V.	Rufus Gibson	2 Mar 1882	
	Alpheus	Juliet Warfield	9 Sep 1805	
	Amanda M.	Samuel Turner	16 Apr 1822	
	Ann C.	Richard Davis	28 Sep 1852	
	Ann M.	John T. Brethard	12 Feb 1838	
	Anna L.	John T. Swailes	31 May 1889	c
	Anne	Washington Waters	5 Jun 1829	
	Annie M.	David J. Reinhart	8 Oct 1877	w
	Arthur	Annie Dawson	13 Jan 1882	w
	Asa M.	Elizabeth Medley	17 Jan 1832	
	Asbury	Annie Pumphrey	2 Jun 1894	c
	Asbury	Mary A. Johnson	28 Dec 1896	c
	Basil E.	Eliza M. McNew	7 Jan 1852	
	Bettie	Thomas M. Pyles	24 Nov 1873	
	Bettie	William G. Offutt	24 Jul 1879	
	Cassandra	Azel Waters	14 Oct 1805	
	Catharine	William Taylor	* Sep 1883	c
	Catharine Amelia	Horatio Willcoxen	19 Feb 1827	
	Catharine L.	Richard J. Bowie	5 May 1833	
	Charles	Elizabeth Shaw	22 Feb 1800	
	Charles	Mary Harris	23 Mar 1874	
	Charlotte J.	James W. Watkins	11 Dec 1872	
	Columbus	Margaret Berry	27 Oct 1879	
	Cora L.	George F. Pollock	15 Oct 1889	w
	Cornelia J.	Marion W. Thompson	30 Jul 1883	
	David	Elizabeth Wise	14 Sep 1871	
	David	Sarah Scott	17 Aug 1888	c
	Downey M.	Frances E. Bolton	31 Dec 1892	w
	Edward H.	Elizabeth Shaw	23 Nov 1829	
	Edward O.	Elizabeth Clagett	3 Dec 1800	
	Edy	Isaac Johnson	4 Nov 1869	
	Eleanor	Rezin Barber	7 Jun 1832	
	Eleanor	Charles Francis Adams	21 Dec 1868	
	Elender	Peter Hawkins	8 Mar 1798	
	Elisha Jr.	Sarah Graham	17 Nov 1812	
	Elisha O.	Emma B. Wallace	5 Jun 1854	
	Elisha W.	Jane Plater	16 Jan 1826	
	Eliza	Peter Brent	5 Dec 1868	
	Elizabeth Ann	Richard Cromwell	9 Sep 1833	
	Elizabeth F.	Horace Coburth	19 Feb 1835	
	Elizabeth Jane	Jonathan R. Shaw	12 Dec 1833	
	Ellen	Philemon W. Dorsey	18 Oct 1879	c
	Ellen G.	Albert C. Guerry	19 Jan 1887	w
	Emma	Horace M. Davis	2 Jul 1878	w
	Emma	Henry Rinehart	25 Feb 1880	c
	Exzeal	William J. Thomas	3 Oct 1886	c
	Fannie D.	Nathaniel P. Moore	28 Jun 1892	w

* Cannot read day; before 19

WILLIAMS,	Fannie L.	Thomas I. Fulks	4 Aug 1897 w
	Fanny	Henry Ridgley	21 Dec 1880
	Florence M.	W. McKendree Williams	27 Jun 1877 w
	Florence M.	Jefferson Duvall	20 Dec 1887 w
	Frances	James I. Williams	11 May 1842
	Francis T.	Georgie Griffith	17 Jan 1882
	Francis T.	Mary L. Dawson	22 Oct 1896 w
	George	Lucy Bowie	5 Jan 1866
	George	Mary Dorsey	5 Jan 1872
	George T.	Nancy S. Plummer	8 Nov 1879 c
	Gustavus	Ida Wallace	6 Oct 1883 c
	Henry McGill	Nellie Smith White	11 Nov 1890 w
	Henrietta	Dennis Nelson	25 May 1868
	Henrietta E.	James W. McAtee	10 Jan 1843
	Henrietta E.	Daniel R. Leaman	5 Nov 1874
	Henry	Louisa Carlisle	24 Oct 1866
	Henry	Theresa Prater	1 May 1891 c
	Henry S.	Jennie McPherson	8 Jan 1880 c
	Hezekiah	Elizabeth M. Mitchell	9 Sep 1867
	Hilliary	Sarah Herbert	10 Jan 1810
	Hollice	William P. Butler	7 Mar 1892 c
	I. Overton	Octavia J. Manakee	20 Feb 1860
	Isaac	Sarah Berry*	5 Aug 1819
	James	Susan Green	27 Nov 1886 c
	James B.	Sarah R. Paxton	9 Feb 1870
	James E.	Sarah J. Burdett	4 Oct 1856
	James I.	Frances Williams	11 May 1842
	Jane E. B.	Henry L. Reynolds	17 Jul 1893 w
	Jane Plater	James Snowden Pleasants	19 Nov 1858
	Jane R.	Jacob W. Dudderor	4 Apr 1865
	Jennie	Arthur B. Elmore	14 Nov 1877 w
	John	Sarah Stone	26 Dec 1799
	John	Sarah Nevitt	25 Dec 1806
	John	Priscilla Lyles	22 Dec 1813
	John	Elizabeth Collins	1 Jan 1821
	John	Rose A. Johnson	3 Dec 1890 c
	John A.	Matilda Spayts	7 Nov 1815
	John H.	Carrie Frazier	9 Oct 1889 c
	John M.	Mary Lewis	28 Mar 1825
	John M. Clayton	Eliza Ellen Renshaw	4 Apr 1887 w
	John T.	Ann Maria Talbott	11 Jun 1841
	John W.	Sadie R. Budd	** Jan 1888 c
	Jonathan C.	Georgia A. Umstead	14 Nov 1882 w
	Joseph F.	Sophronia Anderson	22 Oct 1874
	Julia I. N.	Edwin A. Rye***	20 Nov 1876
	Kate	Granville J. Harding	7 Nov 1887 w
	Kitty	Greenberry L. Miles	3 Jan 1854
	Laura	Charles Thompson	23 Feb 1892 c
	Laura V.	Flodoardo H. Johnson	29 Sep 1896 c
	Lavinia R.	David F. Peter	24 Jun 1891 w
	Leanah	George W. H. Campbell	6 Nov 1890 c
	Leonard	Sarah Scrivner	17 Dec 1814

* Smeared; could be Perry
** Cannot read day; either 25 or 26
*** This could be Rys

WILLIAMS,	Leroy	Lizzie Neal	10 Dec 1868	
	Lewis D.	Hallie Venable	4 Aug 1883	
	Lillie	Patrick H. Lee	20 Dec 1887	c
	Lizzie	Franklin S. King	16 Oct 1876	
	Lizzie	William Luckett	13 Sep 1894	c
	Louisa	Benjamin Lewis	20 Nov 1891	c
	Lucy*	William Magruder	15 Feb 1798	
	Lucy A.	William N. Cole	9 Oct 1884	
	Lucy W.	Joseph N. Allnutt	9 Dec 1890	w
	Mahala	James Hardy	14 Aug 1868	
	Margarett	Thomas Scott, Jr.	8 Aug 1814	
	Margarett Ann	Leonard H. Johns	3 Feb 1801	
	Maria	Thomas Pennyfield	23 Jun 1822	
	Maria	John Henry Clagett	5 Mar 1875	
	Martha Jane	Lloyd Green	23 Feb 1828	
	Martha P.	Nicholas Brewer	3 Sep 1849	
	Mary	Charles Higdon	13 Feb 1809	
	Mary	Henry Brown	21 Aug 1879	c
	Mary	Charles Cook	20 Oct 1879	c
	Mary A.	James M. Etchison	16 Dec 1851	
	Mary Ann S.	David E. Collins	28 Oct 1829	
	Mary E.	John T. Case	14 Jan 1845	
	Mary E.	Benjamin R. Beckwith	24 Mar 1868	
	Mary E.	Hilleary Simms	26 Dec 1895	c
	Mary F.	Michael T. Pyles	14 Nov 1893	w
	Mary Millie	Jacob A. Smith	23 Mar 1898	c
	Massie	Thomas Sedgwick	8 Apr 1868	
	Matilda	Benjamin B. Benson	20 Jan 1840	
	Nancy	Thomas Sibley	23 Feb 1820	
	Nancy	Hezekiah Barber	8 Dec 1831	
	Nettie E.	Edgar O. Harr	13 Aug 1894	w
	Otho B.	Laura L. Bennett	26 Apr 1898	w
	Overton	Mary Young	7 Jan 1824	
	Patty	Willy Janes	8 May 1804	
	Peter	Ellen Bowen	8 Nov 1867	
	Peter	Mary E. Che--y	15 Nov 1883	
	Priscilla	Samuel Belmere	24 Nov 1802	
	Rachel	Ambrose Proctor	26 Oct 1874	
	Rachel	John Prather	12 May 1894	c
	Rachel Sarah	William Cecil	30 Dec 1829	
	Rebecca	George W. Page	17 Dec 1840	
	Rebecca	Alexander E. Soper	5 Jan 1844	
	Rebecca N.	Charles W. Burdette	24 Aug 1878	w
	Richard	Victorine Dove	18 Dec 1867	
	Richard H.	Rosa Anderson	14 Nov 1864	
	Richard W.	Mary Jane Dyson	**17 Dec 1844	
	Richard W.	Hester C. White	29 Oct 1863	
	Robert	Milly Hamelton***	16 Jul 1875	
	Robert D.	Louisa Reddick	18 May 1893	c
	Roberta E.	Edward L. Gantt	9 Apr 1864	
	Rose	Thornton Lewis	26 Mar 1890	c
	Ruth	John Maccubbin	14 Mar 1804	

* Part of last name from earlier reading
** Day reads 17, but is entered after 21
*** This could be Hametton

WILLIAMS,	Samuel N. S.	Ann E. Fisher	20 Dec 1838
	Samuel N. S.	Mary E. C. Fisher	23 Aug 1860
	Sarah	Robert Briggs	22 Dec 1804
	Sarah	Otho James	25 Dec 1809
	Sarah	Walker D. Shoemate	26 Jul 1830
	Sarah	Walter Phelps	21 Dec 1842
	Sarah Ann	Edward D. Tippett	1 Feb 1810
	Sarah E.	Henry S. Thompson	4 Feb 1874
	Sarah M.	Hilleary T. Higgins	17 Dec 1877 w
	Simon H.	Anna R. Shaw	3 Mar 1887 c
	Solomon	Syney Bowie	14 Mar 1871
	Solomon	Rachel Holliday	7 Jan 1886 c
	Somerset T.	Ezar Burditt	9 May 1871
	Sophia	Adam Baker	* Jun 1877 c
	Stephen N. C.	Sadie R. Hall	4 Sep 1888 w
	Susan	Sylvester Matthews	20 Jun 1883
	Theresa	Henry Smallwood	8 Dec 1809
	Thomas	Nannie Bettas	28 May 1884 c
	Thompson	Hetty W. King	25 Apr 1883
	Victorine	Charles G. Alexander	28 Dec 1874
	Virginia	Henry Weldon	13 Jun 1878 c
	Virginia	Abraham Somerville	17 Mar 1892 c
	W. McKendree	Florence M. Williams	27 Jun 1877 w
	Walter	Dolly Belt	6 Jan 1819
	Walter	Anne E. Harwood	18 Mar 1825
	William	Eleanor Holland	20 Nov 1802
	William	Priscilla Lewis	17 Feb 1841
	William	Lucinda Washington	8 Aug 1893 c
	William	Lucinda Bowie	29 Nov 1897 c
	William B.	Ann Dorsey	19 Jun 1817
	William D.	Susan Winpenny	4 Dec 1866
	William H.	Agnes Gaither	4 May 1892 c
	William H.	Gertrude Brown	11 Jul 1895 c
	William Henry	Elizabeth Campbell	29 Apr 1873
	William Henry	Mary J. Lee	14 Aug 1879
	William J.	Elizabeth A. Schaeffer	26 Nov 1883
	William L.	Marietta Miles	15 Nov 1859
	Zachariah	Eleanor Simmons	21 Feb 1805
	Zachariah A.	Vandelia R. Soper	25 Oct 1882
WILLIAMSON,	Collin	Mary Talbott	4 Jun 1798
WILLIG,	Susen A.	William T. Vinsen	23 Nov 1863
WILLIS,	George L.	Louisa Grandison	11 Jun 1892 c
	Mary Y.	Samuel C. Owings	27 Oct 1814
	William L.	Louise K. Imhof	19 Apr 1895 w
WILLSON - also see WILSON			
WILLSON,	Alice Ann	James G. Henning	21 Feb 1844
	Ann	William French	26 Apr 1825
	Ann M.	Artaxerxes Fisher	4 Jul 1816
	B. Jane	W. B. Hunter	17 Mar 1857
	Caroline	Hezekiah Washington	25 May 1866
	Cassandra	George Ward	26 Feb 1802
	Charles	Jane Clarke	5 May 1807
	Charles G.	Elizabeth M. Herbert	30 Nov 1882 w
	Columbia	William Taney	10 Mar 1845

* Day has blot on it; between 12 and 27

WILLSON,	Eliza	Laurence Ball	13 Jan 1824
	Eliza A.	Francis L. Lyddane	30 Jan 1861
	Elizabeth	Thomas Page	18 Jan 1811
	Elizabeth	Trammell Harl	10 Oct 1829
	Elizabeth	Benjamin F. Higgins	20 Mar 1844
	Elizabeth Ann	George E. Pryor	5 Mar 1825
	Franklin	Virginia Reed	12 Jan 1863
	George	Elizabeth Crawford	22 May 1804
	Greenbury	Virlinda Harrison	29 Jun 1812
	Hanson	Matilda Sherman	28 May 1828
	Halkiah W.	Caroline M. Veatch	25 Apr 1821
	Helkiah W.	Henrietta Dillehay	21 Apr 1838
	Henry	Elizabeth Morsell	1 Jul 1803
	Henry	Leah Upton	21 Dec 1815
	Horace	Leah Summers	7 Apr 1818
	James	Verlinda Kisner	13 Dec 1817
	James	Rebecca Fling	21 Jan 1828
	Jane	Edmond Riggs	21 May 1799
	John D.	Mary Ann Wells	7 Jan 1829
	Keziah Ann	William Duhurst	19 Apr 1808
	Linney	Thomas H. Mills	18 Jun 1817
	Lucinda	Richard D. Waters	12 Feb 1818
	Lucinda Maria	Stephen Bailey	2 Dec 1845
	Margaret	Benjamin W. Jones	7 Jan 1802
	Margaret	Irving Underhill	13 Aug 1887 w
	Maria E. L.	William A. Waters	17 Sep 1896 w
	Marian	Mortimer Thompson	2 Jan 1857
	Martha A.	George Smizer	11 Aug 1847
	Martha R.	John L. B. Mines	2 Jun 1849
	Mary	William Simpson	22 May 1800
	Mary	Thomas Watkins	9 Jan 1818
	Mary	Thomas Neele	13 Mar 1843
	Mary	Nathan Doy	30 Jul 1877 c
	Mary Ann	Walter Willson	28 Mar 1832
	Mary E.	William S. Whalen	2 Mar 1854
	Mary Ellen	George W. Beall	9 Sep 1875
	Mary N.	Charles Slemmer	7 Aug 1850
	Mary S.	Edward Winsor	20 Aug 1844
	Mary S.	Luther M. Muncaster	20 Jan 1896 w
	Mary T. D.	Frederick S. Poole	12 Aug 1833
	Milly	James Jarvais	3 Apr 1801
	Mirah	Conrad Maught	16 Oct 1847
	Noah *.	Mary C. Gilpin	2 Nov 1838
	Osborn S.	Elizabeth Richards	4 Jan 1813
	Osborn S. Jr.	Elizabeth A. Ball	28 Feb 1854
	Otho	Anne Clarke	29 Sep 1812
	Otho	Mary C. V. Hall	14 Jun 1825
	Percy H.	Harriet Anne Waters	15 Mar 1897 w
	Richard H.	Amelia A. Brown	26 May 1882 c
	Richard T.	Laura Canby	18 Apr 1853
	Rosa E.	Basil R. Frazier	12 Sep 1877 c
	Ruth Ann	Caleb Calvert	9 Dec 1872
	Sallie	Hervey Brown, Jr.	20 Sep 1892 w
	Samuel	Eleza Dawson	10 Apr 1802

* Initial L or S

WILLSON,	Samuel	Margaret Scholl	25 Mar 1824
	Samuel	Anna Gilpin	30 Dec 1856
	Sarah	Philip Carlon	22 Dec 1804
	Sarah	Levi Sibley	7 Mar 1832
	Sarah A. E.	Thomas Poole	14 May 1832
	Sarah Ellen	John Hodges	7 Jun 1837
	Stephen	Sarah Selby	5 Feb 1812
	Susan	Lewis Magruder	30 Jun 1845
	Susanna	Thomas Lanham	26 Jan 1821
	Tabitha	Robert F. Chew	28 Jun 1820
	Tabitha	Richard M. Downes	6 Jan 1834
	Thomas	Nancy Rankins	24 Sep 1798
	Thomas	Sarah Bonnifant	20 Nov 1850
	Thomas L.	Clara E. Becraft	26 Aug 1889 w
	Thomas O.	Mary Ann Bonifant	20 Apr 1841
	Turner	Mary Ann Richards	25 Jan 1817
	Turner	Amy Stubbs	14 Nov 1864
	Virginia	George Smizer	21 Dec 1857
	Walter	Sarah Galer	3 Mar 1810
	Walter	Mary Ann Willson	28 Mar 1832
	William	Rebecca Magruder	10 Jan 1801
	William	Mary Clarke	13 Jan 1809
	William	Anna Maria Linstid	17 Apr 1817
	William Elson	Eleanor Swearingen	12 Nov 1807
	William M. B.	Martha Wootton	29 Nov 1821
	William S.	Jemima Upton	27 Dec 1825
WILMINGTON,	John	Ann Beall	4 Apr 1816
WILMOTH,	Leonard J.	Mamie M. Iglehart	11 Jan 1897 w
WILMS,	Matilda A.	Gotlieb C. Grammer	18 Mar 1825
WILSON - also see WILLSON			
WILSON,	Alfred	Minnie W. Poole	21 Jun 1892 w
	Anna G..	Thomas J. Lea	13 Jul 1885 w
	Annie	Charles B. Stewart	26 May 1892 c
	Annie E.	Edgar M. Parsley	29 Sep 1898 w
	Cyrus S.	Mary A. Carr	15 Dec 1891 w
	Elenor	Josiah Bean, Jr.	23 Oct 1801
	Helen D.	Edward G. Cissel	26 Jun 1882
	James F.	Clara A. Ray	31 May 1892 w
	James S. C.	Mary V. Davis	19 Nov 1887 c
	Jennie F.	George D. Heider	20 Mar 1878 w
	John C.	Selina D. Pendleton	11 Aug 1863
	John E.	Ella Gilpin	18 Oct 1865
	John H.	Victoria V. Hall	4 Dec 1895 c
	John W.	Henrietta Golden	23 Mar 1869
	Laura	Edward Magruder	6 Feb 1851
	Lucind	George T. Linch	22 Dec 1876
	Lucinda	Robert G. Connell	3 Jan 1871
	Mary E.	Samuel S. Belt	19 Feb 1879 w
	Mollie	A. William Magruder	9 Jan 1882
	Moses	Mary Steward	8 Dec 1879 c
	Nellie E.	William H. ShirCliff	16 Apr 1890 w
	Robert	Elender Shekells	29 Oct 1798
	Sallie P.	Arthur L. Morsell	9 Sep 1892 w
	William M.	Annie E. Dawson	27 Nov 1889 w
	Ralp C.	Amy M. Fuller	6 Jan 1896 w

WIMS - also see WEEMS, WHIMS			
WIMS, Benjamin F.	Hattie Ann Foreman	25 Nov 1897	c
David T.	Mary I. Davis	16 Oct 1888	c
George W.	Lillie M. Doy	4 Oct 1894	c
Manzella U.	Robert P. Foreman	17 Aug 1889	c
Sedonia	Charles W. Mason	4 Jan 1898	c
William Henry	Amanda Brown	16 Dec 1876	
WIMSETT, Joseph	Winny Morgan Carroll	17 Dec 1800	
Mary	John Bradburn	14 Nov 1803	
WINCHELL, Trueman	Mary Haney	22 Jan 1823	
Truman	Julia Ann Gray	11 Oct 1859	
WINCHESTER, Thomas W.	Virginia A. F. Olive	2 May 1846	
WINDEER, Cassie	Solomon J. Dorsey	28 Sep 1892	c
George	Julia Harding	5 Jul 1893	c
Maria E.	John Thomas Weems	19 Sep 1894	c
WINDHAM, Harriet	Camden Riley	7 Feb 1824	
James	Mary Riley	3 Mar 1826	
James M.	Charlotte Heffner	5 May 1840	
James M.	Eliza McDonaugh	19 Jun 1848	
Laura R.	William F. Cramer	27 Nov 1883	
Mary E.	George Knorleine	1 May 1882	
WINDOM, Aquila	Mary E. B. Howard	12 Aug 1815	
Sarah	John White	6 Feb 1817	
WINDSOR - also see WINSOR			
WINDSOR, Elizabeth	William Hodges	6 Feb 1868	
Flora	Travilla E. Peters	31 Dec 1883	
Ida M.	William E. Gibson	5 Nov 1879	w
James S.	Sarah R. Darby	9 Oct 1865	
John H.	Frances M. Crawford	23 Dec 1854	
Keturah A.	Andrew J. Waters	18 Dec 1857	
Livenia	Charles E. Browning	4 Mar 1887	w
Mary	Jeremiah Lewis	13 Dec 1805	
Nancy	Joseph Brown	18 Dec 1799	
Randolph H.	Ida P. Burdett	6 Nov 1888	w
Robert	Elizabeth Thompson	6 May 1805	
Tabitha	James Smith	2 Sep 1812	
William R.	Ann E. Murphy	15 Aug 1861	
Willie	Flora V. Leamon	12 Nov 1895	w
Zadok	Jane Lewis	20 Dec 1803	
WINEBERGER, Elizabeth	Thomas Calclaser	19 May 1800	
WINEMILLER, Clarence M.	Mittie W. Easton	5 Aug 1889	w
Elizabeth	Isaac N. Powers	31 Dec 1828	
Harriett Ann	William Baker Bennett	24 May 1827	
Henry	Eleanor Norris	1 Mar 1806	
John	Elizabeth Harper	17 Jul 1824	
John Henry	Eliza Ann Magruder	4 Dec 1832	
WINFREE, Alta M.	Harry R. Scott	24 Sep 1896	w
WINGATE, Abraham R.	Kittie H. Gilliland	12 Sep 1885	
Ambrus	Sally Mockbee	15 Oct 1808	
WINGFIELD, John	Catharine Grime	26 Feb 1868	c
WINKLER, Maria*	Charles Wise	15 Apr 1819	
WINPENNY, Mary J.	Squire L. Brayshaw	30 May 1871	
Susan	William D. Williams	4 Dec 1866	

* Part of last name from earlier reading

WINROAD, Susannah	Jonathan Browning	31 Nov 1804
WINROD, Frederick	Sophia Hall	7 Feb 1801
Henry	Elizabeth Beall	24 Feb 1819
WINSOR - also see WINDSOR		
WINSOR, Alexander	Rebecca Magruder	5 Nov 1821
Arnold T.	Mary Riley	18 Aug 1818
Catharine	Basil Mobley	11 May 1815
Catharine	Nathan Claggett	6 Dec 1816
Edward	Mary S. Willson	20 Aug 1844
Henry	Mary W. Simmons	17 Nov 1818
Rebecca*	Levi Lewis	18 Dec 1798
Rosana N.	William H. Cline	13 Dec 1830
Sarah	John Claggett	15 Dec 1817
WINTERMYER, Thomas J.	Georgia A. Fox	4 Jul 1891 w
WIRE, Thomas N.	Blanche A. Washington	27 Jul 1892 w
WISE, Bertie	James Davis	23 Jan 1896 c
Charles	Maria Winkler*	15 Apr 1819
Elizabeth	David Williams	14 Sep 1871
Erasmus	Charlotte Tucker	16 Oct 1809
George F.	Mary Ann Robinson	19 May 1873
Jesse	Louisa Proctor	20 Oct 1898 c
John	Elizabeth Sayer	22 Feb 1816
Marcy Ann	John Seaton	4 Jan 1800
Mary	Isaac O'Neale	16 Dec 1853
WIVEL - also see WYVALL		
WIVEL, Nancy	John Gray	12 Aug 1868
WIVELL, Susan	Ephraim Young	22 Mar 1814
WOLF, Elizabeth	Caleb Moxley	22 Jan 1821
WOLFE, Ann C.	Jesse T. Hyatt	6 Jan 1860
Garrett Davis	Lilian G. Cecil	16 Jan 1888 w
George	Mary Davis	26 Feb 1829
John H. R.	Cleorah P. Griffith	15 Oct 1889 w
Kate Davis	Luther Lingon Hyatt	6 Jan 1880 w
William	Sarah E. Eller	20 Nov 1855
WOLFORD, Harry C.	Elizabeth M. Allison	** Jul 1898 w
WOLTZ, Henrietta E.	William Stiles	8 Jun 1825
WOOD, Amanda	William Edward Offutt	7 Oct 1880 c
Charles W.	Columbia Whalan	16 May 1859
Charles Worth	Tracey Cary	8 Nov 1832
Elizabeth A.	Franklin P. Sherrer	4 Dec 1894 w
Henry G.	Mary A. Hipkins	4 Feb 1893 w
John	Sally Quary	11 Nov 1804
John G.	Elizabeth Edmonstone	1 Jan 1825
Louisa	Tasker Newman	16 Jun 1870
Lucy	William H. Dove	27 Dec 1878 c
Maggie	Henry Shelton	1 Nov 1898 c
Mary F.	Andrew Davis	17 Sep 1873
Mary L.	Henry Riggs	18 Oct 1879
Ruth H.	Henry H. Duvall	21 Jan 1807
William A.	Mary E. Ridout	17 Nov 1891 c
William E.	Amelia J. Macgill	16 Jun 1896 w
WOODARD, Downs M.	Mary V. Veitch	20 Aug 1889 w

* Earlier readings have Winn; court records show Winsor to be correct
* Cannot read day: either 15 or 16

WOODBURY, George F.	Augusta S.H.C. Hansmann	12 Sep 1895	w
WOODFIELD, Cedalia V.	David L. Ward	4 Jan 1898	w
Della W.	James R. King	26 Dec 1896	w
Edward	Verlinda Burns	20 Apr 1847	
Edward	Sarah Ann Thompson	11 Jun 1873	
George William	Mary L. Thompson	* Jan 1880	
James M.	Laura S. Waters	19 Sep 1885	w
James M.	Laura V. Green	18 Dec 1896	w
John R.	Nettie Young	22 Mar 1878	w
Joseph	Kezia Riggs	21 Mar 1849	
Ollie M.	Millard A. Jackson	25 Jan 1897	w
Thomas G.	Emma C. Boyer	29 Dec 1886	w
Zacheus	Katie M. Grimes	29 Dec 1883	
WOODJETT, Elizabeth A.	John Robey	6 Jan 1815	
WOODLEY, Charles	Winnie Taylor	18 Nov 1874	
Odo W.	Josephine McCooly	17 Feb 1883	
WOODS, Howard	Harriet Thomas	5 May 1880	
Jane	Henry Magruder	29 Apr 1868	
Laura L.	George Franklin	6 Oct 1887	c
WOODWARD, Alice J.	George W. Book	24 May 1888	c
Annie	John Wesley Gray	19 Jan 1870	
Catharine	John C. Gibson	1 Mar 1889	c
Columbus O.	Laura V. Linthicum	23 Nov 1869	
Edith	Harry L. Johnson	14 Sep 1897	w
Eva V.	Campbell F. Gibson	15 Jul 1889	w
Frank	Elizabeth Spencer	13 Dec 1887	w
John	Helen Johnson	30 Apr 1888	c
Mahlon	Mary Ann Darby	23 May 1825	
Rachel	John T. Stevenson	27 May 1885	
Roszell	Eliza Jane Reed	19 Sep 1867	
WOODY, Edward T.	Maggie Crumbaugh	24 Dec 1867	
WOOLLARD, John	Sarah Anders	7 May 1816	
WOOTTON, Eliza	Lewis Beall	9 Jul 1801	
John	Betsey Lynn Magruder	17 Jun 1806	
Margaret	Ignatius Davis	22 May 1798	
Margaret	Arundel Smith	24 Jul 1832	
Martha	William M. B. Willson	29 Nov 1821	
Martha	Thomas Anderson	7 Feb 1873	
Mary	Daniel B. Kelley	5 Apr 1866	
Nannie	John F. Byers	25 Apr 1885	w
Octavia O.	Watkins Walls	19 oct 1846	
Richard	Octavia Smith	11 Mar 1835	
William H.	Mary J. Hutchison	18 Feb 1865	
WORMWOOD, John D.	Alice G. Marlow	5 Nov 1894	w
WORRELL, Ann Maria	Frederick T. Brown	19 Jan 1856	
Elizabeth	James Harvey	23 Feb 1870	
Rebecca			
Jesse	Ruth Fields	2 Nov 1816	
Joanna	Nathan M. Hobbs	2 Jun 1859	
WORSHAM, Robert F.	Ollie Turpin	5 Jul 1897	w
WORTHINGTON, Achsah	Leonard Young Davis	2 Mar 1801	
Ann	Tilghman Hilliary	31 Oct 1820	
Bradley	Mary W. Griffith	11 Nov 1889	w
Eliza	Henry C. Gaither	28 Jan 1812	

* Cannot read day; either 20 or 21

WORTHINGTON, Elizabeth	Samuel T. Magruder	11 Jan 1844	
Elizabeth H.	Samuel Riggs of R	26 Oct 1875	
John Henry	Ann Hammond Dorsey	1 Mar 1815	
Landon	Louisa Tucker	17 Feb 1829	
Nicholas	S. E. Anderson	18 Oct 1847	
Richard S.	Frances N. Nelson	20 Jun 1889	w
Susan H.	Robert G. Russell	31 Aug 1818	
Thomas of William	Elizabeth H. Bowie	26 Feb 1839	
Upton	Catherine Dorsey	28 Nov 1832	
William	Ruth Perry	9 Mar 1798	
William H.	Ruth Ann Crockett	18 Dec 1839	
WORTHMILLER, John H.	Mary E. Umstead	22 Jan 1889	w
WOTONS, Fannie	Daniel Beall	4 Aug 1891	w
WRAN, John	Julia Lewis	6 Jul 1893	c
WREN, Maggie	Timothy Bennett	31 Aug 1876	
Mary	Smith Shipley	30 Apr 1891	c
WRIGHT, Aletha	John White	25 May 1871	
Ann	John Stafford	3 Nov 1810	
Florence E.	Robert H. Bell	15 Mar 1898	w
George	Florence Johnson	1 May 1894	c
James M. Jr.	Mary E. Hollingsworth	1 Sep 1881	
John	Elizabeth Downes	27 Nov 1799	
John	Mary Selbey	31 Dec 1806	
John H.	Sarah Burress	12 Oct 1825	
Marcellena	Samuel Sedgwick	13 Dec 1866	
Margaret	Eli Powell	23 Sep 1896	c
Mary V.	------ M. Ford	* Apr 1879	
Robert	Peggy Betz	7 Jul 1800	
Rosa Bell	Galveston Mastin	16 Jul 1890	w
Rush L.	Rachel E. Rawlins	29 Dec 1896	w
Samuel	Phebe Robertson	2 Jun 1800	
Verlinder	Basil M. Beall	17 Apr 1850	
William	Ella Riel	12 Oct 1874	
William	Sarah Edwards	** Sep 1883	c
William H.	Edith M. Watkins	13 Mar 1890	w
WYATT, Hattie C.	Eustis B. Johnson	21 Oct 1895	c
WYLIE - also see WILEY			
WYLIE, Mary E.	John R. Abell	23 Dec 1859	
WYNKOOP, Lorena L.	Samuel H. Marshall	19 Sep 1895	w
WYVALL - also see WIVEL, WYVELL, WYVILL, WYVILLE			
WYVALL, Henry C.	Ruth Duvall	15 Jan 1799	
WYVELL, Eleanor	Warner Poole	2 Feb 1813	
Eleanor S.	Alfred J. Oden	13 Apr 1850	
Hale	Ceney Owens	18 Jul 1809	
Jane	John Duvall	6 May 1809	
Sally	Zachariah Thompson	17 Jan 1827	
WYVILL, Asena	William Ford	8 Mar 1822	
Edward	Elizabeth Sprigg	21 Jul 1830	
Edward A.	Debora Jane Sprigg	6 Oct 1879	
Elizabeth Emily	Lloyd R. Duvall	13 Feb 1833	
Priscilla	Willson O. Duvall	18 Sep 1832	
Sarah	Lewis Duvall	2 Feb 1801	

* Cannot read day; between 5 and 25
** Cannot read day; either 27 or 29

WYVILL, Susan A.	Benjamin Robert Fish	20 Dec 1832	
WYVILLE, Dellia	John Henry Tilling	2 Apr 1877	w
YAETAMAN - also see YEATMAN			
YEATAMAN, Bell	Charles S. Hart	6 Apr 1886	w
YAGER, Lewis	Carrie Carroll	15 May 1889	c
YARDLEY, Elizabeth	James Peck	8 Jun 1802	
YATES, Amy L.	William J. Yates	31 Aug 1887	w
John	Mary Norris	22 Feb 1816	
William J.	Amy L. Yates	31 Aug 1887	w
Zachariah	Sarah Murray	9 Dec 1817	
YEATMAN - also see YAETAMAN			
YEATMAN, Susie B.	Harry Straus	17 Apr 1895	w
YEWELL - also see EWELL			
YEWELL, John	Anne Seeders	3 Apr 1804	
Mary Ann	George W. Cashell	22 Mar 1866	
Octavia A.	George W. Cashell	24 Mar 1831	
YOST, Elizabeth	Jacob Young	17 Feb 1818	
Henry	Rosa A. Lavender	10 May 1887	w
John	Mary Harry	19 Jul 1826	
Martha	Guy F. Austin	15 Apr 1834	
YOUNG, Albert	Ella J. Taylor	18 Dec 1895	w
Alethea T.	George Brewer	28 Feb 1849	
Alice	Owen Burgess	30 May 1883	
Alice W.	Benjamin F. Coomes	1 May 1872	
Anna C.	John T. Wilkinson	30 Nov 1887	w
Annie	Luther H. Young	22 Sep 1880	
Arthur	E. Belle Cissel	18 Apr 1870	
Benjamin C.	Mary J. Elgin	29 Dec 1859	
Carrie H.	William H. Nicholson	19 Nov 1883	
Catharine	William J. Dronenburg	24 Mar 1871	
Catharine S.	Benjamin E. Hughes	25 Apr 1849	
Charles	Eleanor Wallace	13 Nov 1806	
Charles L.	Laura F. Nichols	18 Feb 1892	w
Charles T.	Sallie White	21 Feb 1884	
Comforte	John All	12 Jul 1798	
David	Matilda Chilton	11 Apr 1827	
Edward W. O.	Isabelle E. Stevens	3 Apr 1895	c
Eleanor	George W. Bowman	15 Dec 1834	
Eleanor H.	Richard H. Leaman	27 Sep 1865	
Elias	Mary Adams	13 Jun 1891	c
Eliza	John L. Horn	13 Mar 1824	
Eliza	William H. Brown	11 Feb 1898	c
Elizabeth	Richard Fish	17 Dec 1800	
Elizabeth	Mahlon Roach	4 Jan 1810	
Elizabeth	Fielder Darnall	7 Jun 1824	
Elizabeth	Thomas H. Schaffer	14 Feb 1867	
Elizabeth	John P. Sellman	31 Oct 1898	w
Elizabeth Ann	Gayhart Metzgar	18 Sep 1838	
Ella J.	George W. Mulligan	25 Oct 1897	w
Ephraim	Susan Wivell	22 Mar 1814	
Harriet	John Grimes	18 Jan 1839	
Henry	Margaret Chiswell	28 Jan 1823	
Henry	Sarah E. Allnutt	27 Oct 1860	
Henry	Martha Cissel	10 Nov 1871	

YOUNG,	Hilleary	Laura Wallace	18 May 1870
	Hilleary	Lela Warren	30 Sep 1886 c
	Horace E.	Annie L. Warthen	4 Jan 1881
	Howard	Martha Ann Purdom	19 Dec 1834
	Isaac	Margaret Young	14 May 1856
	Jacob	Elizabeth Yost	17 Feb 1818
	Jacob	Sarah Hutchinson	8 Jan 1821
	Jacob	Sarah Warfield	24 Sep 1833
	Jacob	Laura D. Grimes	6 Aug 1874
	James M.	Sarah A. Iglehart	7 Apr 1868
	Jane	Perry Davis	12 Dec 1866
	Jane Eversfield	John Franklin Leaman	10 Jan 1868
	Jesse	Ellen Peake	3 Jun 1879 c
	John	Sarah Jones	30 Mar 1812
	John	Rebecca Poole	27 Dec 1817
	John A.	Henrietta Poole	5 Jun 1893 w
	Laura M.	Reuben H. Riggs	28 Aug 1883
	Levi T.	Mary J. Davis	16 Jan 1867
	Lewald	Betsey Query	2 Jun 1828
	Linda C.	Joseph T. Chiswell	29 Nov 1887 w
	Louisa	Thomas Ranson	1 Jan 1870
	Lucy L.	Edward C. Brice	3 Nov 1894 w
	Ludowick	Catharine Barratt	27 Dec 1817
	Lulie	Wilson H. Powell	14 Dec 1882 c
	Luther	Catherine L. Luckett	15 Oct 1891 c
	Luther H.	Annie Young	22 Sep 1880
	Margaret	Isaac Young	14 May 1856
	Martha S.	Vernon H. Nicholson	12 Dec 1883
	Martha W.	Christian T. Leaman	11 Mar 1863
	Mary	Thomas Dixon	22 Aug 1820
	Mary	Overton Williams	7 Jan 1824
	Mary	Rezin H. Bowman	29 Apr 1845
	Mary Ann	Charles Smith	17 Apr 1827
	Mary E.	Daniel T. Remsburg	11 Apr 1856
	Mary P.	Erastus V. Penn	27 Dec 1854
	Mary R.	Henry M. Thomas	13 Oct 1888 c
	Mary S.	George Washington	8 Oct 1883 c
	Millie	Walter Bailey	20 Sep 1882 c
	Minnie	Ernest Baseman	17 Feb 1888 w
	Mollie	William E. Action	3 Jan 1881
	Mollie E.	Joshua Davis, Jr.	21 Jun 1869
	Mortimer T.	Mary E. A. Shaw	23 Sep 1867
	Nettie	John R. Woodfield	22 Mar 1878 w
	Rebecca*	Samuel Douglass	22 Feb 1808
	Reuben W.	Mary E. Barnesly	29 Dec 1883 w
	Richard	Matilda Riggs	14 Jan 1826
	Richard	Ruth Green	28 Feb 1844
	Richard	Asenath R. Riggs	3 Mar 1847
	Robert L.	Lucy A. Wade	2 Jun 1888 w
	Rosina	Jehu Bowen	27 Dec 1866
	Ruth G.	James H. Gue	24 Feb 1864
	Samuel	Drusilla L.T. Willcoxen	1 Feb 1825
	Samuel C.	Mary Veirs	23 Nov 1831
	Sarah E.	F. M. Getzendanner	12 Mar 1873

* Name from earlier reading

YOUNG, Sarah S.	David T. Cissel	7 Jan 1859	
Sophia	Joseph Harding	3 Mar 1817	
Stephen	Ella Harriss	19 Oct 1892	c
Thomas H.	Charlotte Lewis	21 Dec 1830	
Uriah W.	Leantha J. V. Lee	11 Sep 1897	c
Verlinda C.	Edward Getzendanner	22 Oct 1872	
Victoria	C. R. Hershey	29 Nov 1873	
Wilfred	Eleanor Trail	20 Jan 1824	
William	Rachel Scott	17 Sep 1844	
William	Sarah E. Hilton	25 Nov 1861	
YOUNGER, James	Rebecca Collins	9 Jan 1810	
Margaret B.	James Carroll	13 Jul 1897	c
YOUNT, Fred S.	Oscie L. Amiss	28 Jul 1898	w
ZAHN, Bertha M.	Rufus E. Boyd	31 Aug 1896	w
ZEIGLER, Alice V.	William D. Borum	14 Nov 1882	w
David A.	Ellen A. Hyatt	12 Sep 1835	
Eliza Ann	Jacob Root	2 May 1835	
George H.	Ann E. Sullivan	15 Feb 1871	
Henrietta	Alfred Brown	15 Aug 1848	
Ida J.	Ephraim G. Harris	23 Jan 1877	w
James H.	Annie Bruce Miller	26 Oct 1875	
Mamie	Ernest Richard Cissel	12 Apr 1888	w
Maria E.	Levi Thomas Hyatt	3 Nov 1845	
Mary E.	E. G. Harris	7 Nov 1867	
Sarah C.	William H. Barron	13 May 1873	
ZELLER, Josephine A.	Samuel H. Cator	15 Nov 1894	w
ZEP, Marshal	Martha Golding	15 May 1878	w

www.ingramcontent.com/pod-product-compliance
Lightning Source LLC
Chambersburg PA
CBHW050331230426
43663CB00010B/1814